SECOND EDITION

LEGAL RIGHTS OF TEACHERS AND STUDENTS

NELDA H. CAMBRON-McCABE

Miami University of Ohio

MARTHA M. McCARTHY

Indiana University, Bloomington

STEPHEN B. THOMAS

Kent State University

DISCARD

Boston • New York • San Francisco • Mexico City • Montreal
Toronto • London • Madrid • Munich • Paris • Hong Kong
Singapore • Tokyo • Cape Town • Sydney

Executive Editor and Publisher: *Stephen D. Dragin*
Series Editorial Assistant: *Anne Whittaker*
Marketing Manager: *Darcy Betts*
Production Editor: *Mary Beth Finch*
Composition Buyer: *Linda Cox*
Manufacturing Buyer: *Megan Cochran*
Production Management and Composition: *Progressive Publishing Alternatives*
Cover Administrator: *Linda Knowles*

For related titles and support materials, visit our online catalog at www.pearsonhighered.com.

Between the time website information is gathered and then published, it is not unusual for some sites to have closed. Also, the transcription of URLs can result in typographical errors. The publisher would appreciate notification where these errors occur so that they may be corrected in subsequent editions.

Library of Congress Cataloging-in-Publication Data

Cambron-McCabe, Nelda H.
   Legal rights of teachers and students / Nelda H. Cambron-McCabe, Martha McCarthy, Stephen Thomas. —2nd ed.
      p. cm.
   Rev. ed. of: Legal rights of teachers and students / Martha M. McCarthy, Nelda H. Cambron-McCabe, Stephen B. Thomas. 2004.
   Includes index.
   ISBN-13: 978-0-205-57936-5
   ISBN-10: 0-205-57936-1
   1.   Teachers—Legal status, laws, etc.—United States. 2.   Students— Legal status, laws, etc.—United States.   I. McCarthy, Martha M.   II. Thomas, Stephen B.   III. McCarthy, Martha M. Legal rights of teachers and students.   IV. Title.
   KF4119.M388 2009
   344.73'078—dc22
                                                                   2008027925
Printed in the United States of America

10 9 8 7 6 5 4 3 2 1   HAM   12 11 10 09 08

CONTENTS

Preface   xi

CHAPTER ONE

Legal Framework of Public Education   1

STATE CONTROL OF EDUCATION   1

Legislative Power   2
State Agencies   3
Local School Boards   4
School-Based Councils   5

FEDERAL ROLE IN EDUCATION   6

United States Constitution   6

General Welfare Clause 6 / Obligation of Contracts Clause 7 / First
Amendment 7 / Fourth Amendment 7 / Fourteenth Amendment 7

Federal Legislation   8

Funding Laws 9 / Civil Rights Laws 10

Federal Administrative Agencies   11

FUNCTION AND STRUCTURE OF THE JUDICIAL SYSTEM   11

State Courts   14
Federal Courts   15
Judicial Trends   17

CONCLUSION   18

CHAPTER TWO

Tort Liability   19

NEGLIGENCE   19

Duty   19

Instruction 20 / Supervision 21 / Maintenance of Buildings, Grounds, and
Equipment 23 / Duty to Warn 24

Breach of Duty/Standard of Care   25

Reasonable Person 26 / Invitee, Licensee, and Trespasser 27

Proximate Cause   28
Injury   28
Defenses against Negligence   29

Governmental Immunity 29 / Contributory Negligence 29 / Comparative
Negligence 30 / Assumption of Risk 31

INTENTIONAL TORTS   31
>   Assault and Battery   31
>   False Imprisonment   33
>   Intentional Infliction of Mental Distress   33

DEFAMATION   34
>   Private and Public Persons   35
>   Veracity of Statements   35
>   Fact versus Opinion   36
>   Privilege   37

DAMAGES   37

CONCLUSION   38

POINTS TO PONDER   38

CHAPTER THREE

Church/State Relations   40

CONSTITUTIONAL FRAMEWORK   40

RELIGIOUS INFLUENCES IN PUBLIC SCHOOLS   43
>   Silent Prayer Statutes   43
>   School-Sponsored versus Private Devotionals   44
>>   *Weisman* and Its Progeny   44   /   Student Elections to Authorize Prayers   45   /   Post–*Santa Fe* Rulings   46
>   Pledge of Allegiance   47
>   Religious Displays and Holiday Observances   48
>   Proselytization in the Classroom   49
>   Equal Access for Religious Expression and Groups   51
>>   Equal Access Act   52   /   School Access for Community Groups   53   /   Distribution of Religious Literature   54

ACCOMMODATIONS FOR RELIGIOUS BELIEFS   55
>   Release-Time Programs   55
>   Excusal for Religious Observances   56
>   Religious Exemptions from Secular Activities   56

RELIGIOUS CHALLENGES TO THE SECULAR CURRICULUM   58

STATE AID TO PRIVATE SCHOOLS   61
>   Aid for Student Services   62
>   Aid to Encourage Educational Choice   64
>>   Tax-Relief Measures   64   /   Vouchers   64

CONCLUSION   66

POINTS TO PONDER   66

CHAPTER FOUR

Instructional Issues   67

THE SCHOOL CURRICULUM   67

    Requirements and Restrictions   67
    Censorship of Instructional Materials   69
        Challenges to the Curriculum   69   /   Censorship by Policy Makers   70   /
        Electronic Censorship   72
    Academic Freedom   72
        Curriculum Content   73   /   Teaching Strategies   74

COPYRIGHT COMPLIANCE   76

STUDENT PROFICIENCY TESTING   80

EDUCATIONAL MALPRACTICE/INSTRUCTIONAL NEGLIGENCE   83

INSTRUCTIONAL PRIVACY RIGHTS   85

    Student Records   85
    Pupil Protection and Parental Rights Laws   90

CONCLUSION   91

POINTS TO PONDER   92

CHAPTER FIVE

Student Expression, Association, and Appearance   92

FREEDOM OF SPEECH AND PRESS   93

    Unprotected Conduct and Expression   94
        Defamatory Expression   94   /   Obscene, Lewd, or Vulgar Expression   94   /   Inflammatory
        Expression   95   /   Advocacy of Illegal Activity for Minors   96
    Commercial Expression   97
    School-Sponsored Expression   97
        Type of Forum   97   /   *Hazelwood* and Its Progeny   98
    Protected Private Expression   99
        Prior Restraints   100   /   Postexpression Discipline   102   /   Anti-Harassment
        Policies   103   /   Electronic Expression   106   /   Time, Place, and Manner Regulations   107

STUDENT-INITIATED CLUBS   108

STUDENT APPEARANCE   109

    Hairstyle   110
    Attire   110
        Dress Codes   110   /   Student Uniforms   113

CONCLUSION   114

POINTS TO PONDER   114

CHAPTER SIX

Student Classifications   116

CLASSIFICATIONS BASED ON RACE   116
Plessy and *Brown*   117
De Jure Segregation in the South   118
Distinguishing between *De Jure* and *De Facto* Segregation   120
Fashioning Appropriate Remedies   121
Achieving Unitary Status   122
Postunitary Transfer and School Assignment   124
Race as a Factor in Admission to Private Schools   125
Race Discrimination and Matriculated Students   126

CLASSIFICATIONS BASED ON NATIVE LANGUAGE   127

CLASSIFICATIONS BASED ON SEX   129
Interscholastic Sports   130
Single-Sex Teams   130   /   Fewer Sports Opportunities for Females   132   /   Modified Sports and Separate Seasons for Females   133
Academic Programs   133
Single-Sex Schools   134   /   Sex-Segregated Courses and Programs   135   /   Sex-Based Admission Criteria   135
Sexual Harassment of Students   136
Employee-to-Student Harassment   137   /   Student-to-Student Harassment   137

CONCLUSION   139

POINTS TO PONDER   139

CHAPTER SEVEN

Rights of Students with Disabilities   140

LEGAL CONTEXT   140
Rehabilitation Act   140
Americans with Disabilities Act   143
Individuals with Disabilities Education Act   143

INDIVIDUALIZED EDUCATION PROGRAMS   144
Initial Identification   144
Evaluation   144
IEP Team   146
IEP Preparation   147
Free Appropriate Public Education   148
Least Restrictive Environment   150
Private Schools   151
Public Placement of a Child in a Private School   151   /   Parental Placement of a Child in a Private School   152   /   Services Available in Private Schools   154
Change of Placement   154

RELATED SERVICES   154
   Transportation   155
   Psychological Services   155
   Health and Nursing Services   156

EXTENDED SCHOOL YEAR   156

PARTICIPATION IN SPORTS   157

DISCIPLINE   159
   Suspension   159
   Expulsion   160

PROCEDURAL SAFEGUARDS   162

CONCLUSION   164

POINTS TO PONDER   164

CHAPTER EIGHT

Student Discipline   166

CONDUCT REGULATIONS   167

EXPULSIONS AND SUSPENSIONS   170
   Expulsions   170
         Procedural Requirements   170   /   Zero-Tolerance Policies   172
   Suspensions   173

CORPORAL PUNISHMENT   176
   Constitutional Issues   177
   State Law   178

ACADEMIC SANCTIONS   179
   Absences   179
   Misconduct   180

SEARCH AND SEIZURE   182
   Application of the Fourth Amendment to Students   182
   Lockers   185
   Search of Personal Possessions: Purses, Book Bags, and Other Property   186
   Personal Search of Students   187
   Use of Metal Detectors   189
   Drug-Detecting Canines   190
   Drug Testing   191
   Police Involvement   193

REMEDIES FOR UNLAWFUL DISCIPLINARY ACTIONS   195

CONCLUSION   197

POINTS TO PONDER   197

CHAPTER NINE

Terms and Conditions of Employment   199

LICENSURE   200

EMPLOYMENT BY LOCAL SCHOOL BOARDS   203

Employment Requirements   204
Assignment of Personnel and Duties   205

CONTRACTS   206

Term and Tenure Contracts   208
Supplemental Contracts   209
Domestic Partner Benefits   210
Leaves of Absence   211

PERSONNEL EVALUATIONS   211

PERSONNEL RECORDS   212

REPORTING SUSPECTED CHILD ABUSE   214

COLLECTIVE BARGAINING   216

Teachers' Statutory Bargaining Rights   218
Scope of Negotiations   219
Union Security Provisions   221
Exclusive Privileges   222
Grievances   224
Negotiation Impasse   224

CONCLUSION   226

POINTS TO PONDER   227

CHAPTER TEN

Teachers' Substantive Constitutional Rights   228

FREEDOM OF EXPRESSION   228

Legal Principles   228
Application of the Legal Principles   232
Expression Outside the Classroom   232   /   Prior Restraints and Channel
Rules   235   /   Classroom Expression   237

FREEDOM OF ASSOCIATION   239

Political Affiliations   239
Political Activity   240
Campaigning for Issues and Candidates   240   /   Holding Public Office   241

PERSONAL APPEARANCE   242

CONSTITUTIONAL PRIVACY RIGHTS   243

Search and Seizure   245
Lifestyle Controversies   247

CONCLUSION   249

POINTS TO PONDER   249

CHAPTER ELEVEN

Discrimination in Employment   251

LEGAL CONTEXT   251

Fourteenth Amendment   253
Title VII   253

Disparate Treatment and Impact   253   /   Retaliation   255   /   Relief   255

RACE AND NATIONAL-ORIGIN DISCRIMINATION   256

Hiring and Promotion Practices   256
Adverse Decisions   257
Affirmative Action   258

SEX DISCRIMINATION   259

Hiring and Promotion Practices   260
Compensation Practices   262
Termination, Nonrenewal, and Denial of Tenure   263
Sexual Harassment   263

Quid Pro Quo   264   /   Hostile Environment   264

Pregnancy Discrimination   265
Retirement Benefits   266

RELIGIOUS DISCRIMINATION   266

Hiring and Promotion Practices   267
Accommodation   267

Attire Restrictions   267   /   Personal Leave   268   /   Job Assignments
and Responsibilities   269

Adverse Employment Decisions   269

AGE DISCRIMINATION   270

Hiring and Promotion Practices   271
Compensation and Benefits   271
Adverse Employment Actions   272

Termination, Nonrenewal, Reduction-in-Force   272   /   Retaliation   273

Retirement   273

DISABILITY DISCRIMINATION   274

Qualifying as Disabled   274
Otherwise Qualified   276
Reasonable Accommodation   276
Termination and Nonrenewal   276

CONCLUSION   277

POINTS TO PONDER   277

CHAPTER TWELVE

Termination of Employment   279

PROCEDURAL DUE PROCESS IN GENERAL   279

Dismissal   280
Nonrenewal   281
Establishing Protected Property and Liberty Interests   282
Property Interest   284   /   Liberty Interest   284

PROCEDURAL REQUIREMENTS IN DISCHARGE PROCEEDINGS   285

Notice   287
Hearing   287
Adequate Notice of Hearing   288   /   Waiver of Hearing   288   /   Impartial Hearing   288   /   Evidence   289

DISMISSAL FOR CAUSE   290

Incompetency   291
Immorality   291
Insubordination   293
Unprofessional Conduct   294
Neglect of Duty   295
Other Good and Just Cause   296
Reduction-in-Force   296

REMEDIES FOR VIOLATIONS OF PROTECTED RIGHTS   298

Liability of School Officials   298
Liability of School Districts   300
Remedies   301
Damages   301   /   Reinstatement   302   /   Attorneys' Fees   302

CONCLUSION   303

POINTS TO PONDER   303

CHAPTER THIRTEEN

Summary of Legal Generalizations   305

GENERALIZATIONS   305

CONCLUSION   311

Appendix   312

Glossary   313

Selected Supreme Court Cases   315

Index   317

PREFACE

It has never been more imperative for teachers to understand the law. Since World War II, lawmakers have significantly reshaped educational policy. Most school personnel are aware of the escalating litigation and legislation, and some are familiar with the names of a few landmark Supreme Court decisions. But many educators do not understand basic legal principles that are being applied to educational questions. As a result, they are uncertain about the legality of daily decisions they must make in schools. Information provided in this book should help alleviate concerns voiced by educators who feel that the scales of justice have been tipped against them.

Material in *Legal Rights of Teachers and Students* is drawn from the sixth edition of *Public School Law: Teachers' and Students' Rights* (2009) that the three of us also authored. For this condensed book, we have selected topics particularly pertinent to classroom teachers. In analyzing specific school situations, we have explored the tension between government controls and individual freedoms in the school context. Implications of legal mandates are discussed and guidelines are provided for educators. Throughout the chapters, we have highlighted in bold type or boxes some of the most important legal concepts. Also, we have included a number of tables, figures, and scenarios to make the information more meaningful.

We have attempted to cover the topics thoroughly but in a nontechnical manner, avoiding the extensive use of legal terms. However, the topics are documented in footnotes that appear at the bottom of pages if the reader wants to explore specific cases or points of law in greater detail. These notes provide additional information on selected cases and should assist the reader in understanding specific concepts. Also, a glossary of basic legal terms and a table of selected Supreme Court cases are provided at the end of the book.

A few comments about the nature of the law might assist the reader in using this book. Laws are not created in a vacuum; they reflect the social and philosophical attitudes of society. Moreover, individuals who have personal opinions and biases make laws. Although one may prefer to think that the law is always objective, personal considerations and national political trends do have an impact on the development and interpretation of legal principles.

Also, the law is not static, but rather is continually evolving as courts reinterpret constitutional and statutory provisions and as legislatures enact new laws. In the 1960s and early 1970s, courts and legislative bodies tended to focus on the expansion of personal rights through civil rights laws and constitutional interpretations favoring the individual's right to be free from unwarranted government intrusions. However, since 1975, judicial rulings have supported government authority to impose restraints on individual freedoms in the school context in the interest of the collective welfare. Although the themes of educational equity and individual rights, which dominated litigation earlier, remain important, efforts to attain educational excellence have generated a new genre of legal activity pertaining to teachers' qualifications and performance standards for students.

In this book, much of the discussion of the law focuses on court cases because the judiciary plays a vital role in interpreting constitutional and legislative provisions. Decisions are highlighted that illustrate points of law or legal trends, with particular emphasis on recent litigation. A few cases are pursued in depth to provide the reader with an understanding of the rationale behind the decisions. Reviewing the factual situations that have generated these controversies should make it easier for educators to identify potential legal problems in their own school situations.

As we complete this book, judicial decisions are being rendered and statutes are being proposed that may alter the status of the law vis-a-vis teachers and students. Additionally, some questions confronting school personnel have not yet been addressed by the Supreme Court and have generated conflicting decisions among lower courts. It may be frustrating to a reader searching for concrete answers to learn that in some areas the law is far from clear.

In spite of unresolved issues, certain legal principles have been established and can provide direction in many school situations. It is important for educators to become familiar with these principles and to use them to guide their decisions. Although the issues generating legal concern will change over time, knowledge of the logic underlying the law can make teachers more confident in dealing with questions that have not been clarified by courts or legislatures.

We have attempted to arrange the chapters in logical sequence for those reading the book in its entirety or using it as a text for school law courses. An introductory chapter establishes the legal context for the subsequent examination of students' and teachers' rights, and a concluding chapter provides a summary of the major legal principles. Subheadings appear within chapters to facilitate using this book for reference if a specific issue is of immediate interest. The reader is encouraged, however, to read the entire text because some topics are addressed in several chapters from different perspectives, and many of the principles of law transcend chapter divisions. Taken together, the chapters provide an overall picture of the relationship among issues and the applicable legal principles.

The material will assist school personnel in understanding the current application of the law, but it is not intended to serve as a substitute for legal counsel. Educators confronting legal problems should always seek the advice of an attorney. Also, there is no attempt here to predict the future course of courts and legislatures. Given the dynamic nature of the law, no single text can serve to keep teachers abreast of current legal developments. If we can provide an awareness of rights and responsibilities, motivate educators to translate the basic concepts into actual practice, and generate an interest in further study of the law, our purposes in writing this book will have been achieved.

ACKNOWLEDGMENTS

A number of individuals contributed to the completion of this book. We are extremely grateful to our students who reacted to various drafts of the chapters and assisted in checking citations. Our sincere thanks go to several education graduate students and law students who provided valuable assistance in reviewing drafts of chapters, locating legal materials, and verifying citations: Justin Bathon, Rozlind Gallaspie, Tonya Gendin, Stephen Harper, Lindsy Hitesman, Lisa Lee, Emily Richardson, Janet Rumple, and Lei Wang. In addition, we appreciate the cheerful and conscientious assistance provided by staff members Susan Hanns, Stephanie Maynard, Gloria Sanders, and Cindy Wedemeyer.

This book would not have been completed without the support of our families, who offered constant encouragement as they do in all our professional endeavors. Their contributions simply cannot be measured.

CHAPTER ONE

LEGAL FRAMEWORK
OF PUBLIC EDUCATION

The authority for the establishment and control of American public education, which serves about 48,000,000 students, is grounded in law. State and federal constitutional and statutory provisions provide the framework within which school operational decisions are made. Policies and practices at any level of the educational enterprise must be consistent with legal mandates from higher authorities. The overlapping jurisdictions of federal and state constitutions, Congress and state legislatures, federal and state courts, and various government agencies (including local school boards and school-based councils) present a complex environment for educators attempting to comply with legal requirements. In an effort to untangle the various legal relationships, this chapter describes the major sources of law and how they interact to form the legal basis for public education. This overview establishes a context for subsequent chapters in which legal principles are discussed more fully as they apply to specific school situations.

STATE CONTROL OF EDUCATION

Since the United States Constitution does not authorize Congress to provide for education, the legal control of public education resides with the state as one of its sovereign powers.

The Tenth Amendment to the United States Constitution stipulates that "the powers not delegated to the United States by the Constitution, nor prohibited by it to the states, are reserved to the states respectively, or to the people." The Supreme Court repeatedly has affirmed the comprehensive authority of the states and school officials to control public schools as long as actions are consistent with fundamental federal constitutional safeguards. The state's authority over education is considered comparable to its powers to tax and to provide for the general welfare of its citizens. Although each state's educational system has unique features, many similarities are found across states.

Legislative Power

All state constitutions specifically address the legislative responsibility for establishing public schools. Usually the legislature is charged with providing for a uniform, thorough and efficient, or adequate system of public education. In contrast to the federal government, which has only those powers specified in the United States Constitution, state legislatures retain all powers not expressly forbidden by state or federal constitutional provisions. Thus, **the state legislature has plenary, or absolute, power to make laws governing education.**

At present, all 50 states require that students between specified ages (usually 6 to 16) attend a public or private school or receive equivalent instruction to ensure an educated citizenry. States can authorize exemptions to compulsory attendance (e.g., married students) and can attach conditions to school enrollment (e.g., vaccination against communicable diseases). In addition, legislatures are empowered to create, consolidate, and abolish school districts; raise revenue and distribute educational funds; control teacher certification; prescribe curricular offerings; impose fees for textbooks; establish pupil performance standards; and regulate specific aspects of public school operations.

Legislatures also can authorize other school governance arrangements, such as state-funded charter schools that operate outside many regulations on the basis of a charter granted by the state or local board of education or other entities. The charter school movement has been characterized as one of the fastest growing education reform efforts nationally. **Since 1991, 40 states and the District of Columbia have enacted laws authorizing charter schools, usually specifying a cap on the number of charters granted to existing public or private schools or groups starting new schools.**[1] The number of charter schools ranges from one in a few states to more than 400 in Arizona and California. Charter schools account for less than 2 percent of all students, but their enrollment continues to increase as states approve new legislation and expand existing laws.

In some instances, when state laws are subject to several interpretations, courts are called on to clarify legislative intent or to assess the constitutionality of provisions. A state's attorney general also may be asked to interpret a law or to advise school boards on the legality of their actions, and such opinions are binding unless overruled by the judiciary.

Although the state legislature cannot relinquish its lawmaking powers, it can delegate to subordinate agencies the authority to make rules and regulations necessary to implement laws. These administrative functions must be carried out within the guidelines established by the legislature. Some states are quite liberal in delegating administrative authority, whereas other states prescribe detailed standards that must be followed by subordinate agencies. **It is a widely held perception that local school boards control public education; in reality they have only those powers conferred by the state.** Courts consistently have reiterated that the authority for public education is not a local one, but rather is a central power residing in the state legislature. School buildings are considered state property, local school board members are state officials, and teachers are state employees. Public school funds, regardless of where collected, are state funds.

---

[1]Center for Education Reform, *Charter School Highlights and Statistics*, 2007, available at http://edreform.com/pubs/chglance.htm.

State Agencies

Since it has been neither feasible nor desirable to include in statutes every minor detail governing public schools, all states except Wisconsin have established a state board of education that typically supplies the structural details to implement broad legislative mandates. In most states, members of the state board of education are elected by the citizenry or appointed by the governor, and the board usually functions immediately below the legislature in the hierarchy of educational governance.

Accreditation is an important tool used by state boards to compel local school districts to abide by their directives. School districts often must satisfy state accreditation requirements as a condition of receiving state funds. Though models vary among states, the most common approach involves the establishment of minimum standards in areas such as curriculum, teacher qualifications, instructional materials, and facilities. In some states, different grades of school accreditation exist, with financial incentives in place to encourage local schools to attain the highest level. **Since the mid-1980s, there has been a movement toward performance-based accreditation under which a school's performance is assessed against predicted outcomes calculated for the school in areas such as pupil achievement, absenteeism, and retention.**

Within legislative parameters, the state board of education can issue directives governing school operations. In some states, rules pertaining to such matters as proficiency testing for students and programs for children with disabilities are embodied in state board rules rather than state law. The judiciary generally has upheld decisions made by state boards of education, unless they have violated legislative or constitutional mandates.

State boards of education, however, cannot abrogate powers delegated by law to other agencies. In 1991, the North Carolina Supreme Court held that the state board's prohibition on local board contracts with Whittle Communications interfered with school districts' statutory authority to enter into contracts for supplementary materials.[2] The school board's contract to air daily classroom broadcasts of Channel One (a news program including advertisements) in return for television equipment was within the local board's delegated authority.

In addition to the state board, generally considered a policy-making body, all states have designated a chief state school officer (CSSO), who often is known as the superintendent of public instruction or commissioner of education and functions in an executive capacity. The duties of the CSSO include engaging in research and long-range planning, monitoring reform initiatives, and adjudicating educational controversies. When considering an appeal of a CSSO's decision, courts will not judge the wisdom of the decision or overrule such a decision unless it is clearly arbitrary or against the preponderance of evidence. Each state also has established a state department of education, consisting of educational specialists who provide consultation to the state board, CSSO, and local school boards.

[2]State v. Whittle Communications & Thomasville City Bd. of Educ., 402 S.E.2d 556 (N.C. 1991), *reh'g denied*, 404 S.E.2d 878 (N.C. 1991).

Local School Boards

Although public education in the United States is state controlled, it is for the most part locally administered. All states except Hawaii have created local school boards in addition to state education agencies and have delegated certain administrative authority over schools to these local boards. **Nationwide, there are approximately 14,200 local districts, ranging from a few students to several hundred thousand.** Some states, particularly those with a large number of small school districts, have established intermediate or regional administrative units that perform regulatory or service functions for several local districts.

As with the delegation of authority to state agencies, delegation of powers to local school boards is handled very differently across states. Some states with a deeply rooted tradition of local control over education (e.g., Colorado) give local boards a great deal of latitude in making operational decisions about schools. In states that tend toward centralized control of education (e.g., Florida), local boards must function within the framework of detailed legislative directives. **State legislatures retain the legal responsibility for education and can restrict the discretion of local boards by enacting legislation to that effect.**

The citizenry within the school district usually elects local school board members. The United States Supreme Court has recognized that the Equal Protection Clause of the Fourteenth Amendment to the federal Constitution requires each qualified voter to be given an opportunity to participate in the election of board members, with each vote given the same weight as far as practicable. When board members are elected from geographical districts, such districts must be established to protect voting rights under the "one person, one vote" principle. If "at-large" elections result in a dilution of the minority vote, an abridgment of the federal Voting Rights Act may be found.[3] However, the Supreme Court in 1996 struck down congressional redistricting plans drawn on the basis of race,[4] so the creation of race-based voting districts to ensure that a majority of the voters for designated school board seats are people of color would likely abridge the Fourteenth Amendment.[5]

The state legislature can specify the qualifications, method of selection, terms and conditions, and procedures for removal of local school board members. A local board must act as a body; individual board members are not empowered to make policies or perform official acts on behalf of the board. School boards have some discretion in adopting operational procedures, but they are legally bound to adhere to such procedures once established. **Although courts are reluctant to interfere with decisions made by boards of education and will not rule on the wisdom of such decisions, they will invalidate any board action that is arbitrary, capricious, or outside the board's legal authority (i.e., an *ultra vires* act).**

School board meetings and records must be open to the public. Most states have enacted "sunshine" or "open meeting" laws that specify exceptions, such as allowing school boards to meet in executive session to discuss matters that threaten public safety or pertain to pending or current litigation, personnel matters, collective bargaining, or the disposition of

---

[3] 42 U.S.C. § 1971 *et seq.* (2008). Section 1973 states that "no practice or procedure shall be imposed or applied . . . in a manner which results in a denial or abridgment of the right . . . to vote on account of race." *See, e.g.,* Moore v. Itawamba County, Miss., 431 F.3d 257 (5th Cir. 2005).

[4] Bush v. Vera, 517 U.S. 952 (1996); Shaw v. Hunt, 517 U.S. 899 (1996).

[5] *See, e.g.,* Cannon v. N.C. State Bd. of Educ., 917 F. Supp. 387 (E.D.N.C. 1996) (holding that the creation of race-based single board member voting districts threatened equal protection rights).

real property. Discussion of these matters may take place in closed meetings, but statutes usually stipulate that formal action must occur in open meetings.

Local school boards hold powers specified or implied in state law and other powers considered necessary to achieve the purposes of the express powers. These delegated powers generally encompass the authority to determine the details of the curriculum offered within the school district, raise revenue to build and maintain schools, select personnel, and enact other policies necessary to implement the educational program pursuant to law. Courts have recognized that even without specific enabling legislation, local boards have discretionary authority to enter into contracts and make decisions necessary to operate the schools.[6] But, local school boards cannot delegate their decision-making authority to other agencies or associations.

School-Based Councils

Since the mid-1980s, the notion of decentralizing many operational decisions to the school level (site-based management) has received considerable attention. Several legal controversies have focused on the composition and authority of these councils. In 1995, the Seventh Circuit upheld an Illinois law creating elected school councils, empowered to hire personnel and approve budgets and programs, in the Chicago public schools.[7]

The 1990 Kentucky Education Reform Act entailed major changes in school funding, curriculum, and governance, including the creation of school-based councils with authority for policy decisions affecting school sites. Whereas local school boards retain many of their traditional powers, such as establishing schools, setting tax rates and budgets, and maintaining facilities, school-based councils are authorized to hire the building principal, select textbooks, and make policy decisions in other areas such as curricular offerings, staff assignments, and student discipline. In 1994, teachers challenged a local board's decision to require school-based councils to obtain board approval before implementing school improvement plans. Noting some overlap in duties between local boards and school councils, the Kentucky Supreme Court reasoned that the state did not delegate to local boards approval authority over council decisions pertaining to school improvement plans.[8] The court reasoned that the state law granting school-based councils independent policy-making powers constituted a clear delegation of legislative authority to the school level. Decisions of school-based councils have the force of law and will not be invalidated by the judiciary unless the councils act beyond their scope of delegated authority or impair protected rights.

Local boards of education and, in some jurisdictions, school-based councils are authorized to perform discretionary duties (i.e., those involving judgment), whereas school employees (e.g., superintendents, principals, teachers) can perform only ministerial duties necessary to carry out policies. Hence, a superintendent can recommend personnel to be hired and propose a budget, but the school board, or in some instances the

---

[6]In recent years, corporations such as the Edison Project have attracted substantial attention because of their contracts to manage public schools and school districts. Also, several companies, such as Sylvan Learning Systems, Britannica Learning Centers, and Berlitz Language Schools have more limited contracts with public school districts to provide intensive tutoring or specialized instruction.

[7]Pittman v. Chi. Bd. of Educ., 64 F.3d 1098 (7th Cir. 1995).

[8]Bd. of Educ. v. Bushee, 889 S.W.2d 809 (Ky. 1994).

school council, must make the actual decisions. Although it might appear that educators at the building level retain little decision-making authority, administrators as well as classroom teachers can enact rules and regulations, consistent with policies and laws from higher authorities, to ensure the efficient operation of the school or class under their supervision.

■ ■ ■ ■ ■

FEDERAL ROLE IN EDUCATION

The federal government influences public education through its funding powers and the enforcement of constitutional rights.

Unlike state constitutions, the United States Constitution is silent regarding education; hence, individuals do not have an inherent federally protected right to an education.[9] The Constitution, however, does confer basic rights on individuals, and these rights must be respected by school personnel. Furthermore, Congress exerts control over the use of federal education aid and regulates other aspects of schools through legislation enacted pursuant to its constitutionally granted powers.

United States Constitution

A constitution is a body of precepts providing the system of fundamental laws of a nation, state, or society. The United States Constitution establishes a separation of powers among the executive, judicial, and legislative branches of government. These three branches form a system of checks and balances to ensure that the intent of the Constitution is respected. The Constitution also provides a systematic process for altering the document, if deemed necessary. Article V stipulates that amendments may be proposed by a two-thirds vote of each house of Congress or by a special convention called by Congress at the request of two-thirds of the state legislatures. Proposed amendments then must be ratified by three-fourths of the states to become part of the Constitution.

The United States Constitution is the supreme law in this nation, and state authority over education must be exercised in a manner consistent with its provisions. All federal constitutional mandates affect public education to some degree, but the following provisions have had the greatest impact on public school policies and practices.

General Welfare Clause.   Under Article I, Section 8, of the Constitution, Congress has the power "to lay and collect taxes, duties, imposts and excises, to pay the debts and provide for the common defense and general welfare of the United States." In 1937, the Supreme Court declared that it will not interfere with the discretion of Congress in its domain, unless Congress exhibits a clear display of arbitrary power.[10]

---

[9]San Antonio Indep. Sch. Dist. v. Rodriguez, 411 U.S. 1 (1973) (holding that there is no explicit or implied fundamental right to an education under the United States Constitution).

[10]Helvering v. Dains, 301 U.S. 619, 644–645 (1937).

Using the general welfare rationale, Congress has enacted legislation providing substantial federal support for research and instructional programs in areas such as science, mathematics, reading, special education, vocational education, career education, and bilingual education. Congress also has provided financial assistance for the school lunch program and for services to meet the special needs of various groups of students, such as the educationally and culturally disadvantaged. In addition, Congress has responded to national health and safety concerns with legislation such as the 1980 Asbestos School Hazard Detection and Control Act and the 1988 Indoor Radon Abatement Act, which require the inspection of school buildings and, if necessary, remedial action to assure the safety of students and employees. As addressed in Chapter 4, given the increasing use of the Internet, the federal government has attempted to protect the welfare of minors by policing the suitability of materials made available to them electronically.

Obligation of Contracts Clause.   Article I, Section 10, of the Constitution stipulates that states cannot enact any law impairing the obligation of contracts. Contracted arrangements are common in schools. Administrators, teachers, and noncertified personnel are protected from arbitrary dismissals by contractual agreements. School boards also enter into numerous contracts with individuals and companies in conducting school business. The judiciary often is called on to evaluate the validity of a given contract or to assess whether a party has breached its contractual obligations.

First Amendment.   The Bill of Rights, comprised of the first 10 amendments to the United States Constitution, safeguards individual liberties against government encroachment. The most preciously guarded of these liberties are contained in the First Amendment's protection of speech, press, assembly, and religious liberties. The religion clauses have evoked a number of lawsuits challenging government aid to and regulation of nonpublic schools and contesting public school policies and practices as advancing religion or impairing free exercise rights. Cases involving students' rights to express themselves and to distribute literature have been initiated under First Amendment guarantees of freedom of speech and press. Moreover, teachers' rights to academic freedom and to speak out on matters of public concern have precipitated numerous lawsuits. The right of assembly has been the focus of litigation involving student clubs and employees' rights to organize and engage in collective bargaining.

Fourth Amendment.   This amendment guarantees the right of citizens "to be secure in their persons, houses, papers, and effects against unreasonable searches and seizures." It safeguards individuals against arbitrary government intrusions and has frequently appeared in educational cases involving drug-testing programs and searches of students' lockers, cars, and persons. A few cases also have involved alleged violations of school employees' Fourth Amendment rights by school officials.

Fourteenth Amendment.   The Fourteenth Amendment, adopted in 1868, is the most widely invoked constitutional provision in school litigation since it specifically addresses state action. In part, the Fourteenth Amendment provides that no state shall "deny to any person within its jurisdiction, the equal protection of the laws." This clause has been significant in school cases involving alleged discrimination based on race, sex, ethnic background, and disabilities. In addition, school finance litigation often has been based on the Equal Protection Clause.

The Due Process Clause of the Fourteenth Amendment, which prohibits states from depriving citizens of life, liberty, or property without due process of law, also has played an important role in school litigation. Property rights are legitimate expectations of entitlement created through state laws, regulations, or contracts. Compulsory school attendance laws confer on students a legitimate property right to attend school, and the granting of tenure gives teachers a property entitlement to continued employment. Liberty rights include interests in one's reputation and fundamental rights related to marriage, family matters, and personal privacy. In addition, the Supreme Court has interpreted Fourteenth Amendment liberties as incorporating the personal freedoms contained in the Bill of Rights.[11] Thus, the first 10 amendments, originally directed toward the federal government, have been applied to state action as well. Although the concept of "incorporation" has been criticized, Supreme Court precedent supports the notion that the Fourteenth Amendment restricts state interference with fundamental constitutional liberties. **This incorporation principle is particularly important in school litigation since education is a state function; claims that public school policies or practices impair personal freedoms (e.g., First Amendment free speech guarantees) often are initiated through the Fourteenth Amendment.**

The federal judiciary has identified both procedural and substantive components of due process guarantees. Procedural due process ensures fundamental fairness if the government threatens an individual's life, liberty, or property interests; minimum procedures required by the United States Constitution are notice of the charges, an opportunity to refute the charges, and a hearing that is conducted fairly. Substantive due process requires that state action be based on a valid objective with means reasonably related to attaining the objective. In essence, substantive due process shields the individual against arbitrary government action that impairs life, liberty, or property interests.

Since the Fourteenth Amendment protects personal liberties against unwarranted state interference, private institutions, including private schools, usually are not subject to these restrictions. For practices of private schools and other private entities to be challenged successfully under the Fourteenth Amendment, there must be sufficient government involvement in the private school to constitute "state action." This is difficult, although not impossible, to establish. For example, in 2001, the Supreme Court ruled that private organizations regulating interscholastic sports and other activities among private and public schools are considered state actors if sufficiently involved with state school officials.[12] Thus, private high school athletic associations can be liable for constitutional violations.

Federal Legislation

Congress is empowered to enact laws to translate the intent of the United States Constitution into actual practices. **Laws reflect the will of the legislative branch of government, which, theoretically, in a democracy represents the citizenry.** Because the states have

[11]*See* Cantwell v. Connecticut, 310 U.S. 296, 303 (1940); Gitlow v. New York, 268 U.S. 652, 666 (1925).

[12]Brentwood Acad. v. Tenn. Secondary Sch. Athletic Ass'n, 531 U.S. 288 (2001).

sovereign power regarding education, the federal government's involvement in public schools has been one of indirect support, not direct control.

Funding Laws.   Federal legislation affecting public education was enacted prior to ratification of the Constitution. The Ordinances of 1785 and 1787, providing land grants to states for the maintenance of public schools, encouraged the establishment of public education in many states. However, it was not until the mid-twentieth century that Congress began to play a significant role in stimulating targeted educational reform through its spending powers under the General Welfare Clause.

The most comprehensive law offering financial assistance to schools, the Elementary and Secondary Education Act of 1965 (ESEA), in part supplied funds for compensatory education programs for economically disadvantaged students. With passage of the ESEA, federal aid to education doubled, and the federal government's contribution increased steadily until reaching its high point of over 9 percent of total public education revenue in 1980. The federal share then declined to the 6 to 7 percent range for a period of time, but by 2003–2004 exceeded 9 percent once again.[13]

Congress and federal administrative agencies have exerted considerable influence in shaping public school policies and practices through categorical funding laws and their accompanying administrative regulations. Individual states or school districts have the option of accepting or rejecting such federal assistance, but if categorical aid is accepted, the federal government has the authority to prescribe guidelines for its use and to monitor state and local education agencies to ensure fiscal accountability.

Much of the federal categorical legislation enacted during the 1960s and 1970s provided funds to assist school districts in attaining equity goals and addressing other national priorities. For example, the Bilingual Education Act of 1968 and the Education for All Handicapped Children Act of 1975 (which became the Individuals with Disabilities Education Act of 1990) have provided federal funds to assist education agencies in offering services for students with special needs. Although in the 1980s Congress shifted away from its heavy reliance on categorical federal aid by consolidating some categorical programs into block grants with reduced funding and regulations, aid for economically disadvantaged and English-deficient students and children with disabilities has remained categorical in nature.

In 2002, President George W. Bush signed into law the No Child Left Behind Act (NCLB), the most comprehensive reform of the ESEA since it was enacted in 1965.[14] This law, directed at improving the performance of public schools, pledges that no child will be left in a failing school. Specifically, the law requires states to implement accountability systems with higher performance standards in reading and mathematics along with annual testing of all students in grades 3 through 8. Furthermore, assessment data must be categorized by poverty, ethnicity, race, disability, and limited English proficiency to ensure that no group of children is left behind. The law greatly expands choices for parents of children attending Title I schools (those with high numbers or high percentages of poor children) that do not

[13]National Center for Education Statistics, *Revenues and Expenditures for Public Elementary and Secondary Education* (Washington, DC: U.S. Department of Education, 2006), available at http://nces.ed.gov/programs/digest/d06/tables/dt06_158.asp.

[14]20 U.S.C. § 6301 *et seq.* (2008).

meet state standards. If students are in a school that has been identified as low performing, they must be given the option of attending a better school within the district, including charter schools. For students attending persistently failing schools (failure to make adequate yearly progress in three of the four preceding years), the school district must permit the students to use Title I funds to obtain supplemental educational services (e.g., tutoring, after-school or summer programs) from either public or private providers. Persistently failing schools face mandated reconstitution if they do not make adequate yearly progress.

The NCLB's emphasis on high-stakes testing to assess whether schools have made appropriate annual progress has been the source of controversy,[15] as has the treatment of children with disabilities and English Language Learners (ELLS) in such testing programs. Some critics of the law contend that the public school curriculum has been narrowed to focus too much on the subjects being tested under accountability mandates. Also, variations across states in the rigor of the mandatory exams and the selection of passing scores have been controversial.

Civil Rights Laws.   In addition to laws providing financial assistance to public schools, Congress has enacted legislation designed to clarify the scope of individuals' civil rights. **Unlike the discretion enjoyed by state and local education agencies in deciding whether to participate in federal funding programs, educational institutions must comply with these civil rights laws.** Some federal anti-discrimination laws are enacted to enforce constitutional rights and have general application. Others apply only to recipients of federal financial assistance. Various federal agencies are charged with monitoring compliance with these laws and can bring suit against noncomplying institutions. Under some civil rights laws, individuals also can initiate private suits to compel compliance and, in some instances, to obtain personal remedies.

Several laws enacted in the latter part of the nineteenth century to protect the rights of African American citizens were seldom the focus of litigation until the mid-twentieth century. Since the 1960s, these laws, particularly 42 U.S.C. Section 1983, have been used by students and teachers to gain relief in instances in which their federal rights have been violated by school policies and practices. **Section 1983 provides a private right to bring suit for damages against any person who, acting under color of state law, impairs rights secured by the United States Constitution and certain federal laws.**[16] Although Section 1983 does not confer specific substantive rights, it has been significant in school cases because it allows individuals to obtain damages from school officials and school districts for abridgments of federally protected rights. However, Section 1983 cannot be used to enforce federal laws in situations in which congressional intent to create private rights is not explicit.[17]

Subsequent civil rights laws enacted since the 1960s do confer substantive rights to protect citizens from discrimination. The vindication of employees' rights in school settings has generated substantial litigation under Title VII of the Civil Rights Act of 1964, which prohibits employment discrimination on the basis of race, color, sex, religion, or

---

[15]*See* Sharon L. Nichols and David C. Berliner, *Collateral Damage: How High-Stakes Testing Corrupts America's Schools* (Cambridge, MA: Harvard Education Press, 2007).

[16]School boards as well as school officials are considered "persons" under 42 U.S.C. § 1983 (2008). *See* text accompanying note 84, Chapter 12.

[17]*See* Gonzaga Univ. v. Doe, 536 U.S. 273 (2002) (finding that Congress did not intend to create privately enforceable rights under the Family Education Rights and Privacy Act); text accompanying note 88, Chapter 4.

national origin. Modeled in part after Title VII, the Americans with Disabilities Act of 1990 provides specific protections in employment and public accommodations for individuals with disabilities. Also, the Age Discrimination in Employment Act of 1967 protects employees over age 40 against age-based employment discrimination. Other civil rights laws pertain only to institutions housing programs that receive federal funds, such as Title VI of the Civil Rights Act of 1964 (prohibiting discrimination on the basis of race, color, or national origin), Title IX of the Education Amendments of 1972 (barring sex discrimination against participants in education programs), the Rehabilitation Act of 1973 (prohibiting discrimination against otherwise qualified persons with disabilities), and the Age Discrimination Act of 1975 (barring age discrimination in federally assisted programs or activities). Courts often have been called on to interpret these acts and their regulations as they apply to educational practices.

Still other federal laws offer protections to individuals in educational settings and place responsibilities on school officials. For example, the Family Educational Rights and Privacy Act guarantees parents access to their children's school records and safeguards the confidentiality of such records. Federal laws also protect human subjects in research projects and require parental consent before students participate in federally supported psychiatric or psychological examination, testing, or treatment designed to reveal information in specified sensitive areas. Courts have played an important role in interpreting the protections included in these laws and ensuring compliance with the federal mandates.

Federal Administrative Agencies

Similar to state governments, much of the regulatory activity at the federal level is conducted by administrative agencies. In 1980, the Department of Education was created; its secretary, who serves as a member of the president's cabinet, is appointed by the president with the advice and approval of the Senate. Regulations promulgated by the Department of Education to implement funding laws have had a significant impact on many schools. The department administers regulations for over 100 different programs ranging from services for Native American students to projects for school dropouts.

Through their regulatory activities, numerous federal agencies influence state and local education policies. For example, the Office for Civil Rights and the Equal Employment Opportunity Commission have reviewed claims of discrimination in public schools and initiated suits against school districts that are not in compliance with civil rights laws. The Environmental Protection Agency also has placed obligations on schools in connection with asbestos removal and maintenance of safe school environments. School districts can face the termination of federal assistance if they do not comply with such federal regulations.

FUNCTION AND STRUCTURE OF THE JUDICIAL SYSTEM

Courts do not initiate laws, but they influence the law by interpreting the meaning of constitutional and statutory provisions.

Judicial decisions are usually cited in conjunction with statutory and constitutional provisions as a major source of educational law. As early as 1835, Alexis de Tocqueville noted that "scarcely any political question arises in the United States that is not resolved, sooner or later, into a judicial question."[18] Courts play an important role in applying principles of law to settle disputes. The terms *common law* and *case law* refer to judicially created legal principles that are relied on as precedent when similar factual situations arise.

Although most constitutional provisions and statutory enactments never become the subject of litigation, some provisions require judicial clarification. Since federal and state constitutions set forth broad policy statements rather than specific guides to action, courts serve an important function in interpreting such mandates and in determining the legality of various school policies and practices.

The Supreme Court has articulated specific guidelines for exercising the power of judicial review. The Court will not decide hypothetical cases and will not render an opinion on issues in nonadversarial proceedings. A genuine controversy must be initiated by a party with standing to sue. To achieve such standing, the party must have a "real interest" in the outcome of the case, such as having been adversely affected by the challenged practice. The Court also will not anticipate a constitutional question or decide a case on constitutional grounds if there is some other basis for resolving the dispute. **In applying appropriate principles of law to specific cases, the Court generally follows the doctrine of *stare decisis* (abide by decided cases), and thus relies on precedents established in previous decisions.** On occasion, however, the Court does overrule a prior opinion.

Procedures vary somewhat by type of suit and jurisdiction, but a plaintiff typically initiates a suit by filing a complaint with the appropriate court clerk. After a period of *discovery* when evidence is gathered, the defendant may submit a *motion to dismiss*, arguing that the plaintiff failed to state a legal claim or that the claim was barred by the applicable statute of limitations (i.e., the plaintiff failed to file timely). Furthermore, either party may request *summary judgment*, noting that facts of the case are not in dispute and that the party is entitled to judgment based on applicable law. If summary judgment is not granted, the plaintiff's case then is presented. At that point, a *directed verdict* (state trials) or *judgment as a matter of law* (federal trials) may be awarded if the plaintiff fails to establish a legal violation, or if the defendant is unsuccessful in identifying a proper defense. When a directed verdict is not granted, the defendant's case is then presented.

In cases argued before a judge, the trial judge holds a hearing to make findings of fact based on the evidence presented and then applies legal principles to those facts in rendering a judgment. If the case involves a jury trial, the jury renders a verdict, identifying the prevailing party and appropriate awards. Either party may file a motion for a *judgment notwithstanding the verdict* if believed that the jury made an error as a matter of law. Also, either party may file a motion for a new trial, alleging that proper procedures were not followed, or appeal the decision to a higher court. Figure 1.1 displays the steps (civil procedure) that typically are followed at the trial court level.

If the ruling is appealed, the appellate court must accept the trial court's findings of fact unless they are clearly erroneous. The appeals court reviews the written record of the

[18]Alexis de Tocqueville, *Democracy in America*, rev. ed. (New York: Alfred A. Knopf, 1960), vol. 1, p. 280.

FIGURE 1.1   Civil Procedure

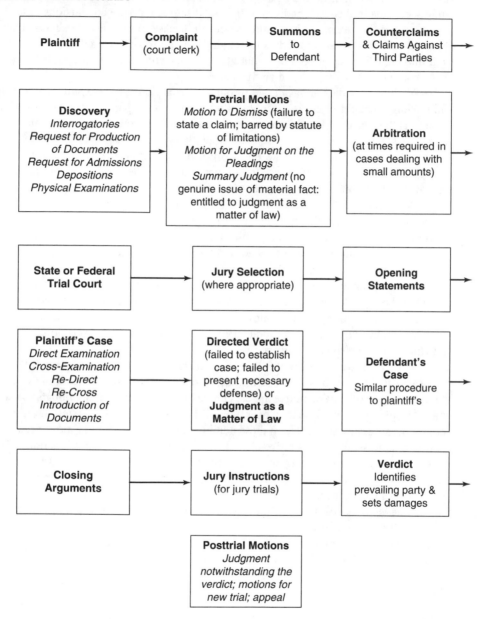

evidence but does not hold a hearing for witnesses to be questioned. The appellate court may accept the trial court's findings of fact but disagree with the conclusions of law.

In addition to individual suits,[19] education cases often involve class-action suits brought on behalf of all similarly situated individuals. To be certified as a class action, the suit must satisfy rules of civil procedure that specify prerequisites to establish class members' commonality of injury and circumstances.

Various remedies are available through court action. In some suits, a court-ordered injunction is sought to compel school officials to cease a particular action or to remove restraints they have imposed on protected freedoms. For a court to issue an injunction, evidence must indicate that the complainant would likely prevail in a trial on the merits of the case. Judicial relief also can take the form of a declaration that specific rights must be respected. In addition, courts can order personal remedies, such as reinstatement and removal of material from school records. Courts also can award damages to compensate individuals for the deprivation of their rights, and punitive damages at times can be assessed against state officials if such deprivations constitute a willful or reckless disregard of protected rights. Under certain circumstances, attorneys' fees can be awarded.

In interpreting constitutional and statutory provisions, courts have developed various criteria to evaluate whether the law has been violated. These judicially created standards or "tests" are extremely important and in some instances appear to go beyond the original intent of the constitutional or statutory provision in question. Judicial standards for assessing claims under various constitutional and statutory provisions are continually evolving and being refined by courts. The judiciary thus occupies a powerful position in shaping the law through its interpretive powers.

Courts, however, will not intervene in a school-related controversy if the dispute can be settled in a legislative or administrative forum. All state educational systems provide some type of administrative appeals procedure for aggrieved individuals to use in disputes involving internal school operations. Many school controversies never reach the courts because they are settled in these administrative forums. Under most circumstances, courts require such administrative appeals to be exhausted before court action is brought. Also, some courts will direct parties to participate in arbitration in an effort to resolve the dispute and avoid a trial.

In evaluating the impact of case law, it is important to keep in mind that a judicial ruling applies as precedent within the geographical jurisdiction of the court delivering the opinion. It is possible for two state supreme courts or two federal courts to render conflicting decisions on an issue, and such decisions are binding in their respective jurisdictions. Only decisions of the United States Supreme Court have national application.

State Courts

State courts are established pursuant to state constitutional provisions, and the structure of judicial systems varies among states. In contrast to federal courts, which have only those

---

[19]Most educational litigation involves civil suits, initiated by individuals alleging injury by another private party. Civil suits often involve claims for damages or requests for specific conduct to cease because it impairs the individual's protected rights. In contrast, criminal suits are brought on behalf of society to punish an individual for committing a crime, such as parents who violate compulsory school attendance laws.

powers granted by the United States Constitution, state courts can review most types of controversies unless restricted by state law. State judicial systems usually include trial courts of general jurisdiction, courts of special jurisdiction, and appellate courts. All states have a court of last resort, and decisions rendered by state high courts can be appealed to the United States Supreme Court.

In most states, the court of last resort is called the supreme court or supreme judicial court. However, in New York and Maryland the highest court is the Court of Appeals, and in West Virginia it is the Supreme Court of Appeals. Courts occupying the next level in the state judicial system usually are referred to as appeals courts or superior courts. State trial courts of general jurisdiction often are called district or circuit courts, but in New York, trial courts are referred to as supreme courts of their respective counties. The most common special jurisdiction courts are juvenile, probate, domestic relations, and small claims. State judges are usually either elected or appointed by the governor.

Federal Courts

Article III, Section I, of the United States Constitution establishes the Supreme Court and authorizes Congress to create other federal courts as necessary. The federal court system contains courts of special jurisdiction such as the Claims Court, Tax Court, and Court of International Trade. There are three levels of federal courts of general jurisdiction: district courts, circuit courts of appeal, and the Supreme Court. The number of federal district courts in a state is based on population. Each state has at least one federal district court; many states have two or three; and California, New York, and Texas have four each. Judgments at the district court level are usually presided over by one judge.

On the federal appeals level, the nation is divided into 12 geographic circuits, each with its own federal circuit court of appeals.[20] A thirteenth federal circuit court has national jurisdiction to hear appeals regarding specific claims (e.g., customs; copyrights, patents, and trademarks; international trade). Most federal circuit courts have from 15 to 20 judges, but the largest (Ninth Circuit) has more than 40 judges. Circuit decisions usually are rendered by a panel of the court, but in some instances the entire court *(en banc)* will rehear a case. Although a federal circuit court decision is binding only in the states within that circuit, such decisions often influence other appellate courts when dealing with similar questions. The jurisdiction of the federal circuits is as follows:

- *First Circuit*: Maine, Massachusetts, New Hampshire, Rhode Island, and Puerto Rico
- *Second Circuit*: Connecticut, New York, and Vermont
- *Third Circuit*: Delaware, New Jersey, Pennsylvania, and the Virgin Islands
- *Fourth Circuit*: Maryland, North Carolina, South Carolina, Virginia, and West Virginia
- *Fifth Circuit*: Louisiana, Mississippi, Texas, and the Canal Zone
- *Sixth Circuit*: Kentucky, Michigan, Ohio, and Tennessee
- *Seventh Circuit*: Illinois, Indiana, and Wisconsin
- *Eighth Circuit*: Arkansas, Iowa, Minnesota, Missouri, Nebraska, North Dakota, and South Dakota

[20]In 1981, the Fifth Circuit was divided into the Fifth and Eleventh Circuits.

- *Ninth Circuit*: Alaska, Arizona, California, Idaho, Hawaii, Montana, Nevada, Oregon, Washington, and Guam
- *Tenth Circuit*: Colorado, Kansas, New Mexico, Oklahoma, Utah, and Wyoming
- *Eleventh Circuit*: Alabama, Florida, and Georgia
- *D.C. Circuit*: Washington, D.C.[21]
- *Federal Circuit*: National jurisdiction on specific claims

The United States Supreme Court is, of course, the highest court in the nation, beyond which there is no appeal. **It has been firmly established that the Supreme Court has the ultimate authority in interpreting federal constitutional guarantees.**[22] If the Supreme Court finds a specific practice unconstitutional (e.g., intentional school segregation), this judicial mandate applies nationwide. If the Court, however, concludes that a given activity does not impair federal constitutional guarantees (e.g., corporal punishment in public schools), states and local school boards retain discretion in placing restrictions on the activity. In the latter instances, legal requirements will vary across jurisdictions.

When the judiciary interprets a statutory enactment contrary to legislative intent, the law can be amended to clarify its purpose. Congress has done so with a number of civil rights laws in response to Supreme Court rulings. However, the legislative branch does not have this discretion in connection with constitutional interpretations. If the Supreme Court rules that a federal law conflicts with a provision of the United States Constitution, the only recourse to keep the law is to amend the Constitution. Given the significance of Supreme Court decisions and the nine justices' lifetime appointments, the composition of the Court is critically important.

The Supreme Court has original jurisdiction in cases in which a state is a party or that involve federal ambassadors and other public ministers. The Court has appellate jurisdiction in other cases arising under the Constitution or federal laws or entailing disputes between states or parties residing in different states.[23] The Supreme Court disposes of approximately 5,000 cases a year, but renders a written opinion on the merits in less than 5 percent of these cases. The Court often concludes that the topic of a case is not appropriate or of sufficient significance to warrant Supreme Court review. It requires concurrence of at least four justices for a case to be accepted, and denial of review (*certiorari*) does not infer agreement with the lower court's decision even though that decision stands. Since the Supreme Court has authority to determine which cases it will hear, many issues are left for resolution by lower courts. Accordingly, precedents regarding some school controversies must be gleaned from federal circuit courts or state supreme courts and may differ from one jurisdiction to another.

An individual need not exhaust state administrative appeals before initiating a federal suit if the abridgment of a federally protected right is involved, but some federal laws specify

---

[21]Washington, D.C., has its own federal district court and circuit court of appeals; only federal laws apply in this jurisdiction.

[22]*See* Marbury v. Madison, 5 U.S. (1 Cranch) 137 (1803).

[23]*See* text accompanying note 94, Chapter 12, for a discussion of Eleventh Amendment restrictions on federal lawsuits brought by citizens against the state.

administrative procedures that must be pursued before commencing court action. Suits involving federal issues also may be heard by state courts, and the United States Supreme Court may review the interpretation of federal rights by the state judiciary. Individuals have a choice whether to initiate a federal or state suit in these circumstances, but they cannot relitigate an issue in federal court if they have been denied relief by the state judiciary. In essence, a federal suit cannot be initiated if the state judiciary has already adjudicated the issue or it could have been raised in the prior state litigation.

Judicial Trends

Traditionally, the federal judiciary did not address educational concerns; fewer than 300 cases involving education had been initiated in federal courts prior to 1954.[24] However, starting with the landmark desegregation decision *Brown v. Board of Education of Topeka* (1954),[25] federal courts assumed a significant role in resolving educational controversies. By 1970, litigation was clearly viewed as an important tool to influence social policies, and more legal challenges to school practices were initiated in the 1970s than had been in the preceding seven decades combined.[26] Since the 1960s, courts have addressed nearly every facet of the educational enterprise. Much of this judicial intervention has involved the protection of individual rights and the attainment of equity for minority groups.

The volume of federal cases pertaining to school issues reached its zenith in the 1970s. Since then, it has stabilized or declined slightly in most areas (e.g., employment concerns, student discipline), except for litigation dealing with church/state issues and the rights of children with disabilities. Indeed, cases involving children with disabilities have increased at a phenomenal rate since 1980.

There has been a notable shift in the posture of the federal judiciary during the past two decades. In the 1960s and early 1970s, federal courts expanded constitutional protections afforded to individuals in school settings, but since the 1980s the federal judiciary has exhibited more deference to the decisions of the legislative and executive branches and greater reluctance to extend the scope of civil rights. **When the Supreme Court strikes down a practice under the Constitution, standards become more uniform nationally, but when the Court defers to local boards, standards vary, reflecting local perspectives.** If the federal judiciary continues to exhibit restraint, volatile political controversies will be assured, because policy makers will have to grapple with issues that formerly were settled through judicial pronouncements.

The Rehnquist Court and Roberts Court, with their strong federalism stance, are redefining the balance of power between the federal government and states. In sharply divided decisions, the Supreme Court has strengthened states' sovereign immunity by precluding federal lawsuits against states unless Congress has abrogated state immunity through legislation enacted to enforce the Fourteenth Amendment. Such congressional intent, however, must be explicit in the federal legislation. For example, in recent cases, the Court held that Congress exceeded its authority in imposing liability on states under the

---

[24]John Hogan, *The Schools, the Courts, and the Public Interest* (Lexington, MA: D.C. Heath, 1985), p. 11.

[25]347 U.S. 483 (1954).

[26]William Bennett, "Excessive Legalization in Education," *Chicago Daily Law Bulletin* (February 22, 1988), p. 2.

Age Discrimination in Employment Act[27] and the Americans with Disabilities Act.[28] Although the new federalism limits suits against states, school districts will not benefit from the immunity unless they are considered an arm of the state for Eleventh Amendment purposes.[29]

The debate will likely continue over whether courts have the competence to play a key role in shaping educational policies and whether it is legitimate for courts to play such a role, but it cannot be questioned that courts influence school policies. Despite some deceleration in federal litigation, the volume of school cases is still substantial, far outstripping school litigation in any other nation.

CONCLUSION

Public schools in the United States are governed by a complex body of regulations that is grounded in constitutional provisions, statutory enactments, agency regulations, and court decisions. Since the mid-twentieth century, legislation relating to schools has increased significantly in both volume and complexity, and courts have played an important role in interpreting statutory and constitutional provisions. Although rules made at any level must be consistent with higher authority, administrators and teachers retain considerable latitude in establishing rules and procedures within their specific jurisdictions. As long as educators act reasonably and do not impair the protected rights of others, their actions will be upheld if challenged in court.

[27]Kimel v. Fla. Bd. of Regents, 528 U.S. 62 (2000).

[28]Bd. of Trs. v. Garrett, 531 U.S. 356 (2001).

[29]*See* text accompanying note 98, Chapter 12.

CHAPTER TWO

TORT LIABILITY

Tort law offers civil rather than criminal remedies to individuals for harm caused by the unreasonable conduct of others. A *tort* is described as a civil wrong, independent of breach of contract, for which a court will provide relief in the form of damages. Tort cases primarily involve state law and are grounded in the fundamental premise that individuals are liable for the consequences of their conduct that result in injury to others. Most school tort actions can be grouped into three primary categories: negligence, intentional torts, and defamation.

NEGLIGENCE

To determine whether an educator is negligent in a given situation, courts determine if a reasonably prudent teacher (with the special skills and training associated with that role) would have acted in a similar manner under like conditions.

Negligence is a breach of one's legal duty to protect others from unreasonable risks of harm. The failure to act or the commission of an improper act, which results in injury or loss to another person, can constitute negligence. To establish negligence, an injury must be avoidable by the exercise of reasonable care. Four elements must be present to support a successful claim (see Figure 2.1):

- The defendant has a *duty* to protect the plaintiff,
- The *duty is breached* by the failure to exercise an appropriate standard of care,
- The negligent conduct is the *proximate or legal cause* of the injury, and
- An actual *injury* occurs.

Duty

School officials have a common law duty to anticipate foreseeable dangers and to take necessary precautions to protect students entrusted in their care.[1] Among the specific duties school personnel owe students are the following:

[1]*See, e.g.*, Carr v. Sch. Bd. of Pasco County, Fla., 921 So. 2d 825 (Fla. Ct. App. 2006).

FIGURE 2.1   Tort Liability

Source: Janet Rumple, J.D. and Associate Instructor, Indiana University

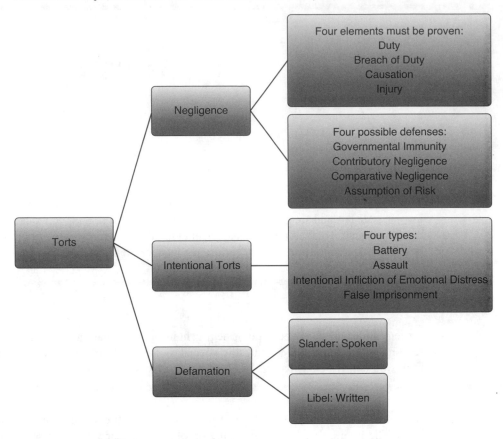

- To give proper instruction,
- To provide adequate supervision,
- To maintain equipment, facilities, and grounds,
- To warn students of known dangers.

Instruction.   Teachers have a duty to provide students with adequate and appropri-ate instruction prior to commencing an activity that may pose a risk of harm—the greater the risk, the greater the need for proper instruction. Following such instruction, effort should be made to determine whether the material was heard and understood. This can be accomplished through assessments such as paper and pencil tests, oral tests, and observations, as appropriate for the activity. Proper instruction was not given when a Nebraska ninth-grader was severely burned in a welding course when his flannel shirt ignited.[2] The school failed to make protective leather aprons available to the students, as was recommended for such activities, and the instructor had informed the students simply

[2]Norman v. Ogallala Pub. Sch. Dist., 609 N.W.2d 338 (Neb. 2000).

to wear old shirts. Perhaps most damaging to the district's case was the testimony of the instructor when he stated on four separate occasions that it was not his responsibility to ensure that students wore protective clothing. "Safety garments" as a topic was briefly mentioned in one of many handouts distributed in class, but no effort was made to determine whether students read or understood the material and on no occasion did the instructor prevent a student from participating based on the type of clothing worn.

Supervision. Although state statutes require educators to provide proper supervision, school personnel are not expected to have every child under surveillance at all times during the school day or to anticipate every possible accident or incident that might occur. Moreover, there is no set level of supervision required under common law (i.e., there is no predetermined student/teacher ratio mandated by courts) for each activity or population. The level of supervision required in any given situation is determined by the aggregate of circumstances, including the age, maturity, and prior experience of the students; the specific activity in progress; and the presence of external threats.

In assessing if adequate supervision has been provided, courts will determine whether the events leading up to the injury foreseeably placed the student at risk and whether the injury could have been prevented with proper supervision.[3] Two student injury cases involving rock-throwing incidents illustrate this point. In one instance in which student rock throwing had continued for almost 10 minutes before the injury occurred, the court found the supervising teacher liable for negligence.[4] But, in a case in which a teacher aide had walked past a group of students moments before one child threw a rock that was deflected and hit another child, no liability was assessed.[5] The court concluded that the teacher aide had provided adequate supervision and had no reason to anticipate the event that caused the injury.

In Georgia, school employees failed to intercede prior to an altercation between two students or to call 911 following the severe beating one of the students received.[6] The teacher had heard part of a verbal exchange between the two, but failed to provide further supervision as he had not been informed that one of the students had an extensive history of explosive violent behavior. Moreover, school officials had not sought emergency aid until the injured student's father, by telephone, demanded immediate medical assistance approximately 49 minutes following the battery. School officials were reluctant to notify the police given administrative directives strongly discouraging the reporting of violence for fear that the school would be classified as "persistently dangerous" under the federal No Child Left Behind Act. The appeals court reasoned that the case should proceed to a jury, as the parents provided support for their claim of willfulness, corruption, and malice.

---

[3]Swan v. Town of Brookhaven, 821 N.Y.S.2d 265 (App. Div. 2006) (determining that no amount of supervision could have prevented injury to an 11-year-old who had attempted to get off a slide when he was only halfway down, caught his foot, and fell to the ground).

[4]Sheehan v. Saint Peter's Catholic Sch., 188 N.W.2d 868 (Minn. 1971).

[5]Fagan v. Summers, 498 P.2d 1227 (Wyo. 1972). *See also* Stephenson v. Commercial Travelers Mut. Ins. Co., 893 So. 2d 180 (La. Ct. App. 2005) (determining that when a soccer player incurred a fractured leg, her injury was not foreseeable or preventable).

[6]Bajjani v. Gwinnett County Sch. Dist., 630 S.E.2d 103 (Ga. Ct. App. 2006). *See also* Wood v. Watervliet City Sch. Dist., 815 N.Y.S.2d 360 (App. Div. 2006) (concluding that fact issues remained regarding foreseeability when a student with an extensive disciplinary record battered a classmate while the teacher stood outside the classroom door).

It is important to note that there may be times when students pass out of the "orbit of school authority," even though they may remain on school property. This often occurs, given the wide range of uses of school buildings and the variety of activities. In one such case, an Indiana appeals court found that a district had no duty to supervise male students who secretly videotaped female lifeguards in their locker room in various stages of undress.[7] The tape later was circulated at the school, and the victims claimed that the school district's negligence caused their emotional distress. The lifeguard class, although held in school facilities, was not part of the public school curriculum (i.e., it was sponsored by the Red Cross after school hours), and school employees neither taught nor supervised the course. When school officials learned what had transpired, they investigated the incident, identified and suspended those responsible, and confiscated the one remaining tape. The taping was found to be unforeseeable, and no special duty was established for the district either to provide security or to supervise the class.

Supervision of students en route to and from school also has generated considerable litigation. Over the years, parents have argued that school officials are responsible for their children from the time they leave home until the time they return.[8] Although such a bright-line test would assist courts in rendering uniform decisions, it clearly would result in the placement of an unrealistic demand on school resources and an unfair burden on personnel. Courts instead focus on whether:

- The events that caused the injury were foreseeable,
- The district had an express or implied duty to provide supervision on and off school grounds both before and after school hours, and
- The child was injured due to a breach of that duty.

In cases in which the district is responsible for providing transportation, officials should ensure that involved staff are properly trained and that district procedures are communicated and practiced. Personnel should strictly adhere to transportation requirements, including those related to licensure; background checks; vehicle maintenance; driving, loading, and unloading practices; conduct during transport; and criteria for the assignment of an aide. Designated procedures were not followed when a Washington school bus driver was found negligent in the death of a 13-year-old who was killed by a car after she had exited the bus.[9] The bus driver failed to use either the stop sign or flashing lights as the student was discharged and then permitted the student to cross behind the bus instead of in front, as required by state law.

In addition, school officials have a duty to provide supervision during school-sponsored off-campus activities. As with other supervisory roles, school officials accompanying the students need to assess foreseeable risks associated with each activity and be aware of the abilities of participating students. However, when the activity is neither curricular nor school sponsored, liability is less likely, given the difficulty of identifying a continuing duty on the part of school officials to provide supervision.

[7]Roe v. N. Adams Cmty. Sch. Corp., 647 N.E.2d 655 (Ind. Ct. App. 1995).

[8]Also, parents have unsuccessfully asserted that their school districts should provide supervision during private transport to school functions. *See, e.g.,* Gylten v. Swalboski, 246 F.3d 1139 (8th Cir. 2001).

[9]Yurkovich v. Rose, 847 P.2d 925 (Wash. Ct. App. 1993).

In those instances in which districts are not responsible for transporting children to and from school, proper supervision still should be provided at the pick-up and drop-off area; crossing guards should be stationed at nearby intersections for walkers; and assistance should be provided to parents and children to help identify safe routes to and from school. Also, parents need to be informed about the earliest time of day that supervision will be provided before school so that students will not arrive prior to school personnel.

As a general rule, school districts are not expected to protect truant and nonattending students, or students who are injured in their homes.[10] This is true for those who never arrive at school as well as for those who exit school grounds during the school day without permission, notwithstanding an appropriate level of surveillance of the school building and grounds as determined by the age and ability of the students. A New York student left school detention to go joyriding with friends. They were involved in a high-speed police chase resulting in a crash at approximately 5:00 p.m., well after school hours. The student lost part of an arm in addition to sustaining other injuries, and the parents sued the school claiming negligent supervision. The court declared that "nothing short of a prison-like atmosphere with monitors at every exit could have prevented [the student] from leaving the school grounds."[11] The court refused to require such extreme measures to detain students or to require the district to provide supervision of truant students off school property and after the school day.

Moreover, extreme measures to keep students at school may themselves result in liability. A Kentucky teacher chained a student by the ankle and later, when he escaped, chained him by the neck to a tree to prevent him from leaving school grounds again. The student had arrived late or had skipped class on numerous occasions. The appeals court determined that the lower court erred in granting a directed verdict to the teacher and that proof of emotional damages should be submitted to the jury on remand.[12]

Maintenance of Buildings, Grounds, and Equipment.   By law, some states protect frequenters of public buildings from danger to life, health, safety, or welfare. These *safe place statutes* may be used by individuals to obtain damages from school districts for injuries resulting from defective conditions of school buildings and grounds. Furthermore, school officials have a common law duty to maintain facilities and equipment in a reasonably safe condition. Districts can be held liable when they are aware of, or should be aware of, hazardous conditions and do not take the necessary steps to repair or correct the conditions.

The duty to provide reasonable maintenance of facilities does not place an obligation on school personnel to anticipate every possible danger or to be aware of and correct every minor defect as soon as the condition occurs. For example, a Louisiana student was unsuccessful in

[10]*See, e.g.*, Maldonado v. Tuckahoe, 817 N.Y.S.2d 376 (App. Div. 2006).

[11]Palella v. Ulmer, 518 N.Y.S.2d 91, 93 (Sup. Ct. 1987). *See also* Doe v. San Antonio Indep. Sch. Dist., 197 Fed. App'x 296 (5th Cir. 2006) (determining that when a student left school without permission and was later sexually assaulted, her injury was not foreseeable and was not due to any disciplinary action taken by the district or to its lack of supervision); Chalen v. Glen Cove Sch. Dist., 814 N.Y.S.2d 254 (App. Div. 2006) (finding no duty to protect a student beyond the boundaries of school property or liability in a wrongful death claim in a case in which a student and family friend ingested poison and died; noting that officials had no knowledge that the visitor posed a danger or that the student would leave campus without permission).

[12]Banks v. Fritsch, 39 S.W.3d 474 (Ky. Ct. App. 2001).

establishing a breach of duty in connection with an injury sustained on a defective door latch.[13] The state appeals court concluded that there was no evidence that any school employee had knowledge of, or should have had knowledge of, the broken latch. Because the risk was unforeseen, a duty to protect the student could not be imposed.

If dangers are known, damages may be awarded when injuries result from unsafe buildings or grounds. For example, a Michigan student was successful in obtaining damages for the loss of sight in one eye; the injury was sustained while playing in a pile of dirt and sand on the playground after school hours.[14] The area was not fenced, and prior to the incident parents had complained to school officials about dirt fights among children. The state appeals court concluded that the school district breached its duty to maintain the school grounds in a safe condition. In contrast, a parent who fell on a sidewalk on school property and was injured was denied damages.[15] Officials did not cancel an athletic contest held in the evening, even though school had been cancelled that day because of the accumulation of ice and snow. In granting immunity to the West Virginia school district, the court distinguished conditions caused by the weather from those caused or exacerbated by the district (e.g., placement of snow on the walkway in an effort to clear the roadway), with liability assigned only in the latter circumstances.

In addition to maintaining buildings and grounds, school personnel also are required to maintain equipment and to use it safely, such as in woodshop, science labs, athletics, or transportation. A Kentucky coach was found liable for the death of a student by electrocution who had been using a whirlpool. The coach had modified the equipment but had failed to install a ground fault interrupter, although one was required by the national electric code. His negligence was found to be the substantial factor causing the student's death.[16] Similarly, the Texas appeals court determined that immunity would be waived in part in a case in which a 5-year-old fell asleep on her way to school and was locked in the bus for the remainder of the school day. The court reasoned that although the district was immune for its alleged failure to supervise the unloading of the children, the district could be sued for the negligent locking of the door, given that such an act did not qualify as the "operation or use of a motor vehicle" for which immunity is granted.[17]

Duty to Warn.   In nearly all states, courts have recognized either a statutory or common law duty to warn students, parents, and at times educators and staff of known risks they may encounter. This duty has been identified in areas such as physical education and interscholastic sports, vocational education, laboratory science, and other occasions when a student uses potentially dangerous machinery or equipment. Informing, if not warning, students and parents of known dangers is necessary so that the participants then may assume the usual risk associated with the activity.

In addition to the somewhat traditional warnings connected with sports or the use of equipment, educators, school psychologists, and counselors have a duty to warn when they learn through advising, counseling, or therapy that students intend to harm themselves or

[13]Lewis v. Saint Bernard Parish Sch. Bd., 350 So. 2d 1256 (La. Ct. App. 1977).

[14]Monfils v. City of Sterling Heights, 269 N.W.2d 588 (Mich. Ct. App. 1978).

[15]Porter v. Grant County Bd. of Educ., 633 S.E.2d 38 (W. Va. 2006).

[16]Massie v. Persson, 729 S.W.2d 448 (Ky. Ct. App. 1987).

[17]Elgin Indep. Sch. Dist. v. R.N., 191 S.W.3d 263 (Tex. App. 2006).

others. Those in receipt of such information are required to inform potential victims or to notify parents if students threaten to injure themselves. This requirement supersedes claims of professional ethics, discretion, therapist/client privilege, or confidentiality.

However, school officials will not typically be found liable when acts of violence are unforeseeable (e.g., the threat of suicide was neither explicitly stated nor apparent), even if they knew that a particular student was under stress or seemed depressed or preoccupied. The Third Circuit found no school district liability when a student committed suicide while at home.[18] The deceased had sent a note to his former girlfriend stating that her new relationship "almost made me want to go kill myself."[19] The counselor discussed the matter with the young man and was satisfied that he showed no indications of committing suicide. As a result, the counselor elected not to inform the school psychologist or the student's parents. A little over a week later, following an altercation with his mother, the youth hanged himself. The school district and its employees were found entitled to immunity, given that the counselor's conduct did not amount to actual malice, willful misconduct, fraud, or a crime. She did not believe the student was at risk, nor did she create or enhance the danger.[20]

School officials also have a duty to warn employees of known dangers, whether structural, environmental, or human. As such, a Florida court reversed a lower court grant of summary judgment in a case in which district officials failed to warn a teacher about a student's propensity for violence.[21] On remand, the court held that the battered teacher will have to show that the employer engaged in conduct substantially certain to result in injury.[22] To aid the lower court in reaching its decision, the appeals court noted that the student had (1) been classified as severely emotionally disabled with a multiple personality disorder, (2) been involved in numerous acts of violence, (3) previously threatened teachers, and (4) been ordered by a court to undergo inpatient treatment for slamming his mother's head against the floor. Moreover, the district had either concealed or misrepresented these facts in its effort to place the student in his current school.

Breach of Duty/Standard of Care

Once a duty has been established, the injured individual must show that the duty was breached by the failure of another to exercise an appropriate standard of care. The degree of care that teachers owe students is determined by:

- The age, experience, and maturity level of the students,
- The environment within which the incident occurs, and
- The type of instructional or recreational activity.

---

[18]Sanford v. Stiles, 456 F.3d 298 (3d Cir. 2006).

[19]*Id.* at 301.

[20]*See also* Carrier v. Lake Pend Oreille Sch. Dist., 134 P.3d 655 (Idaho 2006) (finding no duty to warn as the student's conduct did not qualify as "suicidal tendency" under state law—i.e., a present aim, direction, or trend toward taking one's own life).

[21]Patrick v. Palm Beach County Sch. Bd., 927 So. 2d 973 (Fla. Dist. Ct. App. 2006).

[22]This level of foreseeability is required for the teacher to overcome the general rule of workers' compensation immunity. *See also* Wyble v. Acadiana Preparatory Sch., 956 So. 2d 722 (La. Ct. App. 2007) (determining that a school employee was eligible for workers' compensation when injured at work moving a desk).

For example, primary grade students will generally require closer supervision and more detailed and repetitive instructions than will high school students, and a class in woodwork will require closer supervision than will a class in English literature. Variability in the level of care deemed reasonable is illustrated in a Louisiana case in which a student with disabilities was fatally injured when he darted into a busy thoroughfare while being escorted with nine other classmates to a park three blocks from the school.[23] The state appellate court noted that the general level of care required for all students becomes greater when children with disabilities are involved, particularly when they are taken away from the school campus. The court found the supervision to be inadequate and the selected route to be less safe than alternate routes.

Reasonable Person.   In assessing whether appropriate care has been taken, courts consider whether the defendant acted as a "reasonable person" would have acted under the circumstances. The reasonable person is a hypothetical individual who has:

- The physical attributes of the defendant,
- Normal intelligence, problem-solving ability, and temperament,
- Normal perception and memory with a minimum level of information and experience common to the community, and
- Such superior skill and knowledge as the defendant has or purports to have.

Courts will not assume that a defendant possesses any predetermined physical attributes (e.g., size, strength, agility), but rather will consider each defendant's actual physical abilities and disabilities in determining whether the defendant was responsible in whole or in part for an individual's injury. Accordingly, in cases in which a child requires physical assistance to avoid injury (e.g., when being attacked by another student), a different expectation will exist for a large, physically fit teacher as compared to a small, frail teacher.

Even though defendants' actual physical characteristics and capabilities are used in determining whether their conduct was reasonable, that is not the case when considering mental capacity. Courts will assume all adult individuals have normal intelligence, problem-solving ability, and temperament even when the evidence indicates that they do not possess such attributes.[24] In addition to diminished intelligence, defendants also might argue that consideration should be given to factors such as their inability to make good or quick decisions, lack of perception or concentration, poor attention to detail, confrontational personality, or inability to deal with stress. Trying to determine each person's mental abilities and capabilities would be impractical, if not impossible, given the dearth of valid and reliable assessment instruments or techniques and the ease of those being assessed to misrepresent their abilities.

Furthermore, courts will expect the defendant to have a normal perception of the environment (e.g., being aware that the rear of the school yard is bordered by a small river) and an accurate memory of what has occurred within that environment (e.g., recalling that the playground floods following a heavy rain). In this process, it often is necessary for judges to ascertain whether a defendant "discovered that which was readily apparent."[25]

---

[23]Foster v. Houston Gen. Ins. Co., 407 So. 2d 759, 763 (La. Ct. App. 1981).

[24]W. Page Keeton, Dan B. Dobbs, Robert E. Keeton, and David G. Owen, *Prosser and Keeton on Torts*, 5th ed. (St. Paul, MN: West Publishing, 1984), p. 177.

[25]*Id.* at p. 182.

This requirement does not assume that the defendant will know all facts, foresee all risks, or be aware of all things. Instead, it is based on the premise that a reasonable adult, with normal intellect, should know certain facts.

In an effort to determine whether the defendant acted as a reasonable person, courts also consider whether the individual had or claimed to have had any superior knowledge or skill. Teachers, who are college graduates and state licensed, are expected to act like reasonable persons with similar credentials. In addition, any special training an individual has received may affect whether a given act is considered reasonable. Accordingly, a physical education instructor who is a certified lifeguard or a teacher with an advanced degree in chemistry may be held to higher standards of care than others with lesser skills and knowledge when a student is drowning or when chemicals in a school laboratory are mixed improperly and ignite.

Invitee, Licensee, and Trespasser.   In determining if an appropriate standard of care has been provided, courts consider whether an injured individual was an invitee, licensee, or trespasser, with invitees receiving the greatest level of care and trespassers receiving the least. In a school setting, an *invitee* is one who enters the school premises on the expressed or implied invitation of the school district or one of its agents. The district then has an affirmative duty to exercise reasonable care for the safety of invitees commensurate with the risks and circumstances involved. Furthermore, invitees must be protected against known dangers as well as those that might be discovered with reasonable care. Under most circumstances, students, teachers, and administrators are invitees of the district. Students who break into a school after hours, however, have exceeded the "period of invitation" and become trespassers.[26]

Where permission to be on school premises is requested and granted, the person becomes a *licensee* (e.g., requests by unsolicited visitors, salespersons, parents, newspersons). Even school children may qualify as licensees under certain circumstances (e.g., while engaged in activities of a local nonschool organization that has been permitted evening or weekend use of a school classroom). Such persons enter the building or grounds facing the same conditions and threats as the occupier. Nevertheless, districts still need to warn licensees of known dangers and not injure them intentionally or by willful, wanton, or reckless conduct.

If the individual has neither been invited nor received consent, the person is guilty of *trespass* upon entering school property. Although state laws often blur the distinction between licensee and trespasser, less care has to be provided for the safety of trespassers. Adult trespassers in particular have no right to a safe place and must assume the risk of what they may encounter. Generally, the owner owes no duty to trespassers other than to refrain from willfully or wantonly injuring them (e.g., by setting traps). In selected jurisdictions, however, if the owner knows that trespassers are on the premises (e.g., vagrants living in an abandoned school building), the owner must use reasonable care not to expose the trespasser to an environment that is known to be dangerous. When the trespasser is a child,

[26]*See, e.g.*, Howard County Bd. of Educ. v. Cheyne, 636 A.2d 22 (Md. Ct. Spec. App. 1994) (holding that a 4-year-old was an invitee when she initially entered a gymnasium to attend a sports function, but that a question remained for the jury to determine whether she had exceeded the "scope of her invitation" at the time of the injury; following a school basketball game, the child was injured while retrieving basketballs her mother had shot). *See also* Tincani v. Inland Empire Zoological Soc'y, 875 P.2d 621 (Wash. 1994) (remanding a case in which a student sued a zoo after falling off a cliff during a field trip; the court questioned whether he became a licensee when he strayed beyond the "area of his invitation").

as often is the case on school property, it is prudent to take additional steps to restrict access or to remove known dangers. In such narrow instances, there is little legal distinction between a trespasser and a licensee in regard to the standard of care provided.

Proximate Cause

For liability to be assessed against a school district, the negligent conduct of school personnel must be the proximate or legal cause of injury. ***Proximate cause* has been defined as "that which in a natural and continuous sequence, unbroken by any efficient intervening cause, produces the injury, and without which the result would not have occurred."**[27] In determining proximate cause, courts will:

- Consider factors other than the defendant's conduct that contributed to the injury,
- Ascertain whether the challenged conduct created a force that was in operation up to the time of the injury, and
- Assess the lapse of time between the conduct and the occurrence of the injury.

Accordingly, not every seemingly negligent act results in liability, even when an injury occurs, unless the act was in fact the cause of the injury. A New York appellate court affirmed summary judgment for a school district when the sole proximate cause of the student's injuries was his attempt to do a back flip dismount from the playground equipment while his teacher's back was turned; the act was sudden and unforeseeable.[28] Likewise, the Montana Supreme Court affirmed a jury verdict finding no negligent supervision on the part of a special education assistant when a child let go and fell two to three feet from playground equipment, breaking her leg. Two adult supervisors were overseeing 11 special needs students, but by the time the supervisors saw the child falling, it was too late to intervene. The alleged failure to supervise was not found to be the proximate cause of the child's injury.[29]

Injury

Legal negligence does not exist unless actual injury is incurred either directly by the individual or by the individual's property. Most often, an individual will know of the injury as soon as it occurs; in some instances, however, the individual may not be aware of the injury for many months or even years (e.g., development of asbestosis due to exposure to asbestos 20 years previously). In most states, there is a statute of limitations of one to three years on tort claims, although the actual time can be greater if the limitations period does not begin until the plaintiff reaches the age of majority or becomes aware of the injury.

When students are injured in the school setting, school personnel have a duty to provide reasonable assistance commensurate with their training and experience. Where reasonable treatment is provided, generally no liability will be assessed even if the treatment later is proven to be inappropriate or inadequate.

---

[27]Anselmo v. Tuck, 924 S.W.2d 798, 802 (Ark. 1996).

[28]Ascher v. Scarsdale Sch. Dist., 700 N.Y.S.2d 210 (App. Div. 1999).

[29]Morgan v. Great Falls Sch. Dist., 995 P.2d 422 (Mont. 2000). *See also* Williamson v. Liptzin, 539 S.E.2d 313 (N.C. Ct. App. 2000) (reasoning that the alleged negligence by the psychiatrist was not the proximate cause of plaintiff's actions—i.e., killing two people eight months after his last session).

Defenses against Negligence

Several defenses are available to school districts when employees have been charged with negligence. At times, districts have identified procedural defects (e.g., the failure to adhere to statutory requirements regarding notice of claim), or have proposed that an individual's injury was caused by uncontrollable events of nature (i.e., an act of God) in an effort to thwart liability claims. More commonly, defenses such as immunity, contributory negligence, comparative negligence, and assumption of risk have been asserted.

Governmental Immunity. In rare cases in which governmental immunity is comprehensively applied, governmental entities, including school districts, cannot be sued for any reason. This defense has evolved for two primary reasons: (1) government agencies do not generally collect tax funds for liability purposes, and (2) permitting citizens to file suit against the government is tantamount to filing suit against oneself. This defense is available to employees only when state law specifically confers such immunity for acts within the scope of employment, or courts interpret the law to do so. However, immunity is seldom comprehensively applied today, as nearly all states have limited its use by considering whether:

- The claim was related to the maintenance of the school building or property,[30]
- Acts were proprietary rather than governmental,[31]
- Decisions were ministerial rather than discretionary,[32]
- School property was being used for recreational purposes,[33] or
- The injury was compensable under the state's workers' compensation laws (employees only).[34]

Contributory Negligence. In states that recognize contributory negligence as a defense, plaintiffs are denied recovery if their actions are shown to have been substantially responsible

[30]Moreover, school districts may not maintain an *attractive nuisance* (i.e., a facility, structure, or piece of equipment that entices the public to engage in activity that is potentially dangerous).

[31]*Governmental functions* are those that are performed in discharging the agency's official duties (e.g., hiring faculty) and are generally considered immune from liability. *Proprietary functions* are those that are only tangentially related to the curriculum, can as easily be performed by the private sector, and often require the payment of a fee (e.g., community use of school pool); these activities have been permissible targets for tort actions.

[32]*Discretionary functions* are those that require consideration of alternatives, deliberation, judgment, and the making of a decision (e.g., the discretion used in the selection of a new teacher). In contrast, *ministerial functions* are those performed in a prescribed manner, in obedience to legal authority, and without discretion (e.g., procedures used for stopping a school bus at a railroad crossing). As a rule, districts will be liable for negligence involving ministerial duties but be immune from liability for negligence associated with those that are discretionary. *See, e.g.*, Schnarrs v. Girard Bd. of Educ., 858 N.E.2d 1258 (Ohio Ct. App. 2006).

[33]*Recreational use* immunity statutes were passed to encourage property and landowners to open their lands and waters for public recreational use. Immunity for injuries incurred while on the property is provided unless the entrant was charged a fee for admission or was injured because of the owner's willful or wanton misconduct.

[34]Under workers' compensation, liability exists regardless of negligence or fault on the part of the employer or employee, provided that the injury was accidental *and* arose out of and in the course of employment. However, not all injuries that occur at work are necessarily "work related." *See, e.g.*, Gutierrez v. Artesia Pub. Sch., 583 P.2d 476 (N.M. Ct. App. 1978) (denying workers' compensation benefits to a teacher's widow after her adulterous husband was shot at school by another teacher's jealous husband; the death did not arise out of, was not incident to, and did not occur in the course of the teacher's employment).

for the injury; it makes no difference that the defendant was negligent and also partially at fault. In most jurisdictions today, a slight degree of fault will not prevent a plaintiff from prevailing; typically, the contributory negligence must be significant, although it need not be dominant.

In assessing whether contributory negligence exists, children are not necessarily held to the same standard of care as adults. Rather, their actions must be reasonable for persons of similar age, maturity, intelligence, and experience. Many courts make individualized determinations as to whether a minor plaintiff appreciated the risks involved and acted as a reasonable person of like characteristics and abilities. Other courts have established age ranges in an effort to more objectively and uniformly determine whether children have the capacity to contribute to or cause their own injuries. Although courts vary greatly and designated ages may seem arbitrary (often based on biblical scripture or criminal law, with little or nothing to do with child development), the most commonly used ranges are the following:

- Children below the age of 7 are considered incapable of negligence,
- Youth between the ages of 7 and 14 are considered incapable of negligence, but this presumption can be rebutted,[35] and
- Students age 14 and older are generally presumed capable of negligence, although this presumption too can be rebutted.[36]

When adults are injured on school grounds or at school functions, courts will assess the nature of the risk involved and whether such a risk was known to the injured party or reasonably should have been known. For example, an Indiana court upheld a grant of summary judgment in a case in which a father fell from backless bleachers while watching his son participate in a basketball game. The court found the plaintiff to be contributorily negligent in that he failed to exercise the degree of care that an ordinary, reasonable, and prudent person in a similar situation would exercise.[37]

Comparative Negligence.   With the comparative model, the plaintiff and/or one or more defendants bear responsibility in proportion to fault. For example, a Louisiana school bus driver permitted two girls to exit his bus even though he knew one had threatened to injure the other. He initially exited with them, held them apart, and told a teacher to summon the principal. Instead of waiting for the principal or a teacher to arrive, however, he reentered the bus to move it, because he was blocking traffic. When he pulled away, one student proceeded to stomp the other student's ankle; the injury was so severe that it required three screws to align the broken bones. The court reasoned that the driver should not have left the students unsupervised under the circumstances and assessed 15 percent liability against him and 85 percent liability to the student responsible for the attack.[38]

---

[35]*See, e.g.*, Agnor v. Caddo Parish Sch. Bd., 936 So. 2d 865 (La. Ct. App. 2006) (determining that an 8-year-old was 25 percent liable for the injury she sustained when sliding on the routinely wet floors in the girl's restroom; when she lost her balance and fell, a pencil penetrated her face and lodged beneath her eye).

[36]*See, e.g.*, Doe v. LaFayette Sch. Corp., 846 N.E. 2d 691 (Ind. Ct. App. 2006) (observing that children over the age of 14 generally are responsible for exercising the standard of care of an adult, but a 15-year-old student who was seduced by her teacher was found not to have been engaged in contributory negligence).

[37]Funston v. Sch. Town of Munster, 849 N.E.2d 595 (Ind. 2006).

[38]Bell v. Ayio, 731 So. 2d 893 (La. Ct. App. 1999).

Assumption of Risk.   This defense can be either express or implied. *Express assumption* **occurs when the plaintiff consents in advance to take his or her chances of injury, given a known danger** (e.g., signing an agreement to assume the risks associated with participating in high school football). On the other hand, *implied assumption* **occurs without an express written or oral agreement, yet is logically assumed, given the plaintiff's conduct** (e.g., when spectators at a baseball game elect to sit in unscreened seats; such persons assume the risk of possible injury even if they failed to sign an agreement).

Although inherent risks are associated with athletics or recreation, all participants will not necessarily understand those risks. Understanding risks often is associated with age, maturity, and experience. As a result, school personnel must exercise reasonable care to protect students from unassumed, concealed, or unreasonably high risks. This duty can be met when participation is voluntary and the student is knowledgeable of and assumes the risks associated with the activity.[39]

However, student athletes assume only those risks that occur during normal participation; they do not assume unknown risks associated with a coach's negligence.[40] Moreover, they are not assuming that they will be exposed to intentional torts or conduct that represents a reckless disregard for the safety of others. But, penalties and poor judgment by other participants generally will not qualify as intentional torts and most often will be viewed as occurring commonly, if not routinely, in the sport (e.g., being clipped in football).

■ ■ ■ ■ ■

INTENTIONAL TORTS

School personnel can be liable for intentionally harming others through assault, battery, false imprisonment, or the intentional infliction of mental distress.

To be an intentional tort, the behavior must be purposeful. Qualifying behaviors do not include negligence, acts that occur through happenstance, or events that are due to an act of nature. Each of the more common types of intentional torts is discussed briefly here (see Figure 2.1).

Assault and Battery

Assault **consists of an overt attempt to place another in fear of bodily harm; no actual physical contact need take place.** Examples include threatening with words, pointing a gun, waving a knife, or shaking a fist. For there to be an assault, the plaintiff needs to be aware of the threat, and the person committing the assault needs to be perceived as having

---

[39]*See, e.g.*, Stowers v. Clinton Cent. Sch. Corp., 855 N.E.2d 739 (Ind. Ct. App. 2006) (permitting the admission of a release form signed by a mother giving permission for her son to participate in organized athletics and acknowledging that injuries and even death may result); Ross v. N.Y. Quarterly Meeting of the Religious Soc'y of Friends, 819 N.Y.S.2d 749 (App. Div. 2006) (determining that the athlete had assumed the risks associated with playing softball when she was injured when practicing her slide).

[40]*See, e.g.*, Cotillo v. Duncan, 912 A.2d 72 (Md. Ct. Spec. App. 2006) (concluding that a weightlifter assumed the risks typically associated with the sport, but did not assume that the spotters would fail to intervene or come to his aid unless signaled by an official to do so).

the ability to carry out the threat. In contrast, **a** *battery* **is committed when an assault is consummated.** Examples include being shot, stabbed, beaten, or struck. Actual injury need not result for a battery claim to succeed (e.g., the person could have been punched but not injured due to a comparatively weak blow).

Some school-based assault and battery cases have involved the administration of corporal punishment and other forms of discipline that require physical touching. Generally, courts have been reluctant to interfere with a teacher's authority to discipline students and have sanctioned the use of reasonable force to control pupil behavior.

Although comparatively uncommon, school personnel may initiate battery suits against students who injure them.[41] Suits are not barred simply because the person committing the tort is a minor, although the amount of the award may be capped by state statute. A Wisconsin appeals court awarded damages to a teacher when he was physically attacked outside the school building while attempting to escort a student to the office for violating a smoking ban. The court held that the student, who had five previous fighting violations, acted with malicious intent in striking the teacher numerous times and in pushing the teacher's face into the corner of a building. Both actual and punitive damages were awarded, notwithstanding the fact that the student was a minor at the time of the battery or that the student's psychiatrist purported that a punitive award would not be a deterrent for his impulsive conduct.[42] The court also was unpersuaded by the argument that the student's violence and anger were due to his poor self-control or that he had a learning disability. The court concluded its ruling by noting that if the student expected to continue to live freely in society, he would have to learn to control his assaultive behavior, or "appreciate" the consequences.

Self-defense often has been used to shield an individual from liability for alleged battery. **An individual need not wait to be struck to engage in defensive acts, although reasonable grounds must exist to substantiate that harm is imminent.** The "test" in such cases is to determine whether the defendant's conduct was that in which a reasonable person may have engaged given the circumstances. Consideration should be given to the magnitude of the existing threat, possible alternatives to physical contact, and the time frame available to make a decision (i.e., whether the defendant acted instantaneously or had time for contemplation and deliberation).[43] Even when contact is justified, the defendant must use only force that is reasonably necessary for self-protection. Furthermore, if the alleged aggressor is disarmed, rendered helpless, or no longer capable of aggressive behavior, the defendant may not take the opportunity to engage in revenge or to punish.

In addition to self-defense, individuals accused of battery also may claim that they were acting in the defense of others. This type of tort defense is of particular importance in a school setting in which educators often are called on to separate students who are fighting or to come to the aid of someone being attacked. Most jurisdictions not only permit such action on behalf of others but also consider it to be a responsibility or duty of educators, assuming good faith and the use of reasonable and necessary force.

---

[41]Some negligence suits are filed by school personnel against their districts when they have been battered at work. In most cases, however, courts have found that the incidents were unforeseen and that no special duty existed on the part of the district to prevent the battery.

[42]Anello v. Savignac, 342 N.W.2d 440 (Wis. Ct. App. 1983).

[43]The American Law Institute, *A Concise Restatement of Torts* (St. Paul, MN: American Law Institute, 2000), p. 19.

False Imprisonment

Obviously, all restrictions on the freedom of movement or the effort to enter or exit will not qualify as false imprisonment. For example, the court found no false imprisonment when a student was placed for seven minutes in a holding cell in a county detention facility for continually disrupting a tour of the building—the student's behavior jeopardized the safety of the children and disrupted an otherwise orderly environment.[44] Also, a student who was taken out of class to be questioned by the principal and a magistrate judge regarding sexual activities on the Internet could not claim false imprisonment.[45]

Interestingly, to be falsely imprisoned, one need not be incarcerated; walls, locks, and iron bars are not required. Rather, imprisonment can result from being placed in a closet, room, corner, automobile, or even a circle in the middle of a football field; it can occur when a person is confined to an entire building or when forced to accompany another on a walk or trip. The taking of a purse, car keys, or other property with the intent to force the person to remain also may qualify as imprisonment. *Imprisonment* **results when physical action, verbal command, or intimidation is used to restrain and/or detain persons against their will.** Tone of voice, body language, and what was reasonably understood or even implied from the defendant's conduct will be considered.

In imprisonment cases, the student need not show that physical force was used; it will suffice that the individual submitted given the apprehension of force. The student must be aware of the restraint, but need not show damages beyond the confinement itself to prevail at trial. Accordingly, any time children are unjustifiably restrained against their will, tied or taped to chairs, or bound and gagged, the tort of false imprisonment (as well as other possible violations[46]) may be claimed. Although there are times when the use of physical restraints may be necessary, educators need to document the circumstances requiring such actions and provide a narrative explaining why restraint is an appropriate and reasoned response to the behavior. Also, when behavioral management techniques such as time-out are used, any resulting isolation needs to be imposed for reasonable periods of time, and the confinement area needs to be both safe and clean.

Intentional Infliction of Mental Distress

A tort claim of intentional infliction of mental distress is available to individuals who have experienced severe mental anguish. This claim, however, does not provide a remedy for every trivial indignity, insult, incidence of bad manners, annoyance, or sexist or racist comment, even if disturbing to the plaintiff.

Some forms of communication can result in an assault claim (e.g., a threat to strike another) or defamation suit (e.g., an unfounded claim that a teacher has been sexually involved with students). Other communications might provide a basis for discrimination

---

[44]Harris *ex rel.* Tucker v. County of Forsyth, 921 F. Supp. 325 (M.D.N.C. 1996).

[45]Howard v. Yakovac, No. CV04-202-S-EJL, 2006 U.S. Dist. LEXIS 27253 (Idaho, May 2, 2006).

[46]For example, plaintiffs also may claim a Fourth Amendment "seizure" violation that could be accompanied by 42 U.S.C. §1983. *See* Gray v. Bostic, 458 F.3d 1295 (11th Cir. 2006) (determining that the handcuffing of a compliant 9-year-old girl for the sole purpose of punishing her represented a constitutional violation), *cert. denied*, 127 S. Ct. 2428 (2007).

suits under federal laws (e.g., sexual or racial harassment). **For the conduct to result in intentional infliction of mental distress under tort law, it must be flagrant, extreme, or outrageous; it must go beyond all possible bounds of decency and be regarded as atrocious and utterly intolerable in civilized society.**[47] No person should be expected to endure such conduct (e.g., severe and extreme acts of stalking, harassment, and assault). Moreover, in most instances, the conduct needs to be prolonged and recurring, since single acts seldom meet the necessary threshold.

Given the difficulty of meeting this stringent standard, it is not surprising that few school-based claims succeed. Numerous claims have involved injured feelings or reputations, appearing trivial at best. In one such claim that bordered on disingenuous, a sixth grade Oregon student alleged intentional infliction of mental distress when two of her teachers refused to use her nickname, Boo. "Boo" also is the street name for marijuana and was recognized as such by other students. Neither teacher had ever stated that the student used or condoned the use of drugs. In granting summary judgment for the teachers, the court concluded that no juror could reasonably find that the conduct of the teachers was an "extraordinary transgression of the bounds of socially tolerable conduct."[48]

In contrast, a Florida teacher was found to have supported a claim of intentional infliction of mental distress against two students.[49] The youths had planned, edited, written, printed, copied, and distributed a newsletter that referred to the teacher in racially derogatory and sexually vulgar ways; threatened to rape her, her children, and their cousins; and threatened to kill her. The court distinguished the case from those that involved mere name-calling, embarrassing photos, or harassment and concluded that the conduct was extreme and went beyond all possible bounds of decency.

■ ■ ■ ■ ■

DEFAMATION

Individuals can receive damages for written or spoken injury to their reputations, presuming, of course, that the statements are false.

Most tort actions have involved claims for damages that were due to physical or mental injuries, but plaintiffs also have claimed injury to their reputations in the form of defamation. School districts may be liable for the defamatory acts of their employees, but only when the employees are engaged in district work and their conduct is within the scope of their

[47]Keeton, *et al. supra* note 25, pp. 54–66. *See also* Ott v. Edinburgh Cmty. Sch. Corp., 189 Fed. App'x 507 (7th Cir. 2006) (concluding that a former coach was not defamed when a school board member disclosed to the superintendent that the coach had a criminal record).

[48]Phillips v. Lincoln County Sch. Dist., 984 P.2d 947, 951 (Or. Ct. App. 1999). *See also* Green v. San Diego Unified Sch. Dist., 226 Fed. App'x 677 (9th Cir. 2007) (determining that defendant's conduct was neither extreme nor outrageous and plaintiff failed to meet the standard for emotional distress).

[49]Nims v. Harrison, 768 So. 2d 1198 (Fla. Dist. Ct. App. 2000). *See also* Smith v. Jackson County Bd. of Educ., 608 S.E. 2d 399 (N.C. Ct. App. 2005) (denying defendant's motion to dismiss in a case seeking damages based on emotional distress in which a teacher encouraged a 14-year-old female plaintiff to have a sexual relationship with an 18-year-old male student; made his office, home, and car available for the relationship; and attempted to videotape the two having sex).

authority.[50] Otherwise, claims may be filed only against the individual responsible for the alleged defamation. *Slander* **is the term generally associated with spoken defamation (but also includes sign language), whereas** *libel* **is used to refer to written defamation (but also includes pictures, statues, motion pictures, and conduct carrying a defamatory imputation—e.g., hanging a person in effigy).**[51] In determining whether defamation has occurred, courts will consider whether:

- The targeted individual was a private or public person,
- The communication was false,
- The expression qualified as opinion or fact, and
- The comment was privileged (see Figure 2.1).

Private and Public Persons

To prevail in a defamation case, private individuals need prove only that a false publication by the defendant was received and understood by a third party and that injury resulted. Receipt of potentially defamatory information that is not understood (e.g., receiving an unintelligible encrypted message on a computer, receiving a phone call in an unknown language) cannot adversely affect the plaintiff's reputation, dignity, or community standing and does not qualify as defamation. Individuals considered public figures or officials additionally must show that the publication was made with either malice or a reckless disregard for the truth. Although definitions vary considerably by state, public figures generally are those who are known or recognized by the public (e.g., professional athletes, actors), whereas public officials are those who have substantial control over governmental affairs (e.g., politicians, school board members).

The trend in recent years has been to broaden the class of public officials and figures, but it is fortunate for teachers that the vast majority of courts have not found them to be "public," in large part because their authority typically is limited to school children. Some courts, however, have found school administrators and coaches to be either public officials or figures.[52] This does not mean that all administrators and coaches even within the same jurisdiction will qualify as public persons; such a determination is made on an individual basis and is dependent on the role, responsibility, degree of notoriety, and authority of the specific individual.

Veracity of Statements

In assessing defamation claims, courts also consider whether a statement is true or false. If the statement is found to be true, or at least substantially true, judgment will generally be for the defendant, assuming that critical facts have not been omitted, taken out of context,

---

[50]*See, e.g.,* Henderson v. Walled Lake Consol. Schs., 469 F.3d 479 (6th Cir. 2006).

[51]Keeton *et al. supra* note 25, p. 786.

[52]*See, e.g.,* Jordan v. World Publ'g Co., 872 P.2d 946 (Okla. Civ. App. 1994) (principal); Johnson v. Southwestern Newspapers Corp., 855 S.W. 2d 182 (Tex. App. 1993) (football coach). *But see* O'Connor v. Burningham, 165 P. 3d 1214 (Utah 2007) (determining that a coach was not a public official as school athletics did not affect in any material way the civic affairs of a community).

or otherwise artificially juxtaposed to misrepresent.[53] However, educators must be particularly careful when discussing students and must avoid making comments in bad faith that will result in liability. For example, if a teacher were to comment in class that a particular female student was a "slut," the comments would qualify as defamation *per se*.[54] In such cases no proof of actual harm to reputation is required.

In addition to proving a communication to be false, the individual must show that he or she was the subject addressed. Interestingly, the individual's identity need not be clear to all third parties (i.e., readers, viewers, or hearers of the defamation); as long as at least one third party can identify the individual, the claim is actionable even though the individual is not mentioned by name. Furthermore, the defamatory content need not be explicit; it may be implied or may be understood only by third parties with additional information.

Fact versus Opinion

Most opinions receive constitutional protection, particularly when public figures or officials are involved or the issue is one of public concern. **To qualify as opinion, the communication must not lend itself to being realistically proven as true or false, and must be communicated in such a way as to be considered a personal perspective on the matter.** Parents may express critical opinions about a teacher (verbally or in writing) and may submit such opinions to a principal or school board. Moreover, parents may even express negative views directly to the teacher, assuming that the expression does not amount to "fighting words"[55] or qualify as an assault.

Notwithstanding the above, allegations that "the teacher sold drugs to a student" or that "the superintendent stole school funds" are factual statements that are capable of being substantiated and therefore may qualify as defamation unless proven true. The appeals court in Ohio reversed a lower court dismissal where letters and a news article stated that a football coach had his entire team batter one of the players on the team. On remand, in reexamining the facts of the case, the lower court was directed to assess the totality of circumstances, including the specific language used in the statement, whether the statement was verifiable, and the general context of the statement.[56] Similarly, an Oregon appeals court affirmed a damage award against parents who accused a school bus driver of sexual abuse. Even though there were no facts or evidence that supported the claim, the parents persisted in making accusations over an extended period of time by writing letters, uniting parents in protest, and attending board meetings. Their unsupported claims injured the driver's reputation, adversely affected his employability, and caused him to suffer emotional distress.[57]

---

[53]Determining whether something is true can be difficult, as perspectives and standards will vary. *See, e.g.,* Woodruff v. Ohman, 166 Fed. App'x 212 (6th Cir. 2006).

[54]*See, e.g.,* Smith v. Atkins, 622 So. 2d 795 (La. Ct. App. 1993).

[55]"Fighting words" are by their nature likely to result in an immediate breach of the peace and do not qualify as First Amendment protected speech. *See* text accompanying notes 10–14, Chapter 5.

[56]Rich v. Thompson Newspapers, Inc., 842 N.E.2d 1081 (Ohio Ct. App. 2005).

[57]Kraemer v. Harding, 976 P.2d 1160 (Or. Ct. App. 1999).

Privilege

Whether a communication qualifies as *privileged* also may affect whether defamation is supported. Statements that are considered *absolutely privileged* cannot serve as a basis for defamation under any circumstance, even if they are false and result in injury. An absolute privilege defense has been selectively applied in cases involving superintendents and school board members, although it is less common in education than qualified privilege.

Communication between parties with qualified or *conditional privilege* also may be immune from liability if made in good faith with appropriate motives and content. However, conditional privilege may be lost if *actual malice* exists (i.e., a person made a defamatory statement that was known to be false, acted with a high degree of awareness of probable falsity, or entertained serious doubts about whether the statement was true). Qualified privilege was supported when a board member during a board meeting commented on the suspension of a student for marijuana possession,[58] administrators rated school personnel,[59] and a teacher informed school officials about the inappropriate conduct of another teacher during a European trip.[60]

■ ■ ■ ■ ■

DAMAGES

Tort suits for damages may be filed against school districts and the individuals responsible for the injury.

Damages in tort suits can be either compensatory or punitive, and many include attorneys' fees that are typically calculated as a percent of the total award (often one-third if the case is settled prior to trial and 40 percent if the case is tried). **Compensatory damages include past and future economic loss, medical expenses, and pain and suffering.** These awards are intended to make the plaintiff whole, at least to the degree that money is capable of doing so. If a plaintiff's previous injury has been aggravated, the defendant is generally liable only for the additional loss.

Although damages vary by state, it is common to cap intangibles (e.g., pain, suffering, loss of consortium, mental anguish) but not to cap actual loss. When plaintiffs prevail, it is important to note that school district assets are not subject to execution, sale, garnishment, or attachment to satisfy the judgment. Instead, judgments are paid from funds appropriated specifically for that purpose, acquired through revenue bonds, or available because of insurance. If sufficient funds are not available, it is common for states to require fiscal officers to certify the amount of unpaid judgment to the taxing authority for inclusion in the next

[58]Morrison v. Mobile County Bd. of Educ., 495 So. 2d 1086 (Ala. 1986).

[59]*See, e.g.*, Malia v. Monchak, 543 A.2d 184 (Pa. Commw. Ct. 1988).

[60]Rocci v. Ecole Secondaire MacDonald-Cartier, 755 A.2d 583 (N.J. 2000).

budget. When the amounts are significant, many states permit districts to pay in installments (at times for a period up to 10 years) for damages that do not represent actual loss.[61]

Furthermore, in most states, educators can be sued individually. When they are not "save harmlessed" by their school district and do not have personal insurance coverage, their personal assets (e.g., cars, boats, bank accounts) may be attached, their wages may be garnished, and a lien may be placed on their property. Where a lien is filed, the property may not be sold until the debt is satisfied. Moreover, debtors are not permitted to transfer ownership to avoid attachment (i.e., this would represent *fraudulent conveyance*). It is common for persons in law enforcement (e.g., a county sheriff) to be authorized to seize the property and hold it for sale at public auction. Because the debtor's financial worth is not a factor in calculating actual damages, the award may exceed the debtor's ability to pay. If the debtor is eventually successful in filing for bankruptcy, the plaintiff/creditor is typically paid in the same manner as other creditors.

Finally, punitive damages are awarded to punish particularly wanton or reckless acts and are in addition to actual damages. The amount is at the discretion of the jury and is based on the circumstances, behaviors, and acts. Unlike the calculation of actual damages, the debtor's financial worth may be a factor in determining punitive amounts. When jury verdicts are seemingly out of line, the court may reduce (*remittitur*) or increase (*additur*) the amount where either passion or prejudice is a factor.

CONCLUSION

All individuals, including educators, are responsible for their actions and can be liable for damages if they intentionally or negligently cause injury to others. Educators have a responsibility to act reasonably, but some negligent conduct is likely to occur. Consequently, educators should be knowledgeable about their potential liability under applicable state laws and should ensure that they are either protected by their school districts or have adequate insurance coverage for any damages that might be assessed against them.

Moreover, school personnel should refrain from intentionally injuring others, engaging in assaultive behaviors, detaining students for inappropriate reasons, or participating in conduct that ultimately may result in the emotional distress of another. Educators also should be cautious when sharing information about colleagues or students, as the dissemination of incorrect or confidential information may result in liability.

POINTS TO PONDER

1. During a faculty meeting, a high school principal mentioned that one of the teachers in the building had been arrested for shoplifting and that extra precautions should be taken to safeguard personal belongings. However, the principal failed to mention that although the teacher had been arrested, evidence was inadequate to support her conviction and that she was released soon after her arrest. The principal did not mention the teacher by name, but

---

[61]Jonathan E. Buchter, Susan C. Hastings, Timothy J. Sheeran, and Gregory W. Stype, *Ohio School Law* (Cleveland, OH: West Publishing, 2001), p. 862.

his comments about the make and model of her car left no doubt as to her identity. Her reputation was tarnished and her personal relationships were adversely affected. She sued the principal, claiming defamation of character. Is she likely to win? Explain.

2. A secondary school principal directed a student teacher in social studies to supervise a chemistry class, because the regular science teacher was ill. During lab, a student was injured in an explosion. The parents of the injured child sued the principal (even though he was not present during the explosion, nor had he instructed the class in regard to the chemicals) and the school district. Are the parents likely to prevail in this suit? Explain your reasoning.

3. A physical education instructor requires a student to climb a 30-foot rope in physical education class even though the student informed the teacher that he was afraid of heights (a fact that also is part of his school record). After the instructor threatened the student with corporal punishment, he climbed the rope, but fell when about half way up. He was not injured, but sued the instructor and the district, claiming negligence. Will he succeed in this claim? Why or why not?

4. While on the school bus, two students got into an altercation over a loud radio. The zydeco music emanating from the boom box was more than the second student could tolerate. The owner of the boom box refused to turn off or even turn down the music. As a result, the student informed the boom box owner that if the music was not turned off, the radio would be destroyed and the owner would be struck. Numerous passengers overheard the conversation. The boom box owner was a large, athletic, 18-year-old male; the confronting student was a small, frail, 12-year-old female. She had no special martial arts skill and did not give the impression that she was capable of carrying out the threat. The male student sued the female, claiming assault. Will he succeed in his claim? Why or why not?

CHAPTER THREE

CHURCH/STATE RELATIONS

Efforts to identify the appropriate relationship between government and religion have generated substantial controversy in our nation, and since the mid-twentieth century, schools have provided the battleground for some of the most volatile disputes. This chapter provides an overview of the constitutional framework, the evolution of legal activity, and the current status of church/state relations involving education.

CONSTITUTIONAL FRAMEWORK

The First Amendment's Establishment Clause is used primarily to challenge governmental *advancement* of religion, whereas claims under the Free Exercise Clause usually focus on secular governmental regulations alleged to impair the practice of religious beliefs.

The First Amendment to the United States Constitution stipulates in part that "Congress shall make no law respecting an establishment of religion or prohibiting the free exercise thereof." Although this amendment was directed toward the *federal* government, the Fourteenth Amendment, adopted in 1868, specifically placed restrictions on *state* action impairing personal rights. **In the twentieth century the Supreme Court recognized that the Fourteenth Amendment's fundamental concept of** *liberty* **incorporates First Amendment guarantees and safeguards them against state interference.**[1] Education is primarily a state function, so church/state controversies involving schools usually have been initiated through the Fourteenth Amendment.

In the first major Establishment Clause decision, *Everson v. Board of Education*, the Supreme Court in 1947 concluded that the Establishment Clause (and its Fourteenth Amendment application to states) means:

> Neither a state nor the Federal Government can set up a church. Neither can pass laws which aid one religion, aid all religions, or prefer one religion over another. . . . In the words of Jefferson, the clause against establishment of religion by law was intended to erect "a wall of separation between church and state."[2]

[1]*See* Cantwell v. Connecticut, 310 U.S. 296, 303 (1940); Gitlow v. New York, 268 U.S. 652, 666 (1925).

[2]330 U.S. 1, 15–16 (1947).

41

FIGURE 3.1   Judicial Standards to Evaluate Challenged Government Action under the Establishment Clause.

The government actions or practices will violate the Establishment Clause if they:	
o **Have a religious (sectarian) purpose** o **Advance or impede religion** o **Create excessive government entanglement with religion**	*Lemon Test*
o **Have a purpose or effect endorsing or disapproving religion**	*Endorsement Test*
o **Place direct or indirect government coercion on individuals to profess a faith**	*Coercion Test*

Thomas Jefferson's "wall of separation" metaphor was used widely by the federal judiciary for more than 30 years following *Everson*, even though this phrase does not appear in the First Amendment. During this period, the Establishment Clause seemed to be accorded greater weight than the Free Exercise Clause, with courts often supporting the notion that church/state separation "must be complete and unequivocal."[3]

In a 1971 case, *Lemon v. Kurtzman*, the Supreme Court applied a three-part test to assess Establishment Clause claims.[4] **To withstand scrutiny under this test, often referred to as the *Lemon* test, governmental action must (1) have a secular purpose, (2) have a primary effect that neither advances nor impedes religion, and (3) avoid excessive governmental entanglement with religion** (see Figure 3.1). This test was used consistently in Establishment Clause cases involving school issues until 1992. However, a majority of the current justices has voiced dissatisfaction with the test,[5] and reliance on *Lemon* has been noticeably absent in the Supreme Court's recent Establishment Clause rulings. Support for church/state separation seems to be waning, even in school cases where support for separationist doctrine traditionally has been the strongest.

Some of the current Supreme Court justices favor an *endorsement* standard under which governmental action would be struck down if an objective observer would view it as having the purpose or effect of endorsing or disapproving religion.[6] And on occasion, the Court has applied a *coercion* test, which requires direct or indirect governmental coercion on

[3]*Zorach v. Clauson*, 343 U.S. 306, 312 (1952).

[4]403 U.S. 602 (1971).

[5]In *Lamb's Chapel v. Ctr. Moriches Union Free Sch. Dist.*, 508 U.S. 384, 398 (1993), Justice Scalia, concurring, compared the *Lemon* standard to a "ghoul" that rises from the dead "after being repeatedly killed and buried."

[6]*See, e.g.,* County of Allegheny v. ACLU, 492 U.S. 573, 592 (1989); Lynch v. Donnelly, 465 U.S. 668, 687 (1984) (O'Connor, J., concurring).

individuals to profess a faith.[7] Instead of replacing the *Lemon* test with another standard or a combination of standards, the current Supreme Court will likely continue to draw on various tests depending on the specific circumstances of each case (see Figure 3.1). Some lower courts are attempting to cover all bases by reviewing challenged government action under the three-part *Lemon* test, the endorsement standard, and the coercion test.[8]

Whereas in establishment cases, the legality of the governmental action itself is at issue, in free exercise claims, individuals often accept the secular nature of the government regulation but assert that it burdens their religious exercise. To evaluate free exercise claims, the judiciary traditionally has applied a balancing test that includes an assessment of whether practices dictated by a sincere and legitimate religious belief have been impeded by the governmental action, and if so, to what extent. Finding such an impairment, courts then have evaluated whether the government action serves a compelling interest that justifies the burden imposed on the exercise of religious beliefs. Even if such a compelling interest is shown, the government is expected to attain its objectives through means that are the least burdensome on free exercise rights.

In the most significant school case involving a free exercise claim, *Wisconsin v. Yoder*, the Supreme Court exempted Amish children from compulsory school attendance upon successful completion of the eighth grade.[9] Although noting that the assurance of an educated citizenry ranks at the "apex" of state functions, the Court nonetheless concluded that parents' rights to practice their legitimate religious beliefs outweighed the state's interest in mandating two additional years of formal schooling for Amish youth. The Court cautioned, however, that its ruling was limited to the Amish who offer a structured vocational program to prepare their youth for a cloistered agrarian community rather than mainstream American society.

In 1990, the Supreme Court modified this balancing test, ruling that the government does not have to demonstrate a compelling interest to defend a criminal law that burdens the free exercise of religious beliefs.[10] The Court concluded that without a "hybrid" situation, such as the combination of free exercise rights and parental rights in *Yoder*, individuals cannot rely on the Free Exercise Clause to be excused from complying with a valid criminal law prohibiting specific conduct.

Courts not only apply different criteria to assess claims under the Free Exercise and Establishment Clauses, but also they impose different remedies for violations of the two clauses. **If an Establishment Clause violation is found, the unconstitutional government activity must cease. If government action is found to impair the Free Exercise Clause, accommodations to enable individuals to practice their beliefs may be required, but the secular policy or program would not have to be eliminated.**

Troublesome church/state controversies involve competing claims under the Free Exercise and Establishment Clauses because there is an inherent tension between the two provisions. The controversies become even more complex when Free Speech Clause protections are involved, as has been prevalent in recent cases. This tension among First

---

[7]*See* Lee v. Weisman, 505 U.S. 577 (1992).

[8]*See, e.g.,* Doe v. Beaumont Indep. Sch. Dist., 240 F.3d 462 (5th Cir. 2001); Stark v. Indep. Sch. Dist. No. 640, 123 F.3d 1068 (8th Cir. 1997).

[9]406 U.S. 205 (1972).

[10]Employment Div. v. Smith, 494 U.S. 872 (1990) (upholding the termination of employees who ingested peyote at a religious ceremony of the Native American Church).

Amendment guarantees has complicated the judiciary's task in assessing claims regarding the role of religion in public schools and government relations with sectarian schools.

■ ■ ■ ■ ■

RELIGIOUS INFLUENCES IN PUBLIC SCHOOLS

Devotionals sponsored by public schools violate the Establishment Clause, whereas private religious expression is protected by the Free Exercise and Free Speech Clauses.

From colonial days until the mid-twentieth century, religious (primarily Protestant) materials and observances were prevalent in many public schools. In two precedent-setting decisions in the early 1960s, the Supreme Court prohibited public schools from sponsoring daily prayer and Bible reading, concluding that such activities advance religion in violation of the Establishment Clause.[11] The Court reasoned that the students' voluntary participation in the religious activities was irrelevant to the constitutional impairment. The fact that daily devotional activities were sponsored by the public school was sufficient to abridge the First Amendment. In a number of subsequent decisions, federal appellate courts have struck down various legislative attempts to return state-condoned religious activities to public schools.[12]

However, these rulings have not resolved many issues pertaining to religious influences in public education. Is the constitutional violation lessened if students rather than teachers initiate the devotional activities? Can religious speech be distinguished from other types of speech in applying restrictions? To date, courts have provided only partial answers to these and related questions.

Silent Prayer Statutes

Students have a free exercise right to engage in *private* **devotional activities in public schools as long as they do not interfere with regular school activities.** Indeed, it would be difficult to monitor whether students were engaging in silent prayer. Controversies have focused on state laws or school board policies that condone silent devotionals, thus placing the stamp of public school approval on such activities.

In 1985, the Supreme Court rendered its first and only opinion to date on this issue in *Wallace v. Jaffree*, invalidating an Alabama silent prayer law under the Establishment Clause.[13] Since a 1978 Alabama law already authorized a period of silent meditation in public schools, the Court majority concluded that the only logical reason for adding the phrase "or voluntary prayer" in the 1981 amendment was to encourage students to pray. But the Court indicated that such laws without a legislative intent to impose prayer might withstand scrutiny under the Establishment Clause.

[11]Sch. Dist. of Abington Twp. v. Schempp, 374 U.S. 203 (1963); Engel v. Vitale, 370 U.S. 421 (1962).

[12]*See, e.g.*, Doe v. Sch. Bd., 274 F.3d 289 (5th Cir. 2001); Ingebretsen v. Jackson Pub. Sch. Dist., 88 F.3d 274 (5th Cir. 1996); Doe v. Duncanville Indep. Sch. Dist., 70 F.3d 402 (5th Cir. 1995).

[13]472 U.S. 38 (1985). *See also* Borden v. Sch. Dist., 523 F.3d 153 (3d Cir. 2008) (holding that a coach violated the First Amendment by kneeling and bowing his head during a moment of silence; an objective observer would view his action as endorsing religion, particularly in light of his past encouragement of the team's devotional activities).

The constitutionality of laws calling for a moment of silence for prayer or meditation in public schools, which currently exist in a majority of the states, remains to be resolved on a case-by-case basis, and courts have rejected most recent challenges to such laws. For example, the Eleventh Circuit upheld termination of a high school teacher for refusing to comply with Georgia's law that requires each public school teacher to conduct a minute of quiet reflection at the opening of the school day. The court concluded that the statute has the secular purpose of providing an opportunity for pupils to reflect on the upcoming day.[14] The Fourth Circuit also upheld a Virginia silent prayer statute as being neutral toward religion since students were not encouraged to pray during the moment of silence; the court reasoned that the law was enacted to provide time for quiet reflection, which is a good management strategy to settle students.[15]

School-Sponsored versus Private Devotionals

The most controversial issues currently revolve around what constitutes *private* religious expression in the public school context that does not trigger Establishment Clause restrictions. In short, when is religious expression *not* sponsored by the public school?

Weisman **and Its Progeny.**   A 1992 decision generated a wave of legislative activity pressing the limits of the Establishment Clause. In *Lee v. Weisman*, the divided Supreme Court struck down a Rhode Island school district's policy that permitted principals to invite clergy members to deliver invocations and benedictions at middle and high school graduation ceremonies.[16] The Court majority reasoned that the policy had a coercive effect; students felt peer pressure to participate in the devotionals at the school-sponsored ceremony, and the voluntary nature of graduation exercises did not eliminate the Establishment Clause infraction. According to the Court majority, students should not have to make a choice between attending their graduation ceremony, a milestone event in their lives, and respecting their religious convictions.

Rather than reducing devotional activities in public school graduations, the Supreme Court's decision had the opposite impact. Negative reactions to this ruling resulted in school authorities and students finding creative strategies to include prayers in graduation

---

[14]Bown v. Gwinnett County Sch. Dist., 112 F.3d 1464 (11th Cir. 1997). *See also* Croft v. Perry, 530 F. Supp. 2d 825 (N.D. Tex., 2008) (upholding a Texas law, requiring each school to observe a minute of silence for students to reflect, pray, or meditate). *But see* Sherman v. Twp. High Sch. Dist. 214, No. 070C-6048, 2008 U.S. Dist. LEXIS 25979 (N.D. Ill. Mar. 28, 2008) (reaffirming a preliminary injunction against enforcing an Illinois law requiring all public schools to observe a moment of silence, rejecting school district's motion to dismiss an Establishment Clause challenge to the law, and certifying as classes all students and public schools in Illinois subject to the contested law). According to the National Conference of State Legislatures, in 2007 almost two-thirds of the states authorized a moment of silence in public schools and 12 states required such a daily observance. *See States with Moment of Silence or School Prayer Legislation,* available at www.ncsl.org/magazine/momentofsilence.htm.

[15]Brown v. Gilmore, 258 F.3d 265 (4th Cir. 2001). *See also* the No Child Left Behind Act, 20 U.S.C. § 6061 (2008) (specifying that no federal funds can be appropriated under the act for policies that prevent voluntary prayer and meditation in public schools).

[16]505 U.S. 577 (1992).

ceremonies. In some districts, baccalaureate services were reinstated and sponsored by churches or other groups in space rented from the school district.[17]

Because of the prohibition on *school-sponsored* religious activities, most post-*Weisman* controversies have involved *student-led* devotionals. **Some school districts have given students discretion to include religious messages in their graduation speeches, designating the graduation ceremony a forum for student expression.** Accordingly, students' messages (including any religious references) are not subject to review and do not bear the stamp of school approval. The Ninth Circuit upheld an Idaho school district's policy that prohibited school authorities from censoring students' graduation speeches and allowed student speakers, chosen by academic standing, to select a reading, song, or any other presentation of their choosing.[18] Finding the ceremony a forum for student expression, the court reasoned that the student speakers were selected based on secular criteria and were not advised to include devotionals in their remarks.

In two other Ninth Circuit cases, however, the appeals court upheld school districts in barring proselytizing graduation speeches that students had submitted to their principals for review in accordance with school policy. Unlike the first case, school authorities in these districts clearly maintained control of the graduation ceremony. Thus, the court found censorship of the proposed religious speeches appropriate to avoid an Establishment Clause violation.[19] **The central consideration seems to be whether the school has explicitly created a forum for student expression in the graduation ceremony or has retained control over students' graduation speeches.**

Student Elections to Authorize Prayers. Especially volatile controversies have focused on having students decide by election to include student-led devotionals in graduation ceremonies and other school activities. Federal appellate courts have differed regarding the constitutionality of allowing students to vote on having nonsectarian graduation prayers selected and delivered by students.[20]

In 2000, the Supreme Court in *Santa Fe Independent School District v. Doe* found an Establishment Clause violation in a Texas school district's policy authorizing student-led

---

[17]*See, e.g.,* Shumway v. Albany County Sch. Dist. No. One, 826 F. Supp. 1320 (D. Wyo. 1993) (finding no school sponsorship in students renting the high school gym for a baccalaureate program at which the school band performed and the district's graduation announcements mentioned the baccalaureate program); Verbena United Methodist Church v. Chilton County Bd. of Educ., 765 F. Supp. 704 (M.D. Ala. 1991) (holding that a school board must take all reasonable steps to disassociate itself from a baccalaureate service sponsored by religious organizations and conducted in space rented from the school district).

[18]Doe v. Madison Sch. Dist. No. 321, 147 F.3d 832 (9th Cir. 1998), *vacated and remanded en banc* (because the student had graduated), 177 F.3d 789 (9th Cir. 1999). *See also* Doe v. Sch. Dist., 340 F.3d 605 (8th Cir. 2003) (broadly interpreting what constitutes private, rather than school-sponsored, religious expression in finding no Establishment Clause violation in a school board member's unscheduled recitation of the Lord's Prayer in the graduation ceremony).

[19]Lassonde v. Pleasanton Unified Sch. Dist., 320 F.3d 979 (9th Cir. 2003); Cole v. Oroville Union High Sch. Dist., 228 F.3d 1092 (9th Cir. 2000).

[20]*Compare* ACLU of N.J. v. Black Horse Pike Reg'l Bd. of Educ., 84 F.3d 1471 (3d Cir. 1996) *with* Jones v. Clear Creek Indep. Sch. Dist., 930 F.2d 416 (5th Cir. 1991), *vacated and remanded*, 505 U.S. 1215 (1992), *on remand*, 977 F.2d 963 (5th Cir. 1992).

devotionals before public school football games.[21] The controversial policy and an identical graduation prayer policy authorized two elections—one to determine whether to have invocations and the second to select the student to deliver them. **The Supreme Court limited its ruling to the policy authorizing student-led prayers before football games and declared that student-led expression at a school event on school property and representing the student body under the supervision of school personnel could not be considered private speech.**[22] The degree of school involvement gave the impression that the devotionals at issue represented the school, leading the Court majority to conclude that the practice entailed both perceived and actual endorsement of religion. Noting that the purpose of the Bill of Rights is to shield certain subjects from the political process, the Court held that the use of student elections intensifies the lack of representation of minority views, ensuring that they will never be heard. While rejecting the argument that Establishment Clause concerns can be eliminated by delegating decisions to students, **the majority emphasized that only state sponsorship of devotionals violates the Establishment Clause; nothing in the Constitution prohibits public school students from voluntarily praying at school.**

Post–*Santa Fe* Rulings.   The *Santa Fe* decision has not settled what distinguishes protected private religious expression from unconstitutional school-sponsored devotionals. Indeed, some post–*Santa Fe* federal appellate rulings represent an expansive stance regarding the reach of the Free Speech Clause in protecting students' private religious expression in public schools. For example, the Eleventh Circuit reaffirmed its two pre–*Santa Fe* rulings in which it upheld a school district's policy authorizing seniors to select graduation speakers who could choose religious content[23] and lifted an injunction that had prohibited students from expressing religious views in most public school settings in an Alabama district.[24] The appeals court declared that the Establishment Clause does not *require* and the Free Speech Clause does not *permit* suppressing student-initiated religious expression in public schools or relegating it to whispers or behind closed doors. Distinguishing the Supreme Court's condemnation of school-sponsored student prayer in *Santa Fe*, the Eleventh Circuit reasoned that school censorship of *private* student religious expression also is unconstitutional.[25] The appeals court emphasized that all student religious speech in public schools cannot be equated with expression *representing* the public school. Furthermore, federal guidelines to implement the No Child Left Behind Act expansively interpret what constitutes protected religious expression in public schools.[26]

---

[21]530 U.S. 290 (2000).

[22]*Id.* at 310.

[23]Adler v. Duval County Sch. Bd., 206 F.3d 1070 (11th Cir. 2000), *vacated and remanded*, 531 U.S. 801 (2000), *reinstated on remand*, 250 F.3d 1330 (11th Cir. 2001).

[24]Chandler v. James, 180 F.3d 1254 (11th Cir. 1999), *vacated and remanded*, 530 U.S. 1256 (2000), *reinstated on remand sub nom* Chandler v. Siegelman, 230 F.3d 1313 (11th Cir. 2000).

[25]*Id.,* 230 F.3d at 1315. *See also* Prince v. Jacoby, 303 F.3d 1074 (9th Cir. 2002) (finding that the Free Speech Clause demands equal treatment of student religious and secular clubs); *infra* text accompanying note 62.

[26]*Guidance on Constitutionally Protected Prayer in Public Elementary and Secondary Schools*, U.S. Department of Education, 68 Fed. Reg. 9645-01 (February 28, 2003), interpreting the No Child Left Behind Act, 20 U.S.C. § 6061 (2008).

The Supreme Court undoubtedly will be asked to provide additional clarification regarding how to distinguish private religious expression from prohibited school-sponsored devotionals. **Student religious expression may be considered private if truly student initiated, but the *Santa Fe* decision casts doubt on the legality of holding student elections to determine that student-led devotionals will be included in school-sponsored activities.**

Pledge of Allegiance

More than four-fifths of the states have laws or policies specifying that the Pledge of Allegiance to the American flag will be recited in public schools, and many of these provisions were enacted or amended since the terrorist attacks on September 11, 2001.[27] As discussed later, students have a right to opt out of the Pledge based on their religious or philosophical beliefs,[28] but recent controversies have focused on whether the Pledge can be said in public schools *at all*, given the 1954 addition of the phrase "under God."

The Seventh Circuit upheld an Illinois law requiring daily recitation of the Pledge in public schools, as long as students can decline to participate. Regarding the Establishment Clause claim, the appeals court ruled that the "ceremonial deism" in the Pledge "has lost through rote repetition any significant religious content."[29] A Virginia federal district court reached the same conclusion in rejecting a constitutional challenge to a Virginia law requiring the recitation of the Pledge in public schools, noting that a civic religion has been recognized in the United States.[30] Even though the school district at issue in this case considered recitation of the Pledge in a citizenship reward program, the judge noted that other factors also were considered in making the citizenship awards, so there was no coercion to participate in the Pledge.

In contrast, the Ninth Circuit attracted national attention when it rejected the "ceremonial deism" justification and declared that saying the Pledge in public schools abridges the Establishment Clause by endorsing a belief in monotheism.[31] The appellate panel applied the *Lemon,* coercion, and endorsement tests in finding an Establishment Clause violation and emphasized that the words "under God" had been inserted in the Pledge to promote religion rather than to advance the legitimate secular goal of encouraging patriotism.

The Supreme Court reversed the Ninth Circuit's decision in 2004 without addressing the constitutional claim in *Elk Grove Unified School District v. Newdow*. The majority

---

[27]Peyton Cooke, *Pledge of Allegiance Statutes, State by State* (June 19, 2006), available at www.firstamendmentcenter. org/analysis.aspx?id=17035; Jennifer Piscatelli, "Pledge of Allegiance," *StateNotes: Character/Citizenship Education* (Denver: Education Commission of the States, August 2003).

[28]*See* W. Va. State Bd. of Educ. v. Barnette, 319 U.S. 624 (1943); *infra* text accompanying note 78.

[29]Sherman v. Cmty. Consol. Sch. Dist. 21, 980 F.2d 437, 447 (7th Cir. 1992).

[30]Myers v. Loudoun County Sch. Bd., 251 F. Supp. 2d 1262, 1267–1270 (E.D. Va. 2003) (rejecting also an Establishment Clause challenge to a state law requiring the motto "In God We Trust" to be displayed in public schools). *See also* Myers v. Loudon County School Bd., 500 F. Supp. 2d 539 (E.D. Va. 2007) (holding that the school could reject a parent's proposed vulgar advertisement for school publications that denounced the Pledge and his attempt to distribute leaflets at school, but he could not be prevented from distributing leaflets on the sidewalk adjacent to the school).

[31]Newdow v. U.S. Cong., 292 F.3d 597, 607–613 (9th Cir. 2002), *opinion amended and superseded by* 328 F.3d 466 (2003), *rev'd sub nom.* Elk Grove Unified Sch. Dist. v. Newdow, 542 U.S. 1 (2004).

reasoned that Newdow lacked standing to challenge his daughter's participation in the Pledge because California law deprived him as a noncustodial parent of the right to bring suit as "next friend" on behalf of his daughter.[32] Following the Supreme Court's ruling, a California federal district court again has ruled that the classroom recitation of the Pledge violates the Establishment Clause.[33]

Religious Displays and Holiday Observances

The display of religious documents and the observance of religious holidays in public schools also remain controversial. In 1980, the Supreme Court declined to hear an appeal of a decision in which the Eighth Circuit ruled that given the historical and cultural signifi- cance of Christmas, the prudent and objective observance of this holiday in public schools does not serve to advance religion, even if songs such as "Silent Night" are sung and the nativity scene is temporarily displayed.[34] The appeals court held that the school board's pol- icy, allowing the observance of holidays with both a religious and secular basis, had the nonreligious purpose of improving the overall instructional program.

In contrast, a week later the five-member Supreme Court majority in *Stone v. Graham* struck down a Kentucky law calling for the posting of the Ten Commandments in public schools. Distinguishing the display of religious texts from the permissible use of religious literature in academic courses, the majority held that the Kentucky law's purpose was to advance a particular religious faith in violation of the Establishment Clause. The majority rejected the state judiciary's conclusion that the constitutional impairment was neutralized because the copies were purchased with private donations and carried the disclaimer that "the secular application of the Ten Commandments is clearly seen in its adoption as the fundamental legal code of Western Civilization and the Common Law of the United States."[35]

In spite of this ruling, state efforts to authorize the posting of the Ten Commandments with other historic documents in public buildings including schools continue to generate litigation. The Supreme Court rendered two companion decisions pertaining to displays of the Ten Commandments on government property in 2005. The Court upheld the longstand- ing display of a Ten Commandments monument on the Texas state capitol grounds along with other artifacts that reflect the secular purpose of paying tribute to the state's history.[36] In contrast, the Court struck down the display of framed copies of the Ten Commandments in two Kentucky county courthouses, noting that several attempts to add secular items to the displays did not eliminate their initial religious purpose.[37] Although school displays of

---

[32]*Newdow,* 542 U.S. at 17–18.

[33]Newdow v. U.S. Cong., 383 F. Supp. 2d 1229 (E.D. Cal. 2005).

[34]Florey v. Sioux Falls Sch. Dist. 49-5, 619 F.2d 1311, 1314 (8th Cir.1980). *See also* Sechler v. State Coll. Area Sch. Dist., 121 F. Supp. 2d 439 (M.D. Pa. 2000) (rejecting an Establishment Clause challenge to a holiday obser- vance that allegedly was not "Christian enough"; the program included the menorah and Kwanzaa candelabra as well as a Christmas tree and carols and was designed to celebrate diversity).

[35]Stone v. Graham, 449 U.S. 39, 41 (1980).

[36]The monument was donated by the Fraternal Order of Eagles in 1961. Van Orden v. Perry, 545 U.S. 677 (2005).

[37]McCreary County, Ky. v. ACLU, 545 U.S. 844 (2005).

the Ten Commandments were not at issue in these cases, the Court indicated that *Stone v. Graham* still has precedential value.

Other religious displays also have been controversial. The Sixth Circuit held that the display of a portrait of Jesus in a public secondary school failed all three prongs of the *Lemon* test,[38] and a New York federal district court enjoined the display of a religious painting in a high school auditorium because it conveyed governmental endorsement of religion.[39] However, a federal district court in New Jersey found that inclusion of religious holidays, such as Christmas and Hanukkah, on school district calendars satisfied the *Lemon* test as it was designed to broaden students' sensitivity toward religious diversity and knowledge of the role of religion in the development of civilization.[40]

Courts have not been receptive to parental assertions that public schools are promoting the religion of Wicca by observing Halloween. The Supreme Court declined to review a Florida court's ruling in which the state appeals court held that a display of witches does not promote a nontheistic religion or give any perception of public school endorsement of Wicca.[41] Similarly, an Establishment Clause challenge to using a devil as a public school's mascot has been rejected.[42]

The Supreme Court has condoned the use of public funds or property for certain religious displays in several decisions outside the school domain.[43] Nonetheless, **courts seem likely to continue to strike down the display of sectarian documents in public schools, even though the objective recognition of religious holidays will presumably withstand judicial scrutiny as long as particular faiths are not compromised.**

Proselytization in the Classroom

Public schools must abide by Establishment Clause restrictions on governmental promotion of religious creeds. Because teachers and other personnel in public schools are working with a vulnerable captive audience, their actions have been scrutinized to ensure that classrooms are not used as a forum to indoctrinate sectarian beliefs. To illustrate, the Tenth Circuit held that school officials could order the removal of religiously oriented books from a teacher's classroom library and require the teacher to keep his Bible out of sight and to

---

[38]Washegesic v. Bloomingdale Pub. Schs., 33 F.3d 679 (6th Cir. 1994). *See also* Fleming v. Jefferson County Sch. Dist. R-1, 298 F.3d 918 (10th Cir. 2002) (finding no Establishment or Free Speech Clause violation in not allowing persons connected with the Columbine shootings to paint religious messages on tiles hung in the school). *But see* Kiesinger v. Mex. Acad. & Cent. Sch., 56 Fed. App'x 549 (2d Cir. 2003), *on remand*, 427 F. Supp. 2d 182 (N.D.N.Y. 2006) (finding viewpoint discrimination in a school district's removal of bricks with references to Jesus from a walkway funded by selling bricks that individuals inscribed with personal messages).

[39]Joki v. Bd. of Educ., 745 F. Supp. 823 (N.D.N.Y. 1990). *See also* Gernetzke v. Kenosha Unified Sch. Dist. No. 1, 274 F.3d 464 (7th Cir. 2001) (finding no Equal Access Act violation when a principal barred a student religious group from including a large cross in the group's mural for the school hallway).

[40]Clever v. Cherry Hill Twp. Bd. of Educ., 838 F. Supp. 929 (D.N.J. 1993).

[41]Guyer v. Sch. Bd., 634 So. 2d 806 (Fla. Dist. Ct. App. 1994).

[42]*See* Kunselman v. W. Reserve Local Sch. Dist., 70 F.3d 931 (6th Cir. 1995).

[43]For citations and further explanation of these cases, *see* Stephen Thomas, Nelda Cambron-McCabe, and Martha McCarthy, *Public School Law: Teachers' and Students' Rights*, 6th ed. (Boston: Allyn and Bacon, 2009), Chapter 2.

refrain from silently reading it during school hours.[44] Similarly, the Second Circuit found no free exercise impairment in a New York school board's directive for a teacher to stop using religious references in delivering his instructional program,[45] and a federal district court held that school authorities were reasonable in asking a Connecticut teacher to cover a proselytizing shirt at school.[46] **The judiciary has recognized that the Establishment Clause bars public school teachers' use of the prestige and influence of their positions to lead devotional activities.**

In several cases, teachers have been discharged for proselytizing students or disregarding selected aspects of the curriculum that conflict with their religious values. For example, the Seventh Circuit upheld a school board's dismissal of a kindergarten teacher who literally interpreted the biblical prohibition against worshiping graven images, and thus refused to teach about the American flag, the observance of patriotic holidays, and the importance of historical figures such as Abraham Lincoln. The appellate court noted that the teacher enjoys the freedom to hold such beliefs but has "no constitutional right to require others to submit to her views and to forgo a portion of their education they would otherwise be entitled to enjoy."[47] A New York appeals court also upheld the dismissal of a tenured teacher based on evidence that she had tried to recruit students to join her religious organization, conducted prayer sessions in her office, and used her classroom to promote her religious faith.[48]

Although proselytization of students by public school teachers violates the Establishment Clause, the Supreme Court has emphasized that it is permissible, even desirable, to teach the Bible and other religious documents from a literary, cultural, or historical perspective.[49] The insufficient treatment in textbooks of the role of religion in the development of Western civilization has been partially due to fears of violating the Establishment Clause. Several coalitions of national education, civic, and religious groups as well as the Department of Education have distributed materials addressing permissible methods to teach about the role of religion in society and attempting to clarify the legal status of various church/state issues in public schools.[50]

Comparative religion courses in high schools have seldom been controversial, but the line is not always clear between teaching about religion and instilling religious tenets in other courses. Numerous Bible study courses, particularly at the elementary school level,

[44]Roberts v. Madigan, 921 F.2d 1047 (10th Cir. 1990). However, the court enjoined the school board from removing the Bible from the school library, noting that the Bible has significant literary and historical significance.

[45]Marchi v. Bd. of Coop. Educ. Servs., 173 F.3d 469 (2d. Cir. 1999).

[46]Downing v. W. Haven Bd. of Educ., 162 F. Supp. 2d 19 (D. Conn. 2001). The shirt read "Jesus 2000, J2K."

[47]Palmer v. Bd. of Educ., 603 F.2d 1271, 1274 (7th Cir. 1979). For a discussion of teachers' wearing religious attire in public schools, *see* text accompanying note 67, Chapter 11.

[48]La Rocca v. Bd. of Educ., 406 N.Y.S.2d 348 (App. Div. 1978).

[49]*See* Sch. Dist. of Abington Twp. v. Schempp, 374 U.S. 203, 225 (1963). The Ninth Circuit rejected a claim that role playing activities to teach seventh graders world history promoted Islam; the court did not find the activities to be religious exercises. Eklund v. Byron Union Sch. Dist., 154 Fed. App'x 648 (9th Cir. 2005), *cert. denied,* 127 S. Ct. 86 (2006).

[50]*See Guidance, supra* note 26; Pew Forum on Religion and Public Life and the First Amendment Center, *Teaching about Religion in Public Schools: Where Do We Go from Here?* (Arlington, VA: First Amendment Center, 2003).

have been challenged as a ploy to advance sectarian beliefs. Courts have carefully evaluated curricular materials and have struck down programs designed to inculcate religious tenets rather than to study *about* religion or where private groups have controlled the personnel or curriculum.[51]

Performances of school choirs often have evoked controversies over alleged proselytization. The Tenth Circuit accepted a school district's justification for using religious songs in choir performances, noting that a substantial amount of appropriate choral music is religious in nature.[52] The Fifth Circuit similarly found no endorsement of religion in a choir's use of religious songs.[53]

Some controversies over proselytization in the classroom have not challenged teachers' activities but have entailed requests for students to include sectarian materials in their presentations, artwork, or other school assignments. In most of these cases, the schools have prevailed in denying the students' requests. For example, the Sixth Circuit upheld a school district's prohibition on an elementary school student showing in class a videotape of herself singing a proselytizing religious song.[54] Recognizing that the public school curriculum is supervised by faculty and designed to impart knowledge, the appeals court held that student projects can be censored to ensure that the school is not viewed as endorsing religious content. In contrast, the Second Circuit found the likelihood of unconstitutional viewpoint discrimination in a teacher's refusal to display a kindergarten student's poster and censorship of his replacement poster because of his religious content in portraying what he had learned about the environment.[55]

Equal Access for Religious Expression and Groups

In the 1960s and 1970s, it was generally assumed that the Establishment Clause governed controversies regarding religious speech in government forums. Since then, however, the Supreme Court has reasoned that **singling out religious views for differential treatment**

---

[51]*See, e.g.*, Hall v. Bd. of Sch. Comm'rs, 707 F.2d 464 (11th Cir. 1983); Doe v. Porter, 188 F. Supp. 2d 904 (E.D. Tenn. 2002). *But see* Doe v. Beaumont Indep. Sch. Dist., 240 F.3d 462 (5th Cir. 2001) (*en banc*) (remanding for a trial to determine if use of volunteer clergy counselors in public schools violates the Establishment Clause).

[52]Bauchman v. W. High Sch., 132 F.3d 542 (10th Cir. 1997) (ruling also that two choir performances could be held at religious sites because of their superior facilities).

[53]Doe v. Duncanville Indep. Sch. Dist., 70 F.3d 402 (5th Cir. 1995). However, the court struck down the basketball team's policy of praying before games, practices, and pep rallies with the encouragement of school employees.

[54]DeNooyer v. Merinelli, 12 F.3d 211 (6th Cir. 1993). *See also* Curry v. Hensiner, 513 F.3d 570 (6th Cir. 2008) (finding no violation of a fifth grade student's free speech rights in prohibiting the student from selling candy canes with religious cards as part of a school project); Settle v. Dickson County Sch. Bd., 53 F.3d 152 (6th Cir. 1995) (upholding a junior high school teacher who gave a student a zero on a report, because the student had cleared a different topic with the teacher but then wrote her report on the life of Jesus Christ); Walz v. Egg Harbor Twp. Bd. of Educ., 187 F. Supp. 2d 232 (D.N.J. 2002) (rejecting the contention that a student had a First Amendment right to distribute religious gifts in the classroom; reasonable accommodations were made in that religious materials could be distributed before and after school and during recess).

[55]Peck v. Baldwinsville Cent. Sch. Dist., 426 F.3d 617 (2d Cir. 2005) (remanding for further consideration of the free expression issue but ruling that the lower court properly dismissed the Establishment Clause claim), *cert. denied*, 547 U.S. 1097 (2006). *See also Guidance, supra* note 26 (stipulating that students should not be disadvantaged if they express their religious beliefs in their class assignments).

FIGURE 3.2   The Equal Access Act, 20 U. S. C. §§ 4071–4074 (2008)

Sec. 801(a) It shall be unlawful for any public secondary school which receives federal financial assistance and which has a limited open forum to deny equal access or a fair opportunity to, or discriminate against, any students who wish to conduct a meeting within that limited open forum on the basis of the religious, political, philosophical, or other content of the speech at such meetings.

(b) A public secondary school has a limited open forum whenever such school grants an offering to or opportunity for one or more noncurriculum related student groups to meet on school premises during noninstructional time.

(c) Schools shall be deemed to offer a fair opportunity to students who wish to conduct a meeting within its limited open forum if such school uniformly provides that

   (1) the meeting is voluntary and student-initiated;

   (2) there is no sponsorship of the meeting by the school, the government, or its agents or employees;

   (3) employees or agents of the school or government are present at religious meetings only in a nonparticipatory capacity;

   (4) the meeting does not materially and substantially interfere with the orderly conduct of educational activities within the school; and

   (5) nonschool persons may not direct, conduct, control, or regularly attend activities of student groups.

compared with other private expression would be unconstitutional viewpoint discrimination, which abridges the Free Speech Clause.[56]

Equal Access Act.   The Free Speech Clause was augmented at the secondary school level by the Equal Access Act (EAA) in 1984 (see Figure 3.2).[57] In 1990, the Supreme Court in *Board of Education v. Mergens* held that the EAA does not abridge the Establishment Clause by allowing student religious groups to meet. The Court recognized the law's clear secular purpose of preventing discrimination against religious and other types of private expression.[58] **The Court distinguished government speech promoting religion that is prohibited by the Establishment Clause from private religious expression protected by the Free Speech and Free Exercise Clauses.** In subsequent cases, federal appellate courts have ruled that the EAA:

- Prevails over state constitutional provisions requiring greater separation of church and state than demanded by the Establishment Clause;[59]
- Authorizes student religious meetings during lunch if that is considered noninstructional time;[60]

[56]*See* Widmar v. Vincent, 454 U.S. 263 (1981) (finding no Establishment Clause violation in providing student religious group's access to a forum created for student expression on state-supported college campuses); *infra* text accompanying notes 64–66.

[57]20 U.S.C. §§ 4071–4074 (2008).

[58]496 U.S. 226, 249–250 (1990).

[59]Ceniceros v. Bd. of Trs., 106 F.3d 878 (9th Cir. 1997); Garnett v. Renton Sch. Dist. No. 403, 987 F.2d 641 (9th Cir. 1993).

[60]*Ceniceros*, 106 F.3d 878. *See also* Van Schoick v. Saddleback Valley Unified Sch. Dist., 104 Cal. Rptr. 2d 562 (Ct. App. 2001) (holding that to be protected under the EAA, only the on-campus meetings, and not the religious club itself, would have to be students initiated).

- Authorizes student religious groups to require certain officers to be Christians to preserve the spiritual content of their meetings;[61] and
- Requires student religious groups to be provided equal access to fund-raising activities, school bulletin boards, and other resources available for student clubs.[62]

However, the Ninth Circuit ruled that a school district in Washington state did not violate the EAA by denying recognition to a student Bible club whose charter denied full voting membership to students who did not pledge to abide by the Bible.[63]

Although there are limits on the reach of the EAA, this federal law has provided substantial protection to student religious meetings in secondary schools during noninstructional time. The EAA has codified the concept of equal access and equal treatment of religious expression that is currently guiding First Amendment litigation as well.

School Access for Community Groups. **The EAA applies *only* to secondary students, so community religious groups desiring public school access during noninstructional time cannot use this law; they must instead rely *solely* on First Amendment protections.** Since the early 1990s, the Supreme Court has made some definitive pronouncements about protecting private religious expression from viewpoint discrimination. In *Lamb's Chapel v. Center Moriches Union Free School District*, the Court held that if secular community groups are allowed to use the public school after school hours to address particular topics (e.g., family life, child rearing), a sectarian group desiring to show a film series addressing these topics from religious perspectives cannot be denied public school access.[64] In essence, **school districts cannot enforce policies governing facility use during nonschool time that entail viewpoint discrimination against a religious group's message.**

In 2001, the Supreme Court delivered a seminal decision, *Good News Club v. Milford Central School*, allowing a private Christian organization to hold its meetings in a New York public school after school hours.[65] The Good News Club is affiliated with the Child Evangelism Fellowship, which teaches Christian values to children ages 6 to 12. The Milford School District had denied the Good News Club's request under its community-use policy that allows civic and recreational groups to use the school but not for religious purposes.

Disagreeing with the school district and the lower courts, the Supreme Court in *Milford* held that the school district's policy discriminated against religious viewpoints in violation of the Free Speech Clause. Milford school authorities attempted to distinguish student meetings of the Good News Club that involve religious instruction and prayer from a religious group using the school to show films primarily to adults, which was upheld in

---

[61]Hsu v. Roslyn Union Free Sch. Dist. No. 3, 85 F.3d 839 (2d Cir. 1996).

[62]Prince v. Jacoby, 303 F.3d 1074 (9th Cir. 2002).

[63]Truth v. Kent Sch. Dist., 524 F3d 957 (9th Cir., 2008).

[64]508 U.S. 384 (1993).

[65]533 U.S. 98 (2001). *See also* Culbertson v. Oakridge Sch. Dist. No. 76, 258 F.3d 1061 (9th Cir. 2001) (upholding the Good News Club's right to meet in the public school after school hours, but enjoining teachers from distributing permission slips for the meetings as encouraging the club in violation of the Establishment Clause).

Lamb's Chapel. The Supreme Court did not find the distinction significant, noting that whether moral lessons are taught through live storytelling and prayers or through films is inconsequential from a constitutional standpoint.[66] **Under *Milford*, if a public school establishes a limited forum for community meetings, it cannot bar religious groups, even those involved in worship activities that target students attending the school.** The Court did not find a danger that the community would perceive the Good News Club's access as school district endorsement of religion.

Distribution of Religious Literature.   The Supreme Court has not directly addressed the distribution of religious literature in public schools, and lower courts have rendered a range of opinions. Courts consistently have ruled that school personnel cannot give students Bibles or other religious materials,[67] and most courts have prohibited religious sects, such as the Gideon Society, from visiting the school to distribute materials to captive public school audiences.[68]

Departing from this trend, the Fourth Circuit upheld a West Virginia school district's policy allowing sectarian organizations along with political groups to distribute materials, such as Bibles, in public secondary schools on a designated day because the organizations were considered private entities that do not represent the school.[69] However, the policy was invalidated at the elementary school level because of the impressionability of younger children and their greater difficulty in distinguishing private from school-sponsored speech.

Recent controversies have focused primarily on student requests to distribute religious publications. **Most courts have applied the "equal access" concept in concluding that the same legal principles govern students' distribution of religious and nonreligious literature.**[70]

Yet, even personal expression is subject to reasonable time, place, and manner regulations. For example, an Indiana federal district court supported a school policy requiring students to give the principal advance notice of the distribution and to submit a copy of the literature to the superintendent, but not for approval purposes.[71] Whereas reasonable restrictions on how material is distributed have been upheld, school districts cannot place a blanket ban on students' distribution of religious literature.

---

[66]*Good News Club,* 533 U.S. at 108–110.

[67]*See, e.g.,* Jabr v. Rapides Parish Sch. Bd., 171 F. Supp. 2d 653 (W.D. La. 2001) (finding that a school principal violated the Establishment Clause by distributing New Testament Bibles to public school students).

[68]*See, e.g.,* Doe v. South Iron R-1 Sch. Dist., 498 F.3d 878 (8th Cir. 2007); Doe v. Duncanville Indep. Sch. Dist., 70 F.3d 402 (5th Cir. 1995); Roe v. Tangipahoa Parish Sch. Bd., No. 07-2908, 2008 U.S. Dist. LEXIS 32793 (E.D. La. Apr. 22, 2008).

[69]Peck v. Upshur County Bd. of Educ., 155 F.3d 274 (4th Cir. 1998). *See also* Bacon v. Bradley-Bourbonnais High Sch. Dist. No. 307, 707 F. Supp. 1005 (C.D. III. 1989) (upholding Gideons' right to distribute Bibles on the school-owned sidewalk in front of a high school, because the sidewalk was considered a public forum for use by the general public).

[70]*See, e.g.,* Muller v. Jefferson Lighthouse Sch., 98 F.3d 1530 (7th Cir. 1996); Hedges v. Wauconda Cmty. Unit Sch. Dist. No. 118, 9 F.3d 1295 (7th Cir. 1993). *See also* Rosenberger v. Rector & Visitors, 515 U.S. 819 (1995) (relying on the Free Speech Clause in holding that a public university could not withhold support from a student group wanting to use student activity funds to distribute sectarian materials).

[71]Harless v. Darr, 937 F. Supp. 1351 (S.D. Ind. 1996).

■ ■ ■ ■ ■

ACCOMMODATIONS FOR RELIGIOUS BELIEFS

Religious exemptions from school observances and assignments will be upheld as long as they do not interfere with the management of the school or the excused student's progress.

In addition to challenging sectarian influences in public schools, some students have asserted a right to accommodations so they can practice their religious beliefs. Conflicts over release-time programs for religious education, excusal from public schools for religious observances, and religious exemptions from secular school activities often pit free exercise and free speech protections against prohibitions on religious establishment.

Release-Time Programs

Although the Supreme Court has struck down the practice of using public school classrooms for clergy to provide religious training to public school students during the instructional day,[72] the Court has recognized that the school must not be hostile toward religion so it can release students to receive such religious training off public school grounds.[73] A release-time program was even upheld in a school district in which students received an hour of religious instruction each week in a mobile unit parked at the edge of school property.[74] Confining students to a single choice of attending religious classes or remaining in the public school has not been found to advance religion or to deny nonparticipating pupils their state-created right to an education.

While upholding a release-time program in Utah, the Tenth Circuit enjoined the school's practice of awarding course credit in the public high school for the secular aspects of daily instruction received at a Mormon seminary.[75] More recently, an Indiana federal district court enjoined several features of a release-time program that was held in trailers on public school property, with utilities supported by the school district. Nonparticipating students were required to read silently when their classmates attended the religious instruction to discourage students from remaining in the classroom during the release-time program.[76] Recognizing the legality of release-time programs, the court nonetheless

---

[72]McCollum v. Bd. of Educ., 333 U.S. 203 (1948).

[73]Zorach v. Clauson, 343 U.S. 306, 313–314 (1952).

[74]Smith v. Smith, 523 F.2d 121 (4th Cir. 1975). Programs in which all students are released early from school one day a week might be easier to defend constitutionally because students would not be restricted to either remaining at the public school or attending sectarian classes.

[75]Lanner v. Wimmer, 662 F.2d 1349 (10th Cir. 1981) (holding, however, that time spent by students in the seminary program could satisfy compulsory school attendance and be counted toward the school's eligibility for state aid).

[76]Moore v. Metro. Sch. Dist., No. IP 00-1859-C-M/S, 2001 U.S. Dist. LEXIS 2722 (S.D. Ind. Feb. 7, 2001). *See also* Doe v. Shenandoah County Sch. Bd., 737 F. Supp. 913 (W.D. Va. 1990) (granting a temporary restraining order against Weekday Religious Education classes being held in buses—almost identical to public school buses—parked in front of the school, with instructors going into the school to recruit students).

found Establishment Clause violations in this school district's effort to encourage participation in the program and in the use of school property for the religious classes.

Excusal for Religious Observances

The judiciary has been asked to determine how far public school authorities must go in accommodating religious holidays and how far they can go before such accommodations abridge the Establishment Clause. **Courts have required school districts to accommodate reasonable religious absences, but not excessive absences for religious reasons (e.g., one day a week).** Also, courts have not been receptive to attempts to avoid school attendance altogether on religious grounds, though parents can select private education or home schooling for their children. As discussed previously, the one judicially endorsed exception to compulsory school attendance involves Amish children after completion of the eighth grade.[77]

Religious Exemptions from Secular Activities

Teachers and other school employees have requested exemptions from public school activities that offend their religious beliefs, but most exemptions have been sought for students, because particular school requirements allegedly impair the practice of their religious tenets. In evaluating whether school authorities must honor such requests, courts have attempted to balance parents' interests in directing the religious upbringing of their children against the state's interest in ensuring an educated citizenry.

　　Courts have relied on the First Amendment in striking down required student participation in certain public school activities and observances. In the landmark case, *West Virginia State Board of Education v. Barnette*, the Supreme Court in 1943 ruled that students could not be required to recite the Pledge of Allegiance to the American flag in contravention of their religious beliefs,[78] overturning a precedent established by the Court only three years earlier.[79] In *Barnette*, the Court held that refusal to participate in the flag salute and Pledge of Allegiance does not interfere with the rights of others to do so or threaten any type of disruption.

　　But controversy still surrounds the nature of required exemptions from the Pledge. Courts have struck down laws or policies requiring students to stand during the Pledge or mandating parental notification of nonparticipating students, reasoning that such requirements coerce students into reciting the Pledge.[80] Furthermore, the Eleventh Circuit concluded that paddling a student for silently raising his fist in protest during the Pledge was an unwarranted infringement on the student's expression rights, since his action was not disruptive.

---

[77]*See* Wisconsin v. Yoder, 406 U.S. 205 (1972); *supra* text accompanying note 9.

[78]319 U.S. 624 (1943).

[79]Minersville Sch. Dist. v. Gobitis, 310 U.S. 586 (1940).

[80]*See, e.g.,* Frazier v. Alexandre, 434 F. Supp. 2d 1350 (S.D. Fla. 2006) (enjoining the school district's unconstitutional practices and awarding damages to a student who was publicly reprimanded for not participating in the Pledge and told he would have to get parental permission to opt out and would have to stand when others recited the Pledge); Circle Sch. v. Phillips, 270 F. Supp. 2d 616, 626 (E.D. Pa. 2003) (holding that a state law requiring parental notification of nonparticipating students violated the First Amendment).

Of course, students who opt not to participate can be disciplined if they create a disturbance while others are reciting the Pledge.[81]

Although the Supreme Court has not directly addressed teachers' rights in this regard, it is generally assumed that teachers, like students, have a First Amendment right to refuse to pledge allegiance as a matter of personal conscience. Teachers, however, cannot use their religious beliefs to deny students the opportunity to engage in this observance. If a school district requires the Pledge to be recited daily, teachers must make provisions for this observance to occur in their classrooms.

Patriotic observances have not been the only source of controversy; religious exemptions also have been sought from components of the curriculum. Whereas teachers cannot assert a free exercise right to disregard aspects of the state-prescribed curriculum, the judiciary has been more receptive to students' requests for exemptions from instructional requirements. Students, unlike teachers, are compelled to attend school, and for many this means a public school. Accordingly, the judiciary has been sensitive to the fact that certain public school policies may have a coercive effect on religious practices. In balancing the interests involved, courts consider:

- The extent the school requirement burdens the exercise of sincere religious beliefs,
- The governmental justification for the requirement, and
- Alternative means available to meet the state's objectives.

School authorities must have a compelling justification to deny students an exemption from a requirement that impairs the exercise of sincerely held religious beliefs.
Most requests for religious exemptions are handled at the classroom or school level, but a few have generated legal controversies. Students often have been successful in securing religious exemptions from various instructional activities, such as drug education, sex education, coeducational physical education, dancing instruction, officers' training programs, and specific course assignments if alternatives can satisfy the instructional objectives. Although individual children have been excused, the secular activities themselves have not been disturbed.

Religious exemptions have not been honored if considered unnecessary to accommodate the practice of religious tenets or if the exemptions would substantially disrupt the school or students' academic progress or pose a safety hazard. In a widely publicized 1987 case, the Sixth Circuit rejected fundamentalist Christian parents' request that their children be excused from exposure to the basal reading series used in elementary grades in a Tennessee school district.[82] Reversing the lower court's grant of the exemption, the Sixth Circuit reasoned that the readers did not burden the students' exercise of their fundamentalist religious beliefs, because the students were not required to profess a creed or perform religious exercises. More recently, a federal court rejected a parent's request for his son to be exempted from a Connecticut school district's mandatory health curriculum for

[81]The student was protesting the public chastisement of a classmate for previously not reciting the pledge. Holloman v. Harland, 370 F.3d 1252 (11th Cir. 2004) (denying qualified immunity to the principal and teacher regarding the impermissible punishment and allowing the student's Establishment Clause claim that the teacher encouraged students to pray during the daily moment of silence to proceed against the teacher and the school board).

[82]Mozert v. Hawkins County Bd. of Educ., 827 F.2d 1058 (6th Cir. 1987).

religious reasons.[83] The Court was not persuaded that the state law entitling students to religious exemptions from a family life education program could be used to secure exemptions from the entire health curriculum that provides important information.

As discussed in Chapter 4, conservative parents' organizations have secured federal and state laws allowing students to be excused from public school activities and components of the curriculum for religious and other reasons. Thus, parents may be able to use legislation to secure exemptions for their children,[84] even if they cannot substantiate that particular instructional activities impair free exercise rights.

■ ■ ■ ■ ■

RELIGIOUS CHALLENGES TO THE SECULAR CURRICULUM

Most lawsuits claiming that components of the public school curriculum (e.g., evolution) advance an antitheistic religious belief have not succeeded.

Although courts have been receptive to requests for individual students to be excused from specific public school activities, the judiciary has not been inclined to allow the restriction of the secular curriculum to satisfy parents' religious preferences. The Supreme Court has recognized that "the state has no legitimate interest in protecting any or all religions from views distasteful to them."[85]

Challenges to the curriculum raise complex questions involving what constitutes religious beliefs and practices that are subject to First Amendment protections and restrictions. **In protecting the free exercise of beliefs, the Supreme Court has adopted an expansive view toward religion, but it has not yet found an Establishment Clause violation in connection with a nontheistic creed.** The Third Circuit, however, ruled that a public school curricular offering (instruction in transcendental meditation) unconstitutionally advanced a nontraditional religious belief (the Science of Creative Intelligence).[86] Also, the Ninth Circuit held that taxpayers had standing to raise an Establishment Clause challenge to a school district's magnet school that used the Waldorf approach (emphasizing the arts and alternative teaching methods), which is based on the spiritual science known as anthroposophy.[87] Other courts have suggested that secular religions should be subjected to the same standards that are applied to theistic religions in determining whether the Establishment Clause has been breached.[88]

---

[83]Leebaert v. Harrington, 193 F. Supp. 2d 491 (D. Conn. 2002). *See also* Parker v. Hurley, 514 F.3d 87 (1st Cir. 2008) (holding that parents do not have a First Amendment right for their children to opt out of lessons designed to teach tolerance toward homosexuality); text accompanying note 10, Chapter 4.

[84]*See* Protection of Pupil Rights Amendment to the No Child Left Behind Act of 2001, 20 U.S.C. § 1232h (2008); text accompanying note 108, Chapter 4.

[85]Epperson v. Arkansas, 393 U.S. 97, 107 (1968) (quoting Joseph Burstyn v. Wilson, 343 U.S. 495, 505 (1952)).

[86]Malnak v. Yogi, 592 F.2d 197 (3d Cir. 1979).

[87]Plans v. Sacramento City Unified Sch. Dist., 319 F.3d 504 (9th Cir. 2003).

[88]*See, e.g.,* Sch. Dist. of Abington Twp. v. Schempp, 374 U.S. 203, 225 (1963) (noting that "the state may not establish a 'religion of secularism' in the sense of affirmatively opposing or showing hostility to religion, thus 'preferring those who believe in no religion'").

Even courts that have considered nontheistic creeds "religions" for First Amendment purposes have not ruled that challenged public school courses and materials advance such creeds, often referred to as *secular humanism* or *New Age theology.* In a 1987 case that attracted substantial media attention, the Eleventh Circuit reversed an Alabama federal judge's conclusion that secular humanism was being unconstitutionally advanced in the Mobile County schools.[89] The judge had enjoined the school district's use of several dozen home economics, history, and social studies books found to advance secular humanism. Disagreeing, the appellate court held that the books did not promote an antitheistic creed and rejected the contention that the mere omission of religious facts in the curriculum represented unconstitutional hostility toward theistic beliefs.

Sex education classes have been particularly susceptible to charges that an antitheistic faith is being advanced, but courts consistently have found that the challenged courses present public health information that furthers legitimate educational objectives and do not denounce Christianity.[90] However, **students have a free exercise right to be excused from sex education classes if such instruction conflicts with their sectarian beliefs.**

Because conservative citizen groups have not been successful in getting sex education barred from the public school curriculum, they have lobbied for the adoption of programs that stress abstinence between unmarried people. Courts have struck down the use of programs that include erroneous information or deal with the spiritual implications of premarital sex, contraceptives, and sexually transmitted diseases.[91]

Instruction pertaining to the origin of humanity also has generated continuing legal disputes. Historically, some states by law barred evolution from the curriculum, because it conflicted with the biblical account of creation. In the famous Scopes "monkey trial" in the 1920s, the Tennessee Supreme Court upheld such a law prohibiting the teaching of any theory that denies the Genesis version of creation or suggests "that man has descended from a lower order of animals."[92] In 1968, however, the United States Supreme Court struck down an Arkansas anti-evolution statute under the Establishment Clause, reasoning that evolution is science (not a secular religion) and a state cannot restrict student access to such information simply to satisfy religious preferences.[93]

After creationists were unable to convince the judiciary that evolution unconstitutionally advances an antitheistic faith, they focused on securing laws that require equal emphasis on the biblical account of creation whenever evolution is taught in public schools. In 1987, the Supreme Court invalidated a Louisiana statute that mandated "equal time" for creation science and evolution and required school boards to make available curriculum guides,

[89]Smith v. Bd. of Sch. Comm'rs, 655 F. Supp. 939 (S.D. Ala. 1987), *rev'd,* 827 F.2d 684 (11th Cir. 1987). *See also* Cowan v. Strafford R-VI Sch. Dist., 140 F.3d 1153 (8th Cir. 1998) (sending a "magic rock" home with each student did not advance New Ageism in violation of the Establishment Clause), text accompanying note 43, Chapter 4; Grove v. Mead Sch. Dist. No. 354, 753 F.2d 1528 (9th Cir. 1985) (reasoning that *The Learning Tree* does not advance an antitheistic faith).

[90]*See, e.g.,* Citizens for Parental Rights v. San Mateo County Bd. of Educ., 124 Cal. Rptr. 68 (Ct. App. 1975); Smith v. Ricci, 446 A.2d 501 (N.J. 1982).

[91]*See, e.g.,* ACLU v. Foster, No. 02-1440, 2002 U.S. Dist. LEXIS 13778 (E.D. La. July 25, 2002).

[92]Scopes v. State, 289 S.W. 363, 364 (Tenn. 1927).

[93]Epperson v. Arkansas, 393 U.S. 97 (1968).

teaching aids, and resource materials on creation science.[94] **Reasoning that creationism is not science, the Court concluded that the law was intended to discredit scientific information and advance religious beliefs in violation of the Establishment Clause.**

Despite two Supreme Court decisions, the origin of humanity continues to generate legal activity. Courts have rejected claims that teachers have a right to disregard directives to teach evolution[95] and that biology texts cannot treat evolution as fact.[96] Federal courts also have struck down efforts to include disclaimers (indicating that evolution is not a fact) in instruction or texts as a ploy to convey support for Christian fundamentalists and creationists.[97]

There has been political activity at the school district or state level pertaining to teaching evolution and alternative theories in 40 states during the past decade, and developments in some states, such as Kansas, have made front-page news.[98] In 2004, a Pennsylvania school district attracted national attention when it required high school biology teachers to introduce students to intelligent design (ID), a doctrine specifying that human beings are too complex to have evolved randomly by natural selection, but does not mention God in referring to an unidentified intelligent designer.[99] After several teachers complained, the school board instructed administrators to read a statement that evolution is a theory and to refer students to a book explaining ID as an alternative theory. A federal district court struck down the policy, reasoning that it was a ploy to insert religious beliefs in the public school science curriculum.[100]

In addition to sex education and evolution, other central targets have been values clarification, outcome-based education, and reading series, but few aspects of the public school curriculum remain untouched by claims that antitheistic doctrine is being promoted. For example, the Impressions reading series, published by Harcourt Brace Jovanovich, generated numerous challenges in the late 1980s and early 1990s. The series, employing the whole language approach to reading instruction, was challenged as being morbid and depressing and promoting witchcraft based on the Wicca religion, but federal appellate courts ruled that reading stories about witches or even creating poetic chants does not entail the practice of witchcraft or advance a pagan cult.[101] More recently, inclusion of the popular Harry Potter

---

[94]Edwards v. Aguillard, 482 U.S. 578 (1987).

[95]*See* Peloza v. Capistrano Unified Sch. Dist., 37 F.3d 517 (9th Cir. 1994); LeVake v. Indep. Sch. Dist. No. 656, 625 N.W.2d 502 (Minn. Ct. App. 2001).

[96]*See* Moeller v. Schrenko, 554 S.E.2d 198 (Ga. Ct. App. 2001); Johnson v. City of Chesapeake City Sch. Bd., 52 Va. Cir. 252 (Cir. Ct. 2000).

[97]*See* Freiler v. Tangipahoa Parish Bd. of Educ., 185 F.3d 337, 344–347 (5th Cir. 1999); Selman v. Cobb County Sch. Dist., 390 F. Supp. 2d 1286, 1312 (N.D. Ga. 2005), *vacated with instructions for the district court to conduct new evidentiary proceedings,* 449 F.3d 1320 (11th Cir. 2006).

[98]*See* National Center for Science Education, "News Archive," *Events of 2005–2007* (September 8, 2007), available at www.ncseweb.org/pressroom.asp?branch=statement.

[99]*See* Martha McCarthy, "Instruction about the Origin of Humanity: Legal Controversies Evolve," *Education Law Reporter,* vol. 203 (2006), pp. 453–467.

[100]*See* Kitzmiller v. Dover Area Sch. Dist., 400 F. Supp. 2d 707, 747 (M.D. Pa. 2005).

[101]*See, e.g.,* Brown v. Woodland Joint Unified Sch. Dist., 27 F.3d 1373 (9th Cir. 1994); Fleischfresser v. Dirs. of Sch. Dist. 200, 15 F.3d 680 (7th Cir. 1994). This series was discontinued in 1994 because of the controversies generated.

series in public school libraries has been challenged as advancing the occult/Satanism,[102] but no court to date has barred these books.

The Second Circuit agreed with some New York parents that a teacher's assignment for students to construct images of a Hindu deity abridged the First Amendment. Also, the court reasoned that making worry dolls (Indian dolls supposed to take away problems) amounted to preference of superstition over religion in violation of the Establishment Clause. But the court did not find constitutional violations in celebrating Earth Day or in role-playing as part of a drug prevention program using peer facilitators.[103]

Although courts have not condoned parental attacks on various aspects of the public school curriculum that allegedly conflict with their religious values, more difficult legal questions are raised when policy makers support curriculum restrictions for religious reasons. Since courts show considerable deference to legislatures and school boards in educational matters, conservative parent organizations have worked to elect board members and legislators who are sympathetic to their claims and have pressed for state and federal legislation and school board policies barring certain content from public schools.

STATE AID TO PRIVATE SCHOOLS

The Supreme Court is likely to uphold government aid to religious schools that benefits primarily the child or goes to sectarian schools because of parents' choices.

In addition to disputes over the place of religion in public schools, government relations with private—primarily religious—schools have generated a substantial amount of First Amendment litigation. **In 1925, the Supreme Court afforded constitutional protection to private schools' rights to exist and to parents' rights to select private education as an alternative to public schooling.**[104] Yet, the Court also recognized that the state has a general welfare interest in mandating school attendance and regulating private education to ensure an educated citizenry, considered essential in a democracy. Some disputes have resulted from conflicts between the state's exercise of its *parens patriae* authority[105] and parental interests in having their children educated in settings that reinforce their religious and philosophical beliefs. If the government interferes with parents' child-rearing decisions, it must show that the intervention is necessary to protect the child or the state.[106] Although courts have upheld minimum state requirements for private schools (e.g., prescribed courses, personnel requirements), the recent trend has been toward imposing outcome measures, such as requiring private school students to participate in statewide testing programs.

---

[102]*See* Kathleen K. Manzo, "Charmed and Challenged," *Education Week* (November. 14, 2001), pp. 14–15.

[103]Altman v. Bedford Cent. Sch. Dist., 245 F.3d 49 (2d Cir. 2001). *See also* Eklund v. Byron Union Sch. Dist., 154 Fed. App'x 648 (9th Cir. 2005), *cert. denied*, 127 S. Ct. 86 (2006); *supra* text accompanying note 49.

[104]Pierce v. Soc'y of the Sisters, 268 U.S. 510 (1925).

[105]*Parens patriae* refers to the authority of the state in certain circumstances to usurp the rights of the natural parent in order to protect the interests of the child.

[106]*See* Wisconsin v. Yoder, 406 U.S. 205, 214 (1972); *supra* text accompanying note 9.

About 12 percent of all PK–12 students are enrolled in private schools or home education, but this ratio could change if additional government aid flows to private education. Despite the fact that more than three-fifths of the states specifically prohibit the use of public funds for sectarian purposes, about three-fourths of the states provide public aid to private school students, including those attending sectarian schools, for such things as transportation services, the loan of textbooks, state-required testing programs, and special education services. Some of the most significant Supreme Court decisions interpreting the Establishment Clause have pertained to the use of public funds for private, primarily sectarian, education.

Aid for Student Services

The Supreme Court's support of religious accommodations in terms of allowing government support for parochial school students has been consistent since 1993, with some evidence of the accommodationist trend much earlier. Indeed, the "child benefit" doctrine has been used to justify government aid for transportation and secular textbooks for parochial school students since the mid-twentieth century.[107]

In 1993, the Supreme Court in *Zobrest v. Catalina Foothills School District* found no Establishment Clause violation in publicly supporting sign-language interpreters in parochial schools, reasoning that the aid is going to the child as part of a federal government program that distributes benefits neutrally to qualifying children with disabilities under federal law.[108] The court reasoned that the child is the primary recipient of the aid, and the school receives only an incidental benefit. Four years later, the Court in *Agostini v. Felton* removed the ban on public school personnel providing remedial instruction in religious schools that it had announced 12 years earlier.[109] The Court recognized that in *Zobrest* it had abandoned the presumption that public employees in sectarian schools would be tempted to inculcate religion.[110]

The Supreme Court in *Mitchell v. Helms* subsequently found no Establishment Clause violation in using federal aid to purchase instructional materials and equipment for student use in sectarian schools.[111] The Court reasoned that religious indoctrination could not be attributed to the government when aid, even direct aid:

- Is distributed based on secular criteria and would be appropriate for public schools,
- Is allocated in a nondiscriminatory manner to religious and secular beneficiaries, and
- Flows to religious schools only because of private choices of parents.

[107]*See* Bd. of Educ. v. Allen, 392 U.S. 236 (1968) (finding no Establishment Clause violation in a state law requiring public school districts to loan secular textbooks to all secondary students, including those attending parochial schools); Everson v. Bd. of Educ., 330 U.S. 1 (1947) (rejecting an Establishment Clause challenge to the use of public funds to provide transportation services for nonpublic school students). *See also* Comm. for Pub. Educ. & Religious Liberty v. Regan, 444 U.S. 646 (1980) (upholding government support for state-required testing programs in private schools).

[108]509 U.S. 1 (1993).

[109]521 U.S. 203 (1997) (overturning its ruling that barred the use of public school personnel to provide Title I remedial services on sectarian school premises, Aguilar v. Felton, 473 U.S. 402 (1985), and overruling the portion of its decision that invalidated a shared-time program under which public school classes were provided for parochial school students on parochial school premises, Sch. Dist. v. Ball, 473 U.S. 373 (1985)).

[110]521 U.S. at 223–224.

[111]530 U.S. 793 (2000), *on remand sub nom.* Helms v. Picard, 229 F.3d 467 (5th Cir. 2000).

Six justices agreed that prior Supreme Court rulings barring state aid in the form of providing maps, slide projectors, and other instructional materials and equipment to sectarian schools were no longer good law.

The Supreme Court seems to have dismantled most of the separationist decisions rendered during the heyday of applying the stringent *Lemon* test in the 1970s to strike down various types of public assistance to parochial schools. The only separationist rulings of this period that have not been eroded at least in part by subsequent Supreme Court opinions involved government aid made available *solely* to private schools or their patrons.[112]

However, because courts have interpreted the Establishment Clause as allowing various types of public aid for nonpublic school students does not mean that states must use public funds for these purposes. For example, courts have ruled that transportation aid to private school students violates state constitutional or statutory provisions prohibiting the use of public funds for sectarian purposes.[113] Similarly, some state courts have invalidated lending textbooks to nonpublic school students under their state constitutions.[114] The California Supreme Court called the child-benefit doctrine "logically indefensible" in striking down a state law that provided for the loan of textbooks to nonpublic school students.[115]

In 2004, the Supreme Court delivered a significant decision, *Locke v. Davey,* upholding states' discretion to adopt more stringent antiestablishment provisions than demanded by the First Amendment.[116] Upholding the state of Washington's prohibition on state scholarships for college students to pursue pastoral degrees, the Court reasoned that even though such aid is *permitted* under the Establishment Clause,[117] it is not *required* by the Free Exercise Clause. In short, simply because the Establishment Clause allows an activity does not mean that a state must financially support the activity. The Supreme Court rejected the contention that the restriction emanated from religious bigotry as a so-called Blaine Amendment.[118]

Most of the state constitutional provisions that preclude the use of public funds for religious purposes are more restrictive than the Establishment Clause. The *Locke* decision has provided an impetus for state litigation as the limits of similar provisions are tested in

---

[112]*See, e.g.*, Levitt v. Comm. for Pub. Educ. and Religious Liberty, 413 U.S. 472 (1973) (rejecting direct state aid for teacher-developed tests in religious schools). *See also* Bd. of Educ. v. Grumet, 512 U.S. 687 (1994) (invalidating a legislative attempt to create a separate public school district along religious lines to serve special-needs Satmar Hasidic children).

[113]*See, e.g.*, Pucket v. Rounds, No. 07-2651, 2008 U.S. App. LEXIS 11070 (8th Cir. May 23, 2008); Matthews v. Quinton, 362 P.2d 932 (Alaska 1961); McVey v. Hawkins, 258 S.W.2d 927 (Mo. 1953); Visser v. Nooksack Valley Sch. Dist. No. 506, 207 P.2d 198 (Wash. 1949).

[114]*See, e.g.*, Fannin v. Williams, 655 S.W.2d 480 (Ky. 1983); Elbe v. Yankton Indep. Sch. Dist. No. 63-3, 372 N.W.2d 113 (S.D. 1985).

[115]Cal. Teachers Ass'n v. Riles, 632 P.2d 953, 962 (Cal. 1981).

[116]540 U.S. 712 (2004) (interpreting Wash. Const. Art. I, § 11 (2007)).

[117]*See* Witters v. Wash. Dep't of Servs. for the Blind, 474 U. S. 481 (1986) (holding that the Establishment Clause does not preclude a student with a visual problem from using state rehabilitation aid to study for the ministry at a Christian college).

[118]*Locke*, 540 U.S. at 724, n. 7 (finding that Washington's constitutional prohibition on the use of public funds for religious worship, exercise, or instruction was *not* modeled on a failed constitutional amendment proposed by former House Speaker James Blaine in 1875, which allegedly reflected anti-Catholic sentiment).

other states. Indeed, one of the most significant implications of *Locke* might be its stimulation of an increase in church/state cases initiated in *state* courts.

Aid to Encourage Educational Choice

There also has been legislation to provide indirect aid to make private schooling a viable choice for more families. Tax-relief measures for private school tuition and educational vouchers have received considerable attention in legislative forums. The primary justification for such measures is that the aid flows to religious schools only because of private choices of parents.

Tax-Relief Measures.   Tax benefits in the form of deductions or credits for private school expenses have been proposed at both state and federal levels. Although Congress has not yet endorsed any proposals for federal income tax credits for private school tuition, a few states have enacted tax-relief provisions for educational expenses. The central constitutional question is whether such measures advance religion in violation of the Establishment Clause because the primary beneficiaries are parents of parochial school children and ultimately religious institutions.

In 1983, the Supreme Court upheld a Minnesota tax-benefit program allowing parents of public or private school students to claim a limited state income tax deduction for tuition, transportation, and secular textbook expenses incurred for each elementary or secondary school dependent. The Court majority in *Mueller v. Allen* found the Minnesota law "vitally different" from an earlier New York provision, which violated the Establishment Clause by bestowing tax benefits only on private school patrons.[119] Notwithstanding this ruling, only six states provide such tax benefits. Most efforts to provide state tax relief for educational expenses have been defeated when placed before the voters, possibly because of their significant impact on state revenues.

Vouchers.   There has been debate since the 1970s over the merits of various voucher models. Under a basic voucher plan, the state provides a set amount of money per child that parents can use for their children to attend public or private schools of their choice. There are many modifications that limit student eligibility or vary the voucher amount based on family income. Several New England states for years have had *de facto* voucher plans under which school districts without high schools provide a designated amount for high school tuition in neighboring public school districts or in private schools that the families select. However, very few other plans were adopted until the mid-1990s, and not until 1999 did Florida become the first state to implement a statewide voucher plan targeting students attending failing public schools. Also, a few urban districts have adopted state-funded voucher plans for disadvantaged youth, and privately funded scholarships are available for students to attend private schools in many major cities nationally.

In 2002, the Supreme Court rendered a significant decision, *Zelman v. Simmons-Harris*, resolving the conflict among lower courts regarding the participation of religious schools in state-funded voucher programs.[120] **The Supreme Court in *Zelman* relied heavily on the fact that parents—not the government—make the decision for the**

---

[119]463 U.S. 388, 398 (1983) (contrasting Comm. for Pub. Educ. & Religious Liberty v. Nyquist, 413 U.S. 756 (1973)).

[120]536 U.S. 639 (2002).

scholarship funds to flow to private schools. Considering the program to be one of "true private choice" among public and private options, the Court found no Establishment Clause violation. Even though 96 percent of participating students attended religious schools, the Court reasoned that a neutral program does not become unconstitutional simply because most recipients decide to use the aid in religious schools.

Since there are no federal constitutional issues, the legality of voucher programs will be determined on the basis of state law. The Milwaukee and Cleveland voucher programs have been endorsed by state courts,[121] but recently other programs have not fared well when challenged under state education clauses or state prohibitions on the use of public funds for religious purposes. The Florida Supreme Court relied on the state constitution's education clause, similar to provisions in many other states, to invalidate the statewide voucher program for students attending deficient public schools.[122] The court interpreted the legislature's duty to provide for a uniform system of public schools as requiring all schools that receive state aid to satisfy the same standards, reasoning that the voucher program unconstitutionally diverted public funds into separate, nonuniform, private systems that compete with and reduce funds for public education.

The Colorado Supreme Court also invalidated a pilot voucher program for low-income students attending low-performing schools, concluding that the program violated the "local control" clause of the state constitution by taking away districts' discretion in spending funds for instruction.[123] In addition, federal and state courts have upheld Maine's law that excludes religious schools from the state's tuition reimbursement program for high school students in districts that do not operate public high schools.[124] As discussed, the Supreme Court's 2004 *Locke* decision recognized that states can adopt more stringent antiestablishment measures than included in the First Amendment without exhibiting hostility toward religion, thereby strengthening the state grounds for challenging voucher programs.[125]

Despite recent judicial setbacks, several states are considering targeted voucher proposals, and some have been adopted.[126] Florida, Utah, and Arizona have established voucher programs for children with disabilities to attend private schools. In 2007, the Utah legislature adopted the most comprehensive voucher plan to date, offering all children the opportunity to receive state scholarships that varied by family income, but this program was soundly defeated in a statewide referendum.[127]

[121]*See* Simmons-Harris v. Goff, 711 N.E.2d 203 (Ohio 1999); Jackson v. Benson, 578 N.W.2d 602 (Wis. 1998).

[122]Bush v. Holmes, 919 So. 2d 392 (Fla. 2006).

[123]Owens v. Colo. Congress of Parents, Teachers, and Students, 92 P.3d 933 (Colo. 2004). Florida, Georgia, Kansas, Montana, and Virginia have provisions similar to Colorado's "local control" clause.

[124]*See* Eulitt v. Me. Dep't of Educ., 386 F.3d 344 (1st Cir. 2004); Anderson v. Town of Durham, 895 A.2d 944 (Me. 2006), *cert. denied,* 127 S. Ct. 661 (2006).

[125]*See* Locke v. Davey, 540 U.S. 712 (2004); *supra* text accompanying note 116.

[126]In 2006, Ohio expanded eligibility beyond Cleveland to provide up to 14,000 vouchers for disadvantaged students who have attended failing "academic emergency" public schools for three years. Ohio Rev. Code Ann. § 3310.01 *et seq.* (2008). In addition to state initiatives, the federal government in 2004 approved $14 million for a pilot voucher program for low-income students in Washington, D.C., to attend private schools.

[127]*See* Utah Code Ann. § 53A-1a-801 *et seq.* (2007); Glen Warchol, "Vouchers Go Down in Crushing Defeat," *Salt Lake Tribune* (November 7, 2007). Referenda in other states, such as California, Colorado, Michigan, Oregon, and Washington, also have failed in recent years.

Even where voucher programs that include sectarian schools satisfy state constitutions, fiscal concerns may influence whether large-scale voucher initiatives are implemented, because states currently are not supporting students attending private schools. Voucher proposals will continue to be enacted and challenged, and their legality will depend primarily on state courts' interpretations of state constitutional provisions. Indeed, instead of a national policy, we soon may have 50 standards regarding the legality of school vouchers.

CONCLUSION

For almost a half century, church/state controversies have generated a steady stream of education litigation, and there are no signs of diminishing legal activity in this domain. The principle that the First Amendment demands governmental neutrality toward religion has been easier to assert than to apply. Although some lawsuits have involved claims under the Free Exercise Clause, most school cases have focused on interpretations of Establishment Clause prohibitions.

From the 1960s through the mid-1980s, the federal judiciary seemed more committed to enforcing Establishment Clause restrictions in elementary and secondary school settings than elsewhere. Recently, however, there seems to be greater government accommodation of religion, especially in terms of public funds flowing to religious schools. The Free Speech Clause increasingly seems to prevail over Establishment Clause restrictions in protecting religious expression in public schools. The concepts of equal access and equal treatment for religious groups and expression seem to have replaced the principle of church/state separation.

POINTS TO PONDER

1. Some courts have emphasized that for student-initiated devotional activities in public school to be upheld, prayers must be nonsectarian. Can a prayer be nonsectarian, or is the term "nonsectarian prayer" an oxymoron?

2. A student who attended the middle school was killed in an automobile accident. The next day, a classmate asks you if she can lead the class in saying a prayer for the deceased student. What would be your response and why?

3. The majority of the senior class engaged in a recitation of the Lord's Prayer five minutes before the high school graduation ceremony. School authorities did not lead the prayer, and although they had heard rumors that the student-initiated recitation was planned, they had not been officially informed. Did this activity represent the school? Did it violate an injunction prohibiting school personnel from authorizing, conducting, sponsoring, or intentionally permitting prayers during the graduation ceremony?

4. High school students have requested that their religious club be allowed to hold meetings in the public school during lunch when other student groups are allowed to meet. They also have asked for access to student activity funds to promote their meetings and distribute religious materials, because other student groups can use such funds to support their activities. What would be your response and why?

5. Is "a wall of separation between church and state" still the guiding metaphor. If not, what has replaced it?

CHAPTER FOUR

INSTRUCTIONAL ISSUES

Although U.S. citizens have no federal constitutional right to a public education, each state constitution places a duty on its legislature to provide for free public schooling, thus creating a state entitlement (property right) for all children to be educated at public expense.[1] Substantial litigation has resulted from the collision of state interests in providing for the welfare of all citizens and individual interests in exercising constitutional and statutory rights. This chapter focuses on legal mandates pertaining to various requirements and rights associated with the public school instructional program.

THE SCHOOL CURRICULUM

States and local school boards control the public school curriculum, but they must respect federal constitutional guarantees.

The federal government influences the curriculum through funds it provides for particular initiatives, such as reading instruction in early grades, but such influence is quite limited. In contrast, state legislatures have plenary or complete power over education and thus broad authority to impose curriculum mandates.

Requirements and Restrictions

A few state constitutions include specific curriculum mandates, but more typically, the legislature is given responsibility for curricular determinations. Most states mandate instruction pertaining to the federal Constitution, American history, English, mathematics, drug education, health, and physical education. Some state statutes specify what subjects will be

---

[1]*See* Goss v. Lopez, 419 U.S. 565 (1975); text accompanying note 28, Chapter 8. For a discussion of compulsory education requirements and exceptions, residency requirements, home education, and related issues, *see* Stephen Thomas, Nelda Cambron-McCabe, and Martha McCarthy, *Public School Law: Teachers' and Students' Rights,* 6th ed. (Boston: Allyn and Bacon, 2009), Chapter 3.

taught in which grades, and many states have detailed legislation pertaining to vocational education, bilingual education, and special services for children with disabilities. States also increasingly are requiring character education. State laws usually stipulate that local school boards must offer the state-mandated minimum curriculum, which they may supplement unless there is a statutory prohibition. In about half of the states, local school boards (and, in some instances, school-based councils) are empowered to adopt courses of study, but often they must secure approval from the state board of education.

Despite states' substantial latitude in curricular matters, some legislative attempts to impose curriculum restrictions have impaired federal constitutional rights. The first curriculum case to reach the Supreme Court involved a 1923 challenge to a Nebraska law that prohibited instruction in a foreign language to any public or private school student who had not successfully completed the eighth grade.[2] The state high court had upheld the dismissal of a private school teacher for teaching the subject of reading in German to elementary school students. In striking down the statute, the Supreme Court reasoned that the teacher's right to teach, the parents' right to engage him to instruct their children, and the children's right to acquire useful knowledge were protected liberties under the Due Process Clause of the Fourteenth Amendment.

The Supreme Court on occasion has ruled that other curriculum decisions violate constitutional rights. The Court held in 1968 that under the First Amendment states cannot bar public school instruction—teaching about evolution—simply because it conflicts with certain religious views.[3] Yet, **courts will not interfere with instructional decisions made by state and local education agencies, unless the decisions are clearly arbitrary or impair constitutional rights.** For example, federal appellate courts have rejected allegations that mandatory community service requirements for students force expression of altruistic values in violation of the First Amendment, entail involuntary servitude prohibited by the Thirteenth Amendment, or impair parents' Fourteenth Amendment rights to direct the upbringing of their children.[4] School authorities also have discretion in establishing standards for pupil performance and imposing other instructional requirements, such as prerequisites and admission criteria for particular courses, as long as such criteria are not arbitrary and do not disadvantage certain groups of students.

In addition to having authority over the content of the public school curriculum, states also have the power to specify textbooks and to regulate the method by which such books are obtained and distributed. A list of acceptable books typically is adopted by the state board of education or a textbook commission, and local school boards then select specific texts from the list. However, in some states, such as Colorado, almost complete authority is delegated to local boards to make textbook selections. Courts will not interfere with textbook decisions unless the established procedures are not followed or overtly biased materials are adopted.

[2]Meyer v. Nebraska, 262 U.S. 390 (1923).

[3]Epperson v. Arkansas, 393 U.S. 97 (1968). *See also* Edwards v. Aguillard, 482 U.S. 578 (1987) (invalidating a Louisiana law requiring instruction in the biblical account of creation whenever evolution was introduced as unconstitutionally advancing religion); text accompanying notes 93–94, Chapter 3.

[4]*See, e.g.*, Herndon v. Chapel Hill-Carrboro City Bd. of Educ., 89 F.3d 174 (4th Cir. 1996); Immediato v. Rye Neck Sch. Dist., 73 F.3d 454 (2d Cir. 1996).

Censorship of Instructional Materials

Attempts to remove books from classrooms and libraries and to tailor curricular offerings and methodologies to particular religious and philosophical values have led to substantial litigation. Although most people agree that schools transmit values, there is little consensus regarding *which* values should be transmitted or *who* should make this determination.

Challenges to the Curriculum. Some civil rights and consumer groups have challenged public school materials and programs as allegedly promoting racism, sexism, or bad health habits for students. But most of the challenges come from conservative parent groups, alleging that the use of instructional activities and materials considered immoral and anti-Christian impairs parents' rights to control their children's course of study in public schools.[5] As discussed in Chapter 3, courts have endorsed requests for specific children to be excused from selected course offerings (e.g., sex education) that offend their religious beliefs, as long as the exemptions do not impede the students' academic progress or the management of the school. Challenges to the courses themselves, however, have not found a receptive judiciary.

To date, courts have not allowed mere parental disapproval of instructional materials to dictate the public school curriculum. Federal appellate courts have been unsympathetic to claims that reading series or individual novels used in public schools conflict with Christian doctrine and advance an antitheistic creed, finding the challenged materials to be religiously neutral and related to legitimate educational objectives.[6] Although many challenges have religious overtones, some simply assert parents' rights to determine their children's education. The First Circuit rejected parents' claim that the school district was liable for subjecting their children to a mandatory AIDS-awareness assembly that featured a streetwise, comedic approach to the topic. The appeals court observed that "if all parents had a fundamental constitutional right to dictate individually what the schools teach their children, the schools would be forced to cater a curriculum for each student whose parents had genuine moral disagreements with the school's choice of subject matter."[7] The Ninth Circuit subsequently held that the Oregon law restructuring public schools to impose a rigorous academic program and student assessments did not abridge speech rights or "freedom of the mind," as nothing in the law compelled students to adopt state-approved views.[8] And the same court dismissed African American parents' complaint that their daughter suffered psychological injuries due to being required to read two literary works that contained repeated use of the word *nigger*.[9]

---

[5]Some of the best-known conservative groups are the American Coalition for Traditional Values, the Christian Coalition, Citizens for Excellence in Education, Concerned Women for America, the Eagle Forum, and Focus on the Family.

[6]*See, e.g.*, Monteiro v. Tempe Union High Sch. Dist., 158 F.3d 1022 (9th Cir. 1998); Fleischfresser v. Dirs. of Sch. Dist. 200, 15 F.3d 680 (7th Cir. 1994); Smith v. Sch. Bd. of Sch. Comm'rs, 827 F.2d 684 (11th Cir. 1987); text accompanying note 101, Chapter 3.

[7]Brown v. Hot, Sexy and Safer Prods., 68 F.3d 525, 534 (1st Cir. 1995).

[8]Tennison v. Paulus, 144 F.3d 1285, 1287 (9th Cir. 1998).

[9]*Monteiro*, 158 F.3d 1022 (remanding for further proceedings, however, regarding allegations that school personnel failed to respond to complaints of a racially hostile environment in violation of Title VI of the Civil Rights Act of 1964).

Sometimes school districts have *not* prevailed, if shown that they acted arbitrarily or in violation of parents' or students' protected rights. For example, in a Maryland case, a federal district court enjoined implementation of a school district's pilot sex education program, reasoning that additional investigation was needed to determine if the materials on "sexual variation" constitute viewpoint discrimination by presenting only the perspective that homosexuality is natural and a morally correct lifestyle. The curriculum subsequently was revised and approved by the school board with the directive that teachers must convey that sexual orientation is an innate characteristic. A parental challenge to the new curriculum was rejected by the Maryland State Board of Education and subsequently by a state court.[10]

Censorship by Policy Makers.   Although courts have not been receptive to challenges to school boards' curricular decisions simply because some materials or course content offend the sensibilities of specific students or parents, the legal issues are more complicated when policy makers themselves (e.g., legislators, school board members) support the censorship activity. Bills calling for instructional censorship have been introduced in Congress and numerous state legislatures, and policies have been proposed at the school board level to eliminate "objectionable" materials from public school classrooms and libraries. **The Supreme Court has recognized the discretion of school boards to make decisions that reflect the "legitimate and substantial community interest in promoting respect for authority and traditional values, be they social, moral, or political."**[11] Thus, the judiciary has been reluctant to interfere with school boards' prerogatives in selecting and eliminating instructional materials, unless a board flagrantly abuses its authority.

Courts generally have upheld school boards' authority in determining curricular materials and offerings, but some specific censorship activities have been invalidated. Courts have intervened if the censorship of specific library selections has clearly been motivated by a desire to suppress particular viewpoints or controversial ideas in violation of the First Amendment. To illustrate, the Fifth Circuit remanded a case for a trial to determine whether a Louisiana school board was unconstitutionally suppressing ideas in removing from school libraries all copies of *Voodoo & Hoodoo*, which traces the development of African tribal religion and its evolution in African American communities in the United States.[12] More recently, an Arkansas federal district court found insufficient justification for a school district's policy requiring parental permission for students to check out specific library books allegedly dealing with witchcraft and the occult, concluding that the policy stigmatized the targeted books and abridged students' First Amendment rights to have access to the materials without parental permission.[13] Also, a Florida federal district court

---

[10]Citizens for a Responsible Curriculum v. Montgomery County Pub. Schs., No. AW 05 1194, 2005 U.S. Dist. LEXIS 8130, at *3 (S.D. Md. May 5, 2005); Citizens for a Responsible Curriculum v. Montgomery County Pub. Schs., No. 284980 (Md. Cir. Ct. Jan. 31, 2008). *See also* Parker v. Hurley, 514 F.3d 87 (1st Cir. 2008) (finding no constitutional violation in a program teaching respect for homosexuality and same-sex marriages).

[11]Bd. of Educ. v. Pico, 457 U.S. 853, 864 (1982). *See also* Seyfried v. Walton, 668 F.2d 214 (3d Cir. 1981) (holding that the high school drama club's performances were a part of the school program and therefore the school board could prohibit performance of the musical *Pippin* because of its explicit sexual scenes).

[12]Campbell v. St. Tammany Parish Sch. Bd., 64 F.3d 184 (5th Cir. 1995).

[13]Counts v. Cedarville Sch. Dist., 295 F. Supp. 2d 996 (W.D. Ark. 2003).

enjoined a school board's effort to remove from elementary school libraries *Vamos a Cuba!* along with 23 other books in a series about life in other countries, finding impermissible viewpoint discrimination and lack of compliance with the district's procedures for removing library materials.[14]

Despite substantial activity in lower courts, the Supreme Court has rendered only one decision involving censorship in public schools. This case, *Board of Education v. Pico*,[15] unfortunately did not provide significant clarification regarding the scope of school boards' authority to restrict student access to particular materials, with seven of the nine Supreme Court justices writing separate opinions. At issue in *Pico* was the school board's removal of certain books from junior high and high school libraries, in spite of the contrary recommendation of a committee appointed to review the books. The Supreme Court narrowly affirmed the appellate court's remand of the case for a trial because of irregularities in the removal procedures and unresolved factual questions regarding the school board's motivation. However, even the three justices endorsing the notion that students have a protected right to receive information recognized the broad authority of school boards to remove materials that are vulgar or educationally unsuitable as long as they used regular and unbiased procedures. The *Pico* plurality also emphasized that the controversy involved *library* books, which are not required reading for students, noting that school boards "might well defend their claim of absolute discretion in matters of *curriculum* by reliance upon their duty to inculcate community values."[16]

Further strengthening the broad discretion of school authorities in curriculum-related censorship was the landmark 1988 Supreme Court decision involving students' free speech rights, *Hazelwood School District v. Kuhlmeier*.[17] The Court declared that public school authorities can censor student expression in school-sponsored activities to ensure that the expression is consistent with educational objectives. Relying on *Hazelwood*, the Eleventh Circuit upheld a Florida school board's decision to ban a humanities book because it included Aristophanes' *Lysistrata* and Chaucer's *The Miller's Tale*, which board members considered vulgar. Although not addressing the wisdom of the board's decision, the court deferred to the board's discretion in curricular matters.[18] Also relying on *Hazelwood*, the Fifth Circuit denied a claim by two students and the author of a textbook that the state's rejection of the book from the Texas State Board of Education's approved list of texts implicated the First Amendment. The court reasoned that the selection of curricular materials entails governmental speech, not a forum for expression, and that the state board has wide latitude in making such decisions.[19]

Specific issues may change, but controversies surrounding the selection of materials for the public school library and curriculum will likely persist, reflecting the basic tension

[14]ACLU v. Miami-Dade County Sch. Bd., 439 F. Supp. 2d 1242 (S.D. Fla. 2006).

[15]474 F. Supp. 387 (E.D.N.Y. 1979), *rev'd and remanded*, 638 F.2d 404 (2d Cir. 1980), *aff'd*, 457 U.S. 853 (1982).

[16]*Id.*, 457 U.S. at 869. Following the Supreme Court's decision, the school board voted to return the controversial books to the school libraries, thus averting the need for a trial regarding the board's motivation for the original censorship.

[17]484 U.S. 260 (1988). *See* text accompanying note 24, Chapter 5.

[18]Virgil v. Sch. Bd., 862 F.2d 1517 (11th Cir. 1989).

[19]Chiras v. Miller, 432 F.3d 606 (5th Cir. 2005).

between instilling community values in students and exposing them to new ideas. School boards would be wise to establish procedures for reviewing objections to course content and library materials *before* a controversy arises. Criteria used to acquire and eliminate instructional materials should be clearly articulated and educationally defensible. **Once a process is in place to evaluate complaints relating to the instructional program, school boards should follow it carefully, as courts will show little sympathy when a school board ignores its own established procedures.**

Electronic Censorship.   The next wave of censorship activity is likely to focus on the electronic frontier. It was estimated in 2006 that approximately 87 percent of U.S. teenagers had Internet access.[20] With schools increasingly making online services accessible to students, concerns are being raised about the possible transmission of sexually explicit material to minors and the vulnerability of children to sexual predators via the Internet. Many states as well as the federal government have enacted measures to restrict minors' access to harmful materials over the Internet.

The only federal law that has survived a First Amendment challenge is the Children's Internet Protection Act (CIPA), which received Supreme Court endorsement in 2003.[21] This law requires libraries and school districts that receive technology funds to implement technology protection measures that safeguard students from access to harmful content and to monitor student Internet use.[22] The Supreme Court reasoned that CIPA places a condition on the use of federal funds, which poses a small burden for library patrons, and the law does not penalize those posting materials on the Internet.[23]

Academic Freedom

From its origin in German universities, the concept of academic freedom historically was applied to postsecondary education and embodied the principle that faculty members should be free from governmental controls in conducting research and imparting knowledge to students. **Public school teachers have asserted a similar right to academic freedom, but courts have not extended the protections found in higher education to public elementary and secondary schools.**[24] Although reasoning that teachers possess academic interests, courts have refrained from establishing precise legal principles in this domain. Instead, courts have balanced teachers' interests in academic freedom against school boards' interests in assuring an appropriate instructional program and efficient school operations.

---

[20]*See* Amanda Lenhart, Mary Madden, and Lee Rainie, *Teens and the Internet*, Pew Internet and American Life Project (July 11, 2006), available at www.pewinternet.org/reports.asp.

[21]United States v. American Library Ass'n, 539 U.S. 194 (2003).

[22]20 U.S.C.§ 9134(f) (2008); 47 U.S.C. § 254(h)(5) (2008). For a discussion of two federal laws struck down, *see* Martha McCarthy, "The Continuing Saga of Internet Censorship: The Child Online Protection Act," *Brigham Young University Education and Law Journal* (2005), pp. 83–101.

[23]*American Library Ass'n*, 539 U.S. 194. For information on state laws pertaining to Internet filtering requirements, *see* Lenhart et al., *supra* note 20.

[24]*See, e.g.*, Bates v. Dallas Indep. Sch. Dist., 952 S.W.2d 543 (Tex. App. 1997) (holding that a teacher's refusal to assign a grade to a student, as instructed by his supervisor, is not shielded by academic freedom).

Curriculum Content. Public school teachers do not have a right to determine the content of the instructional program. Recognizing that the state, as employer, controls the curriculum, the Ninth Circuit rejected a vagueness challenge to California legislation holding teachers personally liable for actual damages if they willfully refuse to teach predominantly in English.[25] The court concluded that in the vast majority of instances, it would be clear to teachers when they were dispensing instruction that would be subject to the language restriction.

Despite the state's legal authority to impose such curricular restrictions, state law often delegates to local school boards considerable authority to make instructional decisions. Several courts have declared that school boards are not legally obligated to accept teachers' curricular recommendations in the absence of a board policy to that effect. For example, the Fifth Circuit held that teachers cannot assert a First Amendment right to substitute their own supplemental reading list for the officially adopted list without securing administrative approval.[26] And the Fourth Circuit ruled that a high school teacher did not have complete discretion to select the plays performed by her acting class students, recognizing school officials' legitimate pedagogical interests in regulating the curriculum.[27]

Teachers are not permitted to ignore or omit prescribed course content under the guise of academic freedom. To illustrate, the Seventh Circuit upheld a school board's dismissal of a kindergarten teacher who, for religious reasons, refused to teach patriotic topics.[28] The Supreme Court of Washington found no First Amendment impairment in a school board prohibiting two teachers from team-teaching a history course, finding it within the board's discretion to require teachers to cover course content in a conventional manner.[29] The Third Circuit held that a teacher could not assert a First Amendment right to disregard school board instructions and continue using a classroom management technique, Learnball, that gave students responsibility for establishing class rules and grading procedures.[30] And the Supreme Court of Colorado upheld a policy requiring administrative review of "controversial learning resources," noting the district's legitimate pedagogical interest in shaping its secondary school curriculum.[31]

---

[25]Cal. Teachers Ass'n v. State Bd. of Educ., 271 F.3d 1141 (9th Cir. 2001).

[26]Kirkland v. Northside Indep. Sch. Dist., 890 F.2d 794 (5th Cir. 1989).

[27]Boring v. Buncombe County Bd. of Educ., 136 F.3d 364 (4th Cir. 1998).

[28]Palmer v. Bd. of Educ., 603 F.2d 1271 (7th Cir. 1979).

[29]Millikan v. Bd. of Dirs., 611 P.2d 414, 418 (Wash. 1980). *See also* Fisher v. Fairbanks N. Star Borough Sch. Dist., 704 P.2d 213 (Alaska 1985) (rejecting a teacher's asserted right to disregard a rule, requiring the superintendent's approval of supplementary instructional materials, in selecting materials to teach about homosexual rights in a unit on American minorities); Sch. Admin. Dist. No. 58 v. Mt. Abram Teachers Ass'n, 704 A.2d 349 (Me. 1997) (finding educational policy decisions about selection of novels for the tenth grade curriculum to be within the school board's authority and not subject to grievance and arbitration procedures under the collective bargaining agreement).

[30]Murray v. Pittsburgh Bd. of Educ., 919 F. Supp. 838 (W.D. Pa. 1996), *aff'd mem.*, 141 F.3d 1154 (3d Cir. 1998).

[31]Bd. of Educ. v. Wilder, 960 P.2d 695, 702 (Colo. 1998) (upholding termination of a teacher for showing his high school class portions of a movie that included nudity, profanity, and graphic violence; also rejecting the teacher's due process claim since sufficient notice of the policy had been provided). *See infra* text accompanying note 35.

Educators are not legally vulnerable when they are teaching the prescribed curriculum, even though their superiors instruct them to honor requests from school patrons.[32] For example, the Sixth Circuit ruled in favor of a teacher who was teaching a life science course in compliance with the school board's directives, finding that community protests did not justify school authorities placing restrictions on his course content. Noting that the films and text used by the teacher had been approved by the school board and used for several years, the court found the teacher's classroom behavior appropriate and consistent with the course objectives.[33] More recently, after a Maine teacher received several complaints about his curriculum from members of a Christian church, the school board ordered the teacher to refrain from teaching certain social science subjects pertaining to prehistoric times and Greek, Roman, and Asian history. The teacher challenged the board's action, and the district court denied the board's request for summary judgment, reasoning that the teacher was threatened with termination for teaching "non-Christian" ancient history. The court emphasized that classrooms cannot be used to promote Christian ideology.[34]

Teaching Strategies. State laws and school board policies establish the basic contours of the curriculum, but teachers retain some discretion in choosing *strategies* to convey prescribed content. In reviewing school board restrictions on teachers' classroom activities, the judiciary considers several factors, such as:

- Whether teachers have been provided adequate notice that use of specific teaching methodologies or materials will result in disciplinary action,
- Relevance of the method to the course of study and age and maturity of the students,
- Support of the method by the profession,
- Threat of disruption posed by the method, and
- Impact of the strategy on community norms.

A primary consideration in reviewing the legitimacy of classroom activities is whether instructional strategies are related to course objectives. Relevancy applies also to the age and maturity of the students; a controversial topic appropriate for high school students would not necessarily be suitable for elementary and junior high pupils. Relevance has been found lacking in several cases in which teachers have shown R-rated movies to public school students.[35] Also, the Eighth Circuit upheld termination of a teacher who willfully violated board policy by permitting her students to use profanity in their creative writing assignments.[36]

---

[32]It should also be noted that school counselors may discuss controversial issues in confidence with counselees and provide information as well as referrals. For example, counselors can provide factual information on the legal status of abortions, but they cannot urge or coerce students to have an abortion. *See* Arnold v. Bd. of Educ., 880 F.2d 305 (11th Cir. 1989), *on remand*, 754 F. Supp. 853 (S.D. Ala. 1990).

[33]Stachura v. Truszkowski, 763 F.2d 211 (6th Cir. 1985), *rev'd and remanded* (regarding award of compensatory damages) *sub nom*. Memphis Cmty. Sch. Dist. Stachura v., 477 U.S. 299 (1986).

[34]Cole v. Me. Sch. Admin. Dist. No. 1, 350 F. Supp. 2d 143 (D. Me. 2004).

[35]*See, e.g.*, Fowler v. Bd. of Educ., 819 F.2d 657 (6th Cir. 1987); Borger v. Bisciglia, 888 F. Supp. 97 (E.D. Wis. 1995); Bd. of Educ. v. Wilder, 960 P.2d 695, 702 (Colo. 1998).

[36]Lacks v. Ferguson Reorganized Sch. Dist. R-2, 147 F.3d 718 (8th Cir. 1998). *See also* Oleske v. Hilliard City Sch. Dist., 764 N.E.2d 1110 (Ohio Ct. App. 2001) (upholding dismissal of a teacher who told dirty jokes to middle school students and referred to another teacher by a derogatory name).

The Second Circuit similarly allowed a state college to dismiss a teacher for a classroom exercise in which students uttered sexually profane comments in a word-association exercise.[37]

Teachers, however, cannot be forced to discontinue instructionally relevant activities solely because of parental displeasure. The Fifth Circuit ruled that a teacher's use of a simulation to teach about post–Civil War U.S. history was related to legitimate educational objectives, and therefore dismissal for refusing to stop using the simulation impaired the teacher's academic rights.[38] Relevancy was established in the Sixth Circuit case discussed previously in which the court ordered reinstatement for the teacher who was teaching his life science course in conformance with board-approved objectives.[39]

Among the factors courts examine in assessing restrictions on classroom instruction is whether a teacher's action poses a threat of disruption to the operation of the school. To illustrate, an Oregon federal district court found a school board's policy of banning all political speakers from the high school unreasonable on several grounds, including the fact that no disruptions had occurred or could be anticipated from political discussions.[40] However, an Illinois federal district court recognized that a school board does not necessarily have to show that instructional materials actually caused a disruption to justify nonrenewal of a teacher's contract. Materials may be considered inappropriate for classroom use (e.g., an R-rated film with vulgarity and sexually explicit scenes), even though students "quietly acquiesce" to their use.[41]

Courts have been protective of school boards' authority to design the curriculum to reflect community values. A New York appeals court held that a teacher, who defied warnings that use of certain materials and sexual words in classroom discussions offended community mores, had no First Amendment grounds to challenge his reprimand.[42] Yet, if a particular strategy is instructionally relevant and supported by the profession, it likely will survive judicial review even though it might disturb some school patrons. For example, the Eighth Circuit found sufficient evidence that a teacher's contract was not renewed for impermissible religious reasons after parents complained that she was promoting New Age doctrine by sending a letter and "magic" rock home with her second-graders.[43] The letter indicated that the rocks were unique, like the students, and that if the students rubbed their magic rock and thought good things about themselves, they could achieve their goals. The teacher was awarded two years of pay, but the court did not order reinstatement because of the damaged relationship between the teacher and school principal.

[37]Vega v. Miller, 273 F.3d 460 (2d Cir. 2001).

[38]Kingsville Indep. Sch. Dist. v. Cooper, 611 F.2d 1109 (5th Cir. 1980).

[39]Stachura v. Truszkowski, 763 F.2d 211 (6th Cir. 1985); *supra* text accompanying note 33.

[40]Wilson v. Chancellor, 418 F. Supp. 1358 (D. Or. 1976).

[41]Krizek v. Bd. of Educ., 713 F. Supp. 1131, 1141 (N.D. Ill. 1989). *See also* Solmitz v. Me. Sch. Admin. Dist. No. 59, 495 A.2d 812 (Me. 1985) (upholding a school board's cancellation of a Tolerance Day program for legitimate safety concerns over bomb threats received).

[42]Bernstein v. Norwich City Sch. Dist., 726 N.Y.S.2d 474 (App. Div. 2001).

[43]Cowan v. Strafford R-VI Sch. Dist., 140 F.3d 1153 (8th Cir. 1998); text accompanying note 89, Chapter 3.

■ ■ ■ ■ ■ ▬▬▬▬▬▬▬▬▬▬▬▬▬▬▬▬▬▬▬▬▬▬▬▬▬▬▬▬▬▬▬▬▬▬▬

COPYRIGHT COMPLIANCE

Educators must comply with the federal copyright law; some copyrighted materials may be used for instructional purposes without the publisher's permission if fair use guidelines are followed.

Educators extensively use published materials and various other media in the classroom, and all school personnel are expected to comply with the federal copyright law. Although the law grants the owner of a copyright exclusive control over the protected material, courts since the 1800s have recognized exceptions to this control under the doctrine of "fair use." The fair use doctrine allows those other than the copyright owner to use the copyrighted material in a reasonable manner without the owner's consent.[44]

Congress incorporated the judicially created fair use concept into the 1976 revisions of the Copyright Act. In identifying the purposes of the fair use exception, Congress specifically noted teaching. **The exception provides needed flexibility for teachers but does *not* exempt them from copyright infringements.** The following factors are used in assessing whether copying specific material constitutes fair use or an infringement:

- The purpose and character of the use, including whether such use is of a commercial nature or is for nonprofit educational purposes,
- The nature of the copyrighted work,
- The amount and substantiality of the portion used in relation to the copyrighted work as a whole, and
- The effect of the use upon the potential market for or value of the copyrighted work.[45]

To clarify fair use pertaining to photocopying from books and periodicals, the House and Senate conferees incorporated into their conference report a set of classroom guidelines developed by a group representing educators, authors, and publishers. These guidelines are only part of the legislative history of the Copyright Act and do not have the force of law, but they have been widely used as persuasive authority in assessing the legality of reproducing printed materials in the educational environment. The guidelines permit making single copies of copyrighted material for teaching or research but are quite restrictive on the use of multiple copies. **To use multiple copies of a work, the tests of brevity, spontaneity, and cumulative effect must be met** (see Figure 4.1). Furthermore, the guidelines do not permit copying to substitute for anthologies or collective works or to replace consumable materials such as workbooks.

Publishers have taken legal action to ensure compliance with these guidelines. The Sixth Circuit held that a commercial copy shop violated the fair use doctrine in the reproduction of course packets for faculty at the University of Michigan. The copy shop owner argued that such reproduction of multiple copies for classroom use is a recognized

---

[44]Marcus v. Rowley, 695 F.2d 1171, 1174 (9th Cir. 1983).

[45]17 U.S.C. § 107 (2008).

FIGURE 4.1   Copyright Guidelines for Not-for-Profit Educational Institutions: Multiple Copies

Each copy must include the copyright notice and meet the following criteria:

Brevity

- For poems, not more than 250 words can be copied.
- For prose, a complete article of less than 2,500 words or an excerpt of not more than 1,000 words or 10 percent of the work, whichever is less, can be copied.
- Copies of illustrations can be one chart, graph, diagram, drawing, cartoon, or picture per book or periodical.

Spontaneity

- The copying is initiated by the individual teacher (not an administrator or supervisor).
- The inspiration to use the material occurs in such a manner that does not reasonably permit a timely request for permission.

Cumulative effect

- The copies are for use in one course.
- Not more than one short poem, article, or two excerpts can be copied from a given source or author during one class term.
- Multiple copying in a term is limited to nine instances.

The following practices are prohibited:

- Copying cannot substitute for compilations or collective works.
- Consumable works cannot be copied (e.g., workbooks, standardized tests).
- The same items cannot be copied from term to term.
- Copying cannot replace the purchase of books or periodicals.

statutory exemption. The appellate court disagreed, reasoning that the sale of multiple copies for commercial, not educational, purposes destroyed the publishers' potential licensing revenue, contained creative material, and involved substantial portions of the copyrighted publications (as much as 30 percent of one work).[46] This ruling does not prevent faculty from using course packets or anthologies in the classroom, but it requires them to seek permission from publishers and the possible payment of fees prior to photocopying.

The fair use doctrine and congressional guidelines have been strictly construed in educational settings. Although materials reproduced for the classroom meet the first factor in determining fair use—educational purpose—the remaining factors also must be met. The Ninth Circuit held that fair use was not met in a teacher's use of a copyrighted booklet to make a learning activity packet used for the same purpose as the protected booklet.[47] The absence of personal profit on the part of the teacher did not lessen the violation. Furthermore, half of the packet was a verbatim copy of the copyrighted material, and the copying did not meet the guideline of spontaneity in that it was reproduced several times over two school years.

---

[46]Princeton Univ. Press v. Mich. Document Servs., 99 F.3d 1381 (6th Cir. 1996).

[47]*Marcus*, 695 F.2d at 1171.

An Illinois federal district court ruled that a Chicago teacher and editor of a newspaper called *Substance* committed a copyright violation against the Chicago school board by publishing its copyrighted tests used to assess educational levels of high school freshmen and sophomores. The tests were clearly marked with the copyright notice and included a warning that the material could not be duplicated. In dismissing the teacher's affirmative defenses, the court ruled that he did not possess a First Amendment right to publish the copyrighted tests as the Copyright Act limits First Amendment freedoms, and publication of the material did not fall within the fair use guidelines.[48]

Rapid developments in instructional technology pose a new set of legal questions regarding use of videotapes, digital video disks, and computer software. Recognizing the need for guidance related to recording material, Congress issued guidelines for educational use in 1981.[49] These guidelines specify that recording must be made at the request of the teacher, and the material must be used for relevant classroom activities only once within the first 10 days of recording. Additional use is limited to instructional reinforcement or evaluation, and the tape or disk must be erased after 45 calendar days. A New York federal district court held that a school system violated the fair use standards by extensive off-the-air taping and replaying of entire television programs.[50] The taping interfered with the producers' ability to market the tapes and films. In a subsequent appeal, the school system sought permission for temporary taping; however, because of the availability of these programs for rental or lease, even temporary recording and use violated fair use by interfering with the marketability of the films.[51]

Recording television broadcasts on home video recorders for later classroom use may constitute copyright infringement if off-the-air taping guidelines above are not followed. The Supreme Court ruled that personal video recording for the purpose of "time shifting" is a legitimate, unobjectionable purpose, posing minimal harm to marketability.[52] However, **home recording for broader viewing by students in the classroom would be beyond the purposes envisioned by the Supreme Court and would necessitate careful adherence to the guidelines for limited use.**

Under 1980 amendments to the copyright law, software was included as protected intellectual property.[53] It is clear from the amended law that only one duplicate or backup copy can be made of the master computer program to ensure a working copy of the program if the master copy is damaged. Application of the fair use exception does not alter this restriction for educators. Although duplicating multiple copies would be for educational purposes, other factors of fair use would be violated: The software is readily accessible for purchase, programs can only be duplicated in their entirety, and copying substantially reduces the potential market.

In spite of the amendments, publishers continue to be concerned about illegal copying of computer software in the school environment. Limited school budgets and high costs have led

---

[48]Chi. Sch. Reform Bd. v. Substance, 79 F. Supp. 2d 919 (N.D. Ill. 2000).

[49]Guidelines for Off-Air Recording of Broadcast Programming for Educational Purposes, Cong. Rec. § E4751, October 14, 1981.

[50]Encyclopedia Britannica Educ. Corp. v. Crooks, 542 F. Supp. 1156 (W.D.N.Y. 1982).

[51]Encyclopedia Britannica Educ. Corp. v. Crooks, 558 F. Supp. 1247 (W.D.N.Y. 1983).

[52]Sony Corp. v. Universal City Studios, 464 U.S. 417 (1984).

[53]17 U.S.C. § 117 (2008).

to abuse of copyrighted software. In 1999, the school board of the Los Angeles Unified School District settled what might be the worst case of software piracy discovered in public schools.[54] An investigation by a group of software companies discovered more than 1,400 copies of software, such as Microsoft Word and Adobe Photoshop, allegedly being used without authorization. The school district denied the violation but settled to avoid the costs of a trial.

A question not answered by the copyright law but plaguing schools is the legality of multiple use of a master program. That is, can a program be loaded on many computers in a laboratory for simultaneous use, or can a program be modified for use in a network of microcomputers? Again, application of the fair use concept would indicate that multiple use is not permissible. The most significant factor is that the market for the educational software would be greatly diminished. Several students using the master program one at a time (serial use), however, would appear not to violate the copyright law. **To acquire broad use of particular software, school systems must either purchase multiple copies or negotiate site license agreements with the publishers.**

As schools are developing their capacity to take advantage of the Internet, copyright law also is evolving. Congress amended the law in 1998 with the Digital Millennium Copyright Act, **reinforcing that an individual's copyright is secured when the work is created and "fixed in any tangible medium of expression."**[55] In 2002, greater clarity was provided for educators regarding the use of digital media in distance education with the enactment of the Technology, Education, and Copyright Harmonization (TEACH) Act.[56] The act gives accredited nonprofit educational institutions more flexibility in using the Internet to distribute copyrighted materials in distance education programs. Basically, the act allows copyrighted materials to be used in distance education courses in the same way they can be used in regular classrooms.

Case law clearly indicates that the Internet is not immune from the basic principles of copyright law; material that is created on the Internet or produced in a different format and then converted for use on the Internet is entitled to full legal protections. For example, in 2001 the Ninth Circuit imposed an injunction against Napster Corporation and its distribution of a file-sharing program that allowed individuals to download music files.[57] More recently, the Supreme Court found that two software companies, presenting themselves as "alternatives" to Napster, infringed the rights of songwriters, music publishers, and motion picture studios who had brought suit to prevent unauthorized use of their protected property. Like Napster, the challenged software companies distributed free software products that allowed individuals to share electronic files through peer-to-peer networks, so the companies were "liable for the resulting acts of infringement by third parties."[58] Although the

---

[54]"L.A. School Board Settles Software Copyright Suit," *School Law News* (March 5, 1999), p. 2. The case was settled for $300,000 plus an additional $1.5 million for a task force to monitor software usage over a three-year period.

[55]17 U.S.C. § 1201 *et seq.* (2008).

[56]17 U.S.C. §110 (2008).

[57]A&M Records v. Napster, 239 F.3d 1004 (9th Cir. 2001).

[58]Metro-Goldwyn-Mayer Studios v. Grokster, Ltd., 545 U.S. 913, 919 (2005). The lower courts had ruled that the software companies could be not held liable for unlawful use of the file-sharing programs. The Supreme Court remanded the case to the district court for a trial.

file-sharing software had some lawful uses, its primary purpose and use was to share copyrighted files, which made the software companies culpable.

Extraordinary technological advances have given teachers and their school systems the means to access a wide range of instructional materials and products, but many of them are protected by the federal copyright law that restricts unauthorized reproduction. Because violation of the law can result in school district and educator liability, school boards should adopt policies or guidelines to prohibit infringement and to alert individuals of unlawful practices.[59]

■ ■ ■ ■ ■

STUDENT PROFICIENCY TESTING

Courts have recognized that an educated citizenry is an appropriate government goal and the establishment of minimum performance standards to give value to a high school diploma is a rational means to attain that goal.

The concept of performance assessment is not new, but the use of proficiency tests as a condition of grade promotion or the receipt of a high school diploma has a relatively brief history. In 1976, only four states had enacted student proficiency testing legislation. Now all states have laws or administrative regulations pertaining to statewide performance testing programs, and more than half of the states condition receipt of a high school diploma on test passage. Given the state's authority to establish academic standards, including mandatory examinations, the judiciary traditionally has been reluctant to interfere with assessments of pupil performance.[60]

Recently, other forms of performance assessment, such as portfolios, have received attention, but standardized tests continue to be used in most school districts. Annual student testing is strongly supported by the federal government. Indeed, the No Child Left Behind (NCLB) Act:

- Mandates annual testing in grades 3 through 8 in reading and math and in science at certain grade intervals,
- Requires high school students to take a general test in core subjects at least once, and
- Ties federal assistance and sanctions for schools to student test scores.[61]

High-stakes assessments shape the instructional program, and states increasingly are evaluating educators' performance based on their students' test scores. Not surprisingly,

---

[59]*See* 17 U.S.C. § 511(a) (2008). In response to several appellate court decisions holding that under the Eleventh Amendment states and their agents were not subject to suit in federal courts for the infringement of copyrights, Congress amended the copyright law (Copyright Remedy Clarification) specifically abrogating immunity. *See also* BV Eng'g v. UCLA, 858 F.2d 1394 (9th Cir. 1988); Richard Anderson Photography v. Brown, 852 F.2d 114 (4th Cir. 1988).

[60]*See* Hurd v. Hansen, 230 Fed. App'x 692 (9th Cir. 2007) (holding that a teacher's grading decision did not violate student's equal protection or substantive due process rights).

[61]No Child Left Behind Act of 2001, 20 U.S.C. § 6301 *et seq.* (2008).

claims are being made that teachers are limiting classroom activities to material covered on the tests and/or unfairly coaching students for the exams.[62]

Although the state's authority to evaluate student performance has not been questioned, specific high-stakes assessment programs have been legally challenged as impairing students' rights to fair and nondiscriminatory treatment. In a case still widely cited as establishing the legal standards, *Debra P. v. Turlington*, the Fifth Circuit in 1981 recognized that by making schooling mandatory, Florida created a property interest—a valid expectation that students would receive diplomas if they passed required courses.[63] **This state-created property right to an education requires sufficient notice of conditions attached to high school graduation and a fair opportunity to satisfy them before a diploma can be withheld.** The court found that 13 months was insufficient notice of the test requirement and further held that the state may have administered a fundamentally unfair test covering material that had not been taught in Florida schools. The appeals court also enjoined the state from using the test as a diploma prerequisite for four years to provide time for the vestiges of prior school segregation to be removed and to ensure that all minority students subjected to the requirement started first grade under desegregated conditions. However, the court held that continued use of the test to determine remediation needs was constitutionally permissible, noting that the disproportionate placement of minority students in remedial programs *per se* does not abridge the Equal Protection Clause without evidence of intentional discrimination.

On remand, the district court ruled that the injunction should be lifted, and the appeals court affirmed this decision in 1984.[64] By presenting substantial evidence, including curriculum guides and survey data, the state convinced the judiciary that the test was instructionally valid in that it covered material taught to Florida students. Also, data showed that only students who entered school under desegregated conditions would be subjected to the diploma sanction. Furthermore, there was significant improvement among African American students during the six years the test had been administered.

Other courts have reiterated the principles established in *Debra P.* and have reasoned that despite evidence of higher minority failure rates, such testing and remediation programs are effectively addressing the effects of prior discrimination.[65] Yet, courts have not agreed as to whether individual rights are abridged when students are not allowed to participate in graduation exercises because they failed the statewide proficiency examination used as a prerequisite to receipt of a diploma.[66]

---

[62]*See* Buck v. Lowndes County Sch. Dist., 761 So. 2d 144 (Miss. 2000) (upholding nonrenewal of teachers' contracts for noncompliance with testing procedures that resulted in a reduction in the district's accreditation level).

[63]474 F. Supp. 244 (M.D. Fla. 1979), *aff'd in part, vacated in part*, 644 F.2d 397 (5th Cir. 1981).

[64]Debra P. v. Turlington, 564 F. Supp. 177 (M.D. Fla. 1983), *aff'd*, 730 F.2d 1405 (11th Cir. 1984). The Fifth Circuit was divided into the Fifth and Eleventh Circuits while this case was in progress.

[65]*See, e.g.*, GI Forum v. Tex. Educ. Agency, 87 F. Supp. 2d 667 (W.D. Tex. 2000). Courts also have upheld the practice of conditioning grade promotion on test scores. *See, e.g.*, Parents against Testing before Teaching v. Orleans Parish Sch. Bd., 273 F.3d 1107 (5th Cir. 2001); Bester v. Tuscaloosa City Bd. of Educ., 722 F.2d 1514 (11th Cir. 1984); Sandlin v. Johnson, 643 F.2d 1027 (4th Cir. 1981).

[66]*Compare* Williams v. Austin Indep. Sch. Dist., 796 F. Supp. 251 (W.D. Tex. 1992) (holding that the graduation ceremony can be reserved for students meeting all requirements, assuming that appropriate notice and instruction are provided) *with* Crump v. Gilmer Indep. Sch. Dist., 797 F. Supp. 552 (E.D. Tex. 1992) (requiring a Texas school to permit students who failed the exam but satisfied other graduation requirements to take part in the graduation ceremony, even though they will not receive their diplomas until they pass the test).

A California appeals court rejected a claim that students in an economically challenged community were entitled to diplomas because they had passed all the required courses but had not been provided adequate educational resources to pass the state's high school exit examination. The court found use of the test as a diploma sanction integral to the goal of raising academic standards in the state's schools.[67] Although several school districts have unsuccessfully asserted that the federal government must provide the funds necessary under the NCLB to devise and administer tests, improve test scores, and train teachers before requiring schools to comply with federal requirements, in 2008 the Sixth Circuit ruled that state officials could reasonably interpret the NCLB to mean that states do not have to comply with the law's requirements that are not funded by the federal government.[68] Also, an Alaska court recently ruled that because the state failed to provide sufficient oversight to ensure that local districts were providing students a meaningful opportunity to acquire proficiency in the subjects tested by the state, receipt of a high school diploma could not be conditioned on passage of a proficiency exam.[69]

Given the high stakes attached to some exams, parents have requested access to questions on previously administered tests. The Ohio Supreme Court ruled that the statewide proficiency test fell under the definition of a public record, so previously administered exams must be disclosed to parents, except for portions owned and developed by a private nonprofit corporation.[70] But, a Kentucky appeals court held that parents were not entitled to view the statewide proficiency exam because indiscriminate viewing by the public could jeopardize the test's reliability.[71]

Administering proficiency tests to children with limited mastery of English and to children with disabilities has been controversial. After school districts and others challenged California's failure to make appropriate testing accommodations under the NCLB for students with limited English proficiency,[72] the parties reached a settlement under

[67]O'Connell v. Valenzuela, 47 Cal. Rptr. 3d 147 (Ct. App. 2006) (recognizing that if students receive diplomas without demonstrating mastery of basic skills, they will not be provided the remediation they need to be productive workers and citizens). *See also* Valenzuela v. O'Connell, No. JCCP-4468 (Cal. Super. Ct. Aug. 13, 2007) (approving a settlement agreement that calls for legislation providing two years of academic assistance to students who do not pass the exam).

[68]Sch. Dist. v. Sec'y of the U.S. Dep't of Educ., 512 F. 3d 252 (6th Cir. 2008) (holding that Congress must clarify if such compliance is mandatory regardless of funding). *But see* Connecticut v. Spellings, No.3:05CV1330(MRK), 2008 U.S. Dist. LEXIS 364434 (D. Conn. Apr. 28, 1998); Connecticut v. Spellings, 453 F. Supp. 2d 459 (D. Conn. 2006) (rejecting Connecticut's challenge to the NCLB's unfounded mandates on jurisdictional and procedural grounds, but not addressing the merits of the state's claims).

[69]Moore v. State, No. 3AN-04-9756 (Alaska Super. Ct. June 26, 2007), available at www.law.state.ak.us/unpublished/pdf/mooredecision.pdf.

[70]Rea v. Ohio Dep't of Educ., 692 N.E.2d 596 (Ohio 1998).

[71]Triplett v. Livingston County Bd. of Educ., 967 S.W.2d 25 (Ky. Ct. App. 1997).

[72]Coachella Valley Unified Sch. Dist. v. California, No. C05-02657 WHA, 2005 U.S. Dist. LEXIS 44825 (N.D. Cal. Aug. 5, 2005) (remanding state law challenge to the state judiciary); Coachella Valley Unified Sch. Dist. v. State, No. 05-505334 (Cal. Super. Ct. May 25, 2007) (finding decision to assess all students in English neither arbitrary or capricious, given that students are taught mainly in English and the impracticality of translating all assessment instruments into multiple languages). *See also Assessment and Accountability for Recently Arrived and Former Limited English Proficient (LEP) Students* (Non-Regulatory Guidance) (Washington, DC: U.S. Department of Education, May 2007).

which the U.S. Department of Education changed its classification of schools needing improvement to allow more accommodations for non-English speakers.

Courts in general have ruled that the state does not have to alter its academic standards for students with disabilities; such children can be denied grade promotion or a diploma if they do not meet the specified standards.[73] A child with mental disabilities may be given the option of not taking a proficiency examination if the team planning the individualized education program (IEP) concludes that there is little likelihood of the child mastering the material covered on the test. Children excused from the test requirement usually are awarded certificates of school attendance instead of diplomas. Yet, such children cannot be denied the *opportunity* to satisfy requirements (including tests) for promotion or a diploma.

The Seventh Circuit has suggested that children with disabilities may need earlier notice of a proficiency test requirement than other students to ensure an adequate opportunity for the material on the test to be incorporated into their IEPs.[74] While students with disabilities are entitled to special accommodations in the administration of examinations to ensure that their knowledge, rather than their disability, is being assessed (e.g., braille tests), they are not entitled to accommodations that would jeopardize the validity of the graduation test, such as reading to the student a test measuring reading comprehension.[75] The types of accommodations required for graduation tests remain controversial, especially when accommodations that are part of the student's IEP for classroom instruction are denied for high-stakes tests.[76]

Specific proficiency testing programs will likely continue to be challenged on constitutional and statutory grounds. Educators would be wise to keep in mind the points listed in Figure 4.2.

■ ■ ■ ■ ■

EDUCATIONAL MALPRACTICE/INSTRUCTIONAL NEGLIGENCE

Students have not yet secured damages from school districts for instructional negligence, but detailed proficiency standards and special education requirements may strengthen the grounds for such claims in the future.

---

[73]*See, e.g.*, Brookhart v. Ill. State Bd. of Educ., 697 F.2d 179 (7th Cir. 1983); Anderson v. Banks, 540 F. Supp. 761 (S.D. Ga. 1982); Bd. of Educ. v. Ambach, 457 N.E.2d 775 (N.Y. 1983).

[74]*Brookhart*, 697 F.2d at 187. *But see* Rene v. Reed, 751 N.E.2d 736 (Ind. Ct. App. 2001), *transfer denied*, 774 N.E.2d 506 (Ind. 2002) (reasoning that three years' notice of the test requirement as a prerequisite to a diploma was sufficient for children with disabilities, given ample opportunities to receive remediation and retake the exam). *See* Chapter 7 for a discussion of federal and state protections of children with disabilities.

[75]*See Rene*, 751 N.E.2d 736. The Office for Civil Rights in the U.S. Department of Education has reasoned that states can deny use of reading devices to accommodate children with disabilities on graduation exams, even though their IEPs allow use of such devices. *See* Ala. Dep't of Educ., 29 IDELR 249 (1998).

[76]*See* Smiley v. Cal. Dep't of Educ., 53 Fed. App'x 474 (9th Cir. 2002) (dissolving the parts of the lower court's injunction pertaining to required test waivers and alternative assessments for children with disabilities as not ripe for adjudication).

FIGURE 4.2   High-Stakes Proficiency Testing Programs

Proficiency tests used as a prerequisite to high school graduation will survive legal challenges if:

- Students are advised upon entrance into high school of test requirements as a prerequisite to graduation,
- Students have the opportunity to be adequately prepared for the tests,
- Tests are not intentionally discriminatory and do not perpetuate the effects of past school segregation,
- Students who fail are provided remedial opportunities and the chance to retake the examinations, and
- Children with disabilities receive appropriate accommodations.

A topic prompting litigation since the mid-1970s is instructional negligence, commonly referred to as *educational malpractice*. Initial suits focused on whether students have a right to attain a predetermined level of achievement in return for state-mandated school attendance; parents asserted a right to expect their children to be functionally literate upon high school graduation. More recent cases have involved allegations that school authorities have breached their duty to diagnose students' deficiencies and place them in appropriate instructional programs.

In the first educational malpractice suit to receive substantial attention, a student contended that the school district was negligent in teaching, promoting, and graduating him from high school with the ability to read only at the fifth grade level.[77] He also claimed that his performance and progress had been misrepresented to his mother, who testified that she was unaware of his deficiencies until he was tested by a private agency after high school graduation. Concluding that the school district was not negligent, a California appeals court reasoned that the complexities of the teaching/learning process made it impossible to place the entire burden on the school to ensure that all students, with their varying abilities to learn, attain a specified reading level before high school graduation.

The New York high court has rejected several instructional negligence claims, concluding that it is not the role of the judiciary to make such educational policy determinations that should be handled through the state educational system's administrative appeals.[78] Other courts also have denied instructional malpractice claims, indicating a reluctance to intervene

---

[77]Peter W. v. S.F. Unified Sch. Dist., 131 Cal. Rptr. 854 (Ct. App. 1976). *See* Chapter 2 for an overview of tort law pertaining to negligence suits.

[78]*See* Torres v. Little Flower Children's Servs., 474 N.E.2d 223 (N.Y. 1984) (rejecting the malpractice claim against the child-care agency for a student's failure to receive suitable instruction for him to learn to read; he was incorrectly diagnosed at age 10, after having been tested in English even though he understood only Spanish); Donohue v. Copiague Union Free Schs., 391 N.E.2d 1352 (N.Y. 1979) (dismissing an educational malpractice suit brought by a learning-disabled high school graduate who claimed that because of the school district's negligence he was unable to complete job applications and cope with the problems of everyday life); Hoffman v. Bd. of Educ., 410 N.Y.S.2d 99 (App. Div. 1978), *rev'd*, 400 N.E.2d 317 (N.Y. 1979) (reversing the lower court's conclusion that the student was entitled to damages because school personnel disregarded the school psychologist's report and erroneously instructed the student for 12 years in a program for the mentally retarded—even though the student scored in the 90th percentile on reading readiness tests at ages 8 and 9).

in such educational policy decisions.[79] For example, state courts have denied damages claims for a school district's alleged breach of its duty to evaluate and develop an individualized education plan for a child with multiple disabilities,[80] the alleged misclassification of a student with dyslexia,[81] and a school district's failure to provide students with a quality education resulting in alleged intellectual and emotional harm and diminished future opportunities.[82]

The increasing specificity of legislation pertaining to student proficiency standards and special education placements may strengthen the grounds for tort suits involving *placement negligence*. Moreover, state and federal legislation making school districts accountable for ensuring student mastery of state standards may increase school districts' potential liability. Even though it seems unlikely that public schools in the near future will be held responsible for a specified quantum of student achievement, it is conceivable that schools will be held legally accountable for:

- Diagnosing students' needs,
- Placing them in appropriate instructional programs,
- Reporting their progress to parents, and
- Providing educational options if students are not progressing in their current placements.

INSTRUCTIONAL PRIVACY RIGHTS

Parents are entitled to review their children's records and instructional materials and to have personal information kept confidential.

The protection of students' privacy rights has become an increasingly volatile issue in political forums. State and federal laws place dual duties on the government—to protect the public's First Amendment right to be informed about government activities and to protect the personal privacy of individuals. In addition, laws have been enacted to protect students from mandatory participation in research projects or instructional activities designed to reveal personal information in sensitive areas. This section provides an overview of legal developments pertaining to students' privacy rights in instructional matters.

Student Records

The Supreme Court has recognized that the federal Constitution protects a zone of personal privacy.[83] Thus, there must be a compelling justification for governmental action that

---

[79]*See, e.g.*, Vogel v. Maimonides Acad., 754 A.2d 824 (Conn. App. Ct. 2000); Page v. Klein Tools, 610 N.W.2d 900 (Mich. 2000); Suriano v. Hyde Park Cent. Sch. Dist., 611 N.Y.S.2d 20 (App. Div. 1994).

[80]Keech v. Berkeley Unified Sch. Dist., 210 Cal. Rptr. 7 (Ct. App. 1984).

[81]D.S.W. v. Fairbanks N. Star Borough Sch. Dist., 628 P.2d 554 (Alaska 1981). *See also* Johnson v. Clark, 418 N.W.2d 466 (Mich. Ct. App. 1987) (finding that a student who was reading on a fourth grade level at graduation could not recover damages for the school's failure to assess him annually).

[82]Denver Parents Ass'n v. Denver Bd. of Educ., 10 P.3d 662 (Colo. Ct. App. 2000).

[83]*See* Griswold v. Connecticut, 381 U.S. 479 (1965); text accompanying note 72, Chapter 10.

impairs privacy rights, including the right to have personal information kept confidential. Because of this right, questions about who has access to public school students' permanent files, and the contents of such files have been the source of controversy. Legal challenges to school record-keeping procedures have resulted in courts ordering school officials to expunge irrelevant information from students' permanent folders. In some situations, students have brought successful libel suits for damages against school authorities who allegedly recorded and communicated defamatory information about them.[84]

Due to widespread dissatisfaction with educators' efforts to ameliorate abuses associated with student record-keeping practices, Congress enacted the Family Educational Rights and Privacy Act (FERPA) in 1974.[85] **FERPA stipulates that federal funds may be withdrawn from any educational agency or institution that (1) fails to provide parents access to their child's educational records or (2) disseminates such information (with some exceptions) to third parties without parental permission.** Upon reaching the age of majority, students may exercise the rights previously guaranteed to their parents.[86] Education officials should assume that a parent is entitled to exercise rights under FERPA unless state law or a court order bars a parent's access to his or her child's records under specific circumstances and the education agency has been instructed accordingly.[87]

After reviewing a student's permanent file, the parent or eligible student can request amendments in any information thought to be inaccurate, misleading, or in violation of the student's protected rights. If school authorities decide that an amendment is not warranted, the parent or eligible student must be advised of the right to a hearing. The hearing officer may be an employee of the school district but may not be an individual with a direct interest in the outcome of the hearing. Either party may be represented by counsel at the hearing, and the hearing officer must issue a written decision summarizing the evidence presented and the rationale for the ruling. If the hearing officer concludes that the records should not be amended, the parent or eligible student has the right to place in the file a personal statement specifying objections.

Individuals can file a complaint with the U.S. Department of Education if they believe a school district displays a custom or practice of violating FERPA provisions. The remedy for FERPA violations is the withdrawal of federal funds. The department has advised some school districts to change their practices to conform to FERPA, but no district to date has lost federal funds for noncompliance.

The Department of Education functioned without direction from the Supreme Court until 2002 when the Court rendered two FERPA decisions. **In *Gonzaga University v. Doe*, the Supreme Court held that individuals cannot bring damages suits for FERPA violations, because the law does not create privately enforceable rights.**[88] Resolving the conflict among lower courts, the Supreme Court further held that since FERPA contains no

---

[84]*See, e.g.*, Elder v. Anderson, 23 Cal. Rptr. 48 (Ct. App. 1962). *See also* Chapter 2 for a discussion of tort law.

[85]20 U.S.C. § 1232g (2008); 34 C.F.R. § 99.1 *et seq.* (2008).

[86]The Family Policy Compliance Office was created to investigate alleged FERPA violations, 20 U.S.C. § 1232g(g) (2008). This office reviews complaints and responses from accused agencies and submits written findings with steps the agency must take to comply. *See* 34 C.F.R. §§ 99.65(a)(2), 99.66(b), 99.66(c)(1) (2008).

[87]*See, e.g.*, Fay v. S. Colonie Cent. Sch. Dist., 802 F.2d 21 (2d Cir. 1986) (recognizing that joint custodial parents must have equal access to education information about their child). In some situations, however, one parent may be granted sole legal authority, including all educational decisions, even though the noncustodial parent has visitation rights.

[88]536 U.S. 273 (2002).

rights-creating language, the law cannot be enforced through suits under 42 U.S.C. Section 1983, which provides individuals a damages remedy for the deprivation of federal rights.[89] The Court reiterated that FERPA has an aggregate rather than individual focus and the remedy for violations is the denial of federal funds to schools that exhibit a policy or practice of noncompliance. School personnel were relieved that the Court did not authorize private suits for damages to enforce FERPA, as such a ruling would have provided a significant incentive for parents to challenge student record-keeping practices in court.

In the second 2002 Supreme Court ruling, *Owasso Independent School District v. Falvo*, the Court reversed the Tenth Circuit's conclusion that peer grading practices violate FERPA.[90] The Supreme Court concluded that peer graders are not "maintaining" student records under FERPA, and even though students may call out the scores in class, they are not "acting for" the educational institution.[91] **There may be educational reasons for not having students grade each others' work, but given the *Falvo* ruling, there is no legal barrier under FERPA.** The Supreme Court also hinted that teachers' grade books may not be subject to FERPA, mentioning that records covered by the act are usually kept in a central repository, but it specifically declined to resolve this issue.

A student's records can be released to school authorities authorized to review such information or to officials of a school to which the student is transferring if the parents or eligible student are notified or if the sending institution has given prior notice that it routinely transfers such records. Students' records must be disclosed if subpoenaed by a grand jury or law enforcement agency, and schools may disclose information pursuant to other court orders or subpoenas if a reasonable effort is made to notify the parent or eligible student.[92] Identifiable information also can be disclosed to appropriate authorities or to advocacy groups if necessary to protect the health or safety of the student or others.[93]

---

[89]Civil Rights Act of 1871, § 1, codified as 42 U.S.C. § 1983 (2008). For a discussion of this law, *see* text accompanying note 82, Chapter 12.

[90]534 U.S. 426 (2002), *on remand*, 288 F.3d 1236 (10th Cir. 2002) (granting summary judgment in favor of defendant school district and administrators).

[91]*Owasso*, 534 U.S. at 433. Although peers can call out scores, students' grades cannot be posted or disseminated in any manner that allows individual students to be identified (e.g., by name or listed in alphabetical order).

[92]20 U.S.C. § 1232g(b)(1)(J)(i) and (ii) (2008); 1232g(b)(2)(B) (2008). *See* Ellis v. Cleveland Mun. Sch. Dist., 455 F.3d 690 (6th Cir. 2006) (upholding disclosure of records related to substitute teachers' use of corporal punishment in a suit challenging the use of this disciplinary technique); Commonwealth v. Buccella, 751 N.E.2d 373 (Mass. 2001) (holding that a school district did not violate a student's privacy rights when it shared samples of the student's school work with police to compare his handwriting with graffiti on school property in connection with criminal charges). FERPA specifically exempts from the definition of "education records" the records of law enforcement units that the school maintains (e.g., a unit of commissioned officers or security guards that enforces the law and maintains security). *See* 34 C.F.R. § 99.8 (2008).

[93]*See, e.g.*, Disability Rights Wis. v. State Dep't of Pub. Instruction, 463 F.3d 719 (7th Cir. 2006) (requiring disclosure of names of students to state-designated advocacy agency conducting an investigation of alleged abuse or neglect); Doe v. Woodford County Bd. of Educ., 213 F.3d 921 (6th Cir. 2000) (upholding disclosure to coach of information that student was a hemophiliac and carrier of hepatitis B); 34 C.F.R. § 99.36 (2008). The Department of Education in 2007 issued a series of brochures to clarify that health or safety emergencies permit the disclosure of a student's unique information; *see* Frank Wolfe, "ED Releases FERPA Brochures to Deter School Violence," *Education Daily* (October 31, 2007). p. 2. In 2008, the Department proposed revised FERPA regulations to incorporate the Supreme Court's 2002 decisions and to further clarify the discretion of school authorities to share identifiable student data if safety is at stake. 73 Fed. Reg. 15573 (proposed Mar. 24, 2008 and to be codified at 34 C.F.R. pt. 99).

Under FERPA, certain public directory information—such as students' names, addresses, dates and places of birth, major fields of study, e-mail addresses, pictures, and degrees and awards received—can be released without parental consent.[94] Any educational agency releasing such data must give public notice of the specific categories it has designated as "directory" and must allow a reasonable period of time for parents to inform the agency that any or all of this information on their child should not be released without their prior consent. An NCLB provision requires public secondary schools to provide military recruiters with access to personal contact information for every student.[95] Although parents can request that their records be withheld, some school districts simply submit their student directories to the military recruiters. Directory data about a student cannot be released if accompanied by other personally identifiable information unless it is among the specified exceptions to the general rule against nonconsensual disclosure.

Students' privacy rights do not preclude federal and state authorities from having access to data needed to audit and evaluate federally supported education programs as long as collected in a way that prevents the disclosure of personally identifiable information. However, FERPA was amended in 2001 in accordance with the provisions of the USA PATRIOT (Uniting and Strengthening America by Providing Appropriate Tools Required to Intercept and Obstruct Terrorism) Act to give institutions permission to disclose, without parental or student consent, personally identifiable information to representatives of the U.S. attorney general based on an order from a court of competent jurisdiction in connection with investigations of terrorism crimes.[96]

Composite information on pupil achievement[97] and discipline[98] can be released to the public as long as individual students are not personally identified. Yet, a Florida appeals court ruled that discipline forms about incidents on school buses and surveillance videotapes of such incidents could not be disclosed to a television station even with personally identifying information redacted, because Florida law goes further than FERPA in preventing the release of such information.[99]

---

[94]For a complete list of directory items, *see* 34 C.F.R. § 99.3 (2007).

[95]20 U.S.C. § 1232h(c)(4)(a)(i) (2008). *See also* Rumsfeld v. Forum for Academic & Institutional Rights, 547 U.S. 47 (2006) (finding no First Amendment compelled speech violation by requiring law schools that receive federal aid to accommodate the military's recruitment message).

[96]20 U.S.C. § 1232g(j) (2008). Schools are required to record such disclosures in students' permanent files. *See* USA PATRIOT Act, 18 U.S.C. § 2332b(g)(5)(B) (2008); Susan Stuart, "Lex-Praxis of Educational Informational Privacy for Public Schoolchildren," *Nebraska Law Review*, vol. 84 (2006), pp. 1158–1225.

[97]*See, e.g.*, Laplante v. Stewart, 470 So. 2d 1018 (La. Ct. App. 1985) (finding that the public had the right to examine the rankings of schools participating in a school effectiveness study conducted by the state department of education). *But see* Sargent Sch. Dist. No. RE-33J v. W. Servs., 751 P.2d 56 (Colo. 1988) (holding that student scholastic data were exempt from disclosure under the state's open records law; there was no duty to mark out all identifying information so the data could be released); Fish v. Dallas Indep. Sch. Dist., 170 S.W.3d 226 (Tex. App. 2005) (rejecting open-records request for longitudinal student performance data on the Iowa Test of Basic Skills because the requested information could be traced to students in violation of FERPA).

[98]*See, e.g.*, United States v. Miami Univ., 294 F. 3d 797 (6th Cir. 2002); Hardin County Schs. v. Foster, 40 S.W.3d 865 (Ky. 2001); Bd. of Trs. v. Cut Bank Pioneer Press, 160 P.3d 482 (Mont. 2007).

[99]WFTV v. Sch. Bd. of Seminole, 874 So. 2d 48 (Fla. Dist. Ct. App. 2004).

Several courts have allowed disclosures because they are not educational records under FERPA or have exempted specific items from nondisclosure provisions. For example, the Tenth Circuit concluded that school personnel could advise parents of harassment and assault victims regarding how they dealt with the perpetrator; disclosures to parents of victims or witnesses of the playground assaults did not comprise an educational record that would implicate FERPA.[100] And a Kentucky appeals court ruled that a special education teacher could view videotapes made in her classroom for the purpose of evaluating her own performance and improving her classroom management; both FERPA and the comparable state law provided for an exception for teachers with a legitimate educational interest in the material sought.[101]

FERPA cannot be used by parents to assert a right to review faculty evaluations used to determine which students will be given academic honors, such as membership in the National Honor Society.[102] Additionally, students cannot rely on FERPA to challenge teachers' grading procedures, other than whether grades were accurately calculated and recorded.[103] The Fourth Circuit ruled that FERPA does not entitle students to see an answer key to exams to check the accuracy of their grades, because the key is not part of students' educational records.[104]

Other federal laws provide additional protections regarding the confidentiality and accessibility of student records.[105] Many states also have enacted legislation addressing the maintenance and disclosure of student records. Both state and federal privacy laws recognize certain exceptions to "access and disclosure" provisions. For example, a teacher's daily notes pertaining to pupil progress that are shared only with a substitute teacher are exempt from the laws. Private notes, however, become education records and are subject to legal specifications once they are shared, even among educators who have a legitimate need for access to such information. At times there are conflicts between "freedom of information" or "right to know" provisions and federal and state laws protecting privacy rights, and FERPA protections of personally identifiable educational records generally prevail.[106]

Congress, state legislatures, and the judiciary have indicated a continuing interest in safeguarding students' privacy rights, and school boards would be wise regularly to reassess their policies and practices in this regard. School personnel should use some restraint, however, before purging material that may be necessary to provide continuity in a

---

[100]Jensen v. Reeves, 3 Fed. App'x 905 (10th Cir. 2001). *See also* Cudjoe v. Edmond Pub. Schs., 297 F.3d 1058 (10th Cir. 2002) (finding a teacher's comments about a student during a residents' meeting at her condominium complex did not rise to the level of invading privacy rights protected by FERPA or the federal Constitution).

[101]Medley v. Bd. of Educ., 168 S.W.3d 398 (Ky. Ct. App. 2004). *See also* Bd. of Educ. v. Butcher, 402 N.Y.S.2d 626 (App. Div. 1978) (ruling that the records of students in a teacher's class would have to be disclosed, obliterating identifying data, for the teacher to defend charges pertaining to his reputation and competence).

[102]*See, e.g.,* Moore v. Hyche, 761 F. Supp. 112 (N.D. Ala. 1991); Price v. Young, 580 F. Supp. 1 (E.D. Ark. 1983); Becky v. Butte-Silver Bow Sch. Dist. 1, 906 P.2d 193 (Mont. 1995).

[103]*See, e.g.,* Tarka v. Cunningham, 917 F.2d 890 (5th Cir. 1990). *See also supra* text accompanying note 60.

[104]Lewin v. Cooke, 28 Fed. App'x 186 (4th Cir. 2002).

[105]*See, e.g.,* Individuals with Disabilities Education Act, 20 U.S.C. § 1415(b)(1) (2008).

[106]*See, e.g.,* Chi. Tribune Co. v. Bd. of Educ., 773 N.E.2d 674 (Ill. App. Ct. 2002); *But see* Lindeman v. Kelso Sch. Dist. No. 458, 172 P.3d 329. (Wash. 2007) (holding that a videotape recorded on a school bus for safety reasons was not a record maintained for students, so it did not qualify as exempt from public disclosure under state law); Burlington Free Press v. Univ. of Vt., 779 A.2d 60 (Vt. 2001); Wall v. Fairfax County Sch. Bd., 475 S.E.2d 803 (Va. 1996).

student's instructional program and *should* be included in a permanent record. It is unfortunate that school personnel, fearing federal sanctions under FERPA, have deleted useful information —along with material that should be removed—from student records. Public school officials have a *duty* to record and communicate true, factual information about students to schools to which they are transferring, including institutions of higher learning.

Pupil Protection and Parental Rights Laws

Congress and state legislatures have enacted laws to protect family privacy in connection with school research activities and treatment programs. Under federal law, human subjects are protected in research projects supported by federal grants and contracts in any private or public institution or agency.[107] **Informed consent must be obtained before placing subjects at risk of being exposed to physical, psychological, or social injury as a result of participating in research, development, or related activities.** All education agencies are required to establish review committees to ensure that the rights and welfare of all subjects are adequately protected.

Several amendments to the General Education Provisions Act, most notably the 1978 Hatch Amendment, require all instructional materials in federally assisted research or experimentation projects to be made available for inspection by parents of participating students. Under the more recent Protection of Pupil Rights Amendment, parents must be allowed to review in advance all instructional materials in programs administered by the Department of Education, and such **federally assisted programs cannot require students, without prior written parental consent, to be subjected to surveys or evaluations that reveal information pertaining to personal beliefs, behaviors, and family relationships.**[108] The department is charged with reviewing complaints under this law; if an educational institution is found in violation and does not comply within a reasonable period, federal funds can be withheld.

Some conservative citizen groups have pressed for a broad interpretation of the federal law, but courts usually have not agreed. The Sixth Circuit affirmed without an opinion a Michigan federal district court's ruling that a school district's decision to have a child see a school counselor (because of his problems interacting with classmates) without securing his parents' consent did not violate the parents' rights under the Hatch Amendment.[109] A Kentucky court also rejected a Hatch Amendment challenge to the use of certain questions included in the statewide student assessment program.[110]

The Third Circuit denied New Jersey parents' claim that a voluntary survey asking students sensitive questions about their attitudes and behavior violated federal privacy

[107]42 U.S.C. § 201 *et seq.* (2008); 45 C.F.R. § 46.101 *et seq.* (2008).

[108]20 U.S.C. § 1232h (2008). The sensitive areas pertain to students' or their parents' political affiliations; mental or psychological problems; sexual behavior or attitudes; illegal, antisocial, or demeaning behavior; critical appraisals of family members; legally recognized privileged relationships; religious practices or beliefs; or income. Parents must be notified at least annually of their rights under this law.

[109]Newkirk v. E. Lansing Pub. Schs., No. 1:91:CV:563, 1993 U.S. Dist. LEXIS 13194 (W.D. Mich. 1993), *aff'd mem.*, 57 F.3d 1070 (6th Cir. 1995).

[110]Triplett v. Livingston County Bd. of Educ., 967 S.W.2d 25 (Ky. Ct. App. 1997).

protections or represented compelled speech because written parental permission was not secured for their children to participate.[111] The court reasoned that even if participation in the survey was involuntary, as the parents claimed, there was no violation because the disclosure of personal information occurred only in the aggregate and was properly safeguarded.

California parents, who had granted permission for their elementary school children to participate in a survey regarding psychological barriers to learning, later learned that the survey included some items pertaining to sexual topics and alleged that these items violated their right to privacy and to control the upbringing of their children. The Ninth Circuit affirmed the lower court's conclusion that parents do not have a free-standing fundamental right, or a right encompassed by any other fundamental right, to prevent the school from providing students important information pertaining to sex. The court proclaimed that "schools cannot be expected to accommodate the personal, moral, or religious concerns of every parent," finding the psychological survey to be a reasonable way to advance legitimate state interests.[112]

There is concern among educators that the federal pupil protection requirements and similar provisions being considered or enacted by many states will cause certain instructional activities to be dropped even before legally challenged. Although these measures are couched in terms of protecting students' privacy rights by granting them *exemptions* from particular instructional activities, if a substantial number of exemptions are requested, the instructional activity itself may be eliminated from the curriculum.

CONCLUSION

The state and its agents enjoy considerable latitude in regulating various aspects of public education, but any requirements that restrict students' activities must be reasonable and necessary to carry out legitimate educational objectives. When students' or parents' protected rights are impaired, school authorities must be able to substantiate that there is an overriding public interest to be served. However, parents on behalf of their children or teachers asserting academic freedom do not have a right to determine the public school curriculum. The state and its agencies have the authority to determine public school course offerings and instructional materials, and such curricular determinations will be upheld by courts unless clearly arbitrary or in violation of constitutional or statutory provisions. For example, school personnel cannot censor instructional materials for religious reasons or disregard federal copyright requirements.

Courts defer to school authorities in assessing student performance in the absence of evidence of arbitrary or discriminatory academic decisions. Accordingly, proficiency examinations can be used to determine pupils' remedial needs and as a prerequisite to high school graduation if students are given sufficient notice prior to implementation of the test requirements and are provided adequate preparation for the examinations.

[111]C.N. v. Ridgewood Bd. of Educ., 430 F.3d 159 (3d Cir. 2005).

[112]Fields v. Palmdale Sch. Dist., 427 F.3d 1197, 1206 (9th Cir. 2005).

Public schools do not have a legal duty to ensure that students attain a specified level of achievement. But they do have a duty to provide parents information on their child's progress and to ensure that the confidentiality of such records is maintained. Also, parents have the right to review their children's records and to inspect materials used in federally funded experimental projects or surveys. Moreover, students have a right to be excused from participation in such programs or activities involving psychiatric or psychological testing or treatment designed to reveal sensitive information about them or their families.

POINTS TO PONDER

1. A school board decided to eliminate several books from the English curriculum, including *The Learning Tree, The Adventures of Huckleberry Finn*, and *The Catcher in the Rye*, because of parental complaints. Several teachers contend that they have a right to use these books in their classes, because the books relate to course objectives and their use is supported by the profession. How would the court rule and why?

2. A school district has a policy stipulating that students cannot be promoted from third to fourth grade or from seventh to eighth grade until they demonstrate on proficiency tests that they have mastered specified skills. Parents of children who were promoted at both grade levels based on test passage have brought an instructional negligence suit against the school district. They claim that their children do not have the specified academic skills based on an external evaluation by a licensed psychometrist. Is the testing program vulnerable to a legal challenge? Will the parents prevail in their educational malpractice suit? Why or why not?

3. Is this notation appropriate for a student's permanent record? If not, how would you change it?

   Sam is an extremely troubled child who comes from a broken home. He is lazy, and his work is spotty. He hangs around with the wrong crowd and always seems to be in trouble. He is bright enough to do the assigned work, but he does not seem to apply himself.

4. A school distributed an anonymous survey asking students about their attitudes and behaviors. The students and their parents were informed that participation was completely voluntary and that no student's responses could be identified, but parents were not asked to give written permission for their children to participate. Parents claimed that the survey violated the federal Protection of Pupil Rights Amendment. How should the court rule?

5. A middle school teacher taped several television movies on the Disney Channel to show to her classes. She has shown the movies the past two semesters. Is this protected as fair use? Is there a copyright violation?

CHAPTER FIVE

STUDENT EXPRESSION, ASSOCIATION, AND APPEARANCE

Students continue to test the limits of their personal freedoms in public schools, frequently colliding with educators' efforts to maintain an appropriate school environment. This chapter addresses students' substantive rights regarding First Amendment freedoms of speech and press and closely related association rights.

FREEDOM OF SPEECH AND PRESS

Students have the right to express nondisruptive ideological views at school, but restrictions can be placed on their expression that represents the school.

The First Amendment, as applied to the states through the Fourteenth Amendment, restricts *government* (not private) interference with citizens' free expression rights, which are perhaps the most preciously guarded individual liberties. The government, including public school boards, must have a compelling justification to curtail citizens' freedom of expression. And these rights extend to unpopular viewpoints, such as political protesters' burning of the American flag[1] and the Ku Klux Klan's placement of a cross on public property.[2] The First Amendment also shields the individual's right to remain silent when confronted with an illegitimate government demand for expression, such as mandatory participation in the salute to the American flag in public schools.[3]

Although public school authorities traditionally were allowed to restrict student expression for almost any reason, the Supreme Court has recognized since the mid-twentieth

---

[1]Texas v. Johnson, 491 U.S. 397 (1989).

[2]Capitol Square Review & Advisory Bd. v. Pinette, 515 U.S. 753 (1995). *But see* Virginia v. Black, 538 U.S. 343 (2003) (upholding a statutory prohibition on cross burning with the intent to intimidate).

[3]*See* W. Va. State Bd. of Educ. v. Barnette, 319 U.S. 624 (1943); text accompanying note 78, Chapter 3.

century that students do not give up their constitutional rights as a condition of public school attendance. However, the Court also has acknowledged that students' constitutional rights, which are not the same as the rights of adults in other settings, may be limited by reasonable policies designed to take into account the special circumstances of the public school environment.[4] The collision of individual and governmental interests in the school context has generated a growing body of First Amendment litigation.

Unprotected Conduct and Expression

A threshold question before applying First Amendment standards is whether the behavior at issue constitutes expression *at all*. **Only if conduct is meant to communicate an idea that is likely to be understood by the intended audience is it considered expression for First Amendment purposes.**[5] Even if specific conduct qualifies as expression, it is not assured constitutional protection; the judiciary has recognized that defamatory, obscene, and inflammatory communications are outside the protective arm of the First Amendment. In addition, expression that is lewd or promotes illegal activity is not protected in the public school context.

Defamatory Expression.   Defamation includes spoken (slander) and written (libel) statements that are false, expose another to public shame or ridicule, and are communicated to someone other than the person defamed. Courts have upheld school authorities in banning libelous content from publications distributed at school and imposing sanctions on students responsible for such material, but regulations cannot be vague or grant school officials complete discretion to censor potentially libelous materials.[6]

Obscene, Lewd, or Vulgar Expression.   The judiciary has held that individuals cannot claim a First Amendment right to voice or publish obscenities,[7] but school authorities do not have to prove that student expression is obscene for it to be curtailed. In *Bethel School District No. 403 v. Fraser*, the Supreme Court in 1986 granted school authorities considerable latitude in censoring offensively lewd and indecent student expression that would undermine the school's basic educational mission. Overturning the lower courts, the Supreme Court upheld disciplinary action against a student for using a sexual metaphor in

---

[4]*See, e.g.,* Morse v. Frederick, 127 S. Ct. 2618, 2621–2622 (2007); Tinker v. Des Moines Indep. Sch. Dist., 393 U.S. 503, 506–507 (1969).

[5]For a discussion of these requirements, *see Johnson,* 491 U.S. at 404. In the school context, *see, e.g.*, Jarman v. Williams, 753 F.2d 76 (8th Cir. 1985) (holding that social and recreational dancing in public schools does not enjoy First Amendment protection).

[6]*See* Chapter 2 for a discussion of the principles of tort law governing defamation suits for damages and how these apply to public figures and officials.

[7]*See* Miller v. California, 413 U.S. 15, 24 (1973) (distinguishing obscene material from constitutionally protected material based on whether the work as a whole appeals to prurient interests based on community standards; depicts or describes sexual activity as defined by state law in a patently offensive way; and lacks serious literary, artistic, political, or scientific value). On several occasions, the Supreme Court has recognized the government's authority to adjust the definition of obscenity as applied to minors. *See, e.g.*, Ginsberg v. New York, 390 U.S. 629 (1968) (upholding a state law prohibiting the sale to minors of magazines depicting female nudity).

a nominating speech during a student government assembly.[8] **Concluding that the sexual innuendos were offensive to both teachers and students, the** *Fraser* **majority held that the school's legitimate interest in protecting the captive student audience from exposure to lewd and vulgar speech justified the disciplinary action.** The majority reasoned that the sensibilities of fellow students must be considered and that an important objective of public schools is the inculcation of fundamental values of civility. Furthermore, the Supreme Court held that the school board has the authority to determine what manner of speech is appropriate in classes or assemblies.

Inflammatory Expression. The judiciary also has supported regulations banning the use of inflammatory expression in public schools. **Fighting words or other expression that agitates, threatens, or incites an immediate breach of peace have been distinguished from speech that represents ideological views and leaves an opportunity for calm and reasonable discussion.**

A growing body of First Amendment litigation involves alleged threats made by students toward classmates or school personnel. In determining if a true threat has been made, courts consider several factors, such as:

- Reactions of the recipient and other listeners,
- Whether the maker of the alleged threat had made similar statements to the victim in the past,
- Whether the utterance was conditional and communicated directly to the victim, and
- Whether the victim had reason to believe that the speaker would engage in violence.[9]

In an illustrative case, the Arkansas Supreme Court held that a rap song did not entail fighting words but was a true threat, as it contained an unconditional threat to the life of a classmate and was delivered to the targeted student who perceived it as unequivocally threatening.[10] Similarly finding a true threat, the Eighth Circuit upheld expulsion of a student for writing a letter, threatening to rape and murder his former girlfriend, which he assumed a friend would share with the potential victim.[11] Also, the Fifth Circuit held that a student's notebook, outlining a pseudo-Nazi group's plan to commit a "Columbine shooting," constituted a "terroristic threat" that was not protected by the First Amendment.[12]

---

[8]Bethel Sch. Dist. No. 403 v. Fraser, 478 U.S. 675 (1986). Fraser was suspended for two days and disqualified as a candidate for commencement speaker. However, due to write-in votes, he did eventually deliver a commencement speech, so his claim that the disqualification violated due process rights was not reviewed by the appellate court.

[9]*See* United States v. Dinwiddie, 76 F.3d 913 (8th Cir. 1996).

[10]Jones v. State, 64 S.W.3d 728 (Ark. 2002). *See also* Lovell v. Poway Unified Sch. Dist., 90 F.3d 367 (9th Cir. 1996) (upholding suspension of a student for threatening a teacher, despite conflicting testimony regarding what was actually said).

[11]Doe v. Pulaski County Special Sch. Dist., 306 F.3d 616 (8th Cir. 2002). *See also* S.G. v. Sayreville Bd. of Educ., 333 F.3d 417 (3d Cir. 2003), *infra* text accompanying note 29.

[12]Ponce v. Socorro Indep. Sch. Dist., 508 F.3d 765, 767 (5th Cir. 2007) (relying on the Supreme Court's reasoning that evidence of a disruption is not required when there is a threat of special danger to the safety of students). *See* Morse v. Frederick, 127 S. Ct. 2618 (2007); *infra* text accompanying note 15.

Utterances can be considered inflammatory, and thus unprotected, even if not found to be true threats or fighting words.[13] Courts seem more inclined to uphold school disciplinary action, in contrast to criminal prosecution, for students' alleged threats or other inflammatory expression.[14]

Advocacy of Illegal Activity for Minors.   In its first student expression decision in almost two decades, *Morse v. Frederick*, the Supreme Court in 2007 held that given the special circumstances in public schools, students can be disciplined for expression reasonably viewed as promoting or celebrating illegal drug use.[15] *Morse* focused on a banner containing the phrase "BONG HITS 4 JESUS," which Joseph Frederick and some friends unfurled across the street from their school as the Olympic torch relay passed by. The Court reasoned that the students could be disciplined because they were under the school's control when they were allowed to cross the street and watch the torch relay; it was a school-authorized event supervised by school personnel.

The Supreme Court narrowly reversed the Ninth Circuit's conclusion that the school could *not* censor non-disruptive, off-campus student speech simply for promoting "a social message contrary to the one favored by the school."[16] **The Supreme Court majority emphasized the importance of deterring student drug use and concluded that Frederick's action violated the school board's policy prohibiting expression advocating use of illegal substances.** However, a majority of the justices declined to extend school authorities' discretion to the point that they can curtail any student expression they find "plainly offensive" or at odds with the school's "educational mission," which would allow school officials too much discretion.[17] All justices agreed that students can be disciplined for promoting the use of illegal drugs, but they differed regarding whether the banner at issue actually did so.[18]

---

[13]*See, e.g., In re* Douglas D., 626 N.W.2d 725 (Wis. 2001) (finding no true threat to justify criminal prosecution, but ruling that school authorities had sufficient reason to suspend a student for his creative writing assignment describing a student who was removed from class for being disruptive—as the writer had been—and then returned the next day to behead his teacher). *But see In re* A.S., 626 N.W.2d 712 (Wis. 2001) (finding a student's comments that he intended to kill everyone at his middle school to represent an intent to inflict harm in violation of the disorderly conduct law).

[14]*See, e.g.*, Porter v. Ascension Parish Sch. Bd., 393 F.3d 608 (5th Cir. 2004) (finding no true threat in off-campus expression, but granting the principal qualified immunity for suspending the student speaker). *See also* Cuesta v. Miami-Dade County Sch. Bd., 285 F.3d 962 (11th Cir. 2002) (upholding the principal's compliance with the school's zero tolerance policy by reporting to the police a student's distribution of a threatening pamphlet). *But see* State v. McCooey, 802 A.2d 1216 (N.H. 2002) (overruling a disorderly conduct conviction of a student who said he might "shoot up the school" if a teacher did not give him a hug; finding no evidence that the expression caused a school disruption to justify the conviction).

[15]127 S. Ct. 2618 (2007).

[16]Frederick v. Morse, 439 F.3d 1114, 1118 (9th Cir. 2006).

[17]*See Morse,* 127 S. Ct. at 2629. Justices Alito and Kennedy emphasized that this decision is restricted to the promotion of illegal drug use and does not extend to censorship of expression on social or political issues that may be viewed as inconsistent with the school's mission. *Id.* at 2636 (Alito, J., joined by Kennedy, J., concurring).

[18]*See id.* at 2647 (Stevens, J., joined by Ginsberg & Souter, JJ., dissenting) (arguing that the banner was a nonsensical effort to get on television and promoted nothing).

Commercial Expression

Commercial speech enjoys some constitutional protection but is not afforded the same level of First Amendment protection as speech intended to convey a particular point of view. The Supreme Court has recognized that government restrictions on speech with economic motives do not have to be the least restrictive means to achieve the desired end; rather, there only needs to be a reasonable "fit" between the restrictions and the government goal.[19] Courts generally have upheld regulations prohibiting sales and fund-raising activities in public schools as justified to preserve schools for their educational function and to prevent commercial exploitation of students.

Some controversies focus on students' rights *not* to be exposed to commercial expression in public schools. For example, many school districts nationwide receive free equipment for having students watch Channel One—a daily 10-minute news program containing two minutes of commercials. Although the judiciary has recognized the legal authority of school boards to enter into contracts for supplementary instructional materials that include commercials,[20] some courts have required school boards to excuse students whose parents do not want them exposed to the commercial activities.[21] With an increasing number of companies offering monetary enticements for school boards to air commercials over public address systems and to display advertisements on scoreboards, such commercial activities in public schools seem destined to generate additional legal challenges.

School-Sponsored Expression

In contrast to the categories of unprotected expression, students' airing of political or ideological views in public schools *is* protected by the First Amendment. **Since the mid-1980s, the Supreme Court has emphasized the distinction between student expression that appears to represent the school and *private* student expression that merely occurs at school. The latter commands substantial constitutional protection, but student expression appearing to bear the school's imprimatur can be restricted to ensure its consistency with educational objectives.** The Court's expansive interpretation of what constitutes school-sponsored expression has narrowed the circumstances under which students can prevail in First Amendment claims.

Type of Forum. In Free Speech Clause litigation, an assessment of the type of forum the government has created for expressive activities has been important in determining whether expression can be restricted. The Supreme Court has recognized that public places, such as streets and parks, are traditional public forums for assembly and communication where content-based restrictions cannot be imposed unless justified by a compelling government interest.[22] In contrast, expression can be confined to the government purpose of

---

[19]Bd. of Trs. v. Fox, 492 U.S. 469 (1989). *See also* Bolger v. Youngs Drug Prods. Corp., 463 U.S. 60, 64–75 (1983).

[20]*See, e.g.,* Wallace v. Knox County Bd. of Educ., No. 92-6195, 1993 U.S. App. LEXIS 20477 (6th Cir. Aug. 10, 1993); State v. Whittle Communications, 402 S.E.2d 556 (N.C. 1991).

[21]*See, e.g.,* Dawson v. E. Side Union High Sch. Dist., 34 Cal. Rptr. 2d 108 (Ct. App. 1994).

[22]*See, e.g.,* Cornelius v. NAACP Legal Def. & Educ. Fund, 473 U.S. 788 (1985).

the property in a nonpublic forum, such as a public school. Content-based restrictions are permissible in a nonpublic forum to assure that expression is compatible with the intended government purpose, provided that regulations are reasonable and do not entail viewpoint discrimination.

The government, however, can create a limited public forum for expression on public property that otherwise would be considered a nonpublic forum and reserved for its government function.[23] For example, a student activities program after school might be established as a limited forum for student expression. A limited forum can be restricted to a certain class of speakers (e.g., students) and/or to specific categories of expression (e.g., noncommercial speech). Otherwise, expression in a limited forum is subject to the same protections that govern a traditional public forum.

Hazelwood **and Its Progeny.**   In 1988, the Supreme Court rendered *Hazelwood School District v. Kuhlmeier*, holding that **school authorities can censor student expression in school publications and other school-related activities as long as the censorship decisions are based on legitimate pedagogical concerns.**[24] At issue in *Hazelwood* was a high school principal's deletion of two pages from the school newspaper because of the controversial content of articles on divorce and teenage pregnancy and the fear that individuals could be identified in the articles. The Court ruled that the principal's actions were based on legitimate educational concerns. Rejecting the assertion that the school newspaper had been established as a public forum for student expression, the Court declared that only with school authorities' clear *intent* do school activities become a public forum.[25] The Court acknowledged school authorities' broad discretion to ensure that expression occurring in school publications and all school-sponsored activities (including extracurricular) is consistent with educational objectives, which differs from *private* student expression that the school may be constitutionally required to tolerate under some circumstances.

Echoing the *Hazelwood* rationale, the Ninth Circuit ruled that a school district could reject Planned Parenthood's advertisements in its newspapers, yearbooks, and programs for athletic events because the ads were inconsistent with its educational mission.[26] Similarly

---

[23]*See, e.g.*, Kincaid v. Gibson, 236 F.3d 342 (6th Cir. 2001) (holding that a university's yearbook was created as a limited public forum for student expression; the university's actions in confiscating copies because of objections violated the editors' First Amendment rights). The scope of an open forum is complicated by the electronic age. Page v. Lexington County Sch. Dist. One, No. 3:06-cv-00249-CMC, 2008 WL 2486739 (4th Cir, June 23, 2008) (holding that a school district's use of its Web site and e-mail to urge opposition to a bill proposing tax or credits for private Schooling was government speech; the district's informational distribution system was not a public forum requiring equal access for opposing views).

[24]484 U.S. 260 (1988), *on remand*, 840 F.2d 596 (8th Cir. 1988).

[25]*Id.*, 484 U.S. at 267. In response to this decision, several state legislatures have enacted laws granting student editors of school-sponsored papers specific rights in determining the content of those publications. *See, e.g.*, Cal. Ed. Code § 48907 (2008); Colo. Rev. Stat. Ann. § 22-1-120 (2007); Iowa Code § 280.22 (2008); Kan. Stat. Ann. § 72-1506 (2008); Mass. Gen. Laws Ann. ch. 71, § 82 (2008).

[26]Planned Parenthood v. Clark County Sch. Dist., 887 F.2d 935 (9th Cir. 1989), *rehearing en banc*, 941 F.2d 817 (9th Cir. 1991). *See also* Poling v. Murphy, 872 F.2d 757 (6th Cir. 1989) (holding that a student could be disqualified from running for student council president because his candidacy speech was discourteous, noting that civility is a legitimate pedagogical concern).

reasoning that the school can disassociate itself from expression that conflicts with its objectives, the Fourth Circuit upheld a high school principal's decision to bar the school's use of the Johnny Reb symbol following complaints that it offended African American students.[27] And the Eighth Circuit upheld a principal's decision to disqualify a student council candidate who handed out condoms with stickers bearing his campaign slogan ("Adam Henerey, the Safe Choice"), recognizing that *Hazelwood* grants school authorities broad discretion to control student expression in school-sponsored activities.[28] More recently, the Third Circuit upheld suspension of a kindergarten student for saying, "I'm going to shoot you," while playing cops and robbers during recess, finding a school's prohibition on speech threatening violence and the use of firearms to be based on legitimate pedagogical concerns.[29]

There are limits, however, on school authorities' wide latitude to censor student expression that bears the public school's imprimatur. **Blatant viewpoint discrimination, even in a nonpublic forum, abridges the First Amendment.** For example, the Ninth Circuit held that a school board violated students' First Amendment rights, because it failed to produce a compelling justification for excluding an antidraft organization's advertisement from the school newspaper, while allowing military recruitment advertisements.[30] Similarly, the Eleventh Circuit found no compelling justification for school authorities to exclude a peace activist group from the public school's career day and to bar the group's literature from school bulletin boards and counselors' offices, whereas military recruiters were allowed such access.[31]

Even if viewpoint discrimination is not involved, censorship actions in a nonpublic forum still must be based on legitimate pedagogical concerns. To illustrate, a Michigan federal district court found no legitimate pedagogical reason for the removal from the school newspaper of a student's article on a pending lawsuit alleging that school bus diesel fumes constitute a neighborhood nuisance.[32]

Protected Private Expression

Student expression that does not fall within one of the categories of unprotected expression or represent the school is governed by the landmark Supreme Court decision, *Tinker v. Des Moines Independent School District*, rendered in 1969. In *Tinker*, three students were suspended from school for wearing armbands to protest the Vietnam War. School officials did not attempt to prohibit the wearing of all symbols, but instead prohibited only one type of

---

[27]Crosby v. Holsinger, 852 F.2d 801 (4th Cir. 1988) (noting that the one-day delay in posting students' notices of the upcoming board meeting constituted a minimal impairment of expression rights).

[28]Henerey v. City of St. Charles Sch. Dist., 200 F.3d 1128, 1131 (8th Cir. 1999).

[29]S.G. v. Sayreville Bd. of Educ., 333 F.3d 417 (3d Cir. 2003).

[30]San Diego Comm. Against Registration & the Draft v. Governing Bd., 790 F.2d 1471 (9th Cir. 1986).

[31]Searcey v. Harris, 888 F.2d 1314 (11th Cir. 1989).

[32]Dean v. Utica Cmty. Schs., 345 F. Supp. 2d 799 (E.D. Mich. 2004). *See also* Desilets v. Clearview Reg'l Bd. of Educ., 647 A.2d 150 (N.J. 1994) (finding no legitimate educational reason to exclude a student's reviews of R-rated movies from the junior high school newspaper when such movies were discussed in class and available in the school library).

anti-war expression. Concluding that school authorities punished the students for expression that was not accompanied by any disorder or disturbance, the Supreme Court ruled that "undifferentiated fear or apprehension of disturbance is not enough to overcome the right to freedom of expression."[33] Student expression cannot be curtailed merely because it causes school officials some discomfort. The Court emphasized that "students in school as well as out of school are 'persons' under our Constitution. They are possessed of fundamental rights which the state must respect."[34]

In *Tinker*, the Supreme Court echoed statements made in an earlier federal appellate ruling: A student may express opinions on controversial issues in the classroom, cafeteria, playing field, or any other place, as long as the exercise of such rights does not "materially and substantially interfere with the requirements of appropriate discipline in the operation of the school" or collide with the rights of others.[35] The Supreme Court emphasized that educators have the authority and duty to maintain discipline in schools, but they must consider students' constitutional rights as they exert control. Because school authorities can censor school-sponsored student expression for educational reasons, the *Tinker* standard now applies *only* to protected expression that does *not* give the appearance of representing the school, such as underground (not school-sponsored) student papers distributed at school. As discussed in Chapter 3, most courts have treated students' distribution of religious literature like the distribution of other material that is not sponsored by the school. Figure 5.1 displays questions to guide school personnel in determining when they can regulate student expression.

Prior Restraints.   When determined that protected private expression is at issue, courts then are faced with the difficult task of assessing whether restrictions are justified in particular situations. Under the *Tinker* principle, private expression can be curtailed if it is likely to disrupt the educational process or intrude on the rights of others.[36] The law clearly allows students to be punished after the fact if they cause a disruption, but school authorities have a greater burden of justification when they impose a ban before the expression takes place. Prior restraints on student speech must bear a substantial relationship to an important government interest; contain narrow, objective, and unambiguous criteria for determining what material is prohibited; and include procedures that allow a speedy determination of whether materials meet those criteria.[37]

The burden is on school authorities to justify policies requiring administrative approval of unofficial (underground) student publications, but such prior review is not

---

[33]393 U.S. 503, 508 (1969).

[34]*Id.* at 511.

[35]*Id.* at 513 (quoting Burnside v. Byars, 363 F.2d 744, 749 (5th Cir. 1966)). *See also* Smith v. Novato Unified Sch. Dist., 59 Cal. Rptr. 3d 508 (Ct. App. 2007) (finding a student's provocative editorial criticizing illegal immigration to be protected speech under California law and not expression that would incite unlawful acts or a school disruption).

[36]*See, e.g.,* Guzick v. Drebus, 431 F.2d 594 (6th Cir. 1970) (concluding that a long-standing rule banning the wearing of freedom buttons was lawful in a situation in which the learning environment would be disrupted if pupils were allowed to wear such symbols of their disagreements).

[37]*See, e.g.,* Muller v. Jefferson Lighthouse Sch., 98 F.3d 1530 (7th Cir. 1996).

FIGURE 5.1   Assessing Student Expression Rights.

Source: Adapted from a figure developed by Amy Steketee, Associate Instructor, Indiana University.

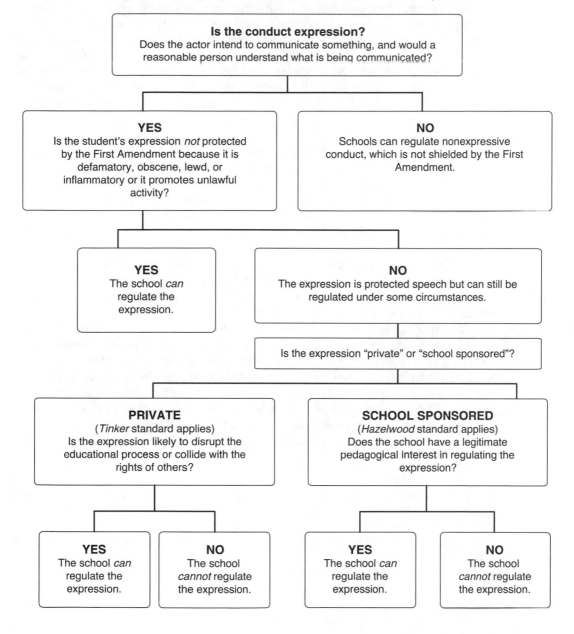

unconstitutional *per se.* The Eighth Circuit rejected a vagueness challenge to a school board's policy requiring administrative review of unofficial student papers distributed at school and barring the distribution of material that advertises anything unlawful, disruptive, obscene, libelous, or pervasively indecent.[38] Several other courts have approved the *concept* of prior review of nonschool publications but have found challenged policies constitutionally defective because they lacked criteria to assess the materials and explicit review procedures.[39] For example, the Ninth Circuit considered a policy subjecting *all* nonschool publications to prior review for the purpose of censorship to be overbroad, and it ruled that suspending students for distributing an unauthorized paper at a school function impaired the First Amendment.[40]

Postexpression Discipline.   Although prior restraints on private expression may be legally vulnerable, courts are inclined to support disciplinary action and confiscation of materials *after* the expression has occurred, if it is considered unprotected (e.g., libelous or lewd comments), fosters a disruption of the educational process, or intrudes on the rights of others. As discussed, the Supreme Court in 2007 upheld a high school principal in disciplining a student and confiscating his banner viewed as promoting illegal drug use without evidence that the expression would lead to a disruption.[41] Much earlier, the Fourth Circuit upheld school administrators in impounding copies of a student publication that contained an advertisement for drug paraphernalia and in banning further distribution on school property.[42] The court emphasized that the literature was not subjected to predistribution approval; copies were impounded only after distribution began.

Students also have been disciplined after the fact for distributing material that is abusive toward classmates or teachers.[43] To illustrate, the Eighth Circuit found no impairment of speech rights in requiring a girls' basketball player, who violated the team handbook by distributing a letter that criticized the girls' varsity basketball coach, to apologize to the coach and teammates as a condition of returning to the team.[44] More recently, the Eleventh Circuit found the *Tinker* standard satisfied in that school authorities could forecast a substantial disruption when a student wrote a story about killing a teacher and brought it to school; her suspension was justified because she shared the story with a classmate.[45] Students additionally

---

[38]Bystrom v. Fridley High Sch. Indep. Sch. Dist. No. 14, 822 F.2d 747 (8th Cir. 1987) (invalidating, however, part of the policy proscribing material that invades others' privacy, reasoning that such expression could not be curtailed unless it would subject the school to a libel suit under state law). *See also* Bystrom v. Fridley High Sch., 686 F. Supp. 1387 (D. Minn. 1987), *aff'd mem.*, 855 F.2d 855 (8th Cir. 1988) (finding no First Amendment infringement in the suspension of students for violating the revised policy).

[39]*See, e.g.*, Quarterman v. Byrd, 453 F.2d 54 (4th Cir. 1971); Eisner v. Stamford Bd. of Educ., 440 F.2d 803 (2d Cir. 1971).

[40]Burch v. Barker, 861 F.2d 1149 (9th Cir. 1988).

[41]Morse v. Frederick, 127 S. Ct. 2618 (2007); *supra* text accompanying note 15.

[42]Williams v. Spencer, 622 F.2d 1200 (4th Cir. 1980) (further holding that the regulation authorizing the principal to halt the distribution of any publication encouraging actions that endanger students' health or safety was not unconstitutionally vague).

[43]*See, e.g.*, Kicklighter v. Evans County Sch. Dist., 968 F. Supp. 712 (S.D. Ga. 1997), *aff'd mem.*, 140 F.3d 1043 (11th Cir. 1998); Donovan v. Ritchie, 68 F.3d 14 (1st Cir. 1995).

[44]Wildman v. Marshalltown Sch. Dist., 249 F.3d 768 (8th Cir. 2001).

[45]Boim v. Fulton County Sch. Dist., 494 F.3d 978 (11th Cir. 2007).

can be disciplined for advocating the destruction of school property in publications they distribute at school. The Seventh Circuit recognized that a "reason to believe" or "reasonable forecast" standard can be applied to punish a student for such expression, even though the anticipated destruction of school property never materializes.[46] In this case, the student was expelled for one year for distributing at school an article in an underground paper that contained information about how to disable the school's computer system.

Courts have condoned disciplinary action against students who have engaged in walkouts, boycotts, sit-ins, or other protests involving conduct that blocks hallways, damages property, causes students to miss class, or in other ways interferes with essential school activities. The Sixth Circuit held that a petition circulated by four football players, denouncing the head coach, justified their dismissal from the varsity football team. The court reasoned that the petition disrupted the team and athletes are subject to greater restrictions than applied to the general student body.[47] The Ninth Circuit also ruled that student athletes could be disciplined for refusing to board the team bus and play in a basketball game to protest actions of their coach; their boycott of the game substantially disrupted a school activity.[48] However, this court departed from the Sixth Circuit in finding that the students' petition requesting that the coach resign because of derogatory remarks he made toward players was protected speech and remanded the case for a determination of whether the students were impermissibly removed from the basketball team in retaliation for their petition. In an earlier Ninth Circuit case, the appeals court overturned the suspension of students for wearing buttons containing the word *scab* in connection with a teachers' strike,[49] reasoning that students could not be disciplined for nondisruptive, nonvulgar private expression that was merely critical of school personnel or policies.

Students also cannot be disciplined for materials distributed off school grounds unless at a school-sponsored event or the off-campus distribution threatens the educational process. The Second Circuit found that school officials overstepped their authority by disciplining high school students who published a satirical magazine in their homes and sold it at a local store.[50] Without evidence that the activity had an adverse impact on the school, the court equated punishment for such expression with disciplining students for watching X-rated movies at home.

Anti-Harassment Policies. Some school districts have adopted policies prohibiting expression that constitutes verbal or physical harassment based on race, religion, color, national origin, sex, sexual orientation, disability, or other personal characteristics.[51] Until recently, these public school policies have not appeared vulnerable to First Amendment challenges, whereas "hate speech" policies have been struck down in municipalities and public

---

[46]Boucher v. Sch. Bd., 134 F.3d 821, 828 (7th Cir. 1998).

[47]Lowery v. Euverard, 497 F.3d 584 (6th Cir. 2007).

[48]Pinard v. Clatskanie Sch. Dist. 6J, 467 F.3d 755 (9th Cir. 2006).

[49]Chandler v. McMinnville Sch. Dist., 978 F.2d 524 (9th Cir. 1992).

[50]Thomas v. Bd. of Educ., 607 F.2d 1043 (2d Cir. 1979).

[51]*See, e.g.,* Fister v. Minn. New Country Sch., 149 F.3d 1187 (8th Cir. 1998) (upholding a policy specifying that fighting, threatening language, other endangerment, or harassment would be grounds for suspension or expulsion).

higher education.[52] Public schools have been considered a special environment in terms of government restrictions on private expression, because of their purpose in educating America's youth and inculcating basic values, such as civility and respect for others with different backgrounds and beliefs.[53]

A growing body of cases interpreting anti-harassment provisions has focused on students displaying Confederate flags, and some courts have upheld restrictions on such displays. To illustrate, the Tenth Circuit upheld disciplinary action against a Kansas middle school student for drawing a Confederate flag during math class in violation of the school district's anti-harassment policy, finding that the drawing might cause a disruption and interfere with the rights of others, as the school district had already experienced some racial incidents related to the Confederate flag.[54] In addition, the Sixth Circuit upheld a school district's ban on students displaying the Confederate flag, finding "ample reason" for school authorities to anticipate a disruption from students wearing the banned symbol, but concluding that evidence of a disruption is *not* required.[55] Other courts, however, have struck down such restrictions on Confederate flag displays in the absence of a link to disruption[56] or if the policies were applied inconsistently.[57]

Several recent cases have focused on the conflict between expressing religious views and promoting civil expression; these cases are particularly sensitive because they pit free speech and free exercise guarantees against the school's authority to instill basic values, including respect for others. The Third Circuit struck down a Pennsylvania school district's anti-harassment policy challenged by plaintiffs who feared reprisals for voicing their

[52]*See, e.g.*, R.A.V. v. St. Paul, 505 U.S. 377 (1992) (invalidating a St. Paul ordinance barring expression that could arouse anger or resentment on the basis of race, color, creed, religion, or gender); Dambrot v. Cent. Mich. Univ., 55 F.3d 1177 (6th Cir. 1995) (striking down the university's policy prohibiting harassing speech as overbroad and vague, but holding that the coach's use of the word *nigger* during locker room talk was not protected by the First Amendment). There is also significant legal activity pertaining to anti-bullying provisions, including cyber bullying, in public schools; *see* Thomas Wheeler, "How Far Is Too Far? Limiting Cyber-Speech by Students," *School Board News* (April 2008), at 5; text accompanying notes 9 and 41, Chapter 8.

[53]*See, e.g.*, Bethel Sch. Dist. No. 403 v. Fraser, 478 U.S. 675 (1986); Charles A. Beard and Mary R. Beard, *New Basic History of the United States* (New York: Doubleday, 1968). School districts' antidiscrimination provisions that conflict with organizations' expression rights also have been controversial. After the Supreme Court upheld the Boy Scouts' constitutional rights to bar homosexuals from being troop leaders, Boy Scouts v. Dale, 530 U.S. 640 (2000), some school districts attempted to deny after-school access to the Boy Scouts to comply with their antidiscrimination policies. *See, e.g.,* Boy Scouts v. Till, 136 F. Supp. 2d 1295 (S.D. Fla. 2001) (finding unconstitutional viewpoint discrimination in the school board's prohibition on the Boy Scouts using school facilities).

[54]West v. Derby Unified Sch. Dist. No. 260, 206 F.3d 1358 (10th Cir. 2000). *See also* Denno v. Sch. Bd., 218 F.3d 1267 (11th Cir. 2000) (holding that school authorities were not liable for disciplining a student for displaying a small Confederate flag to a group of friends during an outdoor lunch break because the display intruded on the school's legitimate function of inculcating manners and habits of civility).

[55]D.B. v. Lafon, 217 Fed. App'x 518 (6th Cir. 2007). *See also* Scott v. Sch. Bd., 324 F.3d 1246 (11th Cir. 2003) (upholding a school's unwritten policy banning the display of Confederate flags because there had been race-based fights in the school and the flag can be viewed as an offensive symbol of racism).

[56]*See, e.g.*, Bragg v. Swanson, 371 F. Supp. 2d 814 (S.D. W. Va. 2005) (overturning disciplinary action against a student for wearing a T-shirt displaying the Confederate flag in observance of his southern heritage and finding the policy prohibiting displays of the Rebel flag within the category of racist symbols to be overbroad).

[57]*See, e.g.*, Castorina v. Madison County Sch. Bd., 246 F.3d 536 (6th Cir. 2001); *infra* text accompanying note 94.

religious views about moral issues, including the harmful effects of homosexuality.[58] Concluding that the policy was unconstitutionally overbroad, the court reasoned that the policy went beyond expression that could be curtailed under civil rights laws or the *Tinker* disruption standard.

The Ninth Circuit in 2006 found the second prong of the *Tinker* standard to be controlling when it ruled that a student wearing a T-shirt degrading homosexuality "'collides with the rights of other students' in the most fundamental way."[59] The court reasoned that the school is allowed to prohibit such expression, regardless of the adoption of a valid anti-harassment policy, as long as it can show that the restriction is necessary to prevent the violation of other students' rights *or* a substantial disruption of school activities. **The court disagreed with the suggestion that injurious slurs interfering with the rights of others cannot be barred unless they *also* are disruptive, reasoning that the two *Tinker* prongs are independent restrictions.**[60]

But other courts have applied the *Tinker* disruption standard in ruling that students have a right to express their religious views that denounce homosexuality in the absence of a substantial disruption. For example, the Seventh Circuit ordered the district court to enter a limited preliminary injunction enjoining defendants from prohibiting high school students from wearing T-shirts with the slogan, "Be Happy, Not Gay." The school had a policy forbidding derogatory comments based on race, ethnicity, religion, gender, sexual orientation, or disability. The court agreed with the plaintiff student that he had a First Amendment right to express negative comments about members of a listed group, including homosexuals, as long as the expression was not inflammatory or fighting words. But the court recognized that the district judge must "strike a careful balance between the limited constitutional right of a high school student to campaign inside the school against the sexual orientation of other students and the school's interest in maintaining an atmosphere in which students are not distracted from their studies by wrenching debates over issues of personal identity."[61]

[58]Saxe v. State Coll. Area Sch. Dist., 240 F.3d 200 (3d Cir. 2001). *See also* Flaherty v. Keystone Oaks Sch. Dist., 247 F. Supp. 2d 698 (W.D. Pa. 2003) (finding that student handbook policies did not adequately define "abusive," "offensive," "harassment," and "inappropriate," so disciplinary action against a student for postings on a Web site message board could not be based on the vague and overbroad policy). *But see* Sypniewski v. Warren Hills Reg'l Bd. of Educ., 307 F.3d 243 (3d Cir. 2002) (upholding a school district's anti-harassment policy enacted to respond to incidents of race-based conflicts, but ordering the phrase banning speech that "creates ill will" to be eliminated as reaching some protected expression); *infra* text accompanying note 92.

[59]Harper v. Poway Unified Sch. Dist., 445 F.3d 1166, 1178 (9th Cir. 2006) (quoting Tinker v. Des Moines Indep. Sch. Dist., 393 U.S. 503, 508 (1969)), *cert. granted, judgment vacated, and case remanded to dismiss as moot*, 127 S. Ct. 1484 (2007).

[60]*Harper*, 445 F.3d at 1180 (citing *Saxe*, 240 F.3d at 217). *See also* Morrison v. Bd. of Educ., 521 F.3d 602 (6th Cir., 2008) (finding that the school board did not take specific action to suppress student expression of religious objections to homosexuality so there was no justiciable controversy that could give rise to nominal damages).

[61]Nuxoll v. Indian Prairie Sch. Dist. No. 204, 523 F.3d 668, 676 (7th Cir., 2008). *See also* Nixon v. N. Local Sch. Dist., 383 F. Supp. 2d 965, 971-974 (S.D. Ohio 2005) (rejecting school administrators' assertion that a shirt denigrating homosexuality, Islam, and abortion was "plainly offensive" under *Fraser*; applying *Tinker* instead and finding no disruption or evidence that the expression interfered with the rights of others); Chambers v. Babbitt, 145 F. Supp. 2d 1068 (D. Minn. 2001) (granting a temporary order allowing a student to wear a sweatshirt bearing the message "straight pride" in the absence of any disruption).

Since the Supreme Court in 2007 declined to review the Ninth Circuit case, the collision of religious views and anti-harassment policies seems destined to generate more litigation. Questions remain regarding the legality of school districts' anti-harassment provisions, especially those adopted in the absence of disruptive incidents.

Electronic Expression.   Another topic generating volatile controversies pertains to students' expression rights involving the Internet. These cases are particularly troublesome because students often prepare and disseminate the materials from their homes, but their expression is immediately available to the entire school population and beyond. With the increasing amount of material posted on Facebook, MySpace, and other social networking sites, legal activity in this arena is bound to increase.[62]

Courts are divided on whether students can be disciplined for Web pages created at home. The key determinant appears to be whether the material created off campus has a direct and detrimental impact on the school. Students have prevailed in several instances when they were disciplined for Web pages they created at home because such an impact was not established. For example, a high school senior successfully challenged his suspension for creating a Web site on which he posted mock obituaries of students and allowed visitors to the site to vote on who would "die" next.[63] In granting the injunction, the Washington federal district court noted that the student's Web site was not produced in connection with any class or school activity, and school personnel failed to substantiate that the material threatened or intended harm to anyone. A Michigan federal district court also found an insufficient connection between the disruption of any school activity and a student's Web site called "Satan's Web Page," containing likes and dislikes, including a list of people he wished would die.[64] And a Pennsylvania federal district court invalidated the suspension of a student for sending an e-mail message to friends that included a discourteous and rude "top 10 list" about the school's athletic director, as school authorities did not produce evidence linking the message to a disruption of classes or the management of the school.[65] More recently, the same court reasoned that disciplinary action against a student who created on MySpace a parody profile of the school principal was not justified because there was no disruption of the high school's daily operations.[66] However, the school policies requiring students to express their ideas in a respectful manner and to refrain from verbal abuse were not found to be overbroad.

In contrast, the Fifth Circuit upheld a student's conviction for his Internet communication threatening to shoot and kill students at his high school. Finding that only general intent was required to constitute a threat in violation of federal law, the court upheld the

---

[62]There are more than 200 social networking sites, and MySpace has approximately 60 million members who share journals, photos, etc. *See* Thomas Wheeler II, "Lessons from the *Lord of the Flies*: The Responsibility of Schools to Protect Students from Internet Threats and Cyber-Hate Speech," *Education Law Reporter*, vol. 215 (2007), pp. 227–244.

[63]Emmett v. Kent Sch. Dist. No. 415, 92 F. Supp. 2d 1088 (W.D. Wash. 2000). *See also* Beussink v. Woodland R-IV Sch. Dist., 30 F. Supp. 2d 1175 (E.D. Mo. 1998) (ordering a preliminary injunction to block a student's suspension for using his home computer to create a home page criticizing school administrators, given the lack of evidence of interference with school discipline).

[64]Mahaffey v. Aldrich, 236 F. Supp. 2d 779 (E.D. Mich. 2002).

[65]Killion v. Franklin Reg'l Sch. Dist., 136 F. Supp. 2d 446 (W.D. Pa. 2001).

[66]Layshock v. Hermitage Sch. Dist., 496 F. Supp. 2d 587 (W.D. Pa. 2007).

student's conviction of knowingly and intentionally transmitting in interstate commerce a threat to injure another.[67] Also, the Pennsylvania Supreme Court upheld a student's expulsion because he created a Web site ("Teacher Sux") on his home computer that contained derogatory comments about teachers and administrators and a graphic depiction of the algebra teacher's death.[68] The court reasoned that the off-campus activities substantially disrupted the school, noting that the algebra teacher was so upset by the material that she had to take a leave of absence. The Second Circuit also upheld a semester expulsion of a student for displaying in his instant messaging buddy icon a drawing of a pistol firing at a person's head, with the caption "Kill Mr. VenderMolen," his English teacher, finding that the icon, although displayed outside of school, violated school rules and disrupted school operations.[69] Students are not likely to prevail if their electronic expression has a negative impact on the school, its employees, or its students.

Time, Place, and Manner Regulations. Although private expression enjoys greater constitutional protection than does school-sponsored expression, the judiciary consistently has upheld reasonable policies regulating the time, place, and manner of private expression. For example, students can be prohibited from voicing political and ideological views and distributing literature during instructional time. Additionally, to ensure that the distribution of student publications does not impinge on other school activities, distribution can be barred near the doors of classrooms while class is in session, near building exits during fire drills, and on stairways when classes are changing.

Time, place, and manner regulations, however, must be reasonable, content neutral, and uniformly applied to expressive activities. Such regulations cannot restrict more speech than necessary to ensure nondisruptive distribution of materials.[70] School officials must provide students with specific guidelines regarding when and where they can express their ideas and distribute materials. Moreover, literature distribution cannot be relegated to remote times or places either inside or outside the school building, and regulations must not inhibit any person's right to accept or reject literature that is distributed in accordance with the rules. Policies governing demonstrations should convey to students that they have the right to gather, distribute petitions, and express their ideas under nondisruptive circumstances.[71] If regulations do not precisely inform demonstrators of what behavior is prohibited, the judiciary may conclude that punishment cannot be imposed.

[67]United States v. Morales, 272 F.3d 284 (5th Cir. 2001) (interpreting 18 U.S.C. § 875(c) (2008)).

[68]J.S. v. Bethlehem Area Sch. Dist., 807 A.2d 847 (Pa. 2002). *See also* J.S. v. Blue Mt. Sch. Dist., No. 3:07cv585, 2007 U.S. Dist. LEXIS 23406 (M.D. Pa. Mar. 29, 2007) (denying restraining order and temporary injunction to prevent suspension of student who created a fake MySpace for the principal, depicting him as bisexual, because the expression disrupted the school).

[69]Wisniewski v. Bd. of Educ., 494 F.3d 34 (2d Cir. 2007), *cert. denied*, 128 S. Ct. 1741 (2008). *See also* Requa v. Kent Sch. Dist. No. 415, 492 F. Supp. 2d 1272 (W.D. Wash. 2007) (denying preliminary injunction to student who was suspended for posting on YouTube a disparaging video he secretly filmed of a teacher).

[70]*See* M.B. v. Liverpool Cent. Sch. Dist., 487 F. Supp. 2d 117 (N.D.N.Y. 2007).

[71]*See, e.g.*, Orin v. Barclay, 272 F.3d 1207 (9th Cir. 2001) (upholding restriction on student anti-abortion demonstration at a community college that interferes with campus activities but invalidating prohibition on demonstrations that entail religious worship in a public forum).

■ ■ ■ ■ ■

STUDENT-INITIATED CLUBS

Public schools can deny access to all noncurriculum student clubs but cannot discriminate against specific groups based on the content of their meetings.

Association and related free expression rights have arisen in connection with the formation and recognition of student clubs. Freedom of association is not specifically included among First Amendment protections, but the Supreme Court has held that associational rights are "implicit in the freedoms of speech, assembly, and petition."[72] The word *association* refers to the medium through which individuals seek to join with others to make the expression of their own views more meaningful.

Public school pupils have not prevailed in asserting that free expression and association rights protect student-initiated social organizations or secret societies that determine their exclusive membership by a vote of the clubs' members. In contrast, prohibitions on student-initiated organizations with *open* membership are vulnerable to First Amendment challenge. Even before Congress enacted the Equal Access Act (EAA), courts recognized that public school access policies for student meetings must be content neutral. **The EAA, enacted in 1984, codified these rulings by stipulating that if federally assisted secondary schools provide a limited open forum for noncurricular student groups to meet during noninstructional time, access cannot be denied based on the religious, political, philosophical, or other content of the groups' meetings.**[73]

The EAA was championed by the Religious Right, but its protection encompasses far more than student-initiated religious expression. As discussed in Chapter 3, the Supreme Court in 1990 rejected an Establishment Clause challenge to the EAA in *Board of Education of the Westside Community Schools v. Mergens*.[74] The Court further held that if a federally assisted high school allows even one noncurricular group to use school facilities during noninstructional time, such as a chess club or scuba-diving club, the EAA guarantees equal access for other noncurricular student groups. Of course, meetings that threaten a disruption can be barred. Moreover, school authorities can decline to establish a limited forum for student-initiated meetings during noninstructional time and thus confine school access to student organizations that are an extension of the curriculum, such as drama groups, language clubs, and athletic teams. School districts can offer special privileges to curriculum organizations, such as access to publication outlets, facilities, and the public address system, as long as all noncurriculum student groups are treated in the same manner.[75]

[72]Healy v. James, 408 U.S. 169, 181 (1972).

[73]20 U.S.C. § 4071 (2008). *See* text accompanying note 57 and Figure 3.2, Chapter 3.

[74]496 U.S. 226 (1990). The Court rejected the contention that only noncurricular, *advocacy* groups are protected under the EAA.

[75]*See* Palmer High Sch. Gay-Straight Alliance v. Colo. Springs Sch. Dist. No. 11, No. 03-M-2535 (CBS), 2005 WL 3244049 (D. Colo. Mar. 30, 2005).

Controversies have surfaced over what constitutes a curriculum-related group since the EAA is triggered only if noncurriculum student groups are allowed school access during noninstructional time. Many of these cases have focused on the Gay-Straight Alliance (GSA), and this group has usually prevailed in gaining school access if other clubs are allowed to meet in public secondary schools.[76] To illustrate, a California federal district court ruled that a school board had established a limited forum by allowing some noncurriculum student groups to meet during noninstructional time and thus could not discriminate against the GSA.[77] The Eighth Circuit also enjoined a Minnesota school district from treating the club, Straights and Gays for Equality, differently from other noncurriculum student groups.[78]

However, departing from the judicial trend, a Texas federal district court upheld school authorities in denying the Gay and Proud (GAP) Youth Group's request to hold meetings and post flyers about their meetings in the school, agreeing with school authorities that some of the materials promoted by the GAP Youth on its Web site were inappropriate for minors and conflicted with the board's promotion of its adopted abstinence policy.[79] In contrast, a Florida federal district court found a substantial likelihood that the GSA would prevail in establishing that it was not a "sex-based club," to which student access can be restricted until age 18 under state law. Finding no conflict between the club's purpose and the school's abstinence-based policy, a preliminary injunction was issued so the school district could not deny the GSA access to the forum it provided for student clubs to meet.[80] **Even if agreed that a secondary school has *not* established a limited forum for noncurriculum student groups, it still cannot exert viewpoint discrimination against particular curriculum-related groups.**

■ ■ ■ ■ ■

STUDENT APPEARANCE

Restrictions can be placed on student grooming and attire if based on legitimate educational and safety objectives and not intended to suppress expression.

Fads and fashions in hairstyles and clothing have regularly evoked litigation as educators have attempted to exert some control over pupil appearance. Courts have been called upon to weigh students' interests in selecting their attire and hairstyle against school authorities' interests in preventing disruptions and promoting school objectives.

---

[76]*Id. See also* E. High Sch. Prism Club v. Seidel, 95 F. Supp. 2d 1239 (D. Utah 2000).

[77]Colin v. Orange Unified Sch. Dist., 83 F. Supp. 2d 1135, 1146 (C.D. Cal. 2000).

[78]Straights & Gays for Equality (SAGE) v. Osseo Area Schs., 471 F.3d 908 (8th Cir. 2006).

[79]Caudillo v. Lubbock Indep. Sch. Dist., 311 F. Supp. 2d 550 (N.D. Tex. 2004). The Equal Access Act stipulates that "nothing in this subchapter shall be construed to limit the authority of the school, its agents or employees, to maintain order and discipline on school premises, to protect the well-being of students and faculty, and to assure that attendance of students at meetings is voluntary." 20 U.S.C. § 4071(f) (2008).

[80]Gay-Straight Alliance v. Sch. Bd., 483 F. Supp. 2d 1224 (S.D. Fla. 2007).

Hairstyle

Substantial judicial activity in the 1970s focused on school regulations governing the length of male students' hair. The Supreme Court, however, declined to review these cases, and federal circuit courts of appeal reached different conclusions in determining the legality of policies governing student hairstyle.[81] If school officials have offered health or safety reasons for grooming regulations, such as requiring hairnets, shower caps, and other hair restraints intended to protect students from injury or to promote sanitation, the policies typically have been upheld. Furthermore, restrictions on male students' hairstyles at vocational schools have been upheld to create a positive image for potential employers visiting the school for recruitment purposes. Special grooming regulations have been endorsed as conditions of participation in extracurricular activities for legitimate health or safety reasons and, in some instances, to enhance the school's image.[82] Of course, students can be disciplined for hairstyles that cause a disruption, such as hair groomed or dyed in a manner that distracts classmates from educational activities. It also appears that different hair-length and hairstyle restrictions can be applied to male and female students to reflect community norms or to deter gang activity.[83]

But hairstyle regulations cannot be arbitrary or devoid of an educational rationale. For example, a Texas federal district court ruled that school officials failed to show a valid justification to impair Native American students' protected expression right to wear long hair that posed no disruption.[84]

Attire

Although public school students' hair length has subsided as a major subject of litigation, other appearance fads have become controversial as students have asserted a First Amendment right to express themselves through their attire at school. Even in situations in which students' rights to govern their appearance have been recognized, the judiciary has noted that attire can be regulated if immodest, disruptive, unsanitary, or if it promotes illegal behavior for minors.

Dress Codes.   Under the principle established in *Fraser*, lewd and vulgar expression is outside the protective arm of the First Amendment. Thus, **indecent attire can be curtailed applying *Fraser*, regardless of whether the attire would meet the *Tinker* test of threatening a disruption.** For example, an Idaho federal district court held that a school could prevent a student from wearing a T-shirt that depicted three high school administrators drunk on school grounds, noting that the student had no free expression right to portray administrators in a fashion that would undermine their authority and compromise the school's efforts to educate students about the harmful effects of alcohol.[85] More recently, a

---

[81]For a discussion of these cases, *see* Stephen Thomas, Nelda Cambron-McCabe, and Martha McCarthy, *Public School Law: Teachers' and Students' Rights*, 6th ed. (Boston: Allyn and Bacon, 2009), Chapter 4.

[82]*See, e.g.*, Davenport v. Randolph County Bd. of Educ., 730 F.2d 1395 (11th Cir. 1984); Menora v. Ill. High Sch. Ass'n, 683 F.2d 1030 (7th Cir. 1982).

[83]For a discussion of these cases, see Thomas et al., *supra* note 81.

[84]Ala. & Coushatta Tribes v. Trs., 817 F. Supp. 1319 (E.D. Tex. 1993), *remanded*, 20 F.3d 469 (5th Cir. 1994).

[85]Gano v. Sch. Dist. No. 411, 674 F. Supp. 796 (D. Idaho 1987). *See also* Broussard v. Sch. Bd., 801 F. Supp. 1526 (E.D. Va. 1992) (upholding a one-day suspension of a middle school student who refused to change her shirt printed with the words "Drugs Suck," because "suck" is offensive and vulgar to many people).

Georgia federal district court upheld the suspension of a student who wore a T-shirt with the phrases "kids have civil rights too" and "even adults lie."[86] The court ruled that wearing the shirt was the last incident in a series of disruptions justifying the student's suspension. Several courts also have upheld dress codes that prohibit male students from wearing earrings to inhibit gang influences and promote community values, rejecting the assertion that jewelry restrictions must be applied equally to male and female students.[87]

An Illinois federal court found no First Amendment right for gifted students to wear a shirt they had designed as their class shirt. The court reasoned that school authorities had legitimate pedagogical concerns that the shirt, depicting in a satirical manner a physically handicapped child with the word "gifties," could be viewed as ridiculing students with disabilities and could threaten school discipline.[88] Also, an Ohio federal court upheld the removal of two students from the high school prom for dressing in clothing of the opposite sex, reasoning that the school board's dress regulations were "reasonably related to the valid educational purposes of teaching community values and maintaining school discipline."[89]

In one of the most expansive interpretations of *Fraser*, the Sixth Circuit upheld a school district's decision to prohibit students from wearing Marilyn Manson T-shirts. The appeals court agreed with school authorities that the shirts were offensive, promoted destructive conduct, and were counter to the school's efforts to denounce drugs and promote human dignity and democratic ideals.[90] The court held that under *Fraser*, schools can prohibit student expression that is inconsistent with its basic educational mission even though such speech might be protected by the First Amendment outside the school environment.

[86]Smith v. Greene County Sch. Dist., 100 F. Supp. 2d 1354, 1357 (M.D. Ga. 2000). *See also* D.B. v. Lafon, 217 Fed. App'x 518 (6th Cir. 2007), *supra* text accompanying note 55; Long v. Bd. of Educ., 121 F. Supp. 2d 621 (W.D. Ky. 2000), *aff'd mem.*, 21 Fed. App'x 252 (6th Cir. 2001) (upholding a restrictive student dress code limiting the colors, materials, and type of clothing that could be worn, as justified to deter gang symbols and student conflicts over clothing).

[87]*See, e.g.*, Olesen v. Bd. of Educ., 676 F. Supp. 820 (N.D. Ill. 1987); Jones v. W.T. Henning Elementary Sch., 721 So. 2d 530 (La. Ct. App. 1998); Barber v. Colo. Indep. Sch. Dist., 901 S.W.2d 447 (Tex. 1995).

[88]Brandt v. Bd. of Educ., 326 F. Supp. 2d 916 (N.D. Ill. 2004). *See also* Bivens *ex rel.* Green v. Albuquerque Pub. Schs., 899 F. Supp. 556 (D.N.M. 1995), *aff'd mem.*, 131 F.3d 151 (10th Cir. 1997) (upholding a student's suspension for wearing "sagging" pants in violation of the school's dress code; finding no evidence that the attire conveyed an African American cultural message in contrast to gang affiliation or simply a fashion fad).

[89]Harper v. Edgewood Bd. of Educ., 655 F. Supp. 1353, 1355 (S.D. Ohio 1987). More recently, Lambda Legal filed suit on behalf of a gay male high school student who was turned away from his school prom in Gary, Indiana, for wearing a gown in violation of the prom's dress code. The suit contends that school officials violated the student's First Amendment rights of freedom of speech and expressive conduct. Lambda Legal, "Lambda Legal Challenges Denial of Rights of Feminine Gay Male Student to Wear Dress to Prom" (December 12, 2007), available at www.lambdalegal.org/news/pr/lambda-legal-challenges-denial-of-rights-kk-logan.html.

[90]Boroff v. Van Wert City Bd. of Educ., 220 F.3d 465 (6th Cir. 2000). *See also* Governor Wentworth Reg'l Sch. Dist. v. Hendrickson, 421 F. Supp. 2d 410 (D.N.H. 2006) (upholding suspension of a gay student for wearing an arm patch with a swastika and the international "no" symbol superimposed over it, given the friction between gay students and students identifying themselves as "rednecks" and the administrators' need to promote safety), *vacated as moot*, 201 Fed. App'x 7 (1st Cir. 2007); Madrid v. Anthony, 510 F. Supp. 2d 425 (S.D. Tex. 2007) (upholding a ban on students, who were mostly Hispanic, wearing T-shirts with "We Are Not Criminals" to protest pending immigration legislation; school authorities instituted the ban to curb the escalating racial tension in the school that threatened student safety).

However, as with hairstyle regulations, school authorities must have an educational rationale for attire restrictions, such as preventing class disruptions, curtailing gang behavior, and/or advancing educational objectives. For example, a Texas federal district court found overly broad and vague a dress code prohibiting students from wearing gang-related apparel. Two students who wore rosaries outside their shirts were advised that they were in violation of the policy, but the court held that wearing rosaries was a well-recognized form of religious expression protected by the First Amendment.[91] The Third Circuit similarly struck down a prohibition on wearing T-shirts with the comedian Jeff Foxworthy's "redneck sayings," as not sufficiently linked to racial harassment or other disruptive activity.[92] A student also prevailed in wearing a T-shirt depicting three black silhouettes holding firearms with "NRA" and "Shooting Sports Camp" superimposed over the silhouettes. Applying *Tinker* instead of *Fraser*, the Fourth Circuit held that the student's free expression rights were overriding because the shirt was not disruptive and did not promote gun use.[93]

In addition, **dress codes must not discriminate based on the content of students' messages or be discriminatorily enforced.** The Sixth Circuit ordered a school district to reconsider suspensions of two students who wore T-shirts with a country singer on the front and the Confederate flag on the back and who refused to turn the shirts inside out or to go home and change.[94] Finding evidence that the dress code had been selectively enforced, as students had been allowed to wear shirts celebrating Malcolm X, the court reasoned that any restriction on private expression cannot be enforced in a content-specific manner. Thus, the court remanded the case to determine if the students' First Amendment rights had been violated.

The Second Circuit relied on *Tinker* in protecting a student's right to wear a shirt expressing political views; the shirt depicted George W. Bush negatively (i.e., calling him "Chicken Hawk in Chief" and linking him to drinking, taking drugs, and being a crook and draft dodger).[95] Reasoning that simply because the expression is in poor taste is not a

---

[91]Chalifoux v. New Caney Indep. Sch. Dist., 976 F. Supp. 659 (S.D. Tex. 1997). *See also* Stephenson v. Davenport Cmty. Sch. Dist., 110 F.3d 1303 (8th Cir. 1997) (finding policy prohibiting gang symbols, which was challenged by a student who was forced to remove a small tattoo of a cross on her hand, to give insufficient notice of what was prohibited, allowing school officials unfettered discretion to decide what constituted gang symbols); Grzywna v. Schenectady Cent. Sch. Dist., 489 F. Supp. 2d 139 (N.D.N.Y. 2006) (allowing claim to proceed that student's free expression rights were violated by school authorities' barring her necklace supporting the war in Iraq).

[92]Sypniewski v. Warren Hills Reg'l Bd. of Educ., 307 F.3d 243 (3d Cir. 2002); *supra* text accompanying note 58. *See also* DePinto v. Bayonne Bd. of Educ., 514 F. Supp. 2d 633 (D.N.J. 2007) (enjoining school authorities from prohibiting the wearing of buttons depicting Hitler youth to protest the school's dress code; the buttons, while in poor taste, were not disruptive, vulgar, or sexually charged).

[93]Newsom v. Albemarle County Sch. Bd., 354 F.3d 249 (4th Cir. 2003). *See also* Griggs v. Ft. Wayne Sch. Bd., 359 F. Supp. 2d 731 (N.D. Ind. 2005) (finding no legitimate pedagogical reason to ban a T-shirt with the Marine Creed and a large picture of an M16 rifle, as the shirt did not threaten violence). *But see* Douglass v. Londonderry Sch. Bd., 413 F. Supp. 2d 1 (D.N.H. 2005) (holding that student yearbook editors could refuse to run a senior portrait of a student in trap shooting attire and holding a shotgun; the editors were not acting under color of state law and had offered to publish the picture in the community sports section of the yearbook).

[94]Castorina v. Madison County Sch. Bd., 246 F.3d 536 (6th Cir. 2001).

[95]Guiles v. Marineau, 461 F.3d 320, 322 (2d Cir. 2006), *cert. denied,* 127 S. Ct. 3054 (2007).

sufficient reason to curtail students' expression rights, the appeals court concluded that for student expression to be censorable as plainly offensive under *Fraser*, it would need to contain sexual innuendos and/or profanity. Since neither was at issue, the court applied the *Tinker* disruption standard and found that the student wearing the controversial shirt was not linked to a disruption of the educational process.

Student Uniforms.   Some student attire controversies since the 1990s have focused on school board policies specifying uniforms for students, and the line is not always clear between restrictive dress codes and student uniforms. Voluntary as well as mandatory student uniforms are gaining popularity in many urban school districts. Advocates assert that student uniforms eliminate gang-related attire, reduce violence and socioeconomic distinctions, and improve school climate by placing the emphasis on academics rather than fashion fads.

The Fifth Circuit has rejected challenges to uniform policies in Louisiana and Texas school districts. **Recognizing that attire can communicate a message entitled to First Amendment protection, the court nonetheless found the student uniform policies justified by substantial government interests unrelated to suppressing expression, such as improving achievement, decreasing disciplinary problems, improving safety, decreasing socioeconomic tensions, and increasing attendance.** In the Louisiana case, the court rejected the parents' claim that the uniforms posed a financial burden, noting that the uniforms were inexpensive and a donation program was available for those who could not afford them.[96] In the Texas case, the court noted that parents could apply for their children to be exempt from wearing the uniform based on philosophical or religious objections or medical necessity; thus, the court found no violation of parents' religious freedom or their Fourteenth Amendment right to direct the upbringing of their children.[97]

After the New York City school board adopted a citywide uniform policy for children in elementary schools, a father brought suit claiming that if his child took advantage of the opt-out provision, the child would "stick out," which would violate the child's rights.[98] But the Second Circuit affirmed the federal district court's conclusion that the opt-out provision adequately addressed parents' rights to direct the upbringing of their children. Courts have not been persuaded that any rights are violated because a stigma is associated with exercising the First Amendment right to be exempt from certain requirements.

Although federal appellate courts have differed in their interpretations of constitutional protections regarding appearance regulations, school officials would be wise to ensure that they have a legitimate educational justification for any grooming or dress code. **Policies designed to protect students' health and safety, reduce violence and discipline problems, and enhance learning usually will be endorsed.** Given the current student interest in tattoos, body piercing, and other fashion fads and school authorities' concerns about attire linked to gangs and violence, continued legal controversies over student appearance in public schools seem assured.

---

[96]Canady v. Bossier Parish Sch. Bd., 240 F.3d 437 (5th Cir. 2001).

[97]Littlefield v. Forney Indep. Sch. Dist., 268 F.3d 275 (5th Cir. 2001).

[98]Lipsman v. N.Y. City Bd. of Educ., 13 Fed. App'x 13 (2d Cir. 2000). *See also* Jacobs v. Barber, No.05-16434, 2008 U.S. App. LEXIS 10203 (9th Cir. May 12, 2008) (holding that mandatory student uniform policy does not entail compelled speech).

CONCLUSION

Courts will continue to be called on to balance students' rights to express views and receive information with educators' duty to maintain an appropriate educational environment. In the latter 1960s and early 1970s, the federal judiciary expanded students' constitutionally protected expression and association rights. Since the mid-1980s, however, courts have emphasized that school officials can restrict student conduct and expression in school-related activities for educational reasons and can curtail expression advocating illegal activities. Concerns over student violence coupled with restrictions imposed on expression in response to terrorism have placed new strains on First Amendment freedoms in public schools. Tensions are exacerbated by students' ability to distribute materials to broad audiences over the Internet.

It appeared that the reach of *Tinker* was narrowing after the Supreme Court ruled that lewd and vulgar student speech and attire are not protected by the First Amendment and that public school authorities can censor school-sponsored expression. Nonetheless, courts still rely on the *Tinker* disruption standard in evaluating student expression rights in connection with student publications that are not sponsored by the school, anti-harassment policies, and postings on personal Web pages. Moreover, students do not need to base claims solely on constitutional protections, as federal and state laws, most notably the Equal Access Act, also protect students' expression and association rights.

Controversies over student appearance, particularly messages on T-shirts, have increased recently, so continued litigation pertaining to student attire seems assured. This may encourage additional school districts to consider adopting student uniforms. Judicial criteria applied in weighing the significant competing interests of students and school authorities in connection with expressive and associational activities continue to be refined.

POINTS TO PONDER

1. Students opposed to the United States' military involvement in the Middle East organized several activities to protest the government's policy. The students:

    a. Distributed flyers condemning the war to classmates at school,
    b. Posted flyers on school bulletin boards that announced an anti-war rally to be held after school,
    c. Led students in walking out of a school assembly to meet with protesting adults who were holding a rally across from the school, and
    d. Held a rally in front of the county courthouse after school.

    Could school authorities legally curtail any of these activities? Which activities implicate students' First Amendment rights?

2. Students developed a newspaper in their homes and distributed it at a local store. The articles were critical of school administrators and contained vulgar language. Can school authorities discipline the students for their expression? Would your conclusion be different if the paper were distributed over the Internet?

3. A high school allows a chess club to meet in a classroom after school. Three other student clubs—the Gay-Straight Alliance, the Fellowship of Christian Athletes, and the Young Neo-Nazis—have asked for similar privileges. Must each of these groups be provided school access? Why or why not?

4. A school-based council has decided to adopt a policy requiring students to wear uniforms. What features should the policy include to survive a legal challenge?

5. Students wore T-shirts condemning homosexuality. Can school authorities ban such attire? Why or why not?

CHAPTER SIX

STUDENT CLASSIFICATIONS

It might appear from a literal translation of equality that once a state establishes an educational system, all students must be treated in the same manner. Courts, however, have recognized that individuals are different and that equal treatment of unequals can have negative consequences. Accordingly, valid classification practices, designed to enhance the educational experiences of children by recognizing their unique needs, generally have been accepted as a legitimate prerogative of educators. Indeed, all schools classify students in some fashion, and state laws often specifically authorize or even require school boards to group students by academic levels, sex, age, and other distinguishing traits.

Although educators' authority to classify students has not been contested, the bases for certain classifications and the procedures used to make distinctions among students have been the focus of substantial litigation. To the extent that school classifications determine a student's access to educational resources, courts and legislatures have looked closely at the practices. This chapter explores differential treatment of students based on race, native language, and sex. Classifications based on disability are discussed in Chapter 7.

CLASSIFICATIONS BASED ON RACE

The Supreme Court declared that separate schools based on race are inherently unequal.

The most prevalent reason for classifying students according to race has been to establish or perpetuate racially segregated schools. Widespread racial segregation in educational institutions existed in this country from the colonial period well into the twentieth century. Even after the adoption of the Fourteenth Amendment in 1868, most schools remained segregated either by state constitution or statute, local ordinance, district policy or practice, or court interpretation, and the separate schools seldom were equal. When such practices were challenged, courts generally mandated only that children be provided with access to public education. They did not require equal access to integrated schools or to equal school facilities, the provision of equal curricular or extracurricular opportunities, instruction by equally trained professionals, or instruction of equal duration (i.e., an equivalent school year or school day).

Today, most former *de jure* segregated schools[1] are already, or are in the process of becoming, integrated. In some instances, costs to desegregate schools have exceeded $200 million, and court supervision has lasted 20 to 30 years or longer. No other area of school law has involved such volatile debate, obligated such a high percentage of a school district's budget, or resulted in greater political and social turmoil than desegregation.

Lawsuits challenging school segregation often claim a violation of the Fourteenth Amendment. **Because race qualifies as a suspect class, the state or local school district must demonstrate a compelling interest in its use of facially discriminatory racial classifications. The public entity must show that its procedures are narrowly tailored if it uses race as a basis to segregate students, to deny equal educational opportunity, or to advantage one student over another.**

Plessy and *Brown*

Perhaps the most infamous case supporting the "separate but equal" standard resulting in the segregation of the races in public schools was *Plessy v. Ferguson* in 1896, in which the Supreme Court upheld racial segregation of passengers in railroad coaches as required by Louisiana law.[2] Following *Plessy*, individuals and groups wishing to equalize educational opportunities or to integrate schools made little progress until the late 1930s and 1940s when courts began looking more closely at "separate" facilities and programs and occasionally concluded that they were not "equal." Several related cases involved the National Association for the Advancement of Colored People (NAACP) under the leadership of Charles Houston and Thurgood Marshall (a future United States Supreme Court justice). Four key higher education appeals reached the Supreme Court between 1938 and 1950. These cases included claims from minority students that there were no separate but equal programs available (two cases), that the separate program was inferior, or that the education received within a previously all-Caucasian institution was unequal due to the student's separation from the rest of the student body.[3] The students in each case prevailed.

Given the success of the higher education students, the time appeared ripe to attack the public elementary and secondary schools' "separate but equal" standard directly. This occurred in 1954 when the Supreme Court combined cases from four states—Kansas, South Carolina, Virginia, and Delaware.[4] Once again, Marshall served as lead attorney for the plaintiffs. Although these cases differed regarding conditions and facts, minority children in each state sought the assistance of the courts under the Fourteenth Amendment to

---

[1]*De jure* segregated schools are those in which the separation of the races was required by law or was the result of other action by the state or its agents.

[2]163 U.S. 537 (1896).

[3]McLaurin v. Okla. State Regents for Higher Educ., 339 U.S. 637 (1950); Sweatt v. Painter, 339 U.S. 629 (1950); Sipuel v. Bd. of Regents, 332 U.S. 631 (1948) (*per curiam*); Missouri *ex rel.* Gaines v. Canada, 305 U.S. 337 (1938).

[4]Brown v. Bd. of Educ., 98 F. Supp. 797 (D. Kan. 1951); Briggs v. Elliott, 98 F. Supp. 529 (E.D.S.C. 1951), *vacated and remanded*, 342 U.S. 350 (1952), *on remand*, 103 F. Supp. 920 (E.D.S.C. 1952); Davis v. County Sch. Bd., 103 F. Supp. 337 (E.D. Va. 1952); Gebhart v. Belton, 87 A.2d 862, *aff'd*, 91 A.2d 137 (Del. 1952).

obtain admission to public schools on a nonsegregated basis. **In the landmark decision, collectively called *Brown v. Board of Education*, Chief Justice Warren, writing for a unanimous Court, declared education to be "perhaps the most important function of state and local governments"[5] and repudiated the separate but equal doctrine, stipulating that racially segregated public schools were "inherently unequal."[6]**

Because of the significant impact of this decision and the difficulty in fashioning an immediate remedy, the Supreme Court delayed an implementation decree for one year, soliciting friend-of-the-court briefs[7] regarding strategies to convert *de jure* segregated dual school districts into integrated unitary districts. **Then, in 1955 the Court in *Brown II* concluded that the conversion from dual to unitary must occur "with all deliberate speed,"[8]** although it gave little guidance on what specific time frame was required or to what extent integration was mandated. As a result, states varied widely in their efforts to comply.

De Jure Segregation in the South

Despite the *Brown* mandate to end segregation, during the next decade the Supreme Court was forced to react to many blatant violations, such as a state's efforts to physically block the desegregation of schools;[9] an attempt to avoid integration by closing public schools in one county, while maintaining public schools in other counties in the state;[10] provisions allowing students to transfer back to their former schools if, after rezoning, they would be assigned to a school where their race would be in the minority;[11] and a one-grade-per-year plan[12] that clearly strained the Court's mandate to integrate with "all deliberate speed."[13] Lower courts also identified violations, but often hesitated to require anything more than the removal of barriers to integration, given the dearth of guidance regarding compliance.[14]

Then, in a trilogy of cases in 1968, the Supreme Court announced that school officials in systems that were segregated by law in 1954 had an affirmative duty to take whatever steps were necessary to convert to unitary school systems and to eliminate the effects of past discrimination.[15] Furthermore, the Court declared that desegregation remedies would be evaluated based on their effectiveness in dismantling dual school systems. **Thus, the notion**

---

[5]*Brown I*, 347 U.S. 483, 493 (1954).

[6]*Id*. at 495.

[7]Friend-of-the-court (*amicus curiae*) briefs are provided by nonparties to inform or perhaps persuade the court.

[8]Brown v. Bd. of Educ. (Brown II), 349 U.S. 294, 301 (1955).

[9]Cooper v. Aaron, 358 U.S. 1 (1958).

[10]Griffin v. County Sch. Bd., 377 U.S. 218 (1964).

[11]Goss v. Bd. of Educ., 373 U.S. 683 (1963).

[12]A one-grade-per-year plan requires the integration of one grade each fall term until the system is unitary and all grades are integrated.

[13]Rogers v. Paul, 382 U.S. 198 (1965) (*per curiam*).

[14]*See* Briggs v. Elliott, 132 F. Supp. 776, 777 (E.D.S.C. 1955) (declaring that the Constitution "does not require integration" but "merely forbids discrimination").

[15]Green v. County Sch. Bd., 391 U.S. 430 (1968); Raney v. Bd. of Educ., 391 U.S. 443 (1968); Monroe v. Bd. of Comm'rs, 391 U.S. 450 (1968).

of state neutrality was transformed into a requirement of affirmative state action to desegregate; the mere removal of barriers to school integration was not sufficient.

In one of these 1968 cases, *Green v. County School Board*, the Court reviewed a freedom-of-choice plan adopted by a small district in Virginia. The district historically operated only two schools, both kindergarten through twelfth grade: one for African Americans, the other for Caucasians. To eliminate race-based assignments within the district, the local board implemented a plan to allow children to attend the school of their choice. During the three-year period immediately following implementation, no Caucasian children enrolled in the historically African American school, while only a few African American children enrolled in the historically Caucasian school. The district contended that any resulting segregation was the result of the choices of individuals, not because of government action, and was therefore permissible, but the Supreme Court disagreed. The problem with this plan was not that it was unconstitutional *per se*; it simply was not achieving school integration. As a result, the district was ordered to come forward with a new plan that promised "realistically to work and to work now."[16] In addition, **the Court ruled that school authorities must eliminate the racial identification of schools in terms of the *composition of the student body, faculty, and staff; transportation; extracurricular activities; and facilities.*** These six elements still are used today and are referred to in the aggregate simply as the *Green* criteria.

In 1971, additional direction was provided when the Supreme Court ruled in *Swann v. Charlotte-Mecklenburg Board of Education* that the elimination of invidious racial distinctions may be sufficient in connection with transportation, support personnel, and extracurricular activities, but that more was necessary in terms of constructing facilities and making faculty and student assignments.[17] The Court endorsed the practice of assigning teachers on the basis of race until faculties were integrated and declared that new schools must be located so that the dual school system would not be perpetuated or reestablished.

Correcting racial imbalance among student populations, however, was more difficult. For the vestiges of segregation to be eliminated, the school district had to achieve racial balance in a sufficient number of schools, although every school did not have to reflect the racial composition of the school district as a whole. The presence of a small number of predominantly one-race schools in the district did not necessarily mean that it continued to practice state-imposed segregation, but the burden of proof was placed on school officials to establish that such schools were not the result of present or past discriminatory action. To achieve the desired racial balance, the Court suggested pairing or consolidating schools, altering attendance zones, and using racial quotas, but rejected the practice of assigning students to the schools nearest their homes if it failed to eliminate *de jure* segregation. The Court also endorsed the use of reasonable busing as a means to integrate schools, yet qualified that endorsement by noting that the soundness of any transportation plan must be evaluated based on the time involved, distance traveled, and age of students.

By applying the criteria established in *Green* and *Swann*, substantial desegregation was attained in southern states during the 1970s. Where unconstitutional segregation was found, federal courts exercised broad power in ordering remedies affecting student and staff assignments, curriculum, school construction, personnel practices, and budgetary

[16]*Green*, 391 U.S. at 439.

[17]402 U.S. 1 (1971).

allocations. Judicial activity was augmented by threats from the former Department of Health, Education, and Welfare to terminate federal funds to school districts not complying with Title VI of the Civil Rights Act of 1964.[18] Title VI, like the Fourteenth Amendment, requires the integration only of *de jure* segregated school districts.

Distinguishing between *De Jure* and *De Facto* Segregation

Since the Supreme Court carefully limited its early decisions to states and school districts with a long history of school segregation by official policy, questions remained regarding what type of evidence—other than explicit legislation requiring school segregation—was necessary to establish unconstitutional *de jure* segregation.[19] That is, what factors would distinguish *de jure* segregation (e.g., intentional acts of the school board in the selection of a new school location) from permissible *de facto* segregation (e.g., community segregation caused by the choices of families in the selection and location of homes)? The answer to this question began to evolve in *Keyes v. School District No. 1, Denver* in which the Supreme Court in 1973 held that if **"no statutory dual system has ever existed, plaintiffs must prove not only that segregated schooling exists but also that it was brought about or maintained by intentional state action."**[20] Some federal courts have assumed that a presumption of unlawful purpose can be established if the natural, probable, and foreseeable results of public officials' acts perpetuate segregated conditions, while others have required evidence that policymakers actually harbored a desire to segregate.

Although courts vary in the processes they use to determine whether school districts are guilty of discriminatory intent, they often consider:

- The impact of the disputed governmental act,
- The history of discriminatory official action,
- Procedural and substantive departures from norms generally followed, and
- Discriminatory statements made publicly or in legislative or administrative sessions.

If intent is proven, courts then are responsible for fashioning appropriate remedies, but, when allegations of discriminatory intent not supported, no action on the part of the district is required. Moreover, **school districts that either have no history of unlawful segregation**[21] **or have become unitary while under court supervision, will not be responsible for correcting any future racial imbalance they have not created.**[22]

---

[18]42 U.S.C. §§ 2000d–2000d-7 (2008).

[19]In the 1960s, some courts reasoned that school segregation did not warrant remedial action in school districts in which segregation was not imposed by law in 1954. *See, e.g.,* Deal v. Cincinnati Bd. of Educ., 369 F.2d 55 (6th Cir. 1966).

[20]413 U.S. 189, 198 (1973).

[21]*See* S.F. NAACP v. S.F. Unified Sch. Dist., 413 F. Supp. 2d 1051 (N.D. Cal. 2005) (refusing to extend an expired consent decree created to integrate the public schools; the district had never been found guilty of *de jure* segregation or in noncompliance with the voluntary decree).

[22]Pasadena City Bd. of Educ. v. Spangler 427 U.S. 424 (1976). *See also* Holton v. City of Thomasville Sch. Dist., 425 F.3d 1325 (11th Cir. 2005) (concluding that the segregation occurring since acquiring unitary status was caused by demographic changes and not official action; although the school district could voluntarily develop a new desegregation plan, federal law did not require it and courts were without the authority to order it).

Fashioning Appropriate Remedies

Because each desegregation case involves a combination of unique circumstances and violations, it is not surprising that each remedy also is unique and at times requires:

- Rezoning and redistricting,
- Providing thematic magnet schools,
- Developing new curricular offerings and specialized learning centers,
- Providing compensatory education programs, bilingual/bicultural programs, and counseling and career guidance services,
- Closing, reopening, renovating, or constructing schools,
- Busing students, or
- Hiring, transferring, or retraining current staff.

Basically, courts can require nearly anything of districts and states to bring about the fulfillment of the primary objective—the integration of public schools. "All deliberate speed" in many instances has taken decades while cost often seemed irrelevant.

One approach to achieving integration that has been closely scrutinized by courts, however, is the use of interdistrict remedies. Many city school districts experienced both real and percentage increases in minority populations because of a variety of reasons, including "white flight" and "zone jumping."[23] Integration in these areas then became problematic, given the presence primarily of one race. As a result, several courts reasoned that if racial integration in a predominantly one-race district is to be achieved, adjacent districts must be involved in student transfer and busing plans. The Supreme Court has not accepted this approach, however, and has concluded that each district involved in a desegregation remedy must have been involved in purposeful discrimination. The Court has reasoned that a remedy must not be broader in scope than warranted by the constitutional violation.[24] Furthermore, the Court has articulated a three-part framework to guide district courts in the exercise of their authority. This framework requires that the nature and scope of the desegregation remedy:

- Be determined by the nature and scope of the constitutional violation,
- Be remedial so as to restore the victims of discriminatory conduct to the position they would have occupied in the absence of such conduct, and
- Take into account the interests of state and local authorities in managing their own affairs.[25]

Accordingly, **an interdistrict remedy may include only those districts that were involved in *de jure* segregation;** courts are not authorized to include districts that were not segregated or were segregated only due to *de facto* circumstances.

---

[23]Zone jumping occurs when a student transfers from the assigned attendance zone to an adjacent zone.

[24]Milliken v. Bradley (Milliken I), 418 U.S. 717 (1974).

[25]Milliken v. Bradley (Milliken II), 433 U.S. 267, 280–281 (1977).

In a 1995 decision involving interdistrict remedies, *Missouri v. Jenkins*, the Supreme Court evaluated Kansas City's 18-year history of desegregation orders. Over this period, the district court ordered approximately $1.5 billion in program improvements, comprehensive magnet schools, transportation, capital improvements, and salary assistance.[26] The Supreme Court noted that racial imbalance within a school district, without additional evidence supporting a Fourteenth Amendment violation, did not infringe the Constitution and that the lower court's plan to attract nonresident nonminority students represented an interdistrict remedy and was therefore beyond the court's authority. The Supreme Court further admonished that the lower court should have determined whether the lower achievement of minority students was attributable to prior *de jure* segregation and, if so, whether it had been remedied to the extent practicable. Once this had been accomplished, control of the schools was ordered to be returned to state and local school officials.

Achieving Unitary Status

Federal courts have found numerous school systems guilty of having engaged in *de jure* segregation and have fashioned a variety of remedies. Some orders required only a few years to demonstrate compliance, while others continue to exist today, even though the original decisions may have been rendered in the 1950s, 1960s, or 1970s. Such lengthy supervision has usurped the traditional roles of trained and licensed school administrators, elected school boards, and state legislatures regarding funding, facilities, personnel, and curriculum. Furthermore, judicial oversight continued in many states when compliance seemingly had occurred. With key decisions in 1991 and 1992, however, the Supreme Court provided complying districts with a means to an end.

In *Board of Education v. Dowell*, the school district had been operating since 1972 under a court-ordered plan that entailed substantial student busing to achieve integration. Five years after the initial decision, the federal district court ruled that the board had complied with the order in good faith and was entitled to pursue its legitimate policies without further court supervision. At that time, judicial monitoring was removed, but the 1972 decree was not dissolved. However, the appeals court reasoned that the district's circumstances had not changed enough to justify modifying the 1972 decree.[27] The court conjectured that compliance alone could not be the basis for dissolving an injunction and concluded that the school board failed to meet its burden of proof.

On appeal, the Supreme Court held that the appellate court's standard for dissolving the original decree was too stringent and emphasized that federal supervision of local school systems was intended only as a temporary measure to remedy past discrimination. The Court reasoned that the intent of a desegregation plan is met upon finding—as the district court had done—that the school system was operating in compliance with the Equal Protection Clause and was not likely to return to its former ways. Furthermore, the Court concluded that **the federal judiciary should terminate supervision of school districts in which school boards have complied with desegregation mandates in good faith and**

[26]515 U.S. 70 (1995).
[27]890 F.2d 1483 (10th Cir. 1989).

have eliminated vestiges of past discrimination "to the extent practicable."[28] In making this determination, the district court on remand was directed to assess the six factors identified in *Green*. The lower court also was instructed to reconsider whether current residential segregation in Oklahoma City was the result of private decision making and economics or a vestige of prior school segregation.

Although the *Dowell* decision gave districts hope to eventually end judicial supervision, many districts have had difficulty proving that they were unitary. Courts have not agreed on how long a district must be in compliance prior to ending court supervision and whether all *Green* criteria had to be met simultaneously. Then, in 1992 the Supreme Court clarified several related issues in *Freeman v. Pitts*, in which it directed that district courts must relinquish supervision and control over those aspects of a school system in which there has been compliance with a desegregation decree even if other aspects of the decree have not been met. Through this approach the Court sought to restore to state and local authorities control over public schools at the earliest possible date and noted that **"[p]artial relinquishment of judicial control . . . can be an important and significant step in fulfilling the district court's duty to return the operations and control of schools to local authorities."**[29] To guide the lower courts in determining whether supervision should be removed, the Court identified three questions:

- Has there been full and satisfactory compliance with the decree in those aspects of the system in which supervision is to be withdrawn?
- Is the retention of judicial control necessary or practicable to achieve compliance with the decree in other facets of the school system?
- Has the district demonstrated good faith commitment to the court's entire decree and relevant provisions of federal law?

With this guidance, numerous districts have been able to show that they have achieved a unitary operation.

In contrast, the Eighth Circuit refused to release the Little Rock School District, although it did acknowledge the district's involvement in desegregation since 1956, a highly detailed district court order that appeared to go beyond the scope of the voluntary agreement, and the fact that plaintiffs failed to show that prior *de jure* segregation was causally linked to the achievement gap between African American and Caucasian students.[30] The court reasoned that continued court supervision was necessary to ensure that the school district complied with the voluntary agreement it had knowingly entered in an effort to address the historically low academic achievement of African American students. The agreement went beyond what the court could order, but nonetheless became a financial obligation (i.e., "a promise made is a debt unpaid").[31]

---

[28]Bd. of Educ. v. Dowell, 498 U.S. 237, 249–250 (1991).

[29]503 U.S. 467, 489 (1992).

[30]Little Rock Sch. Dist. v. N. Little Rock, 451 F.3d 528 (8th Cir. 2006).

[31]*Id.* at 541.

Postunitary Transfer and School Assignment

Litigation will not end simply because the school district has achieved unitary status and been relieved of judicial control and supervision. Any decision that may even potentially result in racial imbalance, whether *de jure* or *de facto*, is likely to be challenged. Accordingly, the placement of a new school or the creation of a new school district will foreseeably be scrutinized, as will policies regarding school transfer, initial school assignment, open enrollment, or charter schools. However, a transfer policy that results in an insignificant change in minority-majority enrollment within the district will not typically justify reasserting judicial supervision.[32]

Furthermore, students have challenged school district policies that were designed and administered to maintain the racial balance accomplished through years of court supervision, to integrate *de facto* segregated communities, or to achieve the goal of a diverse student body. In such instances, students generally were permitted to enroll in schools in which their race was a minority or otherwise underrepresented, but not vice versa. Given the use of race, numerous cases have been filed, with courts rendering mixed opinions. Direction for lower courts began to emerge in 2003 when the Supreme Court, in *Grutter v. Bollinger*,[33] permitted a law school to consider race as one of several factors in determining the composition of its first-year class. In denying the plaintiff's race-based Fourteenth Amendment claim, the Court majority identified a compelling interest (i.e., the benefits derived from a diverse student body) and reasoned that the school's admission procedures were sufficiently narrowly tailored not to adversely affect the rights of rejected Caucasian applicants.[34]

With *Grutter* as justification, if not incentive, school districts once again are considering race in making placement decisions, but this time with the motive to integrate rather than segregate. Nonetheless, numerous questions remain concerning the legality of such practices. A partial answer was provided in a 2007 Supreme Court case, *Parents Involved in Community Schools v. Seattle School District No. 1*. The plurality opinion identified an Equal Protection Clause violation in which both the Seattle, Washington, and Jefferson County, Kentucky, school districts relied on race to determine school assignment, once residence and availability of space were considered.[35] Seattle had never been found guilty of *de jure* segregation or been subjected to court-ordered desegregation, while Jefferson County had its court order dissolved in 2000 after it had eliminated the vestiges of prior segregation to the greatest extent practicable.

The Court reasoned that each district's diversity plan relied on race in a nonindividualized mechanical way even though other means were available to address integration goals

[32]United States v. Texas, 457 F.3d 472 (5th Cir. 2006).

[33]539 U.S. 306 (2003). Since *Grutter*, Michigan voters amended the state constitution to prohibit the consideration of race in making admissions decisions—Mich. Const. art. I, § 26. In 2006 this law was unsuccessfully challenged. *See* Coal. to Defend Affirmative Action v. Granholm, 473 F.3d 237 (6th Cir. 2006).

[34]For a critical review of this opinion, *see* Stephen B. Thomas, "*Grutter v. Bollinger*: The Supreme Court Missed a Stitch," *UCEA Review*, vol. XLVI, no. 1 (2004), pp. 14–17.

[35]127 S. Ct. 2738 (2007). This case combined the claims from Parents Involved in Cmty. Sch. v. Seattle Sch. Dist., No. 1, 426 F.3d 1162 (9th Cir. 2005) and McFarland v. Jefferson County Pub. Schs., 416 F.3d 513 (6th Cir. 2005).

of the *de facto* segregated communities. The plans were neither race neutral nor narrowly tailored. Moreover, they were not designed to result in the achievement of broad-based student diversity, but rather were created to address the racial balancing of "whites" and "non-whites" in Seattle and "blacks" and "others" in Jefferson County.

Although both of these race-based programs were disallowed, only four justices (Roberto, Alito, Scalia, Thomas) appear to foreclose the use of race in making placement decisions where there has been no proven history of race discrimination. The fifth member of the plurality opinion (Kennedy) and the justices in the minority (Breyer, Ginsburg, Souter, Stevens) are willing to consider a school district's use of race in making student assignments even in *de facto* segregated school districts, assuming such practices address a compelling interest (i.e., diversity) and are narrowly tailored. Accordingly, expect to see continued growth in the number of cases regarding student assignment, as school districts go beyond complying with court-ordered desegregation plans and attempt to identify narrowly tailored means to achieve diversity.

Race as a Factor in Admission to Private Schools

When private schools use race as a factor to determine admission, only Title VI of the Civil Rights Act of 1964 and 42 U.S.C. Section 1981 at the federal level will apply, in addition to any related state laws or local ordinances. Title VI forbids race discrimination, but applies only to those schools that receive federal financial assistance. Section 1981 prohibits both race and ethnicity discrimination in entering into and fulfilling contracts and requires compliance of all public and private schools, regardless whether they qualify as recipients of federal aid. The seminal case applying this law to a private education setting is *Runyon v. McCrary*, in which the Supreme Court held that Section 1981 was violated when private school administrators rejected all applicants to their school who were not Caucasian.[36] The Court concluded that the practice violated the right to contract due to race, and purported that its ruling violated neither parents' privacy rights nor their freedom of association.

Notwithstanding, the Ninth Circuit in 2006 found no Section 1981 violation when a private school in Hawaii, founded by the descendents of King Kamehameha I, denied admission to an applicant because he was not of Hawaiian ancestry. In fact, only one non-Hawaiian had previously been admitted, given the highly unusual situation that year in which the pool of Hawaiian applicants was one fewer than the number of available openings.[37] Students were required to pay a modest tuition, thus establishing a contract. In rendering its decision permitting continued use of race in making admissions decisions and distinguishing the present case from *Runyon*, the court reasoned that:

- The preference was remedial in nature; it was targeted to assist native Hawaiian students who were performing less well academically than all other classes of students,
- Non-Hawaiian applicants did not have their rights unnecessarily trammeled nor did they face an absolute bar to their advancement; other schools were available that provided adequate education for non-Hawaiians, and

[36]427 U.S. 160 (1976).

[37]Doe v. Kamehameha Schs., 470 F.3d 827 (9th Cir. 2006), *cert. dismissed*, 127 S. Ct. 2160 (2007).

■ The preference was limited—first, when the number of openings exceeds the number of Hawaiian applicants, non-Hawaiians will be admitted; second, the preference will last only long enough to remedy the current educational effects of past, private, and government-sponsored discrimination as well as existing social and economic deprivation.

The next decade should continue to provide ample case law dealing with racial preferences. Future cases are likely to be similar to those litigated over the past few years and will continue to identify a new class of victims (i.e., those not Hawaiian, African American, etc., depending on the target of affirmative action).

Race Discrimination and Matriculated Students

Although there are several laws that prohibit race discrimination in educational settings, there is no doubt that discrimination continues, even though it is more likely to be subtle and therefore difficult to prove than in prior years. Discrimination has been alleged in such areas as the assignment to ability-based courses or programs (e.g., gifted, advanced, developmental);[38] athletic eligibility;[39] racial profiling;[40] academic dismissal from special programs;[41] sexual harassment and molestation;[42] the creation of a hostile environment;[43] and the like.

In an illustrative case, an African American student was denied a temporary restraining order and preliminary injunction to prevent school authorities from expelling him for the remainder of the current academic year (it was already May) plus the following academic year. On two separate occasions, the freshman brushed his teacher's buttocks with the back of his hand and made inappropriate sexual comments about her to other students. The district court upheld the punishment, notwithstanding some minor procedural violations, and found no evidence that the student had been discriminated against due to race.[44] The court also noted that the severity of the punishment was not extraordinary given the intimate touching and was necessary to ensure a safe learning environment.

Because claims of race discrimination against matriculated students are seldom litigated today, it is unclear the extent or frequency of violations. Nonetheless, from a school district perspective, it is prudent to establish a written policy prohibiting race and other forms of impermissible discrimination; inform educators and staff of their individual responsibilities; promptly and thoroughly investigate claims of impropriety; conduct fair and impartial hearings; and determine an appropriate response (e.g., suspension of a student; termination of an employee) for those who have engaged in discriminatory behavior.

[38]*See, e.g.*, Hobson v. Hansen, 269 F. Supp. 401 (D.D.C. 1967), *aff'd sub nom.* Smuck v. Hobson, 408 F.2d 175 (D.C. Cir. 1969).

[39]*See, e.g.*, Allen-Sherrod v. Henry County Sch. Dist., 248 Fed. App'x 145 (11th Cir. 2007).

[40]*See, e.g.*, Carthans v. Jenkins, No. 04 C 4528, 2005 U.S. Dist. LEXIS 23294 (N.D. Ill. Oct. 6, 2005).

[41]*See, e.g.*, Brewer v. Bd. of Trs. of Univ. of Ill., 479 F.3d 908 (7th Cir. 2007).

[42]*See, e.g.*, Doe v. Smith, 470 F.3d 331 (7th Cir. 2006).

[43]*See, e.g.*, Qualls v. Cunningham, 183 Fed. App'x 564 (7th Cir. 2006).

[44]*See, e.g.*, Brown v. Plainfield Cmty. Consol. Dist. 202, 500 F. Supp. 2d 996 (N.D. Ill. 2007).

CLASSIFICATIONS BASED ON NATIVE LANGUAGE

School districts have the responsibility to remove English language barriers that impede equal participation of non-English-speaking students; educators may use bilingual education or other appropriate methods that assist English Language Learners (ELLS) classrooms in which English is the primary language of instruction.

Among the numerous identifiable "classes" of students in American schools are "linguistic minorities," some of whom have been denied an adequate education due to the failure of the school district to address their language barriers through appropriate instruction. The rights of ELLS are protected by the Fourteenth Amendment,[45] Title VI of the Civil Rights Act of 1964, and the Equal Educational Opportunities Act of 1974 (EEOA).

Title VI stipulates that "[n]o person in the United States shall, on the ground of race, color, or national origin, be excluded from participation in, be denied the benefits of, or be subjected to discrimination under any program or activity receiving [f]ederal financial assistance from the Department of Education."[46] Moreover, this statute requires compliance throughout a school district if *any* activity is supported by federal funds (e.g., special education). Discrimination against linguistic minorities is considered a form of national origin discrimination and is therefore prohibited by Title VI.

In addition, the EEOA requires public school systems to develop appropriate programs for ELLS.[47] The act mandates in part that "[n]o state shall deny equal educational opportunity to an individual on account of his or her race, color, sex, or national origin, by . . . the failure by an educational agency to take appropriate action to overcome language barriers that impede equal participation by its students in its instructional program."[48] The EEOA does not impose any specific type of instruction or teaching methodology on education agencies but rather requires "appropriate action."

In the only United States Supreme Court decision involving the rights of ELLS, *Lau v. Nichols*, Chinese children asserted that the San Francisco public schools failed to provide for the needs of non-English-speaking students. The Supreme Court agreed with the students and held that the lack of sufficient remedial English instruction violated Title VI. The Court reasoned that equality of treatment was not realized merely by providing students with the same facilities, textbooks, teachers, and curriculum, and that requiring children to acquire English skills on their own before they could hope to make any progress in school made "a mockery of public education."[49] The Court emphasized

---

[45]*Strict scrutiny* is applied when the acts are facially discriminatory; *intent* is required when the acts are facially neutral (e.g., when tests administered only in English are used to determine enrollment in gifted programs).

[46]42 U.S.C. § 2000d *et seq.* (2008). Regulations may be found at 34 C.F.R. § 100 *et seq.* (2008).

[47]20 U.S.C. § 1701 *et seq.* (2008).

[48]20 U.S.C. § 1703(f) (2008).

[49]Lau v. Nichols, 414 U.S. 563, 566 (1974).

that "basic English skills are at the very core of what these public schools teach," and, therefore, "students who do not understand English are effectively foreclosed from any meaningful education."[50]

As a rule, courts acknowledge that there are numerous legitimate educational theories and practices that may be used to eliminate language barriers and do not typically require one method over another. In fact, they tend to order the use of bilingual education (often the method preferred by plaintiffs) only when less expensive and less cumbersome options have proven ineffective. In making such determinations, courts will examine:

- The level of resources committed to the various programs,
- The competency and training of the instructors,
- The methods of classifying students for instruction, and
- The procedures for evaluating student progress.

A Colorado federal district court, in assessing compliance of the Denver public schools, concluded that the law does not require a full bilingual education program for ELLS but does place a duty on the district to take action to eliminate barriers that prevent ELLS from participating in the educational program. **Good faith effort is inadequate. What is required, according to the court, is an effort that "will be reasonably effective in producing intended results."**[51] Such an effort was not found in the Denver public schools. Although a transitional bilingual program was selected by district personnel, it was not being implemented effectively, primarily due to poor teacher training, selection, and assignment. Accordingly, an EEOA violation was found. Likewise, the Seventh Circuit, in examining Illinois's compliance, argued that "appropriate action" under the law certainly means more than "no action."[52] Once again, the court found that the selection of transitional bilingual education was appropriate, but that it had not been effectively implemented. The court identified both an EEOA violation and a violation of Title VI regulations.

In contrast, a California school district's Spanish bilingual program and three forms of English as a Second Language were judicially endorsed. District teachers were found to be proficient, qualified, and experienced; native-language academic support was available for 38 languages in all subjects; and a cultural enrichment program was operating for grades PK–3. Plaintiffs claimed a violation of the EEOA and Title VI and requested instruction in the students' native tongue. The court disagreed and found that the program was based on sound theory, implemented in a consistent manner with that theory, and produced satisfactory results (i.e., area ELLS were learning at rates equal to or higher than their English-speaking counterparts).[53]

California has generated a significant amount of case law involving the instruction of non- and limited-English speaking students. Many suits attack Proposition 227, which requires that all children within public schools be taught English through "sheltered English immersion" (SEI). This approach requires the use of specially designed materials and

---

[50]*Id.*

[51]Keyes v. Sch. Dist. No. 1, 576 F. Supp. 1503, 1520 (D. Colo. 1983).

[52]Gomez v. Ill. State Bd. of Educ., 811 F.2d 1030, 1043 (7th Cir. 1987).

[53]Teresa P. v. Berkeley Unified Sch. Dist., 724 F. Supp. 698 (N.D. Cal. 1989).

procedures where "nearly all" classroom instruction is in English. In most instances, the law requires school districts to abandon their use of bilingual education. Notwithstanding the prior use of bilingual programming, immigrant children within the state had experienced a high drop-out rate and were low in English literacy. Only those children who already possess good English language skills or those for whom an alternate course of study would be better suited may be excused from the SEI initiative. Even then, 20 or more exempted students per grade level are required before an alternative program such as bilingual education needs to be provided.

To ensure that the SEI approach is used, the state legislature included a *parental enforcement provision* in the law which gives parents the right to sue to receive SEI instruction, as well as for actual damages and attorneys' fees. Any educator who willfully and repeatedly refuses to teach "overwhelmingly" in English may be held personally liable. The state teachers' association attacked this provision as being unconstitutionally vague. But the Ninth Circuit found terms such as "nearly all" and "overwhelmingly" to be no more vague than other descriptive terms used in the writing of statutes and reasoned that such language was likely to chill only a negligible amount of non-English speech, if any.[54]

Another type of national origin/language discrimination was alleged in Kansas where the principal and several teachers prohibited students from speaking Spanish while on school grounds.[55] Following his suspension for speaking Spanish, a student claimed Fourteenth Amendment, Section 1983, and Title VI violations. The court dismissed the Fourteenth Amendment and Section 1983 claims against the school district, as the district could not be vicariously liable under *respondeat superior* because the principal and teachers were not final decision makers—such authority was held by the school board and could not be delegated. Similar claims against individual defendants also were dismissed, as the educators were entitled to qualified immunity. Moreover, the student failed to establish that there was a clearly established right to speak a foreign language while at a public school. In spite of the above, the court refused to dismiss the student's Title VI claim, given the disparate impact the practice had on Hispanic students.

In light of the significant growth of Hispanic and other populations immigrating to the United States, expect growth in this area of litigation. Claims of discrimination as well as controversies about appropriate programming should become increasingly common, particularly within southern border states.

■ ■ ■ ■ ■

CLASSIFICATIONS BASED ON SEX

Students are protected against discrimination based on sex,[56] including sexual harassment by educators and peers.

---

[54]Cal. Teachers Ass'n v. State Bd. of Educ., 271 F.3d 1141 (9th Cir. 2001).

[55]Rubio v. Turner Unified Sch. Dist. No. 202, 453 F. Supp. 2d 1295 (D. Kan. 2006).

[56]"Sex" typically refers to having male or female reproductive systems, whereas "gender" generally refers to social identity related to one's sex.

Classifications and discriminatory treatment based on sex in public education are as old as public education itself, as the first public schools and colleges primarily served males. When women were eventually allowed to enroll, programs were typically segregated and inferior. Over the years, sex equality in public schools has improved, but at times classifications based on sex have limited both academic as well as extracurricular activities for females. Aggrieved students often turn to federal courts to vindicate their rights. In most cases, students allege a violation of either the Fourteenth Amendment[57] or Title IX of the Education Amendments of 1972.[58] Under Title IX, educational recipients of federal financial assistance are prohibited from discriminating, excluding, or denying benefits because of sex.

In addition, Title IX has been interpreted to prohibit retaliation against both students and staff who themselves are not the target of intentional discrimination but are adversely treated due to their advocacy roles. The Supreme Court addressed this issue in 2005 in *Jackson v. Birmingham Board of Education*, in which a teacher/coach was removed from his coaching position, allegedly because of his complaints about the treatment of the girls' basketball team (i.e., not receiving equal funding, equal access to equipment and facilities, etc.).[59] The Court reasoned that discriminatory treatment against advocates was impliedly prohibited by Title IX and remanded the case for a determination of whether the coach's advocacy was in fact the motivating factor in his removal.

Interscholastic Sports

Sex discrimination litigation involving interscholastic sports has focused on two primary themes: the integration of single-sex teams and the unequal treatment of males and females. Although courts will issue injunctions to correct discriminatory conduct where it is found, they will not award monetary damages unless the school receives actual notice of the violation and then is shown to be deliberately indifferent to the claim.

Single-Sex Teams.   One of the more controversial issues involving high school athletics is the participation of males and females together in contact sports (i.e., wrestling, rugby, ice hockey, football, basketball, and other sports that involve physical contact). Title IX explicitly permits separation of students by sex within contact sports. However, the Sixth Circuit has interpreted the act to give discretion to individual school districts, rather than athletic associations, to determine whether to allow coeducational participation in contact sports in their efforts to provide equal athletic opportunities for males and females.[60] Nonetheless, most school districts have elected to take the less controversial route and prohibit coeducational participation. When exclusion occurs, students have no basis for suit under Title IX against either the school district or the athletic association. The explicit wording of the

---

[57]Under the Fourteenth Amendment, *intermediate scrutiny* is applied in sex-based cases in which facial discrimination exists, while *intent* is used in cases in which facially neutral practices result in alleged discrimination.

[58]20 U.S.C. § 1681 (2008).

[59]544 U.S. 167 (2005).

[60]Yellow Springs Exempted Vill. Sch. Dist. v. Ohio High Sch. Athletic Ass'n, 647 F.2d 651 (6th Cir. 1981).

statute protects the school district, while the athletic association will not qualify as either a direct or indirect recipient of federal financial assistance, thereby exempting it from Title IX requirements.[61] This does not foreclose the athlete's opportunity to participate in coeducational contact sports; Fourteenth Amendment claims still may be filed.

Although most athletic associations that regulate interscholastic competition are private corporations, the Supreme Court has found that they are entwined with their respective state governments and therefore are involved in state action.[62] As a result, athletes who are denied coeducational sports opportunities may sue both their public school district and the state athletic association for perceived constitutional violations. The Fourteenth Amendment does not necessarily require integration of contact sports, as it permits separate teams where such teams are considered equal. But if separate teams are not available or are found unequal, school districts are required to allow the participation of female athletes on traditionally male teams, including those that involve contact.

A federal district court in New York reviewed a female student's request to try out for the junior varsity football squad.[63] The school district was unable to show that its policy of prohibiting mixed competition served an important governmental objective, as is required under Fourteenth Amendment intermediate scrutiny. In rejecting the district's assertion that its policy was necessary to ensure the health and safety of female students, the court noted that no female student was given the opportunity to show that she was as fit as or more fit than the weakest male member of the team.

A Wisconsin federal district court similarly ruled that female students have the constitutional right to compete for positions on traditionally male contact teams, declaring that once a state provides interscholastic competition, such opportunities must be provided to all students on equal terms.[64] The court reasoned that the objective of preventing injury to female athletes was not sufficient to justify the prohibition of coeducational teams in contact sports. If school officials were reluctant to permit sex-integrated play, they had other options available—interscholastic competition in contact sports could be eliminated for all students or separate and equal teams for females could be established. But if comparable sex-segregated programs were provided, female athletes could not assert the right to try out for the male team simply because of its higher level of competition.

In addition to the controversies regarding coeducational participation in contact sports, there have been numerous challenges to policies denying integration of males and females in noncontact sports. Females filed the majority of these suits and prevailed in nearly every instance. **Title IX regulations explicitly require recipient districts to allow coeducational participation in those noncontact sports that are available only to one sex, presuming that athletic opportunities for that sex have been historically limited.** Thus, females tend to succeed in their claims, whereas males tend to fail. As a rule, school districts have been able to show an important governmental interest (e.g., redressing disparate athletic opportunities for females) in support of their decisions to exclude males

[61]*See* NCAA v. Smith, 525 U.S. 459 (1999).

[62]Brentwood Acad. v. Tenn. Secondary Sch. Athletic Ass'n, 531 U.S. 288 (2001).

[63]Lantz v. Ambach, 620 F. Supp. 663 (S.D.N.Y. 1985).

[64]Leffel v. Wis. Interscholastic Athletic Ass'n, 444 F. Supp. 1117 (E.D. Wis. 1978).

from participating on teams traditionally reserved for females, while males have had difficulty supporting the claim that their athletic opportunities have been historically limited.

Fewer Sports Opportunities for Females.   Although athletic opportunities for females have significantly increased since passage of Title IX in 1972, equal opportunity has not been achieved within all school districts. State efforts to provide a greater number of opportunities for females have been weakened significantly by public education budgetary problems. Expenditures for special education, literacy, technology, smaller class size, school safety, and the like have been given priority when dividing a shrinking public purse. Given such financial constraints, equality of athletic opportunities for males and females often has been achieved either by reducing the number of sports traditionally available for males, or by lowering the number of participants on boys' teams (e.g., football) to provide generally equal opportunities for males and females. Also, efforts have been made to disguise the existing inequity (e.g., double counting participants in women's indoor and outdoor track, but not double counting men in fall/spring events such as track, golf, and tennis[65]) to avoid taking corrective action.

At times, female athletes have expressed an insufficient interest in a given sport to have it approved by the state athletic association. In a Kentucky case, high school athletes claimed a Title IX violation when the state athletic association refused to approve females' interscholastic fast-pitch softball. The association's decision was based on its policy of not sanctioning a sport unless at least 25 percent of its member institutions demonstrated an interest in participation. Since only 17 percent indicated an interest, approval was denied. In the original hearing on this controversy, the Sixth Circuit had held that the 25 percent requirement did not violate the Equal Protection Clause, as the facially neutral policy was not proven to entail intentional discrimination.[66] The case then was remanded and later appealed. The court again found no Title IX violation and further concluded that grouping sports by sex did not violate federal law.[67]

In a higher education case, Brown University responded to budget cuts in 1991 by eliminating two interscholastic teams for men and two for women. At the time of the reductions, only 37 percent of the participants in varsity sports, compared to 48 percent of the institution's students, were women. By 1994, the ratio had not significantly changed. The First Circuit found a Title IX violation, concurring with the Office for Civil Rights' policy interpretation that for schools to be in compliance they should:

- Provide interscholastic sports opportunities for both sexes in terms of numbers of participants that are substantially proportionate to the respective enrollments of male and female students,
- Show a history of expanding sports programs for the underrepresented sex, or
- Provide enough opportunities to match the sports interests and abilities of the underrepresented sex.[68]

[65]Miller v. Univ. of Cincinnati, No. 1:05-cv-764, 2007 U.S. Dist. LEXIS 70484 (S.D. Ohio Sept. 21, 2007).

[66]Horner v. Ky. High Sch. Athletic Ass'n, 43 F.3d 265 (6th Cir. 1994).

[67]Horner v. Ky. High Sch. Athletic Ass'n, 206 F.3d 685 (6th Cir. 2000).

[68]Cohen v. Brown Univ., 101 F.3d 155 (1st Cir. 1996).

The court rejected the university's unproven assertion that female students were less interested in sports and viewed the comment as being based on a stereotypical view of women.

Modified Sports and Separate Seasons for Females. Among the equity claims initiated by female athletes are those contesting the use of sex-based modifications in sports. Although federal courts historically have permitted different rules for males and females (e.g., split-court rules for women's basketball), differential treatment of male and female athletes cannot be justified by unfounded and unsupported perceptions about either sex regarding strength, endurance, or ability.

Also, maintaining separate playing seasons for female and male teams has been challenged as a violation of the equal protection clauses of both federal and state constitutions. In some instances, separate seasons have been upheld because of a lack of adequate facilities and general comparability of programs. In other instances, separate seasons have been found to violate equal protection rights. This was the situation in Michigan where the Sixth Circuit upheld a lower court ruling concluding that the difficulty in finding facilities, coaches, and officials did not justify the use of separate seasons for males and females where the girls bore the burden of off-season participation.[69] The court opined that if single-sex seasons were in fact necessary, the burden must be shared. For example, the junior varsity teams of both sexes could be placed into the disadvantageous season; as a result, the varsity teams then could compete during the preferred time period. This plan would result in the same utilization of facilities and staff, yet the advantages and disadvantages of off-season play would be equally divided between the sexes.

Academic Programs

Allegations of sex bias in public schools have not been confined to athletic programs. Differential treatment of males and females in academic courses and schools also has generated litigation. **Because the "separate but equal" principle has been applied in cases alleging a Fourteenth Amendment violation, public school officials are required to show a substantial justification for classifications based on sex that are used to segregate or exclude either males or females in academic programs.** In contrast, Title IX excludes elementary and secondary school admission policies from its coverage (i.e., the operation of a single-sex PK–12 school does not violate Title IX).[70] However, a recipient school district cannot use a single-sex admissions policy to deny a student, because of that student's sex, the opportunity to participate in or benefit from its total districtwide curriculum. Accordingly, if a single-sex school operates the only performing arts program in the district, officials are responsible for acquiring comparable programming elsewhere or for admitting the student of the excluded sex. The Department of Education prefers that when such sex-segregated programming is made available, it should be offered in a single-sex program (i.e., similar to the Fourteenth Amendment standard of separate but equal).[71]

---

[69]Cmtys. for Equity v. Mich. High Sch. Athletic Ass'n, 459 F.3d 676 (6th Cir. 2006).

[70]34 C.F.R. § 106.15(d) (2008).

[71]*See* Office for Civil Rights, *Guidelines Regarding Single Sex Classes and Schools, 2005*, available at www. ed. gov/ about/ offices/ list/ ocr/ t9-guidelines-ss. html.

Legal issues related to single-sex schools, sex-segregated courses and programs, and sex-based admission criteria are reviewed below.

Single-Sex Schools.   The Third Circuit held that the operation of two historically sex-segregated public high schools (one for males, the other for females) in which enrollment is voluntary and educational offerings are essentially equal, is permissible under the Equal Protection Clause, Title IX, and the Equal Educational Opportunities Act of 1974.[72] Noting that Philadelphia's sex-segregated college preparatory schools offered functionally equivalent programs, the court concluded that the separation of the sexes was justified because youth might study more effectively in sex-segregated high schools. The court emphasized that the female plaintiff was not compelled to attend the sex-segregated academic school; she had the option of enrolling in a coeducational school within her attendance zone. Furthermore, the court stated that her petition to attend the male academic high school was based on personal preference rather than on an objective evaluation of the offerings available in the two schools. Subsequently, an equally divided United States Supreme Court affirmed this decision without delivering an opinion.

In contrast, Detroit school officials did not prevail in their attempt to segregate inner-city, African American male students to address more effectively these students' unique educational needs. Three African American male academies (preschool to fifth grade, sixth to eighth grade, and high school) were proposed. The three-year experimental academies were designed to offer an Afrocentric curriculum, emphasize male responsibility, provide mentors, offer Saturday classes and extended classroom hours, and provide individual counseling. No comparable program existed for females, although school authorities indicated that one would be forthcoming. The district court issued a preliminary injunction prohibiting the board from opening the academies, given the likelihood that the practice violated the Equal Protection Clause. Additionally, the court reasoned that failing to provide the injunction could result in irreparable injury to the female students and cause great disruption if the schools were allowed to open and then were forced to close.[73] The court noted that the district failed to show a substantial justification for its actions, as is required under the Fourteenth Amendment for facially discriminatory acts involving sex.

In a higher education case, but one with PK–12 implications, the Supreme Court in 1982 struck down a nursing school's admission policy that restricted admission in degree programs to females without providing comparable opportunities for males.[74] Although the Court acknowledged that sex-based classifications may be justified in limited circumstances when a particular sex has been disproportionately burdened, it rejected the university's contention that its admission policy was necessary to compensate for past discrimination against women. The Court found no evidence that women had ever been denied opportunities in the field of nursing that would justify remedial action by the state. In applying intermediate scrutiny, the Court concluded that the university failed its burden of showing that the facially discriminatory sex classification served an important

[72]Vorchheimer v. Sch. Dist., 532 F.2d 880 (3d Cir. 1976), *aff'd by equally divided court,* 430 U.S. 703 (1977).

[73]Garrett v. Bd. of Educ., 775 F. Supp. 1004 (E.D. Mich. 1991).

[74]Miss. Univ. for Women v. Hogan, 458 U.S. 718 (1982).

governmental objective, or that its discriminatory means were substantially related to the achievement of those objectives.

Similarly, the Fourth Circuit addressed male-only admissions policies in Virginia. The court found such a policy at the Virginia Military Institute (VMI) to be in violation of the Equal Protection Clause because there were no comparable opportunities for females.[75] The appellate court held that VMI's claims that its male-only program provided needed diversity in higher education did not justify exclusion of women. The state was given three options: admit women, establish a parallel institution for women, or abandon state support for VMI. The state chose to establish a parallel program for women at Mary Baldwin College, a small private women-only institution; that decision was initially upheld.[76] On appeal in *United States v. Virginia*, however, the Supreme Court reversed the lower courts and held that the state had violated the Fourteenth Amendment by its failure to provide equal opportunities for women in the area of military training.[77] A new program at Mary Baldwin would never be able to approach the success, quality, and prestige associated with that provided at VMI. Also, the Court refuted the reasons given by VMI for its refusal to admit women. The exclusion of women from VMI failed to further the institution's purported purpose of providing diversity in higher education; VMI's distinctive teaching methods and techniques could be used unchanged in many instances or slightly modified in the instruction of women; and privacy issues were resolvable.

Sex-Segregated Courses and Programs. Unequal educational opportunities for males and females will not be permitted by courts. Although most cases challenging the exclusion of one sex from specific curricular offerings have been settled on constitutional grounds, Title IX regulations also prohibit sex-segregated courses such as physical education (although students may be grouped by skill level), vocational education, and music (although requirements based on vocal range that result in disparate impact are permissible), as well as others.[78] There are two exceptions, however, in which classes *may be* segregated by sex: (1) physical education classes during participation in contact sports;[79] and (2) portions of classes that deal exclusively with human sexuality.[80]

Sex-Based Admissions Criteria. At times, two sets of admissions standards have been used, one for males and the other for females. Without substantial justification, this facially discriminatory practice will not satisfy constitutional scrutiny or provisions of Title IX.[81] For example, the admissions practices of two Boston schools were found to have discriminated against female applicants and were therefore invalidated.[82] Because of

---

[75]United States v. Virginia, 976 F.2d 890 (4th Cir. 1992).

[76]United States v. Virginia, 852 F. Supp. 471 (W.D. Va. 1994), *aff'd*, 44 F.3d 1229 (4th Cir. 1995).

[77]518 U.S. 515 (1996).

[78]34 C.F.R. § 106.34(a)(2), (4) (2008); 34 CFR § 106.35 (2008).

[79]34 C.F.R. § 106.34(a)(1) (2008).

[80]34 C.F.R. § 106.34(a)(3) (2008).

[81]45 C.F.R. § 86.35(b) (2008).

[82]Bray v. Lee, 337 F. Supp. 934 (D. Mass. 1972).

the different seating capacities of the two schools, the Latin School for males required a lower score on the entrance examination than did the school for females. Although permitting the operation of sex-segregated schools, the federal district court was unsympathetic to the school's alleged physical plant problems and ruled that the same entrance requirements had to be applied to both sexes. Similarly, the Ninth Circuit concluded that a school district's plan to admit an equal number of male and female students to a high school with an advanced college preparatory curriculum violated equal protection guarantees because it resulted in unequal admission criteria.[83] The court found the district's policy to be an illegitimate means of reaching its goal of balancing the number of male and female students enrolled in the school.

If the district uses reliable, valid, and bias-free forms of assessment to admit students to special programs or to grant awards or scholarships, decisions will be upheld even if a disparate impact occurs. Moreover, it is recommended that multiple forms of assessment be used and that all personnel involved in assessment have appropriate credentials and training.

Sexual Harassment of Students

Title IX and the Fourteenth Amendment also have been applied in sex-based claims of sexual harassment and abuse of students. However, Title IX does not apply when the harassment is due to sexual preference, transvestism, transsexualism, or other behaviors that are sexual in nature; it applies only when the harassment is due to being male or being female. In an illustrative Tenth Circuit case, Title IX was held not to apply in a case in which a male high school football player was hazed by his teammates, taped while nude to a towel rack, and then subjected to viewing by his former girlfriend, who had been invited into the locker room. He reported the incident, resulting in the eventual cancellation of the final game of the season. Following this altercation, he was subjected to great animosity and verbal threats and harassment from numerous students until he eventually transferred to another school. Nonetheless, because the plaintiff was unable to show that his harassment was due to being male, the Title IX portion of his suit was dismissed.[84]

Historically, charges of sexual harassment against school districts generally were dismissed. But then in 1992 the Supreme Court heard the appeal of a case in which a female student alleged that a coach initiated sexual conversations, engaged in inappropriate touching, and had coercive intercourse with her on school grounds on several occasions. In this case, *Franklin v. Gwinnett County Public Schools*, the Court held that Title IX prohibited the sexual harassment of students and that damages could be awarded where appropriate.[85] Since *Gwinnett*, numerous other cases with mixed results have been filed by current and former students alleging a range of claims. With *Gwinnett* as a starting point, two similar but slightly different standards have evolved: one for employee-to-student harassment and the other for student-to-student harassment.

---

[83]Berkelman v. S.F. Unified Sch. Dist., 501 F.2d 1264 (9th Cir. 1974).

[84]Seamons v. Snow, 84 F.3d 1226 (10th Cir. 1996).

[85]503 U.S. 60 (1992).

Employee-to-Student Harassment. In 1998, the Supreme Court provided further guidance in *Gebser v. Lago Vista Independent School District* regarding the liability of school districts when students are harassed by school employees.[86] In this case, a high school student and a teacher were involved in a relationship that had not been reported to the administration until the couple was discovered having sex and the teacher was arrested. The district then terminated the teacher's employment and the parents sued under Title IX. On appeal, the Supreme Court held that to be liable the district had to have *actual notice* of the harassment. The Court reasoned that allowing recovery of damages based on either *respondeat superior* or *constructive notice* (i.e., notice that is inferred or implied) would be inconsistent with the objective of the act as liability would attach even though the district had no actual knowledge of the conduct or an opportunity to take action to end the harassment.[87] Accordingly, **for there to be an award of damages, an official who has the authority to address the alleged discrimination must have *actual knowledge* of the inappropriate conduct and then fail to ameliorate the problem. Moreover, the failure to respond must amount to *deliberate indifference* to the discrimination.** In the instant case, the plaintiff did not argue that actual notice had been provided and the district's failure to promulgate a policy and grievance procedure failed to qualify as deliberate indifference.

Also of relevance in hostile environment cases in which school personnel are allegedly involved is the fact that, at least for younger children, the behavior does not have to be "unwelcome," as in Title VII (Civil Rights Act of 1964) employment cases.[88] The Seventh Circuit reviewed a case in which a 21-year-old male kitchen worker had a consensual sexual relationship with a 13-year-old middle school female.[89] The court noted that under Indiana criminal law a person under the age of 16 cannot consent to sexual intercourse and that children may not even understand that they are being harassed. To rule that only unwelcome behavior is actionable would permit violators to take advantage of young, impressionable youth who voluntarily participate in requested conduct. Moreover, if welcomeness were an issue properly before the court, the children bringing the suits would be subject to intense scrutiny regarding their degree of fault.

Student-to-Student Harassment. Educators must be in control of the school environment, including student conduct, and eliminate known dangers and harassment. Not all harassment will be known, however, and not all behavior that is offensive will be so severe as to violate Title IX. Also, for student-to-student harassment to be actionable the behavior must be unwelcome.

---

[86]524 U.S. 274 (1998).

[87]*See also* Henderson v. Walled Lake Consol. Schs., 469 F.3d 479 (6th Cir. 2006) (observing that even if administrators had notice that a female soccer player was involved in a relationship with her coach, such awareness did not establish notice that the plaintiff, another member of the team, had been exposed to a hostile environment).

[88]*But see* Escue v. N. Okla. Coll., 450 F.3d 1146 (10th Cir. 2006) (concluding that there was insufficient evidence for a jury to conclude that the professor's conduct was unwelcome or that consent from the college student was not provided).

[89]Mary M. v. N. Lawrence Cmty. Sch. Corp., 131 F.3d 1220 (7th Cir. 1997).

Clarification regarding liability associated with student-to-student harassment was provided in 1999 when the Supreme Court in *Davis v. Monroe County Board of Education*[90] proposed a two-part test to establish:

- Whether the board acted with deliberate indifference to known acts of harassment, and,
- Whether the harassment was so severe, pervasive, and objectively offensive that it effectively barred the victim's access to an educational opportunity or benefit.

The Court remanded the case to determine if these standards were met. The plaintiff's daughter had allegedly been subjected to unwelcome sexual touching and rubbing, as well as sexual talk. On one occasion, the violating student put a doorstop in his pants and acted in a sexually suggestive manner toward the plaintiff. Ultimately, the youth was charged with and pled guilty to sexual battery for his misconduct. The victim and her mother notified several teachers, the coach, and the principal of these incidences. No disciplinary action was ever taken other than to threaten the violating student with possible sanctions.

Neither Eleventh Amendment immunity nor the claim that the violator was engaged in First Amendment protected free speech may be used as defenses to Title IX actions. As a result, damage awards[91] are available from educational institutions receiving federal funds, although not from those persons who were directly responsible for the harassment.[92] "Individuals" are not "recipients" and cannot, therefore, be held liable under this particular law.[93] Whether 42 U.S.C. Section 1983 can be attached to Title IX to increase possible damage awards has not been resolved.[94] However, violators can be sued directly under state tort law for sexual battery or intentional infliction of emotional distress,[95] and criminal charges may be filed against perpetrators when force is used or minors are involved. Moreover, being found guilty of sexual harassment can justify demotion, suspension, or termination, even for tenured educators.

The high volume of sexual harassment litigation will likely continue. Even when administrators deal with claims of sexual harassment in timely and effective ways, parents still may file suit. They will be understandably angry that their child has been subjected to inappropriate behavior and will be looking for someone to blame, if not pay.

[90]526 U.S. 629 (1999).

[91]*See* Doe v. East Haven Bd. of Educ., 200 Fed. App'x 46 (2d Cir. 2006) (affirming award of $100,000 to a victim of student-to-student harassment; finding officials deliberately indifferent to the harassment, taunting, and name calling following plaintiff's rape).

[92]*See, e.g.*, Hartley v. Parnell, 193 F.3d 1263 (11th Cir. 1999); Floyd v. Waiters, 133 F.3d 786 (11th Cir. 1998).

[93]Floyd, 133 F.3d 786.

[94]*Compare* Doe v. Smith, 470 F.3d 331 (7th Cir. 2006) (dismissing § 1983 claims and determining that Title IX provides adequate statutory recourse for the alleged discrimination) *with* Cmtys. for Equity v. Mich. High Sch. Athletic Ass'n, 459 F.3d 676 (6th Cir. 2006) (concluding that § 1983 and the Fourteenth Amendment may be used to supplement the relief sought under Title IX), *cert. denied*, 127 S. Ct. 1912 (2007).

[95]*See, e.g.*, Johnson v. Elk Lake Sch. Dist., 283 F.3d 138 (3d Cir. 2002).

CONCLUSION

A basic purpose of public education is to prepare students for postsecondary life, regardless of their innate characteristics. Accordingly, courts and legislatures have become increasingly assertive in guaranteeing that students have the chance to realize their capabilities while in school. Arbitrary classification practices that disadvantage certain groups are not tolerated. Conversely, valid classifications, applied in the best interests of students, are generally supported. Indeed, some legal mandates require the classification of certain students to ensure that they receive instruction appropriate to their needs.

Sex-based classification schemes and discrimination are likely to continue to be heavily litigated, particularly in the areas of harassment and sports opportunities. Also, the number of cases that claim native language discrimination will likely increase, given the significant number of non-English-speaking persons who immigrate yearly, and race discrimination cases will focus on both desegregation and efforts to achieve diverse student bodies.

POINTS TO PONDER

1. A student and coach had a three-month affair that included sexual involvement. The student is 18 years old and voluntarily participated in all activities; the coach was tenured as a social studies teacher. The parents learned of the affair and informed the superintendent and principal. Both the student and coach admitted to their involvement. The coach was fired following an appropriate hearing; the parents nevertheless sued the district claiming a Title IX violation. How will the court respond?

2. An alternative school has been specially designed to address the unique needs of African American males; a comparable program has been developed for African American females. Both are to begin in the fall. Two suits are filed: one alleging a violation of Title IX, the other claiming a Title VI infraction. Who wins each suit and why?

3. There is only one non-English-speaking child in the school district. Officials refused her parent's request for a bilingual program. The parents then retained the services of three nationally known experts on bilingual education; each provided significant data that supported the use of bilingual education in the elimination of language barriers. Nonetheless, the district still refused to provide the requested program and, in the alternative, offered an English as a Second Language program. This program has been successful in eliminating language barriers in the past (both in this district and throughout the state). School officials were unsure which of the two instructional methods was better, but claim that they were not required to offer the best program. The parents sued the district under Title VI and the Equal Educational Opportunities Act. What will be the outcome of their legal challenge?

4. The local school district has been unitary for 10 years. Recently, however, the state implemented (1) a plan allowing students to enroll in private schools, (2) a program in which students are permitted to transfer to any adjacent public school district, and (3) a transfer program in which students may attend any public school in the state if their home school fails to meet state guidelines. Under these provisions, the district once again becomes racially segregated. A lawsuit was filed under the Fourteenth Amendment and Title VI challenging recent changes that have resulted in resegregation. Will the plaintiffs succeed in this suit?

CHAPTER SEVEN

RIGHTS OF STUDENTS WITH DISABILITIES

Since children with disabilities represent a vulnerable minority group, their treatment has resulted in considerable judicial and legislative concern. Courts have addressed the constitutional rights of such children to attend school and to be classified accurately and instructed appropriately. Federal and state statutes have further delineated the rights of students with disabilities and have provided funds to assist school districts in meeting their special needs.

LEGAL CONTEXT

Education must be made available to all school-age children. Those with qualifying disabilities have additional rights guaranteeing them a free appropriate public education (FAPE).

Case law supporting the inclusion of children with disabilities, lobbying efforts, and changes in state laws eventually helped to pave the way for the passage of federal laws specially designed to protect and enhance the rights of individuals with disabilities—Section 504 of the Rehabilitation Act, the Americans with Disabilities Act (ADA), and the Individuals with Disabilities Education Act (IDEA) (see Table 7.1). Each is reviewed briefly below.

Rehabilitation Act

Section 504 of the Rehabilitation Act of 1973 applies to both public and private recipients of federal financial assistance. Section 504 stipulates that otherwise qualified individuals shall not be excluded from participating in, be denied the benefits of, or be subjected to discrimination by recipient programs or activities, if that treatment is due to their disabilities.[1]

---

[1]29 U.S.C. § 794(a) (2008). *See also* Clark v. Banks, 193 Fed. Appx. 510 (6th Cir. 2006) (finding that plaintiff was not denied the right to transfer schools due solely to her disability; her residence and issues related to funding also were considered).

TABLE 7.1   Applicability of Selected Federal Laws Affecting Students with Disabilities

FEDERAL LAW	PUBLIC RECIPIENT REQUIRED TO COMPLY	PUBLIC NON-RECIPIENT REQUIRED TO COMPLY	PRIVATE RECIPIENT REQUIRED TO COMPLY	PRIVATE NON-RECIPIENT REQUIRED TO COMPLY
Fourteenth Amendment Equal Protection Clause	Yes	Yes	No	No—except state athletic ass'ns
Fourteenth Amendment Due Process Clause	Yes	Yes	No	No—except state athletic ass'ns
42 USC § 1983	Yes	Yes	No	No—except state athletic ass'ns
Rehabilitation Act § 504	Yes	No	Yes	No
ADA—Title II	Yes	Yes	No	No
ADA—Title III	No	No	Yes	Yes
IDEA	Yes, if recipient of IDEA funds	No	No, service contracts do not qualify	No

Under the Rehabilitation Act, an individual with a disability is one who *has a physical or mental impairment*[2] that substantially limits one or more major life activities, *has a record of impairment*, or *is regarded as having an impairment*.[3] These latter two definitions (i.e., "record of" and "regarded as") apply when a person has been subjected to discrimination, such as being terminated as a teacher because of having a record of hospitalization for tuberculosis[4] or excluded from school for being HIV positive.[5] However, only those

---

[2] 34 C.F.R. § 104.3(j)(2)(i)) (2008) (defining physical or mental impairments as including "any physiological disorder or condition, cosmetic disfigurement, or anatomical loss affecting one or more of the following body systems: neurological; musculoskeletal; special sense organs; respiratory, including speech organs; cardiovascular; reproductive, digestive, genito-urinary; hemic and lymphatic; skin; and endocrine; or any mental or psychological disorder, such as mental retardation, organic brain syndrome, emotional or mental illness, and specific learning disorders").

[3] 34 C.F.R. § 104.3(j)(1) (2008).

[4] Sch. Bd. v. Arline, 480 U.S. 273 (1987) (concluding that a teacher suffering from tuberculosis qualified as an individual with a disability because she had a record of physical impairment that limited a major life activity—working).

[5] Ray v. Sch. Dist., 666 F. Supp. 1524 (M.D. Fla. 1987).

children who meet the first definition, in that they have an impairment that is substantially limiting, will be eligible for reasonable accommodations and modifications. Students with only a record of a *past* impairment are not currently in need of accommodation, while students who are only *regarded* as having an impairment have no actual disability to accommodate.

In addition, **the limitation must *substantially limit* a *major life activity*.**[6] In making this determination, courts compare the performance difficulties of the student with those of the theoretical "average person" (or in this discussion "average student") in the general population. **To qualify, the student will have to be either incapable of performing the designated activity or significantly restricted; merely functioning below average will be insufficient. This assessment requires a case-by-case evaluation,** because impairments will vary in severity, affect people differently, and may or may not be restricting given the nature of the life activity. As a result, some students with physical or mental impairments will be substantially limited and others with the same diagnosis will not, with only the former qualifying as disabled under Section 504. Failure to recognize that Section 504 provides protection only for persons who are disabled (in that a life activity is significantly restricted) but not for those who are merely impaired, can lead to the over-classification of students. This may result in increased administrative and instructional costs, greater parental expectations for programming, and the increased likelihood of litigation.

When a student's limitation qualifies as a disability, it still is necessary to determine whether he or she is *otherwise qualified*. At the PK–12 level, children qualify if they are of school age, or if they are eligible for disability services under either state law or the Individuals with Disabilities Education Act (IDEA).[7] Students who qualify under Section 504, but not under the IDEA (e.g., general education children who are wheelchair confined) need to be provided with accommodation plans that will include individualized aids and services that allow participation in the recipient's program.[8] The programs must be delivered in accessible facilities,[9] and programming must be designed and selected to meet the needs of students with disabilities to the same extent that their nondisabled peers' needs are met. Furthermore, children with disabilities should not be segregated from other children unless in the rare instance appropriate services cannot otherwise be provided in the general education classroom. Where such segregation exists, programs must be comparable in materials, facilities, teacher quality, length of school term, and daily hours of instruction.

When the school district and the parents disagree on whether an appropriate education has been provided, the parents have the right to review records, participate in an impartial hearing, and be represented by counsel. Section 504 is not specific about the procedures that must be followed, but does acknowledge the rights to notice and a hearing comparable

---

[6]Major life activities include caring for oneself, performing manual tasks, walking, seeing, hearing, speaking, breathing, learning, working. *See* 34 C.F.R. § 104.3(j)(2)(ii) (2008).

[7]34 C.F.R. § 104.3(l)(2) (2008).

[8]Furthermore, it is the position of the Office for Civil Rights that a student who qualifies under the IDEA is not entitled also to receive a plan formulated consistent with the provisions of § 504. Response to McKethan, 25 IDELR 295 (OCR 1996).

[9]34 C.F.R. § 104.22 (2008). To comply, a recipient need not make each existing facility or every part of a facility accessible, but must operate its programs so that they are accessible to individuals with disabilities.

to those mandated under the IDEA. In addition, parents have the right to file a complaint with the Office for Civil Rights within 180 days of the alleged discrimination. If the school district fails to correct its discriminatory practices, federal funds may be terminated. Moreover, there is a private right of action under Section 504, although IDEA exhaustion requirements have to be met if the relief sought also is available under the IDEA, and damage awards are available where bad faith or gross misjudgment is found in failing to provide accommodations and modifications.[10]

Americans with Disabilities Act

In 1990, Congress passed the Americans with Disabilities Act (ADA).[11] Two titles of that act are of particular importance to students with disabilities: Title II applies to public schools and Title III applies to those that are private. Like Section 504, these titles prohibit discrimination against persons (birth to death) who are disabled. Unlike Section 504, the ADA requires compliance of schools that do not receive federal aid and were not previously federally regulated.

Individuals with Disabilities Education Act

Two years after the passage of the Rehabilitation Act, and 15 years before the passage of the ADA, Part B of the Education of the Handicapped Act was amended by Public Law 94-142. This law, now known as the Individuals with Disabilities Education Act (IDEA),[12] is enforced by the Office of Special Education Programs. States, but not local school districts, have the option of declining IDEA funds, thereby avoiding the myriad compliance requirements. However, states still are required to address the needs of students with disabilities as stipulated in Section 504. All states currently participate in the IDEA financial assistance program.

To qualify for services, a child must be mentally retarded, hard of hearing, deaf, speech or language impaired, visually impaired, blind, emotionally disturbed, orthopedically impaired, autistic, other health impaired, learning disabled, or suffer from traumatic brain injury, *and*, as a result, be in need of special education and related services.[13] Accordingly, it is possible to have a disability but not be in need of special education and, therefore, not qualify for services under the IDEA. Although a child must qualify as "disabled" under one or more of the these categories for the state and district to receive federal funding, it is not necessary to label the child to provide an individualized education program.[14] It is important, however, for the child's needs to be correctly identified and for those needs to be properly addressed.

---

[10]Smith v. Special Sch. Dist. No. 1, 184 F.3d 764 (8th Cir. 1999).

[11]42 U.S.C. §§ 12101–12213 (2008).

[12]20 U.S.C. § 1400 *et seq.* (2008). Revisions of the IDEA at times are referred to as Public Law 94-142, IDEA '97, or IDEA '04 (also known as the Individuals with Disabilities Education Improvement Act (IDEIA)). The name of the law itself, however, has not changed in recent years and will be referred to as the Individuals with Disabilities Education Act.

[13]20 U.S.C. § 1401(3)(A) (2008). Not all children with special needs will qualify as disabled.

[14]20 U.S.C. § 1412 (a)(3)(B) (2008).

The IDEA remains the primary law under which a free appropriate public education (FAPE) is challenged and as a result generates most of the student-disability case law. In the following sections, several of the most important and heavily litigated areas of the IDEA are reviewed.

INDIVIDUALIZED EDUCATION PROGRAMS

Individualized education programs must be designed to provide the child with some educational benefit and be made available in the neighborhood school when appropriate and desirable.

The process of preparing and delivering an appropriate program begins when a child with a disability is identified and ends only when the child withdraws or graduates from school, fails to qualify for services, or reaches the age of 21. To begin this process, the child is identified and evaluated; then an individualized education program (IEP) is written and a placement is prepared.

Initial Identification

Under IDEA's "child find" mandate, states are required to identify, locate, and evaluate all[15] resident children with disabilities (including those who are homeless, limited English proficient, or wards of the state), regardless of the severity of their disability or whether they attend public or private schools.[16] Although federal law requires that children with disabilities be identified, it does not dictate how this is to occur. Nevertheless, courts give deference to districts when their efforts are substantial, in good faith, and ultimately effective.

The screening process may necessitate the use of tests that are administered to all children, not simply those students suspected of having disabilities. Prior to testing, parents must be given notice that identifies the tests to be used and provides a general explanation of their intended purpose. Educators, however, need not acquire consent at this time. When these initial referral and screening efforts have been completed, children potentially in need of special education ideally will be identified and will require additional evaluation.

Evaluation

Next, school districts are responsible for evaluating further those children residing in their respective service areas who may qualify for special education, given referrals or the results of preliminary exams. Although state residency laws vary, generally children who physically live in the district's service area with a custodial parent, legal guardian, or foster parent; are emancipated minors; or have reached the age of majority and live apart from their parents will qualify as "residents."

---

[15]No child with a disability is to be denied an appropriate program ("zero reject"). *See* 20 U.S.C. § 1412(a)(2) (2008). Marcover, the IDEA requires services for children birth to age 21.

[16]20 U.S.C. § 1412(a)(3)(A) (2008); 20 U.S.C. § 1412(a)(10)(A)(ii) (2008).

Prior to placement of a child with disabilities, the IDEA requires the performance of a multifactored evaluation using a variety of technically sound assessment tools and strategies to gather information related to the child's academic, functional, and developmental abilities. No single criterion or procedure may be used to determine a child's eligibility or placement. Assessments must be validated for the purposes they are used, administered by qualified personnel, selected and employed in ways that neither racially nor culturally discriminate, given in accordance with the producer's instructions, and made available in the child's native language or other mode of communication.[17]

Notice must be provided to the parents that the district intends to conduct an evaluation of their child. It must describe any assessments the district proposes to conduct (including each procedure, test, record, or report that will be used), as well as any other relevant information. Generally, informed parental consent[18] must be acquired prior to personalized testing for either an initial evaluation or reevaluation,[19] but consent is not required for curricular, state, or districtwide assessments. However, **if a parent refuses consent for the initial evaluation, or fails to respond to the request to provide consent, the district may undertake due process to authorize an evaluation.**[20] If the hearing officer supports the district's request to perform an assessment, or if reassessment is needed to determine the appropriateness of a contested current placement, the parents are required to make the child available.[21]

When either parental consent is provided or authorization is acquired from a hearing officer, the IEP team and other qualified professionals are responsible for reviewing existing data on the child, including evaluations and information provided by the parents, current classroom-based assessments, and observations by teachers and related services providers.[22] The IEP team then can identify what additional information, if any, is needed. After all relevant input has been aggregated, the team must ascertain whether the child qualifies as disabled and, if so, whether special education and related services will be required. The team should determine the child's present level of academic achievement and developmental needs, and project whether any additions or modifications to the instruction or services are necessary to enable the child to meet measurable annual goals and to participate, as appropriate, in the general education curriculum.[23]

If parents are dissatisfied with the original evaluation or resulting placement decision, they have the right to request an independent second evaluation. The public school pays for the additional evaluation, unless officials contest the need for reassessment

---

[17]20 U.S.C. § 1414(b)(2), (3) (2008).

[18]20 U.S.C. § 1414(a)(1)(D)(i)(I) (2008).

[19]*But see* Shelby S. *ex rel.* Kathleen T. v. Conroe Indep. Sch. Dist., 454 F.3d 450 (5th Cir. 2006) (determining that the district was within its right to reevaluate a child, notwithstanding a lack of parental consent, where such reevaluation was critical to the district preparing an appropriate IEP), *cert. denied*, 127 S. Ct. 936 (2007).

[20]20 U.S.C. § 1414(a)(1)(D)(ii)(I) (2008).

[21]Loren F. v. Atlanta Indep. Sch. Sys., 349 F.3d 1309 (11th Cir. 2003) (observing that the lower court in reaching its decision may consider the delays caused by the parents as well as their failure to make their child available for evaluation).

[22]20 U.S.C. § 1414(c)(1)(A) (2008).

[23]20 U.S.C. § 1414(c)(1)(B) (2008).

through due process or the evaluation already obtained by the parents does not meet district criteria.[24] When the district elects to challenge payment for a second evaluation, it must be prepared to demonstrate that all procedures and appropriate professional practices were followed. If the impartial hearing officer rules in favor of the district, and that decision is not appealed, the parents still may acquire a second, independent evaluation but must pay for it. When additional evaluations are acquired, school personnel are required to consider their results but are not required to follow them.[25]

The 2004 amendments to the IDEA were in part designed to reduce the number of evaluations, the frequency of IEP meetings, and the amount of overall paperwork. Generally, placements must be reviewed annually, or more often as appropriate, and a reevaluation must be performed every three years. However, a reevaluation is not required if the IEP team determines that it is unnecessary, in whole or in part, unless requested by the child's parent. Even when parents make routine requests for reevaluation, they need not be performed more than once per year, unless the district agrees.[26] When a reevaluation supports amendment to the IEP, the IDEA permits the district to make the necessary changes without conducting a full IEP team meeting, if it acquires parental approval.[27]

IEP Team

The school district, through its IEP teams, is responsible for determining whether children qualify under the IDEA for services and, if so, for designing appropriate, least restrictive placements. The team includes:

- The parents or a surrogate,
- Not less than one general and one special education teacher,
- A representative of the local educational agency who is qualified to provide or supervise specially designed instruction and is knowledgeable about the general education curriculum and available resources,
- An individual who can interpret instructional implications of evaluation results,
- Other individuals with special knowledge or expertise, and
- The child, if appropriate.[28]

Some committees consist of 10 or more participants, but all need not be present at every meeting. Excusal is permitted when the parents consent and those members not attending have the opportunity to submit their input in writing prior to the meeting.[29] Failure to acquire written consent, particularly for removal of the general education teacher,

[24]34 C.F.R. § 300.502(a)(1), (b) (2008).

[25]34 C.F.R. § 300.502(c)(1) (2008).

[26]20 U.S.C. § 1414(a)(2)(B)(i) (2008).

[27]20 U.S.C. § 1414(d)(3)(D) (2008).

[28]20 U.S.C. § 1414(d)(1)(B) (2008).

[29]20 U.S.C. § 1414(d)(1)(C) (2008).

has been found to be so significant as to result in an IDEA violation and an inappropriate placement.[30]

IEP Preparation

The parents must agree to the IEP meeting time and location, and the district must ensure that the parents have the opportunity to participate fully, which may require hiring foreign-language translators or sign-language interpreters.[31] Participation may be accomplished through videoconferencing and conference calls when necessary. If no parent is available or willing to attend, school officials should document each effort to encourage parental involvement.

In preparation for the first IEP meeting, the district may elect to prepare a tentative IEP as a basis for discussion. This initial IEP should be presented as a draft and in no way should be represented as final.[32] When agreement is ultimately reached, the IEP should:

- Record the child's present level of academic achievement and functional performance;
- State measurable annual goals;
- Note how performance will be measured and communicated to parents;
- Identify special education, related services, supplementary aids and services, and transition services (beginning at age 16) to be provided;
- Explain the extent, if any, to which the child will not be included in general education activities;
- Specify any accommodations that will be made in performing state or district assessments (or an explanation of why alternate assessments are necessary);
- Describe benchmarks or short-term objectives for children taking alternate assessments;
- Identify the date to initiate services;
- Project the frequency, location,[33] and duration of services; and
- Provide a statement indicating that students have been familiarized with their IDEA rights and informed that such rights transfer to them at the age of majority[34] (except when the student is found to be incompetent under state law).[35]

---

[30]M.L. v. Fed. Way Sch. Dist., 394 F.3d 634 (9th Cir. 2004). *But see* Sanford v. Birmingham Pub. Schs., 70 Fed. App'x 295, 297 (6th Cir. 2003) (finding that the absence of the physician was not fatal to the challenged IEP).

[31]However, this right to participate does not extend to preparatory meetings conducted by the local school district to generate proposals to be discussed with the parents at a later IEP meeting. *In re* D., 32 IDELR 103 (SEA CT, 2000).

[32]*See, e.g.*, Deal v. Hamilton County Bd. of Educ., 392 F.3d 840 (6th Cir. 2004) (determining that the district violated the IDEA by predetermining the child's placement prior to parental involvement and by failing to involve a general education teacher in several relevant discussions).

[33]According to the Fourth Circuit, this requirement includes the obligation to identify the particular school at which the child is to be educated. *See* A.K. v. Alexandria City Sch. Bd., 484 F.3d 672 (4th Cir. 2007).

[34]20 U.S.C. § 1414(d)(1)(A) (2008).

[35]20 U.S.C. § 1415(m)(1) (2008).

Also contributing to the effort to be more cost and time efficient is the provision that requires districts to accept existing IEPs for students who move into the local service area during the school year. The receiving district must provide services comparable to those identified by the former district, whether in state or out of state. This placement should be continued until the district has evaluated the child and developed a new IEP consistent with IDEA procedures.[36]

Free Appropriate Public Education

Once agreement has been reached on the IEP, district personnel must prepare the actual placement and coordinate needed services. Parental consent again is required. Unlike the evaluation phase, however, if the parents refuse the initial placement proposed by the district, educators are not permitted to seek authorization through due process. But if the parents reject a placement, the district is not in violation of the IDEA and is not required to convene an IEP meeting or prepare a placement.[37]

Where consent is provided, **all children ages 3 through 21 with qualifying disabilities must be provided a free appropriate public education that is made available in the least restrictive environment.**[38] The placement must address the unique needs of the child and be delivered by "highly qualified" instructors.[39] Moreover, to qualify as appropriate, the placement must:

- Be provided at public expense and under public supervision and direction (even if the school district selects a private school placement),
- Meet the standards of the state educational agency,
- Include an appropriate preschool, elementary school, or secondary school education, and
- Be delivered in conformity with the IEP.[40]

As needed, students also must be provided supplementary aids and services in the general education classroom to enable children with disabilities to be educated with nondisabled children to the maximum extent appropriate;[41] services to assist in transitioning from school to postschool activities such as postsecondary education, vocational training, integrated employment, continuing and adult education, adult services, independent living, or community participation;[42] and assistive technology devices and services to

---

[36]20 U.S.C. § 1414(d)(2)(C)(i) (2008).

[37]20 U.S.C. § 1414(a)(1)(D)(ii)(II), (III) (2008).

[38]This is true unless students ages 3 to 5 and 18 through 21 are not served within the state. *See* 20 U.S.C. § 1412(a)(1)(B) (2008).

[39]*Highly qualified* is defined in § 9109 of the Elementary and Secondary Education Act of 1965 (20 U.S.C. § 7801 (2008)).

[40]20 U.S.C. § 1401(9) (2008).

[41]20 U.S.C. § 1401(33) (2008).

[42]20 U.S.C. § 1401(34) (2008).

enable the child to increase, maintain, or improve functional capabilities.[43] Moreover, special education and related services should be made available as soon as possible following completion of the IEP, although no specific time line is identified in the IDEA.[44] When services are prepared, they must be provided as close to the child's home as possible, and preferably in the school the child would have attended if not disabled. But it is not realistic to assume that all programs can be made available in every neighborhood school.

Even though IEPs must be "appropriate," they need not be "the best" available or represent "optimum" programs that will maximize learning potential. This issue was addressed in 1982 in *Board of Education v. Rowley*,[45] in which parents had requested that the school district provide a sign-language interpreter for their daughter in her academic classes, given her minimal residual hearing. The child's IEP specified a general education first grade placement with special instruction from a tutor one hour per day and a speech therapist three hours per week, but did not include interpreter services. An interpreter had been provided during a two-week period when she was in kindergarten, but the practice was discontinued based on recommendations by the interpreter and other educators working with the child. Because of this omission, the parents were dissatisfied with the IEP and, after unsuccessful administrative review, filed suit.

On appeal, the Supreme Court rejected the standard proposed by the lower court (i.e., maximization of the potential of children with disabilities commensurate with the opportunity provided to other children[46]) and reasoned that "the intent of the act was more to open the door of public education to [children with disabilities] on appropriate terms than to guarantee any particular level of education once inside."[47] The IDEA was found to guarantee a "basic floor of opportunity,"[48] consisting of access to specialized instruction and related services that are individually designed to provide educational benefit. Applying these principles, the Court held that the plaintiff was receiving an appropriate education in that she was incurring educational benefit from individualized instruction and related services, as evidenced by her better-than-average performance in class, promotion from grade to grade, and positive interpersonal relationships with educators and peers.

The Court also made clear that lower courts are not to define an appropriate education. Rather, their review is limited to two questions:

- **Has the state complied with the procedures identified in the IDEA?**
- **Is the IEP developed through these procedures reasonably calculated to enable the child to receive educational benefit?**[49]

Lower courts have interpreted this latter requirement to mandate educational programs that provide more than "trivial advancement."[50]

[43]20 U.S.C. § 1401(1), (2) (2008).

[44]*See, e.g.*, D.D. v. N.Y. City Bd. of Educ., 465 F.3d 503 (2d Cir. 2006).

[45]458 U.S. 176 (1982).

[46]483 F. Supp. 528, 534 (S.D.N.Y. 1980).

[47]458 U.S. 176, 192 (1982).

[48]*Id.* at 200.

[49]*Id.* at 207.

[50]*See, e.g.*, Ridgewood Bd. of Educ. v. N.E. *ex rel.* M.E., 172 F.3d 238 (3d Cir. 1999).

Courts often defer to state and local educators and administrative review officials regarding the nature of IEPs and matters of pedagogy but still will not uphold proposed placements that are found inappropriate and not supported by the data. In such situations, courts have not been reluctant to direct the development of an appropriate public placement, or to approve a private one. For example, the Ninth Circuit concluded that a California school district failed to provide an appropriate education by placing a child with autism in a program for the "communicatively handicapped." The court noted that the program was not individualized, the student's needs were not being met, and the teacher was not trained to work with autistic children.[51] The district was required to reimburse the parents for the costs of an out-of-district placement, including expenses associated with commuting, lodging, and tuition, as well as attorneys' fees.

Least Restrictive Environment

Children with disabilities are to be educated with children who are not disabled to the maximum extent appropriate. Special classes, separate schooling, or other removal of a child from general education may occur only if the nature or severity of the disability is to the extent that education cannot be achieved satisfactorily.[52] In making least restrictive environment (LRE) decisions, school personnel should determine the types of placements for delivery of the IEP along the continuum of alternative placements and then select the option that is least restrictive. Alternative placements may include:

- A general education classroom with various support services,
- A general education classroom with or without itinerant teachers or resource rooms,
- Self-contained special classes,
- Special schools,
- Home instruction, or
- Instruction in hospitals or residential institutions.[53]

Educational and noneducational benefits for each placement should be assessed, including the effect the child with a disability may have on classmates.[54]

---

[51]Union Sch. Dist. v. Smith, 15 F.3d 1519 (9th Cir. 1994). *But see* M.M. v. Sch. Bd. Miami-Dade County, 437 F.3d 1085 (11th Cir. 2006) (finding that the IDEA does not require that the best program be provided and that the methods employed by the district to address plaintiff's severe bilateral sensorial hearing loss provided an appropriate program).

[52]20 U.S.C. § 1412 (a)(5)(A) (2008). *See* L.E. v. Ramsey Bd. of Educ., 435 F.3d 384 (3d Cir. 2006) (upholding lower court determination that the general education classroom, even with supplemental aids and services, could not provide plaintiff with an appropriate education).

[53]34 C.F.R. § 300.115(b) (2008). If the parents elect not to have their child medicated while at school, the student may not be denied an appropriate placement because of not being medicated. The selection of services and the determination of the least restrictive environment may be affected, however. *See* 20 U.S.C. §1412(a)(25) (2008).

[54]*See* Alex R. v. Forrestville Valley Cmty. Unit Sch. Dist. #221, 375 F.3d 603 (7th Cir. 2004) (upholding the lower court's determination that consideration of a child's regular outbursts and physical attacks of others in identifying the LRE was appropriate).

General education with supplemental aids and services represents the LRE for most children; for a few, however, the LRE will be in a setting that is more restrictive.[55] The IEP team need not select a placement that is entirely in general education or entirely segregated. In some instances it is appropriate to deliver the child's program within a range of LRE settings (e.g., a segregated program to assist in the development of lipreading, but a general education setting for other instructional and noninstructional activities).[56] States are responsible for ensuring that teachers and administrators are fully informed about their LRE responsibilities and for providing them with technical assistance and training.[57]

Moreover, children should not be placed experimentally in the general classroom under the guise of full inclusion,[58] and then provided appropriate placements only after they fail to meet objectives or acquire educational benefit. Inappropriate placements may require the unnecessary expenditure of thousands of dollars, violate the child's right to a free appropriate public education, and, most important, delay the provision of truly appropriate and beneficial education.

Private Schools

Many children with disabilities attend private schools. Some are placed in a private program by the public school district, given the availability of an appropriate program. Other children attend private schools because of parental preference given factors such as the nature of the curriculum, program quality, religious orientation, and convenience.

Public Placement of a Child in a Private School. The IDEA does not necessarily require creation of new programs if a school district cannot effectively address specific individual student needs, appropriate programs are not available within a child's reasonable commute, or existing programs are not age appropriate.[59] In the alternative, placement often may be made in other public schools or in private facilities, including those that are residential. Although the fiscal obligation can be substantial, the school district will be held financially responsible for residential placements that are required to provide an appropriate program. In such instances, the district must cover all nonmedical costs, including room and board. The IDEA's provision for residential care, however, is not intended to compensate for a poor home environment or to serve as a means of delivering social, medical, or incarceration services. Accordingly, if a residential placement is sought by the parents for reasons other than the child's education (e.g., the risk the child poses at home, the inability to shelter or feed the youth, the student being the target of a parent's abuse), then the request may be denied.

---

[55]*See* Beth B. v. van Clay, 282 F.3d 493 (7th Cir. 2002) (supporting selection of a placement that was more restrictive than general education as the child's academic progress was virtually nonexistent and her developmental progress was limited within general education).

[56]*See, e.g.*, Brillon v. Klein Indep. Sch. Dist., 100 Fed. Appx 309 (5th Cir. 2004).

[57]34 C.F.R. § 300.119 (2008).

[58]The term *full inclusion* is used here to refer to placement in general education where the child's educational needs are appropriately addressed through the use of supplemental aids and services.

[59]*See, e.g.*, T.R. *ex rel.* N.R. v. Kingwood Township Bd. of Educ., 205 F.3d 572 (3d Cir. 2000).

When the public school system selects a private placement, a representative of the private school should participate in IEP placement meetings either in person or through a telephone conversation. Subsequent meetings to review and revise the IEP may be initiated and conducted by private school personnel, if approved by district officials. When this occurs, both the parents and a public school representative must be involved in any decision about the child's IEP, and the district must authorize any change prior to implementation. It is important to note that **private schools are not required to implement special programs or to lower their academic standards to permit placement of children with disabilities.**[60] Applicants who cannot participate effectively in the private school's general education curriculum, assuming the availability of "minor adjustments," may be denied admission.

Parental Placement of a Child in a Private School.   In some instances, parents elect to place their children in private schools, either initially or when they perceive public programs to be inappropriate.[61] **Parents always have the option of selecting an alternative program, but such placements will be at parental expense unless the parents can show that the public placement is inappropriate and that their selected placement is appropriate.**

The Supreme Court addressed this issue in 1985 in *School Committee of Burlington v. Department of Education of Massachusetts*.[62] A father had disagreed with the school district's proposed educational placement of his child with learning disabilities and, after seeking an independent evaluation from medical experts and initiating the appeals process, enrolled the child in a private school. The Court rejected the school district's argument that a change in placement without district consent waived all rights to reimbursement. In the Court's opinion, denying relief would defeat the IDEA's major objective of providing an appropriate program. When the school district's proposed placement is ultimately found to be inappropriate, reimbursement is considered necessary since the review process can be quite lengthy. The Court reasoned that children should not be educationally disadvantaged by an inappropriate placement and that parents should not be economically penalized for removing their children.

The Supreme Court, however, issued one caveat: parents who unilaterally seek private placements do so at their own financial risk. If the public school placement is found to be proper, reimbursement will be denied, even if the parentally selected program is shown to be appropriate, better, or even cheaper.[63] Furthermore, reimbursement will be denied when both the public and private placements are shown to be inappropriate.[64] Thus, relief

---

[60]St. Johnsbury Acad. v. D.H., 240 F.3d 163 (2d Cir. 2001).

[61]*Compare* Bd. of Educ. of City of N.Y. v. Tom F., 193 Fed. App'x 26 (2d Cir. 2006) (noting that 20 U.S.C. § 1412(a)(10)(C)(i) did not require reimbursement where children had not previously received special education under public school supervision), *affirmed by an equally divided court,* 128 S. Ct. 1 (2007) *with* Frank G. v. Bd. of Educ., 459 F.3d 356 (2d Cir. 2006) (concluding that prior receipt of services under public supervision is not necessary to seek reimbursement; all that is required is reasonable notice and the intent to reject the proposed placement), *cert. denied,* 128 S. Ct. 436 (2007).

[62]471 U.S. 359 (1985).

[63]L.T. v. Warwick Sch. Comm., 361 F.3d 80 (1st Cir. 2004) (finding the district's proffered placement to be appropriate and noting that the inquiry ends at that point so there is no need to consider whether the program preferred by the parents would be better).

[64]M.S. v. Yonkers Bd. of Educ., 231 F.3d 96 (2d Cir. 2000).

can be acquired only if the public placement is inappropriate and the private placement is appropriate.[65]

A subsequent Supreme Court decision in 1993, *Florence County School District Four v. Carter*, gave additional support to parents seeking reimbursement for private placements.[66] In that case, a child with a learning disability was removed by her parents from what was proven to be an inappropriate public placement and enrolled in an appropriate private program. Controversy developed when the parents sought reimbursement but were denied because the private school was not included on the state-approved list—a list that was not made available to the public, as the district preferred to evaluate each case individually. The Court held that reimbursement could not be denied simply because the school was not state approved. The touchstone was that the public program was inappropriate, while the unilaterally selected program was appropriate. As a result, the reimbursement of reasonable costs was required.

Parental choices are not always found either reasonable or appropriate, however. For example, the Eleventh Circuit upheld a lower court decision denying reimbursement, as the student had been provided an IEP that was reasonably calculated to confer an appropriate education. A parentally requested residential placement was found to be both unnecessary and not least restrictive. The court also rejected the opinion of an expert hired by the parents who had indicated that the family needed someone to take care of their son in their home, because family members had responsibilities other than caretaker and teacher.[67] In another case, the parents sued a school district for failure to provide their child with an appropriate education, notwithstanding the out-of-state placement of the child in a private residential facility and payment for three round-trips home for the child to visit. The parents were demanding that the district pay transportation costs (including airfare for both parents and two siblings), hotel, food, and rental car expenses so that they could visit the child. The court acknowledged that the IEP encouraged the development of family relations, but ruled that the district was not required to "foot the bill for family gatherings."[68]

In an effort to limit district liability for private placements unilaterally selected by parents, the IDEA permits reduction or denial of reimbursement if the parents fail to provide public officials with notification of their intent or if a court finds their conduct unreasonable.[69] Proper notification can be accomplished either by discussing the matter with the IEP team during a formal meeting or by providing the district with written notice, including an explanation of the reasons for the decision, at least 10 days prior to the projected removal of the child. At that point, if the district elects to perform additional student evaluations, then the parent is required to make the child available.

---

[65]*Compare* Montgomery Township Bd. of Educ. v. S.C., 135 Fed. App'x 534 (3d Cir. 2005) (upholding reimbursement for unilaterally selected private education) *with* Houston Indep. Sch. Dist. v. Bobby R., 200 F.3d 341 (5th Cir. 2000) (denying reimbursement for a placement unilaterally selected by the parent given that the district had provided the student with a FAPE that was reasonably calculated to provide educational benefit as evidenced by increased test scores in a range of areas).

[66]510 U.S. 7 (1993).

[67]Devine v. Indian River County Sch. Bd., 249 F.3d 1289 (11th Cir. 2001).

[68]Cohen v. Sch. Bd., 450 So. 2d 1238, 1240 (Fla. Dist. Ct. App. 1984).

[69]*See, e.g.,* Loren F. v. Atlanta Indep. Sch. Sys., 349 F.3d 1309 (11th Cir. 2003).

Services Available in Private Schools.   Students enrolled by their parents in private schools have no individual right to receive special education and related services provided by the school district.[70] Instead, public officials are responsible for meeting with parents and other representatives of the children to decide who is to receive services; what, where, and how services are to be provided; and how services are to be evaluated. In selecting a site for the delivery of services, officials will consider available alternative delivery systems as well as whether provision on campus (e.g., at a religious school) violates state law. If off-campus delivery is selected, eligible children must be transported from the private school to the site and back or to their home.

Funding for private school services is provided in the IDEA at a per-pupil prorated amount equal to the federal funds spent on IEP services provided to children in the public school district.[71] This amount is modest, however, when compared to the dollars contributed by state and local governments. As a result, services that are made available to children enrolled in private schools will tend to be fewer in number or for shorter time periods than those available to children placed or served by the local school district.[72] When parents with children in private schools have challenged this disparity as a violation of the Equal Protection Clause or the Free Exercise Clause, they have been unsuccessful.[73]

Change of Placement

Following an appropriate initial placement in a public or private school, adjustments to a child's IEP may be necessary because of the results of an annual review or reevaluation; discontinuation of a school, program, or service; violent or disruptive behavior; or graduation. Before changing a substantive aspect of a student's program, written notice must be given to the parents of their right to review the proposed alteration, and informed consent generally must be provided. However, if the parent does not respond to efforts to communicate, district personnel should document the date and type of each effort and then may proceed to deliver the program as amended.[74] If the parents later contact the district, they may challenge the placement decision through due process.

■ ■ ■ ■ ■ ■

RELATED SERVICES

When related services are found to be essential elements of a free appropriate public education under the IDEA, they must be provided regardless of cost.

---

[70]Foley v. Special Sch. Dist., 153 F.3d 863 (8th Cir. 1998).

[71]20 U.S.C. § 1412(a)(10)(A)(i)(I) (2008).

[72]*See* Jasa v. Millard Pub. Sch. Dist. No. 17, 206 F.3d 813 (8th Cir. 2000) (concluding that the district had provided the child with a FAPE and need not fund the same services in a private school unilaterally selected by the parents).

[73]*See, e.g.*, Gary S. v. Manchester Sch. Dist., 374 F.3d 15 (1st Cir. 2004).

[74]20 U.S.C. § 1414(c)(3) (2008).

A free appropriate public education may include related services in addition to special education. *Related services* are defined as transportation and such developmental, corrective, and other supportive services (including speech pathology and audiology, psychological services, physical and occupational therapy, recreation, social work services, early identification and assessment, orientation and mobility services, school health services, counseling services, medical services for diagnostic and evaluation purposes, parent counseling and training, school nurse services, and interpreting services) that are necessary for a child with a disability to benefit from special education.[75] The areas of transportation, psychological services, and health services are reviewed briefly here.

Transportation

Federal regulations require the provision of transportation as a related service for qualified children to and from school, within school buildings, and on school grounds, even if specialized equipment is needed in making programs and activities accessible. A child qualifies for transportation if it is provided for other children or included within an IEP or Section 504 plan. Failure to provide the service to qualified students has resulted in courts requiring districts to reimburse parents for transportation costs, time, effort, baby-sitting services, and interest accrued on their expenses. Nonetheless, courts also have concluded that when alternative transportation was provided, the district was not required to reimburse parents who wanted to transport their own child;[76] that a child's hearing impairment did not qualify her for special transportation;[77] and that transportation did not have to be provided following involvement in a privately funded after-school program that was unrelated to the IEP.[78]

Psychological Services

Psychological services are explicitly identified in federal law as related services to be included within IEPs when appropriate. Such services include:

- Administering and interpreting psychological and educational tests as well as other assessment procedures,
- Obtaining, integrating, and interpreting information about the child's behavior and condition,
- Consulting with staff in planning IEPs,
- Planning and managing a program of psychological services, and
- Assisting in the development of positive behavioral intervention strategies.[79]

When psychological services are needed to enable the child to benefit from instruction and are provided by a psychologist or other qualified individual, the services should be included

---

[75] 20 U.S.C. § 1401(a)(26) (2008).

[76] DeLeon v. Susquehanna Cmty. Sch. Dist., 747 F.2d 149 (3d Cir. 1984).

[77] McNair v. Oak Hills Local Sch. Dist., 872 F.2d 153 (6th Cir. 1989).

[78] Roslyn Union Free Sch. Dist. v. Univ. of N.Y., 711 N.Y.S.2d 582 (App. Div. 2000).

[79] 34 C.F.R. § 300.34(c)(10) (2008).

within the IEP. However, if parents request psychiatric and other medical services,[80] or if psychological services are not required to provide a free appropriate public education (FAPE),[81] such requests may be denied.

Health and Nursing Services

Courts have differentiated between medical and health services. As indicated, the IDEA excludes medical services except for diagnostic and evaluative purposes and defines both medical (i.e., those provided by a licensed physician) and health services (i.e., those provided by a school nurse or other qualified person). Health services such as catheterization often are essential in that they enable the child to attend school and thereby benefit from instruction.[82] Nevertheless, the issue of health care has been volatile, given the growing number of medically fragile children now in public schools, the desire of many parents to have their health-impaired child integrated into general education, and the escalating costs of health care.

In *Cedar Rapids Community School District v. Garret F.*,[83] a child had a severed spinal column and was paralyzed from the neck down. To remain in school, he required full-time nursing care (e.g., catheterization, suctioning, ventilator assistance, emergency aid). The school district argued that the services collectively should be viewed as medical, even if individually they qualified as health services, and asserted that it would incur an undue financial burden if required to provide the full-time nursing care. The Court acknowledged the legitimate budgetary concerns of the district, but noted that the IDEA does not allow schools to refuse to pay for services simply because of the financial burden.[84] Moreover, by applying the bright-line test, **the Court ruled that any health service a student may need to participate in a school setting[85] had to be provided, regardless of cost or resulting financial impact on the district.**

EXTENDED SCHOOL YEAR

Federal statutes require that IEPs be both appropriate and designed to provide educational benefit. In meeting these mandates, it may be necessary for a particular child to receive services beyond the traditional nine-month school year. While school districts can prescribe a fixed number of instructional days for students without disabilities, such a determination must be made on an individual basis for children with disabilities. Nonetheless, when extended school year (ESY) services are found "beneficial" or even "maximizing," but are not "essential" to the provision of an appropriate program, they are not required under the

[80]Butler v. Evans, 225 F.3d 887 (7th Cir. 2000).

[81]Nack v. Orange City Sch. Dist., 454 F.3d 604 (6th Cir. 2006).

[82]Irving Indep. Sch. Dist. v. Tatro, 468 U.S. 883 (1984).

[83]526 U.S. 66 (1999).

[84]Although unavailable under the IDEA, the undue burden defense is available under both § 504 and the ADA.

[85]However, some health care services do not have to be provided when the child is home bound. *See, e.g.*, Daniel O. v. Mo. State Bd. of Educ., No. 99-2792, 2000 U.S. App. LEXIS 7032 (8th Cir. April 19, 2000).

IDEA.[86] When ESY services are provided, programs will vary widely. Some mandate the extension of the full IEP for one, two, or three additional months, others utilize new or different services, and yet others utilize all or some of the same services, but in different amounts.[87]

Eligibility decisions should be made annually during the IEP review and be based on:

- Regression-recoupment,
- Individual need,
- The nature and severity of the disability,
- Self-sufficiency and independence,
- Whether educational benefit can be incurred without such services, and
- Whether progress is being made toward the accomplishment of goals.

Receipt of ESY services in previous years, however, is not a factor to consider in making the eligibility decision for the current year.

■ ■ ■ ■ ■

PARTICIPATION IN SPORTS

Athletic association rules that deny or limit the participation of students with disabilities must qualify as reasonable *and* reflect the essential elements of the sport.

Children with disabilities, like many children without disabilities, often are interested in participating in interscholastic sports. However, the requests of these student-athletes to participate have at times been denied because either they failed to meet eligibility requirements or their participation represented too great a risk to themselves or to others. Although most disputes are based on either the Rehabilitation Act or the Americans with Disabilities Act (ADA), a few cases have been filed under the IDEA.

The IDEA has been involved in two types of sports-related disability cases: (1) those in which parents wanted to include sports in the IEP; and (2) those in which the IEP team included sports in the IEP and the state athletic association penalized the school for allowing an ineligible student to participate. Because sports participation is seldom considered essential for students to incur educational benefit, it typically is not included in IEPs. Furthermore, from the school district's perspective, it generally is not prudent to include sports, or any other extracurricular activity, in IEPs. Such a practice establishes an entitlement to team membership (not to participation *per se*, however) and enables sports participation to become a right that can be withdrawn only through due process.

In the second scenario (i.e., in which the team is penalized), state athletic associations do not receive IDEA funds or any other type of federal financial assistance and consequently

[86]*See* Kenton County Sch. Dist. v. Hunt, 384 F.3d 269 (6th Cir. 2004) (remanding and requiring parents to bear the burden of showing that an ESY was needed to avoid something more than adequately recoupable regression and that the current IEP without ESY failed to provide an appropriate program).

[87]*See* J.H. v. Henrico County Sch. Bd., 395 F.3d 185 (4th Cir. 2005) (remanding with instructions for the lower court to have the hearing officer determine the amount of ESY services necessary for the plaintiff's speech, language, and occupational skills acquired during kindergarten not to be placed in jeopardy).

are not required to comply with either the IDEA or Section 504 (although disability discrimination suits under the ADA are possible). Accordingly, if the IEP team were to include sports in the IEP and thereby allow an otherwise ineligible student to participate in an interscholastic contest, then school officials may have created a situation that will result in rules violations and penalties. The Montana Supreme Court "strongly encouraged" educators to be prudent in including sports in IEPs and warned that they might be "making a promise [they] simply cannot keep."[88] Given this situation, the district would have to sue the athletic association (presumably under the Fourteenth Amendment[89]) to terminate whatever remedial actions have been taken against it. In the end, even if the district is to prevail, it will incur substantial expense and have to dedicate considerable personnel time to a problem that could have easily been avoided by not including sports participation in IEPs.

Unlike the IDEA, there are myriad related scenarios and cases regarding athletic participation filed under Section 504 and the ADA. Most claims have alleged discrimination based on facially neutral regulations that disproportionately affect students with disabilities, such as age limitations, grade-point average restrictions, one-year residency and transfer requirements, and eight-semester/four-season limitations. Resulting decisions have been split, even when reviewing seemingly similar claims.[90]

Historically, all students were required to meet eligibility criteria and were allowed to play only when they were otherwise qualified to participate *and* if they made the team. The courts permitted and often required the uniform application of such rules, but that trend may be changing. A related issue reviewed by the Supreme Court in a professional sport context has application to interscholastic sports. In *PGA Tour v. Martin*, the Supreme Court supported a professional golfer's request to ride a cart rather than walk the course, as the event rules required.[91] Walking caused him pain that resulted in fatigue that could lead to hemorrhaging and the development of blood clots or fractures. The Court reasoned that "shot making" was the essence of golf and that walking was neither an essential attribute nor an indispensable feature of the sport, notwithstanding contradictory testimony from golf legends Arnold Palmer, Jack Nicklaus, and Ken Venturi. This decision will have implications for all sports as it requires the evaluation of any rule that disqualifies an otherwise qualified participant with a disability. Review of such rules should reveal whether they are essential features of the sport or are peripheral and therefore subject to alteration or elimination.

---

[88]J.M. v. Mont. High Sch. Ass'n, 875 P.2d 1026, 1032 (Mont. 1994).

[89]Such suits are more likely today given the Supreme Court's ruling in Brentwood Acad. v. Tenn. Secondary Sch. Athletic Ass'n., 531 U.S. 288 (2002), in which the state athletic association was declared a state actor, notwithstanding the fact that it was a private corporation.

[90]*Compare* Washington v. Ind. High Sch. Athletic Ass'n, 181 F.3d 840 (7th Cir. 1999) (determining that a student who had dropped out of school and later reentered and played basketball should not have been declared ineligible under the rule limiting participation during the first eight semesters following commencement of the ninth grade; reasoning that waiver of the rule involving this student would not represent a fundamental alteration or create an undue burden for the association) *with* McPherson v. Mich. High Sch. Athletic Ass'n, 119 F.3d 453 (6th Cir. 1997) (upholding application of an eight-semester rule against a student with attention deficit hyperactivity disorder and a seizure disorder and concluding that its waiver would represent a fundamental alteration of the sports program and create an immense and undue financial burden for the state association).

[91]532 U.S. 661 (2001).

■ ■ ■ ■ ■ ▬

DISCIPLINE

Students with disabilities may be expelled only when it can be shown that the behavior on which the disciplinary action is based is not a manifestation of the child's disability.

Students with disabilities are not exempt from reasonable disciplinary measures. However, at times they are entitled to procedural protections beyond those provided general education students. Also, punishments for children with disabilities may be limited in type and duration. The Supreme Court, in *Honig v. Doe*, held that **an indefinite suspension of two students pending the outcome of expulsion proceedings was a prohibited change in placement and violated the stay-put provision of the IDEA.**[92] The state superintendent of public instruction had urged the Supreme Court to recognize a "dangerousness" exception to the stay-put requirement. Notwithstanding, the Court stated that Congress deliberately stripped schools of the unilateral authority to exclude students with disabilities. The history of exclusion of such students prior to passage of the IDEA and the early litigation that guided the development of the law convinced the Court that the conspicuous absence of an emergency exception was intentional.

The Supreme Court, however, emphasized that school officials are not without options when confronted with a dangerous student. They may use a range of normal procedures (e.g., suspension of up to 10 days, detention, time-out[93]). In addition, the Court indicated that if other forms of discipline are not successful, and the student already has been suspended for the maximum 10-day period but continues to pose a threat, school officials may seek injunctive relief if the parents refuse to agree to a change in placement.

Among the disciplinary options available to school officials, suspension and expulsion have resulted in considerable judicial action. Each is reviewed here in greater detail.

Suspension

The IDEA allows school officials to consider unique circumstances on a case-by-case basis in suspending students with disabilities if there has been a violation of the student conduct code. When officials determine that a *suspension* (i.e., removal of a student from the educational setting for 10 or fewer days) is justified, no procedures beyond those provided for general education students are required. The resulting suspension may be either an in-school assignment to a suspension room or out-of-school, requiring the complete removal from the school setting. **Students with disabilities may not generally be suspended for more than 10 consecutive days or receive repetitive brief suspensions that aggregate to more than 10 days during the school year.** Successive suspensions exceeding the 10-day

---

[92]484 U.S. 305 (1988).

[93]Not all assignment to time-out will be found legal, however. *See, e.g.*, Covington v. Knox County Sch. Sys., 205 F.3d 912 (6th Cir. 2000) (observing that plaintiff had been routinely locked in a small time-out room for up to several hours at a time, denied lunch, required to disrobe on one occasion, and forced to remain in the room following urination that resulted when the confinement period was lengthy).

limit are possible, but only when they do not represent a pattern of removal and are based on separate incidents of misconduct. In the comparatively exceptional circumstance in which removal justifiably exceeds the 10-day limit, services consistent with the IEP must be provided beginning on the eleventh day.[94]

The key in determining whether a day of suspension is to apply toward the total is to assess whether the child has been removed from the IEP, not whether the child has received an in-school or out-of-school suspension. If a student is assigned to a time-out room, rather than an in-school suspension room, and instruction and/or services identified within the IEP continue to be delivered by properly credentialed individuals, it is unlikely that the time removed from the general education classroom will contribute to the 10-day limit. To reduce the likelihood of litigation, however, it is recommended that assignment to time-out be included within the IEPs of students who are likely to require such assignments as a form of behavior modification or intervention. Once the parent has agreed to such a provision, assignment to time-out will be consistent with, rather than removal from, the IEP.

Expulsion

If violations of the conduct code are excessive or severe, school officials have the authority to expel students. *Expulsion* is the removal of a student for more than 10 consecutive days. When students with disabilities are expelled, a change of placement results and procedures that exceed those required for general education students are required. In such instances, an expulsion will be justified only if the district has properly implemented the student's IEP and the contested conduct does not have a direct and substantial relationship to the student's disability.[95] When expulsion is supported, the student may be assigned either to a home placement or to an interim alternative educational setting. The student's record may include reference to the student being expelled and the basis for the expulsion. Notwithstanding the above, if the student is to be removed from his or her current placement for more than 10 days, then services consistent with the IEP need to be delivered in the new environment that will enable the student to make progress toward achieving identified goals and objectives. These services are required, regardless whether the behavior was disability related.[96] In short, **educational services cannot be terminated for children with disabilities for longer than 10 days.**

When there is a determination that the behavior is a manifestation of the student's disability,[97] the IEP team is responsible for conducting a functional behavioral assessment and for implementing a behavioral intervention plan.[98] Interventions should address the conduct that resulted in the disciplinary action and should be modified when needed. Notwithstanding, assignment to an alternative setting for up to 45 days is permissible under

[94]34 C.F.R. § 300.530(b); 34 C.F.R. § 300.536 (2008)

[95]20 U.S.C. § 1415(k)(1)(E)(i) (2008).

[96]20 U.S.C. § 1415(k)(1)(D) (2008).

[97]*See* Peter S. Latham, Patricia H. Latham, and Myrna R. Mandlawitz, *Special Education Law* (Boston: Pearson, 2008), pp. 76–77.

[98]20 U.S.C. § 1415(k)(1)(F)(i) (2008). Failure to provide such a plan can result in the denial of FAPE and an IDEA violation. *See* Metro. Bd. of Pub. Educ. v. Bellamy, 116 Fed. App'x 570 (6th Cir. 2004).

the IDEA, even when the student's behavior is disability related. This may occur only when the student has committed one of the following violations on school grounds or at a school function:

- Carries a weapon,
- Knowingly possesses, uses, sells, or solicits illegal drugs, or
- Inflicts serious bodily injury upon another.[99]

If the parents disagree with a decision to remove their child from school, they may appeal that decision to a hearing officer. Similarly, school officials may appeal when they are concerned that a student's continued presence within the school setting is substantially likely to result in injury to the student or others. The hearing officer has the authority either to return the student to the placement from which he or she was removed or to order placement to an interim alternative educational setting. The hearing should occur within 20 school days of the date of request and a decision must be provided within 10 school days after the hearing. During this period, the student remains in the current placement (i.e., the interim alternative setting), unless the removal period has expired, or the parent and district agree otherwise.[100]

Interestingly, even students who are not yet identified as disabled at times may be protected by the IDEA, but only if school officials had "knowledge" that they may be disabled. Knowledge exists when parents express in writing to administrative or supervisory personnel their concern that their child may be in need of special education and related services or request an evaluation. Knowledge also may be established when an educator expresses concern about a student's behavior directly to supervisory personnel. However, the student is not entitled to IDEA protection in a given disciplinary hearing if:

- Notification of a possible disability occurred following the inappropriate conduct,
- The child was found not to qualify as disabled given the results of an expedited evaluation,
- The parents did not allow the district to conduct the evaluation, or
- The parents previously refused IDEA services.[101]

When an evaluation is conducted and the student does not qualify as both disabled and in need of special education and related services, instruction during the removal period need not be provided, unless available to other general education students who have been removed from school. In contrast, if the student does qualify as disabled, special education and related services consistent with the newly developed IEP need to be provided no later than practical and feasible, and preferably no later than following the tenth day of removal.[102]

The IDEA does not prohibit personnel from reporting to law enforcement authorities any crime a student may commit.[103] Law enforcement officials are not bound by the IDEA

[99]20 U.S.C. § 1415(k)(1)(G) (2008).

[100]20 U.S.C. § 1415(k)(3)(B), (4) (2008).

[101]20 U.S.C. § 1415(k)(5) (2008).

[102]20 U.S.C. § 1415(k)(5)(D)(ii) (2008).

[103]20 U.S.C. §1415(k)(6) (2008).

and may require an unruly or delinquent student to submit to treatment, home detention, or incarceration, in addition to any penalty the district may impose.

■ ■ ■ ■ ■

PROCEDURAL SAFEGUARDS

Whenever parents disagree with the placement committee or an action taken by the district, they are entitled to procedural due process.

School officials generally make good faith efforts to meet the needs of children with disabilities, yet there will be times when the parents disagree with evaluation, program, or placement decisions. Understandably, many parents seek the best possible education for their children. Alternatively, school districts may offer what parents perceive as only a minimally appropriate program, or even less. Where disagreement persists, the IDEA has provided a variety of means by which parents or districts may seek third-party review.

Figure 7.1 provides a flow chart of the procedures. Parents are entitled to receive a copy of IDEA procedural safeguards at least one time per year in addition to the initial referral or request for evaluation, upon filing of a complaint, or upon request. Moreover, during IDEA administrative appeals, the student must be assigned to the then-current educational placement, an interim alternative educational setting (if placed following an appropriate disciplinary hearing), or another placement agreed to by the parents and school officials.[104]

Both informal meetings and mediation must be offered to the parents in an effort to resolve disputes quickly and in a less adversarial manner. Participation is voluntary, and at times is not selected. When a hearing is conducted, parties must disclose any evaluations, recommendations, and evidence that they intend to use. The burden of persuasion is on the party seeking relief in an administrative hearing,[105] while the hearing officer's opinion must be based only on evidence presented by the parties.

If the impartial hearing is conducted at the local level, either party aggrieved by the findings and decision may appeal to the state. At the state level, the review official is responsible for ensuring that the hearing officer followed appropriate procedures, impartially reviewed the record in its entirety, and sought additional evidence, if necessary. Following completion of these procedures, the reviewer must make an independent decision and provide the parties with written findings.

Prior to filing an IDEA suit, parents are required to exhaust administrative remedies (i.e., an impartial hearing and state review where appropriate), unless such remedies would prove futile or fail to provide the required relief, or emergency conditions exist that could result in severe or irreparable harm to the child. The exhaustion requirement helps reduce

[104]20 U.S.C. § 1415(j) (2008); 20 U.S.C. § 1415(k)(4)(A) (2008).

[105]Schaffer v. Weast, 546 U.S. 49 (2005). Prior to this opinion, the Third Circuit had placed the burden on the school district. More recently, the Third Circuit suggested that it might be possible for states to go beyond the IDEA through state statute and put the burden once again on the school district, although it did not indicate why a state would want to do so. L.E. v. Ramsey Bd. of Educ., 435 F.3d 384 (3d Cir. 2006).

FIGURE 7.1   IDEA Complaint Procedure

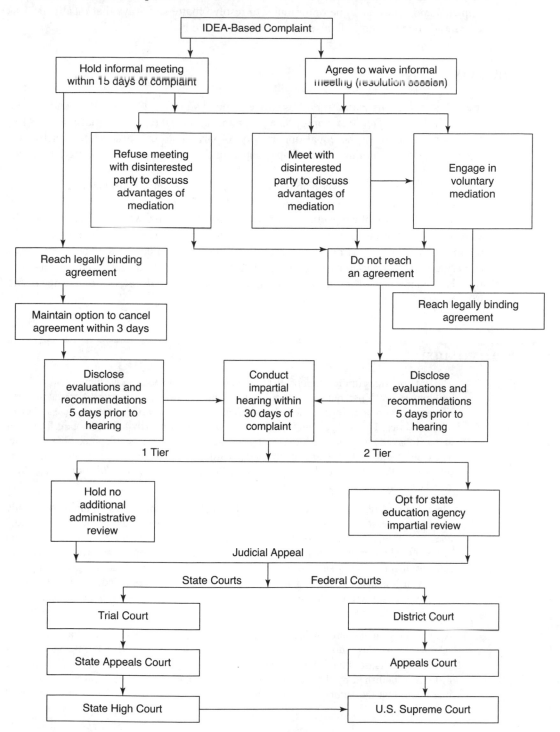

the case load for courts, limits expenditures associated with litigation, and ensures that recipients and states have the opportunity to resolve matters in ways that ideally are less adversarial and more child focused than a lawsuit would be.

CONCLUSION

The rights of students with disabilities have expanded significantly since 1975 and include rights to accessible facilities, appropriate programs, and least restrictive placements. Also, students must be given the equal opportunity to participate in extracurricular activities, including sports, assuming that their participation does not represent a danger to themselves or others.

School districts are responsible for identifying, assessing, and placing all qualified students with disabilities. All placements must be both appropriate and least restrictive; most will require a public placement, although some placements will be in private schools. Also, students with disabilities may be disciplined in the same manner as other students, although there may be additional procedural requirements to meet. Moreover, when expulsion is merited, services consistent with the IEP must continue to be delivered. Understanding what federal laws both allow and require should help educators prepare legal and effective placements for children with disabilities.

POINTS TO PONDER

1. The state provides limited support to children with special needs above that provided for all children ($7,000 per pupil). A family moves into a small, poor, rural community and requests appropriate programs for two children, ages 5 and 6, with severe physical and mental disabilities. The cost per child will be over $100,000, primarily for health care. The services will have to be provided for several years, as neither child's health is likely to improve. The district refuses to pay and claims undue hardship. Following unsuccessful administrative review, the parents sued the district under the IDEA seeking a FAPE for their children. Are the parents likely to win the suit? Why or why not?

2. The school district considers itself to be a "full-inclusion" district. All children are initially placed in general education with supplemental aids and services, as directed by the school administration. Parents, who recently moved into the district, contend that general education is clearly not the appropriate placement for their child with severe disabilities and have significant documentation supporting their position. They request a more segregated placement, which is denied by school authorities based on procedures mandating full inclusion. Following unsuccessful administrative appeals, the parents sued under the IDEA. Which party is likely to prevail? Why?

3. A child in your homeroom has a mild learning disability. He lives one-half mile from school. His parents requested that transportation services be provided, but the request was denied. The district noted that the family lives less than a mile from the school (i.e., the distance established by the state to require the transportation of elementary school children), and that the nature of the student's disability does not necessitate the provision of

transportation. The parents point out that the bus travels in front of their home each day and would merely need to stop to allow their son to board. The district would incur no additional cost. The parents sued under the IDEA and Section 504. Are they likely to win? Why or why not?

4. Your daughter wants to play softball for her school team, but has been denied because of her low grade-point average. You sued the state athletic association under Section 504 when it denied her grade appeal. The association uniformly applies its academic, residency, and other requirements. You contend that the requirements should not apply to her, given that a learning disability is in large part responsible for her low GPA. Are you likely to win this suit? Why?

CHAPTER EIGHT

STUDENT DISCIPLINE

Student misconduct continues to be one of the most persistent and troublesome problems confronting educators. Public concern has focused on school disciplinary problems, particularly those involving use of illicit drugs, alcohol abuse,[1] and violence. In response, schools have directed more efforts toward violence-prevention strategies, including not only stringent security measures but also modification of the curricula to strengthen students' social skills and the training of teachers and administrators to monitor the school climate. States and local school districts also have enacted restrictive laws or policies that call for "zero tolerance" of weapons, drugs, and violence on campus. The efficacy of legislating tougher approaches to create safe schools has evoked volatile debates.[2] This chapter does not address the merits of these measures; rather, it examines the range of strategies employed by educators to maintain a safe and secure learning environment from a legal perspective. The analyses focus on the development of conduct regulations, the imposition of sanctions for noncompliance, and the procedures required in the administration of student punishments.

The law clearly authorizes the state and its agencies to establish and enforce reasonable conduct codes to protect the rights of students and school districts and to ensure that school environments are conducive to learning. Historically, courts exercised limited review of student disciplinary regulations, and pupils seldom were successful in challenging policies governing their behavior. Courts were reluctant to interfere with the judgment of school officials because public education was considered to be a privilege bestowed by the state.

While there has been a quantum leap from this early judicial posture, legal developments have not eroded educators' rights or their responsibilities. The Seventh Circuit noted

---

[1]In March 2007, the U.S. Surgeon General's Office issued its first "call to action" to stop underage drinking, which poses a significant threat to the health and safety of the nation's youth. Kenneth Moritsugu, "The Surgeon General's Call to Action to Prevent and Reduce Underage Drinking" (press conference, March 6, 2007), available at www.surgeongeneral.gov/topics/underagedrinking/moritsugu.html. A national survey reported that there were 11 million underage drinkers in 2005; about 7.2 million of them were binge drinkers. Substance Abuse and Mental Health Services Administration, *Results from the 2005 National Survey on Drug Use and Health: National Findings* (Rockville, MD: U.S. Department of Health and Human Services, 2006).

[2]See Advancement Project, *Education on Lockdown: The Schoolhouse to Jailhouse Track* (Washington, DC: Author, March 2005); Robert C. Johnston, "Federal Data Highlight Disparities in Discipline," *Education Week*, (June 21, 2000), p. 3.

that **the United States Supreme Court "has repeatedly emphasized the need for affirming the comprehensive authority of the states and of school officials, consistent with fundamental constitutional safeguards, to prescribe and control conduct in the schools."**[3] Reasonable disciplinary regulations, even those impairing students' protected liberties, have been upheld if justified by a legitimate educational interest. Educators not only have the authority but also the duty to maintain discipline in public schools. Although rules made at any level (e.g., classroom, building, school board) cannot conflict with higher authorities (e.g., constitutional and statutory provisions), building administrators and teachers retain substantial latitude in establishing and enforcing conduct codes that are necessary for instructional activities to take place. After a brief discussion of conduct regulations, subsequent sections of this chapter address legal issues related to expulsions and suspensions, corporal punishment, academic sanctions, search and seizure, and remedies for unlawful disciplinary actions.

■ ■ ■ ■ ■

CONDUCT REGULATIONS

School boards are granted considerable latitude in establishing and interpreting their own disciplinary rules and regulations.

The Supreme Court has held that the interpretation of a school regulation resides with the body that adopted it and is charged with its enforcement.[4] Disciplinary policies, however, have been struck down if unconstitutionally vague. Policies prohibiting "improper conduct" and behavior "inimical to the best interests of the school" have been invalidated because they have not specified the precise nature of the impermissible conduct.[5] Although policies should be precise, courts have recognized that disciplinary regulations do not have to satisfy the stringent criteria or level of specificity required in criminal statutes. The Eighth Circuit noted that the determining factor is whether a regulation's wording is precise enough to notify an individual that specific behavior is clearly unacceptable.[6]

In addition to reviewing the validity of the conduct regulation on which a specific punishment is based, courts evaluate the nature and extent of the penalty imposed in relation to the gravity of the offense. Courts also consider the age, sex, mental condition, and

---

[3]Boucher v. Sch. Bd., 134 F.2d 821, 827 (7th Cir. 1998).

[4]*See* Bd. of Educ. v. McCluskey, 458 U.S. 966 (1982); Wood v. Strickland, 420 U.S. 308 (1975).

[5]*See* Killion v. Franklin Reg'l Sch. Dist., 136 F. Supp. 2d 446, 459 (W.D. Pa. 2001) (finding school district's retaliatory policy against verbal or other abuse of teachers unconstitutionally vague—"devoid of any detail"); Flaherty v. Keystone Oaks Sch. Dist., 247 F. Supp. 2d 698 (W.D. Pa. 2003) (ruling that handbook policies were overbroad and vague in violation of a student's First Amendment rights). *But see* Fuller v. Decatur Pub. Sch. Bd. of Educ., 252 F.3d 662 (7th Cir. 2001) (concluding that a prohibition of ganglike behavior was not overly vague when the students' conduct clearly violated the regulation).

[6]Woodis v. Westark Cmty. Coll., 160 F.3d 435 (8th Cir. 1998).

past behavior of the student in deciding whether a given punishment is appropriate. The judiciary has sanctioned punishments such as the denial of privileges, suspension, expulsion, corporal punishment, and detention after school. Any of these punishments, however, could be considered unreasonable under a specific set of circumstances. Consequently, courts examine each unique factual situation; they do not evaluate the validity of student punishments in the abstract.

Litigation challenging disciplinary practices often has focused on the procedures followed in administering punishments rather than on the substance of disciplinary rules or the nature of the sanctions imposed. Implicit in all judicial declarations regarding school discipline is the notion that severe penalties require more formal procedures whereas minor punishments necessitate only minimal due process (e.g., notice of the charges and an opportunity to refute them). Nonetheless, **any disciplinary action should be accompanied by some procedure to ensure the rudiments of fundamental fairness and to prevent mistakes in the disciplinary process.** The Fifth Circuit noted that "the quantum and quality of procedural due process to be afforded a student varies with the seriousness of the punishment to be imposed."[7]

The judiciary has recognized that punishment for student conduct off school grounds must be supported by evidence that the behavior has a detrimental impact on other pupils, teachers, or school activities.[8] This has become a much more contentious area with students' increased use of the Internet at home. Personal Web sites and use of social networks such as MySpace and Facebook raise difficult First Amendment issues for school officials attempting to discipline students for off-campus conduct.[9]

Generally, school officials can regulate student conduct outside of school hours and off school property only if such conduct interferes with school operations. Courts have upheld sanctions imposed on students for engaging in assault or criminal acts away from school grounds;[10] making and using explosive devices off campus;[11] compiling a "shit list" of other students noting derogatory characteristics;[12] making threatening, harassing remarks on a Web site created at home;[13] writing a threatening letter over the summer break to another student;[14] and shooting a student with a BB gun near a school bus stop.[15]

---

[7]Pervis v. LaMarque Indep. Dist., 466 F.2d 1054, 1057 (5th Cir. 1972).

[8]For a synthesis of applicable case law on conduct off school grounds, *see* Perry A. Zirkel, "Disciplining Students for Off-Campus Misconduct," *Education Law Reporter*, vol. 163 (2002), pp. 551–553.

[9]*See* "School Safey," NSBA Legal Clips (August 24, 2006) (reporting a national poll indicating that more than 13 million students, ages 6 to 17, have been "cyberbullied" through Web pages, text messages, e-mails, or cell phones); Alan Gomez, "Students, Officials Locking Horns over Blogs," *U.S.A. Today* (October 26, 2006) (noting that some districts are adopting policies that warn students they can be disciplined for comments online).

[10]Pollnow v. Glennon, 757 F.2d 496 (2d Cir. 1985); Nicholas v. Sch. Comm., 587 N.E.2d 211 (Mass. 1992).

[11]Collins v. Prince William County Sch. Bd., 142 Fed. App'x 144 (4th Cir. 2005)

[12]Donovan v. Ritchie, 68 F.3d 14 (1st Cir. 1995).

[13]J.S. v. Bethlehem Area Sch. Dist., 807 A.2d 847 (Pa. 2002). *But see* Beussink v. Woodland R-IV Sch. Dist., 30 F. Supp. 2d 1175 (E.D. Mo. 1998) (concluding that a Web site created off-campus did not materially and substantially interfere with the educational process). *See also* text accompanying notes 62–69, Chapter 5.

[14]Doe v. Pulaski County Special Sch. Dist., 306 F.3d 616 (8th Cir. 2002).

[15]S.K. and Z.K. v. Anoka-Hennepin Indep. Sch. Dist. No. 11, 399 F. Supp. 2d 963 (D. Minn. 2005).

FIGURE 8.1   Guidelines for the Development of a Student Conduct Code

- Rules must have an explicit purpose and be clearly written to accomplish that purpose.
- Any conduct regulation adopted should be necessary in order to carry out the school's educational mission; rules should not be designed merely to satisfy the preferences of school board members, administrators, or teachers.
- Rules should be publicized to students and their parents.
- Rules should be specific and clearly stated so students know what behaviors are expected and what behaviors are prohibited.
- Student handbooks that incorporate references to specific state laws should also include the law or paraphrase the statutory language.
- Regulations should not impair constitutionally protected rights unless there is an overriding public interest, such as a threat to the safety of others.
- A rule should not be *ex post facto*; it should not be adopted to prevent a specific activity that school officials know is being planned or has already occurred.
- Punishments should be appropriate to the offense, taking into consideration the child's age, gender, disability, and past behavior.
- Some procedural safeguards should accompany the administration of all punishments; the formality of the procedures should be in accord with the severity of the punishment.
- A process for periodic review of the student handbook should be established that involves students and school staff members in the revisions and refinement.

Courts, however, have prohibited school authorities from punishing students for misbehavior off school grounds if they had not been informed that such conduct would result in sanctions or if the misbehavior had no direct relationship to the welfare of the school.

School personnel must be careful not to place unnecessary constraints on student behavior. In developing disciplinary policies, all possible means of achieving the desired outcomes should be explored, and means that are least restrictive of students' personal freedoms should be selected (see Figure 8.1 for general guidelines).[16] Once it is determined that a specific conduct regulation is necessary, the rule should be clearly written so that it is not open to multiple interpretations. Each regulation should include the rationale for enacting the rule as well as the penalties for infractions. Considerable discretion exists in determining that certain actions deserve harsher penalties (i.e., imposing a more severe punishment for the sale of drugs as opposed to the possession or use of drugs). **To ensure that students are knowledgeable of the conduct rules, it is advisable to require students to sign a form indicating that they have read the conduct regulations.** With such documentation, students would be unable to plead ignorance of the rules as a defense for their misconduct.

[16]*See* Thomas Baker, "Construing the Scope of Student Conduct Codes," *Education Law Reporter*, vol. 174 (2003), pp. 555–588, for an extensive discussion of the development of conduct codes.

In designing and enforcing student conduct codes, it is important that school personnel bear in mind the distinction between students' substantive and procedural rights. If a disciplinary regulation or the administration of punishment violates substantive rights (e.g., restricts protected speech), the regulation cannot be enforced nor the punishment imposed. When only procedural rights are impaired, however, the punishment generally can be administered if determined at an appropriate hearing that the punishment is warranted.

■ ■ ■ ■ ■

EXPULSIONS AND SUSPENSIONS

Some type of procedural due process should be afforded to students prior to the imposition of expulsions or suspensions.

Expulsions and suspensions are among the most widely used disciplinary measures. Courts uniformly have upheld educators' authority to use such measures as punishments, but the procedural requirements (i.e., notice, hearing, etc.) discussed below must be provided to ensure that students are afforded fair and impartial treatment. Although most states have recognized that students have a property right to an education, they may be deprived of this right if they violate school rules. This section focuses on disciplinary action in which students are removed from the regular instructional program.

Expulsions

State laws and school board regulations are usually quite specific regarding the grounds for *expulsions*—that is, the removal of students from school for a lengthy period of time (in excess of 10 days). Such grounds are not limited to occurrences during school hours and can include infractions on school property immediately before or after school, at school-sponsored activities on or off school grounds, or en route to or from school. Although specific grounds vary from state to state, infractions typically considered legitimate grounds for expulsion include:

- Engaging in violence,
- Stealing or vandalizing school or private property,
- Causing or attempting to cause physical injury to others,
- Possessing a weapon,
- Possessing or using drugs or alcohol, and
- Engaging in criminal activity or other behavior forbidden by state laws.

Procedural Requirements.   State statutes specify procedures for expulsion and the limitations on their length. Except for the possession of weapons, a student generally cannot be expelled beyond the end of the current academic year unless the expulsion takes place near the close of the term. A teacher or administrator may initiate expulsion proceedings,

FIGURE 8.2 Procedural Due Process for Student Expulsions

- Written notice of the charges; the intention to expel; the place, time, and circumstances of the hearing; and sufficient time for a defense to be prepared
- A full and fair hearing before an impartial adjudicator
- The right to legal counsel or some other adult representation
- The right to be fully apprised of the proof or evidence
- The opportunity to present witnesses or evidence
- The opportunity to cross-examine opposing witnesses
- Some type of written record demonstrating that the decision was based on the evidence presented at the hearing

but usually only the school board can expel a student. **Prior to expulsion, students must be provided procedural protections guaranteed by the United States Constitution; however, school officials can remove students immediately if they pose a danger or threat to themselves or others.**[17] No duty exists to provide an educational alternative for a properly expelled student unless the school board policies or state mandates specify that alternative programs must be provided or the student is receiving special education services.[18]

Although the details of required procedures must be gleaned from state statutes and school board regulations, courts have held that students facing expulsion from public school are guaranteed at least minimum due process under the Fourteenth Amendment (see Figure 8.2 for procedural elements). Procedural safeguards required may vary, depending on the circumstances of a particular situation. In a Mississippi case, a student and his parents claimed that prior to an expulsion hearing they should have been given a list of the witnesses and a summary of their testimony.[19] Recognizing that such procedural protections generally should be afforded prior to a long-term expulsion, the Fifth Circuit nonetheless held that they were not requisite in this case. The parents had been fully apprised of the charges, the facts supporting the charges, and the nature of the hearing. Consequently, the court concluded that the student suffered no material prejudice from the school board's failure to supply a list of witnesses; the witnesses provided no surprises or interference with the student's ability to present his case. In a later case involving expulsion for possession of drugs, the same court found no impairment of a student's rights when he was denied an opportunity to confront and rebut witnesses who accused him of selling drugs.[20] The names of student witnesses had been withheld to prevent retaliation against them. Similarly, the

---

[17]*See, e.g.,* Lavine v. Blaine Sch. Dist., 257 F.3d 981 (9th Cir. 2001).

[18]*See* Gun-Free Schools Act, 20 U.S.C. § 7151 (2008) (allows school officials to place students expelled for gun possession in alternative instructional programs). *See also* text accompanying note 92, Chapter 7, for a discussion of the expulsion of children with disabilities.

[19]Keough v. Tate County Bd. of Educ., 748 F.2d 1077 (5th Cir. 1984).

[20]Brewer v. Austin Indep. Sch. Dist., 779 F.2d 260 (5th Cir. 1985).

Sixth Circuit noted that it is critical to protect the anonymity of students who blow the whistle on classmates involved in serious offenses such as drug dealing.[21]

State laws and school board policies often provide students facing expulsion with more elaborate procedural safeguards than the constitutional protections noted. Once such expulsion procedures are established, courts will require that they be followed.

Zero-Tolerance Policies.   The concern about school safety led to specific federal and state laws directed at the discipline of students who bring weapons onto school campuses. Under the Gun-Free Schools Act of 1994, all states enacted legislation requiring at least a one-year expulsion for students who bring firearms to school.[22] In expanding the scope of the law, states have added to the list of prohibitions weapons such as knives, explosive devices, hand chains, and other offensive weapons as well as drugs and violent acts. The federal law also requires states to permit the local school superintendent to modify the expulsion requirement on a case-by-case basis.

Severe criticism has been directed at zero-tolerance policies when school officials fail to exercise discretion and flexibility. The American Bar Association and others have called for an end to such policies that require automatic penalties without assessing the circumstances.[23] Recent cases underscore the harsh consequences when students encounter inflexible policies. In a Virginia case, a 13-year-old student, attempting to save a suicidal friend's life, took the friend's binder containing a knife and placed it in his own locker. Upon hearing about the knife, the assistant principal asked the student to retrieve it from his locker. Although the assistant principal felt that the student was attempting to save his friend's life and at no time posed a threat to anyone, he was expelled from school for four months. The Fourth Circuit, in upholding the expulsion, noted its harshness but found no violation of the student's due process rights.[24]

Some courts, however, have held that invoking mandatory expulsion policies may implicate constitutional rights if administrators fail to take into consideration the individual student's history and the circumstances surrounding the conduct. For example, the Sixth Circuit noted that expelling a student for weapons possession when the student did not know that the weapon was in his car could not survive a due process challenge.[25] Other courts, however, have been reluctant to impose the *knowing possession* standard that would require the determination of a student's intent.[26]

---

[21]Newsome v. Batavia Local Sch. Dist., 842 F.2d 920 (6th Cir. 1988). *See also* Scanlon v. Las Cruces Pub. Schs., 172 P.3d 185 (N.M. Ct. App. 2007) (ruling that a student's procedural due process rights were not violated when school officials did not disclose the names of student informants).

[22]20 U.S.C. § 7151 (2008). Additionally, most states have enacted gun-free or weapons-free school zone laws restricting possession of firearms in or near schools.

[23]Report to the ABA House of Delegates, February 19, 2001, American Bar Association, Chicago, Ill.

[24]Ratner v. Loudoun County Pub. Schs., 16 Fed. App'x 140, 143 (4th Cir. 2001). *See also* S. Gibson Sch. Bd. v. Sollman, 768 N.E.2d 437 (Ind. 2002) (ruling that the judiciary's role is to determine whether a school board acted arbitrarily or capriciously and not to assess the harshness of zero-tolerance policies).

[25]Seal v. Morgan, 229 F.3d 567 (6th Cir. 2000).

[26]*See, e.g.,* Bundick v. Bay City Indep. Sch. Dist., 140 F. Supp. 2d 735, 740 (S.D. Tex. 2001); *In re* B.N.S., 641 S.E.2d 411 (N.C. Ct. App. 2007).

Suspensions

Suspensions are frequently used to punish students for violating school rules and standards of behavior when the infractions are not of sufficient magnitude to warrant expulsion. Suspensions include short-term removals (usually 10 days or less) from school as well as the denial of participation in regular courses and activities (in-school suspension). Most legal controversies have focused on out-of-school suspensions, but it is advisable to apply the same legal principles to any disciplinary action that separates the student from the regular instructional program, even for a short period of time.

Historically, state laws and judicial decisions differed widely in identifying and interpreting procedural safeguards for suspensions. In 1975, the Supreme Court provided substantial clarification regarding the constitutional rights of students confronting short-term suspensions. In *Goss v. Lopez*, the Court held that minimum due process must be provided before a student is suspended for even a brief period of time.[27] **Recognizing that a student's state-created property right to an education is protected by the Fourteenth Amendment, the Court ruled that such a right cannot be impaired unless the student is afforded notice of the charges and an opportunity to refute them before an impartial decision maker**[28] (see Figure 8.3). The Supreme Court also emphasized that suspensions implicate students' constitutionally protected liberty interests because of the potentially damaging effects that the disciplinary process can have on a student's reputation and permanent record.

The *Goss* majority strongly suggested that its holding applied to all short-term suspensions, including those of only one class period. Consequently, many school boards have instituted policies that require informal procedures for every brief suspension and more formal procedures for longer suspensions.

The Supreme Court's *Goss* decision established the rudimentary procedural requirements for short-term suspensions, but students continue to seek expansion of their procedural rights. The Court specifically noted that such formal procedures as the right to secure counsel, to confront and cross-examine witnesses, and to call witnesses are not constitutionally required. The Court reiterated this stance in a later case by noting that a

FIGURE 8.3   Procedural Due Process for Student Suspensions

- Oral or written notification of the nature of the violation and the intended punishment
- An opportunity to refute the charges before an objective decision maker (such a discussion may immediately follow the alleged rule infraction)
- An explanation of the evidence on which the disciplinarian is relying

---

[27]419 U.S. 565 (1975). Individuals posing a danger or threat may be removed immediately, with notice and a hearing following as soon as possible.

[28]The requirement of an impartial decision maker does not mean that an administrator or teacher who is familiar with the facts cannot serve in this capacity either for the informal or formal hearings. The decision maker simply must judge the situation fairly and on the basis of valid evidence.

two-day suspension "does not rise to the level of a penal sanction calling for the full panoply of procedural due process protections applicable to a criminal prosecution."[29]

Decisions by lower state and federal courts indicate a reluctance to impose additional requirements unless mandated by state law. The *right to remain silent* has been advanced, with students arguing that school disciplinary proceedings should be governed by the Supreme Court's ruling in *Miranda v. Arizona* (that persons subjected to custodial interrogation must be advised of their right to remain silent, that any statement made may be used against them, and that they have the right to legal counsel).[30] Courts have readily dismissed these claims, finding that discussions with school administrators are noncustodial. In the *Miranda* decision, the Supreme Court was interpreting an individual's Fifth Amendment right against self-incrimination when first subjected to police questioning in connection with criminal charges. A Maine student claimed a violation of procedural due process because the school administrator denied him permission to leave during questioning and failed to advise him of his right to remain silent or to have his parents present during the interrogation. The court rejected all claims, noting that there was no legal authority to substantiate any of the asserted rights.[31] The court reasoned that to rule otherwise would, in fact, contradict the informal procedures outlined in *Goss* allowing for immediate questioning and disciplinary action. Also relying on *Goss*, the Third Circuit ruled that the suspension of a 5-year-old kindergartener for telling his friends, "I'm going to shoot you" while playing a game of cops and robbers satisfied required informal procedures even though the parents contended that they should have been present to help him understand the process.[32]

Although the Supreme Court in *Goss* recognized the possibility of "unusual situations" that would require more formal procedures than those outlined, little guidance was given about what these circumstances might be. The only suggestion offered in *Goss* was that a disciplinarian should adopt more extensive procedures in instances involving factual disputes "and arguments about cause and effect."[33] Courts have declined to expand on this brief listing. The Sixth Circuit rejected a student's contention that drug charges constituted such an "unusual situation" because of the stigmatizing effect on his reputation. The court did not believe that an eighth grade student suspended for 10 days for possessing a substance that resembled an illegal drug was "forever faced with a tarnished reputation and restricted employment opportunities."[34] More extensive procedures also have been found unnecessary when students are barred from interscholastic athletics and other activities.[35]

---

[29]Bethel Sch. Dist. No. 403 v. Fraser, 478 U.S. 675, 686 (1986).

[30]384 U.S. 436 (1966).

[31]Boynton v. Casey, 543 F. Supp. 995 (D. Me. 1982). *But see In re* R.H., 791 A.2d 331 (Pa. 2002) (holding that school police officers were required to give a student *Miranda* warnings prior to interrogation since they exercised the same powers as municipal police and the interrogation led to charges by the police, not punishment by school officials).

[32]S.G. *ex rel.* A.G. v. Sayreville Bd. of Educ., 333 F.3d 417 (3d Cir. 2003). *But see In re* Andre M., 88 P.3d 552 (Ariz. 2004) (finding that a 16-year-old student's rights were violated when *police* interrogated him at school and refused to permit his parent to be present).

[33]Goss v. Lopez, 419 U.S. 565, 583–584 (1975).

[34]Paredes v. Curtis, 864 F.2d 426, 429 (6th Cir. 1988).

[35]*See, e.g.*, Donovan v. Ritchie, 68 F.3d 14 (1st Cir. 1995); Taylor v. Enumclaw Sch. Dist., 133 P.3d 492 (Wash. Ct. App. 2006).

Students have asserted that suspensions involving loss of course credit or occurring during exam periods require greater due process than outlined in *Goss*. The Fifth Circuit, however, did not find persuasive the argument that the loss incurred for a 10-day suspension during final examinations required more than a mere give-and-take discussion between the principal and the student. In refusing to require more formal proceedings, the court noted that *Goss* makes no distinction as to when a short-term suspension occurs, and a contrary ruling would "significantly undermine, if not nullify, its definitive holding."[36] Similarly, the Seventh Circuit rejected a student's claim that additional procedures were required because a suspension occurred at the end of the school year and precluded the student from taking his final exams and graduating.[37]

In-school suspensions or isolation may entitle students to minimal due process procedures if they are deprived of instruction or the opportunity to learn. A Tennessee federal district court found that a student's placement in a classroom "time-out box" did not require due process because he continued to work on class assignments and could hear and see the teacher from the confined area.[38] The court emphasized that teachers must be free to administer minor forms of classroom discipline such as time-out, denial of privileges, and special assignments. Similarly, the Sixth Circuit held that a one-day suspension in which a student completed school work and was counted as in attendance did not implicate a property interest in educational benefits or a liberty interest in reputation; it was simply too *de minimis*.[39]

Closely related to suspensions are *involuntary transfers* of students to alternative educational placements for disciplinary reasons. Such transfers generally do not involve denial of public education, but they may implicate protected liberty or property interests. Legal challenges to the use of disciplinary transfers have addressed primarily the adequacy of the procedures followed. Recognizing that students do not have an inherent right to attend a given school, some courts nonetheless have held that pupils facing involuntary reassignment are entitled to minimal due process if such transfers are the result of misbehavior.[40]

Suspensions have frequently been imposed to discipline students for bullying behavior. New state laws are now formalizing the school's responsibility for disrupting and deterring bullying behavior.[41] Oregon law is typical, requiring that policies include consequences for bullying behavior, but it also goes further than some states by specifying that remedial measures should be taken with the students who bully.[42] Although not addressing initial

[36]Keough v. Tate County Bd. of Educ., 748 F.2d 1077, 1081 (5th Cir. 1984).

[37]Lamb v. Panhandle Comm. Unit Sch. Dist. No. 2, 826 F.2d 526 (7th Cir. 1987).

[38]Dickens v. Johnson County Bd. of Educ., 661 F. Supp. 155 (E.D. Tenn. 1987). *See also* Rasmus v. Arizona, 939 F. Supp. 709 (D. Ariz. 1996) (holding that denying a student the ability to work on class assignments during a 10-minute time-out was *de minimis* and did not violate a property right).

[39]Laney v. Farley, 501 F.3d 577 (6th Cir. 2007).

[40]*See, e.g.,* McCall v. Bossier Parish Sch. Bd., 785 So. 2d 57 (La. Ct. App. 2001).

[41]Since 2000, more than 20 states have enacted anti-bullying legislation because of concerns about connections between school violence and bullying. Like the mandate under the federal zero-tolerance law, these state laws require local school districts to include an anti-bullying policy in their discipline codes. Most of the state laws provide a broad definition of what constitutes bullying behavior. The laws refer to intentional, aggressive behavior, repeated over time, that involves an imbalance of power and strength. Typically, proscribed verbal or written behavior includes name-calling, teasing, intimidation, ridicule, humiliation, physical acts, and taunts.

[42]Or. Rev. Stat. § 339.356(1) (2008).

consequences, Georgia law specifies student assignment to an alternative school after three bullying offenses.[43] Since the anti-bullying state laws are relatively new, case law is quite limited in interpreting students' rights and school districts' liability.[44] Nonetheless, in developing and administering anti-bullying policies, school officials must take into consideration students' procedural due process rights. Policies imposing short-term suspensions must comply at least with the minimum requirements of *Goss*;[45] more extensive disciplinary measures for bullying behavior will necessitate formal hearings.

Fundamental fairness requires at least minimal due process procedures when students are denied school attendance or removed from the regular instructional program. Severity of the separation dictates the amount of process due under the United States Constitution and state laws. Permanent expulsion from school triggers the most extensive process, whereas minor infractions may involve a brief give-and-take between school officials and students. Simply providing students the opportunity to be heard not only reduces mistakes but also preserves trust in the school system.

■ ■ ■ ■ ■

CORPORAL PUNISHMENT

If not prohibited by law or school board policy, reasonable corporal punishment can be used as a disciplinary measure.

Many states have banned educators' use of corporal punishment either by law or state regulation. In 1971, only one state prohibited corporal punishment; today, more than half proscribe its use.[46] Generally, when state law and school board policy permit corporal punishment, courts have upheld its reasonable administration and have placed the burden on the aggrieved students to prove otherwise. **In evaluating the reasonableness of a teacher's actions in administering corporal punishment, courts have assessed the child's age, maturity, and past behavior; the nature of the offense; the instrument used; any evidence of lasting harm to the child; and the motivation of the person inflicting the punishment.** This section provides an overview of the constitutional and state law issues raised in the administration of corporal punishment.

---

[43]Ga. Code Ann. § 20-2-751.4(b) (2008).

[44]In addition to state laws, victims of bullying also may rely on federal civil rights laws if they are in a protected class (i.e., race, sex, national origin, or religion) or seek a remedy for negligence against the aggressor and the school district under state tort law.

[45]*See supra* text accompanying notes 27–35.

[46]Corporal punishment is the use of physical force (i.e., paddling) to punish students for misbehavior. *See Global Initiative to End All Corporal Punishment of Children*, available at www.endcorporalpunishment.org/pages/frame.html, for the status of corporal punishment laws in each state and country in the world. The American Academy of Pediatrics has recommended that corporal punishment be abolished in all states because of its detrimental effect on students' self-image and achievement as well as possible contribution to disruptive and violent behavior. American Academy of Pediatrics, "Corporal Punishment in Schools," *Pediatrics*, vol. 106 (August 2000), p. 343; reaffirming 2000 statement, *Pediatrics*, vol. 118 (September 2006), p. 1266.

Constitutional Issues

In 1977 the Supreme Court addressed the constitutionality of corporal punishment that resulted in the severe injury of two students. The Court held in *Ingraham v. Wright* that **the use of corporal punishment in public schools does not violate either the Eighth Amendment's prohibition against the government's infliction of cruel and unusual punishment or the Fourteenth Amendment's procedural due process guarantees.**[47] While recognizing that corporal punishment implicates students' constitutionally protected liberty interests, the Court emphasized that state remedies are available, such as assault and battery suits, if students are excessively or arbitrarily punished by school personnel. In essence, the Court majority concluded that state courts under provisions of state laws should handle cases dealing with corporal punishment. The majority distinguished corporal punishment from a suspension by noting that the denial of school attendance is a more severe penalty that deprives students of a property right and thus necessitates procedural safeguards. Furthermore, the majority reasoned that the purpose of corporal punishment would be diluted if elaborate procedures had to be followed prior to its use.

The Supreme Court's ruling in *Ingraham*, however, does not foreclose a successful constitutional challenge to the use of *unreasonable* corporal punishment. Most federal appellate courts have held that students' substantive due process right to be free of brutal and egregious threats to bodily security might be impaired by the use of shockingly, excessive corporal punishment.[48] The Fourth Circuit concluded that although *Ingraham* bars federal litigation on procedural due process issues, excessive or cruel corporal punishment may violate students' substantive due process rights, which protect individuals from arbitrary and unreasonable governmental action. According to the appellate court, the standard for determining if such a violation has occurred is "whether the force applied caused injury so severe, was so disproportionate to the need presented, and was so inspired by malice or sadism rather than a merely careless or unwise excess of zeal that it amounted to a brutal and inhumane abuse of official power literally shocking to the conscience."[49] Clearly, student challenges to the reasonable use of ordinary corporal punishment are precluded by this standard.

Substantive due process claims generally are evaluated by examining the need for administering corporal punishment, the relationship between the need and the amount of punishment administered, whether force was applied to maintain or restore discipline or used maliciously with the intent of causing harm, and the extent of a student's injury.[50] Courts allowing substantive due process claims, however, have found the threshold for recovery for the violation of a student's rights to be high. Minor pain, embarrassment, and

---

[47]430 U.S. 651 (1977).

[48]*See, e.g.,* Johnson v. Newburgh Enlarged Sch. Dist., 239 F.3d 246 (2d Cir. 2001); Neal v. Fulton County Bd. of Educ., 229 F.2d 1069 (11th Cir. 2000).

[49]Hall v. Tawney, 621 F.2d 607, 613 (4th Cir. 1980).

[50]The Fifth and Seventh Circuits, disagreeing with the stance of the majority of the appellate courts, concluded that substantive due process claims cannot be raised if states prohibit unreasonable student discipline and provide adequate postpunishment civil or criminal remedies for abuse. Moore v. Willis Indep. Sch. Dist., 233 F.3d 871 (5th Cir. 2000); Wallace v. Batavia Sch. Dist. 101, 68 F.3d 1010 (7th Cir. 1995).

hurt feelings do not rise to this level; actions must literally be *shocking to the conscience*. Actions that courts have found *not* to rise to this level include requiring a 10-year-old boy to clean out a stopped-up toilet with his bare hands,[51] pushing a student's shoulder causing her to fall against a door jam,[52] restraining by force a sixth grade student who was violently kicking a vending machine,[53] and slapping a student's face once.[54] In contrast, the Tenth Circuit ruled that substantive due process rights were implicated when a 9-year-old girl was paddled with a split paddle while she was held upside down by another teacher, resulting in severe bruises, cuts, and permanent scarring.[55] Similarly, other conscience-shocking behavior involved a coach knocking a student's eye out of the socket with a metal weight lock,[56] a teacher physically restraining a student until he lost consciousness and fell to the floor suffering significant injuries,[57] and a wrestling coach initiating and encouraging team members to repeatedly beat a student.[58]

State Law

Although the Supreme Court has ruled that the United States Constitution does not prohibit corporal punishment in public schools, its use may conflict with state law provisions or local administrative regulations. As noted, the majority of states now prohibit corporal punishment and others have established procedures or conditions for its use. Teachers can be disciplined or discharged for violating these state and local provisions regulating corporal punishment. Courts have upheld dismissals based on insubordination for failure to comply with reasonable school board requirements in administering corporal punishment. In a typical case, a Michigan teacher was dismissed because he violated board policy by using corporal punishment after having been warned repeatedly to cease.[59] Teachers also have been dismissed under the statutory grounds of "cruelty" for improper use of physical force with students. In Illinois, a tenured teacher was dismissed on this ground for using a cattle prod in punishing students.[60] Other disciplinary measures also may be taken against teachers. A Nebraska teacher who "tapped" a student on the head was suspended without pay for 30 days under a state law that prohibits the use of corporal punishment.[61]

Beyond statutory or board restrictions, other legal means exist to challenge the use of unreasonable corporal punishment in public schools. Teachers can be charged with criminal

---

[51]Harris v. Robinson, 273 F.3d 927 (10th Cir. 2001).

[52]Gottlieb v. Laurel Highlands Sch. Dist., 272 F.3d 168 (3d Cir. 2001).

[53]Golden v. Anders, 324 F.3d 650 (8th Cir. 2003).

[54]Lilliard v. Shelby County Bd. of Educ., 76 F.3d 716 (6th Cir. 1996).

[55]Garcia v. Miera, 817 F.2d 650 (10th Cir. 1987).

[56]Neal v. Fulton County Bd. of Educ., 229 F.3d 1069 (11th Cir. 2000).

[57]Metzger v. Osbeck, 841 F.2d 518 (3d Cir. 1988).

[58]Meeker v. Edmundson, 415 F.3d 317 (4th Cir. 2005).

[59]Tomczik v. State Tenure Comm'n, 438 N.W.2d 642 (Mich. Ct. App. 1989).

[60]Rolando v. Sch. Dirs. of Dist. No. 125, 358 N.E.2d 945 (Ill. App. Ct. 1976).

[61]Daily v. Bd. of Educ., 588 N.W.2d 813 (Neb. 1999).

assault and battery, which might result in fines and/or imprisonment. Civil assault and battery suits for monetary damages also can be initiated against school personnel (see Chapter 2).

When corporal punishment is allowed, educators should use caution in administering it since improper use can result in dismissal, monetary damages, and even imprisonment. Corporal punishment should never be administered with malice, and the use of excessive force should be avoided. Teachers would be wise to keep a record of incidents involving corporal punishment and to adhere to minimum procedural safeguards such as notifying students of behavior that will result in a paddling, asking another staff member to witness the act, and providing parents on request written reasons for the punishment. Moreover, teachers should become familiar with relevant state laws and school board policies before attempting to use corporal punishment in their classrooms.

■ ■ ■ ■ ■

ACADEMIC SANCTIONS

Academic sanctions for nonacademic reasons should be reasonable; related to perform-ance, absences, or other academic concerns; and serve a legitimate school purpose.

It is indisputable that school authorities have the right to use academic sanctions for poor academic performance. Consistently, courts have been reluctant to substitute their own judgment for that of educators in assessing students' academic accomplishments. Failing grades, denial of credit, academic probation, retention, and expulsion from par-ticular programs have been upheld as legitimate means of dealing with poor academic performance.

Although courts have granted broad discretionary powers to school personnel in establishing academic standards, there has been less agreement regarding the use of grade reductions or academic sanctions as punishments for student absences and misbehavior. More complex legal issues are raised when academic penalties are imposed for nonacade-mic reasons. These issues are explored next in connection with grade reductions for absences and misconduct.

Absences

Excessive student absenteeism is a growing concern and has led many school boards to impose academic sanctions for absences. These practices have generated legal challenges related to students' substantive due process rights. To meet the due process requirements, the sanction must be reasonable—that is, rationally related to a valid educational purpose. Since students must attend class to benefit from the educational program, most courts have found that academic penalties for absenteeism serve a valid educational goal.

In an illustrative case, a student claimed that a school regulation stipulating that grades would be lowered one letter grade per class for an unexcused absence impaired protected rights.[62] In defending the rule, Illinois school officials asserted that it was the most appropriate punishment for the serious problem of truancy. They argued that students could not perform satisfactorily in their class work if they were absent, since grades reflected class participation in addition to other standards of performance. The appeals court was not persuaded by the student's argument that grades should reflect only scholastic achievement, and therefore concluded that the regulation was reasonable.

Similarly, the Supreme Court of Connecticut drew a sharp distinction between academic and disciplinary sanctions, noting that the school board's policy of reducing grades for unapproved absences was academic, rather than disciplinary, in intent and effect. Specifically, the court found that a board's determination that grades should reflect more than examinations and papers "constitutes an academic judgment about academic requirements."[63]

Some courts have upheld the imposition of academic penalties even though policies do not differentiate between excused and unexcused absences. For example, the Supreme Court of Arkansas upheld a board policy that disallowed course credit and permitted expulsion of students who accumulated more than 12 absences per semester.[64] The court, in refusing to substitute its judgment for the school board's, concluded that under state law this action was within the board's power to make reasonable rules and regulations. Similarly, a New York appellate court found that a policy denying course credit for absences in excess of nine classes for semester courses and 18 absences for full-year courses was rational; students were permitted and encouraged to make up the classes before they exceeded the limit.[65]

Given the serious truancy problem confronting many school districts, it seems likely that school boards will continue to consider the imposition of academic sanctions. The legality of such policies will depend primarily on judicial interpretation of applicable state law.

Misconduct

Academic sanctions imposed for student misconduct also have been challenged. It is generally accepted that students can be denied credit for work missed while suspended from school. In fact, if students could make up such work without penalty, a suspension might be viewed as a vacation rather than a punishment. More controversy has surrounded policies that impose an additional grade reduction for suspension days, and courts have not agreed regarding the legality of this practice.

For example, a Kentucky appeals court voided a regulation whereby grades were reduced because of unexcused absences resulting from student suspensions.[66] The school board policy stated that work missed because of unexcused absences could not be made up,

---

[62]Knight v. Bd. of Educ., 348 N.E.2d 299 (Ill. App. Ct. 1976).

[63]Campbell v. Bd. of Educ., 475 A.2d 289, 294 (Conn. 1984).

[64]Williams v. Bd. of Educ., 626 S.W.2d 361 (Ark. 1982).

[65]Bitting v. Lee, 564 N.Y.S.2d 791 (App. Div. 1990).

[66]Dorsey v. Bale, 521 S.W.2d 76 (Ky. Ct. App. 1975).

and that five points would be deducted for every unexcused absence from each class during the grading period. The court held that the use of suspensions or expulsions for misconduct was permissible, but the additional lowering of grades as a punitive measure was not. A Pennsylvania court also agreed with this reasoning and found grade reductions for suspensions to be beyond a school board's authority.[67] In the court's opinion, it was a clear misrepresentation of students' scholastic achievement, the penalty went beyond the five-day suspension and downgraded achievement for a full grading period. The Mississippi Supreme Court, relying on a state law mandating the maintenance of alternative schools for suspended students, concluded that students attending these schools are not absent from school.[68] Under this law, a school board cannot count suspension days as unexcused for grading purposes unless the student fails to attend the alternative school.

In contrast, the Supreme Court of Indiana upheld the denial of course credit for a high school junior expelled three days before the end of a semester after the discovery of a small amount of marijuana in his truck. The court noted that although state law did not mandate loss of credit, the board could impose such a penalty.[69] A Texas appellate court upheld a school system's right to lower course grades for suspension days imposed for misconduct in addition to giving zeros on graded class work during the suspension.[70] Relying on a state attorney general's opinion approving grade reductions, the court found the pivotal question to be whether the board had actually adopted a policy that would authorize grade reductions. According to the court, oral announcements in school assemblies explaining grade penalties constituted a valid policy. Moreover, the court noted that the grade reduction did not impair constitutionally protected property or liberty rights.

Generally, courts have ruled that academic course credit or high school diplomas cannot be withheld solely for disciplinary reasons. As early as 1921, the Supreme Court of Iowa held that students who had completed all academic requirements had the right to receive a high school diploma even though they refused to wear graduation caps during the ceremony.[71] The court ruled that the school board was obligated to issue a diploma to a pupil who had satisfactorily completed the prescribed course of study and who was otherwise qualified to graduate from high school. More recently, a Pennsylvania court held that a student who completed all coursework and final exams while expulsion proceedings were pending could not be denied a diploma, because state law specifies that a diploma must be issued once all requirements are met.[72]

Although the use of academic sanctions for student misconduct and truancy is prevalent, students will likely continue to challenge such practices. To ensure fairness, any regulation stipulating that grades will be lowered should be reasonable, related to absences from class, and serve a legitimate school purpose. Furthermore, students must be informed of these rules through the school's official student handbook or similar means.

---

[67]Katzman v. Cumberland Valley Sch. Dist., 479 A.2d 671 (Pa. Commw. Ct. 1984).

[68]Bd. of Trs. v. T.H., 681 So. 2d 110 (Miss. 1996).

[69]S. Gibson Sch. Bd. v. Sollman, 768 N.E.2d 437 (Ind. 2002).

[70]New Braunfels Indep. Sch. Dist. v. Armke, 658 S.W.2d 330 (Tex. Civ. App. 1983).

[71]Valentine v. Indep. Sch. Dist., 183 N.W. 434 (Iowa 1921).

[72]Ream v. Centennial Sch. Dist., 765 A.2d 1195 (Pa. Commw. Ct. 2001); 24 Pa.Stat.Ann. § 16-1613 (2008).

■ ■ ■ ■ ■ ■

SEARCH AND SEIZURE

School personnel can search students' lockers or personal effects based on reasonable suspicion that the students possess contraband that is either illegal or in violation of school policy.

Search and seizure cases continue to arise in the public schools, with the majority resulting from the confiscation of either illegal drugs or weapons. Students have asserted that warrantless searches conducted by school officials impair their rights under the Fourth Amendment of the United States Constitution. Through an extensive line of decisions, the Supreme Court has affirmed that the basic purpose of the Fourth Amendment is to "safeguard the privacy and security of individuals against arbitrary invasions by governmental officials."[73] This amendment protects individuals against unreasonable searches by requiring state agents to obtain a warrant based on probable cause prior to conducting a search. Under the *probable cause standard*, a governmental official must have reasonable grounds of suspicion, supported by sufficient evidence, to cause a cautious person to believe that the suspected individual is guilty of the alleged offense and that the search will produce evidence of the crime committed (see Figure 8.4). Governmental officials violating Fourth Amendment rights may be subject to criminal or civil liability, but the most important remedy for the aggrieved individual is the exclusionary rule.[74] This rule renders evidence of an illegal search inadmissible in criminal prosecutions. Also, under the *fruit of the poisonous tree doctrine*, additional evidence obtained later, resulting from the events set in motion by the illegal search, may be excluded.

Application of the Fourth Amendment to Students

Since Fourth Amendment protections apply only to searches conducted by agents of the state, a fundamental issue in education cases is whether school authorities function as private individuals or as state agents. Most courts have found the Fourth Amendment applicable to public schools, but it was not until 1985 in *New Jersey v. T.L.O.* that the Supreme Court finally ruled that **school officials are state agents, and all governmental actions— not merely those of law enforcement officers—come within the constraints of the Fourth Amendment.**[75]

Although the Fourth Amendment is applicable, the Court in *T.L.O.* concluded that educators' substantial interest in maintaining discipline required "easing" the warrant and probable cause requirements imposed on police officers (see Figure 8.4). The Court reasoned that requiring educators to obtain a warrant before searching students suspected of violating school rules or criminal laws would interfere with the administration of prompt and informal disciplinary procedures needed to maintain order. In modifying the level of

[73]Camara v. Mun. Ct., 387 U.S. 523, 528 (1967).

[74]*See* Mapp v. Ohio, 367 U.S. 643 (1961).

[75]469 U.S. 325 (1985).

FIGURE 8.4   **Standards for Searches**

Probable Cause Standard

- Police officers must secure a warrant prior to conducting a search.
- Facts or evidence must indicate that a person has committed, is committing, or will be committing a crime. Evidence may include witnesses, credible informants, victims of a crime, police officer observations, etc.
- A judge issues a warrant describing the place to be searched and the individual or items to be seized.

Reasonable Suspicion Standard

- School officials are not required to obtain a warrant to search students.
- The legality of a search of a student depends "simply on the reasonableness, under all the circumstances, of the search."*
- Two tests are used to determine reasonableness.
  - Is the search justified at its inception?

    Reasonable suspicion exists that the student has violated, is violating, or will be violating the law or the school discipline code.
  - Is the scope of the search reasonable?

    The type of search (lockers, personal possessions, cars, etc.) is reasonably related to the reason for the search and not overly intrusive for the nature of the suspected infraction and the age and sex of the student.

---

* New Jersy v. T.L.O., 469 U.S. 325, 341 (1985).

suspicion required to conduct a search, the Court found the public interest was best served in the school setting with a standard less than probable cause. Accordingly, **the Court held that the legality of a search should depend "simply on the reasonableness, under all the circumstances, of the search."**[76]

The Court in *T.L.O.* advanced two tests for determining reasonableness. First, is the search justified at its inception? That is, are there "reasonable grounds for suspecting that the search will turn up evidence that the student has violated or is violating either the law or the rules of the school?"[77] Second, is the scope of the search reasonable? In the Court's words, are "the measures adopted reasonably related to the objectives of the search and not excessively intrusive in light of the age and sex of the student and the nature of the infraction?"[78]

The "reasonableness" standard allows courts substantial latitude in interpreting Fourth Amendment rights. Among factors that courts have considered in assessing reasonable grounds for a search are the child's age, history, and record in the school; prevalence

[76]*Id.* at 341.

[77]*Id.* at 342.

[78]*Id.*

and seriousness of the problem in the school to which the search is directed; exigency to make the search without delay and further investigation; probative value and reliability of the information used as a justification for the search; the school officials' experience with the student and with the type of problem to which the search is directed; and the type of search. Clearly, reasonable suspicion requires more than a hunch, good intentions, or good faith. The Supreme Court, in upholding an exception to the warrant requirement for a "stop and frisk" search for weapons by police officers, concluded that to justify the intrusion the police officer must be able to point to "specific and articulable facts."[79] In recognizing an exception for school searches, it appears that, at a minimum, the judiciary will require searches of students to be supported by objective facts.

Informants often play an important role in establishing the "specific and articulable facts" necessary to justify a search. Reliability of informants can be assumed unless school officials have reason to doubt the motives of the reporting student, teacher, parent, citizen, or anonymous caller. The amount of detail given by an informant adds to the veracity of the report—that is, identifying a specific student by name, what the student is wearing, and the specific contraband and where it is located will support a decision to search. Additionally, even with limited information, the level of danger presented by an informant's tip may require an immediate response. A California appellate court commented that "the gravity of the danger posed by possession of a firearm or other weapon on campus was great compared to the relatively minor intrusion involved in investigating" the accused students.[80]

A further requirement of reasonableness is individualized suspicion. The Supreme Court in *T.L.O.* did not address individualized suspicion, but the Court did state that "exceptions to the requirement of individualized suspicion are generally appropriate only where the privacy interests implicated by a search are minimal and where 'other safeguards' are available 'to assure that the individual's reasonable expectation of privacy is not subject to the discretion of the official in the field.' "[81] **Courts have been reluctant to support personal searches lacking individualized suspicion unless the safety of the students necessitates an immediate search.**

In assessing the constitutionality of searches in the public schools, two questions are central: What constitutes a search, and what types of searches are reasonable? According to the Supreme Court's rulings, essential considerations in determining whether an action is a search are an individual's reasonable expectation of privacy (reasonable in the sense that society is prepared to recognize the privacy)[82] and the extent of governmental intrusion.[83] The reasonableness of a specific type of search must be evaluated in terms of all the circumstances surrounding the search. This would include variables such as who initiated the search, who conducted the search, need for the search, purpose of the search, information or factors prompting the search, what or who was searched, and use of the evidence. In the next sections, various types of school searches are examined within this context.

---

[79]Terry v. Ohio, 392 U.S. 1, 21 (1968).

[80]*In re* Alexander B., 270 Cal. Rptr. 2d 342, 344 (Ct. App. 1990).

[81]New Jersey v. T.L.O., 469 U.S. 325, 342 n.8 (1985).

[82]*Id.* at 361 (Harlan, J., concurring).

[83]United States v. Chadwick, 433 U.S. 1, 7 (1977).

Lockers

Courts have singled out school lockers as generating a *lower* expectation of privacy, frequently distinguishing locker searches on the basis that a locker is school property, and students do not retain exclusive possession. This is particularly likely when they have signed a form acknowledging that the locker is school property and subject to inspection. **Under the view of joint control, school officials have been allowed to inspect lockers or even to consent to locker searches by law enforcement officers.**[84]

A Kansas case illustrates the general judicial view toward locker searches. The Supreme Court of Kansas held that the right of inspection is inherent in the authority granted to school officials to manage schools.[85] The court maintained that it is a proper function of school personnel to inspect the lockers under their control and to prevent the use of lockers in illicit ways or for illegal purposes. The Tenth Circuit also concluded that "school authorities have, on behalf of the public, an interest in these lockers and a duty to police the school, particularly where possible serious violations of the criminal laws exist."[86] An important point in both of these cases, however, is that school officials retained a list of the combinations and had occasionally inspected the lockers. These points have been emphasized in other cases to support the nonexclusive nature of lockers.

Most student conduct codes and some state laws specify guidelines for locker searches. These codes or laws may establish that reasonable suspicion is required prior to conducting a search. In a Pennsylvania case, the state supreme court relied on the *T.L.O.* decision and the student code in establishing a legitimate expectation of privacy in lockers. The code specified: "Prior to a locker search a student shall be notified and given an opportunity to be present. However, where school authorities have a *reasonable suspicion* that the locker contains materials which pose a threat to the health, welfare, and safety of students in the school, students' lockers may be searched without prior warning [emphasis added]."[87] The court held that students possessed a reasonable expectation of privacy in their lockers; yet, in balancing students' privacy interests and school officials' concerns, the court found a schoolwide blanket search reasonable based on the heightened awareness of drug activity that permeated the entire school and the compelling concern about drug use.

Because of recent incidents of school violence, some states have enacted broad laws eliminating any presumption of privacy in school lockers. For example, a Michigan law states: "A pupil who uses a locker that is the property of a school district . . . is presumed to have no expectation of privacy in that locker or that locker's content."[88] Furthermore, Michigan school officials can search the lockers at any time and can request the assistance of the local law enforcement agency. Based on judicial interpretations of students' privacy rights, it is likely that statutes such as these will be challenged regarding the expectation of privacy in the contents of the lockers as well as the use of law enforcement personnel.

[84]*But see infra* text accompanying note 122, for cases addressing the involvement of law enforcement personnel.

[85]State v. Stein, 456 P.2d 1, 2 (Kan. 1969).

[86]Zamora v. Pomeroy, 639 F.2d 662, 670 (10th Cir. 1981).

[87]Commonwealth v. Cass, 709 A.2d 350, 353 (Pa. 1998).

[88]Mich. Comp. Laws Ann. § 380.1306 (2008).

Search of Personal Possessions: Purses, Book Bags, and Other Property

Students have a greater expectation of privacy in their personal property or effects than in their school lockers. In the *T.L.O.* case, a teacher had reported a student for smoking in the restroom. Upon questioning by the assistant principal, the student denied smoking and, in fact, denied that she even smoked. The assistant principal then opened the student's purse seeking evidence to substantiate that she did smoke. In the process of removing a package of cigarettes, he spotted rolling papers and subsequently found marijuana and other evidence implicating her in drug dealing. Using the "reasonable suspicion" test, the Supreme Court found that the search in *T.L.O.* was reasonable. The school official had a basis for suspecting that the student had cigarettes in her purse. Although possession was not a violation of a school rule, it was not irrelevant; discovery of cigarettes provided evidence to corroborate that she had been smoking and challenged her credibility. Characterizing this as a "common sense" conclusion, the Court noted that "the requirement of reasonable suspicion is not a requirement of absolute certainty: 'sufficient probability, not certainty, is the touchstone of reasonableness under the Fourth Amendment.' "[89]

Other courts have noted that searches of students' personal possessions—such as wallets, purses, and book bags—do violate students' subjective expectations of privacy and, as such, require individualized suspicion that a violation of a law or school rule has occurred. The Fourth Circuit found that a Little Rock school district policy permitting school officials to conduct full-scale, random, periodic inspections of students' book bags and other personal possessions without any individualized suspicion constituted a major invasion of students' expectation of privacy.[90] The court held that school officials could not argue that under the policy students waived their privacy rights when they brought their possessions onto school property. Finding lack of individualized suspicion, the Supreme Court of California declined to uphold the search of a student's calculator case in the absence of articulable facts to support the search.[91] The vice principal's search was based on the student's tardiness for class, his "furtive gestures" to hide the calculator, and his comment that the principal needed a warrant. These actions alone did not point to the possible violation of any specific rule or law.

Conversely, the New York high court concluded that a security officer's investigation of a student's book bag was reasonable based on hearing an "unusual metallic thud" when the student tossed the bag on a metal shelf. Following the sound, the security officer ran his fingers over the outside of the book bag and detected the outline of a gun. The court noted that the sound alone was insufficient to justify searching the bag, but the discovery of the presence of a gunlike shape established reasonable suspicion for him to open the bag.[92]

---

[89]New Jersey v. T.L.O., 469 U.S. 325, 346 (1985).

[90]Doe v. Little Rock Sch. Dist., 380 F.3d 349 (4th Cir. 2004). *But see* H.Y. *ex rel.* K.Y. v. Russell County Bd. of Educ., 490 F. Supp. 2d 1174 (M.D. Ala. 2007) (holding that the classroom search of students' book bags and personal possessions for missing money was justified even though individualized suspicion did not exist; school officials had an important interest in promoting order and discipline).

[91]*In re* Willaim G., 709 P.2d 1287 (Cal. 1985).

[92]*In re* Gregory M., 627 N.E.2d 500 (N.Y. 1993). *See also* DesRoches v. Caprio, 156 F.3d 571 (4th Cir. 1998) (concluding that the student had a legitimate expectation of privacy in his backpack, necessitating individualized suspicion to search).

In a Massachusetts case, the state high court assessed whether a student had a legitimate expectation of privacy in his handwriting.[93] The charges against the student grew out of several incidents of graffiti on school property containing obscenities and racial slurs, some directed toward one teacher. Because prior occurrences made the student a potential suspect, several of his homework assignments, along with two other students' papers, were analyzed to determine if they matched the graffiti. Based on a match with the student's writing, he was charged with malicious destruction of property and violation of the targeted teacher's civil rights. The court refused to suppress the handwriting analyses and samples, finding that it was reasonable for school authorities to suspect the student and that the inspection of the papers involved minimal intrusion.

A student's car, like other personal possessions, may be searched if reasonable suspicion can be established. A Texas federal district court, however, declined to uphold a general dragnet search of a school parking lot.[94] The school's interest in the contents of the cars was viewed as minimal since students did not have access to their cars during the school day. Furthermore, the search was indiscriminate, lacking any evidence of individualized suspicion. In contrast, a Florida district court upheld the search of a student's car after a school aide, who regularly patrolled the parking lot during students' lunch break, observed in plain view a water pipe, commonly used to smoke marijuana.[95] In the court's opinion, patrolling the lot fell within the school's duty to maintain order and discipline, and the search was based on individualized suspicion.

Personal Search of Students

Warrantless searches of a student's person raise significant legal questions. Unlike locker searches, it cannot be asserted that there is a lower expectation of privacy. **Students have a legitimate expectation of privacy in the contents of their pockets and their person.** The Fifth Circuit noted that "the Fourth Amendment applies with its fullest vigor against any intrusion on the human body."[96] In personal searches, not only is it necessary to have reasonable cause to search, but also the search itself must be reasonable. Reasonableness is assessed in terms of the specific facts and circumstances of a case.

A Washington appellate court declined to support the search of a student's pockets because he was in the school parking lot during the school day, a violation of the closed campus policy. The court emphasized that "there must be a nexus between the item sought and the infraction under investigation."[97] In the absence of other suspicious factors about the student, violation of the school's closed campus rule did not justify the automatic search

---

[93]Commonweatlh v. Buccella, 751 N.E.2d 373 (Mass. 2001).

[94]Jones v. Latexo Indep. Sch. Dist., 499 F. Supp. 223 (E.D. Tex. 1980).

[95]State v. D.T.W., 425 So. 2d 1383 (Fla. Civ. App. 1983). *See also* Covington County v. G.W., 767 So. 2d 187 (Miss. 2000) (holding that report of a student drinking beer in the school parking lot justified search of his truck; no warrant was required).

[96]Horton v. Goose Creek Indep. Sch. Dist., 690 F.2d 470, 478 (5th Cir. 1982).

[97]State v. B.A.S., 13 P.3d 244, 246 (Wash. Ct. App. 2000). *See also* Commonwealth v. Damian D., 752 N.E.2d 679 (Mass. 2001) (finding that a student's truancy did not establish reasonable suspicion to support school officials' search).

that led to the discovery of marijuana. The Alabama Supreme Court, however, found the search of two fifth grade students for the alleged theft of nine dollars reasonable based on the fact that they had been alone in the classroom at the time the money disappeared.[98]

Personal searches of students are permitted, but strip searches usually cannot be justified on the basis of reasonable suspicion. The Second Circuit noted that "as the intrusiveness of the search intensifies, the standard of Fourth Amendment 'reasonableness' approaches probable cause, even in the school context."[99] The Seventh Circuit, in a strongly worded statement, proclaimed in an Indiana case: "It does not require a constitutional scholar to conclude that a nude search of a 13-year-old child is an invasion of constitutional rights of some magnitude. More than that: it is a violation of any known principle of human decency."[100]

Unless exigent circumstances necessitate an immediate search to protect the safety of other students, a warrantless strip search is generally impermissible. In the absence of such a threat, the West Virginia high court found the strip search of a 14-year-old eighth-grader suspected of stealing $100 excessively intrusive, and thus unreasonable in scope.[101] Similarly, the New Mexico Supreme Court ruled that the strip search of two high school students to find a missing ring did not involve an immediate threat or individualized suspicion, which violated clearly established law.[102]

A few strip searches have been upheld with sufficient evidence of individualized suspicion, specifically related to drug use. The Sixth Circuit found the strip search of a female high school student suspected of possessing drugs permissible.[103] Among the significant facts establishing reasonable suspicion were a call from another student's mother, who described a glass vial containing a white powdery substance, a student informant's tip, a teacher's report of strange behavior, and an incriminating letter detailing drug use. Similarly, the Seventh Circuit found that substantial evidence existed to search a high school student with an "unusual bulge" in his sweatpants.[104] Acknowledging that the potential impact of a strip search is substantial, the court, however, emphasized that with the administrators' suspicion that the student was "crotching drugs," a strip search was the least intrusive way to proceed. Both circuit courts considered the nature of the contraband sought and the likelihood of it being hidden on the body in determining that the scope of the searches was reasonable.

Although courts have not prohibited strip searches of students, enough caveats exist to alert school officials of the inherent risks of such intrusive personal searches.

---

[98]Wynn v. Bd. of Educ., 508 So. 2d 1170 (Ala. 1987). *See also* D.L. v. State, 877 N.E.2d 500 (Ind. Ct. App. 2007) (finding that a pat-down search of a student that produced drugs was justified at its inception because the student was discovered in the hallway without identification or a pass during a nonpassing time); *In re* Juvenile, 931 A.2d 1229 (N.H. 2007) (finding student reports that the accused juvenile possessed a "large pot pipe" justified an assistant principal's search of the juvenile's locker).

[99]M.M. v. Anker, 607 F.2d 588, 589 (2d Cir. 1979).

[100]Doe v. Renfrow, 631 F.2d 91, 92–93 (7th Cir. 1980).

[101]State *ex rel.* Galford v. Mark Anthony B., 433 S.E.2d 41 (W. Va. 1993).

[102]Kennedy v. Dexter Consol. Schs., 10 P.3d 115 (N.M. 2000).

[103]Williams v. Ellington, 936 F.2d 881 (6th Cir. 1991).

[104]Cornfield v. Consol. High Sch. Dist. No. 230, 991 F.2d 1316 (7th Cir. 1993).

The judicial trend indicates that reasonable suspicion alone may be inadequate to justify most strip searches; rather, the required standard approaches probable cause necessitating specific evidence of a violation linked to an individual student. Except for emergency situations posing immediate danger to the safety of students, few circumstances appear to necessitate such intrusions.

Use of Metal Detectors

With concern about the high rate of violence in schools, metal detectors have become more commonplace as school officials seek to maintain a safe educational environment. Moreover, the use of metal detectors is no longer limited to secondary schools. In 2000, the Chicago chief education officer approved metal detectors for all the district's 489 elementary schools.[105] Although metal detectors are used in airports and many public buildings, their use does constitute a search for Fourth Amendment purposes. Such public searches have been found to be reasonable in balancing the threat of violence against the minimally intrusive nature of the search. As challenges have been raised about the use of metal detectors in schools, similar reasoning has been applied. **General scanning of students with metal detectors is only minimally intrusive on students' Fourth Amendment rights when weighed against school officials' interest in providing a safe school environment.**

The Pennsylvania high court upheld a general, uniform search of all students for weapons as they entered the high school building; each student's personal belongings were searched, and then a security officer scanned each student with a metal detector.[106] Individualized suspicion was not required in light of the high rate of violence in the school district. The court concluded that the search involved a greater intrusion on students' privacy interests than the search of a locker, but with the nonintrusive nature of the search, it remained a minimal intrusion. Similarly, the Eighth Circuit found a search of all male students from grades 6 to 12 for dangerous weapons to be minimally intrusive based on reasonable suspicion that weapons had been brought to school that day.[107] Students were scanned with a metal detector after they removed their shoes and the contents of their pockets. If the metal detector sounded, a subsequent "pat-down" search was conducted.

An Illinois appellate court assessed the reasonableness of the use of metal detectors from the perspective of schools' "special needs."[108] In the first year of using the detectors, Chicago school officials confiscated over 300 weapons (including 15 guns) from the high schools. With continued use of these devices, they showed a reduction of about 85 percent in weapons confiscated. The court, in concluding that individualized suspicion was not required to use metal detectors, noted that the purpose of the screening was to ensure a safe school environment for all students, not to secure evidence of a crime.

In each of the cases litigated, courts pointed to the violent context that led school officials to use metal detectors and the minimally intrusive nature of these devices. With

---

[105]Jessica Portner, "Girl's Slaying Elicits Calls for Metal Detectors," *Education Week* (March 15, 2000), p. 3.

[106]*In re* F.B., 726 A.2d 361 (Pa. 1999).

[107]Thompson v. Carthage Sch. Dist., 87 F.3d 979 (8th Cir. 1996).

[108]People v. Pruitt, 662 N.E.2d 540 (Ill. App. Ct. 1996).

increasing use, it can be expected that courts will continue to review the constitutional issues raised by metal detectors in school searches.

Drug-Detecting Canines

The use of drug-detecting dogs in searches raises several controversial questions regarding Fourth Amendment rights. Does the presence of a dog sniffing students constitute a search? Must reasonable suspicion exist to justify the use of dogs? Does the alert of a dog establish reasonable suspicion? A few courts have addressed these issues.

The Tenth Circuit upheld the use of trained police dogs in the sniffing of lockers but did not directly address the constitutional issues presented by the canine searches. Rather, the court discussed generally the school administrator's duty to inspect, even to the point that an inspection may violate Fourth Amendment rights. Under this broad grant of authority, the alert of a dog three times at a locker established reasonable suspicion to conduct a search.[109]

The Fifth Circuit, conversely, confronted the question of whether sniffing by a dog is a search in terms of an individual's reasonable expectation of privacy.[110] The appellate court noted that most courts, including the United States Supreme Court, have held that law enforcement use of canines for sniffing objects does not constitute a search.[111] Specifically, the court referenced cases involving checked luggage, shipped packages, public lockers, and cars on public streets. According to the court, a reasonable expectation of privacy does not extend to the airspace surrounding these objects. The court maintained that what has evolved is a doctrine of "public smell," equivalent to the "plain view" theory (that is, an object in plain view can be seized under certain circumstances). This point was illustrated by the example of a police officer detecting the odor of marijuana from an object or property. No search is involved because the odor is considered to be in "public view" and thus unprotected.

From this line of reasoning, the Fifth Circuit noted that the use of canines has been viewed as merely enhancing the ability to detect an odor, as the use of a flashlight improves vision. Accordingly, the court concluded that sniffing of student lockers and cars in public view was not a search, and therefore the Fourth Amendment did not apply. Although permitting the use of dogs to detect drugs, the court held that reasonable suspicion is required for a further search of a locker or car by school officials, and that such suspicion can be established only on showing that the dogs are reasonably reliable in detecting the actual presence of contraband.[112]

[109]Zamora v. Pomeroy, 639 F.2d 662, 670 (10th Cir. 1981).

[110]Horton v. Goose Creek Indep. Sch. Dist., 690 F.2d 470 (5th Cir. 1982).

[111]The Supreme Court concluded that the brief detention of a passenger's luggage at an airport for the purpose of subjecting it to a "sniff" test by a trained narcotics detection dog did not constitute a search under the Fourth Amendment. Use of canines was characterized as unique, involving a very limited investigation and minimal disclosure. United States v. Place, 462 U.S. 696 (1983).

[112]Subsequently, in denying a rehearing, the court clarified the issue of the dogs' reliability. According to the court, a school district does not have to establish with "reasonable certainty that contraband is present . . . or even that there is probable cause to believe that contraband will be found." Rather, there must be some evidence to indicate that the dogs' performance is reliable enough to give rise to a reasonable suspicion. Horton v. Goose Creek Indep. Sch. Dist., 693 F.2d 524, 525 (5th Cir. 1982).

In most instances, judicial support for the use of dogs has been limited to the sniffing of objects. The Seventh Circuit, however, concluded that the presence of dogs in a classroom was not a search.[113] In this Indiana case, school officials with the assistance of police officers conducted a schoolwide inspection for drugs in which trained dogs were brought into each classroom for approximately five minutes. When a dog alerted beside a student, school officials requested that the student remove the contents of his or her pockets or purse. A continued alert by the dog resulted in a strip search. The appellate court, in weighing the minimal intrusion of the dogs against the school's desire to eliminate a significant drug problem, concluded that sniffing of the students by the dogs did not constitute a search invoking Fourth Amendment protections. The search of pockets and purses, did involve an invasion of privacy but was justified because the dog's alert constituted reasonable cause to believe that the student possessed drugs. However, as discussed previously, the court drew the line at conducting a strip search based on a dog's alert.

In contrast to the reasoning of the Seventh Circuit, the Fifth Circuit held that sniffing of students by dogs significantly intrudes on an individual's privacy, thereby constituting a search.[114] Although recognizing that the sniffing of a person is a search, the court did not prohibit such searches but held that their intrusiveness must be weighed against the school's need to conduct the search. The court concluded that even with a significant need to search, individualized suspicion is required prior to the use of dogs because of the degree of intrusion on personal dignity and security. The Ninth Circuit concurred, noting that the significant intrusion on a student's expectation of privacy posed by dogs requires individualized suspicion.[115]

Given the concern about drugs in schools, it seems likely that school districts will continue to consider the use of drug-detecting canine units. Until the Supreme Court addresses whether such a practice constitutes a search in schools (requiring individualized suspicion) or whether a dog alert can establish reasonable grounds for a personal search, different interpretations among lower courts seem destined to persist.

Drug Testing

In an effort to control drug use among students,[116] some districts have considered schoolwide drug-testing programs. Such programs raise serious questions about students' privacy rights. In 1989, the Supreme Court held that urinalysis, the most frequently used means for drug testing, is a search under the Fourth Amendment.[117] Although the Court upheld the

---

[113]Doe v. Renfrow, 631 F.2d 91 (7th Cir. 1980).

[114]*Horton*, 690 F.2d 470.

[115]B.C. v. Plumas Unified Sch. Dist., 192 F.3d 1260 (9th Cir. 1999).

[116]The National Center on Addiction and Substance Abuse in its annual back-to-school survey of 12- to 17-year-olds in 2007 reported that 80 percent of high school students and 44 percent of middle school students would return that fall to schools in which drugs were used, kept, or sold. This is a substantial increase from its findings in 2002 (an increase of 39 percent for high school students and 63 percent for middle school). National Center on Addiction and Substance Abuse, *National Survey of American Attitudes on Substance Abuse XII: Teens and Parents* (New York: Columbia University, 2007), available at http://casacolumbia.org.

[117]Skinner v. Ry. Labor Executives' Ass'n, 489 U.S. 602 (1989); Nat'l Treasury Employees Union v. Von Raab, 489 U.S. 656 (1989).

testing of government employees for drug use in two decisions, the holdings were narrowly drawn and based on compelling governmental interests in ensuring public safety and national security. Individualized suspicion was not a precondition for conducting the urinalysis in these cases, but the narrow circumstances justifying the testing programs minimized the discretion of supervisors and the potential for arbitrariness.

The Supreme Court has rendered two decisions regarding the drug testing of students. **In 1995, the Court in** *Vernonia School District 47J v. Acton* **upheld a school district's drug policy authorizing random urinalysis drug testing of students participating in athletic programs.**[118] Emphasizing the district's "custodial and tutelary" responsibility for children, the Court recognized that school personnel can exercise a degree of supervision and control over children that would not be permitted over adults. This relationship was held to be pivotal in assessing the reasonableness of the district's drug policy—a policy undertaken "in furtherance of the government's responsibilities, under a public school system, as guardian and tutor of children entrusted to its care."[119] Addressing students' legitimate privacy expectations, the court noted that the lower privacy expectations within the school environment are reduced even further when a student elects to participate in sports.

In 2002, the Supreme Court in *Board of Education v. Earls* again reviewed a drug-testing policy but one that applied to students in all extracurricular activities, including athletics.[120] The policy required students to take a drug test prior to participation, to submit to random drug testing while involved in the activity, and to agree to be tested at any time when reasonable suspicion existed. Acknowledging that athletes' lower expectation of privacy was noted in *Vernonia*, the Court emphasized that the critical element in upholding the earlier policy was the school context. In sustaining the drug-testing policy in *Earls*, the Court reasoned that the collection procedures, like *Vernonia*, were minimally intrusive, information was kept in confidential files with limited access, and test results were not given to law enforcement authorities. Based on these factors, the Court concluded that the drug-testing policy was not a significant invasion of students' privacy rights. Although the students had argued that no pervasive drug problem existed to justify an intrusive measure like drug testing, the Court responded that it had never required such evidence before allowing the government to conduct suspicionless drug testing. Moreover, in light of the widespread use of drugs nationally and some evidence of increased use in this school, the Court found it entirely reasonable to enact this specific drug-testing policy.

It is clear that specific subgroups of students, such as athletes and participants in extracurricular activities, can be subjected to drug testing, but courts have not permitted blanket testing of *all* students. A Texas federal district court did not find exigent circumstances or other demonstrated compelling interests to justify a mandatory testing program of *all* students in grades 6 through 12.[121] Accordingly, the federal court held the

---

[118]515 U.S. 646 (1995).

[119]*Id*. at 665.

[120]536 U.S. 822 (2002). *See also* Linke v. N.W. Sch. Corp., 763 N.E.2d 972 (Ind. 2002) (finding a school's policy of random drug testing of students participating in athletics, extracurricular, and cocurricular activities permissible under state law).

[121]Tannahill *ex rel*. Tannahill v. Lockney Indep. Sch. Dist., 133 F. Supp. 2d 919 (N.D. Tex. 2001).

program unreasonable and unconstitutional under the Fourth Amendment. The Seventh Circuit rejected a school district's policy requiring drug and alcohol testing of all students suspended for three or more days for violating any school rule.[122] In this case, the student was suspended for fighting, and upon his return to school was informed that he was required to submit to a test for drug and alcohol use. When he refused, school officials suspended him again; refusal to take the test was treated as admission of unlawful drug use. In ruling that the policy violated the Fourth Amendment, the court did not find a connection between fighting and use of drugs. Furthermore, the suspension procedures in Indiana require school officials to meet with students prior to suspension. At that point, it is possible to determine if individualized suspicion exists to support testing a particular student for drugs or alcohol.

Although blanket or random drug testing of *all* students is not likely to withstand judicial challenge, **many schools subject students to urinalysis based on individualized suspicion, and such practices have not been invalidated by courts.**[123] Any drug-testing program, however, must be carefully constructed to avoid impairing students' Fourth Amendment privacy rights. The policy must be clearly developed, specifically identifying reasons for testing. Data collection procedures must be precise and well defined. Students and parents should be informed of the policy, and it is advisable to request students' consent prior to testing. If the test indicates drug use, the student must be given an opportunity to explain the results. Providing for the rehabilitation of the student rather than punishment strengthens the policy.

Police Involvement

A "reasonable suspicion" or a "reasonable cause to believe" standard is invoked in assessing the legality of school searches, but a higher standard generally is required when police officers are involved. The nature and extent of such involvement are important considerations in determining whether a search is reasonable. **If the police role is one of finding evidence of a crime, a warrant based on probable cause would be required.** However, searches by trained police officers employed by, or assigned to, a school district generally are governed by the *T.L.O.* reasonable suspicion standard rather than the probable cause standard.

Since the 1970s, decisions have tended to draw a sharp distinction between searches with and without police assistance. In an illustrative Illinois case, a school principal received a call that led him to suspect that three girls possessed illegal drugs.[124] On advice from the superintendent, he called the police to assist in the investigation. After the police arrived, the school nurse and the school psychologist searched each girl; however, no drugs were discovered. Subsequently, the students filed suit alleging that their civil rights had been violated. The court found that the police were not called merely to assist in maintaining school discipline but to search for evidence of a crime. Under the circumstances, the

---

[122]Willis v. Anderson Cmty. Sch., 158 F.3d 415 (7th Cir. 1998).

[123]*See* Gruenke v. Seip, 225 F.3d 290 (3d Cir. 2000) (concluding under the *Vernonia* standard that compelling a student athlete to submit to a pregnancy test, absent a legitimate health concern, was an unreasonable search).

[124]Picha v. Wielgos, 410 F. Supp. 1214 (N.D. Ill. 1976).

court concluded that the students had a constitutional right not to be searched unless the police had a warrant based on probable cause.

In contrast, the same Illinois court held that a police officer's involvement in persuading a student to relinquish the contents of his pockets did not violate Fourth Amendment rights under the *T.L.O.* standard.[125] The police officer's role was quite limited in this case. He was in the school building on another matter, and his role in the search was restricted simply to asking the student to empty his pockets. There was no police involvement in the investigation that led to detaining the student, nor was the evidence used for criminal prosecution. Similarly, the Eighth Circuit held that the assistance of a police officer assigned as a liaison officer in a high school did not subject a search for stolen property to the Fourth Amendment's probable cause standard.[126]

When police simply provide information regarding possible criminal conduct in a school, subsequent searches initiated by school administrators generally are not considered "police action" or "joint action." For example, a Pennsylvania court held that a student's Fourth Amendment rights were not violated when the principal conducted an investigation based on a report from the police.[127] Although the police informed the principal about an anonymous tip indicating that a student had brought a gun to school, school officials were not acting as agents of the police or at the request of the police. Rather, they were carrying out their duty to protect the safety and welfare of the student body.

In several decisions applying the reasonable suspicion standard to school searches, courts have specifically noted or implied that this lower standard is not applicable if law enforcement officials are involved. A Florida district court stated: "The reasonable suspicion standard does not apply in cases involving a search directed or participated in by a police officer."[128] Similarly, a Kentucky appellate court found the lower standard appropriate for searches in school settings in the absence of police participation. [129]

Courts have recognized the special role of school liaison or resource officers, noting that the "reasonable under the circumstances" standard applies when officers are working with school officials to maintain a safe school environment.[130] In an Eleventh Circuit case, the court, however, ruled that the actions of a deputy sheriff (assigned as a school resource officer) were not reasonable when he handcuffed a compliant 9-year-old girl solely to punish her for being disrespectful to a coach. The student was not viewed as a threat to the coach or anyone else. The court commented that any reasonable officer of the law would have known that this action was unreasonable.[131]

Although students possess Fourth Amendment rights against unreasonable searches, educators can search when suspicion exists that a student is violating a school rule or the

---

[125]Martens v. Dist. No. 220, 620 F. Supp. 29 (N.D. Ill. 1985).

[126]Cason v. Cook, 810 F.2d 188 (8th Cir. 1987).

[127]*In re* D.E.M., 727 A.2d 570 (Pa. Super. Ct. 1999).

[128]State v. D.T.W., 425 So. 2d 1838, 1385 (Fla. Civ. App. 1983).

[129]Rone v. Daviess County Bd. of Educ., 655 S.W.2d 28 (Ky. Ct. App. 1983).

[130]*See, e.g.,* Wilson *ex rel.* Adams v. Cahokia Sch. Dist., 470 F. Supp. 2d 897 (S.D. Ill. 2007); *In re* Randy G., 28 P.3d 239 (Cal. 2001); *In re* Josue T., 989 P.2d 431 (N.M. Ct. App. 1999).

[131]Gray *ex rel.* Alexander v. Bostic, 458 F.3d 1295 (11th Cir. 2006), *cert. denied,* 127 S. Ct. 2428 (2007).

FIGURE 8.5 Degree of Suspicion Required to Conduct Student Searches

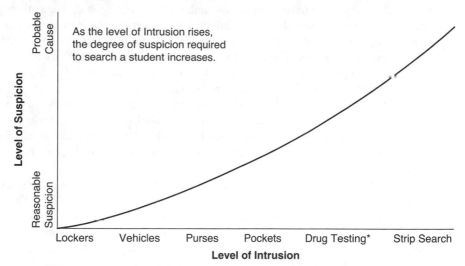

As the level of Intrusion rises, the degree of suspicion required to search a student increases.

Level of Suspicion (y-axis): Reasonable Suspicion to Probable Cause

Level of Intrusion (x-axis): Lockers, Vehicles, Purses, Pockets, Drug Testing*, Strip Search

* Under school district drug-testing policies, athletes and students participating in extracurricular activities can be subjected to suspicionless drug tests.

law. Searches that are highly intrusive, however, must be supported by a greater degree of suspicion (see Figure 8.5). Additionally, school personnel can protect themselves by adhering to a few basic guidelines.

- Students and parents should be informed at the beginning of the school term of the procedures for conducting locker and personal searches.
- Any personal search conducted should be based on "reasonable suspicion" that the student possesses contraband that may be disruptive to the educational process.
- The authorized person conducting a search should have another staff member present who can verify the procedures used in the search.
- School personnel should refrain from using strip searches or mass searches of groups of students.
- If police officials conduct a search in the school, either with or without the school's involvement, it is advisable to ensure that they first obtain a search warrant.

■ ■ ■ ■ ■ ▬▬▬▬▬▬▬▬▬▬▬▬▬▬

REMEDIES FOR UNLAWFUL DISCIPLINARY ACTIONS

If students are unlawfully punished, they are entitled to be restored (without penalty) to their status prior to the imposition of the punishment and to have their records expunged of any reference to the illegal punishment.

Several remedies are available to students who are unlawfully disciplined by school authorities. When physical punishment is involved, students can seek damages through assault and battery suits against those who inflicted the harm. For unwarranted suspensions or expulsions, students are entitled to reinstatement without penalty to grades and to have their school records expunged of any reference to the illegal disciplinary action. Remedies for violation of procedural due process rights may include reversal of a school board's decision rather than remand for further proceedings. If academic penalties are unlawfully imposed, grades must be restored and transcripts altered accordingly. For unconstitutional searches, illegally seized evidence may be suppressed, school records may be expunged, and damages may be awarded if the unlawful search results in substantial injury to the student. Courts also may award court costs when students successfully challenge disciplinary actions.

The Supreme Court has held that school officials can be sued for monetary damages in state courts as well as in federal courts under 42 U.S.C. Section 1983 if they arbitrarily violate students' federally protected rights in disciplinary proceedings.[132] In *Wood v. Strickland*, the Court declared that ignorance of the law is not a valid defense to shield school officials from liability if they should have known that their actions would impair students' clearly established federal rights.[133] Under *Wood*, a showing of malice is not always required to prove that the actions of school officials were taken in bad faith, but a mere mistake in carrying out duties does not render school authorities liable. The Court also recognized in *Wood* that educators are not charged with predicting the future direction of constitutional law. Other courts have reiterated school officials' potential liability in connection with student disciplinary proceedings, but to date students have not been as successful as teachers in obtaining monetary awards for constitutional violations. Courts have been reluctant to delineate students' "clearly established" rights, the impairment of which would warrant compensatory damages.

In 1978, the Supreme Court placed restrictions on the amount of damages that could be awarded to students in instances involving the impairment of procedural due process rights. In *Carey v. Piphus*, **the Court declared that students who were suspended without a hearing, but were not otherwise injured, could recover only nominal damages (not to exceed one dollar).**[134] This case involved two Chicago students who had been suspended without hearings for allegedly violating school regulations. The Supreme Court ruled that substantial damages could be recovered only if the suspensions were unjustified. Accordingly, the case was remanded for the district court to determine whether the students would have been suspended if correct procedures had been followed. This decision may appear to have strengthened the position of school boards in exercising discretion in disciplinary proceedings, but the Supreme Court indicated that students might be entitled to substantial damages if suspensions are proven to be unwarranted. In addition to damages, students also may be awarded attorneys' fees.

Educators should take every precaution to afford fair and impartial treatment to students. School personnel would be wise to provide at least an informal hearing if in doubt as

[132]Howlett v. Rose, 496 U.S. 356 (1990).

[133]420 U.S. 308 (1975).

[134]435 U.S. 247 (1978).

to whether a particular situation necessitates due process. Liability never results from the provision of too much due process, but damages can be assessed if violations of procedural rights result in unjustified suspensions, expulsions, or other disciplinary actions. Although constitutional and statutory due process requirements do not mandate that a specific procedure be followed in every situation, courts will carefully study the record to ensure that any procedural deficiencies do not impede the student's efforts to present a full defense.

CONCLUSION

In 1969, Justice Black noted that "school discipline, like parental discipline, is an integral and important part of training our children to be good citizens—to be better citizens."[135] Accordingly, school personnel have been empowered with the authority and duty to regulate pupil behavior in order to protect the interests of the student body and the school. Reasonable sanctions, such as suspensions and expulsions, can be imposed if students do not adhere to legitimate conduct regulations. Courts, however, will intervene if disciplinary procedures are arbitrary or impair students' protected rights.

Some type of procedural due process should be afforded to students prior to the imposition of punishments. For minor penalties, an informal hearing suffices; for serious punishments, more formal procedures are required (e.g., notification of parents, representation by counsel, opportunity to cross-examine witnesses). Legitimate punishments include suspensions, expulsions, academic sanctions, and transfer to other programs or schools. If state law or school board policy does not prohibit, reasonable corporal punishment also can be used as a disciplinary technique. Additionally, school personnel can search students if reasonable suspicion exists that the students possess contraband that will disrupt the school.

School authorities should ensure that constraints placed on student conduct are necessary for the proper functioning of the school. If students are unlawfully punished, school officials can be held liable for damage. Educators, however, have considerable latitude in controlling student behavior to maintain an appropriate educational environment and should not feel that the judiciary has curtailed their authority to discipline students. As noted in *Goss*, courts "have imposed requirements that are, if anything, less than a fair-minded principal would impose."[136]

POINTS TO PONDER

1. Under a school district's zero-tolerance discipline policy, a middle school student was expelled for one year for the possession of a knife on school property. A teacher discovered the knife when the student dropped his unzipped backpack and several items fell out, including a small Boy Scout pocketknife. The student claimed he had used the backpack for a camping trip the prior weekend and had forgotten to remove the knife. The parents filed suit,

[135]Tinker v. Des Moines Indep. Sch. Dist., 393 U.S. 503, 524 (1969) (Black, J., dissenting).
[136]Goss v. Lopez, 419 U.S. 565, 583 (1975).

arguing that the automatic one-year expulsion was arbitrary and violated their son's due process rights. What issues will the court consider? What is the likely outcome of the case?

2. A high school honor student was suspended for five days at the end of the fall semester. The suspension period included two days of the final exam period, and his request to make up three exams was denied. He asserted that the detrimental impact on his overall grade point average demanded greater due process than an informal conversation with the principal. What procedural protections are due in this suspension?

3. A 13-year-old student, who was in the hallway without a pass, belligerently responded when a teacher ordered him to return to his classroom. The teacher reacted by grabbing the student and throwing him against a locker. The boy suffered a cut to the forehead requiring stitches. He filed suit, claiming that the teacher's action impaired his substantive due process right to be free from unreasonable physical punishment. What issues are involved in this claim? Will the student succeed in his challenge?

4. A high school student discovered that his small, digital recorder was missing from his backpack. He had left the backpack open at his desk while he worked in a small group across the room. The teacher asked everyone to look around the classroom for the recorder. When it was not found, the teacher requested that the students bring their backpacks and jackets to the front of the room to be searched. All students' possessions were searched, but the recorder was not found. The next day one student's parents filed a complaint with the school principal, protesting the search of their son. Was this search reasonable under the circumstances? Explain.

■ ■ ■ ■ ■

CHAPTER NINE

TERMS AND CONDITIONS
OF EMPLOYMENT

Maintenance of a uniform system of public schools is one of the preeminent functions of the state legislature. The judiciary has clearly recognized the plenary power of the state in establishing, conducting, and regulating all public education functions. The legislature, through statutory law, establishes the boundaries within which educational systems operate; however, the actual administration of school systems is delegated to state boards of education, state departments of education, and local boards of education. These agencies enact rules and regulations pursuant to legislative policy for the operation of public schools.

Although state statutes and regulations are prominent in defining school personnel's employment rights, they cannot be viewed independently of state and federal constitutional provisions, civil rights laws, and negotiated agreements between school boards and teacher unions. These provisions may restrict or modify options available under the state school code. For example, the authority to transfer teachers may be vested in the school board, but the board cannot use this power to discipline a teacher for exercising protected constitutional rights. The board's discretion may be further limited if it has agreed in the master contract with the teachers' union (known as a collective bargaining agreement) to follow certain procedures prior to transferring an employee.

Among the areas affected by state statutory and regulatory provisions are the terms and conditions of educators' employment. With the intense public pressure to improve students' academic performance to meet annual yearly progress (AYP) under the No Child Left Behind (NCLB) Act,[1] most states have enacted education reform legislation demanding greater accountability from public schools. These efforts have had an impact not only on the curriculum and operation of schools but also on expectations for educators. NCLB demands that students be taught only by highly qualified educators in core subjects in each elementary and secondary school in all districts. At a minimum, highly qualified teachers hold a bachelor's degree, possess full state certification or licensure, and have demonstrated competence in their subject areas. Local school boards must ensure that these new demands are met, and courts have recognized the boards' expansive authority to fulfill

---

[1]20 U.S.C. § 6301 *et seq.* (2008).

these responsibilities. This chapter presents an overview of state requirements pertaining to licensure, employment, contracts, tenure, collective bargaining, and other related aspects of employment. Specific job requirements that implicate constitutional rights or anti-discrimination mandates are addressed in subsequent chapters.

■ ■ ■ ■ ■

LICENSURE

The state establishes minimum qualifications for licensure, which may include professional preparation as well as other prerequisites.

To qualify for a teaching position in public schools, **prospective teachers must acquire a valid license or certificate[2] from their state.** Licenses are issued according to each state's statutory provisions. States have not only the right but also the duty to establish minimum qualifications and to ensure that teachers meet these standards. Although the responsibility for licensing resides with state legislatures, administration of the process has been delegated to state boards of education and departments of education. In addition to state licensure, many teachers seek National Board Certification, involving an intensive assessment of teaching knowledge and skills by the National Board for Professional Teaching Standards. States and local school districts often provide financial support for teachers seeking this designation and also may provide annual stipends for National Board Certified Teachers.[3]

Licenses are granted primarily on the basis of professional preparation. In most states, educational requirements include a college degree, with minimum credit hours or courses in various curricular areas. Other prerequisites to licensure may include a minimum age, U.S. citizenship, signing of a loyalty oath, and passage of an academic examination. In addition, an applicant for certification may be required to have "good moral character." The definition of what constitutes good character often is elusive, with several factors entering into the determination. Courts generally will not rule on the wisdom of a certifying agency's assessment of character; they will intervene only if statutory or constitutional rights are abridged.

Certification of teachers by examination was common prior to the expansion of teacher education programs in colleges and universities. Then, for many years, only a few southern states required passage of an exam. With the emphasis on improving the quality of teachers and the strong movement toward standards-based licensure, most states now require some type of standardized test or performance-based assessment for teacher education programs, initial license, and/or license renewal.[4] **If a state establishes a test or**

---

[2]The words *licensure* and *certification* are used interchangeably in this chapter.

[3]*See* National Board for Professional Teaching Standards, available at www.nbpts.org/resources/state_local_ information, for state and local information regarding each state.

[4]Almost half the states have set up professional standards boards to govern and regulate standards-based criteria and assessment for licenses. The principal purpose of these boards, whose membership is composed primarily of teachers, is to address issues of educator preparation, licensure, and relicensure.

assessment process as an essential eligibility requirement, it can deny a license to individuals who do not pass. States using standardized tests often employ the Praxis exam. The United States Supreme Court has upheld the use of tests even though some have been shown to disproportionately disqualify minority applicants.[5]

Signing a loyalty oath may be a condition of obtaining a teaching license, but such oaths cannot be used to restrict association rights guaranteed under the United States Constitution. The Supreme Court has invalidated oaths that require teacher applicants to swear that they are not members of subversive organizations;[6] however, teachers can be required to sign an oath pledging faithful performance of duties and support for the federal Constitution and their state's constitution.[7] According to the Supreme Court, these oaths must be narrowly limited to affirmation of support for the government and a pledge not to act forcibly to overthrow the government.[8] Following the September 11, 2001, terrorist attacks, many states began enforcing the signing of existing loyalty oaths for public employment or enacted new laws. For example, Ohio's PATRIOT Act requires applicants for public employment to swear they are not terrorists and have no involvement with terrorist groups; refusal to sign the oath can result in exclusion from employment consideration.[9] Several of these new loyalty oaths potentially could be challenged as too broad under the Supreme Court's earlier rulings.

Some litigation has focused on legislative efforts to alter licensure standards by imposing new or additional requirements as prerequisites to renew a license. The Supreme Court of Texas held that teachers possessing life certificates could be required to pass an examination as a condition of continued employment.[10] Since the certificate was found to be a "license" rather than a "contract," the court held that new conditions for retention of the certificate could be imposed. Under statutory law, however, the Supreme Court of Rhode Island found that the State Board of Regents for Elementary and Secondary Education could not revoke valid five-year certificates for teachers' failure to meet new agency requirements.[11] Since state law provided that certificates were valid for a specified period of time and could be revoked only for cause, teachers could not be required to meet a state agency's new requirements until their certificates expired.

Licenses are issued for designated periods of time under various classifications such as emergency, temporary, provisional, professional, and permanent. Renewing or upgrading a license may require additional university course work, other continuing education activities, or passage of an examination. Licenses also specify professional position

---

[5]United States v. South Carolina, 445 F. Supp. 1094 (D.S.C. 1977), *aff'd sub nom.* Nat'l Educ. Ass'n v. South Carolina, 434 U.S. 1026 (1978). In challenges alleging discrimination, consent decrees between states and plaintiffs have contained agreements for the development of tests that reduce the discriminatory impact on minority candidates. *See, e.g.,* Allen v. Ala. State Bd. of Educ., 164 F.3d 1347 (11th Cir. 1999), *on remand,* 190 F.R.D. 602 (M.D. Ala. 2000).

[6]Keyishian v. Bd. of Regents, 385 U.S. 589 (1967).

[7]Ohlson v. Phillips, 397 U.S. 317 (1970).

[8]Cole v. Richardson, 405 U.S. 676 (1972); Connell v. Higginbotham, 403 U.S. 207 (1971).

[9]Ohio Rev. Code 119 § 2909.34 (2008).

[10]State v. Project Principle, 724 S.W.2d 387 (Tex. 1987).

[11]Reback v. R.I. Bd. of Regents for Elementary and Secondary Educ., 560 A.2d 357 (R.I. 1989).

(e.g., teacher, administrator, librarian), subject areas (e.g., history, English, math), and grade levels (e.g., elementary, high school). Where licensure subject areas have been established, a teacher must possess a valid license to teach a specific subject. A school district's failure to employ licensed teachers may result in the loss of state accreditation and financial support.

A license indicates only that a teacher has satisfied minimum state requirements; no absolute right exists to acquire a position. It does not entitle an individual to employment in a particular district or guarantee employment in the state, nor does it prevent a local school board from attaching additional prerequisites to employment. For example, an Iowa appellate court upheld a local school board's authority to require physical education teachers to complete training in cardiopulmonary resuscitation and water-safety instruction.[12] If a local board imposes additional standards, however, the requirements must be uniformly applied.

Teaching credentials must be in proper order to ensure full employment rights. Under most state laws, teachers must file their licenses with the district where they are employed. Failure to renew a license prior to expiration or to meet educational requirements necessary to maintain or acquire a higher-grade license can result in loss of employment. Without proper licensure, a teaching contract is unenforceable.

The state is empowered not only to license teachers but also to suspend or revoke licensure. Although a local board may initiate charges against a teacher, only the state can alter the status of a teacher's license. Revocation is a harsh penalty, generally foreclosing future employment as a teacher. As such, it must be based on statutory causes with full procedural rights provided to the teacher.[13] The most frequently cited grounds for revoking licenses are immorality, incompetency, contract violation, and neglect of duty. Examples of actions justifying revocation include misrepresenting experience and credentials in a job application and altering license to misrepresent areas of licensure (immorality);[14] theft of drugs and money (conduct unbecoming a teacher);[15] abusive comments to students and threats made in a letter of resignation (unprofessional conduct);[16] and assault on a minor female (lack of good moral character).[17]

When revocation or suspension of a license is being considered, assessment of a teacher's competency encompasses not only classroom performance but also actions outside the school setting that may impair his or her effectiveness. A Florida appellate court ruled that the state's Education Practices Commission did not violate a teacher's rights in

[12]Pleasant Valley Educ. Ass'n v. Pleasant Valley Cmty. Sch. Dist., 449 N.W.2d 894 (Iowa Ct. App. 1989).

[13]*See also* text accompanying notes 20–35, Chapter 12, for details of procedural due process.

[14]Nanko v. Dep't of Educ., 663 A.2d 312 (Pa. Commw. Ct. 1995). *See also* Patterson v. Superintendent of Pub. Instruction, 887 P.2d 411 (Wash. Ct. App. 1995) (supporting a six-month suspension of certificate for falsifying and omitting information from application).

[15]Crumpler v. State Bd. of Educ., 594 N.E.2d 1071 (Ohio Ct. App. 1991).

[16]Knight v. Winn, 910 So. 2d 310 (Fla. Dist. Ct. App. 2005). *See also* Prof'l Standards Comm'n v. Valentine, 603 S.E.2d 792 (Ga. Ct. App. 2004) (upholding a six-month suspension of a teacher's license for verbal altercations on school grounds; the teacher was being monitored by the commission because of an earlier DUI arrest).

[17]*In re* Morrill, 765 A.2d 699 (N.H. 2001). *See also* Boguslawski v. Dep't of Educ., 837 A.2d 614 (Pa. Commw. Ct. 2003) (finding that a teacher's improper touching of fourth grade male students supported revocation for immorality and intemperance).

permanently revoking her certificate for sending sexually explicit material over the Internet to her seventh grade middle school students.[18] In an Arizona case, the appellate court upheld license revocation of a teacher who had been in numerous altercations with neighbors and had been charged on several occasions with disorderly conduct and criminal damage. His tendency to act with violence and aggression was deemed to affect his fitness to teach.[19] Courts will not overturn the judgment of state boards regarding an educator's fitness to teach unless evidence clearly establishes that the decision is unreasonable or unlawful.

■ ■ ■ ■ ■

EMPLOYMENT BY LOCAL SCHOOL BOARDS

School boards are vested with the power to appoint teachers and to establish professional and academic employment standards above the state minimums.

As noted, a license does not guarantee employment in a state; it attests only that educators have met minimum state requirements. The decision to employ a licensed teacher or administrator is among the discretionary powers of local school boards. Although such powers are broad, school board actions may not be arbitrary, capricious, or violate an individual's statutory or constitutional rights.[20] Furthermore, boards must comply with mandated statutory procedures as well as locally adopted procedures.[21] Employment decisions also must be neutral as to race, religion, national origin, and sex.[22] Unless protected individual rights are abridged, courts will not review the wisdom of a local school board's judgment in employment decisions made in good faith.

The responsibility for hiring teachers and administrators is vested in the school board as a collective body and cannot be delegated to the superintendent or board members individually. In most states, binding employment agreements between a teacher or an administrator and the school board must be approved at legally scheduled board meetings. Most state laws specify that the superintendent must make employment recommendations to the board; however, the board is not compelled to follow these recommendations unless mandated to do so by law.

School boards possess extensive authority in establishing job requirements and conditions of employment for school personnel. The following sections examine the school board's power to impose specific conditions on employment and to assign personnel.

---

[18]Wax v. Horne, 844 So. 2d 797 (Fla. Dist. Ct. App. 2003).

[19]Winters v. Ariz. Bd. of Educ., 83 P.3d 1114 (Ariz. Ct. App. 2004). *But see* Prof'l Standards Comm'n v. Peterson, 643 S.E.2d 899 (Ga. Ct. App. 2007) (determining that failure of two teachers to supervise underage drinking at a party in their home did not justify a short suspension of certificates; it did not affect their effectiveness in the classroom).

[20]*See generally* Chapter 10 for a discussion of teachers' constitutional rights.

[21]*See, e.g.,* Swanson v. Bd. of Educ. County of Putnam, 600 S.E.2d 299 (W. Va. 2004).

[22]*See generally* Chapter 11 for a discussion of discriminatory employment practices. Under limited circumstances, sex may be a *bona fide* occupational qualification (e.g., supervision of the girls' locker room).

Employment Requirements

The state's establishment of minimum licensure standards for educators does not preclude the local school board from requiring higher professional or academic standards as long as they are applied in a uniform and nondiscriminatory manner. For example, school boards often establish continuing education requirements for teachers, and a board's right to dismiss teachers for failing to satisfy such requirements has been upheld by the Supreme Court.[23] The Court concluded that school officials merely had to establish that the requirement was rationally related to a legitimate state objective, which in this case was to provide competent, well-trained teachers.

School boards can adopt reasonable health and physical requirements for school personnel. Courts have recognized that such standards are necessary to safeguard the health and welfare of students and other employees. For example, the First Circuit held that a school board could compel an administrator to submit to a psychiatric examination as a condition of continued employment because a reasonable basis existed for the board members to believe that the administrator might jeopardize the safety of students.[24] Similarly, the Sixth Circuit ruled that a school board could justifiably order a teacher to submit to mental and physical examinations when his aberrant behavior affected job performance.[25] Health and physical requirements imposed on school personnel, however, must not be applied in an arbitrary manner. In a Second Circuit case, the court held that it was reasonable to request that a teacher undergo a psychiatric examination prior to returning to work after an extended sick leave, but the demand to release the teacher's medical records to the examining physician as well as the school board was arbitrary.[26] School officials were not competent to assess the records, thus the request served no legitimate purpose. School board standards for physical fitness also must be rationally related to the ability to perform teaching duties. In addition, regulations must not contravene various state and federal laws designed to protect the rights of persons with disabilities.[27]

Under state laws, most school boards are required to conduct a criminal records check of all employees prior to employment. The screening process may require individuals to consent to fingerprinting. Concern for students' safety also has led some school districts to require teacher applicants to submit to drug testing. The Sixth Circuit upheld such testing, noting that teachers occupy safety-sensitive positions in a highly regulated environment with diminished privacy expectations.[28]

Unless prohibited by law, school boards may require school personnel to live within the school district as a condition of employment. Typically, residency requirements have

---

[23]Harrah Indep. Sch. Dist. v. Martin, 440 U.S. 194 (1979) (upholding a policy requiring teachers to earn an additional five semester hours of college credit every three years while employed).

[24]Daury v. Smith, 842 F.2d 9 (1st Cir. 1988).

[25]Sullivan v. River Valley Sch. Dist., 197 F.3d 804 (6th Cir. 1999). *See also* Gardner v. Niskayuna Cent. Sch. Dist., 839 N.Y.S.2d 317 (App. Div. 2007) (finding that a school board is charged with determining that teachers are fit to teach; thereby, teachers may be required to submit to physical or mental exams).

[26]O'Connor v. Pierson, 426 F.3d 187 (2d Cir. 2005).

[27]*See* Chapter 11 for a discussion of discrimination based on disabilities.

[28]Knox County Educ. Ass'n v. Knox County Bd. of Educ., 158 F.3d 361 (6th Cir. 1998). For further discussion of Fourth Amendment rights of employees, *see* text accompanying notes 80–92, Chapter 10.

been imposed in urban communities and encompass all city employees including educators. Proponents contend that the policy builds stronger community relationships and stabilizes the city tax base. The Supreme Court upheld a municipal regulation requiring all employees hired after a specified date in Philadelphia to be residents of the city, finding no impairment of Fourteenth Amendment equal protection rights or interference with interstate and intrastate travel.[29] Those already employed were not required to alter their residence. In upholding the regulation, the Court distinguished a requirement of residency of a given duration prior to employment (which violates the right to interstate travel) from a continuing residency requirement applied after employment. Lower courts have applied similar reasoning in upholding residency requirements for public educators.[30] Although residency requirements after employment do not violate the Constitution, they may be impermissible under state law.[31]

Unlike residency requirements, school board policies requiring employees to send their children to public schools have been declared unconstitutional. Parents have a constitutionally protected right to direct the upbringing of their children that cannot be restricted without a compelling state interest. The Eleventh Circuit held that a school board policy requiring employees to enroll their children in public schools could not be justified to promote an integrated public school system and good relationships among teachers when weighed against the right of parents to direct the education of their children.[32]

Assignment of Personnel and Duties

The authority to assign teachers to schools within a district resides with the board of education. As with employment in general, these decisions must not be arbitrary, made in bad faith, or in retaliation for the exercise of protected rights. Within the limits of a license, a teacher can be assigned to teach in any school at any grade level. Assignments designated in the teacher's contract, however, cannot be changed during a contractual period without the teacher's consent. That is, a board cannot reassign a teacher to a first grade class if the contract specifies a fifth grade assignment. If the contract designates only a teaching assignment within the district, the assignment still must be in the teacher's licensure area. Also, objective, nondiscriminatory standards must be used in any employment or assignment decision. Assignments to achieve racial balance may be permitted in school districts that have not eliminated the effects of school segregation. Any racial classification, however, must be temporary and necessary to eradicate the effects of prior discrimination.

School boards retain the authority to assign or transfer teachers, but such decisions often are challenged as demotions requiring procedural due process. Depending on statutory law, factors considered in determining whether a reassignment is a demotion may

[29]McCarthy v. Phila. Civil Serv. Comm'n, 424 U.S. 645 (1976).

[30]*See, e.g.,* Wardwell v. Bd. of Educ., 529 F.2d 625 (6th Cir. 1976); Providence Teachers' Union Local 958 v. City Council, 888 A.2d 948 (R.I. 2005).

[31]*See, e.g.,* Ind. Code Ann. § 20-28-10-13 (2008); Mass. Gen. Laws ch. 71 § 38 (2008). As urban school systems face difficulty in recruiting teachers, some (e.g., Philadelphia and Pittsburgh) have abolished their residency requirements. *See* Jeff Archer, "City Districts Lifting Rules on Residency," *Education Week* (January 16, 2002), pp. 1, 13.

[32]Stough v. Crenshaw County Bd. of Educ., 744 F.2d 1479 (11th Cir. 1984).

include reduction in salary, responsibility, and stature of position. A transfer from one grade level to another is not usually considered a demotion. Courts recognize the pervasive authority of the superintendent and board to make teaching assignments, as long as the assignments are not in conflict with state law, federal rights, or the collective bargaining contract.[33]

Administrative reassignments frequently are challenged as demotions because of reductions in salary, responsibility, and status of the position. Again, as in the assignment of teachers, statutory law defines an individual employee's rights. The South Carolina appellate court concluded that the reassignment of an assistant superintendent to a principal position was within the school board's discretion when it did not involve a reduction in salary or violate the district's regulations.[34] Similarly, the Seventh Circuit found that the reassignment of a principal to a central office position did not involve an economic loss requiring an opportunity for a hearing.[35] A Wisconsin principal was not removed from her position, but the school board reassigned many of her duties and responsibilities. She resigned her position and claimed that violation of her property interests in the position precipitated the resignation. The Seventh Circuit concluded that under Wisconsin law no right existed to performing specific duties as a principal.[36] Moreover, reassignment from an administrative to a teaching position because of financial constraints or good faith reorganization is not a demotion requiring due process unless procedural protections are specified in state law.

The types of noninstructional duties that can be assigned to teachers are typically specified in a teacher's contract or the master contract negotiated between the school board and the teachers' union. In the absence of such specification, school officials can make reasonable and appropriate assignments, such as activities that are an integral part of the school program and related to the employee's teaching responsibilities. Reasonableness of an assignment is typically evaluated in terms of time involvement, teachers' interests and abilities, benefits to students, and the professional nature of the duty. Refusal to accept reasonable assigned duties can result in dismissal.

■ ■ ■ ■ ■ ▬▬▬

CONTRACTS

Teacher contracts must satisfy the general principles of contract law as well as conform to any additional specifications contained in state law.

The employment contract defines the rights and responsibilities of the teacher and the school board in the employment relationship. The general principles of contract law apply to this contractual relationship. Like all other legal contracts, it must contain the basic

---

[33]*See, e.g.,* Kodl v. Bd. of Educ., 490 F.3d 558 (7th Cir. 2007) (finding that an older middle school teacher's transfer to an elementary school did not violate any federal rights).

[34]Barr v. Bd. of Trs., 462 S.E.2d 316 (S.C. Ct. App. 1995).

[35]Bordelon v. Chi. Sch. Reform Bd. of Trs., 233 F.3d 524 (7th Cir. 2000).

[36]Ulichny v. Merton Cmty. Sch. Dist., 249 F.3d 686 (7th Cir. 2001).

elements of (1) offer and acceptance, (2) competent parties, (3) consideration, (4) legal subject matter, and (5) proper form.[37] Beyond these basic elements, it also must meet the requirements specified in state law and administrative regulations.

The authority to contract with teachers is an exclusive right of the board. The school board's offer of a position to a teacher—including (1) designated salary, (2) specified period of time, and (3) identified duties and responsibilities—creates a binding contract when accepted by the teacher. In most states, only the board can make an offer, and this action must be approved by a majority of the board members in a properly called meeting. In a Washington case, the coordinator of special services extended a teacher an offer of employment at the beginning of the school year, pending a check of references from past employers. The recommendations were negative, and the teacher was not recommended to the board even though she had been teaching for several weeks. The state appellate court held that no enforceable contract existed; under state law, hiring authority resides with the board.[38]

Contracts also can be invalidated because of lack of competent parties. To form a valid, binding contract, both parties must have the legal capacity to enter into an agreement. The school board has been recognized as a legally competent party with the capacity to contract. A teacher who lacks a license or is under the statutorily required age for licensure is not considered a competent party for contractual purposes. Consequently, a contract made with such an individual is not enforceable.

Consideration is another essential element of a valid contract. *Consideration* is something of value that one party pays in return for the other party's performance. Teachers' monetary compensation and benefits are established in the salary schedule adopted by the school board or negotiated between the school board and the teachers' association.[39] The contract also must involve a legal subject matter and follow the proper form required by law. Most states prescribe that a teacher's contract must be in writing to be enforceable, but if there is no statutory specification, an oral agreement is legally binding on both parties.

In addition to employment rights derived from the teaching contract, provisions of any collective bargaining agreement (master contract) are part of the employment contract. Statutory provisions and school board rules and regulations also may be considered part of the terms and conditions of the contract. If not included directly, the provisions existing at the time of the contract may be implied. Moreover, the contract cannot be used as a means of waiving teachers' statutory or constitutional rights.[40]

---

[37]For a discussion of contract elements, *see* Kern Alexander and M. David Alexander, *American Public School Law*, 6th ed. (Belmont, CA: West/Thomson Learning, 2005).

[38]McCormick v. Lake Wash. Sch. Dist., 992 P.2d 511 (Wash. Ct. App. 2000).

[39]*See* Sherwood Nat'l Educ. Ass'n v. Sherwood-Cass R-VIII Sch. Dist., 168 S.W.3d 456 (Mo. Ct. App. 2005) (finding the payment of commitment fees to teachers for the early return of their signed contracts, in which they agreed to work two years in the district "off salary schedule" to be invalid); Davis v. Greenwood Sch. Dist., 620 S.E.2d 65 (S.C. 2005) (holding that the reduction of a 10 percent incentive annual payment to teachers for acquiring national board certification to a $3,000 flat rate per year did not violate the teachers' contracts and was within the board's discretion to manage the district's finances).

[40]*See, e.g.,* Denuis v. Dunlap, 209 F.3d 944 (7th Cir. 2000) (holding that a teacher was not required to relinquish constitutional privacy rights regarding medical or financial records for an employment background check).

Term and Tenure Contracts

Two basic types of employment contracts are issued to teachers: term contracts and tenure contracts. *Term contracts* are valid for a fixed period of time (e.g., one or two years). At the end of the contract period, renewal is at the discretion of the school board; nonrenewal requires no explanation unless mandated by statute. Generally, a school board is required only to provide notice prior to the expiration of the contract that employment will not be renewed. *Tenure contracts*, created through state legislative action, ensure teachers that employment will be terminated only for adequate cause and that procedural due process will be provided. **After the award of tenure or during a term contract, school boards cannot unilaterally abrogate teachers' contracts. At a minimum, the teacher must be provided procedural protections consisting of notice of the dismissal charges and a hearing.**[41]

Since tenure contracts involve statutory rights, specific procedures and protections vary among the states. Consequently, judicial interpretations in one state provide little guidance in understanding another state's law. Most tenure statutes specify requirements and procedures for obtaining tenure and identify causes and procedures for dismissing a tenured teacher. In interpreting tenure laws, courts have attempted to protect teachers' rights while simultaneously preserving school officials' flexibility in personnel management.

Prior to a school board's awarding a tenure contract to a teacher, most states require a probationary period of approximately three years to assess a teacher's ability and competence. During this probationary period, teachers receive term contracts, and there is no guarantee of employment beyond each contract. Tenure statutes generally require regular and continuous service to complete the probationary period.

The authority to grant a tenure contract is a discretionary power of the local school board that cannot be delegated. Although the school board confers tenure, it cannot alter the tenure terms established by the legislature; the legislature determines the basis for tenure, eligibility requirements, and the procedures for acquiring tenure status. Thus, if a statute requires a probationary period, this term of service must be completed prior to the school board's awarding tenure. A board may be compelled to award tenure if a teacher completes the statutory requirements and the school board does not take action to grant or deny tenure. Unless specified in statute, however, tenure is not transferable from one school district to another. This ensures that school officials are provided an opportunity to evaluate teachers before granting tenure.

States often limit the award of tenure to teaching positions, thereby excluding administrative, supervisory, and staff positions. Where tenure is available for administrative positions, probationary service and other specified statutory terms must be met. Although tenure as a teacher usually does not imply tenure as an administrator, most courts have concluded that continued service as a certified professional employee, albeit as an administrator, does not alter tenure rights acquired as a teacher. The Supreme Court of Wyoming noted, "It is desirable—and even important—to have people with extensive classroom teaching experience in administrative positions. It would be difficult to fill administrative

---

[41]*See* text accompanying notes 20–25, Chapter 12, for discussion of procedural due process requirements.

positions with experienced teachers if the teachers would have to give up tenure upon accepting administrative roles."[42]

Supplemental Contracts

School boards can enter into supplement contracts with teachers for duties beyond the regular teaching assignments. As with teaching contracts, authority to employ resides with the school board. Generally, these are limited contracts specifying the additional duties, compensation, and time period. Extra duties often relate to coaching, chairing a department, supervising student activities or clubs, and other special assignments.

Supplemental service contracts are usually considered outside the scope of tenure protections. Coaches, in particular, have asserted that supplemental contracts are an integral part of the teaching position and thereby must be afforded the procedural and substantive protections of state tenure laws. Generally, tenure rights apply only to employment in licensure areas and the lack of licensure requirements for coaches in a state often negates tenure claims for such positions. Some courts also have distinguished coaching and various extra duties from teaching responsibilities based on the extracurricular nature of the assignment and supplemental compensation. In denying the claim of a 10-year veteran baseball coach who was fired, the Ninth Circuit held that the coach did not have a protected interest in his coaching position, since California law specified that extra-duty assignments could be terminated by the school board at any time.[43] When both classroom teaching and extra-duty assignments are covered in the same contract, however, protected property interests may be created. Accordingly, the teacher would be entitled to due process prior to the termination of the extra-duty assignment.

Because coaching assignments typically require execution of a supplemental contract, a teacher can resign from a coaching position and maintain the primary teaching position. School boards having difficulty in filling coaching positions, however, may tender an offer to teach on the condition that an individual assume certain coaching responsibilities. If a single teaching and coaching contract is found to be indivisible, a teacher cannot unilaterally resign the coaching duties without relinquishing the teaching position.[44] Individual state laws must be consulted to determine the status of such contracts.

When teaching and coaching positions are combined, a qualified teaching applicant who cannot assume the coaching duties may be rejected. This practice, however, may be vulnerable to legal challenge if certain classes of applicants, such as women, are excluded from consideration. In an Arizona case, female plaintiffs successfully established that a school district was liable for sex discrimination by coupling a high school biology teaching position with a football coaching position. The school board was unable to demonstrate a business necessity for the practice that resulted in female applicants for the teaching position being eliminated from consideration.[45]

---

[42]Spurlock v. Bd. of Trs., 699 P.2d 270, 272 (Wyo. 1985).

[43]Lagos v. Modesto City Schs. Dist., 843 F.2d 347 (9th Cir. 1988). *See also* Bd. of Educ. v. Code, 57 S.W.3d 820 (Ky. 2001) (ruling that the basketball coach was not entitled to a formal evaluation prior to nonrenewal of his contract).

[44]*See, e.g.,* Smith v. Petal Sch. Dist., 956 So. 2d 273 (Miss. Ct. App. 2006), *cert. denied*, 957 So. 2d 1004 (2007).

[45]Civil Rights Div. of the Ariz. Dep't of Law v. Amphitheater Unified Sch. Dist. No. 10, 706 P.2d 745 (Ariz. Ct. App. 1985).

Domestic Partner Benefits

Increasingly, legal challenges are being brought to secure health, retirement, and other benefits for domestic partners of gay, lesbian, bisexual, and transgendered (GLBT) employees. Rights for GLBT employees may exist under state constitutional and statutory provisions or institutional policies. Only Vermont and Connecticut have sanctioned same-sex civil unions by law, and the Massachusetts's high court has held that denial of civil marriage to same-sex couples violates the state constitution.[46] Several other states—California, Hawaii, Maine, and New Jersey—have enacted domestic partnership laws. Rights under these laws, however, vary significantly, being only symbolic in some instances and in others conferring full rights and benefits.[47] In reviewing claims for benefits, some courts have held that the denial of benefits discriminates on the basis of marital status or that unmarried partners have been treated differently by benefits policies and denial is unrelated to any legitimate governmental interest.[48]

Yet, other courts have firmly upheld the denial of benefits, finding no discrimination.[49] With the federal Defense of Marriage Act (DOMA) and subsequent adoption of mini-DOMAs in 42 states, employees will continue to face significant challenges in achieving equality of benefits for their domestic partners.[50] For example, in 2007 the Michigan Court of Appeals interpreted the state's constitutional marriage amendment as precluding employers from providing same-sex domestic partner benefits. The court ruled that the law, which provides that "the union of one man and one woman in marriage shall be the only agreement recognized as a marriage or similar union for any purpose," blocks the recognition of domestic partnership agreements because it is a status *similar* to marriage.[51] If other state courts follow the Michigan reasoning, the state DOMAs will render many existing domestic partnership programs invalid.

---

[46]Goodridge v. Dep't of Pub. Health, 798 N.E.2d 941 (Mass. 2003). *See also* Varnum v. Brien, No. CV5965 (Iowa Dist. Ct. Aug. 30, 2007) (ruling that it is unconstitutional under the Iowa Constitution for the state to deny same-sex couples the right to marry).

[47]*See* Janice McClendon, "A Small Step Forward in the Last Civil Rights Battle: Extending Benefits under Federally Regulated Benefit Plans to Same-Sex Couples," *New Mexico Law Review,* vol. 36 (Winter 2006), pp. 99–123.

[48]*See, e.g.,* Univ. of Alaska v. Tumeo, 933 P.2d 1147 (Alaska 1998); Snetsinger v. Mont. Univ. Sys., 104 P.3d 445 (Mont. 2004); Tanner v. Or. Health Scis. Univ., 971 P.2d 435 (Or. Ct. App. 1998); Baker v. State, 744 A.2d 864 (Vt. 1999). *See also* Devlin v. City of Phil., 862 A.2d 1234 (Pa. 2004) (holding that a city did not exceed its authority in extending benefits to life partners of its employees); Pritchard v. Madison Metro. Sch. Dist., 625 N.W.2d 613 (Wis. Ct. App. 2001) (denying plaintiffs' challenge that the school system was in violation of state law by providing insurance coverage for unmarried partners of a school district employee).

[49]*See, e.g.,* Rutgers Council of AAUP Chapters v. Rutgers State Univ., 689 A.2d 828 (N.J. Super. Ct. App. Div. 1997); Funderburke v. Uniondale Union Free Sch. Dist. No. 15, 660 N.Y.S.2d 659 (Sup. Ct. 1997). *See also* Donna Euben, *Domestic Partnership Benefits on Campus:A Litigation Update* (Washington, DC: American Association of University Professors, 2002).

[50]McClendon, *supra* note 47, p. 101. *See also* Defense of Marriage Act, 1 U.S.C. § 7 (2008); 28 U.S.C. § 1738C (2008). Congress passed the DOMA in reaction to growing concern about states recognizing same-sex marriages.Under the federal law, marriage is defined as a union between a man and a woman. Furthermore, the act states that individual states are not required to recognize same-sex marriages sanctioned by other states.

[51]Nat'l Pride at Work v. Gov. of Mich., 732 N.W.2d 139, 143 (Mich. Ct. App. 2007), *appeal granted,* 731 N.W.2d 405 (Mich. 2007).

Leaves of Absence

Contracts may specify various types of leaves of absence. Within the parameters of state law, school boards have discretion in establishing requirements for these leaves. A school board may place restrictions on when teachers can take personal leave—for example, no leaves on the day before or after a holiday, or no more than two consecutive days of personal leave.[52] This topic often is the subject of collective negotiations, with leave provisions specified in bargained agreements. School boards, however, cannot negotiate leave policies that impair rights guaranteed by the United States Constitution and various federal and state anti-discrimination laws.[53] Similarly, when state law confers specific rights, local boards do not have the discretion to deny or alter these rights. Generally, statutes identify employees' rights related to various kinds of leaves such as sick leave, personal leave, pregnancy or child-care leave, sabbatical leave, disability leave, family leave, and military leave. State laws pertaining to leaves of absence usually specify eligibility for benefits, minimum days that must be provided, whether leave must be granted with or without pay, and restrictions that may be imposed by local school boards. If a teacher meets all statutory and procedural requirements for a specific leave, a school board cannot deny the request.

■ ■ ■ ■ ■

PERSONNEL EVALUATIONS

A school board's broad authority to determine teacher performance standards may be restricted by state-imposed evaluation requirements.

To ensure a quality teaching staff, many states have enacted laws requiring periodic appraisal of teaching performance. Beyond the purposes of faculty improvement and remediation, results of evaluations may be used in a variety of employment decisions, including retention, tenure, dismissal, promotion, salary, reassignment, and reduction-in-force. When adverse personnel decisions are based on evaluations, legal concerns of procedural fairness arise. Were established state and local procedures followed? Did school officials employ equitable standards? Was sufficient evidence collected to support the staffing decision? Were evaluations conducted in a uniform and consistent manner?

School systems have broad discretionary powers to establish teacher performance criteria, but state statutes may impose specific evaluation requirements. More than half of the states have enacted laws governing teacher evaluation. Content and requirements vary substantially across states, with some states merely mandating the establishment of an appraisal system and others specifying procedures and criteria to be employed.[54] Iowa law notes only that the local board must establish an evaluation system.[55] In contrast,

---

[52]*See, e.g.,* Amaral-Whittenberg v. Alanis, 123 S.W.3d 714 (Tex. App. 2003).

[53]Charges of discrimination in connection with leave policies pertaining to pregnancy-related absences and the observance of religious holidays are discussed in Chapter 11.

[54]*See* Perry Zirkel, "Legal Boundaries for Performance Evaluation of Public School Professional Personnel," *Education Law Reporter*, vol. 172, no. 1 (2003), pp. 1–15.

[55]Iowa Code Ann. § 279.14 (2008).

California specifies the intent of evaluations, areas to be assessed, frequency of evaluations, notice to employees of deficiencies, and an opportunity to improve performance.[56] Florida requires the superintendent of schools to establish criteria and procedures for appraisal, including evaluation at least once a year, a written record of assessment, prior notice to teachers of criteria and procedures, and a meeting with the evaluator to discuss the results of the evaluation.[57] Although a few evaluation systems are established at the state level, state laws usually require local officials to develop evaluation criteria, often in conjunction with teachers or other professionals. Unless prohibited by law, it also may be negotiable with the teachers' union.

Courts generally require strict compliance with evaluation requirements and procedures identified in statutes, board policies, or employment contracts. When school boards have been attentive to these requirements, courts have upheld challenged employment decisions. For example, a California appellate court found that a teacher's dismissal comported with state evaluation requirements because he received periodic appraisals noting specific instances of unsatisfactory performance.[58] The evaluation reports informed the teacher of the system's expectations, his specific teaching weaknesses, and actions needed to correct deficiencies.

Courts are reluctant to interject their judgment into the teacher evaluation process. Judicial review generally is limited to the procedural issues of fairness and reasonableness. Several principles emerge from case law to guide educators in developing equitable systems: standards for assessing teaching adequacy must be defined and communicated to teachers; criteria must be applied uniformly and consistently; an opportunity and direction for improvement must be provided; and procedures specified in state laws and school board policies must be followed.

■ ■ ■ ■ ■

PERSONNEL RECORDS

Maintenance, access, and dissemination of personnel information must conform to federal and state laws and contractual agreements.

Because several statutes in each state as well as employment contracts govern school records, it is difficult to generalize about the specific nature of teachers' privacy rights regarding personnel files. State privacy laws that place restrictions on maintenance and access to the school records typically protect personnel information. Among other provisions, these laws usually require school boards to maintain only necessary and relevant information, provide individual employees access to their files, inform employees of the various uses of the files, and establish a procedure for challenging the accuracy of information.

[56]Cal. Educ. Code Ann. §§ 44660–44665 (2008).

[57]Fla. Stat. § 231.29 (2008).

[58]Perez v. Comm'n on Prof'l Competence, 197 Cal. Rptr. 390 (Ct. App. 1983). *See also* Tippecanoe Educ. Ass'n v. Tippecanoe Sch. Corp., 700 N.E.2d 241 (Ind. Ct. App. 1998) (finding that the evaluator adequately informed the teacher of deficiencies).

Collective bargaining contracts may impose additional and more stringent requirements regarding access and dissemination of personnel information.

A central issue in the confidentiality of personnel files is whether the information constitutes a public record that must be reasonably accessible to the general public. Public record, freedom of information, or right-to-know laws that grant broad access to school records may directly conflict with privacy laws, requiring courts to balance the interests of the teacher, the school officials, and the public. The specific provisions of state laws determine the level of confidentiality granted to personnel records.[59] The federal Freedom of Information Act (FOIA),[60] which serves as a model for many state FOIAs, often is used by courts in interpreting state provisions. Unlike the federal law, however, many states do not exempt personnel records.

In the absence of a specific exemption, most courts have concluded that **any doubt concerning the appropriateness of disclosure should be decided in favor of public disclosure.** The Supreme Court of Michigan held that teachers' personnel files are open to the public because they are not specifically exempt by law.[61] The Supreme Court of Washington noted that the public disclosure act mandated disclosure of information that is of legitimate public concern.[62] As such, the state superintendent of public instruction was required to provide a newspaper publisher records specifying the reasons for teacher certificate revocations. The Supreme Court of Connecticut interpreted the state Freedom of Information Act exemption, prohibiting the release of information that would constitute an invasion of personal privacy, to include employees' evaluations[63] but not their sick-leave records.[64] In the termination of a teacher for conducting pornographic Internet searches on his work computer, the Supreme Court of Wisconsin held that a memorandum and CD created from a forensic analysis of the teacher's computer were "records" subject to release under the state's Open Records Law after the school district completed its investigation.[65] **In general, information that must be maintained by law is a public record (i.e., personal directory information, salary, employment contracts, leave records, and teaching license) and must be released.**

Educators have not been successful in asserting that privacy interests in personnel records are protected under either the Family Educational Rights and Privacy Act (FERPA)

---

[59]*See* Wakefield Teachers Ass'n v. Sch. Comm., 731 N.E.2d 63 (Mass. 2000) (concluding that a disciplinary report is personnel information that is exempt under the state's public records law); Bangor Area Educ. Ass'n v. Angle, 720 A.2d 198 (Pa. Commw. Ct. 1998) (confirming that teachers' personnel files are not public records); Abbott v. N.E. Indep. Sch. Dist., 212 S.W.3d 364, 367 (Tex. App. 2006) (concluding that a principal's memorandum to a teacher about complaints and providing her directions for improvement was "a document evaluating the performance of a teacher" and thus exempt from release under the state's public information act).

[60]5 U.S.C. § 552 (2008).

[61]Bradley v. Bd. of Educ., 565 N.W.2d 650 (Mich. 1997).

[62]Brouillet v. Cowles Pub. Co., 791 P.2d 526 (Wash. 1990).

[63]Chairman v. Freedom of Info. Comm'n, 585 A.2d 96 (Conn. 1991).

[64]Perkins v. Freedom of Info. Comm'n, 635 A.2d 783 (Conn. 1993).

[65]Zellner v. Cedarburg Sch. Dist., 731 N.W.2d 240 (Wis. 2007). *See also* Navarre v. S. Wash. County Schs., 652 N.W.29 (Minn. 2002) (finding that the release of information about a disciplinary matter before *final* disposition violated the counselor's rights under state law protecting private personnel data); Williams v. Bd. of Educ., 747 A.2d 809 (N.J. Super. Ct. App. Div. 2000) (holding that documents related to termination are a public record).

or the United States Constitution. FERPA applies only to students and their educational records, not to employees' personnel records. Similarly, employees' claims that their constitutional privacy rights bar disclosure of their personnel records have been unsuccessful. In a case in which a teacher's college transcript was sought by a third party under the Texas Open Records Act, the Fifth Circuit ruled that even if a teacher had a recognizable privacy interest in her transcript, that interest "is significantly outweighed by the public's interest in evaluating the competence of its school teachers."[66]

Access to personnel files also has been controversial in situations involving allegations of employment discrimination.[67] Personnel files must be relinquished if subpoenaed by a court. The Equal Employment Opportunity Commission (EEOC) also is authorized to subpoena relevant personnel files to investigate thoroughly allegations that a particular individual has been the victim of discriminatory treatment. The Supreme Court held that confidential peer review materials used in university promotion and tenure decisions were not protected from disclosure to the EEOC. The Court ruled that under Title VII of the Civil Rights Act of 1964, the EEOC must only show relevance, not special reasons or justifications, in demanding specific records. Regarding access to peer review materials, the Court noted that "if there is a 'smoking gun' to be found that demonstrates discrimination in tenure decisions, it is likely to be tucked away in peer review files."[68]

With respect to the maintenance of records, information clearly cannot be placed in personnel files in retaliation for the exercise of constitutional rights. Courts have ordered letters of reprimand expunged from files when they have been predicated on protected speech and association activities.[69] Reprimands, although not a direct prohibition on protected activities, may present a constitutional violation because of their potentially chilling effect on the exercise of constitutional rights.

■ ■ ■ ■ ■

REPORTING SUSPECTED CHILD ABUSE

All states have laws requiring teachers to report suspected child abuse and granting them immunity from liability if reports are made in good faith.

---

[66]Klein Indep. Sch. Dist. v. Mattox, 830 F.2d 576, 580 (5th Cir. 1987).

[67]The Federal Procedural Rules, approved by the Supreme Court in April 2006 and effective December 1, 2006, require employers to be more aware about the storage of electronic information. When school officials are involved in the discovery phase of litigation, they must be able to produce e-mails, instant messages, and other digital communications created in their system. The rules send a clear message that digital and electronic communications must be preserved as other documents are preserved. *See* Corey Murray, "High Court: Don't Delete That E-Mail," *eSchool News online* (January 1, 2007), available at http://eschoolnews.org/news/showstory.cfm?ArticleID=6748.

[68]Univ. of Pa. v. EEOC, 493 U.S. 182, 193 (1990). *See* Univ. of Pittsburgh v. Dep't of Labor and Indus., 896 A.2d 683 (Pa. Commw. Ct. 2006) (ruling under the state's Personnel Files Act that a faculty member did not have the right to inspect external letters written for his promotion file; letters were considered references rather than personnel evaluations that would have been open to inspection).

[69]*See* Aebisher v. Ryan, 622 F.2d 651 (2d Cir. 1980) (concluding that a letter of reprimand for speaking to the press about violence in the school implicated protected speech); Columbus Educ. Ass'n v. Columbus City Sch. Dist., 623 F.2d 1155 (6th Cir. 1980) (holding that a letter of reprimand issued to a union representative for zealous advocacy of a fellow teacher violated the First Amendment).

Among a teacher's many responsibilities is the reporting of suspected child abuse. Child abuse and neglect are recognized as national problems, with reported cases remaining at a high level.[70] States, recognizing that teachers are in a unique role to detect signs of potential abuse, have enacted legislation identifying teachers among the professionals required to report signs of child abuse. Most state laws impose criminal liability for failure to report suspected abuse. Penalties may include fines ranging from $500 to $5,000, prison terms up to one year, and/or public service. Civil suits also may be initiated against teachers for negligence in failing to make such reports.[71] In addition, school systems may impose disciplinary measures against a teacher who does not follow the mandates of the law. The Seventh Circuit upheld the suspension and demotion of a teacher-psychologist for not promptly reporting suspected abuse.[72] The court rejected the teacher's claim to a federal right of confidentiality, noting the state's compelling interest to protect children from mistreatment.

Although specific aspects of the laws may vary from one state to another, definitions of abuse and neglect often are based on the federal Child Abuse Prevention and Treatment Act (CAPTA), which provides funds to identify, treat, and prevent abuse. The CAPTA identifies *child abuse* and *neglect* as:

> the physical or mental injury, sexual abuse or exploitation, negligent treatment, or maltreatment of a child under the age of eighteen, or the age specified by the child protection law of the state in question, by a person who is responsible for the child's welfare under the circumstances which indicate that the child's health or welfare is harmed or threatened thereby.[73]

Several common elements are found in state child abuse statutes. The laws mandate that certain professionals such as doctors, nurses, and educators report suspected abuse. Statutes do not require that reporters have absolute knowledge, but rather "reasonable cause to believe" or "reason to believe" that a child has been abused or neglected. Once abuse is suspected, the report must be made immediately to the designated child protection agency, department of welfare, or law enforcement unit as specified in state law. All states grant immunity from civil and criminal liability to individuals if reports are made in good faith.

---

[70]In 2005, 3.3 million referrals (involving approximately 6 million children) were made to child protection agencies, and almost 900,000 children were found to be victims of abuse. U.S. Department of Health and Human Services, Administration for Children and Families, *Child Maltreatment 2005* (Washington, DC: U.S. Government Printing Office, 2007). Over half of the reports were made by professionals, including educators, police, lawyers, and social services staff. *See also* Charol Shakeshaft, *Educator Sexual Misconduct: A Synthesis of Existing Literature* (Washington, DC: U.S. Office of Education, 2004).This report is a national study of child abuse in schools conducted under the requirements of § 5414 of the Elementary and Secondary Education Act of 1965, amended by the No Child Left Behind Act of 2001 (20 U.S.C. § 6301 *et seq.* (2008)).

[71]The Supreme Court of Ohio ruled that a school system and its employees did not have sovereign immunity for damages when state law expressly imposed liability for failure to report suspected abuse. Campbell v. Burton, 750 N.E.2d 539 (Ohio 2001). In a subsequent ruling, the Ohio high court held that a school board may be held liable if it fails to file a sexual abuse report and the suspected teacher later abuses another student.Yates v. Mansfield Bd. of Educ., 808 N.E.2d 861 (Ohio 2004). *See also* Chapter 2 for a discussion of the elements of negligence.

[72]Pesce v. J. Sterling Morton High Sch. Dist. 201, 830 F.2d 789 (7th Cir. 1987).

[73]42 U.S.C. § 5101 (2008).

School districts often establish reporting procedures that require teachers to report suspected abuse to their principal or school social worker. However, if statutory provisions specify that teachers must promptly report suspected abuse to another agency or to law enforcement, teachers are not relieved of their individual obligation to report to state authorities. Some state laws, however, do relieve teachers of the obligation to report if someone else has already reported or will be reporting the incident. But teachers should always follow up to be sure the report was made to the appropriate agency.

State laws are explicit on reporting requirements for suspected child abuse, but it is difficult to prove that a teacher had sufficient knowledge of abuse to trigger legal liability for failure to report. Therefore, it is desirable for school officials to establish policies and procedures to encourage effective reporting. The pervasiveness of the problem and concern about the lack of reporting by teachers also indicate a need for in-service programs to assist teachers in recognizing signs of abused and neglected children.

■ ■ ■ ■ ■

COLLECTIVE BARGAINING

Teachers have a constitutionally protected right to form and join a union; specific bargaining rights are conferred through state statutes or judicial interpretations of state constitutions, thus creating wide divergence in teachers' bargaining rights across states.

Although basic differences in employment exist between the public and private sectors, collective bargaining laws (specifically, the National Labor Relations Act[74] and the Taft-Hartley Act[75]) in the private sector have been significant in shaping statutory and judicial regulation of public negotiations. Similarities between the two sectors can be noted in a few areas, such as unfair labor practices, union representation, and impasse procedures. However, several basic differences distinguish bargaining in the public and private sectors. First, the removal of decision-making authority from public officials through bargaining has been viewed as an infringement on the government's sovereign power, which has resulted in the enactment of labor laws strongly favoring public employers. Public employees' rights have been further weakened by prohibitions of work stoppages. Whereas employees' ability to strike is considered *essential* to the effective operation of collective decision making in the private sector, this view has been rejected in the public sector because of the nature and structure of governmental services.

Bargaining rights developed slowly for public employees who historically had been deprived of the right to organize and bargain collectively. It was not until the late 1960s that public employees' constitutional right to join a union was firmly established. A large number of public employees actively participated in collective bargaining, but statutes and regulations in some states prohibited union membership. These restrictions against union

---

[74]The act states that "employees shall have the right to self-organization, to form, join or assist labor organizations, to bargain collectively through representatives of their own choosing, and to engage in concerted activities, for the purpose of collective bargaining or other mutual aid or protection." 29 U.S.C. § 157 (2008).

[75]29 U.S.C. § 141 *et seq.* (2008).

membership were challenged as impairing association freedoms protected by the First Amendment. Although not addressing union membership, **the Supreme Court held in 1967 that public employment cannot be conditioned on the relinquishment of free association rights.**[76] In a later decision, the Seventh Circuit clearly announced that "an individual's right to form and join a union is protected by the First Amendment."[77] Other courts followed this precedent by invalidating state statutory provisions that blocked union membership. School officials have been prohibited from retaliating against teachers, imposing sanctions, or denying benefits to discourage protected association rights.

Diversity in labor laws and bargaining practices among the states makes it difficult to generalize about collective bargaining and teachers' labor rights. State labor laws, state employment relations board rulings, and court decisions must be consulted to determine specific rights, because there is no federal labor law covering public school employees. Over two-thirds of the states have enacted bargaining laws, ranging from very comprehensive laws controlling most aspects of negotiations to laws granting the minimal right to meet and confer. Still other states, in the absence of legislation, rely on judicial rulings to define the basic rights of public employees in the labor relations arena. This section provides a general overview of public school teachers' employment rights under the collective bargaining process.

Although the United States Constitution has been interpreted as protecting public employees' rights to organize, the right to form and join a union does not ensure the right to bargain collectively with a public employer; individual state statutes and constitutions govern such bargaining rights. Whether identified as professional negotiations, collective negotiations, or collective bargaining, **the process entails bilateral decision making in which the teachers' representative and the school board attempt to reach mutual agreement on matters affecting teacher employment.** The judiciary has been reluctant to interfere with legislative authority to define the collective bargaining relationship between public employers and employees unless protected rights have been compromised.

Because of the variations in labor laws, as well as the lack of such laws in some states, substantial differences exist in bargaining rights and practices. A few states, such as New York, have a detailed, comprehensive collective bargaining statute that delineates specific bargaining rights. In contrast, negotiated contracts between teachers' organizations and school boards are prohibited in North Carolina. Under North Carolina law, all contracts between public employers and employee associations are invalid.[78]

In contrast to North Carolina, other states without legislation have permitted negotiated agreements. The Kentucky Supreme Court ruled that a public employer may recognize an employee organization for the purpose of collective bargaining, even though state law is silent regarding public employee bargaining rights.[79] The decision does not impose a duty on local school boards to bargain but merely allows a board the discretion to negotiate.

[76]Keyishian v. Bd. of Regents, 385 U.S. 589 (1967).

[77]McLaughlin v. Tilendis, 398 F.2d 287, 289 (7th Cir. 1968).

[78]N.C. Gen. Stat. § 95-98 (2008).

[79]Bd. of Trs. v. Pub. Employees Council No. 51, 571 S.W.2d 616 (Ky. 1978). *See also* Independence-Nat'l Educ. Ass'n v. Independence Sch. Dist., 223 S.W.3d 131 (Mo. 2007), *overruling* City of Springfield v. Clouse, 206 S.W.2d 539, 542 (Mo. 1947) (holding that the state constitutional provision guaranteeing "employees" the right to organize and bargain collectively includes both public and private employees).

This ruling is consistent with several other judicial decisions permitting negotiated contracts in the absence of specific legislation. The board's authority to enter into contracts for the operation and maintenance of the school system has been construed to include the ability to enter into negotiated agreements with employee organizations. Once a school board extends recognition to a bargaining agent and commences bargaining, the board's actions in the negotiation process are governed by established judicial principles.

Teachers' Statutory Bargaining Rights

In states with laws governing teachers' bargaining rights, school boards must negotiate with teachers in accordance with the statutorily prescribed process. Generally, public employee bargaining laws address employer and employee rights, bargaining units, scope of bargaining, impasse resolution, grievance procedures, unfair labor practices, and penalties for prohibited practices. Many states have established labor relations boards to monitor bargaining under their statutes. Although the specific functions of these boards vary widely, their general purpose is to resolve questions arising from the implementation of state law. Functions assigned to such boards include determination of membership in bargaining units, resolution of union recognition claims, investigation of unfair labor practices, and interpretation of the general intent of statutory bargaining clauses. Usually, judicial review cannot be pursued until administrative review before labor boards is exhausted. Thus, decisions of labor boards are an important source of labor law, since many of the issues addressed by boards are never appealed to courts. When the labor boards' decisions are challenged in court, substantial deference is given to their findings and determinations.[80]

Like the National Labor Relations Act (NLRA) in the private sector, state statutes require bargaining "in good faith." ***Good faith bargaining* has been interpreted as requiring parties to meet at reasonable times and attempt to reach mutual agreement without compulsion on either side to agree.** Many states have followed the federal law in stipulating that this "does not compel either party to agree to a proposal or to require the making of a concession."[81] Failure of the school board or teachers' organization to bargain in good faith can result in the imposition of penalties.

Statutes impose certain restrictions or obligations on both the school board and the employee organization. Violation of the law by either party can result in an unfair labor practice claim. Allegations of unfair labor practices are brought before the state public employee relations board for a hearing and judgment. Specific unfair labor practices, often modeled after those in the NLRA, are included in state statutes. The most common prohibited labor practice is that an employer or union cannot interfere with, restrain, or coerce public employees in exercising their rights under the labor law.[82] Among other prohibited

---

[80]*See, e.g., In re* Laconia Sch. Dist., 840 A.2d 800 (N.H. 2004).

[81]29 U.S.C. § 158(d) (2008). *See also* Bd. of Educ. v. Sered, 850 N.E.2d 821 (Ill. App. Ct. 2006) (finding that a tentative oral agreement made by the board's representatives was valid; the board could not disregard or modify the terms of the agreement).

[82]*See* Fort Frye Teachers Ass'n v. SERB, 809 N.E.2d 1130 (Ohio 2004) (ruling the nonrenewal of teacher's contract for union activities constitutes an unfair labor practice; SERB was directed to act on the court's finding); Uniontown Area Sch. Dist. v. Pa. Labor Relations Bd., 747 A.2d 1271 (Pa. Commw. Ct. 2000) (concluding that the school district committed an unfair labor practice when it did not promote a teacher to principal because of her union activities).

employer practices are interference with union operations, discrimination against employees because of union membership, refusal to bargain collectively with the exclusive representative, and failure to bargain in good faith. *Unions* are prevented from causing an employer to discriminate against employees on the basis of union membership, refusing to bargain or failing to bargain in good faith, failing to represent all employees in the bargaining unit, and engaging in unlawful activities, such as strikes or boycotts, identified in the bargaining law.

Upon completion of the negotiation process, the members of the bargaining unit and the school board must ratify the written agreement (usually referred to as the *master contract*). These agreements often contain similar standard contract language and clauses, beginning with recognition of the exclusive bargaining representative and union security issues (i.e., fair share fees). Management rights and association rights also are detailed. Management clauses emphasize the board's control over the establishment of educational policies, and union clauses may include the right to use school facilities or communication systems. Other provisions relate to the scope of bargaining, which is defined by the state's labor law or common law. These items include not only salary and fringe benefits but also may address grievance procedures, employee evaluations, preparation time, length of workday, class size, procedures for employee discipline, transfers, layoff and recall procedures, assignment of duties, and processes for filling vacancies.

Scope of Negotiations

Should the teachers' organization have input into class size? Who will determine the length of the school day? How will extra-duty assignments be determined? Will reductions-in-force necessitated by declining enrollment be based on seniority or merit? These questions and others are raised in determining the scope of negotiations. *Scope* refers to the range of issues or subjects that are negotiable, and determining scope is one of the most difficult tasks in public-sector bargaining. Public employers argue that issues must be narrowly defined to protect the government's policy-making role, whereas employee unions counter that bargaining subjects must be defined broadly to have meaningful negotiations.

Restrictions on scope of bargaining vary considerably among states. Consequently, to determine negotiable items in a particular state, the state's collective bargaining law, other statutes, and litigation interpreting these laws must be examined. The specification of negotiable items in labor laws may include broad guidelines or detailed enumeration of specific issues. As noted, many states have modeled their bargaining statutes after the NLRA, which stipulates that **representatives of the employer and employees must meet and confer "with respect to wages, hours, and other terms and conditions of employment."**[83] A few states deal directly with the scope of bargaining by identifying each item that must be negotiated. Some states specify prohibited subjects of bargaining. For example, Michigan's prohibited subjects include decisions related to the establishment of the starting date for the school year, composition of site-based decision-making bodies, interdistrict and intradistrict open enrollment opportunities, authorization of public school academies, and establishment and staffing of experimental programs.[84] Generally, statutory mandates cannot be

[83]29 U.S.C. § 158(d) (2008).

[84]Mich. Comp. Laws Ann. § 423.215(3)(4) (2008).

preempted by collective bargaining agreements;[85] however, in a few states, the negotiated agreement prevails over conflicting laws, unless the laws are specifically exempted.

All proposed subjects for negotiation can be classified as mandatory, permissive, or prohibited. *Mandatory* items must be negotiated.[86] Failure of the school board to meet and confer on such items is evidence of lack of good faith bargaining. *Permissive* items can be negotiated if both parties agree; however, there is no legal duty to consider the items. Furthermore, in most states, permissive items cannot be pursued to the point of negotiation impasse, and an employer cannot unilaterally change these items if no agreement is reached. *Prohibited* items are beyond the power of the board to negotiate; an illegal delegation of power results if the board agrees to negotiate these items. Since most statutory scope provisions are general in nature, courts or labor relations boards often have been asked to differentiate between negotiable and nonnegotiable items.

Defining managerial rights is a key element in establishing limitations on negotiable subjects at the bargaining table. **State laws specify that public employers cannot be required to negotiate governmental policy matters, and courts have held that it is impermissible for a school board to bargain away certain rights and responsibilities in the public policy area.**[87] Generally, educational policy matters are defined through provisions in collective bargaining statutes, such as "management rights" and "scope of bargaining" clauses. Policy issues—such as class size, teacher evaluation criteria, and the award of tenure—are excluded as negotiable items in a few states; however, most states stipulate only that employers are not *required* to bargain such policy rights.

Public employee labor laws requiring the negotiation of "conditions of employment" can include far-reaching policy matters, since most school board decisions either directly or indirectly affect the teacher in the classroom. The Maryland high court noted the difficulty in distinguishing between educational policy and matters relating to teachers' employment: "Virtually every managerial decision in some way relates to 'salaries, wages, hours, and other working conditions,' and is therefore arguably negotiable. At the same time, virtually every such decision also involves educational policy considerations and is therefore arguably nonnegotiable."[88] In many states, the interpretation of what is negotiable resides with the labor relations board. Often, a balancing test is employed by these boards as well as courts, beginning with an inquiry into whether a particular matter involves wages, hours, and terms and conditions of employment. If so, then the labor board or court must determine if the matter also is one of inherent managerial policy. If not, the matter is a mandatory subject of bargaining. However, if the issue also pertains to

---

[85]Furthermore, collective bargaining agreements cannot deprive individuals of rights guaranteed by federal laws. Abrahamson v. Bd. of Educ., 374 F.3d 66 (2d Cir. 2004).

[86]Wages definitely fall within the mandatory category. A wage-related area that has received recent attention is the payment of "signing bonuses" to attract teachers for difficult to fill positions. Failure to bargain these payments may constitute an unfair labor practice. *See, e.g.,* Ekalaka Unified Bd. of Trs. v. Ekalaka Teachers' Ass'n, 149 P.3d 902 (Mont. 2006); Crete Educ. Ass'n v. Salie County Sch. Dist., 654 N.W.2d 166 (Neb. 2002).

[87]*See* City Univ. of N.Y. v. Prof. Staff Cong., 837 N.Y.S.2d 121 (App. Div. 2007) (holding that the employer could not bargain away its right to inspect teacher personnel files; the agreement was against public policy to investigate discrimination complaints).

[88]Montgomery County Educ. Ass'n v. Bd. of Educ., 534 A.2d 980, 986 (Md. 1987).

educational policy, the benefits of bargaining on the decision-making process must be balanced against the burden on the employer's authority. Accordingly, this process entails a fact-specific analysis.

Judicial decisions interpreting negotiability illustrate the range in bargainable matters. The Supreme Court of New Jersey narrowly interpreted *conditions of employment* to mean wages, benefits, and work schedules, thereby removing governmental policy items such as teacher transfers, course offerings, and evaluations.[89] Other courts, however, have construed the phrase in broader terms. For example, the Nevada Supreme Court ruled that items *significantly* related to wages, hours, and working conditions are negotiable.[90] Similarly, the Pennsylvania Supreme Court concluded that an issue's *impact* on conditions of employment must be weighed to determine whether it should be considered outside the educational policy area.[91]

Although courts agree that school boards cannot be *required* to negotiate inherent managerial rights pertaining to policy matters, some states view these rights as *permissive* subjects of bargaining. That is, the board may agree to negotiate a particular "right" in the absence of statutory or judicial prohibitions. **If the board does negotiate a policy item, it is bound by the agreement in the same manner as if the issue were a mandatory item.**

Union Security Provisions

To ensure their strength and viability, unions attempt to obtain various security provisions in the collective bargaining contract. The nature and extent of these provisions will depend on state laws and constitutional limitations. When bargaining with employees, unions seek to gain provisions that require all employees either to join the association or to pay fees for its services. Since a union must represent all individuals in the bargaining unit, it is argued that such provisions are necessary to eliminate "free riders" (i.e., the individuals who receive the benefits of the union's work without paying the dues for membership).

Union security provisions take several forms. The *closed shop*, requiring an employer to hire only union members, does not exist in the public sector and is unlawful in the private sector. The *union shop* agreement requires an employee to join the union within a designated time period after employment to retain a position. Although union shop agreements are prevalent in the private sector, they are not authorized by most public-sector laws and are limited or proscribed in some states under "right-to-work" laws.[92] The security provisions most frequently found in the public sector are *agency shop* and *fair share* agreements—terms that often are used interchangeably. An agency shop provision requires an

---

[89]Ridgefield Park Educ. Ass'n v. Ridgefield Park Bd. of Educ., 393 A.2d 278 (N.J. 1978). *See also* Polk County Bd. of Educ. v. Polk County Educ. Ass'n, 139 S.W.3d 304 (Tenn. Ct. App. 2004) (ruling that a dress code policy constituted a "working condition" not a managerial prerogative).

[90]Clark County Sch. Dist. v. Local Gov't Employee-Management Relations Bd., 530 P.2d 114 (Nev. 1974). *See also* Oak Hills Educ. Ass'n v. Oak Hills Local Sch. Dist., 821 N.E.2d 616 (Ohio Ct. App. 2004) (ruling that a tuition reimbursement program for university course work could not be unilaterally implemented by a school board).

[91]Pa. Labor Relations Bd. v. State Coll. Area Sch. Dist., 337 A.2d 262 (Pa. 1975).

[92]Twenty-two states specifically declare that an individual cannot be required to join a union or pay fees to a union. *See* National Right to Work Legal Defense Foundation, http://nrtw.org/rtws.htm.

employee to pay union dues but does not mandate membership, whereas a fair share arrangement requires a nonmember simply to pay a service fee to cover the cost of bargaining activities.

Nonunion teachers have challenged mandatory fees as a violation of their First Amendment speech and association rights. The Supreme Court, however, upheld the payment of fair share fees by public employees in *Abood v. Detroit Board of Education*.[93] The Court rejected the nonunion members' First Amendment claims, noting the importance of ensuring labor peace and eliminating "free riders." Yet, the Court concluded that **employees cannot be compelled to contribute to the support of ideological causes they oppose as a condition of maintaining employment as public school teachers.** Accordingly, the fee for nonmember teachers who object to forced contributions to a union's political activities must reflect only the costs of bargaining and contract administration.[94]

Although the Supreme Court has upheld fair share arrangements, they may not be permitted under some state laws. The Maine high court held that forced payment of dues was "tantamount to coercion toward membership."[95] The Maine statute ensures employees the right to join a union *voluntarily*, and the court interpreted this provision as including the right to *refrain* from joining. Similarly, the Vermont Supreme Court held that fees were prohibited under the Vermont Labor Relations for Teachers Act, which specified that teachers have the right to join or not to join, assist, or participate in a labor organization.[96] Under some state labor laws, collection of fees may be forbidden. For example, Indiana amended its labor law to prohibit the payment of fair share fees or any other representation fees.[97]

Exclusive Privileges

The designated employee bargaining representative gains security through negotiating exclusive rights or privileges, such as dues checkoff, the use of the school mail systems, and access to school facilities. Although exclusive arrangements strengthen the majority union and may make it difficult for minority unions to survive, courts often support them as a means of promoting labor peace and ensuring efficient operation of the school system.

The exclusive privilege most often included in collective bargaining contracts is dues checkoff, a provision that authorizes employers to deduct union dues and other fees when authorized by employees. Over half of the states with public employee bargaining laws specify dues checkoff as a mandatory subject for bargaining. The Supreme Court, however, has held that **employee unions have no constitutional right to payroll deductions.**[98]

---

[93]431 U.S. 209 (1977).

[94]The Supreme Court ruled in 2007 that a state law requiring unions to obtain affirmative authorization from non-members prior to spending agency fees for election-related purposes is not unconstitutional. The state gave the unions the right to collect the fees and could also place limitations on their use. Davenport v. Wash. Educ. Ass'n, 127 S. Ct. 2372 (2007).

[95]Churchill v. Sch. Adm'r Dist. No. 49 Teachers Ass'n, 380 A.2d 186, 192 (Me. 1977).

[96]Weissenstein v. Burlington Bd. of Sch. Comm'rs, 543 A.2d 691 (Vt. 1988). *But see* Nashua Teachers Union v. Nashua Sch. Dist., 707 A.2d 448 (N.H. 1998) (interpreting a state law that permits negotiation of "other terms and conditions of employment" as authorizing agency fees to promote labor peace).

[97]Ind. Code § 20-7.5-1 (2008).

[98]City of Charlotte v. Local 660, Int'l Ass'n of Firefighters, 426 U.S. 283 (1976).

The Fourth Circuit ruled that state legislation permitting payroll deductions for charitable organizations but not labor unions was not an infringement of the First Amendment; the law did not deny the union members the right to associate, speak, publish, recruit members, or express their views.[99] Unless prohibited by state law, checkoff rights can be reserved for the exclusive bargaining unit and denied to revival unions.

In 1983, the Supreme Court clarified one of the most controversial security rights—exclusive access to school mail facilities.[100] The case focused on an agreement between the exclusive bargaining representative and an Indiana school board denying all rival unions access to the interschool mail system and teacher mailboxes. One union challenged the agreement as a violation of the First and Fourteenth Amendments. The Supreme Court upheld the arrangement, reasoning that the First Amendment does not require "equivalent access to all parts of a school building in which some form of communicative activity occurs."[101] **The Court concluded that the school mail facility was not a public forum for communication and thereby its use could be restricted to official school business.** The fact that several community groups (e.g., Boy Scouts, civic organizations) used the school mail system did not create a public forum. The Court noted that, even if such access by community groups created a limited public forum, access would be extended only to similar groups—not to labor organizations. The Court's emphasis on the availability of alternative channels of communication (e.g., bulletin boards and meeting facilities), however, indicates that total exclusion of rival unions would not be permitted.

In most states, school boards negotiate only with the designated bargaining representative. Under this exclusive recognition, other unions and teacher groups can be denied the right to engage in official exchanges with an employer. The Supreme Court has held that nonmembers of a bargaining unit or members who disagree with the views of the representative have no constitutional right "to force the government to listen to their views."[102] The Court concluded that a Minnesota statute requiring employers to "meet and confer" only with the designated bargaining representative did not violate other employees' speech or associational rights as public employees or as citizens, because these sessions were not a public forum. According to the Court, "The Constitution does not grant to members of the public generally a right to be heard by public bodies making decisions of policy."[103]

However, in a public forum, such as a school board meeting, **a nonunion teacher has a constitutional right to address the public employer, even concerning a subject of negotiation.** The Supreme Court concluded that a Wisconsin nonunion teacher had the right to express concerns to the school board.[104] In this case, negotiation between the board

[99]S.C. Educ. Ass'n v. Campbell, 883 F.2d 1251 (4th Cir. 1989). *See also* San Leandro Teachers Ass'n v. Governing Bd., 65 Cal. Rptr. 3d 288 (Ct. App. 2007) (ruling that state law prohibits unions from using school mailboxes to distribute political endorsement information); Unified Sch. Dist. No. 233 v. Kan. Ass'n of Am. Educators, 64 P. 3d 372 (Kan. 2003) (finding that a school district could not permit a rival professional association to distribute its membership materials through the district's internal mail system when the collective bargaining representative had negotiated exclusive use of the mail system).

[100]Perry Educ. Ass'n v. Perry Local Educators' Ass'n, 460 U.S. 37 (1983). *See* text accompanying note 35, Chapter 10.

[101]*Id.* at 44.

[102]Minn. State Bd. for Cmty. Colls. v. Knight, 465 U.S. 271, 283 (1984).

[103]*Id.*

[104]City of Madison v. Wis. Employment Relations Comm'n, 429 U.S. 167 (1976).

and union had reached a deadlock on the issue of an agency shop provision. A nonunion teacher, representing a minority group of teachers, addressed the board at a regular public meeting and requested postponement of a decision until further study was made. The Court reasoned that the teacher was not attempting to negotiate, but merely to speak on an important issue before the board—a right every citizen possesses. The Court further noted that teachers have never been "compelled to relinquish their First Amendment rights they would otherwise enjoy as citizens to comment on matters of public interest in connection with the operation of the public school in which they work."[105]

Grievances

Disputes concerning employee rights under the terms of a collective bargaining agreement are resolved through the negotiated grievance procedures, which generally must be exhausted before pursuing review by state labor relations boards or courts. The exhaustion requirement ensures the integrity of the collective bargaining process, encouraging orderly and efficient dispute resolution at the local level. Grievance procedures usually provide for a neutral third party, generally an arbitrator, to conduct a hearing and render a decision. *Grievance* arbitration, which addresses enforcement of contract rights, differs from *interest* arbitration, which may take place in resolving an impasse between parties in the bargaining process.

Depending on state law and the negotiated contract, grievance arbitration decisions may be advisory or binding. Public employers, adhering to the doctrine of the sovereign power of government, have been reluctant to agree to procedures that might result in a loss of public authority. Allowing grievance procedures to include final decision making by a third party significantly lessens a school board's power, effectively equating the positions of the teachers' organization and the school board. Nevertheless, as bargaining has expanded, **legislative bodies have favored binding arbitration to settle labor disputes.** About half of the states have enacted laws permitting school boards to negotiate grievance procedures with binding arbitration, and several states require binding arbitration as the final step in the grievance procedure.[106] With the widespread acceptance of grievance arbitration, it has become one of the most contested areas in collective bargaining. Suits have challenged the arbitrator's authority to render decisions in specific disputes as well as the authority to provide certain remedies.

Negotiation Impasse

An impasse occurs in bargaining when an agreement cannot be reached and neither party will compromise. When negotiations reach such a stalemate, several options are available for resolution—mediation, fact-finding, and arbitration. As discussed below, the most effective means for resolving negotiation impasse—the strike—is not legally available to the majority of public employees. Most comprehensive state statutes address impasse procedures, with provisions ranging from allowing impasse procedures to be negotiated to mandating detailed steps that must be followed.

[105]*Id.* at 175 (quoting Pickering v. Bd. of Educ., 391 U.S. 563, 568 (1968)).

[106]States requiring binding grievance arbitration are Alaska, Florida, Illinois, Minnesota, and Pennsylvania.

Mediation is often the first step to reopening negotiations. A neutral third party assists both sides in working toward an agreement. The mediator serves as a facilitator rather than a decision maker, thus enabling the school board's representative and the teachers' association jointly to reach an agreement. Mediation may be optional or required by law; the mediator is selected by the negotiation teams or, upon request, appointed by a public employee relations board.

Failure to reach agreement through mediation frequently results in fact-finding (often called advisory arbitration). The process may be mandated by law or may be entered into by mutual agreement of both parties. Fact-finding involves a third party investigating the causes for the dispute, collecting facts and testimony to clarify the dispute, and formulating a judgment. Because of the advisory nature of the process, proposed solutions are not binding on either party. However, since fact-finding reports are made available to the public, they provide an impetus to settle a contract that is not present in mediation.

In many states, the final step in impasse procedures is fact-finding, which may leave both parties without a satisfactory solution. A few states permit a third alternative—binding interest arbitration. This process is similar to fact-finding except that the decision of the arbitrator, related to the terms of the negotiated agreement, is binding on both parties. States that permit binding arbitration often place restrictions on its use.[107] For example, Ohio, Oregon, and Rhode Island permit binding arbitration on matters of mutual consent;[108] Maine allows binding arbitration on all items except salaries, pensions, and insurance.[109]

Although it is argued there can be no true collective bargaining without the right to withhold services, which characterizes the bargaining process in the private sector, **state statutes or common law prohibit most teachers from striking.** In those states that grant public employees a limited right to strike, certain conditions, specified in statute, must be met prior to the initiation of a work stoppage.[110] Designated conditions vary but usually include: (1) the exhaustion of statutory mediation and fact-finding steps, (2) expiration of the contract, (3) elapse of a certain time period prior to commencing the strike, (4) written notice of the union's intent to strike, and (5) evidence that the strike will not constitute a danger to public health or safety. In contrast to the few states permitting strikes, most states with public employee collective bargaining statutes have specific "no-strike" provisions, and courts have generally denied the right to strike unless affirmatively granted by the state.

A strike is more than simply a work stoppage; states define the term broadly to include a range of concerted activities such as work slowdowns, massive absences for "sick" days, and refusal to perform certain duties. For example, the Massachusetts high

---

[107]To avoid strikes among certain groups of public employees, interest arbitration may be mandatory. *See, e.g.,* Ohio Rev. Code § 4117.14 (D)(l) (2008).

[108]Ohio Rev. Code § 4117 (C) (2008); Or. Rev. Stat. § 243.712 (2)(e)(2008); R.I. Gen. Laws § 28-9.3-9 (2008).

[109]Me. Rev. Stat. tit. 26 § 979.D(4) (2008). *But see* Conn. Gen. Stat. § 10-153f (2008) (provides for submission of unresolved issues to "last best offer" arbitration).

[110]A statutory limited right to strike exists for public employees in Alaska, Colorado, Hawaii, Illinois, Minnesota, Montana, Ohio, Oregon, Pennsylvania, Vermont, and Wisconsin. Alaska law has been interpreted as prohibiting teachers from striking even though most other public employees are permitted to strike. Anchorage Educ. Ass'n v. Anchorage Sch. Dist., 648 P.2d 993 (Alaska 1982).

court found that refusing to perform customary activities, such as grading papers and preparing lesson plans after the end of the school day, constituted a strike.[111] A Missouri appellate court upheld the right of the St. Louis school superintendent to request documentation from 1,190 teachers that a "sick" day was not related to a labor dispute surrounding the negotiation of a new contract.[112] Without documentation from the teachers, the school district could deny payment for the day.

State laws, in addition to prohibiting work stoppages, usually identify penalties for involvement in strikes. Such penalties can include withholding compensation for strike days, prohibiting salary increases for designated periods of time (e.g., one year), and dismissal. Penalties for illegal strikes also are imposed on unions. Sanctions may include fines, decertification of the union, and loss of certain privileges such as dues checkoff.

Despite statutory prohibitions on strikes, many teachers, as well as other public employees, participate in work stoppages each year. Public employers can seek a court injunction against teachers who threaten to strike or initiate such action. Most courts have granted injunctions, concluding as did the Supreme Court of Alaska that the "illegality of the strike is a sufficient harm to justify injunctive relief."[113] Failure of teachers and unions to comply with such a restraining order can result in contempt of court charges and resulting fines and/or imprisonment. For example, in South Bend, Indiana, refusal to comply with an injunction resulted in a contempt-of-court charge and fines totalling $200,000 against two unions.[114]

Teachers illegally participating in a strike are subject to court-imposed penalties and, in most states, to statutory penalties. Refusal of teachers to return to the classroom can result in dismissal.

CONCLUSION

More so than in the other areas of law that have been discussed, individual state laws, school board regulations, and master contracts must be consulted to determine the specific terms and conditions of teachers' employment. Except for certain limitations imposed by constitutional provisions and federal civil rights laws, state statutes govern educators' employment. The state prescribes general requirements for licensure, contracts, tenure, and employment. Local school boards are vested with the power to appoint teachers and to establish professional and academic employment standards above the state minimums. Also, a school board may assign or transfer a teacher to any school or grade at its discretion, as long as the assignment is within the teacher's licensure area and not limited by contract terms. Under state laws, school boards confer tenure, which ensures that dismissal is based on adequate cause and accompanied by procedural due process.

[111]Lenox Educ. Ass'n v. Labor Relations Comm'n, 471 N.E.2d 81 (Mass. 1984).

[112]Franklin v. St. Louis Bd. of Educ., 904 S.W.2d 433 (Mo. Ct. App. 1995).

[113]Anchorage Educ. Ass'n v. Anchorage Sch. Dist., 648 P.2d 993, 998 (Alaska 1982). *But see* Wilson v. Pulaski Ass'n of Classroom Teachers, 954 S.W.2d 221 (Ark. 1997) (requiring proof of irreparable harm to issue a preliminary injunction).

[114]Nat'l Educ. Ass'n-S. Bend v. S. Bend Cmty. Sch. Corp., 655 N.E.2d 516 (Ind. Ct. App. 1995).

In some states, employment is further defined by negotiated collective bargaining agreements (often called master contracts) between school boards and teacher unions, which limit the discretionary power of school boards to make unilateral employment decisions. Specific bargaining rights are conferred through state statutes or judicial interpretations of state constitutions, thus creating wide divergence in teachers' bargaining rights across states. Although all teachers have a constitutionally protected right to form and join a union, school boards are not required to bargain with employee organizations unless mandated to do so by state law. Negotiated agreements typically include the specification of salary and fringe benefits but also may address management and association rights, grievance procedures, employee evaluations, and procedural due process for employee discipline and reduction-in-force.

POINTS TO PONDER

1. After a two-year recruitment effort, a prominent, successful basketball coach moved across the state to accept a position to coach the boys' varsity basketball team and teach science in a well-known high school program. His failure to produce a championship basketball team led the school board to terminate his coaching contract four years later. Although he retained his teaching position, he challenged the board's decision, arguing that he was recruited primarily to coach basketball and that he had moved, at great expense, to the community for the coaching opportunity. What are the teacher-coach's legal rights? For two perspectives, see *Lagos v. Modesto City School District,* 843 F.2d 347 (9th Cir. 1988) and *Kingsford v. Salt Lake City School District,* 247 F.3d 1123 (10th Cir. 2001).

2. You have been offered employment in a school district for next fall. With the offer of employment, the superintendent notes several requirements that must be met prior to final school board approval. In addition to the typical physical examination, the board requires that all new appointees consent to fingerprinting, a criminal records check, and a drug test. Do these requirements implicate protected privacy rights?

3. A high school principal refused to appoint a teacher, former president of the teachers union, as department chair of history. The teacher questioned the decision, claiming that the denial was based on her union activities. What are the teacher's protected rights?

4. Invoking the state Freedom of Information Act, a group calling itself Concerned Citizens for Improving Our Schools requested extensive financial data as well as personnel data from the local school district. Teachers objected to the release of personal data related to their sick leave records, teaching licenses, and annual evaluations. Does this request violate teachers' privacy rights? How do freedom of information laws affect these privacy rights?

5. After several weeks of noticing bruises on a 10-year-old boy, a teacher expressed her concern to the principal. The principal responded that she had no cause to worry, particularly since the boy's parents were prominent citizens in the community. What is the teacher's legal responsibility in this situation?

CHAPTER TEN

TEACHERS' SUBSTANTIVE CONSTITUTIONAL RIGHTS

Although statutory law is prominent in defining specific terms and conditions of employment, the federal Constitution also grants substantive rights to public employees. These rights cannot be abridged by legislation or school board action without an overriding government interest. This chapter presents an overview of the scope of public school teachers' constitutional rights as defined by the judiciary in connection with freedom of expression and association and privacy rights. Other chapters address constitutional rights pertaining to equal protection, due process, and religious guarantees as well as remedies available to aggrieved individuals when their rights have been abridged.

FREEDOM OF EXPRESSION

Public employees' comments on matters of public concern are protected expression if they are made as a citizen and not pursuant to official job duties.

Until the mid-twentieth century, it was generally accepted that public school teachers could be disciplined for expressing views considered objectionable by the school board. The private-sector practice of firing such employees was assumed to apply to public employment as well. Since the late 1960s, however, the Supreme Court has recognized that free expression rights are not forfeited by accepting public school employment, even though such rights must be weighed against the school district's interest in maintaining effective and efficient schools. This section reviews the evolution of legal principles and their application to specific school situations.

Legal Principles

Similar to student free speech cases, an initial determination must be made regarding whether the public employee's claim involves expression *at* all. An action constitutes expression for First Amendment purposes only if it attempts "to convey a particularized message" that will likely be understood by those receiving the message.[1]

In the landmark 1968 decision, *Pickering v. Board of Education*, the Supreme Court recognized that teachers have a First Amendment right to air their views on matters of public concern.[2] The school board had dismissed Pickering for writing a letter to a local newspaper in which he criticized the school board's fiscal policies. The Illinois courts upheld Pickering's dismissal for the letter, which included false statements allegedly damaging the reputations of school board members and district administrators.

Reversing the state courts, the Supreme Court first identified expression pertaining to matters of public concern as constitutionally protected and reasoned that the funding and allocation issues raised by Pickering were clearly questions of public interest requiring free and open debate. **The Court then applied a balancing test, weighing the teacher's interest in expressing his views on public issues against the school board's interest in providing educational services.** The Court recognized that the school board would prevail if Pickering's exercise of protected expression impaired classroom performance, jeopardized relationships with his immediate supervisor or coworkers, or impeded school operations. Concluding that Pickering's letter did not have a detrimental effect in any of these areas, the Court found no justification for limiting his contribution to public debate. Indeed, the Court noted that a teacher's role provides a special vantage point from which to formulate an informed opinion on the allocation of school district funds, thus making it essential for teachers to be able to speak about public issues without fear of reprisal, unless the false statements are intentionally or recklessly made.

In 1977, the Supreme Court established the principle that even if a teacher's expression is constitutionally protected, school officials are not prevented from discharging the employee if sufficient cause exists *independent* of the protected speech. In *Mt. Healthy City School District v. Doyle*, a school board voted not to renew the contract of a nontenured teacher who had made a telephone call to a local radio station concerning a proposed teacher grooming code. The teacher had been involved in several previous incidents, but in not renewing his contract the board cited "lack of tact in handling professional matters," referring only to the radio call and obscene gestures made to several female students.[3] The lower courts ruled in favor of the teacher, but the Supreme Court reversed. The Court held that on remand **the burden of proof is on the employee to show that the expression is constitutionally protected and a substantial or motivating factor in the school board's adverse action. Once established, the burden then shifts to the school board to show by a preponderance of evidence that it would have reached the same decision in the absence of the teacher's exercise of protected speech.** The Court

---

[1]Texas v. Johnson, 491 U.S. 397, 404 (1989). *See also* Montanye v. Wissahickon Sch. Dist., 218 Fed. App'x 126 (3d Cir. 2007) (finding a teacher's actions in scheduling a student's therapy sessions, transporting the student to those sessions, and attending some of the sessions did not involve intent to convey any message deserving First Amendment protection).

[2]391 U.S. 563 (1968). *See also* Givhan v. W. Line Consol. Sch. Dist., 439 U.S. 410 (1979) (concluding that as long as the expression pertains to matters of public concern, rather than personal grievances, statements made in private or through a public medium are constitutionally protected; the forum where the expression occurs does not determine whether it is of public or private interest).

[3]429 U.S. 274, 282 (1977), *on remand*, 670 F.2d 59 (6th Cir. 1982).

reasoned that the exercise of protected expression should not place a public employee in a better or worse position with regard to continued employment. In short, dismissal or nonrenewal is not negated by the employee making comments on matters of public concern as long as the personnel action is warranted on other grounds. On remand, the board established that there were sufficient grounds other than the radio station call to justify the teacher's nonrenewal.

In a significant 1983 decision, *Connick v. Myers*, the Supreme Court narrowed the circumstances under which public employees can prevail in free expression cases.[4] The case involved an assistant district attorney, dissatisfied with her proposed transfer, who circulated among coworkers a questionnaire concerning office operations and morale and was subsequently terminated. The Court ruled that the questionnaire related primarily to a personal employment grievance, which is not protected by the First Amendment, rather than to matters of public interest. Of particular importance was the Court's conclusion that **the *form* and *context* as well as the *content* of the expression should be considered in assessing whether it relates to public matters.** Thus, the Court indicated that the factors applied under the *Pickering* balancing test to determine if speech adversely affects government interests can be considered in the *initial* assessment of whether the expression informs public debate or is simply part of a private employment grievance that is not constitutionally protected.

In 2006, the Supreme Court rendered *Garcetti v. Ceballos*, adding another threshold question in assessing constitutional protection of public employees' expression and making it even more difficult for public employees to prevail in free expression claims (see Figure 10.1).[5] The Court established a bright-line rule that expression related to official job responsibilities is not protected. Thus, **whether the employee is speaking as a private citizen or as an employee pursuant to job duties is the first consideration, because if speaking as an employee, there is no further constitutional assessment.** The Court ruled five-to-four that the district attorney's office did not impair the free speech rights of Ceballos, an assistant district attorney, by allegedly retaliating against him for writing a memorandum indicating that the arresting deputy sheriff may have lied in a search warrant affidavit. Ceballos also informed the defense counsel of his concerns, and the defense subpoenaed Ceballos to testify at the hearing in which the warrant was unsuccessfully challenged. Ceballos alleged he subsequently was mistreated by superiors, denied a promotion, given an undesirable transfer, and retaliated against in other ways.

Reversing the Ninth Circuit, the Supreme Court reasoned Ceballos was speaking about a task he was paid to perform and concluded that "when public employees make statements pursuant to their official duties, . . . the Constitution does not insulate their communications from employer discipline."[6] The majority reiterated that where the comments

---

[4]461 U.S. 138 (1983). *See also* Waters v. Churchill, 511 U.S. 661 (1994) (concluding that the government employer can reach its factual conclusions without being held to the evidentiary rules followed by courts; as long as the employer conducts an investigation and acts in good faith, it can discharge an employee for remarks *believed* to have been made); Rankin v. McPherson, 483 U.S. 378 (1987) (assessing the context, form, and content of a public employee's pejorative statement to a coworker following the assassination attempt on President Reagan and finding no basis for dismissal in the absence of interference with work relationships or performance).

[5]547 U.S. 410 (2006).

[6]*Id.* at 421. But the Court specifically left open whether its analysis would apply to speech related to instruction. *Id.* at 425, *infra* text accompanying note 47.

FIGURE 10.1   Analyzing Public Educators' Expression Rights

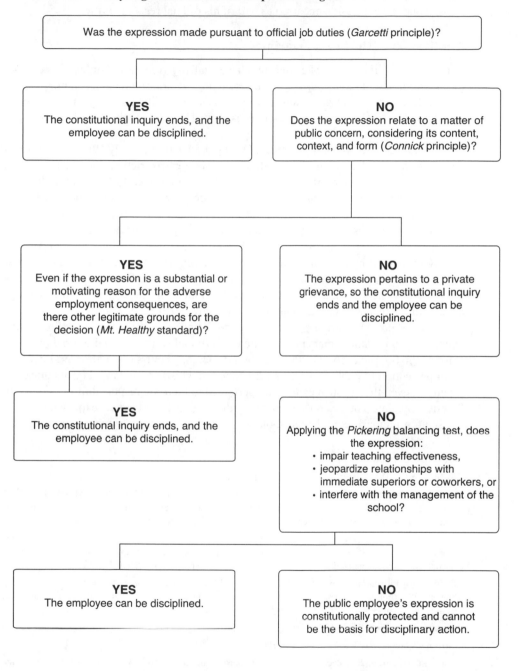

Was the expression made pursuant to official job duties (*Garcetti* principle)?

YES
The constitutional inquiry ends, and the employee can be disciplined.

NO
Does the expression relate to a matter of public concern, considering its content, context, and form (*Connick* principle)?

YES
Even if the expression is a substantial or motivating reason for the adverse employment consequences, are there other legitimate grounds for the decision (*Mt. Healthy* standard)?

NO
The expression pertains to a private grievance, so the constitutional inquiry ends and the employee can be disciplined.

YES
The constitutional inquiry ends, and the employee can be disciplined.

NO
Applying the *Pickering* balancing test, does the expression:
• impair teaching effectiveness,
• jeopardize relationships with immediate superiors or coworkers, or
• interfere with the management of the school?

YES
The employee can be disciplined.

NO
The public employee's expression is constitutionally protected and cannot be the basis for disciplinary action.

were made—inside the workplace—was not the central consideration; the controlling factor was that the expression occurred as part of his official responsibilities.

Application of the Legal Principles

In the majority of cases, public educators have challenged reprisals for their speech outside the classroom. Some courts also have addressed *prior restraints* on public employees' expression and restrictions on communication channels. In addition, during the past couple of decades, educators' classroom expression has evoked litigation under the Free Speech Clause.

Expression Outside the Classroom.   During the 1970s and early 1980s, courts relied on the *Pickering* guidelines in striking down a variety of restrictions on teachers' rights to express views on matters of public interest. Then from the early 1980s until 2006, many courts applied *Connick*[7] in broadly interpreting employee expression that constitutes private grievances in contrast to matters of public concern. To illustrate, courts considered the following expression to be unprotected: discussing salaries during a lunch break;[8] filing a grievance about being assigned a job-sharing teaching position;[9] accusing the superintendent of inciting student disturbances;[10] criticizing harassment and retaliation at the high school in a faculty newsletter;[11] commenting about students' test scores after being instructed by the superintendent not to speak publicly on this topic;[12] and filing a grievance with the teachers' union about the individual's performance rating.[13]

Some courts, however, applied the public/private distinction and found specific expression to pertain to matters of public concern and warrant constitutional protection.[14] Prior to the Supreme Court's 2006 *Garcetti* decision,[15] courts often afforded First Amendment protection to public educators who blew the whistle on unlawful or unethical school practices, even though such expression pertained to their job responsibilities. For example, federal appellate courts considered the following to be protected expression: a former assistant principal's complaints about a suspected cheating scheme involving student

[7]461 U.S. 138 (1983).

[8]Koehn v. Indian Hills Cmty. Coll., 371 F.3d 394 (8th Cir. 2004).

[9]Renfroe v. Kirkpatrick, 722 F.2d 714 (11th Cir. 1984). *See also* Ferrara v. Mills, 781 F.2d 1508 (11th Cir. 1986) (holding that complaints about a policy allowing students to select their own subjects and teachers and about the hiring of coaches to teach social studies did not implicate public concerns).

[10]Stevenson v. Lower Marion County Sch. Dist. No. 3, 327 S.E.2d 656 (S.C. 1985). *See also* Ifill v. District of Columbia, 665 A.2d 185 (D.C. 1995) (holding that an employee's communication with school officials regarding dissatisfaction with overcrowding in her special education classroom dealt with a private grievance).

[11]Sanguigni v. Pittsburgh Bd. of Educ., 968 F.2d 393 (3d Cir. 1992). *See also* Patterson v. Masem, 774 F.2d 251 (8th Cir. 1985) (holding that denial of a promotion to a supervisory role was not retaliation for the teacher recommending that an allegedly racially offensive play not be performed).

[12]Partee v. Metro. Sch. Dist., 954 F.2d 454 (7th Cir. 1992).

[13]Griffin v. Thomas, 929 F.2d 1210 (7th Cir. 1991).

[14]The Sixth Circuit in 2001 declared that "the key question is not whether a person is speaking in his role as an employee or a citizen, but whether the employee's speech in fact touches on matters of public concern." Cockrel v. Shelby County Sch. Dist., 270 F.3d 1036, 1052 (6th Cir. 2001) (citing *Connick v. Myers*, 461 U.S. 138, 148–149 (1983)), *infra* text accompanying note 46.

[15]547 U.S. 410 (2006); *supra* text accompanying note 5.

achievement tests;[16] a special education teacher's assertions that the adapted physical education program violated federal law;[17] a school nurse's criticisms of immunization practices, the heavy nursing caseload, and student safety;[18] and an athletic director's criticism of hazing on the football team.[19] In all of these pre-*Garcetti* cases, the expression at issue related to the employee's job, but none of the courts found the expression unprotected simply because it occurred pursuant to work responsibilities. However, the continued vitality of these rulings under the *Garcetti* precedent is uncertain.

  Garcetti calls into question the public/private distinction as the guiding consideration. If the expression is made pursuant to official job responsibilities, it is not protected and thus unnecessary to establish that the expression pertains to a private grievance or has a negative impact on agency operations (see Figure 10.1). **Whether the content of the expression pertained to a public concern or a private grievance appeared to be the crucial consideration prior to the *Garcetti* ruling, but the role of the speaker now seems to trump the content.**[20] The broad protection once given to public educators' expression under *Pickering* now is available only if the expression (1) does not occur pursuant to official duties, (2) relates to a public concern (considering its context and form as well as its content), and (3) is the motivating factor in the adverse employment action. *Pickering* has not been overturned, but far fewer circumstances trigger its balancing test.

  In post-*Garcetti* decisions, whistle-blowers have not been as successful in securing legal redress for retaliation as they were prior to 2006. For example, the Eleventh Circuit found that a teacher's questions about the fairness of cheerleading tryouts pertained to her duties as a cheerleading sponsor and were not protected expression relating to educational

[16]Canary v. Osborn, 211 F.3d 324 (6th Cir. 2000). *See also* Taylor v. Keith, 338 F.3d 639 (6th Cir. 2003) (finding officers' report written in the course of their employment to be protected speech because it was intended to communicate potential wrongdoing of a fellow officer, which was a matter of public concern); Delgado v. Jones, 282 F.3d 511 (7th Cir. 2002) (holding that a public employee was retaliated against in violation of the First Amendment for a memorandum alleging criminal activities involving a close relative of an elected official).

[17]Settlegoode v. Portland Pub. Schs., 371 F.3d 503 (9th Cir. 2004) (denying defendants' request for qualified immunity and entitling the teacher to the full jury award, including punitive damages, assessed against the school administrators for the violation of her constitutional rights). For additional cases in which public educators prevailed in establishing that their expression pertained to protected matters of public concern, *see* Stephen Thomas, Nelda Cambron-McCabe, and Martha McCarthy, *Public School Law: Teachers' and Students' Rights* (Boston: Allyn and Bacon, 2009), Chapter 9.

[18]Stever v. Indep. Sch. Dist. No. 625, 943 F.2d 845 (8th Cir. 1991). *See also* McGreevy v. Stroup, 413 F.3d 359 (3d Cir. 2005) (finding that a school nurse's low ratings were in retaliation for speaking out on behalf of two students with disabilities and objecting to pesticide spraying by an unlicensed person).

[19]Cioffi v. Averill Park Cent. Sch. Dist., 444 F.3d 158 (2d Cir. 2006), *cert. denied,* 127 S. Ct. 382 (2006) (vacating summary judgment for the school district and board, but granting summary judgment for the board president and superintendent on immunity grounds).

[20]Even prior to *Garcetti,* courts recognized that public employees in policy-making roles relinquished some free speech rights because of the impact of their expression on agency operations. *See, e.g.*, Sharp v. Lindsey, 285 F.3d 479 (6th Cir. 2002) (finding that a tension-free superintendent/principal relationship justified reassigning a principal to a teaching role after a public disagreement regarding the district's new dress code); Vargas-Harrison v. Racine Unified Sch. Dist., 272 F.3d 964 (7th Cir. 2001) (upholding demotion of a principal, who occupied a policy-making role, for expression critical of superiors' policies); Pahmeier v. Marion Cmty. Schs., No. 1:04-CV-365-TS, 2006 U.S. Dist. LEXIS 24048 (N.D. Ind. Mar. 17, 2006) (holding that a high school principal's wearing a red sweatshirt in solidarity with teachers at a public meeting to protest closing her school was not protected expression, since the principal occupied a policy-making role).

quality issues as she claimed.[21] The Tenth Circuit also ruled that a superintendent's comments about the Head Start program and possible violations of federal law were not protected as they were made in the course of her job duties,[22] and a Delaware federal district court ruled that a school psychologist's complaints about the school's noncompliance with the Individuals with Disabilities Education Act pertained to his job assignment and were not protected by the First Amendment.[23] Even if whistle-blowing is not at issue, public school personnel often have not prevailed in their recent free speech claims because courts have concluded that the expression at issue was pursuant to official job duties.[24]

Some employees, however, have succeeded in their expression claims in post-*Garcetti* cases. For example, the Tenth Circuit held that charter school teachers' grievances pertaining to alleged retaliation for meeting off campus to discuss concerns about the operation of the school were not made pursuant to the teachers' official duties and pertained to matters of public concern.[25] Thus, the expression was protected by the First Amendment and subject to the *Pickering* and *Mt. Healthy* standards of review.

[21]The teacher voiced her concerns in responding to a questionnaire her principal asked her to complete. Gilder-Lucas v. Elmore County Bd. of Educ., 186 Fed. App'x 885 (11th Cir. 2006). *See also* Posey v. Lake Pend Oreille Sch. Dist. No. 84, No. CV05-272-N-EJL, 2007 U.S. Dist. LEXIS 7829 (D. Idaho Feb. 2, 2007) (holding that a school district parking lot attendant's complaints about safety issues were pursuant to his job so he could not allege that his position was eliminated in retaliation for his expression); Cole v. Anne Arundel County Bd. of Educ., No. CCB-05-1579, 2006 U.S. Dist. LEXIS 89426 (D. Md. Nov. 30, 2006) (holding that a school bus driver who complained about bus safety was speaking pursuant to her official duties and could not claim retaliation for the expression).

[22]Casey v. W. Las Vegas Indep. Sch. Dist., 473 F.3d 1323 (10th Cir. 2007) (holding, however, that her comments about the New Mexico Open Meetings Act made to the state attorney general were outside the scope of her job, so her claim of retaliation for those comments may be legally viable). *See also* Williams v. Dallas Indep. Sch. Dist., 480 F.3d 689 (5th Cir. 2007) (holding that an athletic director who wrote a letter to the school's office manager about appropriations for athletic activities was speaking pursuant to his official duties and could not claim retaliation for his contract not being renewed); Trujillo v. Bd. of Educ., 212 Fed. App'x 760 (10th Cir. 2007), *on remand,* No. CIV 02-1146 JB/LFG, 2007 U.S. Dist. LEXIS 56500 (D.N.M. June 5, 2007) (finding unprotected a teacher's complaints that his supervisor lacked proper certification for his position and abused students as the teacher had spoken pursuant to official job duties).

[23]Houlihan v. Sussex Technical Sch. Dist., 461 F. Supp. 2d 252 (D. Del. 2006) (holding, however, that the school psychologist stated a valid cause of action for retaliation under the federal Rehabilitation Act, so the school district's motion to dismiss her claim under this law was denied). *See also* Pagani v. Meriden Bd. of Educ., No. 3:05-CV-01115 (JCH), 2006 U.S. Dist. LEXIS 92267 (D. Conn. Dec. 19, 2006) (finding a teacher's report to the Department of Children and Families that a substitute teacher showed middle school students photos of himself with two females, all of whom were nude, was made under the auspices of official responsibilities; the teacher could not claim retaliation for making the report after superiors advised him not to contact the agency).

[24]*See, e.g.,* D'Angelo v. Sch. Bd., 497 F.3d 1203 (11th Cir. 2007) (ruling that a principal was speaking in his professional role in urging his teachers to support conversion of their school to a charter school; his expression was not protected and could be the basis for dismissal).

[25]Brammer-Hoelter v. Twin Peaks Charter Acad., 492 F.3d 1192 (10th Cir. 2007) (reasoning that although some topics discussed at the off-campus meetings pertained to official job duties, the teachers had no supervisory or reporting responsibilities in connection with a number of the problems being discussed). *See also* McGuire v. Warren, 207 Fed. App'x 34 (2d Cir. 2006), *on remand,* 490 F. Supp. 2d 331 (S.D.N.Y. 2007) (allowing the public employee to amend her complaint to establish that termination of her contract to provide services for special-needs students was in retaliation for protected speech pertaining to criticism of school district practices in this regard); Wilcoxon v. Red Clay Consol. Sch. Dist., 437 F. Supp. 2d 235 (D. Del. 2006) (finding that a teacher's journal documenting his coteacher's tardiness and other unprofessional conduct was not written pursuant to official duties and pertained to a matter of public concern).

If determined that protected speech is involved, courts have relied on *Mt. Healthy* to uphold terminations or transfers when other legitimate reasons justify the personnel actions. In an illustrative case, the Seventh Circuit ruled that a teacher failed to prove that her critical expression pertaining to the need for additional textbooks at her school was a substantial or motivating factor in disciplinary action against her, given well-documented incidents of her misconduct and insubordination.[26] The Tenth Circuit similarly found that a director of bilingual education could not establish that speaking about the program's non-compliance with state guidelines and writing a letter to the editor of the local newspaper were the motivating factors in her termination and held instead that poor job performance justified the action.[27]

School authorities cannot rely on *Mt. Healthy* to justify termination or other disciplinary action if the school officials' stated reasons for personnel decisions are merely a pretext to restrict protected expression. For example, the Seventh Circuit held that a jury reasonably could find that a counselor, allegedly dismissed for 14 incidents of insubordination and unprofessional misconduct, was actually fired in retaliation for writing articles for the local paper, commenting to the media about violations of the open-meetings law by the school board, and engaging in other protected expression.[28]

Once determined that expression is protected, the employee then has the burden of demonstrating that it was a key factor in the dismissal or disciplinary decision. Even if shown that expression on matters of public concern was the sole basis for adverse action, the public employer still may prevail under the *Pickering* balancing test. In short, **if established that expression on a matter of public concern that is not pursuant to job duties is the motivating or sole basis for adverse action, the public employer still has the opportunity to establish that its interests in maintaining efficient school operations outweigh the individual's free speech rights.**

Prior Restraints and Channel Rules.   The judiciary is less likely to condone prior restraints on expression than it is to uphold disciplinary action after the expression has occurred. **The key is whether the prior restraint is content based, which requires strict judicial scrutiny, or whether it is content neutral, thus receiving a "less rigorous examination."**[29] For example, the Tenth Circuit struck down a portion of an Oklahoma law authorizing the termination of teachers for "advocating . . . public or private homosexual activity in a manner that creates a substantial risk that such conduct will come to the

---

[26]Smith v. Dunn, 368 F.3d 705 (7th Cir. 2004). *See also* Love v. Chi. Bd. of Educ., 241 F.3d 564 (7th Cir. 2001) (finding that three teachers' dismissals were based on poor performance rather than on criticism of an academic program and of the principal's interactions with teachers).

[27]Deschenie v. Bd. of Educ., 473 F.3d 1271 (10th Cir. 2007) (holding that the time between the expression and termination was too attenuated to show a causal connection). *See also* Phelps v. Fullenwider, 126 Fed. App'x 381 (9th Cir. 2005) (rejecting claim that protected speech was the motivating reason for a school employee's dismissal; finding that parental complaints of inappropriate behavior with students justified the personnel decision); Painter v. Campbell County Bd. of Educ., 417 F. Supp. 2d 854 (E.D. Ky. 2006) (finding no evidence that a principal's speech at a public hearing expressing opposition to closing a school was the motivating factor in his demotion to a teaching position).

[28]Dishnow v. Sch. Dist., 77 F.3d 194 (7th Cir. 1996).

[29]Eclipse Enter. v. Gulotta, 134 F.3d 63, 66 (2d Cir. 1997).

attention of school children or school employees."[30] The Fifth Circuit also invalidated a school board policy requiring prior approval of all political, sectarian, or special-interest materials distributed in the schools. The board had invoked the policy to prevent distribution of documents that were critical of a proposed teacher testing program, while the school board's literature supporting the program had been distributed in the schools.[31]

Policies limiting teachers' access to the school board also have generated legal disputes. In 1976, the Supreme Court held that a nonunion teacher has a free speech right to comment on a bargaining issue at a public school board meeting.[32] Also, the Ninth Circuit awarded a teacher damages for his suspension as a coach, which occurred because he did not advise the superintendent before writing a letter to school board members about the district's athletic policies, an issue of public debate and concern.[33] Similarly, the Seventh Circuit struck down a policy requiring all communication to the school board to be directed through the superintendent and ordered a reprimand for violating the policy to be removed from a teacher's personnel file.[34]

But, some constraints on employee communication in public schools have been upheld. In a significant 1983 decision, *Perry Education Association v. Perry Local Educators' Association*, the Supreme Court ruled that a school district is not constitutionally obligated to allow a rival teachers' union access to internal school mailboxes although the exclusive bargaining agent is granted such access. **Holding that a public school's internal mail system is not a public forum for expression, the Court declared that "the state may reserve the forum for its intended purposes, communicative or otherwise, as long as the regulation on speech is reasonable and not an effort to suppress . . . the speaker's view."**[35] The Court determined that alternative communication channels were available to the rival union. However, under certain circumstances, a school's mail system might be designated as a limited public forum by school officials and thus selective access to the forum could not be denied.[36]

Some more recent controversies have focused on electronic communication. The Fourth Circuit held that public employees do not have a free speech right to use state computers for purposes not related to the agency's business and upheld restrictions on use

---

[30]Nat'l Gay Task Force v. Bd. of Educ., 729 F.2d 1270, 1274 (10th Cir. 1984), *aff'd by an equally divided court*, 470 U.S. 903 (1985).

[31]Hall v. Bd. of Sch. Comm'rs, 681 F.2d 965 (5th Cir. 1982).

[32]City of Madison v. Wis. Employment Relations Comm'n, 429 U.S. 167 (1976); text accompanying note 104, Chapter 9.

[33]Anderson v. Cent. Point Sch. Dist., 746 F.2d 505 (9th Cir. 1984).

[34]Knapp v. Whitaker, 757 F.2d 827 (7th Cir. 1985).

[35]460 U.S. 37, 46 (1983). *See also* Tex. State Teachers Ass'n v. Garland Indep. Sch. Dist., 777 F.2d 1046 (5th Cir. 1985), *aff'd mem.*, 479 U.S. 801 (1986) (finding no public forum so the school district could deny representatives of teachers' organizations school access during school hours and use of the school mail system, but teachers could not be prohibited from discussing employee organizations during nonclass time or using mail facilities for communications that simply mention such organizations); Fla. Family Ass'n v. Sch. Bd., 494 F. Supp. 2d 1311 (M.D. Fla. 2007) (holding that the school board did not deprive a family organization of its First Amendment rights by blocking its mass e-mail campaign criticizing the board's removal of religious holidays from the school calendar).

[36]*See, e.g.*, Ysleta Fed'n of Teachers v. Ysleta Indep. Sch. Dist., 720 F.2d 1429 (5th Cir. 1983). In a limited forum, any content-based policy must be narrowly drawn to achieve a compelling government interest.

of such equipment for state employees to access sexually explicit Internet materials.[37] Also, the Fifth Circuit reiterated that a state university's internal mail system is not a public forum and thus declined to interfere with an institution's use of e-mail spam guards and cancellation of adjuncts' e-mail accounts during semesters they are not teaching.[38] And the Seventh Circuit concluded that a part-time university employee could be required to remove a quotation she affixed to work-related e-mail messages, because the employer considered a word in the quotation to be vulgar and inappropriate for workplace language.[39]

Although prior restraints on teachers' free speech rights are vulnerable to legal attack, courts have upheld reasonable policies regulating the time, place, and manner of expression. Such restrictions must not be based on the content of speech, and they must serve significant government interests and leave alternative communication channels open.

Classroom Expression.   Traditionally, it has been assumed that restrictions can be placed on teachers' expressing their personal views to captive student audiences in their classrooms—a nonpublic forum. Since 1988, many courts have applied *Hazelwood v. Kuhlmeier* to assess the constitutionality of teachers' classroom expression,[40] holding that such expression could be curtailed for legitimate pedagogical reasons, an easy standard for school districts to satisfy. For example, the First Circuit held that a teacher's discussion of aborting fetuses with Down syndrome could be censored, noting that the school board may limit a teacher's classroom expression in the interest of promoting educational goals.[41] The Tenth Circuit relied on *Hazelwood* in upholding disciplinary action against a teacher who made comments during class about rumors that two students had engaged in sexual intercourse on the school tennis court during lunch hour, reasoning that the ninth grade government class was not a public forum.[42] More recently, a Missouri appeals court upheld termination of a teacher for making disparaging classroom comments about interracial relationships, finding no protected expression and noting that the teacher was aware of the district's anti-harassment policy.[43]

In several cases, public school teachers have not prevailed in their efforts to express their views through materials posted in their classrooms or on the adjacent hall walls. To illustrate, school authorities were upheld in censoring material a teacher posted outside his classroom that denounced homosexuality and extolled traditional family values to offset

---

[37]Urofsky v. Gilmore, 216 F.3d 401 (4th Cir. 2000).

[38]Faculty Rights Coal. v. Shahrokhi, 204 Fed. App'x 416 (5th Cir. 2006). *See also* Educ. Minn. Lakeville v. Indep. Sch. Dist. No. 194, 341 F. Supp. 2d 1070 (D. Minn. 2004) (rejecting union's argument that the school district's policy prohibiting the use of internal communication channels to distribute literature endorsing political candidates violated the First Amendment); Herbert v. Pub. Disclosure Comm'n, 148 P.3d 1102 (Wash. Ct. App. 2006) (finding that teachers violated state law by using school mail and e-mail, which are both nonpublic forums, to collect signatures on petitions for ballot measures).

[39]Pichelmann v. Madsen, 31 Fed. App'x 322 (7th Cir. 2002).

[40]484 U.S. 260 (1988). *See* text accompanying note 24, Chapter 5.

[41]Ward v. Hickey, 996 F.2d 448 (1st Cir. 1993).

[42]Miles v. Denver Pub. Schs., 944 F.2d 773 (10th Cir. 1991).

[43]Loeffelman v. Bd. of Educ., 134 S.W.3d 637 (Mo. Ct. App. 2004).

the school district's materials recognizing Gay and Lesbian Awareness Month.[44] Reasoning that the teacher was speaking for the school, the Ninth Circuit concluded that teachers are not entitled to express views that are counter to the adopted curriculum. The Fourth Circuit also upheld a school board's instructions for a teacher to remove religious materials from his classroom bulletin boards, which are not public forums. The court concluded that the items removed (e.g., poster of George Washington praying, an article outlining religious differences among presidential candidates) were curricular in nature and constituted school-sponsored speech, so their removal did not implicate the First Amendment.[45]

The Sixth Circuit seemed to depart from the prevailing judicial stance when it upheld a teacher's right to invite a guest speaker (actor Woody Harrelson) to present information on the industrial and environmental benefits of hemp to her fifth grade class. Even though the teacher was speaking as an employee, the court concluded that the content of her speech involved political and social concerns in the community.[46] Thus, the court found genuine issues of material fact regarding whether the school district's proffered grounds for terminating the teacher based on insubordination, conduct unbecoming a teacher, and other grounds were a pretext for the dismissal based on protected expression. The court recognized that the school district's interest in efficient and harmonious school operations did not outweigh the teacher's interests in speaking to her students about an issue of substantial concern in the state.

It is unclear how the *Garcetti* ruling will affect litigation pertaining to classroom expression. The *Garcetti* majority emphasized that "we need not, and for that reason do not, decide whether the analysis we conduct today would apply in the same manner to a case involving speech related to scholarship or teaching."[47] Yet, the Seventh Circuit relied on *Garcetti* in ruling that classroom expression clearly is part of public educators' official duties and can be censored to protect the captive student audience.[48] Accordingly, the court held that a teacher's expression of pro-peace sentiments regarding the war in Iraq during a current events session was not constitutionally protected under *Garcetti*, as the current events lesson was an assigned classroom task.

Also, a Michigan federal district court held that a teacher wearing a T-shirt in his classes with a printed message about the teachers' union not being under contract caused or had the potential to cause disharmony in the workplace.[49] While recognizing that the issue of labor negotiations touches on a matter of public concern, the court ruled that the school district's interest in ensuring a professional workplace outweighed the teacher's rights in

---

[44]Downs v. L.A. Unified Sch. Dist., 228 F.3d 1003 (9th Cir. 2000). *See also* Newton v. Slye, 116 F. Supp. 2d 677 (W.D. Va. 2000) (finding no First Amendment right for a teacher to post outside his classroom door the American Library Association's pamphlet listing banned books).

[45]Lee v. York County Sch. Div., 484 F.3d 687 (4th Cir. 2007), *cert. denied*, 128 S. Ct. 387 (2007).

[46]Cockrel v. Shelby County Sch. Dist., 270 F.3d 1036 (6th Cir. 2001).

[47]Garcetti v. Ceballos, 547 U.S. 410, 425 (2006).

[48]Mayer v. Monroe County Cmty. Sch. Corp., 474 F.3d 477 (7th Cir. 2007), *cert. denied,* 128 S. Ct. 160 (2007). *See also* Calef v. Budden, 361 F. Supp. 2d 493 (D.S.C. 2005) (upholding a school board in declining to use a substitute teacher who had worn an anti-war button to school and criticized U.S. involvement in Iraq and Panama to impressionable middle school students).

[49]Montle v. Westwood Heights Sch. Dist., 437 F. Supp. 2d 652, 654 (E.D. Mich. 2006).

this instance. The court noted that under *Garcetti,* "government employers, like private employers, need a significant degree of control over their employees' words and actions; without it, there would be little chance for the efficient provision of public services."[50] Whether courts apply *Garcetti* or *Hazelwood* may have little practical significance, because teachers' classroom expression has always been subject to restrictions to protect students from proselytization.

■ ■ ■ ■ ■

FREEDOM OF ASSOCIATION

A public educator's participation in political activities outside the classroom cannot be the basis for adverse employment decisions, unless the employee has policy-making responsibilities or such activities negatively affect job performance.

Although freedom of association is not specifically addressed in the First Amendment, the Supreme Court has recognized that associational rights are "implicit in the freedoms of speech, assembly, and petition."[51] The Court has consistently declared that infringements on the right to associate for expressive purposes can be justified only by a compelling government interest, unrelated to suppressing ideas, that cannot be achieved through less restrictive means.[52] Accordingly, public educators cannot be disciplined for forming or joining political, labor, religious, or social organizations.

Associational activities can be limited, however, if they disrupt school operations or interfere with teachers' professional duties. This section presents an overview of teachers' associational rights in connection with political affiliations and activities. Public educators' rights to intimate association are discussed in the section on privacy rights, and labor union issues are addressed in Chapter 9.

Political Affiliations

Conditioning public employment on partisan political affiliation has been controversial. Historically, the patronage system governed public employment; when the controlling political party changed, non-civil service employees belonging to the defeated party lost their jobs. In 1976, the Supreme Court ruled that the patronage system in an Illinois sheriff's office placed a severe restriction on political association and belief.[53] The constant threat of replacing non–policy-making individuals, who cannot undermine the administration's policies, was considered detrimental to government effectiveness and efficiency. The Court subsequently extended the principle established in the political firing cases to all

---

[50]*Id.* at. 654 (quoting Garcetti v. Ceballos, 547 U.S. 410, 418 (2006)).

[51]Healy v. James, 408 U.S. 169, 181 (1972).

[52]*See, e.g.*, NAACP v. Button, 371 U.S. 415 (1963).

[53]Elrod v. Burns, 427 U.S. 347 (1976).

aspects of public employment, ruling that party affiliation cannot influence promotion, transfer, recall, and other decisions pertaining to employees who do not establish policies.[54]

Despite being insulated from partisan politics, in some instances public educators have asserted that employment decisions have been based on their party affiliation. In such cases, the school employee has the burden of substantiating that protected political affiliation was the motivating factor in the board's employment decision.[55] If an employee satisfies this burden, then the board must demonstrate by a preponderance of evidence that it would have reached the same decision in the absence of the political association.

Public educators have substantial protection against politically based dismissals, but school authorities can question teachers about activities that may adversely affect teaching. In *Beilan v. Board of Public Education*, the Supreme Court held that questions regarding a teacher's involvement in the Communist Party were relevant to an assessment of his classroom activities and fitness to teach and that refusal to answer the superintendent's inquiries could result in dismissal.[56] **Although organizational membership *per se* is protected, a teacher must respond to queries about associational activities that are related to teaching fitness.**

Political Activity

Teachers, like all citizens, are guaranteed the right to participate in the political process. First Amendment associational as well as free speech rights have been invoked to protect public educators in expressing political views, campaigning for candidates, and running for office.

Campaigning for Issues and Candidates.   Public employees are constitutionally protected from retaliation for political participation at the local, state, and federal levels. For example, the Sixth Circuit held that the coordinator of gifted education, which was not a policy-making position, could not be reassigned for the exercise of constitutionally protected political expression and association in actively supporting an unsuccessful superintendent candidate.[57] The superintendent did not demonstrate that political loyalty was essential to the duties of this position. Of course, public employees in policy-making positions may be vulnerable to adverse employment consequences for their political activities that may preclude an effective relationship with the school board.[58]

[54]Rutan v. Republican Party, 497 U.S. 62 (1990). *See also* McCloud v. Testa, 97 F.3d 1536 (6th Cir. 1996) (rejecting public employer's immunity for violating lower level employees' constitutional protections against discrimination based on their political speech and association).

[55]*See* Piazza v. Aponte Roque, 909 F.2d 35 (1st Cir. 1990) (finding that nonrenewal of teachers' aides because of their political party affiliation impaired associational rights).

[56]357 U.S. 399 (1958).

[57]Hager v. Pike County Bd. of Educ., 286 F.3d 366 (6th Cir. 2002). *See also* Pocatello Educ. Ass'n v. Heideman, 504 F.3d 1053 (9th Cir. 2007), *cert. granted*, 128 S. Ct. 1762 (2008) (finding no compelling justification for banning public employee payroll deductions for political activities). *But see* Beattie v. Madison County Sch. Dist., 254 F.3d 595 (5th Cir. 2001) (finding insufficient causal link between employee's termination and her support for the nonincumbent candidate for school superintendent).

[58]*See, e.g.,* Dabbs v. Amos, 70 F.3d 1261 (4th Cir. 1995); Kinsey v. Salado Indep. Sch. Dist., 950 F.2d 988 (5th Cir. 1992).

Political activity that would cause divisiveness within the school district always can be restricted.[59] A California appeals court concluded that teachers could be prohibited from wearing union buttons while delivering instruction because the buttons fell within the definition of "political activity" under state law.[60] **Making campaign speeches in the classroom is clearly prohibited; teachers cannot take advantage of their position of authority with an impressionable captive audience to impose their political views.**[61] However, if campaign issues are related to the class topic, a teacher can present election issues and candidates in a nonpartisan manner.

Holding Public Office. Certain categories of public employees have been prevented from running for political office.[62] In 1973, the Supreme Court upheld the Hatch Act, a federal law that prevents *federal* employees from holding formal positions in political parties, playing substantial roles in partisan campaigns, and running for partisan office.[63] The Court recognized that legitimate reasons exist for restricting political activities of public employees, such as ensuring impartial and effective government, removing employees from political pressure, and preventing employee selection based on political factors.

Yet, laws or policies prohibiting *all* public employees from running for *any* political office have been struck down as overly broad.[64] Several courts have held that public educators, unlike public employees who are directly involved in the operation of government agencies, have the right to hold public office. The Utah Supreme Court, for example, ruled that public school teachers and administrators were not disqualified from serving in the state legislature.[65]

Restrictions can be imposed, however, to protect the integrity of the educational system. If campaigning would interfere with job responsibilities, public educators can be required to take a leave of absence while running for a public office.[66] Courts also have recognized that certain offices are incompatible with public school employment, especially if they involve an employer–employee relationship. Common law has established that such incompatibility exists when a teacher seeks a position on the school board where

---

[59]*See, e.g.,* State Bd. for Elementary and Secondary Educ. v. Howard, 834 S.W.2d 657 (Ky. 1992).

[60]Turlock Joint Elementary Sch. Dist. v. Pub. Employment Relations Bd., 5 Cal. Rptr. 3d 308 (Ct. App. 2003) (unpublished decision). Although political buttons have been prohibited in instructional settings, courts have ruled that school employees can wear such buttons outside the presence of students. *See, e.g.,* Green Twp. Educ. Ass'n v. Rowe, 746 A.2d 499 (N.J. Super. Ct. App. Div. 2000); Cal. Teachers Ass'n v. Governing Bd., 53 Cal. Rptr. 2d 474 (Ct. App. 1996).

[61]*See* Mayer v. Monroe County Cmty. Sch. Corp., 474 F.3d 477 (7th Cir. 2007), *cert. denied,* 128 S. Ct. 160 (2007); *supra* text accompanying note 48.

[62]*See* Brazil-Breashears v. Bilandic, 53 F.3d 789 (7th Cir. 1995) (finding no First or Fourteenth Amendment infractions in prohibiting certain judicial branch employees from being candidates for public office or engaging in specified political activities).

[63]U.S. Civil Serv. Comm'n v. Nat'l Ass'n of Letter Carriers, 413 U.S. 548 (1973) (interpreting 5 U.S.C. § 7324 (2008)). *See also* Broadrick v. Oklahoma, 413 U.S. 601 (1973) (upholding an Oklahoma law forbidding classified civil servants from running for paid political offices).

[64]*See, e.g.,* Minielly v. State, 411 P.2d 69 (Or. 1966); Cranston Teachers Alliance v. Miele, 495 A.2d 233 (R.I. 1985).

[65]Jenkins v. Bishop, 589 P.2d 770 (Utah 1978) (per curiam).

[66]*See, e.g.,* White v. Dougherty County Bd. of Educ., 579 F. Supp. 1480 (M.D. Ga. 1984), *aff'd,* 470 U.S. 1067 (1985).

employed.[67] Of course, a teacher would not be prevented from serving on the school board of another school district.

School boards must be certain that constraints on employees' freedom of association are not based on mere disagreement with the political orientation of the activities. Personnel actions must be justified as necessary to protect the interests of students and the school. Although school boards must respect employees' associational rights, they are obligated to ensure that the political activities of public school personnel do not adversely affect the school. Employees can be disciplined if they:

- Neglect instructional duties to campaign,
- Use the classroom as a political forum, or
- Disrupt school operations because of their political activities.

■ ■ ■ ■ ■

PERSONAL APPEARANCE

School officials can place constraints on educators' personal appearance if there is a rational basis for such restrictions.

Historically, school boards often imposed rigid grooming restrictions on teachers. In the 1970s, such attempts to regulate teachers' appearance generated considerable litigation, as did grooming standards for students. Controversies have subsided somewhat, but constraints on school employees' appearance continue to be challenged. School boards have defended their efforts to regulate teacher appearance on the perceived need to set an appropriate tone in the classroom and enforce similar appearance and dress codes for students. Teachers have contested these requirements as abridgments of their constitutionally protected privacy, liberty, and free expression rights.

Most courts since the mid-1970s have supported school officials in adopting reasonable grooming and dress restrictions for teachers. The Supreme Court provided some clarification in a 1976 decision upholding a hair-grooming regulation for police officers.[68] The Court placed the burden on the individual to demonstrate the lack of a rational connection between the regulation and a legitimate public purpose. This reasoning has been followed by lower courts in assessing dress and appearance restrictions for teachers. The Second Circuit upheld a Connecticut school board's requirement that all male teachers must wear ties as a rational means to promote respect for authority, traditional values, and classroom discipline.[69] Because of the uniquely influential role of teachers, the court noted

---

[67]*See, e.g.,* Unified Sch. Dist. No. 501 v. Baker, 6 P.3d 848 (Kan. 2000) (invalidating election of a teacher to the school board when state legislature had not negated the common law doctrine prohibiting employees from holding incompatible offices).

[68]Kelley v. Johnson, 425 U.S. 238 (1976).

[69]E. Hartford Educ. Ass'n v. Bd. of Educ., 562 F.2d 838 (2d Cir. 1977).

that they may be subjected to restrictions in their professional lives that otherwise would not be acceptable. The First Circuit similarly upheld a school board's dismissal of a teacher for wearing short skirts.[70] More recently, a federal court ruled that a school board did not violate a teacher's rights by instructing her to cover her T-shirt displaying the words *Jesus 2000—J2K* or to change into another top.[71]

Restrictions will not be upheld, however, if found to be unrelated to a legitimate government concern. Although courts generally acknowledge that individuals have a protected interest in governing their appearance, this interest has not been declared a fundamental right requiring heightened judicial scrutiny. School officials thus can restrict employees' appearance as long as the regulations advance legitimate school objectives and are not arbitrary.

■ ■ ■ ■ ■

CONSTITUTIONAL PRIVACY RIGHTS

Sanctions cannot be imposed solely because school officials disapprove of teachers' private conduct, but restrictions can be placed on unconventional behavior that is detrimental to job performance or harmful to students.

Public employees have asserted constitutional and statutory rights to be free from unwarranted government intrusions in their personal activities. The federal Constitution does not explicitly enumerate personal privacy rights, but the Supreme Court has recognized that certain *implied* fundamental rights warrant constitutional protection because of their close relationship to explicit constitutional guarantees. For example, protected privacy rights have been interpreted as encompassing personal choices in matters such as marriage, contraception, procreation, and family relations.[72] Employment decisions cannot be based on relinquishing such rights without a compelling justification. Litigation covered in this section focuses on constitutional privacy claims initiated under the Fourth Amendment (protection against unreasonable searches and seizures), the Ninth Amendment (personal privacy as an unenumerated right reserved to the people), and the Fourteenth Amendment (protection against state action impairing personal liberties without due process of law).

In some instances, public employees have asserted that government action has impaired their privacy right to intimate association related to creating and maintaining a

---

[70]Tardif v. Quinn, 545 F.2d 761 (1st Cir. 1976). *See also* Zalewska v. County of Sullivan, 316 F.3d 314 (2d Cir. 2003) (upholding a uniform policy for van drivers to project a professional appearance and ensure safety of vans with chair lifts).

[71]Downing v. W. Haven Bd. of Educ., 162 F. Supp. 2d 19 (D. Conn. 2001).

[72]*See, e.g.,* Roe v. Wade, 410 U.S. 113 (1973) (right to have an abortion); Loving v. Virginia, 388 U.S. 1 (1967) (right to interracial marriage); Griswold v. Connecticut, 381 U.S. 479 (1965) (right to use birth control measures); Skinner v. Oklahoma, 316 U.S. 535 (1942) (right to procreate). *But see* Gonzales v. Carhart, 127 S. Ct. 1610 (2007) (upholding a federal prohibition on performing partial-birth abortions).

family.[73] To illustrate, public educators cannot be deprived of their jobs because of the politics or other activities of their partners or spouses. The Sixth Circuit found an inference that the superintendent's nonrenewal recommendation for an employee, whose husband was a principal at another school, and disagreed with some school district directives, was impermissibly based on the employee's marital relationship.[74]

However, employees have not been successful in using privacy rights to challenge anti-nepotism policies that prohibit teachers from reporting to their spouses or working in the same building as their spouses. The Sixth Circuit reasoned that such an anti-nepotism policy did not interfere with the fundamental right to marry, because the policy affected working conditions, not the marriage itself.[75] The fact that such policies do not apply to employees who are cohabiting or dating has not nullified anti-nepotism provisions.

Teachers also have not succeeded in asserting a privacy right to refuse physical examinations as a prerequisite to employment or as a condition of returning from medical leave.[76] Furthermore, courts have found no privacy impairments in required observations by superiors and other strategies, such as videotaping lessons, used to assess teaching competence.[77] The Supreme Court of Wisconsin held that a teacher's privacy rights did not outweigh the public's interest in knowing about the teacher's conduct in allegedly conducting Internet searches on his school computer to locate pornographic material.[78]

Although regulations are far less restrictive today than in the early 1900s, when some school districts prohibited female teachers from marrying or even dating, school boards still attempt to proscribe aspects of teachers' personal lives that conflict with community values. **School officials have defended constraints on some behaviors on the grounds that teachers serve as role models for students and therefore should conform to community norms to ensure an appropriate educational environment.** Recognizing that teachers are held to a higher standard of conduct than general citizens, the judiciary has upheld dismissals for behavior that jeopardizes student welfare, even if it takes place during the summer break.[79]

---

[73]Although the Fifth Circuit held that a school board would have to produce a compelling justification to prohibit a teacher from breast-feeding her child at school during noninstructional time, Dike v. Sch. Bd., 650 F.2d 783 (5th Cir. 1981), the Eleventh Circuit subsequently reasoned that strict judicial scrutiny is not required in reviewing such intimate association claims, Shahar v. Bowers, 114 F.3d 1097, 1102 (11th Cir. 1997).

[74]Adkins v. Bd. of Educ., 982 F.2d 952 (6th Cir. 1993). *But see* Finnegan v. Bd. of Educ., 30 F.3d 273 (2d Cir. 1994) (finding inadequate evidence that a probationary teacher was removed from a coaching position and denied tenure because he married a former member of his volleyball team shortly after the student graduated).

[75]Montgomery v. Carr, 101 F.3d 1117 (6th Cir. 1996).

[76]*See, e.g.,* Strong v. Bd. of Educ., 902 F.2d 208 (2d Cir. 1990); Daury v. Smith, 842 F.2d 9 (1st Cir. 1988).

[77]*See* Roberts v. Houston Indep. Sch. Dist., 788 S.W.2d 107 (Tex. App. 1990). *See also* Brannen v. Bd. of Educ., 761 N.E.2d 84 (Ohio Ct. App. 2001) (holding that a board's use of surveillance cameras to videotape school custodians in their break room to identify unauthorized breaks was not unreasonable and did not constitute an unlawful search).

[78]Zellner v. Cedarburg Sch. Dist., 731 N.W.2d 240 (Wis. 2007). *See also* Urofsky v. Gilmore, 216 F.3d 401 (4th Cir. 2000); *supra* text accompanying note 37.

[79]*See, e.g.,* Bd. of Educ. v. Wood, 717 S.W.2d 837 (Ky. 1986).

Search and Seizure

Public educators, like all citizens, are shielded by the Fourth Amendment against unreasonable government invasions of their person and property. This amendment usually requires police officers and other state agents to secure a search warrant (based on probable cause that evidence of a crime will be found) before conducting personal searches. The Supreme Court has not addressed teachers' rights in connection with searches initiated by public school authorities, but it has upheld warrantless personal searches of students based on *reasonable suspicion* that contraband detrimental to the educational process is concealed.[80] The Court also has upheld a warrantless search by state hospital supervisors of an employee physician's office that was necessary to identify improprieties in managing the residency program.[81]

Although case law in the public school context is scant, the judiciary has recognized that the reasonableness of a job-related search or seizure by a supervisor rests on whether educational interests outweigh the employee's expectation of privacy. **The Fourth Amendment prohibits *arbitrary* invasions of teachers' personal effects by school officials, but in some situations courts have ruled that the school's interests are overriding.** For example, the Second Circuit upheld the search of a teacher's classroom after he had been suspended for alleged sexual harassment of a student and was provided two opportunities to remove personal items from the classroom.[82] The court further held that the teacher had no valid claim to materials he prepared during his employment.

Drug-screening programs in schools have become increasingly controversial. School boards can require employees to have physical examinations as a condition of employment, but mandatory screening for drugs has been challenged as impairing Fourth Amendment privacy rights. Several courts have struck down random or blanket urinalysis screening of public school employees, holding that school boards must have *individualized suspicion* of conduct detrimental to the school environment to subject employees to drug tests.[83]

In contrast to *blanket* testing of all personnel, support for drug testing of public employees in *safety-sensitive roles* can be found in two 1989 Supreme Court decisions upholding the mandatory drug testing of railroad employees involved in accidents[84] and customs employees who carry firearms or intercept illegal drugs.[85] The Court found that the safety and security interests served by the programs outweighed employees' privacy concerns. The District of Columbia Circuit subsequently upheld the school district's policy

---

[80]New Jersey v. T.L.O., 469 U.S. 325 (1985). *See* text accompanying note 76, Chapter 8, for a discussion of the reasonable suspicion standard.

[81]O'Connor v. Ortega, 480 U.S. 709 (1987).

[82]Shaul v. Cherry Valley-Springfield Cent. Sch. Dist., 363 F.3d 177 (2d Cir. 2004). *See also* Soderstrand v. Oklahoma *ex rel.* Bd. of Regents, 463 F. Supp. 2d 1308 (W.D. Okla. 2006) (upholding university authorities in seizing a laptop computer from an employee's desk during an investigation of workplace misconduct involving child pornography).

[83]*See, e.g.,* Ga. Ass'n of Educators v. Harris, 749 F. Supp. 1110 (N.D. Ga. 1990); Patchogue-Medford Cong. of Teachers v. Bd. of Educ., 510 N.E.2d 325 (N.Y. 1987).

[84]Skinner v. Ry. Labor Executives' Ass'n, 489 U.S. 602 (1989) (upholding alcohol testing of employees as well).

[85]Nat'l Treasury Employees Union v. Von Raab, 489 U.S. 656 (1989). *See also* Bd. of Educ. v. Earls, 536 U.S. 822 (2002); Vernonia Sch. Dist. 47J v. Acton, 515 U.S. 646 (1995) (upholding suspicionless drug testing of students who participate in sports or other extracurricular activities); text accompanying notes 118–120, Chapter 8.

requiring all employees whose duties affect child safety, such as bus attendants, to submit to a drug test as part of routine medical examinations.[86] And, the Fifth Circuit ruled that a school custodian, whose performance affected almost 900 students, was in a safety-sensitive role justifying suspicionless drug testing.[87]

What constitutes safety-sensitive roles in the school context, however, remains contested, and some courts seem more inclined than they were in the past to interpret expansively the positions in this category. The Sixth Circuit upheld a school district's policy requiring suspicionless drug testing for all individuals who apply for, transfer to, or are promoted to safety-sensitive positions, including teachers who are entrusted with the care of children and are on the front line of school security. The court also upheld drug testing of any individual for whom there was reasonable suspicion of drug possession or use, but it remanded the case for additional factual inquiry regarding the provision calling for alcohol testing of all employees.[88] A Kentucky federal district court subsequently upheld random, suspicionless drug testing of a school district's employees in safety-sensitive roles, including teachers, as justified to comply with the Drug-Free Workplace Act of 1988, designed to ensure that recipients of federal grant funds maintain a drug-free work environment.[89] But the Fifth Circuit struck down policies in two Louisiana school districts that required employees injured in the course of employment to submit to urinalysis, finding an insufficient nexus between such injuries and drug use.[90]

Of course, employees, like students, can be subjected to alcohol and drug testing when there is reasonable suspicion that the individual is under the influence of these substances. Employees can be dismissed for refusing to submit to such a test,[91] but in some instances, reasonable suspicion has not been established to justify targeting particular individuals.[92] **The law is still evolving regarding what constitutes individualized**

[86]Jones v. McKenzie, 833 F.2d 335 (D.C. Cir. 1987), *vacated sub nom.* Jones v. Jenkins, 490 U.S. 1001 (1989*), on remand*, 878 F.2d 1476 (D.C. Cir. 1989).

[87]Aubrey v. Sch. Bd., 148 F.3d 559 (5th Cir. 1998). *See also* English v. Talladega County Bd. of Educ., 938 F. Supp. 775 (N.D. Ala. 1996) (upholding random drug testing of school bus mechanics).

[88]Knox County Educ. Ass'n v. Knox County Bd. of Educ., 158 F.3d 361, 375 (6th Cir. 1998) (remanding this issue for the district court to determine whether the low level of alcohol impairment identified, .02, was reasonably related to the purpose of the testing program). In 2007, the Hawaii State Teachers Association approved a collective bargaining agreement stipulating that all public school teachers will be subject to random as well as suspicion-based drug and alcohol testing, but the Hawaii State Board of Education did not fund the program. *See* American Civil Liberties Union, "ACLU Applauds Hawaii Board of Education's Rejection of Random Teacher Drug Testing and Condemns Governor's Threat to Withhold Wages" (January 25, 2008), available at www.aclu. org/drugpolicy/testing/33833prs20080125.html.

[89]Crager v. Bd. of Educ., 313 F. Supp. 2d 690 (E.D. Ky. 2004) (citing 41 U.S.C. § 702 (2008)). This law stipulates that federal grant and contract recipients cannot receive federal funds unless they implement policies to ensure drug-free workplaces and provide education and employee assistance programs.

[90]United Teachers v. Orleans Parish Sch. Bd., 142 F.3d 853 (5th Cir. 1998).

[91]*See, e.g.,* Hearn v. Bd. of Pub. Educ., 191 F.3d 1329 (11th Cir. 1999) (upholding termination of a teacher who refused to undergo urinalysis after a drug-detecting dog identified marijuana in her car).

[92]*See, e.g.,* Warren v. Bd. of Educ., 200 F. Supp. 2d 1053 (E.D. Mo. 2001) (finding genuine issues about whether the teacher's behavior suggested drug use and whether she consented to the drug test); Best v. Dep't of Health & Human Servs., 563 S.E.2d 573 (N.C. Ct. App. 2002) (overturning public employees' dismissals for refusal to submit to a drug test in the absence of reasonable cause for a public employer to believe they were using a controlled substance).

suspicion of drug use and the circumstances under which certain public employees can be subjected to urinalysis without such suspicion.

Lifestyle Controversies

In recent years, teachers frequently have challenged school officials' authority to restrict their personal lives. Although the right to such personal freedom is not an enumerated constitutional guarantee, it is a right implied in the concept of personal liberty embodied in the Fourteenth Amendment. Constitutional protection afforded to teachers' privacy rights is determined not only by the *location* of the conduct, but also by the *nature* of the activity. The judiciary has attempted to balance teachers' privacy interests against the school board's legitimate interests in providing role models for students and safeguarding the welfare of the school. Teachers can suffer adverse employment consequences for behavior that impairs job performance. Educators can be terminated based on evidence that would not be sufficient to support criminal charges,[93] but they cannot be dismissed for unsubstantiated rumors about their activities.[94] Since some cases dealing with dismissals for alleged immorality are discussed in Chapter 12 in connection with dismissals based on charges of immorality, the following discussion is confined to an overview of the constitutional issues.

Recognizing that decisions pertaining to marriage and parenthood involve constitutionally protected privacy rights, courts have been reluctant to support dismissal actions based on teachers' unwed, pregnant status without evidence that the condition impairs fitness to teach. Compelled leaves of absence for such employees similarly would violate constitutional privacy rights. Most courts also have reasoned that public employees, including educators, have a privacy right to engage in consenting sexual relationships out of wedlock and that such relationships cannot be the basis for dismissal unless teaching effectiveness is impaired. To illustrate, the Sixth Circuit ruled that a school board's nonrenewal of a teacher's contract, because of her involvement in a divorce, abridged constitutional privacy rights.[95]

Some courts, however, have upheld dismissals or other disciplinary actions based on public employees' lifestyles that involve adulterous or other unconventional sexual relationships or activities that impaired job performance. For example, the U.S. Supreme Court upheld dismissal of a police officer for selling videotapes of himself stripping off a police uniform and masturbating.[96] A New York federal court also upheld termination of a teacher for actively participating in a group supporting consensual sexual activity between men and boys, reasoning that his activities in this organization were likely to impair teaching effectiveness and disrupt the school.[97]

---

[93]*See, e.g.,* Montefusco v. Nassau County, 39 F. Supp. 2d 231 (E.D.N.Y. 1999) (holding that while the criminal investigation did not result in criminal charges, the school board could suspend the teacher with pay and remove extracurricular assignments for his possession of candid pictures of female teenagers taken without their consent at his home).

[94]*See, e.g.,* Peaster Indep. Sch. Dist. v. Glodfelty, 63 S.W.3d 1 (Tex. App. 2001) (holding that gossip triggered by unproven allegations of sexual misconduct could not be the basis for nonrenewal of teachers' contracts).

[95]Littlejohn v. Rose, 768 F.2d 765 (6th Cir. 1985). *See also* Bertolini v. Whitehall City Sch. Dist. Bd. of Educ., 744 N.E.2d 1245 (Ohio Ct. App. 2000); text accompanying note 42, Chapter 12.

[96]City of San Diego v. Roe, 543 U.S. 77 (2004) (finding no protected expression involved).

[97]Melzer v. Bd. of Educ., 196 F. Supp. 2d 229 (E.D.N.Y. 2002).

Conditioning employment decisions on a teacher's sexual orientation has become increasingly controversial, and the scope of constitutional protections afforded to gay, lesbian, bisexual, and transgendered (GLBT) educators continues to evolve. Among factors that courts consider are whether the conduct is public or private, the notoriety surrounding the conduct, and its impact on teaching effectiveness. The law is clear that educators can be dismissed for immorality if they engage in *public* sexual activity, whether heterosexual or homosexual in nature.[98]

However, *private* sexual behavior enjoys Fourteenth Amendment protection. In 2003, the Supreme Court in *Lawrence v. Texas* struck down a Texas law prohibiting persons of the same gender from engaging in certain sexual conduct in their own homes as violating liberty rights of consenting adults.[99] Overturning a 1986 ruling in which the Supreme Court upheld a Georgia law criminalizing consensual sodomy,[100] the *Lawrence* Court reasoned that the earlier decision did not recognize the substantial constitutional protection afforded to adults in private matters pertaining to sexual activity.

Dismissals of public school employees based solely on sexual orientation, in the absence of criminal charges, have evoked a range of judicial interpretations. During the 1970s and 1980s, a few courts permitted school districts to dismiss GLBT teachers or reassign them to nonteaching roles even when there was no link to teaching effectiveness.[101] More recently, however, **courts have required a nexus between sexual orientation and impaired teaching effectiveness to justify dismissal.** To illustrate, a federal district court in Utah ruled that the community's negative response to a teacher's homosexuality was not sufficient justification to remove the teacher as the girl's volleyball coach and instruct her not to mention her sexual orientation to students, parents, or staff.[102] Also, an Ohio federal court awarded a teacher reinstatement, back pay, and damages for his nonrenewal that was impermissibly based on his sexual orientation rather than on his teaching deficiencies as the board contended.[103]

In addition to asserting protected privacy rights, some GLBT employees have claimed discrimination under the Equal Protection Clause of the Fourteenth Amendment. A few teachers have prevailed in claims that they have been harassed by teachers and students and treated differently from other non-GLBT educators.[104] However, the Seventh Circuit

---

[98]*See, e.g.*, Nat'l Gay Task Force v. Bd. of Educ., 729 F.2d 1270 (10th Cir. 1984), *aff'd by an equally divided court*, 470 U.S. 903 (1985) (upholding Oklahoma law allowing teachers to be discharged for public homosexual activity, but not for mere advocacy of homosexual rights), *supra* text accompanying note 30; Morgan v. State Bd. of Educ., 2002 Ohio 2738 (Ct. App. 2002) (upholding revocation of teaching certificate for disorderly conduct conviction stemming from his participation in a public sex act).

[99]539 U.S. 558 (2003).

[100]Bowers v. Hardwick, 478 U.S. 186 (1986).

[101]*See Thomas* et al., *supra* note 17, Chapter 9.

[102]Weaver v. Nebo Sch. Dist., 29 F. Supp. 2d 1279 (D. Utah 1998).

[103]Glover v. Williamsburg Local Sch. Dist., 20 F. Supp. 2d 1160 (S.D. Ohio 1998).

[104]*See, e.g.,* Curcio v. Collingswood Bd. of Educ., No. 04-5100 (JBS), 2006 U.S. Dist. LEXIS 46648 (D.N.J. June 28, 2006); Lovell v. Comsewogue Sch. Dist., 214 F. Supp. 2d 319 (E.D. N.Y. 2002); Murray v. Oceanside Unified Sch. Dist., 95 Cal. Rptr. 2d 28 (Ct. App. 2000). *See* Chapter 11 for a discussion of legal principles governing discrimination in employment.

held that a school had not violated a teacher's equal protection rights in connection with parental and student harassment of the teacher based on sexual orientation, because school officials took some action to respond to the teacher's complaints of harassment and treated the allegations as they would treat harassment complaints filed by other teachers.[105]

In recent cases, courts generally have not been convinced that teachers become poor role models simply because of their alternative lifestyles. The case law suggests that courts have shifted from condoning dismissals for merely being GLBT to requiring evidence that an individual's sexual orientation has an adverse impact on job performance or management of the school.

CONCLUSION

The United States Constitution places constraints on government, not private, action. Thus, public employees, but not usually those working in the private sector, can challenge employment decisions as violating their constitutional rights. If public employees can show that they have suffered adverse employment consequences because of the exercise of protected expression, association, or privacy rights, then the burden shifts to the employer to justify the restriction on protected rights as necessary to carry out the work of the government agency. In the school context, this means that the employee's action has impaired teaching effectiveness, relations with superiors, or school operations. The public employer also can prevail by showing that there are legitimate reasons for the personnel action aside from the exercise of protected expression or other constitutional rights. In short, under certain circumstances, restrictions on constitutional freedoms can be justified by overriding government interests.

POINTS TO PONDER

1. A nontenured teacher has received mediocre evaluations for two years. The principal has provided him some instructional assistance but feels that the teacher is not making sufficient progress. Thus, the principal recommends that the teacher's contract not be renewed. Before the school board acts on the recommendation, the teacher writes a letter to the newspaper criticizing the school board's adoption of a new math program for elementary grades. Is protected expression involved? Can the school board decide not to renew the teacher's contract?

2. A teacher complained to her principal that children with disabilities were being placed in the regular classroom for fiscal reasons, when the children needed more restrictive placements. Does such expression pertain to the teacher's job duties? Can the teacher be disciplined for the expression?

3. A school board is concerned about the mounting drug problem in the community and particularly in the public schools. To address the problem, the school has instituted a drug-education program and a drug-testing program for all students who participate in extracurricular activities. Now the board wants to adopt a requirement that all new teachers as part

[105]Schroeder v. Hamilton Sch. Dist., 282 F.3d 946 (7th Cir. 2002).

of their preemployment medical exams must submit to urinalysis screening for drug use. Are teachers in safety-sensitive roles? Can such a drug-screening program be justified without individualized suspicion?

4. A tenured homosexual middle school teacher has not mentioned his sexual orientation to his students. Yet, he has been prominent in gay rights rallies and has been a guest on a radio talk show to advocate a law authorizing same-sex marriages. As a result, several parents have complained to the principal and asked that the teacher be dismissed. Can the teacher be removed from the classroom?

CHAPTER ELEVEN

DISCRIMINATION IN EMPLOYMENT

All persons and groups are potential victims of discrimination in employment. People of color and women claim discrimination in traditionally segregated job categories, whereas Caucasians and men claim that affirmative action has denied them the right to compete on equal grounds. The young argue that the old already hold the good jobs and that entry is nearly impossible, and the old contend that they often are released when downsizing occurs and that reemployment at the same level and salary is unlikely. Religious minorities might not be allowed to dress the way they please or may be denied leave for religious observance, and religious majorities (particularly in private schools) have concerns about governmental intrusion into their homogeneous work environments. Likewise, persons with disabilities often complain that they are not given the opportunity to show what they can do, whereas employers often contend that the costs of accommodating those with disabilities could be significant and never ending. Given these diverse and conflicting interests, it is not surprising that literally hundreds of employment discrimination claims are filed each year.

LEGAL CONTEXT

Extending constitutional protections, numerous federal laws prohibit discrimination in public and private employment.

Most, but not all, forms of employment discrimination violate either federal or state law. Foremost among these mandates are the Fourteenth Amendment to the United States Constitution and Title VII of the Civil Rights Act of 1964; both are discussed here, given their broad application. Other, more narrowly tailored statutes are reviewed in the respective sections addressing discrimination based on race and national origin, sex, religion, age, and disability (see Table 11.1).

TABLE 11.1 Selected Federal Laws Prohibiting Employment Discrimination

FEDERAL LAW	PUBLIC SCHOOLS	PRIVATE SCHOOLS	RECIPIENTS OF FEDERAL FINANCIAL ASSISTANCE	NUMBER OF EMPLOYEES NECESSARY FOR LAW TO APPLY	RACE	NATIONAL ORIGIN, ALIENAGE	SEX	AGE	RELIGION	DISABILITY
Fourteenth Amendment to the U.S. Constitution	X				X	X	X	X	X	X
42 U.S.C. § 1983	X				X	X	X	X	X	X
42 U.S.C. § 1981	X	X			X	X (i.e., ethnicity)				
Title VII of Civil Rights Act of 1964	X	X		15	X	X	X		X	
Equal Pay Act of 1963	X	X		20			X			
Section 504 of Rehabilitation Act of 1973	X		X							X
Americans with Disabilities Act	X	X		15						X
Age Discrimination in Employment Act	X	X		20				X		

Fourteenth Amendment

The Fourteenth Amendment to the United States Constitution mandates that no state shall deny to any person within its jurisdiction equal protection of the laws. This provision has been interpreted as prohibiting intentional discrimination and applies to subdivisions of the state, including public school districts. Districts may be found guilty of facial discrimination (e.g., when an administrative position is reserved for a female applicant), or facially neutral discrimination (e.g., when the district's use of standardized test scores in hiring results in disparate impact based on race) (see Appendix Figure 1).

Title VII

Title VII is enforced by the Equal Employment Opportunity Commission (EEOC) and prohibits employers with 15 or more employees from discriminating on the basis of race, color, religion, sex, or national origin and covers hiring, promotion, and compensation practices as well as fringe benefits and other terms and conditions of employment.[1] However, protection against discriminatory employment practices is not absolute for individuals within these classifications as Congress has expressly permitted employers to facially discriminate based on religion, sex, or national origin (but not on race or color) if they can show the existence of a *bona fide occupational qualification* (BFOQ) that is reasonably necessary to the normal operation of their particular enterprise. Additionally, courts have specified that employers may use facially neutral employment practices that result in disparate impact on a protected class, but only if a *business necessity* is identified in the use of that practice and there are no less discriminatory ways of meeting that need. And, it is possible for an employee to file a Title VII complaint based on retaliation.

Disparate Treatment and Impact.   When evaluating Title VII claims, courts have developed two legal theories: disparate treatment and disparate impact. *Disparate treatment* is applied when the individual claims less favorable treatment when compared to other applicants or employees. *Disparate impact* is used when an employer's ostensibly neutral practice has a discriminatory impact on the class the claimant represents.

In proving disparate treatment, plaintiffs may use direct and/or circumstantial evidence. *Direct evidence* is rarely available and results only when the employer has provided a written or spoken statement that:

- Is clear,
- Comes from an individual involved in making employment decisions,
- Refers specifically to the individual denied the employment opportunity, and
- Is expressed close in time to when the employment decision was made.[2]

Examples include an employer denying an employee a requested raise because he was "just a white guy,"[3] and a supervisor who fired an older female employee with the stated desire to replace her with "a young chippie" with large breasts.[4]

[1]42 U.S.C. § 2000e *et seq.* (2008).

[2]David J. Walsh, *Employment Law for Human Resource Practice,* 2nd ed. (Mason, OH: Thomson Southwestern, 2006), p. 69.

[3]Gagnon v. Sprint Corp., 284 F.3d 839, 846 (8th Cir. 2002).

[4]Glanzman v. Metro. Mgt. Corp., 391 F.3d 506, 510 (3d Cir. 2004).

Nonetheless, plaintiffs usually do not have direct evidence of discrimination, so they often rely on circumstantial evidence to substantiate that they received less favorable treatment and that such conduct, if otherwise unexplained, is "more likely than not based on the consideration of impermissible factors."[5] To support a circumstantial claim, the plaintiff must show that he or she:

- Was a member of a protected class,
- Applied for and was qualified for the job, and
- Was denied the position, while the employer continued to seek applicants with the plaintiff's qualifications.

These criteria were articulated by the Supreme Court in *McDonnell Douglas Corporation v. Green*[6] and, with some modification, are applied beyond claims of hiring discrimination to alleged disparate treatment in areas such as promotion, termination, and tenure.

If the claim is supported, the burden shifts to the employer to state a reason for its action that does not violate Title VII. If the employer is unable to produce a nondiscriminatory reason for the action, a directed verdict for the plaintiff would be granted. But given the ease of presenting a nondiscriminatory reason, employers in nearly every instance provide a response. After the employer provides a rebuttal, the plaintiff then has the burden of proving not only that the proffered reason was false but also that it served as a pretext for prohibited intentional discrimination.[7] In most instances of alleged discrimination, the plaintiff is unable to show that the employer's purported nondiscriminatory basis was pretextual.

In contrast to disparate treatment claims, **to prove disparate impact the plaintiff is not initially required to support discriminatory intent but must establish that an employer's facially neutral practice had a disproportionate impact on the plaintiff's protected class.** This generally is accomplished through the use of statistics. Once disparate impact is established, the employer then must show that the challenged policies or practices (or its employment practices in the aggregate) are job related and justified by a business necessity. Accordingly, an employer's nondiscriminatory reason for the act is insufficient to rebut a claim of discriminatory impact. Moreover, even if a business necessity is identified, a plaintiff still may prevail by showing that the employer's facially neutral practice had a discriminatory purpose.

---

[5]Furnco Constr. Corp. v. Waters, 438 U.S. 567, 577 (1978). *See also* Glover v. Bd. of Educ. of Rockford Pub. Schs., 187 Fed. App'x 614 (7th Cir. 2006) (finding no evidence that supported the use of a discriminatory motive on the part of the employer).

[6]411 U.S. 792, 802 (1973).

[7]*See, e.g.*, St. Mary's Honor Ctr. v. Hicks, 509 U.S. 502, 514–515 (1993). *See also* Riley v. Birmingham Bd. of Educ., 154 Fed. App'x 114 (11th Cir. 2005) (determining that the Caucasian plaintiff was unable to show that race was a factor in the selection of a head coach; testimony that the African American principal had stated "we have to take care of our own" was found insufficient to show pretext); Sarmiento v. Queens Coll., 153 Fed. App'x 21 (2d Cir. 2005) (finding that a rejected applicant for a teaching position failed to support race discrimination; noting that although at least one of the defendants confirmed animosity toward the plaintiff, there was no proof that such animosity was due to race).

The Supreme Court has recognized, however, that mere awareness of a policy's adverse impact on a protected class does not constitute proof of unlawful motive.[8] Nonetheless, foreseeably discriminatory consequences can be considered by courts in assessing intent, although more will be needed to substantiate unlawful motive. Furthermore, the employee may prevail if it is shown that the employer refused to adopt an alternative policy identified by the employee that realistically would have met the employer's business needs without resulting in disparate impact.

Retaliation.   By the time a complaint is filed with the EEOC or a state or federal court, the working relationship between the employer and the employee is strained, sometimes beyond repair. In response to filing, an employee may not be terminated, demoted, or harassed, but less extreme acts such as rudeness will not typically violate Title VII. When actionable behavior occurs, the employee may file a second claim alleging retaliation. To support this type of case, the employee is required to show that:

- He or she participated in statutorily protected activity (i.e., the filing of a complaint or suit),
- An adverse employment action was taken by the employer, and
- A causal connection existed between the protected activity and the adverse action.[9]

If the employee can show that filing the complaint was the basis for the adverse employment decision, even if the original complaint of discrimination fails, the court will provide appropriate relief.[10] It also is critical to show that the retaliatory action followed soon after engagement in the protected activity and that the administrator responsible for the adverse action knew of the filing of the original complaint.[11]

Relief.   If it is proved that the employee was a victim of prohibited discrimination, then courts have the authority to require a *make-whole remedy* in which the person is placed in the same position he or she otherwise would have been, absent discriminatory activity. In meeting this objective, courts may:

- Provide injunctive and declaratory relief;
- Require that a person be reinstated, hired, tenured, or promoted;
- Direct the payment of back pay, interest on back pay, or front pay;[12]
- Assign retroactive seniority;

---

[8]Pers. Adm'r of Mass. v. Feeney, 442 U.S. 256 (1979).

[9]*See, e.g.*, Valdes v. Union City Bd. of Educ., 186 Fed. App'x 319 (3d Cir. 2006).

[10]*See, e.g.*, Nye v. Roberts, 145 Fed. App'x 1 (4th Cir. 2005).

[11]*See, e.g.*, Boynton v. W. Wyo. Cmty. Coll., 157 Fed. App'x 33 (10th Cir. 2005).

[12]For example, if a teacher is denied a principalship because of race, the court may direct the district to hire the teacher for the next available position. If the principalship line provided greater compensation than did the teacher line, the court could require that the difference in salary be awarded to the teacher up to the time of promotion. That portion of the salary paid in the future is termed *front pay*, while that portion due for the period between the failure to hire and the court's ruling is termed *back pay*.

- Provide attorneys' fees and court costs; and,
- In cases in which intentional discrimination is proved, provide compensatory and punitive damages.

However, an employer may not be held liable for the discriminatory acts of its managerial staff when their decisions are contrary to the employer's good faith efforts to comply with Title VII.[13]

■ ■ ■ ■ ■

RACE AND NATIONAL-ORIGIN DISCRIMINATION

Without a proven history of prior discrimination, an employer may not use race as a factor in making employment decisions.

Race and national-origin discrimination in employment continues in spite of nearly 140 years of protective statutes and constitutional amendments. Lawsuits are filed under the Fourteenth Amendment,[14] Title VII, and 42 U.S.C. Section 1981.

Section 1981 originally was Section 1 of the Civil Rights Act of 1866. At one time, this statute prohibited only race discrimination in making and enforcing contracts, but now Section 1981 applies when either race or ethnicity discrimination is alleged in making, performing, modifying, and terminating contracts, as well as in the enjoyment of all benefits, privileges, terms, and conditions of the contractual relationship.[15]

Hiring and Promotion Practices

Unless a school district is under a narrowly tailored court order to correct prior proven acts of race discrimination, it may not advantage or disadvantage an applicant or employee because of that individual's race. When unsuccessful candidates believe that race played a role in the decision-making process, they will generally allege disparate treatment, requiring the heightened proof of discriminatory intent. In attempting to support such a claim, many plaintiffs have difficulty overcoming employers' purported nondiscriminatory reasons for their decisions,[16] even when a person of a different race ultimately is hired.[17]

[13]Kolstad v. Am. Dental Ass'n, 527 U.S. 526 (1999).

[14]The Fourteenth Amendment requires the application of strict scrutiny in cases in which race or national-origin discrimination is facial and proof of intent in cases in which the alleged discrimination is facially neutral.

[15]See, e.g., Amini v. Oberlin Coll., 440 F.3d 350 (6th Cir. 2006).

[16]See, e.g., Barber v. Univ. of Med. and Dentistry of N.J., 118 Fed. App'x 588 (3d Cir. 2004).

[17]See, e.g., Goodman v. Georgia S.W. State Univ., 147 Fed. App'x 888 (11th Cir. 2005). But see Taylor v. Bd. of Educ., 240 Fed. App'x 717 (6th Cir. 2007) (reversing summary judgment for the board; noting that questions remained as to whether the African American applicants were better qualified than the Caucasian counselors who were selected). See also Hammons v. George C. Wallace State Cmty. Coll., 174 Fed. App'x 459 (11th Cir. 2006) (finding that an employee was unable to show she was replaced by someone of another race). Note, however, that it is not always dispositive of a discrimination claim when the successful applicant and the plaintiff are of the same class. The selected candidate may have been chosen only after the employer learned that a suit had been filed.

Because most qualifications for initial employment (e.g., degree, licensure) in educational settings are required to perform jobs satisfactorily and to meet state standards and account-ability mandates, disparate impact claims also are difficult to win. To do so, the plaintiff will have to show that:

- One group succeeded at a rate that was less than 80 percent of that achieved by the group with the highest passing rate (e.g., adverse impact results if 90 percent of Cau-casians pass a test, but fewer than 72 percent of African Americans do so), *or*
- For small populations, the difference in performance between the two groups is sta-tistically significant.

When tests are used, they must be reliable and valid, and must qualify as a business neces-sity.[18] Tests may not be discriminatorily administered, nor may their results be discrimina-torily used. Moreover, employers may not use different cutoff scores for different racial groups or adjust scores based on race.

Adverse Decisions

Employers cannot dismiss, decline to renew, or demote employees on the basis of race or national origin.[19] The Supreme Court rendered a significant decision in a race-based termi-nation case, *St. Mary's Honor Center v. Hicks*,[20] in which a minority employee of a halfway house was demoted and eventually fired. In response to plaintiff's claims, the employer argued that the suspension, letter of reprimand, and demotion were necessary because of the employee's poor supervision of his subordinates, his failure to conduct a proper investigation of a brawl between inmates, and the use of threatening words with his immediate superior. Given this response, the burden shifted back to the employee to show both that the proffered reasons were not to be believed *and* that the true basis for the termination was race.

The district court had determined that the employer's reasons were untrue, noting that the plaintiff was the only supervisor disciplined for violations committed by his subordi-nates and that similar, and at times more severe, violations by others were either treated more leniently or disregarded. The district court noted, and the Supreme Court agreed, however, that even though the employee was able to show that the purported reasons were false, he failed to show that race was a factor in his termination. Because the plaintiff was unable to meet his entire burden of persuasion, he could not prove a Title VII violation. Similar decisions have been reached by other courts when adverse decisions were based on legitimate nonpretextual factors such as assault and battery, stalking and rape, unprofes-sional conduct, and the like.[21]

---

[18]Griggs v. Duke Power Co., 401 U.S. 424, 432 (1971).

[19]*See, e.g.,* Seagrave v. Dean, 908 So. 2d 41 (1st Cir. 2005). Title VII also prohibits race-motivated harassment in the workplace. *But see* Sallis v. Univ. of Minn., 408 F.3d 470 (8th Cir. 2005) (concluding that rude and insensitive racial remarks that were infrequently used did not create a hostile work environment).

[20]509 U.S. 502 (1993).

[21]*See, e.g.,* Silvera v. Orange County Sch. Bd., 244 F.3d 1253 (11th Cir. 2001) (assault and battery); Shaw v. Monroe, 20 Fed. App'x 563 (7th Cir. 2001) (stalking and rape); Conward v. Cambridge Sch. Comm., 171 F.3d 12 (1st Cir. 1999) (unprofessional conduct).

Often employees have difficulty showing that the conduct of their employers qualified as adverse actions (e.g., change of school, grade level, teaching assignment).[22] In the Eleventh Circuit, an African American was given poor performance evaluations by a relatively new principal as well as an independent observer. However, her nonrenewal notice was not delivered in a timely manner. As a result, she was offered a contract, but elected to decline it. The court reasoned that because a new contract had been proffered, plaintiff failed to show that she was subjected to an adverse employment act. The threat of nonrenewal and close supervision were insufficient to qualify as adverse acts.[23]

Affirmative Action

Affirmative action has been defined as "steps taken to remedy the grossly disparate staffing and recruitment patterns that are the present consequences of past discrimination and to prevent the occurrence of employment discrimination in the future."[24] Correcting such imbalances requires the employer to engage in activities such as:

- Expanding its training programs,
- Becoming actively involved in recruitment,
- Eliminating invalid selection criteria that result in disparate impact, and
- Modifying collective bargaining agreements that impermissibly restrict the promotion and retention of minorities.

Courts will uphold most strategies that the EEOC identifies as affirmative action, but will prohibit the use of plans that provide a discriminatory "preference" rather than an "equal opportunity," unless there is a proven history of institutional discrimination.

In 1989, the Supreme Court began to question a variety of public-sector practices that provided racial preferences.[25] **In the aggregate, these cases applied strict scrutiny to race-based affirmative action programs operated at federal, state, and local levels of government; discredited societal discrimination as a justification for such programs; required showing specific discriminatory action to impose a race-based remedy; and allowed only narrowly tailored plans that would further a compelling interest.** Given this precedent, existing public-sector affirmative action plans that provide racial preferences without a proven history of discrimination or are based only on underrepresentation are likely to be found unconstitutional.

In addition to affirmative action in hiring and promotion, there also have been efforts to protect the diversity gained through court order and voluntary affirmative action by providing a preference in organization downsizing. When a reduction in school staff is necessary because of financial exigency, declining enrollment, or a change in education priorities, it generally is based, at least in part, on tenure and seniority within teaching areas. Accordingly, it is impor-

[22]*See, e.g.*, Pipkin v. Bridgeport Bd. of Educ., 159 Fed. App'x 259 (2d Cir. 2005).

[23]Christian v. Cartersville City Schs., 167 Fed. App'x 89 (11th Cir. 2006).

[24]United States Commission on Civil Rights, *Statement of Affirmative Action for Equal Employment Opportunities* (Washington, DC: U.S. Commission on Civil Rights, 1973).

[25]*See, e.g.,* Adarand Constructors v. Pena, 515 U.S. 200 (1995); N.W. Fla. Chapter of the Associated Gen. Contractors of Am. v. City of Jacksonville, 508 U.S. 656 (1993); Martin v. Wilks, 490 U.S. 755 (1989).

tant for all employees to be in their rightful place on the seniority list. To obtain their rightful place, employees have been awarded varying levels of retroactive seniority (i.e., time between rejection of the application due to impermissible discrimination and court ordered initial employment), in addition to those years they have accrued while actually on the job.[26]

In some cases, employers have proposed the modification of seniority systems to give an overall preference to all minorities regarding eligibility for promotion and other job benefits or in protection from a reduction-in-force (RIF). Such affirmative action plans are similar to awards of retroactive seniority, but in contrast to seniority adjustments for individual discrimination victims, class remedies benefit class members who may not have been the victim of prior acts of discrimination. Courts will prohibit such practices, even if the employer is found guilty of a pattern or practice of racial discrimination.[27] The appropriate form of relief is to award competitive seniority to individual victims to restore them to their rightful place. Moreover, courts may not disregard a seniority system in fashioning a class remedy,[28] notwithstanding societal discrimination, the need for role models, or perceived underrepresentation of a particular class.

Case law involving affirmative action and racial preference may increase given the Supreme Court's decision in *Grutter v. University of Michigan*[29] and the desire of many educational entities to increase the diversity of their instructional and administrative staff. At this time, however, it is questionable whether the compelling interest identified in *Grutter* (i.e., the benefits derived from a diverse student body) will expand to include employees and whether the justices' five-to-four decision will effectively negate years of Supreme Court precedent prohibiting the explicit use of race without showing prior institutional discrimination. Even then, the district's affirmative action plan would have to be narrowly tailored.

For example, in a case from the Seventh Circuit, a white female college instructor was not selected for a full-time teaching position.[30] The selected candidate was an African American male who had been evaluated second lowest of all finalists; moreover, he had not been a finalist until an administrator placed him within the group to be interviewed. Standard procedures were not followed and there were numerous examples of suspicious timing, ambiguous statements, and questionable practices. The college defended its position by noting that *Grutter* permitted such race-conscious decision making. Nonetheless, the Third Circuit concluded that the plaintiff provided significant evidence of both race and sex discrimination and remanded the case.

■ ■ ■ ■ ■

SEX DISCRIMINATION

Sex generally may not be used as a basis in determining whom to hire, what salary to provide, or any other term or condition of employment.

---

[26]*See, e.g.*, Franks v. Bowman Trans. Co., 424 U.S. 747 (1976).

[27]Firefighters Local Union No. 1784 v. Stotts, 467 U.S. 561 (1984).

[28]Wygant v. Jackson Bd. of Educ., 476 U.S. 267 (1986).

[29]539 U.S. 306 (2003).

[30]Rudin v. Lincoln Land Cmty. Coll., 420 F.3d 712 (7th Cir. 2005).

Prior to 1963, there were no federal statutes prohibiting discrimination based on sex. Women were commonly denied employment if a qualified male applicant was in the pool, were offered less money for the same or similar job, or were expected to do work that would not have been asked of a man. Today, most forms of sex discrimination are prohibited, including those associated with hiring, promotion, and virtually all terms and conditions of employment. The Fourteenth Amendment,[31] Title VII of the Civil Rights Act of 1964, and other federal and state laws have played significant roles in allowing victims of sex discrimination to vindicate their rights in court. Note, however, that laws prohibiting sex discrimination do not apply in cases in which the discrimination is based on either being transsexual, homosexual, or transvestite, or falls within other "sex" categories. For example, in a Fifth Circuit case, the employee claimed that although he was better qualified, he was not selected for a technology position, in large part because the successful female candidate was having an affair with a high-ranking university administrator.[32] In finding no Title VII violation, the Fifth Circuit noted that the law prohibited sex discrimination (i.e., based on being male or female), not paramour favoritism. Such a basis, although perhaps unfair, results in discrimination against both males and females who were not paramours and, accordingly, is not centered on the employee's sex.

Hiring and Promotion Practices

Sex discrimination is facial when an employer openly seeks a person of a particular sex (e.g., the posting of a position for a female guidance counselor). It becomes illegal discrimination when being male or female is unrelated to meeting job requirements (e.g., hiring only males as basketball coaches). At other times, employment practices are facially neutral (e.g., requiring head coaching experience in football in order to qualify as athletic director), but nevertheless result in nearly the same level of exclusion as when the discrimination is facial. When this occurs, an action will be upheld only if found to qualify as a business necessity and other less discriminatory options do not meet the needs of the organization.

If applicants or employees have been treated unfairly solely because of their sex, plaintiffs typically file a Title VII suit alleging disparate treatment. The standards for a sex-based *prima facie* case are similar to those used for race. Also, assuming that a claim is supported, the employer then must identify a basis other than sex for its decision, such as showing that the successful applicant was equally or better qualified or that the plaintiff was unqualified.[33] When a nondiscriminatory basis has been identified, applicants still may obtain relief if the reasons are shown to be pretextual.[34] For example, rejected applicants could prevail when employers base their decisions on stereotypic attitudes

---

[31]The Fourteenth Amendment requires the application of intermediate scrutiny in cases in which sex discrimination is facial and proof of intent in cases in which the alleged discrimination is facially neutral.

[32]Wilson v. Delta State Univ., 143 Fed. App'x 611 (5th Cir. 2005).

[33]*See, e.g.*, Straughter v. Vicksburg Warren Sch. Dist., 152 Fed. App'x 407 (5th Cir. 2005).

[34]*See, e.g.,* Goodwin v. Bd. of Trs. Univ. of Ill., 442 F.3d 611 (7th Cir. 2006).

about the capabilities of men or women; when job advertisements include phrases, *prefer male* or *prefer female*; or when job descriptions are specifically drafted to exclude qualified applicants of a particular sex.

To illustrate, the Eighth Circuit found that a female teacher who was passed over eight times for promotion to an administrative position was the victim of intentional sex discrimination.[35] The court was concerned about how the superintendent assessed the leadership abilities of male and female applicants as well as his statement that he was "leery" about assigning a female as principal of a junior high school. The applicant was able to show that both sex (the need for male disciplinarians) and race (the need for minority role models) were considered in selecting Caucasian and African American males to fill the positions.[36]

In addition, it is important that employers follow established procedures and use published criteria as the bases for identifying the successful candidate. In a Third Circuit case, the search committee used an unpublished criterion in selecting the plaintiff for a community college position.[37] An unsuccessful male applicant complained that "interpersonal skills" was not mentioned in the job description or in the vacancy announcement. The president of the institution proposed that although he felt that the committee had selected the best-qualified person from the pool of applicants, a new search should be conducted, given the prior failure to base the selection on published criteria. Accordingly, a new search was performed, but a candidate not in the first pool was selected who had better overall experience and preparation. The court determined that (1) it was within the discretionary authority of the president, as set forth in the college's hiring procedures, to void the first search and to conduct a second; and (2) the second posting resulted in hiring the best-qualified candidate.[38] The plaintiff (i.e., the female applicant who was originally selected) failed to show both that the president's proffered reason for the second search (i.e., procedural error) was so plainly wrong that it could not have been the true reason *and* that the president intended to discriminate based on sex and age.

Not all sex-based distinctions are prohibited as Title VII explicitly allows for a *bona fide occupational qualification* (BFOQ) exception. For a BFOQ to be upheld, it needs to be narrowly defined and applied only when necessary to achieve the employer's objectives. There have been few school-based BFOQ cases, since the vast majority of jobs in education can be performed by either males or females. The only readily identifiable BFOQ in education would be the hiring of a female to supervise the girls' locker room and the hiring of a male to supervise the boys' locker room.

---

[35]Willis v. Watson Chapel Sch. Dist., 899 F.2d 745 (8th Cir. 1990), *on remand*, 749 F. Supp. 923 (E.D. Ark. 1990).

[36]*But see* Gore v. Ind. Univ., 416 F.3d 590 (7th Cir. 2005) (concluding that plaintiff failed to show he was discriminated against because of his sex when a university committee failed to hire him as a lecturer).

[37]Morrissey v. Luzerne County Cmty. Coll., 117 Fed. App'x 809 (3d Cir. 2004).

[38]*See also* Mella v. Mapleton Pub. Schs., 152 Fed. App'x 717 (10th Cir. 2005) (finding that plaintiff failed to show pretext in the district's failure to promote her to manager of technology, and noting that the panel making the decision found two other applicants to be better qualified).

Compensation Practices

Claims of sex-based compensation discrimination involving entry salaries, raises, supplemental or overtime opportunities, or other perquisites and benefits are not uncommon within business and industry, and even occur at times in higher education. However, because most PK–12 salary decisions are based on objective criteria such as seniority and degree level, the number of public school cases has been small.

The Fourteenth Amendment, Title VII, and the Equal Pay Act (EPA) of 1963 may be used where plaintiffs claim that their salaries are based in whole or in part on sex. The EPA applies only when the dispute involves sex-based wage discrimination claims of unequal pay for equal work.[39] As a result, the act does not apply when race-based or age-based salary differences are challenged, or when the work is unequal.[40] The plaintiff need not prove that the employer intended to discriminate, as with Title VII disputes; proof that the compensation is different and not based on factors other than sex will suffice. Furthermore, the law prohibits the lowering of the salaries for the higher-paid group and instead requires the salaries for the lower-paid group to be raised. It is important to note that relief under the EPA is not barred by Eleventh Amendment immunity.

Because the EPA is limited to equal work controversies, its application is restricted to those circumstances in which male and female employees perform substantially the same work but for different pay. Accordingly, if no male secretaries are employed for a salary comparison, there can be no EPA violation, regardless of how abysmal the salaries of female secretaries may be. In determining whether the jobs in question are equal, courts look at more than position titles and will examine the comparative skills, effort, responsibilities, and working conditions associated with each job and the nature of required tasks. In situations in which jobs are found to be substantially equal but garner unequal pay, the employer then must show that the different salaries were based on seniority, merit, quantity or quality of production, or any factor other than sex. If the employer purports to use a merit system, it should be uniformly applied and be based on established criteria.

Sex-based wage discrimination claims, however, are not confined exclusively to violations of the EPA; they also may be filed under Title VII.[41] As with race-based cases, intent will have to be proven in a disparate treatment case, while salary differences will have to be significant for plaintiffs to prevail in a disparate impact case. When statistics are used to substantiate a claim, identifiable variables that affect salary must be included (e.g., seniority, degree level, merit, administrative assignments, supplemental duties). The Fourth Circuit ruled in favor of male faculty members who claimed Title VII and EPA violations when their university voluntarily increased the salaries of female faculty, allegedly to eliminate salary inequities.[42] The study did not include performance criteria used for merit, consider the impact of prior administrative experience on salary, or provide any type of adjustment for career interruptions when measuring academic experience.

---

[39]29 U.S.C. § 206(d) (2008). *See also* Ghirardo v. Univ. of S. Cal., 156 Fed. App'x 914 (9th Cir. 2005) (finding no EPA violation when plaintiff failed to show her total compensation or annual raises were based on her sex rather than her refusal to attend retreats and other instances of recalcitrance).

[40]*See, e.g.,* Vasquez v. El Paso County Cmty. Coll., 177 Fed. App'x 422 (5th Cir. 2006).

[41]*See, e.g.,* Farrell v. Butler Univ., 421 F.3d 609 (7th Cir. 2005).

[42]Smith v. Va. Commonwealth Univ., 84 F.3d 672 (4th Cir. 1996).

Termination, Nonrenewal, and Denial of Tenure

Title VII prohibits arbitrary removal of employees and the denial of tenure if based on sex or other prohibited bases.[43] In disparate treatment cases, the employee is required to prove that the employer elected to terminate or not renew the employee's contract based on sex rather than job performance, inappropriate conduct, interpersonal relationships, or other just cause. As in most cases in which proof of intent is required, employees alleging sex discrimination often have difficulty supporting their claims. Occasionally, however, corroborating evidence will be inadvertently provided by officials responsible for making personnel decisions. In the Tenth Circuit, a female former principal was "bumped" by an associate superintendent, who assumed her position as well as his own. The district initially proposed that the RIF was necessary because of financial exigency but later claimed that the female principal had continuing difficulty with her faculty, which allegedly was the basis for her contract not being renewed. The appeals court found the evidence to be contradictory, including the superintendent's annual evaluation of the principal in which she received high marks for establishing and maintaining staff cooperation and creating an environment conducive to learning. Given such discrepancies, the appeals court reversed the lower court's grant of summary judgment for the school district.[44]

In contrast, in a Third Circuit case, a female served as an athletic administrator, program head, and professor.[45] She worked for the college for approximately 10 years, but eventually was terminated. She alleged that her removal was because of her support of equity in sports for women. Nonetheless, the Third Circuit determined that the administration provided sufficient documentation showing that the plaintiff had alienated others in her leadership role, and that her ineffective interpersonal skills created low morale within her unit.

Sexual Harassment

Sexual harassment generally refers to repeated and unwelcome sexual advances, sexually suggestive comments, or sexually demeaning gestures or acts. Both men and women have been victims of sexual harassment from persons of the opposite or same sex.[46] The harasser may be a supervisor, an agent of the employer, a coworker, a nonemployee, or even a student. Critical to a successful claim is proof that the harassment is indeed based on sex, rather than sexual preference, being transsexual, transvestism, or anther factor.[47] There are two types of harassment cognizable under Title VII:[48] *quid pro quo* and hostile environment.

---

[43]Weinstock v. Columbia Univ., 224 F.3d 33 (2d Cir. 2000). *Moreover*, Title VII also prohibits behaviors that would result in the constructive discharge of employees. *See, e.g.*, Palomo v. Trs. of Columbia Univ., 170 Fed. App'x 194 (2d Cir. 2006).

[44]Cole v. Ruidoso Mun. Sch., 43 F.3d 1373 (10th Cir. 1994).

[45]Atkinson v. LaFayette Coll., 460 F.3d 447 (3d Cir. 2006).

[46]*See, e.g.*, Oncale v. Sundowner Offshore Servs., 523 U.S. 75 (1998).

[47]Succar v. Dade County Sch. Bd., 229 F.3d 1343 (11th Cir. 2000) (concluding that an adulterous male teacher was not harassed by his former lover because of being male, but for terminating the relationship).

[48]In addition to filing a Title VII claim, educators may file charges under state employment law or state tort law. Tort claims may include intentional infliction of emotional distress, assault and battery, invasion of privacy, and defamation.

Quid Pro Quo. *Quid pro quo* **harassment literally means giving something for something.** To establish a *prima facie* case of *quid pro quo* harassment against an employer, the employee must show that:

- He or she was subjected to unwelcome sexual harassment in the form of sexual advances or requests for sexual favors,
- The harassment was based on the person's sex, and
- Submission to the unwelcome advances was an express or implied condition for either favorable actions or avoidance of adverse actions by the employer.

Although only a preponderance of evidence is required in such cases, acquiring the necessary 51 percent can be difficult, particularly given that the violator is unlikely to provide corroborating testimony. If the employee succeeds, however, the law imposes strict liability on the employer, because of the harasser's authority to alter the terms and conditions of employment.

Hostile Environment. **To prevail under this theory, the plaintiff must show that the environment in fact was hostile. The harassment needs to be severe or pervasive,[49] unreasonably interfere with an individual's work performance (actual physical or psychological injury is not required),[50] and be either threatening or humiliating. A single offensive utterance generally will be insufficient.[51]** If the victims are able to substantiate their claims, the employer may be vicariously liable for the acts of its supervisors with immediate authority over an alleged victim.[52] However, the employer may raise an affirmative defense to liability if the employee suffered no tangible employment loss. Such a defense requires that the employer exercise reasonable care to prevent or promptly correct harassing behavior *and* that the employee failed to take advantage of preventive and corrective opportunities provided by the employer. Accordingly, to guard against liability, school districts should:

- Prepare and disseminate sexual harassment policies,
- Provide appropriate in-service training,
- Establish appropriate grievance procedures, including at least two avenues for reporting in case one avenue is blocked by the harasser or supportive colleague,
- Take claims seriously and investigate promptly,
- Take corrective action in a timely manner, and
- Maintain thorough records of all claims and activities.

---

[49]*But see* Whittaker v. N. Ill. Univ., 424 F.3d 640 (7th Cir. 2005) (concluding that offensive comments that were unknown to plaintiff until after her employment did not contribute to the creation of a hostile environment), *cert. denied*, 126 S. Ct. 2986 (2006).

[50]Meritor Savs. Bank v. Vinson, 477 U.S. 57 (1986).

[51]Harris v. Forklift Sys., 510 U.S. 17 (1993).

[52]Faragher v. City of Boca Raton, 524 U.S. 775 (1998).

Furthermore, investigators should have no stake in the outcome of the proceedings, and both male and female investigators should be available.

Pregnancy Discrimination

Under the Pregnancy Discrimination Act (PDA),[53] an amendment to Title VII enacted in 1978, employers may not discriminate based on pregnancy, childbirth, or related medical conditions.[54] As such, pregnancy may not be used as a basis for refusing to hire an otherwise qualified applicant; denying disability, medical, or other benefits; or terminating or nonrenewing employment. To succeed, the employee must show that the employer knew she was pregnant prior to the adverse action and that pregnancy, rather than some other factor, was the basis of an adverse decision. The Sixth Circuit remanded a case to determine whether a private religious school terminated the employment of a teacher because of engaging in premarital sex (in violation of religious tenants) or becoming pregnant. The court determined that termination for having engaged in sex was a permissible basis for the adverse employment decision, but that termination could not be based on pregnancy.[55]

Before passage of the PDA, the Fourth Circuit relied on the Fourteenth Amendment in striking down a school board's practice of not renewing teachers' contracts when a foreseeable period of absence could be predicted for the ensuing year.[56] The policy had been applied only to pregnant employees, thus imposing a disproportionate burden on female teachers. The Supreme Court also has held that women of childbearing age cannot be denied equal access to what the employer perceives as "high risk" forms of employment, if they are otherwise qualified for the jobs (e.g., janitorial jobs requiring the use of strong chemicals).[57]

If an employer requires a doctor's statement for other conditions, it also may require one for pregnancy prior to granting leave or paying benefits. And, when employees are unable to perform their jobs because of pregnancy, the employer is required to treat them the same as any other temporarily disabled person. Possible forms of accommodation may be to modify tasks, give alternate assignments, or provide disability leave (with or without pay). If a pregnant employee takes a leave of absence, her position must be held open the same length of time that it would be if she were sick or disabled. Moreover, maternity leave cannot be considered an interruption in employment for the purposes of accumulating credit toward tenure or seniority if employees retain seniority rights when on leave for other disabilities.[58] Finally, mandatory pregnancy leave policies requiring teachers to take a leave of absence prior to the birth of their children and specifying a return date also violate the Due Process Clause by creating an *irrebuttable presumption* that all pregnant teachers are

---

[53]42 U.S.C. § 2000e(k) (2008).

[54]The PDA was passed in response to two Supreme Court decisions in which the denial of benefits for pregnancy-related conditions was found not to violate either Title VII or the Fourteenth Amendment. Gen. Elec. Co. v. Gilbert, 429 U.S. 125 (1976); Geduldig v. Aiello, 417 U.S. 484 (1974).

[55]Cline v. Catholic Diocese, 206 F.3d 651 (6th Cir. 1999).

[56]Mitchell v. Bd. of Trs., 599 F.2d 582 (4th Cir. 1979).

[57]Int'l Union, United Auto., Aerospace, & Agric. Implement Workers of Am. v. Johnson Controls, 499 U.S. 187 (1991).

[58]Nashville Gas Co. v. Satty, 434 U.S. 136 (1977).

physically incompetent as of a specified date.[59] School boards, however, may establish maternity leave policies that are justified by a business necessity, such as the requirement that the employee notify the administration of her intended departure and return dates, assuming this is required for other forms of extended personal leave.

Retirement Benefits

Although the longevity figures for men and women have narrowed over the past 35 years, it remains true that women on average live longer than men. Recognition of female longevity historically resulted in differential treatment of women with respect to retirement benefits; employers either required women to make a higher contribution or awarded them lower annual benefits upon retirement. **However, the Supreme Court rejected the use of sex-segregated actuarial tables in retirement benefits programs when it invalidated a retirement program requiring women to make a higher contribution to receive equal benefits on retirement.**[60] Moreover, the Court has prohibited a state from administering a deferred compensation program by contracting with insurance companies that used sex-segregated actuarial tables to determine benefits.[61] In the latter case, female employees received lower monthly annuity payments than did males who contributed the same amount. Discrimination based on sex will foreseeably continue, notwithstanding federal and state laws making such practices illegal.

■ ■ ■ ■ ■

RELIGIOUS DISCRIMINATION

An employee's religion may not be used as a basis for negative employment decisions; however, neither may it be used by the employee to acquire benefits or opportunities that are rightfully determined by seniority or negotiated agreement.

The United States is now more culturally and religiously diverse than at any time in its history. When discrimination occurs, or the employer fails to provide reasonable accommodations, First and Fourteenth Amendment[62] claims are filed as well as those under Title VII.

The first issue in these cases is whether the discrimination is based on sincerely held religious beliefs. A person's religion does not have to be organized, recognized, or well known. Curiously, even opposition to abortion, the draft, and nuclear power have qualified

---

[59]Cleveland Bd. of Educ. v. LaFleur, 414 U.S. 632 (1974).

[60]City of L.A. Dep't of Water & Power v. Manhart, 435 U.S. 702 (1978).

[61]Ariz. Governing Comm. for Tax Deferred Annuity & Deferred Comp. Plans v. Norris, 463 U.S. 1073 (1983).

[62]If a public employee claims an Equal Protection Clause violation because of religion-based facial discrimination, rational-basis scrutiny would apply. Intent must be proved in cases involving facially neutral discrimination.

as "religious" beliefs,[63] although a belief in veganism has not.[64] Nonetheless, employers generally should accept an employee's representation of a sincerely held belief, at least for accommodation purposes. In situations in which the employee suffers an adverse employment outcome because of religion, the employer then must show either that an accommodation was offered, but not taken, or that no reasonable accommodation existed that would not result in hardship.

Hiring and Promotion Practices

Private religious organizations are exempt from First and Fourteenth Amendment claims and in large part from the religious restrictions imposed by Title VII.[65] As a result, they are not generally prohibited from establishing religion as a *bona fide occupational qualification* (BFOQ) (e.g., when a Methodist theological seminary requires that its instructors be Methodists) or from making employment decisions that are consistent with the tenants of their particular faith.

In contrast, **religion will never qualify as a BFOQ in public education, and public employers may not inquire as to an applicant's religious beliefs, use the interview process as an opportunity to indoctrinate, or require prospective employees to profess a belief in a particular faith or in God.**[66] A person's religious affiliation or practice, if any, should not be considered in making an employment decision.

Accommodation

Recommended forms of religious accommodation include activities such as accepting voluntary substitutions and assignment exchanges, using a flexible schedule, and modifying job assignments. Tests, interviews, and other selection procedures should not be scheduled at times when an applicant cannot attend for religious reasons. However, if requested accommodations would compromise the constitutional, statutory, or contractual rights of others (e.g., interfere with a *bona fide* seniority system) or result in undue hardship, Title VII does not require the employer to make the accommodation. **Undue hardship results when extensive changes are required in business practices or when the costs of religious accommodations are more than minimal.** Some of the more often litigated controversies regarding religious accommodation in public education involve attire restrictions, personal leave, and job assignments and responsibilies.

Attire Restrictions. As a general rule, public school district restrictions on the wearing of religious apparel, even if also purportedly cultural, will be upheld in situations in which young and impressionable students would perceive the garment as religious. In an

---

[63]Wilson v. U.S. W. Commc'ns, 58 F.3d 1337 (8th Cir. 1995); Am. Postal Workers Union v. Postmaster Gen., 781 F.2d 772 (9th Cir. 1986); Best v. Cal. Apprenticeship Council, 207 Cal. Rptr. 863 (Ct. App. 1984).

[64]Veganism is a philosophy and lifestyle that avoids using animals and animal products for food, clothing, and other purposes. *See* Friedman v. S. Cal. Permanente Med. Group, 125 Cal. Rptr. 2d 663 (Ct. App. 2002).

[65]42 U.S.C. § 2000e-1(a) (2008).

[66]Torcaso v. Watkins, 367 U.S. 488 (1961).

illustrative case, the Third Circuit held that a district's refusal to accommodate a Muslim teacher who sought to wear religious attire in the classroom did not violate Title VII.[67] The district's action was pursuant to a state statute that regarded the wearing of religious clothing as a significant threat to the maintenance of a religiously neutral public school system.

Personal Leave.   Although most public school calendars allow time off for Christmas and Easter to coincide with semester and spring breaks, holy days of religions other than Christianity are not so routinely accommodated. However, when a school district serves a significant number of students or employs a large number of teachers or staff of another religion, it is not uncommon for schools to be closed on several of the more significant days of worship for that religion as well. The "secular purpose" of such an act is the need to operate the school efficiently. If schools were to remain open when large numbers of persons are not in attendance, administrators would be required to hire numerous substitutes, and teachers would have to prepare a burdensome level of make-up work. When districts elect to remain open in spite of the absence of a large number of students or teachers, substitute teachers often are instructed not to present new material in order to reduce the need to provide repetitive lessons.

The aforementioned approach may provide satisfactory results when attempting to accommodate one or two faiths, but it is unrealistic to assume that public schools will be closed for the holy days of every religion. Alternatively, school districts often provide a variety of accommodations to avoid unduly burdening the religious beliefs of their employees (e.g., use of personal leave days, flexible schedules), depending on the nature of their employment.

Modest requests for religious absences are typically met, but others may result in hardship both for the district as well as for students. School officials often have difficulty in determining appropriate limits and procedures. Some guidance is found in *Trans World Airlines v. Hardison*, in which a member of the Worldwide Church of God challenged his dismissal for refusing to work on Saturdays in contravention of his religious beliefs.[68] The employer asserted that the plaintiff could not be accommodated because shift assignments were based on seniority in conformance with the collective bargaining agreement. Evidence also showed that supervisors had taken appropriate steps in meeting with the plaintiff and in attempting to find other employees to exchange shifts. The Supreme Court found no Title VII violation and reasoned that an employer was not required to bear more than minimal costs in making religious accommodations or to disregard a *bona fide* seniority system in the absence of proof of intentional discrimination.

When leave has been provided, some employees have been satisfied when allowed to have the day off without adverse impact; others have requested that leave be accompanied with full or partial pay. In *Ansonia Board of Education v. Philbrook*, a teacher asserted that the negotiated agreement violated Title VII by permitting employees to use only three days of paid leave for religious purposes, whereas three additional days of paid

[67]United States v. Bd. of Educ., 911 F.2d 882 (3d Cir. 1990).

[68]432 U.S. 63 (1977).

personal business leave could be used for specified secular activities.[69] The plaintiff proposed either permitting the use of the paid personal business leave days for religious observances or allowing employees to receive full pay and cover the costs of substitute teachers for each additional day missed for religious reasons. The Supreme Court, in upholding the agreement, held that the employer was not required to show that each of plaintiff's proposed alternatives would result in undue hardship, and noted that the employer could satisfy Title VII by offering a reasonable accommodation, which may or may not be the one that the employee preferred. Moreover, if leave is restricted to religious purposes, the nonreligious employee who can never qualify for the leave might assert discrimination.

Job Assignments and Responsibilities.   If employees are hired to perform certain jobs, they must be willing and able to perform all of the essential functions of the job. In a somewhat unique case, an interpreter for the hearing impaired refused to translate or sign any cursing or bad language and used her religious beliefs as a basis for the refusal.[70] Given her willing violation of district policy and administrative directives, her contract was terminated. A Missouri appeals court upheld her termination under state law and concluded that the teacher could not have been accommodated without compromising the educational entitlements of her students and that requiring a literal translation of classroom dialogue was not unreasonable.[71]

Adverse Employment Decisions

Employees at times have claimed religious discrimination when they have been transferred, demoted, nonrenewed, terminated, or denied tenure. As with other claims of employment discrimination, the burden is on the plaintiff to prove that the adverse action was motivated by an impermissible reason—in this case, the employee's religious beliefs, practices, or affiliation. Employees experience difficulty in winning such cases, as employers typically can identify one or more legitimate bases for the adverse action (e.g., lack of commitment, excessive absenteeism). In a private-sector employment case reviewed by the Ninth Circuit, a former employee claimed religious discrimination when terminated.[72] To support its slogan that "diversity is our strength," the employer displayed posters, some including gays. The employee believed that homosexual activity violated strict interpretation of the Bible and began posting within his work cubicle passages from the Bible in large type that could be interpreted as condemning homosexuality. After he refused to remove the postings unless his employer removed its displays regarding gays, he was terminated for insubordination. The court reasoned that the employee failed to support his claim of discrimination and that to permit him to maintain his postings, as a religious accommodation, would result

[69]757 F.2d 476 (2d Cir. 1985), *aff'd*, 479 U.S. 60 (1986).

[70]Sedalia No. 200 Sch. Dist. v. Mo. Comm'n on Human Rights, 843 S.W.2d 928 (Mo. Ct. App. 1992).

[71]*See also* Bruff v. N. Miss. Health Servs., 244 F.3d 495 (5th Cir. 2001) (upholding termination of a Christian counselor who refused to work with homosexuals or persons living together outside marriage).

[72]Peterson v. Hewlett-Packard Co., 358 F.3d 599 (9th Cir. 2004).

in undue hardship on the employer as the material was demeaning and degrading to members of the work force.

■ ■ ■ ■ ■

AGE DISCRIMINATION

Under the Age Discrimination in Employment Act, persons age 40 and over may claim age discrimination in employment; they may not, however, claim age discrimination when the criteria used to make the adverse decision are only correlated with age (e.g., seniority, vesting in retirement).

Unlike other characteristics that generate charges of discrimination, age is unique in that everyone is subject to the aging process and eventually will fall within the age-protected category. The mean age of the U.S. population has climbed steadily in recent years; this trend will eventually result in a significant portion of the population that will be age protected in employment and eligible for a range of public services, Medicare, and eventually retirement. Age discrimination employment claims may be filed under the Equal Protection Clause (any age),[73] the Age Discrimination in Employment Act (ADEA) of 1967 (over age 40),[74] and state statutes. The Equal Employment Opportunity Commission (EEOC) is responsible for the enforcement of the ADEA.

The purpose of the ADEA is to promote the employment of older persons based on their ability, to prohibit arbitrary age discrimination in employment, and to find ways of addressing problems arising from the impact of age on employment. The ADEA specifically stipulates that "it shall be unlawful for an employer . . . to fail or refuse to hire or to discharge any individual or otherwise discriminate . . . with respect to . . . compensation, terms, conditions, or privileges of employment, because of such individual's age."[75] However, if the employment decision is based on any reasonable factor other than age (e.g., merit, seniority, vesting in a retirement plan), even though correlated with or associated with age, there is no violation of the ADEA. For a violation to be substantiated, age must play a role in the decision-making process *and* have a determinative influence on the outcome.[76]

The ADEA applies to most employers that have 20 or more employees for 20 or more weeks in the current or preceding calendar year. In cases in which violations of the ADEA are found, courts may provide for injunctive relief; compel employment, reinstatement, or promotion; and provide back pay (including interest), liquidated damages, and attorneys' fees. Punitive damages, however, are not available.[77]

[73]Facially discriminatory procedures and practices that classify individuals on the basis of age can satisfy the Equal Protection Clause if they are rationally related to a legitimate governmental objective, whereas facially neutral criteria may be successfully challenged only with proof of discriminatory intent.

[74]29 U.S.C. § 621 *et seq.* (2008).

[75]29 U.S.C. § 623(a)(1) (2008).

[76]*See, e.g.*, Hazen Paper Co. v. Biggins, 507 U.S. 604, 617 (1993).

[77]29 U.S.C. § 626(b) (2008).

Future application of the ADEA in public school cases may be limited at times, however, because the Supreme Court in *Kimel v. Florida Board of Regents* held that Eleventh Amendment immunity may be claimed as a defense when money damages to be paid out of the state treasury are sought in federal court.[78] Accordingly, immunity may be claimed when state laws consider school districts to be "arms of the state" rather than political subdivisions. But even when the Eleventh Amendment is used as a defense, plaintiffs can sue under comparable state statutes to vindicate their rights.

Hiring and Promotion Practices

Under the ADEA, except in those circumstances in which age qualifies as a *bona fide occupational qualification* (BFOQ), selection among applicants for hiring or promotion may be based on any factor other than age.[79] Although a BFOQ defense in an educational setting is unlikely in cases involving staff, teachers, or administrators, claims could conceivably be made for school bus drivers and pilots. When a BFOQ is applied, the employer carries the burden of persuasion to demonstrate that there is reasonable cause to believe that all, or substantially all, applicants beyond a certain age would be unable to perform a job safely and efficiently.

As with Title VII cases, most employers who are alleged to have engaged in age discrimination simply respond that a better-qualified applicant was hired, irrespective of age. In the effort to show pretext, a plaintiff need not discredit each and every proffered reason for the rejection, but must cast substantial doubt on many, if not most, of the purported bases so that a fact-finder then could rationally disbelieve the remaining reasons given the employer's loss of credibility. In an illustrative Second Circuit case, a less experienced, unqualified, younger teacher was selected over the plaintiff.[80] The district purported that the selected applicant performed better during the interview and was chosen largely on that basis. In ruling that pretext had been shown, the court noted that the successful candidate did not possess the specified degree and had submitted an incomplete file; that the employer had made misleading statements and destroyed relevant evidence; and that the plaintiff possessed superior credentials, except perhaps as to the interview.

Compensation and Benefits

Few public school employees have alleged age-based salary discrimination. In large part, this is because teachers and staff primarily are paid on salary schedules based on seniority and/or degree level. As employees become older, they concomitantly gain seniority and receive a higher scheduled salary. When age discrimination is alleged, the burden of proof remains with the employee to prove that age—rather than performance, longevity, or other factors—was used to determine the level of compensation.

---

[78]528 U.S. 62 (2000).

[79]*See, e.g.,* Stone v. Bd. of Educ. of Saranac Cent. Sch. Dist., 153 Fed. App'x 44 (2d Cir. 2005) (unfamiliarity with newer teaching methods); Herbick v. Salem City Sch. Dist., 151 Fed. App'x 463 (6th Cir. 2005) (need to combine two part-time teaching positions to create one full-time position).

[80]Byrnie v. Town of Cromwell, Bd. of Educ., 243 F.3d 93 (2d Cir. 2001).

In addition to the prohibition on age-based compensation discrimination, school districts may not spend less on the benefits package of older employees than they do on those who are younger. The cost of the benefits package must be the same, even though the benefits derived from an equal expenditure may represent a lower level of benefits for an older worker (e.g., health and life insurance benefits for older workers at times are less, unless a higher premium is paid).[81]

Adverse Employment Actions

Courts often are asked to determine whether an employee's age was used as a basis to terminate, nonrenew, downsize, fail to rehire following a layoff, or demote an employee.[82] However, every action by an employer that the employee perceives as "adverse" might not qualify as such under law (e.g., mere inconvenience or an alteration of job responsibilities will not typically be enough to constitute adverse action).[83] In contrast, **when a challenged act qualifies as adverse, a plaintiff must show that the reason submitted by the employer is false *and* that age was the basis for the adverse action.**

Termination, Nonrenewal, Reduction-in-Force.   The termination of at-will employees[84] is comparatively simple, as are the removal of nontenured teachers and the elimination of unnecessary teaching and administrative positions, assuming strict adherence to approved policy. In contrast, to terminate tenured employees, as well as those working within a long-term contract, a "for cause" hearing will be required to permit the school district to show why the removal of the employee is necessary. Although many factors may be considered in making such decisions (e.g., morality, efficiency), the employee's age may not be used, unless age qualifies as a BFOQ. In a Supreme Court case, *Reeves v. Sanderson Plumbing Products*, a 57-year-old former employee was terminated and replaced with a person in his thirties.[85] In ruling that the company was not entitled to summary judgment, the Court noted that the plaintiff was able to establish a claim, create a jury issue concerning the falsity of the employer's basis for the action, and introduce additional evidence showing that the director was motivated by age-related animus.

In comparison, summary judgment was awarded in an Eleventh Circuit case in which a teacher failed to support her claim of age discrimination, among others, when she was not offered a fifth one-year contract or tenure.[86] She failed to provide documentation regarding the age of those selected, other than her general claim that they were younger, and stated in her own deposition that she had no personal knowledge that hiring decisions were made on the basis of age. As a result, the lower court ruling on behalf of the school district was affirmed.

---

[81]29 C.F.R. § 1625.10(a)(1) (2008).

[82]*See, e.g.*, Prater v. Joliet Jr. Coll., 148 Fed. App'x 550 (7th Cir. 2005).

[83]Mitchell v. Vanderbilt Univ., 389 F.3d 177 (6th Cir. 2004).

[84]At-will employees have no contract or job expectation and may leave or be terminated at any time.

[85]530 U.S. 133 (2000).

[86]Bartes v. Sch. Bd. of Alachua County, No. 04-15459, 2005 U.S. App. LEXIS 23386 (11th Cir. Oct. 26, 2005).

In addition to termination and nonrenewal cases, at times employees allege that they were constructively discharged because of their age. To succeed, the employee must show that the conditions created by the employer (e.g., arbitrary alteration of the job to ensure poor job performance; harassment) were such that a reasonable person similarly situated would find the work intolerable and that the employer acted with the intent of forcing the employee to quit.[07]

Retaliation   As with cases filed under Title VII, employers under the ADEA may not retaliate against employees when they file complaints or suits. An employee need not establish the validity of the original complaint in order to succeed in a case claiming retaliation, but it would be helpful to show that the person responsible for the adverse decision at least knew of the prior charges of discrimination. Furthermore, the plaintiff shoulders the burden to show that the adverse action was an act of retaliation, and not otherwise justified because of incompetence, insubordination, immorality, or the like.

Retirement

Given that the mandatory retirement of school employees has been eliminated, districts have attempted to entice older employees to retire through attractive retirement benefits packages. **Under the ADEA, employers can follow the terms of a *bona fide* retirement plan as long as the plan is not a subterfuge to evade the purposes of the act.** Also, employers may not reduce annual benefits or cease the accrual of benefits after employees attain a certain age as an inducement for them to retire.[88] Furthermore, legal challenges also may occur when an employee is terminated prior to becoming eligible for full retirement benefits (i.e., prior to becoming vested). In *Hazen Paper Co. v. Biggins*, the employee was fired at age 62, only a few weeks before completing 10 years of service and being vested in his pension plan.[89] In a unanimous opinion, the Supreme Court made it clear, however, that **disparate treatment is not supported when the factor motivating the employer is something other than the employee's age, even if it is correlated with age (e.g., vesting or pension status).** Because age and years of service are distinctly different factors, an employer may take one into account, yet ignore the other. In cases in which violations are found and liquidated damages are sought, the Supreme Court iterated that the plaintiff bears the burden to show that the act was willful in that the employer knew or showed reckless disregard for whether its conduct would violate the ADEA.

Although it is difficult to prevail in an age discrimination claim, expect the number of cases to remain high as the "baby boomers" become sexagenarians over the next decade. Some will be denied employment, promotion, or vesting, while others may be disappointed in their retirement packages. Employees will allege age discrimination, but in most instances that claim will be successfully rebutted by employers.

[87]*See, e.g.*, Dirusso v. Aspen Sch. Dist. No. 1, 123 Fed. App'x 826 (10th Cir. 2004).

[88]29 U.S.C. § 623(i)(1) (2008).

[89]507 U.S. 604 (1993).

■ ■ ■ ■ ■

DISABILITY DISCRIMINATION

Federal disability law protects only those individuals who can show that they qualify as disabled and are otherwise qualified for the job.

Two primary federal statutes prohibit disability discrimination in employment: Section 504 of the Rehabilitation Act of 1973,[90] which applies to recipients of federal financial assistance, and Title I of the Americans with Disabilities Act of 1990 (ADA),[91] which applies to most employers with 15 or more employees. These statutes require nondiscrimination against the disabled involving any term, condition, or privilege of employment. When education employers are involved, Section 504 complaints are submitted to the Office for Civil Rights within the Department of Education. In comparison, the Equal Employment Opportunity Commission and the Department of Justice have enforcement rights under the ADA.

ADA cases filed in federal court seeking monetary awards from educational entities that are found to be state agencies or arms of the state will be dismissed, given the state's Eleventh Amendment immunity.[92] Nonetheless, even within those jurisdictions, persons who have been subjected to disability discrimination are not powerless to vindicate their rights. The ADA still prescribes standards that are applicable to state employers. These standards could be enforced by the United States in federal judicial actions for monetary damages and by employees in actions seeking injunctive relief. Also, many state disability laws provide identical or at least similar coverage to that mandated by the ADA and permit monetary damages under certain circumstances. Furthermore, because all (or nearly all) public schools are recipients of federal financial assistance, they must meet substantially similar obligations under the Rehabilitation Act—a law that at times permits the awarding of money damages.

Qualifying as Disabled

When cases are filed, courts often are asked to resolve questions regarding whether the employee is in fact disabled and, if so, what accommodations are required. A person qualifies as disabled under Section 504 and the ADA if he or she:

- Has a physical or mental impairment that substantially limits one or more major life activities,
- Has a record of impairment, or
- Is regarded as having an impairment.

[90]29 U.S.C. § 794 (2008).

[91]42 U.S.C. § 12101 et seq. (2008).

[92]Bd. of Trs. v. Garrett, 531 U.S. 356 (2001).

However, more is required than simple knowledge of a condition that is physically or mentally limiting for the plaintiff to establish that the employer regarded the employee as disabled. Additionally, suggesting that an employee see a psychologist before returning to work does not establish the fact that the employer regarded the employee as a person with a mental disability.[93]

Although federal regulations define physical or mental impairment broadly,[94] persons who currently are involved in the use of illegal drugs, are unable to perform the duties of the job because of continuing alcohol use, have a contagious disease, or otherwise represent a direct threat to the safety or health of themselves or others do not qualify as disabled. Likewise, persons claiming discrimination based on transvestism, transsexualism, pedophilia, exhibitionism, voyeurism, gender identity disorders not resulting from physical impairments, other sexual behavior disorders, compulsive gambling, kleptomania, pyromania, and psychoactive substance use disorders resulting from current illegal drug use are not protected by either the ADA or Section 504.

Qualifying as "disabled" requires a two-step process: identifying a physical or mental impairment and determining whether the impairment substantially limits a major life activity (i.e., walking, seeing, hearing, speaking, breathing, learning, working, caring for oneself, sitting, standing, lifting, concentrating, thinking, interacting with others, reproducing, and performing manual tasks). In assessing whether an applicant or employee is disabled, mitigating and corrective measures (both positive and negative)[95] must be considered.[96] Not all impairments limit major life activity (e.g., a hearing-impaired employee may have average or near-average hearing by using a hearing aid). **Performance is substantially limited when an employee is unable to perform, or is significantly restricted in performing, a major life activity that can be accomplished by the average person in the general population.** The nature, severity, duration, and long-term impact of the impairment are considered when determining whether a condition is substantially limiting.[97] Also, an impairment that is substantially limiting for one person may not be for another. To qualify, it must prevent or restrict an individual from performing tasks that are of central importance to most people's daily lives. If the life activity claimed is working, impairments are not substantially limiting unless they restrict the ability to perform a broad range of jobs and not just a single or specialized job.[98] In such cases, courts will consider the geographic area to which the plaintiff has reasonable access and the nature of the job from which the individual was disqualified, as well as other jobs that require similar training, knowledge, ability, or skill.[99]

[93]Sullivan v. River Valley Sch. Dist., 197 F.3d 804 (6th Cir. 1999).

[94]34 C.F.R. § 104.3(j)(2)(i) (2008).

[95]For example, corrected vision through use of contact lenses is a positive mitigating measure; side effects of medication represents a negative one.

[96]*See, e.g.*, Sutton v. United Airlines, 527 U.S. 471 (1999).

[97]29 C.F.R. § 1630.2(j)(1), (2) (2008).

[98]*See, e.g.*, Samuels v. Kansas City Mo. Sch. Dist., 437 F.3d 797 (8th Cir. 2006).

[99]29 C.F.R. § 1630.2 (j)(2), (3) (2008).

Otherwise Qualified

If a person qualifies as disabled, it then must be determined whether he or she is "otherwise qualified." **To be an otherwise qualified individual with a disability, the applicant or employee must be able to perform the essential functions of the job in spite of the disability, although reasonable accommodation at times may be necessary**. Generally, employers should not impose a blanket exclusion of persons with particular disabilities, but rather should provide individual review of each person. Only in rare instances will a particular disability disqualify an applicant (e.g., when federal or state law establishes health or ability requirements for particular types of employment).

In identifying the essential functions of the job, courts will give consideration to what the employer perceives to be essential. As long as each identified requirement for employment is either training related (for initial employment) or job related, the employer should not have difficulty in substantiating its claim of business necessity. For example, being on time to work and being at work on a regular daily basis can qualify as a business necessity for most positions in education as well as elsewhere. Nevertheless, the burden will be on the district to show that the absences are excessive, that the requested accommodations are unreasonable, or that undue hardship would result if the employee were reinstated.

Reasonable Accommodation

Persons with disabilities must be able to perform all of the essential functions of the position, although reasonable accommodations may be necessary. Employers are responsible for providing accommodations, such as making necessary facilities accessible and usable, restructuring work schedules, acquiring or modifying equipment, and providing readers or interpreters. Federal law does not require the employer to bump a current employee to allow a person with a disability to fill the position, to fill a vacant position it did not intend to fill, to violate seniority rights, to refrain from disciplining an employee for misconduct, to eliminate essential functions of the job, or to create a new, unnecessary position. Such forms of accommodation may be theoretically possible but would result in undue hardship to the employer and discriminate against other employees. Courts determine whether undue hardship results after a review of the size of the program and its budget, the number of employees, the type of facilities and operation, and the nature and cost of accommodation. Because there is no fixed formula for calculations, courts have differed markedly in identifying what they consider reasonable.

In selecting reasonable accommodations, the employer should engage in an ongoing *interactive process* with the employee with a disability and should consult state and federal agencies when needed.[100] However, the employee does not choose the accommodations; the employer has the right to select among effective reasonable accommodations.

Termination and Nonrenewal

More individuals with disabilities are in the workplace today than ever before, with many achieving leadership positions. Not all persons with disabilities have fared well, however,

---

[100]*See, e.g.*, Cutrera v. Bd. of Supervisors, 429 F.3d 108 (5th Cir. 2005).

as some have not been selected for initial employment, not granted tenure, not been promoted, not paid fairly, arbitrarily discharged, or forced to resign or retire.[101] At times, such adverse decisions were the result of inadequate qualifications or skills, better-qualified applicants, poor job performance, posing a risk, or criminal wrongdoing. At other times, the employee's disability was found to be the basis for the adverse decision, or the environment had become so hostile that the employee's decision to quit qualified as being constructively discharged.

To support a disparate treatment adverse action claim, employees must show that they:

- Have a disability that substantially limits a major life activity compared with the average person in the population,
- Were the target of an action that qualified as adverse, and
- Were denied employment or retention in employment due to disability.[102]

There should continue to be ample case law dealing with termination and other claims filed by employees with disabilities. Such claims are likely to focus on the ADA rather than Section 504, given its broader application. Expect school officials to continue to struggle in their efforts to provide effective, cost-efficient accommodations, but also generally expect good faith efforts as educators attempt to comply with federal and state disability laws.

CONCLUSION

Federal law requires that employment decisions be based on qualifications, performance, merit, seniority, and the like, rather than factors such as race, national origin, sex, religion, age, or disability. Statutes vary considerably, however, about what they require. Moreover, federal regulations are extensive, complex, and at times confounding. As a result, courts differ in applying the law.

When preparing a policy related to personnel, it will be important to consider (1) whether it facially discriminates only in legal and appropriate ways and (2) whether it adversely affects a protected class, even though the policy may be facially neutral. Treating all persons the same may not accommodate individual needs and may inadvertently result in subtle forms of discrimination. In the alternative, treating persons differently may advantage some over others. The bottom line is that there is no simple solution.

POINTS TO PONDER

1. A math and science teacher at an elite (selective admissions) public magnet school had a knowledge base measured at the 99th percentile of all persons taking a standardized math test. He was hired because of his knowledge of math and his ability to teach (as evidenced by the exceptional evaluations he received at his former school in China, his native country).

---

[101]*See e.g.*, Cigan v. Chippewa Falls Sch. Dist., 388 F.3d 331 (7th Cir. 2004).

[102]*See, e.g.*, Macy v. Hopkins County Sch. Bd. of Educ., 484 F.3d 357 (6th Cir. 2007).

Unfortunately, little effort was made to determine his English-language speaking skills, although his written-English proficiency scores were satisfactory. After two semesters of unsuccessful teaching, his contract was not renewed. He was not tenured and did not have the guarantee of employment beyond the one-year contract that had just expired. He then sued the school under Title VII and the Fourteenth Amendment. School officials claimed that he was not renewed because of his horrible teaching evaluations (based overwhelmingly on poor verbal communication skills) and not because of national origin. Two other Chinese teachers remained on staff. Is the nonrenewed teacher likely to win this suit? Why or why not?

2. All candidates for promotion are required to take a standardized test. Only persons scoring in the top 10 percent make the first cut and are allowed to proceed to the interview portion of the promotion process. You did poorly on the test, as did several others within your racial group. In fact, only 2 percent of those within your racial classification were in the top 10 percent, notwithstanding the fact that your race represents 25 percent of those in the pool of candidates with the seniority to be considered for promotion. Performance on the test has been shown to be predictive of success on the job. You sued under Title VII, claiming disparate impact. Will you be successful in this suit? Why or why not?

3. A physically disabled school maintenance worker was terminated because of poor job performance. As a form of accommodation, he had requested either additional time (with additional compensation) to perform the job or an assistant to do a portion of the work for him—he can perform two-thirds of the daily work assignment within an eight-hour day. Following his termination, he filed suit under Section 504 of the Rehabilitation Act of 1973. The school district, which receives federal funds, claimed that he was not otherwise qualified to meet the essential functions of the job. How will this legal challenge be decided? Why?

4. A well-qualified male applicant for a first grade teaching position was not hired, admittedly because of sex. There were no other applicants for the position. The male principal made it clear that only females historically had been first grade teachers and that they, by their nature, were better suited for such positions. Moreover, he encouraged the male to apply for a middle school position, for which he also was licensed, and virtually guaranteed the applicant that he would be selected. Following his initial rejection, the male applicant filed suit against the district under Title VII. Is he likely to win this case? Why or why not?

CHAPTER TWELVE

TERMINATION OF EMPLOYMENT

State laws delineate the authority of school boards in terminating school personnel. Generally, these laws specify the causes for which a teacher may be terminated and the procedures that must be followed. The school board's right to determine the fitness of teachers is well established; in fact, courts have declared that school boards have a duty as well as a right to make such determinations.

The first section of this chapter provides an overview of due process in connection with nonrenewal and dismissal. Since due process is required only if a teacher is able to establish that a constitutionally protected property or liberty interest is at stake, this section explores the dimensions of teachers' property and liberty rights in the context of employment termination. In the next section, specific procedural requirements are identified and discussed. A survey of judicial interpretations of state laws regarding causes for dismissal is presented in the third section. The concluding section provides an overview of remedies available to teachers for violation of their protected rights.

PROCEDURAL DUE PROCESS IN GENERAL

A teacher is entitled to procedural due process if termination of employment impairs a property or liberty interest.

Basic due process rights are embodied in the Fourteenth Amendment, which guarantees that no state shall "deprive any person of life, liberty, or property without due process of law."[1] Due process safeguards apply not only in judicial proceedings but also to acts of governmental agencies such as school boards. As discussed in Chapter 1, constitutional due process entails *substantive* protections against arbitrary governmental action and

---

[1]As noted in Chapter 1, the Fourteenth Amendment restricts state, in contrast to private, action. The Supreme Court has recognized that mere regulation by the state will be insufficient to evoke constitutional protections in private school personnel matters. The Court rejected a suit for damages against a private school for allegedly unconstitutional dismissals, reasoning that there was no "symbiotic relationship" between the private school and the state. Rendell Baker v. Kohn, 457 U.S. 830 (1982).

procedural protections when the government threatens an individual's life, liberty, or property interests. Most teacher termination cases have focused on procedural due process requirements.

The individual and governmental interests at stake and applicable state laws influence the nature of procedural due process required. **Courts have established that a teacher's interest in public employment may entail significant "property" and "liberty" rights necessitating due process prior to employment termination.** A *property interest* is a legitimate claim of entitlement to continued employment that is created by state law.[2] The granting of tenure conveys such a right to a teacher. Also, a contract establishes a property right to employment within its stated terms. A property interest in continued employment, however, does not mean that an individual cannot be terminated; it simply means that an employer must follow the requirements of due process and substantiate cause.

The judiciary has recognized that Fourteenth Amendment *liberty rights* encompass fundamental constitutional guarantees, such as freedom of speech. Procedural due process is always required when a termination implicates such fundamental liberties. A liberty interest also is involved when termination creates a stigma or damages an individual's reputation in a manner that forecloses future employment opportunities. If protected liberty or property interests are implicated, the Fourteenth Amendment entitles the teacher at least to notice of the reasons for the school board's action and an opportunity for a hearing.

Employment terminations are classified as either dismissals or nonrenewals. The distinction between the two has significant implications for teachers' procedural rights. In this section, the procedural safeguards that must be provided the tenured teacher and the nontenured teacher are distinguished. Specific attention is given to the conditions that may give rise to a nontenured teacher's acquiring a protected liberty or property interest in employment, thereby establishing a claim to procedural due process.

Dismissal

The word *dismissal* refers to the termination for cause of any tenured teacher or a probationary teacher within the contract period. Both tenure statutes and employment contracts establish a property interest entitling teachers to full procedural protection.[3] Beyond the basic constitutional requirements of appropriate notice and an opportunity to be heard, state laws and school board policies often contain detailed procedures that must be followed. Failure to provide these additional procedures, however, results in a violation of state law, rather than constitutional law. Statutory procedures vary as to specificity, with some states enumerating detailed steps and others identifying only broad parameters. In addition to complying with state law, a school district must abide by its own procedures, even if they

---

[2]*See* Bd. of Regents v. Roth, 408 U.S. 564 (1972).

[3]If a statute conferring specific property rights (e.g., tenure) is rescinded or amended to eliminate those rights, individuals are not entitled to procedural due process related to that deprivation; statutory benefits can be revoked without due process unless the change impairs contractual rights. *See, e.g.*, Indiana *ex rel.* Anderson v. Brand, 303 U.S. 95 (1938); Pittman v. Chi. Bd. of Educ., 64 F.3d 1098 (7th Cir. 1995). However, school boards generally cannot amend, repeal, or circumvent statutory rights (e.g., entitlement to procedural due process) through the employment contract. *See, e.g.*, Parker v. Indep. Sch. Dist. No. I-003, 82 F.3d 952 (10th Cir. 1996).

exceed state law. For example, if school board policy provides for a preliminary notice of teaching inadequacies and an opportunity to correct remediable deficiencies prior to dismissal, the board must follow these steps.

A critical element in dismissal actions is a showing of justifiable cause for termination of employment. If causes are identified in state law, a school board must base dismissal on those grounds. Failure to relate the charges to statutory grounds can invalidate the termination decision. Because statutes typically list broad causes—such as incompetency, insubordination, immorality, unprofessional conduct, and neglect of duty—notice of discharge must indicate specific conduct substantiating the legal charges. Procedural safeguards ensure not only that a teacher is informed of the specific reasons and grounds for dismissal but also that the school board bases its decision on evidence substantiating those grounds. Detailed aspects of procedural due process requirements and dismissal for cause are addressed in subsequent sections of this chapter.

Nonrenewal

Unless specified in state law, procedural protections are not accorded the probationary teacher when the employment contract is not renewed. At the end of the contract period, employment can be terminated for any or no reason, as long as the reason is not constitutionally impermissible (e.g., denial of protected speech).[4] The most common statutory requirement is notification of nonrenewal on or before a specified date prior to the expiration of the contract. When a statute designates a deadline for nonrenewal, a school board must notify a teacher on or before the established date. The timeliness of nonrenewal notices is strictly construed. The fact that the school board has set in motion notification (e.g., mailed the notice) generally does not satisfy the statutory requirement; the teacher's actual receipt of the notice is critical. A teacher, however, cannot avoid or deliberately thwart delivery of notice and then claim insufficiency of notice. Failure of school officials to observe the notice deadline may result in a teacher's reinstatement for an additional year or even the granting of tenure in some jurisdictions.

In the nonrenewal of teachers' contracts, some states require a written statement of reasons and may even provide an opportunity for a hearing at the teacher's request. Unlike evidentiary hearings for dismissal of a teacher, the school board is not required to show cause for nonrenewal; a teacher is simply provided the reasons underlying the nonrenewal and an opportunity to address the school board. When a school board is required to provide reasons, broad general statements such as "the school district's interest would be best served," "the district can find a better teacher," or "the term contract has expired" will not suffice. When state law establishes specific requirements and procedures for nonrenewal, failure to abide by these provisions may invalidate a school board's decision. Also, a school board must follow not only state law but also must comply substantially with its own nonrenewal procedures.

Although state laws may not provide the probationary teacher with specific procedural protections, a teacher's interest in continued public employment may be constitutionally

---

[4]*See, e.g.*, Grossman v. S. Shore Pub. Sch. Dist., 507 F.3d 1097 (7th Cir. 2007); Back v. Hastings, 365 F.3d 107 (2d Cir. 2004); Flaskamp v. Dearborn Pub. Schs., 385 F.3d 935 (6th Cir. 2004). *See also* Chapter 10 for a discussion of teachers' constitutional rights.

protected if a liberty or property right guaranteed by the Fourteenth Amendment has been abridged. Infringement of these interests entitles a probationary teacher to due process rights similar to the rights of tenured teachers.

Establishing Protected Property and Liberty Interests

The United States Supreme Court addressed the scope of protected interests encompassed by the Fourteenth Amendment in two significant decisions in 1972: *Board of Regents v. Roth*[5] and *Perry v. Sindermann*.[6] These decisions addressed whether the infringement of a liberty or property interest entitles a probationary teacher to due process rights similar to the rights of tenured teachers. The cases involved faculty members at the postsecondary level, but the rulings are equally applicable to public elementary and secondary school teachers.

In *Roth*, the question presented to the Court was whether a nontenured teacher had a constitutional right to a statement of reasons and a hearing prior to nonreappointment. Roth was hired on a one-year contract, and the university elected not to rehire him for a second year. Since Roth did not have tenure, there was no entitlement under Wisconsin law to an explanation of charges or a hearing. Roth challenged the nonrenewal, alleging that failure to provide notice of reasons and an opportunity for a hearing impaired his due process rights.

The Supreme Court held that nonrenewal does not require procedural protection unless impairment of a protected liberty or property interest can be shown. To establish infringement of a liberty interest, the Court held that the teacher must show that the employer's action (1) resulted in damage to his or her reputation and standing in the community or (2) imposed a stigma that foreclosed other employment opportunities. The evidence presented by Roth indicated that there was no such damage to his reputation or future employment. Accordingly, the Court concluded, "It stretches the concept too far to suggest that a person is deprived of 'liberty' when he simply is not rehired in one job but remains as free as before to seek another."[7]

The Court also rejected Roth's claim that he had a protected property interest to continued employment. The Court held that **in order to establish a valid property right, an individual must have more than an "abstract need or desire" for a position; there must be a "legitimate claim of entitlement."**[8] Property interests are not defined by the federal Constitution, but rather by state laws or employment contracts that secure specific benefits. An abstract desire or unilateral expectation of continued employment alone does not constitute a property right. The terms of Roth's one-year appointment and state law precluded any claim of entitlement.

On the same day it rendered the *Roth* decision, the Supreme Court in the *Sindermann* case explained the circumstances that might create a legitimate expectation of reemployment

[5]408 U.S. 564 (1972).

[6]408 U.S. 593 (1972).

[7]*Roth*, 408 U.S. at 575.

[8]*Id*. at 577. *See also* Lautermilch v. Findlay City Schs., 314 F.3d 271 (6th Cir. 2002) (finding that a substitute teacher without a contract did not have a protected property interest in continued employment).

for a nontenured teacher.[9] Sindermann was a nontenured faculty member in his fourth year of teaching when he was notified, without a statement of reasons or an opportunity for a hearing, that his contract would not be renewed. He challenged the lack of procedural due process, alleging that nonrenewal deprived him of a property interest protected by the Fourteenth Amendment and violated his First Amendment right to freedom of speech.

In advancing a protected property right, Sindermann claimed that the college, which lacked a formal tenure system, had created an informal, or *de facto*, tenure system through various practices and policies. Specifically, Sindermann cited a provision in the faculty guide stating that "the College wishes the faculty member to feel that he has permanent tenure as long as his teaching services are satisfactory."[10] The Supreme Court found that Sindermann's claim, unlike Roth's, might have been based on a legitimate expectation of reemployment promulgated by the college. According to the Court, the lack of a formal tenure system did not foreclose the possibility of an institution fostering entitlement to a position through its personnel policies.

In assessing Sindermann's free speech claim, **the Supreme Court confirmed that a teacher's lack of tenure does not void a claim that nonrenewal was based on the exercise of constitutionally protected conduct.** Procedural due process must be afforded when a substantive constitutional right is violated. In a later case, however, the Supreme Court held that if a constitutional right is implicated in a nonrenewal, the teacher bears the burden of showing that the protected conduct was a substantial or motivating factor in the school board's decision.[11] Establishing an inference of a constitutional violation then shifts the burden to the school board to show that it would have reached the same decision in the absence of the protected activity.

The *Roth* and *Sindermann* cases are the legal precedents for assessing the procedural rights of nontenured teachers. To summarize, the Supreme Court held that a nontenured teacher does not have a constitutionally protected property right to employment requiring procedural due process before denial of reappointment. Certain actions of the school board, however, may create conditions entitling a nontenured teacher to notice and a hearing similar to the tenured teacher. Such actions would include:

- Nonrenewal decisions damaging an individual's reputation and integrity,
- Nonrenewal decisions foreclosing other employment opportunities,
- Policies and practices creating a valid claim to reemployment, and
- Nonrenewal decisions violating fundamental constitutional guarantees (e.g., freedom of expression).

Because the Supreme Court has held that impairment of a teacher's property or liberty interests triggers procedural protections, the question arises concerning what constitutes a violation of these interests. Courts have purposely avoided precisely defining the concepts of liberty and property, preferring to allow experience and time to shape their

[9]408 U.S. 593 (1972).

[10]*Id.* at 600.

[11]Mt. Healthy City Sch. Dist. Bd. of Educ. v. Doyle, 429 U.S. 274 (1977). *See* text accompanying note 3, Chapter 10, for a discussion of the First Amendment issue in this case.

meanings. Since 1972, the Supreme Court and federal appellate courts have rendered many decisions that provide guidance in understanding these concepts.

Property Interest.   In general, a nontenured employee does not have a property claim to reappointment unless state or local governmental action has clearly established such a right. Protected property interests are not created by mere longevity in employment. Issuing an employee a series of annual contracts does not constitute a valid claim to continued employment in the absence of a guarantee in state law, local policy, or an employment contract.[12] Similarly, a statute or collective bargaining agreement providing a teacher, upon request, a hearing and statement of reasons for nonrenewal does not confer a property interest in employment requiring legally sufficient cause for termination. Such a provision simply gives the teacher an opportunity to present reasons why the contract should be renewed.

Liberty Interest.   As noted previously, liberty interests encompass fundamental constitutional guarantees such as freedom of expression and privacy rights. If governmental action in the nonrenewal of employment threatens the exercise of these fundamental liberties, procedural due process must be afforded. Most nonrenewals, however, do not overtly implicate fundamental rights, and thus, the burden is on the aggrieved employee to prove that the proffered reason is pretextual to mask impermissible grounds.

   A liberty interest also may be implicated if the nonrenewal of employment damages an individual's reputation. The Supreme Court established in *Roth* that damage to a teacher's reputation and future employability could infringe Fourteenth Amendment liberty rights. In subsequent decisions, the Court identified prerequisite conditions for establishing that a constitutionally impermissible stigma has been imposed. According to the Court, procedural protections must be afforded only if stigma or damaging statements are related to loss of employment, publicly disclosed, alleged to be false, and virtually foreclose opportunities for future employment.[13]

   Under this *stigma-plus test*, governmental action damaging a teacher's reputation, standing alone, is insufficient to invoke the Fourteenth Amendment's procedural safeguards.[14] While many employment actions may stigmatize and affect a teacher's reputation, they do not constitute a deprivation of liberty in the absence of loss of employment.[15] As the Ninth Circuit noted, "nearly any reason assigned for dismissal is likely to be to some

---

[12]*See* Halfhill v. N.E. Sch. Corp., 472 F.3d 496 (7th Cir. 2006) (concluding that a nontenured teacher could not assert a property interest in continued employment based on a principal's positive mid-year evaluation that indicated the teacher's contract would be renewed; the teacher demonstrated a lack of professionalism in handling several incidents with students after the evaluation).

[13]Codd v. Velger, 429 U.S. 624 (1977). *See, e.g.,* O'Connor v. Pierson, 426 F.3d 187 (2d Cir. 2005); Bordelon v. Chi. Sch. Reform Bd. of Trs., 233 F.3d 524 (7th Cir. 2000).

[14]State constitutions, however, may provide greater protection of due process rights encompassing damage to reputation alone. *See, e.g.,* Kadetsky v. Egg Harbor Twp. Bd. of Educ., 82 F. Supp. 2d 327 (D.N.J. 2000).

[15]*See, e.g.,* Brown v. Simmons, 478 F.3d 922 (8th Cir. 2007); Ulichny v. Merton Cmty. Sch. Dist., 249 F.3d 686 (7th Cir. 2001). *But see* Winegar v. Des Moines Indep. Cmty. Sch. Dist., 20 F.3d 895 (8th Cir. 1994) (holding that a teacher's disciplinary transfer to another school because of the physical abuse of a student involved a significant liberty interest necessitating an opportunity to be heard).

extent a negative reflection on an individual's ability, temperament, or character," but circumstances giving rise to a liberty interest are narrow.[16] Charges must be serious implications against character, such as immorality and dishonesty, to create a stigma of constitutional magnitude that virtually forecloses other employment. According to the Fifth Circuit, a charge must give rise to "a 'badge of infamy,' public scorn, or the like."[17]

Among accusations that courts have found to necessitate a hearing are a serious drinking problem, emotional instability, mental illness, immoral conduct, child molestation, and extensive professional inadequacies.[18] Reasons held to pose no threat to a liberty interest include job-related comments such as personality differences and difficulty in working with others, hostility toward authority, incompetence, aggressive behavior, ineffective leadership, and poor performance.[19] Charges relating to job performance may have an impact on future employment but do not create a stigma of constitutional magnitude.

■ ■ ■ ■ ■

PROCEDURAL REQUIREMENTS IN DISCHARGE PROCEEDINGS

When a liberty or property interest is implicated, the Fourteenth Amendment requires that a teacher be notified of charges and provided with an opportunity for a hearing that usually includes representation by counsel, examination and cross-examination of witnesses, and a record of the proceedings.

Since termination of a tenured teacher or a nontenured teacher during the contract period requires procedural due process, the central question becomes, what process is due? Courts have noted that no fixed set of procedures apply under all circumstances. Rather, due process entails a balancing of the individual and governmental interests affected in each situation. Minimally, the Fourteenth Amendment requires that dismissal proceedings be based on established rules or standards. Actual procedures will depend on state law, school board regulations, and collective bargaining agreements, but they cannot drop below constitutional minimums. For example, a statute requiring tenured teachers to pay half the cost of a hearing that the school board must provide was found to impair federal rights.[20]

---

[16]Gray v. Union County Intermediate Educ. Dist., 520 F.2d 803, 806 (9th Cir. 1975).

[17]Ball v. Bd. of Trs., 584 F.2d 684, 685 (5th Cir. 1978).

[18]Donato v. Plainview-Old Bethpage Cent. Sch. Dist., 96 F.3d 623 (2d Cir. 1996); Vanelli v. Reynolds Sch. Dist. No. 7, 667 F.2d 773 (9th Cir. 1982); Carroll v. Robinson, 874 P.2d 1010 (Ariz. Ct. App. 1994).

[19]Lybrook v. Members of Farmington Mun. Schs. Bd., 232 F.3d 1334 (10th Cir. 2000); Hayes v. Phoenix-Talent Sch. Dist. No. 4, 893 F.2d 235 (9th Cir. 1990); Gilder-Lucas v. Elmore County Bd. of Educ., 186 Fed. App'x 885 (11th Cir. 2006).

[20]Rankin v. Indep. Sch. Dist. No. I-3, 876 F.2d 838 (10th Cir. 1989). *See also* Cal. Teachers Ass'n v. State, 975 P.2d 622, 643 (Cal. 1999) (concluding that imposing cost of hearing "chills the exercise of the right to a hearing and vigorous advocacy on behalf of the teacher").

FIGURE 12.1   Procedural Due Process Elements in Teacher Termination Proceedings

- Notification of charges
- Opportunity for a hearing
- Adequate time to prepare a rebuttal to the charges
- Access to evidence and names of witnesses
- Hearing before an impartial tribunal
- Representation by legal counsel
- Opportunity to present evidence and witnesses
- Opportunity to cross-examine adverse witnesses
- Decision based on evidence and findings of the hearing
- Transcript or record of the hearing
- Opportunity to appeal an adverse decision

In assessing the adequacy of procedural safeguards, the judiciary looks for the provision of certain basic elements to meet constitutional guarantees.[21] Courts generally have held that **a teacher facing a severe loss such as termination must be afforded full procedural due process** (see Figure 12.1 for elements).[22] Beyond the constitutional considerations, courts also strictly enforce any additional procedural protections conferred by state laws and local policies. Examples of such requirements might be providing detailed performance evaluations prior to termination, notifying teachers of weaknesses, and allowing an opportunity for improvement before dismissal. Although failure to comply with these stipulations may invalidate the school board's action under state law, federal due process rights *per se* are not violated if minimal constitutional procedures are provided. Except in limited circumstances, individuals are required to exhaust administrative procedures, or the grievance procedures specified in the collective bargaining agreement, prior to seeking judicial review. Pursuing an administrative hearing promotes resolution of a controversy at the agency level.

Various elements of due process proceedings may be contested as inadequate. Questions arise regarding issues such as the sufficiency of notice, impartiality of the board members, and placement of the burden of proof. The aspects of procedural due process that courts frequently scrutinize in assessing the fundamental fairness of school board actions are examined next.

---

[21]At the same time, courts will not find a deprivation of procedural due process rights if educators do not avail themselves of the offered safeguards. *See, e.g.,* Segal v. N.Y. City, 459 F.3d 207 (2d Cir. 2006); Christensen v. Kingston Sch. Comm., 360 F. Supp. 2d 212 (D. Mass. 2005).

[22]This chapter focuses on procedural protections required in teacher terminations. It should be noted, however, that other school board decisions (e.g., transfers, demotions, or mandatory leaves) may impose similar constraints on decision making.

Notice

In general, **a constitutionally adequate notice is timely, informs the teacher of specific charges, and allows the teacher sufficient time to prepare a response.** Beyond the constitutional guarantees, state laws and regulations as well as school board policies usually impose very specific requirements relating to form, timeliness, and content of notice.[23] In legal challenges, the adequacy of a notice is assessed in terms of whether it meets constitutional as well as other requirements. Failure to comply substantially with mandated requisites will void school board action.

The form or substance of notice is usually stipulated in state statutes. In determining appropriateness of notice, courts generally have held that substantial compliance with form requirements (as opposed to strict compliance required for notice deadlines) is sufficient. Under this standard, the decisive factor is whether the notice adequately informs the teacher of the pending action. For example, if a statute requires notification by certified mail and the notice is mailed by registered mail or is personally delivered, it substantially complies with the state requirement. However, oral notification will not suffice if the law requires written notification. If the form of the notice is not specified in statute, any timely notice that informs a teacher is adequate.

Although form and timeliness are important concerns in issuing a notice, the primary consideration is the statement of reasons for an action. **With termination of a teacher's contract, school boards must bring specific charges against the teacher,** including not only the factual basis for the charges but also the names of accusers. State laws may impose further specifications, such as North Dakota's requirement that reasons for termination in the notice must be based on issues raised in prior written evaluations.[24] If the state law identifies grounds for dismissal, charges also must be based on the statutory causes. But a teacher cannot be forced to defend against vague and indefinite charges that simply restate the statutory categories, such as incompetency or neglect of duty. Notice must include specific accusations to enable the teacher to prepare a proper defense. Finally, only charges identified in the notice can form the basis for dismissal.

Hearing

In addition to notice, **some type of hearing is required *before* an employer makes the initial termination decision;** posttermination hearings do not satisfy federal constitutional due process requirements.[25] Courts have not prescribed in detail the procedures to be

---

[23]*See* Hoschler v. Sacramento City Unified Sch. Dist., 57 Cal. Rptr. 3d 115 (Ct. App. 2007) (concluding that a statute silent on the method of delivery required personal delivery rather than certified mail); Clark County Sch. Dist. v. Riley, 14 P.3d 22 (Nev. 2000) (finding that only four days' notice with no mention of the right to a hearing violated a statute requiring 15 days' notice and the right to a hearing); Morrison v. Bd. of Educ., 47 P.3d 888 (Okla. Civ. App. 2002) (ruling that notice did not conform to statutory requirements; notice was sent by the superintendent rather than the school board, and it was received on April 10 rather than prior to that date).

[24]Hoffner v. Bismarck Pub. Sch. Dist., 589 N.W.2d 195 (N.D. 1999).

[25]Cleveland Bd. of Educ. v. Loudermill, 470 U.S. 532 (1985). *See, e.g.*, Belas v. Juniata County Sch. Dist., 202 Fed. App'x 585 (3d Cir. 2006); Jefferson v. Jefferson County Pub. Sch. Sys., 360 F.3d 583 (6th Cir. 2004); Finch v. Fort Bend Indep. Sch. Dist., 333 F.3d 555 (5th Cir. 2003).

followed in administrative hearings. Basically, the fundamental constitutional requirement is fair play—that is, an opportunity to be heard at a meaningful time and in a meaningful manner. Beyond this general requirement, the specific aspects of a hearing are influenced by the circumstances of the case, with the potential for grievous losses necessitating more extensive safeguards. According to the Missouri Supreme Court, a hearing generally should include a meaningful opportunity to be heard, to state one's position, to present witnesses, and to cross-examine witnesses; the accused also has the right to counsel and access to written reports in advance of the hearing.[26] Implicit in these rudimentary requirements are the assumptions that the hearing will be conducted by an impartial decision maker and will result in a decision based on the evidence presented. This section examines issues that may arise in adversarial hearings before the school board.

Adequate Notice of Hearing.   As noted, due process rights afford an individual the opportunity to be heard at a meaningful time. This implies sufficient time between notice of the hearing and the scheduled meeting. Unless state law designates a time period, the school board can establish a reasonable date for the hearing, taking into consideration the specific facts and circumstances. In a termination action, the school board would be expected to provide ample time for the teacher to prepare a defense; however, the teacher bears the burden of requesting additional time if the length of notice is insufficient to prepare an adequate response.

Waiver of Hearing.   Although a hearing is an essential element of due process, a teacher can waive this right by failing to request a hearing, refusing to attend, or walking out. Voluntary resignation of a position also waives an individual's entitlement to a hearing.[27] In some states, a hearing before the school board may be waived by an employee's election of an alternative hearing procedure such as a grievance mechanism or an impartial referee. For example, the Third Circuit held that an employee's choice of *either* a hearing before the school board *or* arbitration under the collective bargaining agreement met the constitutional requirements of due process; the school board was not required to provide the individual a hearing in addition to the arbitration proceeding.[28]

Impartial Hearing.   A central question raised regarding hearings is the school board's impartiality as a hearing body. This issue arises because school boards often perform multiple functions in a hearing; they may investigate the allegations against a teacher, initiate the proceedings, and render the final judgment. Teachers have contended that such expansive involvement violates their right to an unbiased decision maker. Rejecting the idea that combining the adjudicative and investigative functions violates due process rights, courts

---

[26]Valter v. Orchard Farm Sch. Dist., 541 S.W.2d 550 (Mo. 1976). *See also* McClure v. Indep. Sch. Dist. No. 16, 228 F.3d 1205 (10th Cir. 2000) (holding that a teacher was deprived of due process rights when she was not allowed to cross-examine witnesses who provided testimony by affidavit at her termination hearing).

[27]*See, e.g.*, Kirkland v. St. Vrain Valley Sch. Dist. No. RE1J, 464 F.3d 1182 (10th Cir. 2006); Cross v. Monett R-I Bd. of Educ., 431 F.3d 606 (8th Cir. 2005).

[28]Pederson v. S. Williamsport Area Sch. Dist., 677 F.2d 312 (3d Cir. 1982).

generally have determined that prior knowledge of the facts does not disqualify school board members.[29] In addition, the fact that the board makes the initial decision to terminate employment does not render subsequent review impermissibly biased. Neither is a hearing prejudiced by a limited, preliminary inquiry to determine if there is a basis for terminating a teacher. Since hearings are costly and time consuming, such a preliminary investigation may save time as well as potential embarrassment

In *Hortonville Joint School District No. 1 v. Hortonville Education Association*, the United States Supreme Court firmly established that **the school board is a proper review body to conduct dismissal hearings.**[30] The Court held that a school board's involvement in collective negotiations did not disqualify it as an impartial hearing board in the subsequent dismissal of striking teachers. The Court noted that "a showing that the Board was 'involved' in the events preceding this decision, in light of the important interest in leaving with the board the power given by the state legislature, is not enough to overcome the presumption of honesty and integrity in policymakers with decision-making power."[31]

Although the school board is the proper hearing body, bias on the part of the board or its members is constitutionally unacceptable. A teacher challenging the impartiality of the board has the burden of proving actual, not merely potential, bias. This requires the teacher to show more than board members' predecision involvement or prior knowledge of the issues.[32] A high probability of bias, however, can be shown if a board member has a personal interest in the outcome of the hearing or has suffered personal abuse or criticism from a teacher.

Evidence.   Under teacher tenure laws, the burden of proof is placed on the school board to show cause for dismissal. The standard of proof generally applied to administrative bodies is to produce a *preponderance of evidence*. Administrative hearings are not held to the more stringent standards applied in criminal proceedings (i.e., clear and convincing evidence beyond a reasonable doubt). Proof by a preponderance of evidence simply indicates that the majority of the evidence supports the board's decision or, as the New York high court stated, "such relevant evidence as a reasonable mind might accept as adequate to support a conclusion."[33] If the board fails to meet this burden of proof, the judiciary will not uphold the termination decision. For example, the Nebraska Supreme Court, in overturning a school board's dismissal decision, concluded that dissatisfaction of parents and school board members was not sufficient evidence to substantiate incompetency charges against a

---

[29]*See* Withrow v. Larkin, 421 U.S. 35 (1975). *See also* Yukadinovich v. Bd. of Sch. Trs., 278 F.3d 693 (7th Cir. 2002) (concluding that a teacher did not establish bias in a termination hearing held in front of the school board that he had publicly criticized); Moore v. Bd. of Educ., 134 F.3d 781 (6th Cir. 1998) (finding that a superintendent's dual roles as presiding officer at the hearing and investigator did not deprive the teacher of due process).

[30]426 U.S. 482 (1976).

[31]*Id.* at 496–497.

[32]*See, e.g.,* Beischel v. Stone Bank Sch. Dist., 362 F.3d 430 (7th Cir. 2004); Martin v. Sch. Dist. No. 394, 393 F. Supp. 2d 1028 (D. Idaho 2005).

[33]Altsheler v. Bd. of Educ., 464 N.E.2d 979, 980 (N.Y. 1984).

teacher who had received above-average performance evaluations during her entire term of employment.[34]

Only relevant, well-documented evidence presented at the hearing can be the basis for the board's decision. Unlike formal judicial proceedings, hearsay evidence may be admissible in administrative hearings. Courts have held that such evidence provides the background necessary for understanding the situation. Comments and complaints of parents have been considered relevant, but hearsay statements of students generally have been given little weight.[35]

■ ■ ■ ■ ■ ▬▬▬▬▬▬▬▬▬▬▬▬▬▬▬▬▬▬▬▬▬▬▬▬

DISMISSAL FOR CAUSE

Causes for dismissal vary widely among the states, but usually include such grounds as incompetency, immorality, insubordination, unprofessional conduct, neglect of duty, and other good and just cause.

Tenure laws are designed to assure competent teachers continued employment as long as their performance is satisfactory. **With the protection of tenure, a teacher can be dismissed only for cause, and only in accordance with the procedures specified by law.**[36] Tenure rights accrue under state laws and therefore must be interpreted in light of each state's provisions.

When grounds for dismissal of a permanent teacher are identified by statute, a school board cannot base dismissal on reasons other than those specified. To cover unexpected matters, statutes often include a catchall phrase such as "other good and just cause." Causes included in statutes vary considerably among states and range from an extensive listing of individual grounds to a simple statement that dismissal must be based on cause. The most frequently cited causes are incompetency, immorality, and insubordination.

Since grounds for dismissal are determined by statute, it is difficult to provide generalizations that apply to all teachers. The causes are broad in scope and application; in fact, individual causes often have been attacked for impermissible vagueness. It is not unusual to find dismissal cases with similar factual situations based on different grounds. In addition, several grounds often are introduced and supported in a single termination case. Illustrative case law is examined here in relation to the more frequently cited grounds for dismissal.

[34]Schulz v. Bd. of Educ., 315 N.W.2d 633 (Neb. 1982). *See also* Weston v. Indep. Sch. Dist. No. 35, 170 P.3d 539 (Okla. 2007) (ordering the school district to reinstate a teacher because officials did not prove by a preponderance of evidence that dismissal was warranted).

[35]*See, e.g.*, Daily v. Bd. of Educ., 588 N.W.2d 813 (Neb. 1999).

[36]*See* Michael Long, "Studying the 'Dismissal Gap': Research on Teacher Incompetence and Dismissals," *Macro International* (March 2007). In a paper presented at the National Center for Education Statistics's (NCES) Symposium on Data Issues in Teacher Supply and Demand, Long synthesized research on teacher dismissals and reported on his analysis of NCES's Schools and Staffing Survey with both showing that less than 1 percent of teachers are terminated each year.

Incompetency

Incompetency is legally defined as the "lack of ability, legal qualifications, or fitness to discharge the required duty."[37] Although incompetency has been challenged as unconstitutionally vague, courts have found the word sufficiently precise to give fair warning of prohibited conduct. These cases often involve issues relating to teaching methods, grading procedures, classroom management, and professional relationships.

Dismissals for incompetency are generally based on several factors or a pattern of behavior rather than isolated incidents. In a Minnesota case, indicators of incompetency included poor rapport with students, inappropriate use of class time, irrational grading of students, and lack of student progress.[38] A Pennsylvania court interpreted incompetency as deficiencies in personality, composure, judgment, and attitude that have a detrimental effect on a teacher's performance.[39] Incompetency in this case was supported by evidence that the teacher was a disruptive influence in the school; could not maintain control of students; and failed to maintain her composure in dealing with students, other professionals, and parents.

Termination for incompetency usually requires school officials systematically to document a teacher's performance. Providing opportunities and support for a teacher to achieve expected performance standards can be an important component in substantiating that a teacher had adequate notice of deficiencies.

Immorality

Immorality, one of the most frequently cited causes for dismissal, is typically not defined in state laws. The judiciary, in defining the word, has tended to interpret *immorality* broadly as unacceptable conduct that affects a teacher's fitness. **The teacher is viewed as an exemplar whose conduct is influential in shaping the lives of young students, so educators are held to a higher level of discretion than required for the general public.**

Sexually related conduct *per se* between a teacher and student has consistently been held to constitute immoral conduct justifying termination of employment. The Supreme Court of Colorado stated that when a teacher engages in sexually provocative or exploitative conduct with students, "a strong presumption of unfitness arises against the teacher."[40] Similarly, a Washington appellate court found that a male teacher's sexual relationship with a minor student justified dismissal.[41] The court declined to hold that an adverse effect on fitness to teach must be shown. Rather, the court concluded that when a teacher and a minor student are involved, the board might reasonably decide that such conduct is harmful to the school district.

---

[37]Henry Black, *Black's Law Dictionary*, 8th ed. (St. Paul, MN: West, 2004).

[38]Whaley v. Anoka-Hennepin Indep. Sch. Dist. No. 11, 325 N.W.2d 128 (Minn. 1982).

[39]Hamburg v. N. Penn Sch. Dist., 484 A.2d 867 (Pa. Commw. Ct. 1984).

[40]Weissman v. Bd. of Educ., 547 P.2d 1267, 1273 (Colo. 1976).

[41]Denton v. S. Kitsap Sch. Dist. No. 402, 516 P.2d 1080 (Wash. Ct. App. 1973). *See also* DeMichele v. Greenburgh Cent. Sch. Dist. No. 7, 167 F.3d 784 (2d Cir. 1999) (ruling that termination of a teacher for sexual misconduct with students occurring 24 years earlier did not violate his due process rights).

In addition to sexual improprieties with students, which clearly are grounds for dismissal, other conduct that sets a bad example for students may be considered immoral under the "role model" standard. Courts, however, generally have required school officials to show that misconduct or a particular lifestyle has an adverse impact on fitness to teach. They have recognized that allowing dismissal merely based on a showing of immoral behavior without consideration of the nexus between the conduct and fitness to teach would be an unwarranted intrusion on a teacher's right to privacy. For example, an Ohio appellate court found that school officials had not produced evidence to show that an adulterous affair with another school employee constituted immorality when it did not have a hostile impact on the school community.[42]

Teachers' sexual orientation has been an issue in several controversial dismissal cases. Although these cases often have raised constitutional issues related to freedom of expression and privacy, courts also have confronted the question of whether sexual orientation *per se* is evidence of unfitness to teach or whether it must be shown that this lifestyle impairs teaching effectiveness.[43] Courts have rendered diverse opinions regarding gay, lesbian, bisexual, and transgender (GLBT) educators. According to the Supreme Court of California, immoral or unprofessional conduct or moral turpitude must be related to unfitness to teach to justify termination.[44] Yet, the Supreme Court of Washington upheld the dismissal of a teacher based simply on the knowledge of his homosexuality.[45] The court feared that public controversy could interfere with the teacher's classroom effectiveness. In recent years, however, courts have been reluctant to support the dismissal of a GLBT educator simply because the school board does not approve of a particular private lifestyle. For example, an Ohio federal court concluded that the nonrenewal of a teacher because of his homosexuality did not bear a rational relationship to a legitimate government purpose, thereby violating the Equal Protection Clause.[46]

Whereas many teacher terminations for immorality involve sexual conduct, immorality is broader in meaning and scope. As one court noted, it covers conduct that "is hostile to the welfare of the school community."[47] Such hostile conduct has included, among other things, dishonest acts, criminal conduct, and drug-related conduct. Specific actions substantiating charges of immorality have included misrepresenting absences from school as illness,[48] being involved in the sale of illegal drugs,[49] pleading guilty to

---

[42]Bertolini v. City Sch. Dist. Bd. of Educ., 744 N.E.2d 1245 (Ohio Ct. App. 2000). *But see* Parker-Bigback v. St. Labre Sch., 7 P.3d 361 (Mont. 2000) (upholding termination of a counselor for cohabitation with a man to whom she was not married).

[43]*See* text accompanying note 32, Chapter 11, for a discussion of claims of discrimination based on sexual orientation; note 93, Chapter 10, for a discussion of constitutionally protected privacy rights.

[44]Morrison v. State Bd. of Educ., 461 P.2d 375 (Cal. 1969).

[45]Gaylord v. Tacoma Sch. Dist. No. 10, 559 P.2d 1340 (Wash. 1977).

[46]Glover v. Williamsburg Local Sch. Dist., 20 F. Supp. 2d 1160 (S.D. Ohio 1998).

[47]Jarvella v. Willoughby-Eastlake City Sch. Dist., 233 N.E.2d 143, 145 (Ohio 1967).

[48]Riverview Sch. Dist. v. Riverview Educ. Ass'n, 639 A.2d 974 (Pa. Commw. Ct. 1994).

[49]Woo v. Putnam County Bd. of Educ., 504 S.E.2d 644 (W. Va. 1998).

grand larceny,[50] altering student transcripts,[51] and reporting to school under the influence of marijuana.[52]

Although *immorality* is an abstract concept that can encompass broad-ranging behavior, it is understood to refer to actions that violate moral standards and render a teacher unfit to teach. Courts consistently hold that school officials must link the challenged conduct to impairment of the teacher's effectiveness in the classroom to justify termination for immorality.

Insubordination

Insubordination is generally defined as the willful disregard of or refusal to obey school regulations and official orders. Teachers can be dismissed for violation of administrative regulations and policies even though classroom performance is satisfactory; school officials are not required to establish a relationship between the conduct and fitness to teach.

With the plethora of regulations enacted by school districts, wide diversity is found in types of behavior adjudicated as insubordination. Dismissals based on insubordination have been upheld in cases involving refusal to abide by specific school directives, unwillingness to cooperate with superiors, unauthorized absences, and numerous other actions. Since conduct is measured against the existence of a rule or policy, a school board may more readily document insubordination than most other legal causes for dismissal.

Many state laws and court decisions require that acts be "willful and persistent" to be considered insubordinate. A Florida teacher's continued refusal to provide lesson plans during school absences resulted in termination for insubordination. A Florida appellate court, upholding the dismissal, noted insubordination under state law as "constant or continuing intentional refusal to obey a direct order, reasonable in nature, and given by and with proper authority."[53] In some instances, however, a severe or substantial single incident may be adequate for dismissal action. For example, state courts upheld a Missouri teacher's termination for refusal to teach an assigned course[54] and a Colorado teacher's dismissal for showing an R-rated movie without submitting a request for approval under the district's "controversial materials" policy.[55]

Teachers cannot ignore reasonable directives and policies of administrators or school boards. If the school board has prohibited corporal punishment or prescribed procedures for its administration, teachers must strictly adhere to board requirements. In upholding the termination of a Colorado teacher, the state supreme court ruled that tapping a student on the head with a three-foot pointer supported termination when the teacher had been warned and disciplined previously for using physical force in violation of school

---

[50]Green v. N.Y. City Dep't of Educ., 793 N.Y.S.2d 405 (App. Div. 2005).

[51]Hill v. Indep. Sch. Dist. No. 25, 57 P.3d 882 (Okla. Civ. App. 2002).

[52]Younge v. Bd. of Educ., 788 N.E.2d 1153 (Ill. App. Ct. 2003).

[53]Dolega v. Sch. Bd., 840 So. 2d 445, 446 (Fla. Dist. Ct. App. 2003).

[54]McLaughlin v. Bd. of Educ., 659 S.W.2d 249 (Mo. Ct. App. 1983).

[55]Bd. of Educ. v. Wilder, 960 P.2d 695 (Colo. 1998).

district policy.[56] The Eleventh Circuit found that insubordination was established when a teacher refused to undergo a urinalysis drug test within two hours of the discovery of marijuana in her car in the school parking lot as required by school board policy.[57] The Eighth Circuit upheld the dismissal of a teacher for violating a school board policy that prohibited students' use of profanity in the classroom; students had used profanity in various creative-writing assignments such as plays and poems.[58] The key determinant generally is whether the teacher has persisted in disobeying a *reasonable* school policy or directive.

Unprofessional Conduct

Some states identify either unprofessional conduct or conduct unbecoming a teacher as cause for dismissal. A teacher's activities both inside and outside of school can be used to substantiate this charge when it interferes with teaching effectiveness. Dismissals for unprofessional conduct, neglect of duty, and unfitness to teach often are based on quite similar facts. Facts that establish unprofessional conduct in one state may be deemed neglect of duty in another state. Most courts have defined *unprofessional conduct* as actions directly related to the fitness of educators to perform in their professional capacity. The working definition adopted by the Supreme Court of Nebraska specified unprofessional conduct as breaching the rules or ethical code of a profession or "unbecoming a member in good standing of a profession." Under this definition, the court reasoned that a teacher engaged in unprofessional conduct when he "smacked" a student on the head hard enough to make the student cry, thereby violating the state prohibition against corporal punishment.[59]

Courts have upheld dismissal for unprofessional conduct based on several grounds, such as taking photos of a female student nude above the waist,[60] engaging in sexual harassment of female students,[61] wrapping a student in an electrical cord and verbally humiliating him in front of other students,[62] losing complete control of the classroom,[63] showing a sexually explicit film to a classroom of adolescents without previewing it,[64] and stealing pills labeled methylphenidate (generic name for Ritalin) from the school office.[65] As with dismissals based on incompetency, **courts often require prior warning that the behavior may result in dismissal.**

---

[56]Bd. of Educ. v. Flaming, 938 P.2d 151 (Colo. 1997).

[57]Hearn v. Bd. of Pub. Educ., 191 F.3d 1329 (11th Cir. 1999).

[58]Lacks v. Ferguson Reorganized Sch. Dist. R-2, 147 F.3d 718 (8th Cir. 1998).

[59]Daily v. Bd. of Educ., 588 N.W.2d 813, 824 (Neb. 1999). Following a hearing to consider termination of employment, the school board instead gave the teacher a 30-day suspension.

[60]Dixon v. Clem, 492 F.3d 665 (6th Cir. 2007).

[61]Conward v. Cambridge Sch. Comm., 171 F.3d 12 (1st Cir. 1999).

[62]Johanson v. Bd. of Educ., 589 N.W.2d 815 (Neb. 1999).

[63]Walker v. Highlands County Sch. Bd., 752 So. 2d 127 (Fla. Dist. Ct. App. 2000).

[64]Fowler v. Bd. of Educ., 819 F.2d 657 (6th Cir. 1987).

[65]Lannom v. Bd. of Educ., No. M1999-00137-COA-R3-CV, 2000 Tenn. Ct. App. LEXIS 133 (Mar. 6, 2000).

Neglect of Duty

Neglect of duty arises when an educator fails to carry out assigned duties. This may involve an intentional omission or may result from ineffectual performance. In a Colorado case, neglect of duty was found when a teacher failed to discipline students consistent with school policy.[66] Similarly, the Louisiana high court ruled that a teacher repeatedly sending unescorted students to the principal's office in violation of school policy substantiated willful neglect of duty.[67] The Oregon appellate court concluded that a teacher's failure to maintain "harmonious relations with students, parents, staff and other teachers" constituted neglect of duty.[68]

The United States Supreme Court upheld the dismissal of an Oklahoma teacher for "willful neglect of duty" in failing to comply with the school board's continuing education requirement.[69] For a period of time, lack of compliance was dealt with through denial of salary increases. Upon enactment of a state law requiring salary increases for all teachers, the board notified teachers that noncompliance with the requirement would result in termination. Affirming the board's action, the Supreme Court found the sanction of dismissal to be rationally related to the board's objective of improving its teaching force through continuing education requirements.

The Nebraska high court, however, held that a superintendent's failure to file a funding form did not constitute neglect of duty to support the termination of his contract.[70] Similarly, a Louisiana appellate court held that a teacher's showing of an R-rated film did not warrant dismissal for neglect of duty and incompetence.[71] The Louisiana Supreme Court concluded that a teacher bringing a loaded gun to school in his car did not substantiate willful neglect of duty to support termination.[72] The court commented that his action was certainly a mistake and possibly endangered students, but it did not involve a failure to follow orders or an identifiable school policy required for dismissal under state law.

Teachers can be discharged for neglect of duty when their performance does not meet expected professional standards in the school system. Often charges relate to a failure to perform but also can be brought for ineffective performance. Again, as with other

---

[66]Bd. of Educ. v. Flaming, 938 P.2d 151 (Colo. 1997). *See also* Flickinger v. Lebanon Sch. Dist., 898 A.2d 62 (Pa. Commw. Ct. 2006) (concluding that the principal's failure to respond immediately to a report of a gun in the middle school established willful neglect of duty; school procedures specified that such a crisis situation must be handled without delay).

[67]Wise v. Bossier Parish Sch. Bd., 851 So. 2d 1090 (La. 2003).

[68]Bellairs v. Beaverton Sch. Dist., 136 P.3d 93 (Or. Ct. App. 2006).

[69]Harrah Indep. Sch. Dist. v. Martin, 440 U.S. 194 (1979).

[70]Boss v. Fillmore Sch. Dist. No. 19, 559 N.W.2d 448 (Neb. 1997). *But see* Smith v. Bullock County Bd. of Educ., 906 So. 2d 938 (Ala. Civ. App. 2004) (ruling that a principal's failure to establish procedures to prevent the theft of about $25,000 of athletic funds was neglect of duty).

[71]Jones v. Rapides Parish Sch. Bd., 634 So. 2d 1197 (La. Ct. App. 1993).

[72]Howard v. W. Baton Rouge Parish Sch. Bd., 793 So. 2d 153 (La. 2001). *But see* Spurlock v. E. Feliciana Parish Sch., 885 So. 2d 1225 (La. Ct. App. 2004) (ruling that a teacher could be terminated for willful neglect of duty for making misbehaving second grade students simulate a sex act in front of the class—the teacher did not violate a specific policy or fail to follow orders; however, the court opined that she should have known that her egregious behavior was improper).

efforts to terminate employment, documentation must substantiate that performance is unacceptable.

Other Good and Just Cause

Not unexpectedly, *other good and just cause* as grounds for dismissal often has been challenged as vague and overbroad. Courts have been faced with the task of determining whether the phrase's meaning is limited to the specific grounds enumerated in the statute or whether it is a separate, expanded cause. An Indiana appellate court interpreted it as permitting termination for reasons other than those specified in the tenure law, if evidence indicated that the board's decision was based on "good cause."[73] As such, dismissal of a teacher convicted of a misdemeanor was upheld even though the teacher had no prior indication that such conduct was sufficient cause. A Connecticut court found *good cause* to be any ground that is put forward in good faith that is not "arbitrary, irrational, unreasonable, or irrelevant to the board's task of building up and maintaining an efficient school system."[74] Terminating a teacher for altering students' responses on state mandatory proficiency tests was held to be relevant to that task.

The Supreme Court of Iowa applied a statute permitting teachers to be terminated during the contract year for "just cause" to support the termination of a teacher for shoplifting.[75] Although the teacher claimed that her compulsion to shoplift was related to a mental illness, the court found substantial evidence to terminate the teacher's employment, weighing the teacher's position as a role model, the character of the illness, and the school board's needs. In a subsequent case, the Iowa high court ruled "just cause" existed to terminate a teacher who had knowledge of her son and his high school friends drinking at a campsite on her property. She failed to monitor their activities, and four students who left to buy more beer died in a car crash. The court agreed with the school board that the teacher's effectiveness as a role model was significantly diminished.[76]

Reduction-in-Force

In addition to dismissal for causes related to teacher performance and fitness, legislation generally permits the release of teachers for reasons related to declining enrollment, financial exigency, and school district consolidation. Whereas most state statutes provide for such terminations, some states have adopted legislation that specifies the basis for selection

[73]Gary Teachers Union, Local No. 4, AFT v. Sch. City of Gary, 332 N.E.2d 256, 263 (Ind. Ct. App. 1975). *See also* Hierlmeier v. N. Judson-San Pierre Bd., 730 N.E.2d 821 (Ind. Ct. App. 2000) (ruling that sexual harassment of female students and other inappropriate conduct toward students substantiated good and just cause for termination). *But see* Trs. Lincoln County Sch. Dist. No. 13 v. Holden, 754 P.2d 506 (Mont. 1988) (concluding that two instances of calling students crude names did not support good cause for dismissal).

[74]Hanes v. Bd. of Educ., 783 A.2d 1, 6 (Conn. App. Ct. 2001). *See also* Oleske v. Hilliard City Sch. Dist., 764 N.E.2d 1110, 1116 (Ohio Ct. App. 2001) (concluding that a teacher's dismissal for telling dirty jokes and calling another teacher an offensive name in front of students constituted a "fairly serious matter" supporting good and just cause for dismissal).

[75]Bd. of Dirs. v. Davies, 489 N.W.2d 19 (Iowa 1992).

[76]Walthart v. Bd. of Dirs., 694 N.W.2d 740 (Iowa 2005).

of released teachers, procedures to be followed, and provisions for reinstatement. These terminations, characterized as *reductions-in-force* (RIF), also may be governed by board policies and negotiated bargaining agreements.

Unlike other termination cases, the employee challenging a RIF decision shoulders the burden of proof. There is a presumption that the board has acted in good faith with permissible motives. Legal controversies in this area usually involve questions related to the necessity for the reductions, board compliance with mandated procedures, and possible subterfuge for impermissible termination (such as denial of constitutional rights, subversion of tenure rights, discrimination).

If statutory or contractual restrictions exist for teacher layoffs, there must be substantial compliance with the provisions. One of the provisions most frequently included is a method for selecting teachers for release. **In general, reductions are based on seniority, and a tenured teacher, rather than a nontenured teacher, must be retained if both are qualified to fill the same position.** State statutes usually require that both licensure and seniority be considered; a teacher lacking a license in the area would not be permitted to teach, while a permanent teacher with proper credentials, but less seniority, was dismissed. Along with seniority, merit-rating systems may be included in the determination of reductions. School districts in Pennsylvania use a combination of ratings and seniority; ratings are the primary determinant unless no substantial difference exists in ratings, and then seniority becomes the basis for the layoff.[77] Both the Montana and Nebraska high courts concluded that school boards have broad discretion in deciding what factors to use in their RIF policies and how to weight those factors.[78] Guidelines or criteria established by state or local education agencies, however, must be applied in a uniform and nondiscriminatory manner. For example, under New Mexico law, the school board must determine that no other positions exist for teachers targeted for release.[79]

The Fourteenth Amendment requires procedural protections in dismissals for cause, but courts have not clearly defined the due process requirements for RIF. The Eighth Circuit noted that tenured teachers possess a property interest in continued employment, and thereby must be provided notice and an opportunity to be heard.[80] Specific procedural protections for employees vary according to interpretations of state law, bargaining agreements, and board policy. The court emphasized that the law protected the released teacher, who, subject to qualifications, was entitled to the next vacancy. Similarly, a Pennsylvania commonwealth court held that a hearing must be provided to assure the teacher (1) that termination was for reasons specified by law and (2) that the board followed the correct statutory procedures in selecting the teacher for discharge.[81]

State law or other policies may give preference to teachers who are released because of a reduction-in-force. Typically, under such requirements, a school board cannot hire a nonemployee until each qualified teacher on the preferred recall list is reemployed.

---

[77]Pa. Stat. Ann. tit. 24 § 11-1124 (2008).

[78]Scobey Sch. Dist. v. Radakovich, 135 P.3d 778 (Mont. 2006); Nickel v. Saline County Sch. Dist. No. 163, 559 N.W.2d 480 (Neb. 1997).

[79]Aguilera v. Bd. of Educ., 132 P.3d 587 (N.M. 2006).

[80]Boner v. Eminence R-1 Sch. Dist., 55 F.3d 1339 (8th Cir. 1995).

[81]Fatscher v. Bd. of Sch. Dirs., 367 A.2d 1130 (Pa. Commw. Ct. 1977).

Although statutes often require that a teacher be appointed to the first vacancy for which licensed and qualified, courts have held that reappointment is still at the board's discretion. In addition, a board is generally not obligated to realign or rearrange teaching assignments to create a position for a released teacher.

■ ■ ■ ■ ■

REMEDIES FOR VIOLATIONS OF PROTECTED RIGHTS

Wrongfully terminated employees may be entitled to compensatory and punitive damages, reinstatement with back pay, and attorneys' fees for the violation of their constitutional rights.

When it is established that school districts or officials have violated an employee's rights protected by federal or state law, several remedies are available to the aggrieved individual. In some situations, the employee may seek a court injunction ordering the unlawful action to cease. This remedy might be sought if a school board has unconstitutionally imposed restraints on teachers' expression. Where terminations, transfers, or other adverse employment consequences have been unconstitutionally imposed, courts will order school districts to return the affected employees to their original status with back pay.

In addition to these remedies, educators are increasingly bringing suits to recover damages for actions that violate their federally protected rights. Suits are usually based on 42 U.S.C. Section 1983, which provides that any person who acts under color of state law to deprive another individual of rights secured by the federal Constitution or laws is subject to personal liability. This law, which was originally enacted in 1871 to prevent discrimination against African American citizens, has been broadly interpreted as conferring liability on school personnel and school districts, not only for racial discrimination but also for actions that may result in the impairment of other federally protected rights.[82]

Suits alleging Section 1983 violations can be initiated in federal or state courts, and exhaustion of state administrative remedies is not required before initiating a federal suit. When a federal law authorizes an exclusive nondamages remedy, however, a Section 1983 suit is precluded.[83] This section focuses on the liability of school officials and districts for the violation of protected rights and on the types of damages available to aggrieved employees.

Liability of School Officials

Under Section 1983, **public school employees acting under color of state law can be held personally liable for actions abridging students' or teachers' federal rights.** The Supreme Court, however, has recognized that government officials cannot be held

---

[82]Maine v. Thiboutot, 448 U.S. 1 (1980).

[83]*See, e.g.*, Gonzaga Univ. v. Doe, 536 U.S. 496 (2002); Blessing v. Freestone, 520 U.S. 329 (1997).

liable under Section 1983 for the actions of their subordinates, thus rejecting the doctrine of *respondeat superior*, even when school officials have general supervisory authority over the activities of the wrongdoers. In order to be held liable, the officials must have personally participated in, or had personal knowledge of, the unlawful acts or promulgated official policy under which the acts were taken.[84] Furthermore, the Supreme Court in 1998 ruled that public officials are absolutely immune from suit under Section 1983 for their legislative activities.[85] These actions involve discretionary policy-making decisions and enactment of regulations, often with budgetary implications. Subsequently, courts have clarified that employment decisions related to individual employees (such as hiring, dismissal, or demotions) are administrative, not legislative, in nature.[86]

The Supreme Court has recognized that in some circumstances school officials can claim qualified immunity to shield them from personal liability when they have acted in good faith. The Court has declared that "government officials performing discretionary functions generally are shielded from liability for civil damages insofar as their conduct does not violate clearly established statutory or constitutional rights of which a reasonable person would have known."[87] The Second Circuit, noting that unlawfulness must be apparent, stated:

> A right is clearly established if the contours of the right are sufficiently clear that a reasonable official would understand that what he or she is doing violates that right. The question is not what a lawyer would learn or intuit from researching case law, but what a reasonable person in the [school official's] position should know about the constitutionality of the conduct.[88]

The Seventh Circuit emphasized that the individual alleging violation of a clearly established right bears the burden of demonstrating the existence of the right.[89] In determining whether a right is clearly established, the appellate court stated that first it examines controlling Supreme Court precedent and its own circuit decisions related to the case and then reviews all relevant case law. According to the court, a split among courts in assessing similar conduct points to unsettled law.

School officials have been denied qualified immunity when they disregard well-established legal principles in areas such as due process, protected expression, and privacy.[90]

---

[84]*See* Am. Mfrs. Mut. Ins. Co. v. Sullivan, 526 U.S. 40 (1999); Rizzo v. Goode, 423 U.S. 362 (1976).

[85]Bogan v. Scott-Harris, 523 U.S. 44 (1998).

[86]*See, e.g.*, Canary v. Osborn, 211 F.3d 324 (6th Cir. 2000); Harhay v. Town of Ellington Bd. of Educ., 323 F.3d 206 (2d Cir. 2003).

[87]Harlow v. Fitzgerald, 457 U.S. 800, 818 (1982). More recently, the Supreme Court has emphasized that the overriding issue is whether the law at the time that an individual acted gave "clear and fair warning" that rights were established. Hope v. Pelzer, 536 U.S. 730 (2002).

[88]McCullough v. Wyandanch Union Free Sch. Dist., 187 F.3d 272 (2d Cir. 1999).

[89]Denius v. Dunlap, 209 F.3d 944 (7th Cir. 2000). *See, e.g.*, Beard v. Whitmore Lake Sch. Dist., 402 F.3d 598 (6th Cir. 2005); Thomas v. Roberts, 323 F.3d 950 (11th Cir. 2003).

[90]*See, e.g.*, Evans-Marshall v. Bd. of Educ., 428 F.3d 223 (6th Cir. 2005); Baird v. Bd. of Educ., 389 F.3d 685 (7th Cir. 2004); Merkle v. Upper Dublin Sch. Dist., 211 F.3d 782 (3d Cir. 2000).

Liability of School Districts

In 1978, the Supreme Court ruled that local governments are considered "persons" under Section 1983.[91] In essence, **school districts can be assessed damages when action taken pursuant to official policy violates federally protected rights.**

The governmental unit (like the individual official), however, cannot be held liable under the *respondeat superior* doctrine for the wrongful acts committed solely by its employees. Liability under Section 1983 against the agency can be imposed only when execution of official policy by an individual with final authority impairs a federally protected right.[92] The Supreme Court has held that a single egregious act of a low-level employee does not infer an official policy of inadequate training and supervision,[93] but an agency can be liable if "deliberate indifference" in ensuring adequately trained employees is established.[94]

Although school officials can plead good faith immunity, this defense is not available to school districts. The Supreme Court has ruled that school districts and other governmental subdivisions cannot claim qualified immunity based on good faith actions of their officials. The Court acknowledged that under certain circumstances sovereign immunity can shield municipal corporations from state tort suits, but concluded that Section 1983 abrogated governmental immunity in situations involving the impairment of federally protected rights.[95]

To avoid liability for constitutional violations, school districts have introduced claims of Eleventh Amendment immunity. The Eleventh Amendment, explicitly prohibiting citizens of one state from bringing suit against another state without its consent, has been interpreted also as precluding federal lawsuits against a state by its own citizens.[96] A state can waive this immunity by specifically consenting to be sued, and Congress can abrogate state immunity through legislation enacted to enforce the Fourteenth Amendment. Such congressional intent, however, must be explicit in the federal legislation.[97]

School districts have asserted Eleventh Amendment protection based on the fact that they perform a state function. Admittedly, education is a state function, but it does not necessarily follow that school districts gain Eleventh Amendment immunity against claims of constitutional abridgments. For the Eleventh Amendment to be invoked in a suit against a

---

[91]Monell v. Dep't of Soc. Servs., 436 U.S. 658 (1978).

[92]*See, e.g.*, Collins v. City of Harker Heights, 503 U.S. 115 (1992); Langford v. City of Atl. City, 235 F.3d 845 (3d Cir. 2000); Seamons v. Snow, 206 F.3d 1021 (10th Cir. 2000).

[93]Okla. City v. Tuttle, 471 U.S. 808 (1985). *See, e.g.*, Back v. Hastings on Hudson Union Free Sch. Dist., 365 F.3d 107 (2d Cir. 2004); Wilson *ex rel.* Adams v. Cahokia Sch. Dist. No. 187, 470 F. Supp. 2d 897 (S.D. Ill. 2007).

[94]City of Canton, Ohio v. Harris, 489 U.S. 378 (1989).

[95]Owen v. City of Independence, Mo., 445 U.S. 622 (1980). *See* text accompanying note 30, Chapter 2, for a discussion of governmental immunity under tort law.

[96]*See* Hans v. Louisiana, 134 U.S. 1 (1890). *See also* Will v. Mich. Dep't of State Police, 491 U.S. 58 (1989) (holding that § 1983 does not permit a suit against a state; Congress did not intend the word *person* to include states).

[97]For example, the Supreme Court held that the Family Educational Rights and Privacy Act of 1974 does not explicitly confer individually enforceable rights. Gonzaga Univ. v. Doe, 536 U.S. 273 (2002). Also, in ruling that an individual cannot sue a state for money damages in federal court under the Americans with Disabilities Act of 1990, the Supreme Court reasoned that Congress did not act within its constitutional authority when it abrogated Eleventh Amendment immunity under that law. Bd. of Trs. v. Garrett, 531 U.S. 356 (2001).

school district, the state must be the "real party in interest." In many states, the Eleventh Amendment question with respect to school district immunity was resolved in the *Mt. Healthy* case.[98] The Supreme Court concluded that the issue in this case hinged on whether, under Ohio law, a school district is considered an arm of the state as opposed to a municipality or other political subdivision. Considering the taxing power and autonomy of school district operations, the Supreme Court found school districts to be more like counties or cities than extensions of the state. As a result, Eleventh Amendment immunity does not apply.

Remedies

Judicial remedies for the violation of protected rights depend on employment status, federal and state statutory provisions, and the discretion of courts. Federal and state laws often identify damages that may be recovered or place limitations on types of awards. Unless these provisions restrict specific remedies, courts have broad discretionary power to formulate equitable settlements.

Damages.   When a school official or school district is found liable for violating an individual's protected rights, damages are assessed to compensate the claimant for the injury. **Actual injury, however, must be shown for the aggrieved party to recover damages; without evidence of monetary or mental injury, the plaintiff is entitled only to nominal damages (not to exceed one dollar), even though an impairment of protected rights is established.**[99] Significant monetary damages, however, may be awarded for a wrongful termination if a teacher is able to demonstrate substantial losses. At the same time, individuals must make an effort to mitigate damages by seeking appropriate employment.

In some instances, aggrieved individuals have sought punitive as well as compensatory damages. The judiciary has ruled that school officials can be liable for punitive damages (to punish the wrongdoer) if a jury concludes that the individual's conduct is willful or in reckless and callous disregard of federally protected rights.[100] Punitive and compensatory damages were assessed against a principal and superintendent who, without authority, discharged a teacher in retaliation for the exercise of protected speech.[101]

[98]Mt. Healthy City Sch. Dist. v. Doyle, 429 U.S. 274 (1977). *But see* Belanger v. Madera Unified Sch. Dist., 963 F.2d 248 (9th Cir. 1992) (holding that California school boards are indivisible agencies of the state and thus entitled to Eleventh Amendment immunity).

[99]*See* Farrar v. Hobby, 506 U.S. 103 (1992) (concluding that an award of nominal damages is mandatory when a procedural due process violation is established but no actual injury is shown); Carey v. Piphus, 435 U.S. 247 (1978) (holding that pupils who were denied procedural due process in a disciplinary proceeding would be entitled only to nominal damages unless it was established that lack of proper procedures resulted in actual injury to the students).

[100]*See* Smith v. Wade, 461 U.S. 30 (1983). In 1991, the Supreme Court refused to place a limit on the amount of punitive damages that properly instructed juries may award in common-law suits, but it did note that extremely high awards might be viewed as unacceptable under the Due Process Clause of the Fourteenth Amendment. Pac. Mut. Life Ins. Co. v. Haslip, 499 U.S. 1 (1991).

[101]Fishman v. Clancy, 763 F.2d 485 (1st Cir. 1985). *See also* Ciccarelli v. Sch. Dep't, 877 N.E.2d 609 (Mass. App. Ct. 2007) (upholding a $50,000 punitive damages award to a provisional teacher who was not rehired after her name appeared on a witness list for another teacher who had filed a sex discrimination complaint).

In 1981, the Supreme Court ruled that **Section 1983 does not authorize the award of punitive damages against a municipality.**[102] Recognizing that compensation for injuries is an obligation of a municipality, the Court held that *punitive* damages were appropriate only for the *individual* wrongdoers and not for the municipality itself. The Court also noted that punitive damages constitute punishment against individuals to deter similar conduct in the future, but they are not intended to punish innocent taxpayers. This ruling does not bar claims for punitive damages for violations of federal rights in school cases, but such claims must be brought against individuals rather than against the school district itself.

Reinstatement.   Whether a court orders reinstatement as a remedy for school board action depends on the protected interests involved and the discretion of the court, unless specific provision for reinstatement is specified in state law. If a tenured teacher is unjustly dismissed, the property interest gives rise to an expectation of reemployment; reinstatement in such instances is usually the appropriate remedy. A nontenured teacher, wrongfully dismissed during the contract period, however, is normally entitled only to damages, not reinstatement.

A valid property or liberty claim entitles a teacher to procedural due process, but the teacher can still be dismissed for cause after proper procedures have been followed. If a teacher is terminated without proper procedures and can establish that the action is not justified, reinstatement will be ordered. If proven that the actual reason for the nonrenewal of a teacher's contract is retaliation for the exercise of constitutional rights (e.g., protected speech), reinstatement would be warranted, although substantiation of such a claim is difficult.

The failure to comply with statutory requirements in nonrenewals and dismissals may result in reinstatement. When statutory dates are specified for notice of nonrenewal, failure to comply strictly with the deadline provides grounds for reinstatement of the teacher. Courts may interpret this as continued employment for an additional year or reinstatement with tenure if nonrenewal occurs at the end of the probationary period. In contrast to the remedy for lack of proper notice, the remedy for failure to provide an appropriate hearing is generally a remand for a hearing, not reinstatement.

Attorneys' Fees.   Attorneys' fees are not automatically granted to the teacher who prevails in a lawsuit, but are dependent on statutory authorization. At the federal level, the Civil Rights Attorneys' Fees Award Act gives federal courts discretion to award fees in civil rights suits.[103] In congressional debate concerning attorneys' fees, it was stated that "private citizens must be given not only the right to go to court but also the legal resources. If the citizen does not have the resources, his day in court is denied him."[104]

To receive attorneys' fees, the teacher must be the prevailing party; that is, damages or some form of equitable relief must be granted to the teacher. The Supreme Court has held that a prevailing party is one who is successful in achieving some benefit on any significant issue in the case, but not necessarily the primary issue. At a minimum, the

---

[102]City of Newport v. Fact Concerts, 453 U.S. 247 (1981).

[103]42 U.S.C. § 1988 (2008).

[104]122 Cong. Rec. 33,313 (1976).

Court ruled that "the plaintiff must be able to point to a resolution of the dispute which changes the legal relationship between itself and the defendant."[105] If a plaintiff achieves only partial success, the fees requested may be reduced.

Although it has been established that the plaintiff who prevails in a civil rights suit may, at the court's discretion, be entitled to attorneys' fees, the same standard is not applied to defendants. The Supreme Court has held that such fees cannot be imposed on a plaintiff unless the claim was "frivolous, unreasonable, or groundless."[106] Although awards of damages to prevailing defendants have not been common, in some situations such awards have been made to deter groundless lawsuits.

CONCLUSION

Through state laws and the federal Constitution, extensive safeguards protect educators' employment security. Most states have adopted tenure laws that precisely delineate teachers' employment rights in termination and disciplinary proceedings. Furthermore, in the absence of specific state guarantees, the Fourteenth Amendment ensures that teachers will be afforded procedural due process when property or liberty interests are implicated. At a minimum, the employee is entitled to notice of the charges and an opportunity to be heard. Legal decisions interpreting both state and federal rights in dismissal actions have established broad guidelines about when due process is required, the types of procedures that must be provided, and the legitimate causes required to substantiate dismissal action.

Causes for dismissal vary widely among the states, but usually include such grounds as incompetency, neglect of duty, immorality, insubordination, unprofessional conduct, and other good and just cause. These causes relate not only to classroom performance but also to other conduct that may have a negative impact on a teacher's effectiveness in the school system. If educators' constitutional rights are impaired in connection with termination actions, school officials and school districts can be held liable for damages. An individual, however, can recover only nominal damages for such impairment unless monetary, emotional, or mental injury can be proven.

POINTS TO PONDER

1. An elementary school teacher was not renewed for failure to meet the school district's teaching expectations as she completed her third year of employment. A mentor teacher had worked closely to assist the teacher in pedagogical and classroom management issues, but little progress had been made. Her sixth grade students consistently scored lower than other students in the school district, and parents frequently complained to the principal about her teaching. Upon receipt of the nonrenewal notice, the teacher asked for a hearing, claiming that the school board's decision had severely damaged her reputation and affected her ability to obtain another position. Is she entitled to a hearing? Does the school board's action violate her protected liberty interests?

[105]Tex. State Teachers Ass'n v. Garland Indep. Sch. Dist., 489 U.S. 782, 792 (1989).
[106]Christiansburg Garment Co. v. EEOC, 434 U.S. 412, 422 (1978).

2. A school board sent a tenured teacher a notice of its intent to terminate him for insubordination after he repeatedly refused to develop a personal growth plan as required by school district policy. Even though he had not complied with the policy, the principal had given the teacher good teaching evaluations each year. Can the school board terminate his employment? What are the teacher's rights if the school board pursues termination?

3. A tenured veteran teacher received a notice from the school board of its intent to terminate her employment for lack of teaching effectiveness. The brief letter cited the statutory language permitting teacher termination for cause and indicated that a hearing would be held in 10 days. Does this constitute adequate notice?

4. After two convictions for driving while intoxicated, a tenured middle school teacher was dismissed on grounds of immorality. The teacher argued that the convictions did not relate to his teaching effectiveness, the students had been unaware of the incidents until his termination, and he was in a treatment program for his drinking problem. Do you think his termination will be upheld? Support your answer.

5. A male teacher was arrested and charged with propositioning a male undercover police officer. Subsequently, the charges were dropped, but the school board, with no statement of reasons, did not renew the teacher's contract at the end of the school year. Although state law and local policies do not provide for a hearing in nonrenewals, the teacher requested an opportunity to appear before the school board. Is he entitled to such a hearing? Why or why not?

CHAPTER THIRTEEN

SUMMARY OF LEGAL GENERALIZATIONS

━━━━━

In the preceding chapters, principles of law have been presented as they relate to specific aspects of teachers' and students' rights and responsibilities. Constitutional and statutory provisions, in conjunction with judicial decisions, have been analyzed in an effort to depict the current status of the law. Many diverse topics have been explored, some with clearly established legal precedents and others about which the law is still evolving.

The most difficult situations confronting school personnel are those without specific legislative or judicial guidance. In such circumstances, educators must make judgments based on their professional training and general knowledge of the law as it applies to education. The following broad generalizations, synthesized from the preceding chapters, are presented to assist educators in making such determinations.

GENERALIZATIONS

The Legal Control of Public Education Resides with the State as One of its Sovereign Powers.   In attempting to comply with the law, school personnel must keep in mind the scope of the state's authority to regulate educational activities. Courts consistently have held that state legislatures possess plenary power in establishing and operating public schools; only federal and state constitutions and civil rights laws restrict this power. Of course, when the federal judiciary has interpreted the United States Constitution as prohibiting a given practice in public education, such as racial discrimination, the state or its agents can not enact laws or policies that conflict with the constitutional mandate. In contrast, if the federal Constitution and civil rights laws have been interpreted as permitting a certain activity, states retain discretion in either restricting or expanding the practice. Under such circumstances, standards vary across states, and legislation becomes more important in specifying the scope of protected rights. For example, the Supreme Court has rejected the assertion that probationary teachers have an inherent federal right to due process prior to contract nonrenewal, but state legislatures have the authority to create such a right under state law. Similarly, the Supreme Court has found no Fourth Amendment violation in blanket or random drug testing of public school students who participate in extracurricular activities; however, state law may place restrictions on school authorities in conducting such searches. Also, the Supreme Court has found no Establishment Clause violation in the participation of sectarian schools in state-supported voucher programs to fund education, but these programs might run afoul of state constitutional provisions prohibiting the use of public funds for religious purposes.

Unless constitutional rights are at stake, courts defer to the will of legislative bodies in determining educational matters. State legislatures have the authority to create and redesign school districts; to collect and distribute educational funds; and to determine teacher qualifications, curricular offerings, and minimum student performance standards. With such pervasive control vested in the states, a thorough understanding of the operation of a specific educational system can be acquired only by examining an individual state's statutes, administrative regulations, and judicial decisions interpreting such provisions.

Certain prerequisites to public school employment are defined through statutes and state board of education regulations. For example, all states stipulate that a teacher must possess a valid teaching license based on satisfying specified requirements. State laws also delineate the permanency of the employment relationship, dismissal procedures for tenured and nontenured teachers, and the extent to which teachers can engage in collective bargaining.

State laws similarly govern conditions of school attendance. Every state has enacted a compulsory attendance statute to ensure an educated citizenry. These laws are applicable to all children, with only a few legally recognized exceptions. In addition to mandating school attendance, states also have the authority to prescribe courses of study and instructional materials. Courts will not invalidate such decisions unless constitutional rights are abridged.

Comparable reasoning also is applied by courts in upholding the state's power to establish academic standards and graduation requirements. To determine whether students and school districts are progressing consistent with state standards and federal expectations, students are being subjected to more testing than ever before. Examinations determine the level and type of instruction provided; whether the child should be promoted from grade to grade or is eligible for graduation; and if the local school district has achieved required outcomes.

It is a widely held perception that local school boards control public education in this nation, but local boards hold only those discretionary powers conferred by state law. Depending on the state, a local board's discretionary authority may be quite broad, narrowly defined by statutory guidelines, or somewhere in between. School board regulations enacted pursuant to statutory authority are legally binding on employees and students. For example, school boards can place conditions on employment (e.g., continuing education requirements, residency requirements) beyond state minimums, unless prohibited by law.

In some states, policy-making authority in certain domains (e.g., curriculum, personnel) has been delegated to school-based councils, and the relationship between local boards and school-based councils is still being defined. Courts will not overturn decisions made by school boards or site-based councils unless clearly arbitrary, discriminatory, or beyond their scope of authority.

School board and/or council discretion, however, may be limited by negotiated contracts with teachers' associations. Negotiated agreements may affect terms and conditions of employment in areas such as teacher evaluation, work calendar, teaching loads, extra-duty assignments, and grievance procedures. It is imperative for educators to become familiar with all these sources of legal rights and responsibilities.

All School Policies and Practices That Impinge on Protected Personal Freedoms Must Be Substantiated as Necessary to Advance the School's Educational Mission.   The state and its agents have broad authority to regulate public schools, but policies that impair federal constitutional rights must be justified by an overriding public interest. Although courts do not enact laws as legislative bodies do, they significantly influence educational policies and practices by interpreting constitutional and statutory provisions. Both school attendance and public employment traditionally were considered privileges bestowed at the will of the state, but the Supreme Court has recognized that teachers and students do not shed their constitutional rights at the schoolhouse door. The state controls education, but this power must be exercised in conformance with the federal Constitution.

It is important to keep in mind that the Bill of Rights places restrictions on governmental, not private, action that interferes with personal freedoms. To illustrate, the public schools may have to tolerate private student expression under certain circumstances, but expression representing the school can be censored for educational reasons. Similarly, the Establishment Clause prohibits public school employees from directing or condoning devotional activities in public education. However, student-initiated religious groups in secondary schools must be treated like other student groups in terms of school access during noninstructional time. Furthermore, community religious groups, even those involved in religious instruction targeting elementary school children, must be treated like other community groups during nonschool hours.

In balancing public and individual interests, courts weigh the importance of the protected personal right against the governmental need to restrict its exercise. For example, courts have reasoned that there is no overriding public interest to justify compelling students to salute the American flag if such an observance conflicts with religious or philosophical beliefs. In contrast, mandatory vaccination against communicable diseases has been upheld as a prerequisite to school attendance, even if opposition to immunization is based on religious grounds. Courts have reasoned that the overriding public interest in safeguarding the health of all students justifies such a requirement.

Restrictions can be placed on students' activities if necessary to advance legitimate school objectives. For example, the judiciary has recognized that students' constitutional rights must be assessed in light of the special circumstances of the school. Consequently, school authorities can bar attire that is disruptive. They also can impose dress codes, and even uniforms, if shown to advance legitimate educational objectives, such as reducing disciplinary problems and gang influences, and the requirement is not intended to stifle expression. School authorities, although considered state officials, can conduct warrantless searches of students based on reasonable suspicion that contraband posing a threat to the school environment is concealed. Similarly, vulgar speech or expression promoting illegal activity that might be protected by the First Amendment for adults can be curtailed among public school students to further the school's legitimate interest in maintaining standards of decency. As noted, student expression that gives the appearance of representing the school also can be censored to ensure its consistency with educational objectives. And even personal student expression of ideological views that merely happens to take place at school can be restricted if linked to a disruption of the educational process or if it collides with the rights of others.

Similarly, constraints can be placed on school employees if justified by valid school objectives. Prerequisites to employment, such as examinations and residency requirements, can be imposed if necessary to advance legitimate governmental interests. Furthermore, restrictions on teachers' rights to govern their appearance and their lifestyle outside the classroom can be justified when appearance or lifestyle impinges on their effectiveness in the classroom. Although teachers enjoy a First Amendment right to express views on matters of public concern, expression pursuant to job responsibilities is not protected by the First Amendment. Even if educators are speaking as citizens and not employees, expression relating to private employment grievances, rather than a public concern, can be the basis for disciplinary action. And even teachers' expression on public issues can be curtailed if it impedes the management of the school, work relationships, or teaching effectiveness.

Every regulation that impairs individual rights must be based on valid educational considerations and be necessary to carry out the school's mission. Such regulations also should be clearly stated and well publicized so that all individuals understand the basis for the rules and the penalties for infractions.

School Policies and Practices Must Not Disadvantage Selected Individuals or Groups.   The inherent personal right to remain free from governmental discrimination has been emphasized throughout this book. Strict judicial scrutiny has been applied in evaluating state action that creates a suspect classification, such as race. In school desegregation cases, courts have charged school officials with an affirmative duty to take whatever steps are necessary to overcome the lingering effects of past discrimination. Similarly, intentional racial discrimination associated with testing methods, suspension procedures, employee hiring, and promotion practices has been disallowed. Whether voluntary race-based school/program assignments that further the goal of diversity will be upheld in *de facto* segregated school districts will depend on the ability of school officials to devise narrowly tailored means to achieve their desired objective.

In contrast, neutral policies, uniformly applied, are not necessarily unconstitutional, even though they may have a disparate impact on minorities. For example, prerequisites to employment, such as tests that disqualify a disproportionate number of minority applicants, have been upheld as long as their use is justified by legitimate employment objectives and not accompanied by discriminatory intent. Also, the placement of a disproportionate number of minority students in lower instructional tracks is permissible if such assignments are based on legitimate educational criteria that are applied in the best interests of students. Likewise, school segregation that results from natural causes rather than intentional state action does not implicate constitutional rights.

In addition to racial classifications, other bases for distinguishing among employees and students have been invalidated if they disadvantage individuals. Federal civil rights laws, in conjunction with state statutes, have reinforced constitutional protections afforded to various segments of society that traditionally have suffered discrimination. Indeed, the judiciary has recognized that legislative bodies are empowered to go beyond constitutional minimums in protecting citizens from discriminatory practices. Accordingly, laws have been enacted that place specific responsibilities on employers to ensure that employees are not disadvantaged on the basis of gender, age, religion, national origin, or disabilities. If an inference of discrimination is established, employers must produce legitimate nondiscriminatory reasons to justify their actions.

Federal and state mandates also stipulate that students cannot be denied school attendance or otherwise disadvantaged based on characteristics such as race, sex, disability, national origin, marriage, or pregnancy. Eligibility for school activities, such as participation on interscholastic athletic teams, can be restricted only narrowly because of factors such as age, sex, or disability. In addition, disciplinary procedures that disproportionately disadvantage identified groups of students are vulnerable to legal challenge. Educators should ensure that all school policies are applied in a nondiscriminatory manner.

Courts will scrutinize grouping practices to ensure that they do not impede students' rights to equal educational opportunities. Nondiscrimination, however, does not require identical treatment. Students can be classified according to their unique needs, but any differential treatment must be justified in terms of providing more appropriate services. Indeed, judicial rulings and federal and state laws have placed an obligation on school districts to provide appropriate programs and services to meet the needs of children with disabilities and to eliminate the language barriers of those with English-language deficiencies.

Due Process Is a Basic Tenet of the United States System of Justice—the Foundation of Fundamental Fairness.   The notion of due process, embodied in the Fifth and Fourteenth Amendments, has been an underlying theme throughout the discussion of teachers' and students' rights. The judiciary has recognized that due process guarantees protect individuals against arbitrary governmental action impairing life, liberty, or property interests and ensure that procedural safeguards accompany any governmental interference in these interests.

In the absence of greater statutory specificity, courts have held that the United States Constitution requires, at a minimum, notice of the charges and a hearing before an impartial decision maker when personnel actions impair public educators' property or liberty rights. A property claim to due process can be established by tenure status, contractual agreement, or school board action that creates a valid expectation of reemployment. A liberty claim to due process can be asserted if the employer's action implicates constitutionally protected rights, damages the teacher's reputation, or imposes such a stigma that the opportunity to obtain other employment is foreclosed.

Many state legislatures have specified procedures beyond constitutional minimums that must be followed before a tenured teacher is dismissed. The provision of due process does not imply that a teacher will not be dismissed or that sanctions will not be imposed. But it does mean that the teacher must be given the opportunity to refute the charges and that the decision must be made fairly and supported by evidence.

Students, as well as teachers, have due process rights. Students have a state-created property right to attend school that cannot be denied without procedural requisites. If this right to attend school is withdrawn for disciplinary reasons, due process is required. The nature of the proceedings depends on the deprivation involved, with more serious impairments necessitating more formal proceedings. If punishments are arbitrary or excessive, students' substantive due process rights may be implicated. Children with disabilities have due process rights in placement decisions as well as in disciplinary matters. Since school authorities are never faulted for providing too much due process, at least minimum procedural safeguards are advisable when making any nonroutine change in a student's status.

Inherent in the notion of due process is the assumption that all individuals have a right to a hearing if state action impinges on personal freedoms. Such a hearing need not be elaborate in every situation; an informal conversation can suffice under some circumstances, such as brief student suspensions from school. The crucial element is for all affected parties to have an opportunity to air their views and present evidence that might alter the decision. Often, an informal hearing can serve to clarify issues and facilitate agreement, thus eliminating the need for more formal proceedings.

Educators Are Expected to Follow the Law, to Act Reasonably, and to Anticipate Potentially Adverse Consequences of Their Actions.   Public school personnel are presumed to be knowledgeable of federal and state constitutional and statutory provisions as well as school board policies affecting their roles. The Supreme Court has emphasized that ignorance of the law is no defense for violating clearly established legal principles. For example, ignorance of the Supreme Court's interpretation of Establishment Clause restrictions would not shield educators from liability for conducting devotional activities in public schools.

Educators hold themselves out as having certain knowledge and skills by the nature of their special training and licenses. Accordingly, they are expected to exercise sound professional judgment in the performance of their duties. To illustrate, in administering student punishments, teachers are expected to consider the student's age, mental condition, and past behavior as well as the specific circumstances surrounding the rule infraction. Failure to exercise reasonable judgment can result in dismissal or possibly financial liability for impairing students' rights.

Teachers also are expected to make reasonable decisions pertaining to the academic program. Materials and methodology should be appropriate for the students' age and educational objectives. If students are grouped for instructional purposes, teachers are expected to base such decisions on legitimate educational considerations.

In addition, educators are held accountable for reasonable actions in supervising students, providing appropriate instructions, maintaining equipment in proper repair, and warning students of any known dangers. Teachers must exercise a standard of care commensurate with their duty to protect students from unreasonable risks of harm. Personal liability can be assessed for negligence if a school employee should have foreseen that an event could result in injury to a student.

Educators also are expected to exercise sound judgment in personal activities that affect their professional roles. Teachers do not relinquish their privacy rights as a condition of public employment, but private lifestyles that impair teaching effectiveness or disrupt the school can be the basis for adverse personnel action. As role models for students, teachers and other school personnel are held to a higher level of discretion in their private lives than is expected of the general public.

CONCLUSION

One objective of this book, as noted in the introduction, has been to alleviate educators' fears that the scales of justice have been tipped against them. It is hoped that this objective has been achieved. In most instances, courts and legislatures have not imposed on school personnel any requirements that fair minded educators would not impose on themselves. Courts have consistently upheld reasonable policies and practices based on legitimate educational objectives. If anything, legislative and judicial mandates have clarified and supported the authority as well as the duty of school personnel to make and enforce regulations that are necessary to maintain an effective and efficient educational environment.

The federal judiciary in the late 1960s and early 1970s expanded constitutional protection of individual liberties against governmental interference. Since the 1980s, however, federal courts have exhibited more restraint and reinforced the authority of state and local education agencies to make decisions necessary to advance the school's educational mission, even if such decisions impinge on protected personal freedoms. Courts do continue to invalidate school practices and policies if they are arbitrary, unrelated to educational objectives, or impair protected individual rights without an overriding justification.

Because reform is usually easier to implement when designed from within than when externally imposed, educators should become more assertive in identifying and altering those practices that have the potential to generate legal intervention. Internet censorship, peer sexual harassment, anti-harassment policies, bullying, hazing, and other intimidating behavior are a few issues now requiring educators' attention. Furthermore, school personnel should stay abreast of legal developments, since new laws are enacted each year and courts are continually reinterpreting constitutional and statutory provisions.

In addition to understanding basic legal rights and responsibilities, educators are expected to transmit this knowledge to students. Students also need to understand their constitutional and statutory rights, the balancing of interests that takes place in legislative and judicial forums, and the rationale for legal enactments, including school regulations. Only with increased awareness of fundamental legal principles can all individuals involved in the educational process develop a greater respect for the law and for the responsibilities that accompany legal rights.

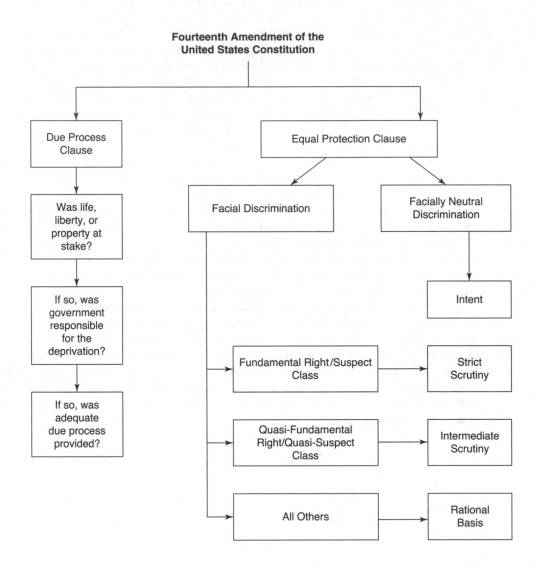

absolute privilege protection from liability for communication made in the performance of public service or the administration of justice.

additur the trial court's power to assess damages or increase the amount of an inadequate jury award, which can be a condition of denying a motion for a new trial.

appeal a petition to a higher court to alter the decision of a lower court.

appellate court a tribunal having jurisdiction to review decisions on appeal from inferior courts.

arbitration (binding) a process whereby an impartial third party, chosen by both parties in a dispute, makes a final determination regarding a contested issue.

assault the placing of another in fear of bodily harm.

battery the unlawful touching of another with intent to harm.

certiorari a writ of review whereby an action is removed from an inferior court to an appellate court for additional proceedings.

civil action a judicial proceeding to redress an infringement of individual civil rights, in contrast to a criminal action brought by the state to redress public wrongs.

civil right a personal right that accompanies citizenship and is protected by the Constitution (e.g., freedom of speech, freedom from discrimination).

class action suit a judicial proceeding brought on behalf of a number of persons similarly situated.

common law a body of rules and principles derived from usage or from judicial decisions enforcing such usage.

compensatory damages monetary award to compensate an individual for injury sustained (e.g., financial losses, emotional pain, inconvenience) and restore the injured party to the position held prior to the injury.

concurring opinion a statement by a judge or judges, separate from the majority opinion, that endorses the result of the majority decision but offers its own reasons for reaching that decision.

consent decree an agreement, sanctioned by a court, that is binding on the consenting parties.

consideration something of value given or promised for the purpose of forming a contract.

contract an agreement between two or more competent parties that creates, alters, or dissolves a legal relationship.

criminal action a judicial proceeding brought by the state against a person charged with a public offense.

damages an award made to an individual because of a legal wrong.

declaratory relief a judicial declaration of the rights of the plaintiff without an assessment of damages against the defendant.

de facto segregation separation of the races that exists but does not result from action of the state or its agents.

defamation false and intentional communication that injures a person's character or reputation; slander is spoken and libel is written communication.

defendant the party against whom a court action is brought.

de jure segregation separation of the races by law or by action of the state or its agents.

de minimis something that is insignificant, not worthy of judicial review.

de novo a new review.

dictum a statement made by a judge in delivering an opinion that does not relate directly to the issue being decided and does not embody the sentiment of the court.

directed verdict the verdict provided when a plaintiff fails to support a prima facie case for jury consideration or the defendant fails to produce a necessary defense.

discretionary power authority that involves the exercise of judgment.

dissenting opinion a statement by a judge or judges who disagree with the decision of the majority of the justices in a case.

en banc the full bench; refers to a session where the court's full membership participates in the decision rather than the usual quorum of the court.

fact finding a process whereby a third party investigates an impasse in the negotiation process to determine the facts, identify the issues, and make a recommendation for settlement.

fraudulent conveyance a transfer of property intended to defraud or hinder a creditor or to put such property beyond the creditor's reach.

friend-of-the-court briefs   briefs provided by nonparties to inform or perhaps persuade the court (also termed *amicus curiae* briefs).

governmental function   activity performed in discharging official duties of a federal, state, or municipal agency.

governmental immunity   the common law doctrine that governmental agencies cannot be held liable for the negligent acts of their officers, agents, or employees.

impasse   a deadlock in the negotiation process in which parties are unable to resolve an issue without assistance of a third party.

injunction   a writ issued by a court prohibiting a defendant from acting in a prescribed manner.

in loco parentis   in place of parent; charged with rights and duties of a parent.

liquidated damages   contractual amounts representing a reasonable estimation of the damages owed to one of the parties for a breach of the agreement by the other.

mediation   the process by which a neutral third party serving as an intermediary attempts to persuade disagreeing parties to settle their dispute.

ministerial duty   an act that does not involve discretion and must be carried out in a manner specified by legal authority.

negligence   the failure to exercise the degree of care that a reasonably prudent person would exercise under similar conditions; conduct that falls below the standard established by law for the protection of others against unreasonable risk of harm.

per curiam   a court's brief disposition of a case that is not accompanied by a written opinion.

plaintiff   the party initiating a judicial action.

plenary power   full, complete, absolute power.

precedent   a judicial decision serving as authority for subsequent cases involving similar questions of law.

preponderance of evidence   a standard that requires more evidence to support than refute a claim; it also is termed the *51 percent rule*.

prima facie   on its face presumed to be true unless disproven by contrary evidence.

probable cause   reasonable grounds, supported by sufficient evidence, to warrant a cautious person to believe that the individual is guilty of the offense charged.

procedural due process   the fundamental right to notice of charges and an opportunity to rebut the charges before a fair tribunal if life, liberty, or property rights are at stake.

proprietary function   an activity (often for profit) performed by a state or municipal agency that could as easily be performed by a private corporation.

punitive damages   a monetary punishment where the defendant is found to have acted with either malice or reckless indifference.

qualified immunity   an affirmative defense that shields public officials performing discretionary functions from civil damages if their conduct does not violate clearly established statutory or constitutional rights.

qualified privilege   protection from liability for communication made in good faith, for proper reasons, and to appropriate parties.

reasonable suspicion   specific and articulable facts, which, taken together with rational inferences from the facts, justify a warrantless search.

remand   to send a case back to the original court for additional proceedings.

remittitur   the trial court's power to reduce a jury's excessive award of damages, which may be a condition of denying a motion for a new trial.

respondeat superior   a legal doctrine whereby the master is responsible for acts of the servant; a governmental unit is liable for acts of its employees.

save harmless clause   an agreement whereby one party agrees to indemnify and hold harmless another party for suits that may be brought against that party.

stare decisis   to abide by decided cases; to adhere to precedent.

statute   an act by the legislative branch of government expressing its will and constituting the law within the jurisdiction.

substantive due process   requirements embodied in the Fifth and Fourteenth Amendments that legislation must be fair and reasonable in content as well as application; protection against arbitrary, capricious, or unreasonable governmental action.

summary judgment   disposition of a controversy without a trial when there is no genuine dispute over factual issues.

tenure   a statutory right that confers permanent employment on teachers, protecting them from dismissal except for adequate cause.

tort   a civil wrong, independent of contract, for which a remedy in damages is sought.

ultra vires   beyond the scope of authority to act on the subject.

vacate   to set aside; to render a judgment void.

verdict   a decision of a jury on questions submitted for trial.

SELECTED SUPREME COURT CASES

Agostini v. Felton, 62
Ansonia v. Bd. of Educ., 268

Beilan v. Bd. of Pub. Educ., 240
Bethel Sch. Dist. No. 403 v. Fraser, 94–95, 104, 110–114
Bd. of Educ. v. Dowell, 122–123
Bd. of Educ. v. Earls, 192, 245
Bd. of Educ. v. Mergens, 52, 108
Bd. of Educ. v. Pico, 70–71
Bd. of Educ. v. Rowley, 149
Bd. of Regents v. Roth, 280, 282–283
Bd. of Trs. v. Fox, 97
Bowers v. Hardwick, 248
Boy Scouts v. Dale, 104
Brown v. Bd. of Educ. (I), 17, 118
Brown v. Bd. of Educ. (II), 118

Capitol Square Review & Advisory Bd. v. Pinette, 93
Carey v. Piphus, 196
Cedar Rapids Comty. Sch. Dist. v. Garret F., 156
City of Madison v. Wis. Employment Relations Comm'n, 236
City of San Diego v. Roe, 247
Connick v. Meyers, 230–232
Cornelius v. NAACP Legal Def. & Educ. Fund, 97

Davis v. Monroe County Bd. of Educ., 138

Edwards v. Aguillard, 59–60, 68
Elk Grove Unified Sch. Dist. v. Newdow, 47–48
Elrod v. Burns, 239
Employment Div. v. Smith, 42
Engel v. Vitale, 43
Epperson v. Arkansas, 58–59, 68
Everson v. Bd. of Educ., 40, 62

Florence County Sch. Dist. Four v. Carter, 153
Franklin v. Gwinnett County Pub. Schs., 136
Freeman v. Pitts, 123

Garcetti v. Ceballos, 230–234, 238–239
Gebser v. Lago Vista Indep. Sch. Dist., 137
Gonzaga Univ. v. Doe, 86

Good News Club v. Milford Cent. Sch., 53–54
Goss v. Lopez, 67, 173–175, 197
Green v. County Sch. Bd., 119, 123
Griswold v. Connecticut, 85, 243
Grutter v. Bollinger, 124, 259

Harrah Indep. Sch. Dist. v. Martin, 204
Hazelwood Sch. Dist. v. Kuhlmeier, 71, 98–99, 101, 237–239
Hazen Paper Co. v. Biggins, 273
Healy v. James, 108, 239
Honig v. Doe, 159

Ingraham v. Wright, 177

Jackson v. Birmingham Bd. of Educ., 130

Keyes v. Sch. Dist. No. 1, Denver, 120
Kelley v. Johnson, 242
Keyishian v. Bd. of Regents, 201, 217
Kimel v. Florida Bd. of Regents, 271

Lamb's Chapel v. Ctr. Moriches Union Free Sch. Dist., 41, 53–54
Lau v. Nichols, 127
Lawrence v. Texas, 248
Lee v. Weisman , 42,44
Lemon v. Kurtzman, 41–42, 49
Locke v. Davey, 63–65

McCollum v. Bd. of Educ., 55
McCreary County, Ky. v. ACLU, 48
McDonnell Douglas Corp. v. Green, 254
Metro-Goldwyn-Mayer Studios v. Grokster, Ltd., 79
Meyer v. Nebraska, 68
Miller v. California, 94
Minersville Sch. Dist. v. Gobitis, 56
Missouri v. Jenkins, 122
Mitchell v. Helms, 62
Morse v. Frederick, 94, 95, 96,102
Mt. Healthy City Sch. Dist. v. Doyle, 229–231, 234–235, 283, 301
Mueller v. Allen, 64

Nat'l Gay Task Force v. Bd. of Educ., 236, 248
Nat'l Treasury Employees Union v. Von Raab, 245
New Jersey v. T.L.O., 182–184, 186, 245

O'Connor v. Ortega, 245
Owasso Indep. Sch. Dist. v. Falvo, 87

Parents Involved in Community Schs. V. Seattle Sch.
    Dist. No. 1, 124
Perry v. Sindermann, 282–283
Perry Educ. Ass'n v. Perry Local Educators' Ass'n,
    223, 236
PGA Tour v. Martin, 158
Pickering v. Bd. of Educ., 229, 231–235
Pierce v. Soc'y of Sisters, 61
Plessy v. Ferguson, 117

Reeves v. Sanderson Plumbing Prods., 272
Runyon v. McCrary, 125
Rutan v. Republican Party, 240

Santa Fe Indep. Sch. Dist. v. Doe, 45–46
Sch. Comm. of Burlington v. Dep't of Educ., 152
Sch. Dist of Abington Twp. v. Schempp, 43, 50,
    58(FO)
Sch. Dist. v. Ball, 62(FO)
Skinner v. Oklahoma, 243(FO)
Skinner v. Ry. Labor Executives' Ass'n, 245

Sony Corp. v. Universal City Studios, 78
St. Mary's Honor Ctr. v. Hicks, 257
Stone v. Graham, 48
Swann v. Charlotte-Mecklenburg Bd. of Educ., 119

Texas v. Johnson, 93, 229
Tinker v. Des Moines Indep. Sch. Dist., 94, 99–102,
    105, 110–114, 197
Transworld Airlines v. Hardison, 268

U.S. Civil Serv. Comm'n v. Nat'l Ass'n of Letter
    Carriers, 241
United States v. Am. Library Ass'n, 72
United States v. Virginia, 135

Van Orden v. Perry, 48
Vernonia Sch. Dist. 471 v. Acton, 192, 245

W. Va. State Bd. of Educ. v. Barnette, 47, 56, 93
Wallace v. Jaffree, 43
White v. Dougherty County Bd. of Educ., 241
Widmar v. Vincent, 51–52
Wisconsin v. Yoder, 42, 56, 61
Wood v. Strickland, 196

Zelman v. Simmons-Harris, 64
Zobrest v. Catalina Foothills Sch. Dist., 62
Zorach v. Clauson, 41, 55

INDEX

Ability grouping, 126
Academic freedom (see also
        Censorship)
    community objections to classroom
        materials, 58–61, 69–70
    in general, 72
    selection of course content, 73–74
    teaching strategies, 74–75
Academic sanctions
    absences, 179–180
    misconduct, 180–181
Accidents, 21
Accreditation of schools, 3
Actual knowledge, 137
Actual notice, 130, 137
Additur, 38
Advertising in public schools, 3, 97
Affirmative action
    employees, 272–273
    students, 126
Age classifications (see also
        Discrimination in
        employment), 116
Age discrimination (see Discrimination
        in employment)
Age Discrimination in Employment Act
        of 1967, 11, 18, 252, 270
Agency shop/fair share agreements,
        221–222
Americans with Disabilities Act of
        1990, 11, 18, 140, 143, 156,
        252
Amicus Curiae, friend of the court, 118
Appearance, grooming, and dress codes
    students, 109–113
    teachers, 242–243
Arbitration, 225
Arm of the state, 301
Asbestos, 28
Assault and battery (see Tort Liability)
Assignment of teachers, 205–206
Association
    in general, 239
    loyalty oaths, 201
    political activity, 240–242
    political affiliation, 239–240

student clubs, 52–53, 108–109
    union membership, 217
Assumption of risk, 31
Athletics (see Extracurricular activities)
Attendance (see Compulsory
        attendance)
Attorneys' fees, 129, 302–303
At-will employee, 272

Background check, 204
Bargaining (see Collective bargaining)
Basic floor of opportunity, 149
Benefits, for domestic partners, 210
Bible
    distribution of, 54
    objective study of, 50–51
    reading of, 43
Bilingual/bicultural education
    application of Title VI Civil Rights
        Act of 1964, 127–129
    Equal Educational Opportunities Act,
        127
    in general, 121, 127–129
Bill of Rights, in general, 7–8
Boards of education (see also
        School-based councils)
    local
        appointment of teachers, 203
        curriculum decisions, 67–68,
            70–74
        elections, 4
        meetings, 4–5
        membership, 4
        powers, in general, 4–5
    state
        authority, in general, 3
        membership, 3
Bona fide occupational qualification,
        253, 267, 271–272
Breach of contract, 7
Brown mandate, 117–118
Bullying, 104, 175–176
Burden of proof/persuasion, 119, 122,
        162, 254, 271
Business necessity standard, 253–254,
        257, 260, 276

Censorship (see also Academic
        freedom)
    course content, 58–61, 69–70
    electronic media, 72, 106–107
    instructional materials, 58–61, 70–72
    removal of library books and
        materials, 70–72
    student expression, 93–107
Certification/licensure, 200–203
Certiorari, writ of, 16
Charter schools, 2
Child abuse, molestation, 214–215
Children's Internet Protection
        Act, 72
Choice plans, 64–66
Church/State relations
    Bible reading, 43
    Bible study courses, 50–51
    Blaine Amendment, 63
    child-benefit doctrine, 62
    coercion test, 41–42
    community religious groups, school
        access, 53–54
    creation science, 59–60
    curriculum challenges, 58–61
    distribution of religious literature, 54
    endorsement test, 41
    Equal Access Act, 52–53
    Establishment Clause, in general,
        40–41
    evolution, teaching of, 59–60
    financial aid to private schools,
        61–66
    Free Exercise Clause, in general, 42
    graduation ceremonies, 44–46
    Halloween observances, challenges
        to, 49
    instruction about religion, 50–51
    intelligent design, 60
    Lemon test, 41
    New Age theology, 59
    Pledge of Allegiance, 47–48, 56–57
    prayer, 43–47
    proselytization in the classroom,
        49–51
    reading series, challenges to, 60

Church/State relations (*continued*)
   regulation of private schools, 61
   release time for religious instruction, 55–56
   religion, defined, 58
   religious displays, 48–49
   religious exemptions from public school activities, 56–58
   religious holiday observances, 48–49, 268
   religious materials in course assignments, 58–61
   secular humanism, 59
   sex education, challenges to, 59
   sexual orientation, teaching about, 70
   silent meditation or prayer, 43–44
   student absences for religious reasons, 56
   student-initiated devotional meetings, 52–53
   student-initiated religious expression, 45–47
   tax relief measures for private school costs, 64
   Ten Commandments, posting of, 48–49
   vouchers, 64–66
Circumstantial evidence, 253–254
Civil procedure, 12–14
Civil Rights Act of 1964, Title VI, 120, 127–129
Civil Rights Act of 1871, Section 1983, 129, 138, 252, 298–300
Civil Rights Act of 1866, Section 1981, 125, 252, 256
Class action suits, 14
Collective bargaining
   agency shop/fair share agreement, 221–222
   bargaining laws, in general, 217–218
   dues check-off, 222–223
   exclusive privileges, 222–224
   First Amendment protection, 217
   good-faith bargaining, 218
   governmental policy, 219–220
   grievances, 224
   impasse procedures, 224–226
   injunctions, 226
   labor relations boards, 218
   managerial rights,219–220
   master contracts, in general, 219
   National Labor Relations Act, 216, 218
   scope of negotiations, 219–221

   state legislation, 217–218
   strikes, 225–226
   unfair labor practices, 218–219
   union shop, 221
   use of school mail facilities, 223
Community groups, use of public schools, 53–54
Community service requirements, 68
Compensatory education, 121
Competency testing (see Proficiency testing)
Compulsory attendance, 134
Conduct regulations
   development of, 169–170
   imposing constraints on students, 167–168
   punishment, conduct off school grounds, 168–169
Conservative citizen groups, 69–70, 90–91
Copyrighted material
   computer software, 78–80
   Copyright Act, 76
   fair use guidelines, 76–77
   video recording, 78
Corporal punishment
   assault and battery, 32, 178–179
   federal constitutional issues, 177–178
   guidelines, 179
   reasonableness, 176
   remedies for inappropriate use, 178–179
   shocking to the conscious, 177–178
   state laws, 178–179
   teacher dismissal, for inappropriate use of, 293
Courts (see Judicial system)
Creation science, teaching of, 59–60
Curriculum (see also Instruction)
   Afrocentric, 134
   censorship, 58–61, 69–72
   college preparatory, 136
   evolution, challenges to, 59–60
   No Child Left Behind, 46, 80, 82
   pupil protection and parental rights laws, 90–91
   religious conflicts, 56–61
   requirements for public schools, 67–68
   sex education, challenges to, 59

Defamation (see Tort Liability)
Defense of Marriage Act of 1996, 210

Deliberate indifference, 130, 137–138
Department of Education, 127, 133, 274
Department of Justice, 274
Desegregation
   affirmative action, 119
   Brown/ Brown mandate, 117–118
   de facto segregation, 120–121, 124–125
   de jure segregation, 117, 120–124
   disparate impact, 253–255, 257–258
   disparate treatment, 253, 256, 260, 262–263, 277
   ending judicial supervision, 123
   Green criteria, 119, 122
   higher education, 117
   in general, 116–125
   inherently unequal, 116, 118
   options (permissible and impermissible)
      altering attendance zones, rezoning, 119
      busing, 119, 121–122
      consolidating schools/districts, 119
      dual school system, 118–120
      freedom of choice/open enrollment, 119–120
      interdistrict remedies, 121–122
      magnet schools, 121–122
      neighborhood schools, 119
      one-grade-per-year, 118
      open enrollment, 124
      pairing schools, 119
      racial quotas, 119
      rezoning, 118, 121
      voluntary transfer, 118, 124
   racial balance/balance, 122
   separate but equal, 117
   staff desegregation, 119, 121
   standards for assessing plans, 121–125
   unitary status, 118, 120, 122–124
   vestige of past discrimination, 123
   white flight, 121
   with all deliberate speed, 118, 121
   zone jumping, 121
Direct evidence, 253–254
Directed verdict, 12, 23, 254
Disabilities (see Students with disabilities; Discrimination in employment)

Discipline
  academic sanctions, 179–181
  alternative educational placements, 175
  bullying, 104, 175–176
  conduct codes, in general, 169–170
  conduct off school grounds, 168–169
  corporal punishment, 176–179
  expulsions
    children with disabilities, 160–162
    due process requirements, 170–171
    guidelines, in general, 171
    grounds, 170
    Gun-Free Schools Act of 1994, 172
    weapons, possession of, 172
    zero-tolerance policies, 172
  Internet, abuse of, 72, 106–107
  remedies for violations of protected rights, 195–197
  suspensions
    children with disabilities, 159–160
    due process requirements, 173
    Goss requirements, 173–174
    in-school suspension, 175
  time-out, 33, 159
  transfers, 175
Discrimination against students (see Desegregation; Students with disabilities; Sex-based classifications)
Discrimination in employment
  age
    adverse actions, 272–273
    Age Discrimination in Employment Act of 1967, 252, 270
    compensation and benefits, 271–272
    early retirement incentive programs, 273
    hiring and promotion, 271
    reasonable factor other than age standard, 273
    retaliation, 273
    retirement, 273
  disabilities
    Americans with Disabilities Act of 1990, 274
    average person in the general population, 275
    essential functions of the job, 276

    interactive process, 276
    major life activity, 275, 277
    mitigating or corrective measures, 275
    otherwise qualified, 274–276
    qualifying as disabled, 274–275
    reasonable accommodation, 276
    substantially limits, 274–275
    termination and nonrenewal, 276–277
  in general
    adverse actions, 257–258
    adverse impact, 255, 257, 268
    affirmative action, 258–259
    bona fide occupational qualification, 261
    burden of proof, 257
    business necessity standard, 253–254, 257, 260, 276
    diversity, 269
    make-whole remedy, 255
    McDonnell Douglas test, 254
    retaliation, 255
    role models/role model theory, 259
  race or national origin
    adverse decisions, 257–258
    harassment, 257
    hiring and promotion, 256–257
  religious
    accommodations, 267, 269
    adverse employment, 269
    attire restrictions, 267–268
    hiring and promotion, 267
    in general, 266–270
    job assignments and responsibilities, 269
    leave, 268
  sex
    compensation, 262
    hiring and promotion, 260–261
    pregnancy-related policies, 265–266
    retirement benefits, 266
    sexual harassment, 263–265
    termination and nonrenewal, 263
  sexual orientation
    access to benefits, 210
    adverse employment decisions, 248–249
    harassment, 248–249
Dismissal (see Teacher dismissal)
Diversity, 135
Domestic partner benefits, 210
Downsize, 258

Dress (see Appearance)
Dress Codes, 110–113
Drugs, possession of, 161
Drug testing
  employees, 245–247
  students, 191–193
Drug-Free Workplace Act of 1988, 246
Due process (see also Teacher dismissal; Discipline)
  defined, 8
  elements, 171, 173, 286
  hearing, 173, 287–290
  in general, 279–285
  notice, 287
  procedural, 279–280
  substantive, 279–280
  students
    expulsion, 170–172
    suspension, 173–176
  teachers
    contract nonrenewal, 281–282
    dismissal, 280–281
    liberty interests, 280, 282–285
    procedures, in general, 285–286
    property interests, 280, 282–284

Education Amendments of 1972, Title IX, 130–138
Educational malpractice, 84–85
Elementary and Secondary Education Act of 1965, 9
Eleventh Amendment, 18, 138, 262, 271, 274, 300–301
Employment (see also Teacher dismissal)
  assignment, 205–206
  contracts, 206–209
  demotion, 206
  evaluation, 211–212
  health/physical requirements, 204
  hiring, 203
  leaves of absence, 211
  licensure, 200–203
  loyalty oaths, 201
  noninstructional duties, 206
  records, 212–214
  requirements for employment, 204–205
  residency requirements, 204–205
  revocation of license, 202–203
English as a second language, 128
English language learners, 127–128
Equal Access Act, 52–53, 108–109

Equal Educational Opportunities Act of
    1974, 127–128, 134
Equal educational opportunity, 117
Equal Employment Opportunity
    Commission, 253, 258, 270,
    274
Equal Pay Act of 1963, 252, 262
Equal Protection Clause
    compelling interest, 117, 125
    in general, 122, 136, 266
    substantial justification, 133–134
    suspect classification, 117
    standards
        intent, 127, 130, 132, 260–261,
            263, 266, 270
        intermediate scrutiny, 130–131,
            134, 260
        rational-basis test, 266, 270
        strict scrutiny, 127, 254, 256, 258
Evaluation of teachers/principals,
    211–212
Evidence
    direct, 253–254
    circumstantial, 253–254
    in general, 289–290
Evolution, teaching of, 59–60
Exhaustion of administrative remedies
    (see also Students with
    Disabilities, procedural
    safeguards),
Expression (see Freedom of expression)
Expulsion (see Discipline)
Extracurricular activities
    drug testing,
    in general, 157
    sports, 130–133
    students with disabilities,
        participation of, 157–158
    Title IX Education Amendments of
        1972, application of, 130–133

Facebook, 106, 168
Facial discrimination, 117, 134–135,
    253, 260,
    266
Facially neutral discrimination, 132,
    253–254, 260, 266
Facilities, public school
    access for community religious
        groups, 53–54
    access for student-led groups, 51–53,
        108–109
Fair share agreement, 221–222
False imprisonment, 33

Family Educational Rights and Privacy
    Act
    access and confidentiality, 11, 86–90
    directory information, 88
    peer grading, 87
    personnel records, 213–214
Federal Constitution
    in general, 6
    major provisions affecting education,
        6–8
Federal courts
    courts of appeal, 15–16
    district courts, 15
    structure, 15
    United States Supreme Court, 16–17
Federal legislation
    civil rights laws, in general, 10–11
    funding laws, in general, 9–10
Field trips, liability for negligence, 27
Fighting words, 36, 95–96
First Amendment (see Association,
        Freedom of Expression,
        Church/State relations)
Flag salute (see Pledge of Allegiance)
For cause hearing, 272
Fourteenth Amendment
    Due Process Clause, 265
    Equal Protection Clause,
    in general, 7–8, 116–117, 127,
        129–136, 138, 251–253
Fourth Amendment, 7, 33, 182–184
Fraudulent conveyance, 38
Free Exercise Clause, 42
Freedom of association (see
        Association)
Freedom of expression (see also
        Academic freedom; Equal
        Access Act; Student clubs;
        Student publications)
    in general (includes speech, press),
        93–94, 228
    students
        anti-harassment policies, 103–106
        commercial speech, 97
        confederate flag, challenges to,
            104
        defamation, 94
        demonstrations, 103
        electronic expression, 106–107
        expression advocating illegal
            activities, 96
        expression resulting in harassment,
            138
        fighting words, 95–96

forums, types of, 97–98
        Gay-Straight Alliance meetings,
            109
        Hazelwood principle, 98–99, 101
        inflammatory expression, 95–96
        lewd and vulgar expression, 94–95
        obscene expression, 94
        prior restraints, 100, 102
        private expression, 99–107
        school-sponsored expression,
            97–99
        student-initiated clubs, 51–53,
            108–109
        threats, 95–96, 106–107
        time, place, and manner
            restrictions, 107
        Tinker principle, 99–101
        unprotected conduct and
            expression, 94–96
        viewpoint discrimination, 99
    teachers
        application of constitutional
            principles, 232–239
        channel rules, 235–237
        expression in the classroom,
            237–239
        expression pursuant to job duties,
            230–234
        Pickering balancing test, 229, 231
        political expression, 240–241
        prior restraints, 235–237
        private expression to superiors,
            229
        private grievances, 230–232
        protected expression on issues of
            public concern, 229, 232–234
        time place and manner restrictions,
            237
Freedom of Information Act, 213
Freedom of press (see Student
        publications)
Freedom of religion (see Church/State
        relations)
Friend of the court brief, 118

Gay, lesbian, bisexual, and
        transgendered (GLBT)
        individuals, 248–249
Gender, defined, 129
General Welfare Clause, 6–7
Good faith, 299
Goss requirements, 173
Governmental immunity, 25, 29,
        300–301

Green criteria, 119, 122
Grievance procedures, 224
Gun-Free Schools Act of 1994, 172

Hairstyle
    students, 110
    teachers, 242
Hatch Act (employment), 241
Hatch Amendment (student privacy), 90
Hazelwood principle, 98–99, 101
Hearings in employee dismissal
    adequate notice, 287
    evidence, 289–290
    impartial hearing, 288–289
    in general, 287–288
    name-clearing hearing, 284–285
    waiver of hearing, 288
Hearsay evidence, 290
Honor societies, selection for, 89
Human subjects, 11, 90

Immorality (see Teacher dismissal)
Immunity
    Eleventh Amendment immunity, 138,
        262, 271, 274, 300–301
    governmental immunity for tort
        actions, 25, 29
Inclusion, 140, 151
Incompetency (see Teacher dismissal)
Individual with disability
    defined, 141, 143
    has a physical or mental impairment,
        141
    has a record of impairment, 141
    is regarded as having an impairment,
        141–142
Individuals with Disabilities Education
        Act
    funding issues, 143
    in general, 140
Individuals with Disabilities Educa-tion
        Improvement Act, 143
Injury (see Tort liability)
In-school suspensions, 159–160, 175
Instruction (see also Curriculum)
    academic achievement, 80–83
    curricular requirements, 67–68
    prescribed textbooks, 68
    proper instruction, tort action, 21–21
Instructional negligence (see
        Educational malpractice)
Insubordination (see Teacher dismissal)
Intentional infliction of mental distress,
        33–34, 138, 263

Internet
    abuse by employees, 33, 236–237
    abuse by students, 33, 106–107, 168
    materials, use of, 72
Irrebuttable presumption, 265

Judicial system
    federal courts, 15–17
    powers of review, 16
    state courts, 14–15
    trends, in general, 17–18

Labor relations (see Collective
        bargaining)
Labor unions (see also Collective
        bargaining)
    exclusive privileges, 222–224
    right to join, 219
    security provisions, 221–222
Language barriers, 127
Least restrictive environment, 146, 148,
        150–151, 153
Leave, personal, 268
Lewd and vulgar student expression,
        94–95
Liability (see also Immunity; Tort
        liability)
    school districts
        damages, 300
        Eleventh Amendment immunity,
            300–301
        Section 1983, Civil Rights Act of
            1871, 10
    school officials
        damages, 298–299
        Section 1983, Civil Rights Act of
            1871, 10, 299
Libel, 35
Liberty rights, 280, 282–284
Licensure (see also Testing of
        employees)
    revocation, 202–203
    types of, 201–202
Linguistic minorities, 127
Liquidated damages, 270
Local boards of education (see Boards
        of education, local)
Loyalty oaths, 201

Malpractice (see Educational
        malpractice)
Major life activity, 141–142
Make-whole remedy, 255
Maximize a child's potential, 149

McDonnel Douglas test, 254
Mediation
    employment, 224–225
    students with disabilities, 163
Mental impairment, defined, 141
Minimum competency testing (see
        Proficiency testing)
Minority role models, 259, 261
Mitigating or corrective measures, 275
Mockery of public education, 127
MySpace, 106, 168

Narrowly tailored (employment), 117,
        251, 256, 258–259
National Association for the
        Advancement of Colored
        People (NAACP), 117
National Labor Relations Act, 216, 218
National origin discrimination (see
        Discrimination in
        Employment)
Native language, 127–129
Neglect of duty (see Teacher dismissal)
Negligence (see Tort liability)
Negotiations (see Collective
        bargaining)
Nepotism policies, 244
Newspapers (see Student publications)
No Child Left Behind Act of 2001,
        9–10, 21, 46, 80, 82, 88
Nonpublic schools (see Private schools)
Nonrenewal of teachers, 281–282

Obligation of Contracts Clause, 7
Obscene expression, 94
Office of Special Education Programs,
        143
Office for Civil Rights, 11, 132–133,
        142–143, 274
Otherwise qualified, under Section 504,
        142

Parental choice, 153
Parental consent, 144–146, 154
Parental rights laws, 90–91
PATRIOT Act, USA, 96, 201
Peer grading, 87
Personnel records, 212–214
Physical or mental impairment, 141
Pickering balancing test, 229, 231
Pledge of Allegiance
    exemption from reciting, 56–57
    challenges to "under God," 47–48
Political activity, employees, 239–242

Prayer (see Church/State relations)
Precedent, defined, 12
Pregnancy
    employees, 265–266
    Pregnancy Discrimination Act of
        1978, 265
    maternity leave, 265
Preponderance of evidence, 264, 289
Privacy rights (see also Search and
        seizure)
    students
        Family Educational Rights and
            Privacy Act, 86–90
        Hatch Amendment, 90–91
        Protection of Pupil Rights
            Amendment, 90–91
        records, 85–90
    teachers
        drug testing, 245–247
        evaluation, 211–212
        health-related issues, 204
        in general, 243–244
        personnel files, 212–214
        sexual orientation, 248–249
        sexual relationships, 247
        unwed, pregnant status, 247
Private right of action, 86–87
Private schools
    government aid to, 62–63
    tax relief measures, 64
    voucher plans, 64–66
Probable cause, 182–183
Procedural due process (see Due
        process, procedural)
Proficiency testing
    students, in general, 80–83
    students with disabilities, 82–83
Property rights
    employees, 279–284
    students, 170
Proselytization of students, 49–51
Proximate cause, 28
Public record laws. 212–213
Publications (see Student publications)
Punitive damages, 32, 270
Pupil protection and parental rights
        laws, 90–91

Quantity or quality of production, 262
Quota, 119

Race discrimination (see
        Discrimination in
        employment; Desegregation)

Racial profiling, 126
Reasonable force, 177–178
Reasonable suspicion, defined, 183
Record of impairment, 141
Records
    Family Educational Rights and
        Privacy Act, 86–90, 214
    personnel, 212–214
    students, 85–90
Reduction-in-force/layoff/downsize,
        296–298
Regression and recoupment, 157
Rehabilitation Act of 1973,
    in general, 149, 157, 252, 274–277
    Section 504, 140, 158, 274–277
Religion (see Church/State relations)
Religious discrimination in
        employment (see
        Discrimination in
        employment)
Religious exemptions, 56–58
Religious influences in public schools,
        43–51
Remedies for violating protected rights
        (see also Liability)
    students, 195–197
    teachers
        attorneys' fees, 302–303
        civil rights legislation, 298–300
        damages, 301–302
        reinstatement, 302
Remittitur, 38
Respondeat superior, 137, 299
Retirement, 266, 270
Retroactive seniority, 255, 259
Revocation of license, 202–203
Right-to-know laws, 213
Rightful place, employment
        discrimination, 259
Role model, 259

Safe place, 23
Save-harmless laws, 38
School-based councils, 5–6
School boards (see Boards of
        education)
School districts, 4–5
Search and seizure
    employees
        drug testing, 245–247
        reasonableness standard, 245
    students
        drug-detecting canines, 190–191
        drug testing, 191–193

Fourth Amendment, 182
    guidelines, 195
    individualized suspicion, in
        general, 184
    informants, 184
    locker searches, 185
    metal detectors, 189–190
    personal possessions, 186–187
    personal searches, 187–189
    police involvement, 193–195
    random drug testing, 192
    reasonableness standard, 182–183
    strip searches, 188–189
    T.L.O. tests, 182–183
    warrants, 182–183
Secret societies, 108
Segregation (see Desegregation)
Self-defense, 32
Separate but equal, 133
Sex-based classifications (see also
        Discrimination in
        employment)
    admission criteria, 133–136
    athletics (see also Extracurricular
        activities)
        contact sports, 130–131, 135
        fewer opportunities for women,
            132
        modified sports for women, 133
        noncontact sports, 131
        sex-segregated teams, 130–131
    sex, defined, 129
    sex-segregated programs and
        schools, 133–135
Sex education, challenges to, 59
Sexual battery, 138
Sexual harassment (see also
        Discrimination in
        employment)
    appropriate official, reporting to, 137
    employees, 263–265
    hostile environment, 126, 263–264
    quid-pro-quo, 263–264
    same sex, 263
    students, 136–138
    unwelcome advance, 264
Sexual molestation or abuse of students,
        126, 214–216
Sheltered English immersion, 128
Sign language/Sign-language
        interpreter, 147, 149
Slander, 35
Special education (see Students with
        disabilities)

Speech (see Freedom of expression)
Sports (see Extracurricular activities)
Stare decisis, 12
State board of education (see Boards of
    education, state)
State department of education, 3
State judicial system, 14–15
State legislative power, 2
Stereotypical view of women, 133
Stigma, nonrenewal of employment,
    284–285
Strikes, 225–226
Student achievement
    educational malpractice, 84–85
    proficiency testing, 80–83
Student appearance
    attire, 110–113
    hairstyle, 110
Student discipline (see Discipline)
Student-initiated clubs, 52–53, 108–109
Student publications (see also Freedom
    of expression)
    prior review, 100, 102
    school sponsorship, 98–99
Student records (see Records)
Students with disabilities
    assistive technology devices,
        services, 148
    behavioral management/
        intervention/modification,
        155, 160
    child find, 144
    contagious disease as a disability,
        141
    constitutional rights, 140
    disability, defined, 141
    discipline, 159–162
    evaluation/reevaluation/independent
        evaluation/multifactor
        evaluation, 145–146
    extended school year, 156–157
    free appropriate public education, 144,
        148, 154, 160
    identification of, 143–144
    parent/parental
        consent/approval, 144–146, 154
        surrogate, 146
    placement
        bright-line test, 156
        change of placement, 159
        continuum of alternative
            placements, 150
        extended school year, 156–157
        financial issues, 154

full inclusion, defined, 151
health services, 156
highly qualified instructors, 148
individualized education program,
    143, 147–158
individualized education program
    team, 146
interim alternative educational
    setting, 160–162
least restrictive environment, 146,
    148, 150–151, 153
maximum extent appropriate, 150
medical evaluation, 156
neighborhood school, 149
private placement/private school,
    151–154
related services
    health services, 156
    in general, 149, 154–156, 161
    psychological services, 155–156
    sign language interpreter, 147,
        149
    speech therapist, 149
    transportation services, 153, 155
residential placement, 151, 153
sports, 157–158
standards
    appropriate, 149–150
    basic floor of opportunity, 149
    best program, 149
    maximize potential, 149
    more than trivial advancement,
        149
    state and districtwide assessment,
        145
    supplemental aids and services,
        148, 150–151
    then current placement, 161
    transitional services, 148
    unilateral placement by parents,
        152–153
procedural safeguards
    administrative hearings, 163
    exhaustion of administrative
        remedies, 162–163
    hearing officer, 162–163
    judicial review, 162–163
    manifestation determination, 159
    mediation, 163
    notice, 153
    state review, 162–163
    stay-put provision, 159
    tier system, 163
reimbursement, 152

Subdivision of the state/political
    subdivision, 300–301
Substantive due process (see Due
    process, substantive)
Substantially limits a major life activity,
    141, 274–275, 277
Suicide, liability for, 25
Summary judgment, defined, 12
Sunshine laws, 4–5
Suspension of students (see Discipline)
Suspicion required, student searches,
    182–183

Teacher dismissal (see also Remedies
        for violating protected rights)
    causes
        immorality, 291–293
        incompetency, 291
        insubordination, 293–294
        neglect of duty, 295–296
        other just cause, 296
        reduction-in-force, 296–298
        statutory provisions, in general,
            290
        unprofessional conduct, 294
    defined, 280, 290
    due process
        defined, 280
        dismissal, 280–281
        liberty interests, 282, 284–285
        nonrenewal, 281–282
        property interests, 284
    remedies for wrongful dismissal,
        attorneys' fees, 302–303
        damages, 301–302
        liability of school districts,
            300–301
        liability of school officials,
            298–299
        reinstatement, 302
Teacher evaluation (see Evaluation of
        teachers)
Teachers' bargaining rights (see
        Collective bargaining)
Technology, Education, and Copyright
        Harmonization Act, 79
Tenth Amendment, in general, 1
Tenure, 208–209
Testing (see Proficiency testing)
Threats by students, 95–96, 106–107
Tinker principle, 99–101
Title IX Education Amendments of
        1972 (see Education
        Amendments of 1972)

Title I Elementary and Secondary
Education Act, 9
T.L.O. tests, 182–183
Tort liability (see also Educational
malpractice)
accidents, 21
attractive nuisance, 29
damages, 32–33, 36–38
defamation
fact versus opinion, 36
in general, 33, 263
libel, 35
malice, 37
privileged communication, 37
public versus private persons, 35
slander, 35
veracity of statements, 35–36
defined, 19
discretionary functions/duties, 29
governmental functions, 29
intentional tort
assault, 23, 31, 33–34, 36, 138,
263
battery, 21, 31, 263
false imprisonment, 33
intentional infliction of mental
distress/emotional distress,
33–34, 138, 263
ministerial functions, 29

negligence
assumption of risk, 31
breach of duty, 22, 24–26
comparative, 30
contributory, 29–30
defenses, 29–31
defined, 19
duties
instruction, 20, 26
maintenance of equipment,
facilities, and grounds, 20, 24
supervision, 20–23, 26, 28
to warn, 20, 24–25
foreseeability, 21–25, 28
injury, 22, 28
instructional (see Educational
malpractice)
invitee, licensee, trespasser, 27
proximate cause, 28
reasonable person, 26–27
safe place statutes, 23
save harmless statutes, 38
standard of care, 25, 27–28
propriety functions, 29
recreational use, 29
Tracking schemes (see Ability
grouping)
Transfer of students, 140, 175
Transfer of teachers, 205–206

Truancy, academic sanctions,
179–180
Tuition tax credits and deductions, 64

Unconstitutionally vague, 129
Undue burden/hardship, 158, 267, 269
Uniforms for students, 113
United States Constitution (see Federal
Constitution)
Unions (see Collective bargaining)
United States Supreme Court, 12–14
Unwelcome advances, 137
Urinalysis (see Drug testing)

Veganism, 267
Vesting, 270, 273
Virginia Military Institute, 135
Voting Rights Act, 4
Vouchers, 64–66

Weapons, possession of, 161
Workers' compensation, 25, 29

YouTube, 106

Zero reject, 144
Zero-tolerance discipline policies,
172
Zone jumping (see Desegregation)